D0414725

WITHDRAWN

WITHDRAWN

CARLISLE LIBRARY
ST MARTINS SERVICES LTD.

Designing for the Disabled
The New Paradigm

Designing for the Disabled
The New Paradigm

Selwyn Goldsmith

Architectural Press

Architectural Press
An imprint of Butterworth-Heinemann
Linacre House, Jordan Hill, Oxford OX2 8DP
225 Wildwood Avenue, Woburn MA 01801-2041
A division of Reed Educational and Professional Publishing Ltd

A member of the Reed Elsevier plc group

OXFORD AUCKLAND BOSTON
JOHANNESBURG MELBOURNE NEW DELHI

First published 1997
Reprinted 1999
Transferred to digital printing 2001

British Library Cataloguing in Publication Data
A catalogue record for this book is available from the British Library

Library of Congress Cataloguing in Publication Data
A catalogue record for this book is available from the Library of Congress

ISBN 0 7506 3442 1

Printed in Great Britain by Antony Rowe Ltd, Eastbourne

www.architecturalpress.com

Contents

Annex A The proposed Built Environment (Accessibility) Act: Draft Model for Authorized Guidance Document

Contents

Preface

'The disabled' is an ambiguous term. It can mean, as it usually does, people with disabilities, those who have got something wrong with them which a physician can describe. That is the medical model. Or it can mean people, whether or not they be 'medically' disabled, who are in some other way disabled – who are financially disabled, for example, or socially disabled, or architecturally disabled. It is architecturally disabled people with whom this book is concerned, those who when using or attempting to use buildings can find themselves confronted by impediments which prevent them from doing so, or allow them to do so only with difficulty and inconvenience. They are disabled because the architect who designed the building did not anticipate their needs, or did not care about them. Congregately, they are people whom the architect *can* disable but whom he need not disable, or not disable as severely as he commonly does.

My aim in this book is to present on my terms a coherent, logical and sound methodology of designing for the disabled. I reject the prevailing orthodoxy of designing-for-the-disabled practice which, rooted in the treat-as-different tradition, is represented in Britain by the Part M building regulation. To illustrate my thesis I draw extensively on my own experiences as a person with a severe physical disability, and my own ethical stance. I wish when I use buildings to do so in the same way as others, to be integrated rather than segregated, to be treated as a normal and not as a peculiar person. I wish to be able, for example, to use normal toilet facilities, and not to be told that a special toilet has been provided for people like me, and I can use it if I have got the special key which opens its door.

Why is it that we in Britain have an access regulation – the Part M building regulation – which insists that disabled people must be treated differently from others? Why is it that we have an access regulation which is *only* for disabled people? Why do we not have an access regulation which takes account of other building users with special needs? Why do we not have an access regulation which ensures that public toilets in buildings are accessible to mothers (or fathers) with infants in pushchairs? Why is it that we do not have an access regulation which ensures that when toilets are planned in public buildings the established practice of discrimination against women is outlawed? Why, in short, do we not have a comprehensive *for everyone* access regulation? Why, relatedly, do we have a Disability

Discrimination Act, which, with its provisions relating to the accessibility of buildings, reinforces the idea that only medically disabled people are vulnerable to architectural discrimination? Why do we have legislation which would permit only medically disabled people to complain that buildings discriminate against them and seek redress through the courts?

The answer to these questions is that over the course of history Britain has persistently strived to follow the line that America had taken. Two questionable beliefs have governed its endeavours: first, that Britain *ought* to be like America, and second, that Britain *could* be like America. In the first part of the narrative material in this book I report the story of history, of how Britain sought to do what America had done, and why what suited America did not suit Britain. I explain why the confused tangle of for-the-disabled accessibility controls which Britain has built up over 25 years cannot be sustained. My theme is that to generate buildings which are convenient for everyone to use there ought to be new control mechanisms, with appropriate new legislation and associated regulations.

The Royal Institute of British Architects published three editions of my book *Designing for the Disabled.* The first came in 1963, the second in 1967 and the third in 1976; for the quality of the presentation of the 1976 edition I owed much to Ron McKie, the then managing director of RIBA Publications. A year or two later he was already encouraging me to busy myself with the preparation of a fourth edition. I was reluctant to do so, first because the production of another encyclopaedia would be a daunting chore, and second because I was troubled that the third edition had no secure ethical base; if there were to be a fourth edition it would need to be informed by a sound and coherent methodology of designing for the disabled. Not until the late 1980s, by which time Mr McKie had retired, did I begin to formulate a clear picture of the ideological stance which would underpin a successor to the third edition, a stance which I was well aware was politically provocative.

The kind of book I had in mind did not, however, appeal to RIBA Publications, and the decision they made in July 1992 was to decline to publish it. For me this was a disappointment, but it was not long before the bonuses which came with it were apparent. With no tie to any publisher and no deadlines to constrain me, I was free, on my own terms, to let the form and character of my proposed book develop and change. It evolved unhurriedly through four versions, and it was only when I was satisfied with its whole content and structure that I sought a publisher. When I did, the book I had drafted was, very gratifyingly, accepted for publication by Architectural Press, the architecture division of Butterworth-Heinemann.

There was now an entirely new book in a new form, and, while there was agreement with the publisher that *Designing for the Disabled* could be retained in its title, it needed a subtitle to distinguish it from its predecessors and confirm that this was not a 'fourth edition'. It was Maritz Vandenberg who came up with the idea of *The New Paradigm.* In the early 1970s he had, with me, been an assistant editor with the *Architects' Journal,* and as the book was being drafted had been a frequent source of sensible advice. Had *The New Paradigm* been my idea, I would, as the book's author, perhaps have dismissed it as being overly pretentious. But Maritz was right – it was concise and it suited well.

The kernel of the book, its salient feature, comes not in the main body of the text but in a tacked-on annex, the Annex A document. It is Annex A which translates the ideology of the new paradigm into practicalities; in it I set out my suggested terms for new legislation which would control the accessibility of the built environment in Britain, specifically the terms of a new Part M regulation which would cover both new buildings and alterations to existing ones. The material which precedes it, a narrative in three parts, is effectively an extended foreword to it.

The first and most substantial part of the narrative is the story of history. It moves to and fro between America and Britain with, apart from a sideways look at Europe towards the end, the rest of the world being ignored. The exclusivity has to do with the story's theme, of how America set the mould for controlling the accessibility of the built environment on behalf of disabled people (and then, associatedly, anti-discrimination legislation), of how Britain attempted to follow the path which America had taken, and of how, as a result, Britain got itself into a tangle.

At this point I have an apology to make, most importantly to Scotland. The prime purpose of the book is to indicate how, on the British side, new access legislation and regulations might sensibly be reformulated. I have certain credentials for tackling the task with regard to England and Wales, but could not do the same for Scotland. Scottish legislation and regulations to do with the accessibility of buildings are currently different from those for England and Wales, and they would doubtless still be different were there to be reformulations on both sides. Relatedly, I apologize for not taking into account the practices and procedures of countries such as Canada, Australia, New Zealand and the Scandinavian countries. A regrettable effect of this is that the valuable contribution they have made to the overall corpus of documentation on designing for the disabled and associated legislative action passes unrecorded.

As I have noted, this book is not an encyclopaedia. It does not purport to be a comprehensive design guidance manual for architects. So far as it tackles design guidance, it is in the context of the terms of the Annex A document and the means by which the proposed legislative mandates would be enforced. Owing to the way I have structured the book the design guidance material is unavoidably scattered, and for the architect reader who is looking for 'how to do it' information, the effect of this will, I am afraid, be confusing, with recourse needing to be taken to the index at the back of the book.

To avoid disturbing the narrative, footnotes are not placed with the text. The references to source material cited in each chapter (and in this preface and the annexes and appendices) are stacked at the back of the book, with numbered cross-references to items in the bibliography which follows. The bibliography, as well as including all cited source material, presents an overview of the literature which has informed the drafting of the whole book, and to better inform the reader it is broken into subject sections and subsections.

The concentrated focus of the book, on public buildings and means of controlling their accessibility, leaves a range of topics uncovered. Egress provision, where it is a matter for building managers is one, as is signage and the particularities of building types such as hospitals and schools. By comparison with the coverage of the third edition of *Designing for the Disabled*, it is, however, design guidance to do with housing which is the most notable gap. For the sake of coherency, housing issues could have been dropped entirely. That they have not been was because I felt that the examination of accessibility controls in respect of public buildings ought to be complemented by a review of the scope there is for mandating access provision when new housing is designed. This is the subject of Annex B, with the issues involved being considered in the context of the possibility that the Department of the Environment will in the near future be presenting new proposals for extending the Part M regulation to cover new housing.

On the detailed practicalities of housing designed to accommodate disabled people, whether special housing, suitable new housing or adaptable ordinary housing, the technical information in the third edition of *Designing for the Disabled* remains virtually as reliable in 1997 as it was in 1976. As a comprehensive design guidance manual the 1976 book continues to hold its place. Practising architects who have been accustomed to referring to it will, I assume, retain it, and, so long as it remains in print and available from RIBA bookshops, those looking to acquire it will be able to do so; it will not be made obsolete by the arrival of *Designing for the Disabled: The New Paradigm.*

On one topic only, public toilets, is there a great deal more design guidance in this book than its 1976 predecessor. A feature of the book is its absorption with public toilets, a recurring theme being the lamentable character of public toilets as they are currently planned and designed by architects, and what ought to be done about public toilet provision for people with disabilities and other building users. The topic figures prominently in the history story and then in subsequent parts of the book; more than any other, it is the issue which informs and illuminates the book's thesis.

A feature of the book is the quantity of its autobiographical content, and for this there are three principal reasons. First, my links with history: I was involved when the idea of British accessibility controls was first mooted in

1962, and I continued until 1986 to have a role in their development. Second, my associations with government: from 1972 until 1992 I served in the Department of the Environment, where I advised on housing and other matters to do with disabled people. Third, my experiences when using buildings as a person with a severe physical disability: I recount in Chapter 21 how I have managed as an ambulant disabled person, as a wheelchair user and as an electric scooter user.

The advice I was given by Jack Lynn, an architect colleague who has long been a valued friend, is a fourth reason. When much of the second version of the book had been drafted, he was among those to whom I copied the text with a request for comments and criticisms. At that time the narrative began with Tim Nugent. No, he said, it must open with Selwyn Goldsmith. So the first part (and all the rest) was restructured, and an effect was to make the entire book into more of an autobiography than I had initially intended it should be.

My life as a person with a disability since age 23 has been privileged. While it was only briefly that I was a practising architect, my professional career has been rewarding. Relatedly, opportunities to engage actively in social affairs have come more readily to me than they do to the generality of severely disabled people. A reason, in my view much the most important reason, is that my disability was caused by poliomyelitis. A feature of the story in Part 1 of this book is the regularity with which the disabled people who made a mark on history were polio-disabled people. That was no coincidence, and I briefly divert to examine the matter.

Among all people with a disability of one kind or another, those affected by polio were historically the elite – I say 'were' because polio as a disabling disease is now practically extinct in western countries. First, because polio, uniquely among all disability conditions, caused motor impairments only, and had no other damaging effects, save for those whose lung muscles were affected and were obliged to wear respiratory equipment. Second, because it was correlated with social status; in Britain its prevalence was disproportionately high among people in the managerial and professional social classes. During the 1920s, 1930s and 1940s notifications of it in Britain hovered around an annual 700. In 1947, a year when there was an uncommonly hot summer, the figure soared to 9000, and, with the virus attacking young adults as frequently as small children, stayed at epidemic level until vaccination, first introduced in 1956, extinguished the disease. In England and Wales in recent years few cases of paralytic polio have been notified; for the years 1988 to 1994 the annual numbers have been 1, 1, 1, 2, 2, 1 and 0[1].

The polio virus randomly targeted motor nerve cells in the spinal cord which transmit messages from the brain to the muscles. Associated muscle functions could be weakened or completely destroyed, the outcome ranging from no significant disability to total paralysis. The virus did not attack adjacent sensory nerve cells, and a polio-disabled person, unlike someone paralysed on account of a spinal injury, is not troubled by any loss of sensation. Nor did polio have related damaging effects such as impaired mental faculties, acute pain, incontinence, impaired hearing or vision, impotence, communication problems, a progressive deterioration of bodily functions or an unpredictable prognosis from one day to the next[2].

As it has been by vaccination, immunization against the polio virus is assured by acquiring a small non-damaging dose of it. During the epidemic years personal cleanliness and hygiene affected proneness to the disease, with natural immunization against it being more widespread among people who were unconcerned about cleanliness and hygiene than those who were. Among small children attacked by the virus there was no correlation with the social class of the family, whereas among young adults there clearly was[3]. It also happened that the residual effects of the disease tended to be more severely disabling for those who were young adults at the time that the virus attacked than those who were small children, and more disabling for those in the higher than the lower social classes[4]. The relatively high prevalence in the 1960s and 1970s of polio-disabled professional people is thus explained.

From the 1950s through to the 1970s there were active members of the architectural profession, as there were of other professions such as law and medicine, who were polio-disabled people. I recall the half dozen or so that I knew, among whom the most notable, both for the quality of his buildings and the severity of his disability, was Sir Richard Sheppard. He, like the others, was a mainstream architect; he resisted the idea that because he had a disability he ought to engage himself in the business of designing for the disabled, and it was only on very rare occasions that he could be encouraged to attend conferences or meetings on disability topics. It was not until the late 1960s that disability affairs began to offer increasing opportunities for disabled people to achieve recognition as professional experts in the disability field, and among them polio people were prominent. In 1996 they still are, even though most of the few who are left are elderly.

As director of the Polio Research Fund, it was Duncan Guthrie who in 1961 prompted my initiation into the field of disability; he died in June 1994, but before then he had read and commented on the draft piece of this book I had written about him. Following him, many hundreds of people have in one way or another contributed to shaping this book, most of them unknowingly. Predominantly they have been people with disabilities, people with whom at meetings, social events and chance encounters I have talked about how they cope with disablement, their mobility when going out and about, and their experiences when using buildings. I mention in particular the numerous blind people I have talked with and guided when walking along streets or within buildings; my understandings of the problems, and non-problems, which blind people come up against have been valuably informed by conversations with them and learning at first hand how they manage.

As a former civil servant I needed to obtain government consent for this book to be published, and a succession of drafts went to government officials for checking. It was by no means the case that they agreed with all that I had written, and that was understandable. They felt, however, that my right as the book's author to my personal views, ideas and arguments should be respected, and on a range of issues we agreed to disagree. The advice and criticisms they offered were none the less invaluable, the regret that I have being that it is not in order for me to name them individually, for their diligence on my behalf I thank them all anonymously. Relatedly, the members of parliament and former ministers to whom I copied draft pages cannot be personally cited. Again anonymously, I thank them all for their help and encouragement.

One person, Tim Nugent of the University of Illinois, dominates the story that I tell. Early in the production process I copied my draft account of his work and achievements to him, and in September 1994 when he was in London we spent a full day reviewing it. Subsequently, by way of correspondence and telephone calls, it was checked, elaborated and refined, and in writing this book it has been my privilege to record the remarkable contribution he made to history. On the American side I am also most grateful to Hugh Gallagher who helped with the history report, and to David Capozzi and his colleagues on the staff of the US Access Board. And John Salmen of Universal Designers and Consultants, who on my two bookwork-associated trips to Washington DC arranged meetings and visits for me, has been an immensely reliable source of useful information.

On the British side I express my gratitude to Murray Denham, who produced the book's diagrams, and did so with much patience and a willing readiness to amend and redraft. I record in the book my valuable association over many years with the Centre on Environment for the Handicapped, now the Centre for Accessible Environments; to Sarah Langton-Lockton, the chief executive, I owe much for her consistently wise counsel over many years. Her staff and others associated with the Centre have also helped, to John Miller I am particularly grateful for his valuable advice on building and planning controls. Elsewhere, three academic colleagues have been among the many people with disabilities who have advised me: Mike Oliver, Professor of Disability Studies at the University of Greenwich, debated my ideas with me at a series of meetings, and there were also informative discussions with Vic Finkelstein of the Open University and Colin Low of the City University.

Maritz Vandenberg and Jack Lynn I have mentioned already. Among others on the British side to whom I owe thanks for commenting on drafts, permitting me to quote from certain documents, assisting with the accumulation of material and illuminating particular topics are Richard Best, David Bonnett, Colin Boyne, Peter Crane, Quentin Crewe, Denny Denly, Richard Dibben, John Dobinson, Mike Donnelly, Lady Hamilton, Peter Holland, Roger Humber, Jack Insley, Val Insley, George Meredith, Peter Mitchell, Cliff Pepper, Peter Phippen, Peter Randall, Tony Shoults, Diana Staples, Claire Tomalin and John West. As well as those in America who have already been mentioned, I am indebted to Bob Funk, Paul Grayson, Judy Heumann, Alexander Kira, Ed Leonard, Ruth Lusher, Jake Pauls, Mark Scher, Ed Steinfeld, Sharon Wilkin, John Wodatch and Marty Yeakel.

On the government front I am grateful for the permission given me to draw on Crown copyright material, and I owe thanks to the Department of the Environment for allowing me to use its library, enabling me to check material such as Hansard records of parliamentary debates. The RIBA library was also a useful source of information, as were a number of municipal and specialist libraries I called on.

For her constant practical help, support, encouragement, it is to my wife Becky that I owe most, and I cannot now imagine how the book could ever have been produced without her being with me. She gave me much practical help with survey work, and I recall her good humour on the many occasions when our days out were disturbed by my absorption with counting people in shopping centres or wc compartments in public toilets. Regularly, her criticisms of what I was drafting were wise and pertinent.

Now for the postscript. For the record of events presented in the main body of this book the cut-off point came in March 1997, to be precise on 16 March, the day that the complete final draft was passed to the publishers to be prepared for printing. The preface was able to wait for a while, and now, in early August 1997 when this is written, there is a changed scenario in the political arena into which the book is thrust. Out of office has gone John Major's Conservative government, and in its place has come Tony Blair's new Labour administration.

To take account of the changeover I made no attempt to revise the text at pageproof stage, and there were in any event two important reasons for letting it remain as it had been set on 16 March. The first was that the timing was propitious, marking as it did the pause between the close of one era and the opening of another. The second was that on the legislative front the switch in political management did not disturb the book's thesis.

Britain, as I have noted, has got its legislation aimed at countering architectural disability (or, meaning the same thing, architectural discrimination) into a mess. To remedy the matter the concentration should, I suggest, be on reconstituting the Part M building regulation, whose extended remit would cover all building users. With local control procedures, it could deal with alterations to existing buildings and perhaps satisfy the intentions of the Disability Discrimination Act.

On taking office, Tony Blair made a series of new policy dispositions for departmental territories and ministerial responsibilities. One of them, the high profile which women's issues would have, was particularly significant with regard to the broad role that a reconstituted Part M could potentially play in countering architectural disability.

As I point out in Chapter 17, architectural disability is a version of the social model of disability. In recent years the campaigning chorus from disability organizations and consumer activists has been that the medical model of disability must be condemned and discarded; in its place the social model must be promoted and acted upon. That is what, in this book, I have aimed to do. A crucial realization has been that, as a social version of disability, architectural disability does not 'belong' only to people with medical disabilities – it can afflict everyone who uses buildings. Importantly, it can affect women and pushchair users and, as relevant material in Chapters 17 to 19 indicates, women are frequently the victims of architectural discrimination.

'We will seek to end unjustifiable discrimination wherever it exists' was a commitment made by the Labour Party in its manifesto for the 1997 general election. Programmes aimed at ending discrimination against women will therefore, we may assume, be on the new government's agenda. Harriet Harman, the Secretary of State for Social Security, is now the Minister for Women, and Joan Ruddock, with a remit to deal only with women's issues, is her junior minister. With backing from lobbyists, they might together urge their ministerial colleagues in the Department of the Environment (in its merged form now DETR, the Department of the Environment, Transport and the Regions) to extend the Part M building regulation to cover women and pushchair users.

The Government's determination to end unjustifiable discrimination wherever it existed was, however, prompted more by deference to the disability lobby. The election manifesto continued 'For example, we support comprehensive enforceable civil rights for disabled people against discrimination in society or at work, developed in partnership with all interested parties'. To cope with this, the task of dealing with the Disability Discrimination Act was transferred from the Department of Social Security to the Department for Education and Employment.

David Blunkett, a blind person who has never previously associated himself with the militant stance of disability lobbyists, is the new Secretary of State for Education and Employment. With equal opportunities being his Department's guiding policy axiom, two of his Ministers in the Commons, Andrew Smith and Alan Howarth, are responsible for handling equal opportunities for disabled people. Neither of them has the title Minister for Disabled People, and for disability organizations that has been a matter for dismay. No longer, after twenty-five years, do they have 'their' Minister.

In the House of Lords, Baroness Blackstone is Minister of State for Education and Employment, and in the debate on the Queen's Speech on 20 May she referred to the Disability Discrimination Act. The Government recognized, she said, that it was flawed, and was neither comprehensive nor easily enforceable; there were, however, lessons to be learnt from the early stages of its implementation, and it would remain in place until the Government introduced new legislation.

My expectation is that the Government will fail in its endeavours to introduce legislation which would mandate comprehensive enforceable civil rights for disabled people. It could well, for example, encounter intractable obstacles in the way of giving disabled people rights of access to public buildings. Confronted by the predicament, the strategy it might sensibly adopt would be to employ the Part M building regulation as the prime instrument for countering architectural discrimination against disabled people.

It could be – we shall have to wait and see – that this book when published will irritate the government ministers responsible for handling issues concerned with disabled people, discrimination and the accessibility of buildings. But were its effect be to prompt constructive legislative action rather than obstinate procrastination, that would be welcome.

Thanks to Neil Warnock-Smith, Mike Cash, Diane Chandler, Sarah Leatherbarrow and others at Architectural Press who worked on its production, the book will surely look well when it arrives. The form in which it is presented means, however, that there will not be a second edition of it. For such misapprehensions, errors and inaccuracies as are to be found in its pages, the responsibility is mine. Corrections could be made should this edition be reprinted, and I shall be grateful to readers who advise the publishers of them.

Part 1

The evolution of accessibility controls

1 Where I came in

The bug was lurking, I suspect, in the polluted seawater off the beach at Amalfi where we went swimming while on holiday in Italy. But whether it was bred in Amalfi or elsewhere, it was around the middle of September 1956 that I acquired my polio virus. Three weeks later, having brought it home with me, I was removed to hospital and transformed from being a regular able-bodied person into a cripple. I was 23 at the time and had just completed my five years at architectural school.

For the first six days or so that I spent in hospital in Nottingham I was literally mindless. Whether I kept going or not was outside my control. I had no comprehension of what had happened to me, and I could not gallantly have proclaimed that I was determined to beat whatever it was. By the time my sanity was restored the critical phase had passed. Five weeks later I was transferred to Harlow Wood Orthopaedic Hospital near Mansfield, where for the next eight months ward four was my home. The initial stage was one of near-total incapacitation and discomforting pain, but it did not last long. As I began to recover, life in hospital became enjoyable.

A feature of polio was that progress towards recovery was unpredictable – it could be steady and considerable, or it could be stalled. I was the only substantially damaged polio patient in Harlow Wood that year, and from day one all the staff in the hospital knew about me. Messages about my progress were relayed each day, and because there was frequently an exciting advance to report the news spread happiness. The pleasure that I was able to give to those whose vocation was to care for their patients was the principal reason why my time in hospital was so rewarding. Another was that life on the ward was fun. Dorothy Aitchison was the ward sister, and 40 years on we still keep in touch; what she wished, she told me when we talked recently, was that everyone was happy and cheerful when she came on duty each morning.

From early on it was evident that my right arm and hand would not, apart from some flexion in the elbow and fingers, recover at all. The left upper limb performed more encouragingly and, aside from the bit used to throw darts at a board, recovered completely. What my legs might be able to do was a more bothersome matter. When I left hospital I could, using a stick, walk with callipers on both legs. My walking technique continued to improve with exercise, so that first one and then the other calliper was discarded, and then the stick. But both knees were permanently unstable, and either could collapse without warning. A slight trip could cause me to topple over and fall flat. In the early years I bounced – I could fall relaxedly without injuring myself. With increasing age the tissues became less resilient, and my falls less comfortable.

Occasional leg fractures put me into hospital, once in the 1960s and twice in the 1970s. In the 1980s they became more frequent. When the leg is healing following a fracture I resort to my wheelchair because I cannot, owing to the useless right arm, manage shoulder crutches. Walking on two legs continues, however, to be my normal means of getting around. For 12 years or so following the time (around 1965) that mobility functions were maximally restored I could get up and down stairs without a stick, walk unaided for miles and climb little mountains, subject to their having grassy terrain and not being steep. With ongoing age, the gradual dilution of muscle power and the battering to bits of my anatomy that has come with all the fractures, I am not now, when walking, as vigorous as I once was. And because any fall that I have is bruising, I have to be much more careful to check where I put my feet. Since 1980 I have regularly taken a walking stick with me when I go travelling, and since 1988 have always used a stick when walking, both outside and within the flat where I live. Virtually all my travelling away from home is done by car, driven either by my wife or myself. In the cause of keeping fit I do not take as much physical exercise as I would wish, and my tummy protrudes more than it should. My major concern being the muscles in my right leg, I sometimes climb the stairs in a public building rather than using the lift. The only regular exercise I now take is at the Latchmere swimming pool down the road from where I live in Battersea.

The experience of becoming disabled was not for me traumatic. I was not devastated by it, and nor was it distressing. In the early weeks after my mind had been restored I had no idea what the consequences might be. When it eventually occurred to me that I would be permanently disabled I was not unduly troubled. It was simply a matter of coping with what had happened and carrying on. Following my return home in July 1957 I carried on as the same person as I had been before, as a normal, active, 'in the mainstream' person. On many occasions I needed help to do things that I had previously been able to manage on my own. I could not run, jump, skip or ride a bicycle. I could no longer write with my right hand. My left hand had to undertake duties where two hands had served before. But my life was not blighted by disability.

I can only speculate as to how, had I remained a regular able-bodied person, my life and professional career might have evolved. I could have spent my years practising as a third-rate architect. Or, benefiting incidentally from the letters RIBA after my name, I could have found a niche on the periphery of the profession. Or I could have moved into a quite different arena. I do not know. What I cannot conceive is that without the disability my professional career would have been anywhere near as rewarding as it has been.

By the rules of what in Britain today makes an architect, there was none in the family before me, although in Bournemouth before the First World

War two of my mother's uncles practised as 'Architects and Surveyors', and in more recent years another relative on my mother's side managed an estate agency business there. My father, from a Norfolk farming family with a record of staunch non-conformism, Methodist lay preaching and diligent public service, was from 1926 a general practitioner in Newark-on-Trent, and it was in the family home there that I was born in December 1932, some 20 minutes before my non-identical twin brother. At an early age I displayed a capability for putting wooden building bricks on top of each other, a flair for mental arithmetic, an absorption with toy construction kits and some talent for drawing and painting pictures. There was also a phase when I avidly collected the numbers of railway engines. Through my later school years my scholastic performance did not shine, but was sufficient to get me to Cambridge in 1951, where for three years I read architecture. I transferred to the Bartlett School in University College London in 1954 for the final two years. In neither school was the architecture course rigorous, and when I emerged in 1956 I was patently ill-equipped to be a practitioner.

My inadequacies were not exposed in the course of the next two months. I was employed by an architect in Plymouth who in turn was employed by a speculative housebuilder; what he wanted, and I could deliver, was plan drawings of retirement bungalows that were as small and cheap as they could be without being unmarketable. When they were built there was no way that a wheelchair could get into them, but wheelchair access was not then an item which anyone would have thought to put on the agenda. Towards the end of that summer I left to go with a friend on the Italian holiday that took us to the beach at Amalfi and the encounter with my polio bug.

A year later, with recovery continuing at home in Newark after the stay in hospital, I faced the prospect of relaunching my professional career. Gordon Benoy, a local architect who had long been a family friend, was keen to help me on my way. At that time, a year before he set up his own practice, which flourished after I had gone, he was staff architect to a national firm of land agents. A specialism of the practice was the production of pigsties and cowsheds, and it was on those that I exercised my nascent professional skills. A feature of them which was not considered was whether the pigs or the cows might be disabled.

I returned to London in early 1959, my choice of architectural employment being governed by the availability of on-street parking outside the offices where I might work. The firm that I joined, Llewellyn Smith and Waters in South Kensington, produced efficient industrial and commercial buildings, and while I successfully dealt with the professional practice examination which permitted me to put ARIBA after my name, it became increasingly apparent that I was not cut out to be a practising architect. I looked around for what I might do instead, and talked with sympathetic architects, academics and others about where I might go. The advice was clear: the ARIBA letters I had acquired were valuable, and for lack of any other appealing track I should exploit them. 'How about research?', I was asked.

Neither at Cambridge nor at the Bartlett had any of my tutors imparted to me any understandings at all of research techniques or scientific method, but 'research' sounded attractive by comparison with the daunting chores of architectural practice. Among all the well-informed people whose advice I sought there was none, however, who hit upon the idea that, taking account of my own disability, the disability patch might yield something promising.

It was in the field of hospital building that opportunities to join the research business were on offer. The government had just, in early 1960, proclaimed a ten-year expansion drive which would generate great new hospitals all across the country, and it was to the South-East Metropolitan Regional Hospital Board and its research and development group, whose only member needed an assistant, that I moved. We spent our days imagining the hospitals that would appear in ten years' time, and devising clever things to put into them. But at no time did anyone in the hospital board's offices, or at conferences and meetings where visions of fine new hospitals were glowingly painted, think to enquire 'what about the disabled?' Certainly I did not; I happened to have a disability, but I was in the mainstream and I wanted no one giving me the idea that I was a second-class citizen for whom special arrangements ought to be made in buildings. Wheelchairs were not on the menu; it simply had not occurred to anyone in the hospital-building business that access for wheelchair users into and around hospitals, and the generality of public buildings as well, should be a paramount planning and design consideration. And no one came up with the idea that for wheelchair users there ought to be special toilet facilities. I did not wait until it did – after a little over a year my sojourn in the realm of hospital architecture was over.

The story of how the *Designing for the Disabled* research project came about can be traced back to the day that 18-month-old Janet Guthrie contracted polio in 1949[1]. Her father Duncan, who during the Second World War had served in special operations behind enemy lines, was working at the time on the Festival of Britain for the Arts Council. Troubled as he was to discover that in Britain no national voluntary organization was committed to defeating polio by raising funds for the medical research which would find a cure for it, he left the Arts Council and worked briefly with the Infantile Paralysis Fellowship (now the British Polio Fellowship). Its style did not suit him; with his entrepreneurial talents he decided in 1952 to operate independently and set up the National Fund for Research into Poliomyelitis. But it was in America, where massive charitable funding went into the research programmes on which Jonas Salk and Albert Sabin worked to produce their vaccines, that polio was beaten.

Following the introduction of vaccination in Britain in 1956, Guthrie's fund, which by then was securely established, became the National Fund for Research into Poliomyelitis and other Crippling Diseases – in 1997 it is known as Action Research. With a remit that covered rehabilitation research, an innovative project which it funded in 1957 was the planning and construction of Mary Marlborough Lodge, a daily living research unit in the grounds of the Nuffield Orthopaedic Centre at Oxford. Opened in 1960, it was a pioneering venture to which severely disabled people could come as residents for a week or more, to be equipped by technicians and trained by experienced therapists for the challenging task of managing daily living activities on their own.

The success of Mary Marlborough Lodge and the vision it offered of independent living for disabled people encouraged Guthrie to look for further initiatives he could promote in the housing field. In early 1961 he approached Gordon Ricketts, the then Secretary of the Royal Institute of British Architects, to discuss possibilities. One idea was an architectural competition for the design of a bungalow suitable for a housewife in a wheelchair, but what might be better, Mr Ricketts suggested, would be funding for research aimed at the production of a comprehensive practical guidance manual on designing for the disabled. Negotiations followed, the outcome, with support from the Building Exhibition and the Building Centre, being a project which was to be directed by Bill Allen, newly appointed head of the Architectural Association School of Architecture. I learnt of it, put in my application and, very gratifyingly, was appointed. The understanding was that I had a brief to produce a book for architects which would be called *Designing for the Disabled*, but I was given no instructions as to how it was to be structured or what its scope might be. The clear presumption, however, was that it would be focused on domestic environments and the design and equipping of houses suitable for disabled people to live in.

From the day I took up the appointment at the beginning of October 1961 I was thrust onto the stage of the theatre of disability. My role was to perform in scenes to do with buildings and disabled people, on a stage that in Britain had not been set. In Scandinavia it had been, and it was to Stockholm that I was sent first, to participate in a conference on the physically disabled and their environment. In Sweden and Denmark projects had been undertaken on the planning and furnishing of kitchens and bathrooms geared to the special needs of wheelchair users, research reports had been published and exemplary new housing could be visited and examined. A new realm of architecture was to be demonstrated to me; from being wholly uninformed about it one week I was to become a national expert the next.

The October 1961 Stockholm event, the first of the many hundreds of conferences and meetings on disability topics that I would attend in the course of my professional career, was a landmark in the history of designing for the disabled in Britain and Europe. It comprised two parallel conferences. One, of some 25 participants including myself, was on the topic Problems of handicapped homemakers. The other, of some 15 participants, was on Problems of handicapped persons in respect of community planning and transport. The first made sense to me – I was there to learn about housing for the disabled. The second I did not understand – I recall wondering what connection there could be between disabled people and community planning. It was, I supposed, a sideshow. I was wrong. The person who had been invited to contribute the principal paper to the conference on community planning, and then to deliver the keynote speech at a public meeting in Stockholm, was an American, Tim Nugent. He was the star of the event, and he came bearing with him the final draft of a document that was to change the world.

2 Tim Nugent - the idealist who changed the world

In the flat lands of midwest America, on the campus of the University of Illinois at Champaign-Urbana, Tim Nugent worked from 1959 through to 1961 on its production. The imaginative idea that had set it on its way had been conceived at meetings held in Washington DC in 1957, but he, on his own terms, engineered it. It was a sensational product, one that would benefit everyone everywhere. Around the world governments bought it, and translated it into the law of their land. It was American Standard A117.1 *American Standard Specifications for Making Buildings and Facilities Accessible to, and Usable by, the Physically Handicapped.* In America it would be the instrument for energising civil rights legislation for disabled people, culminating in the Americans with Disabilities Act of 1990. In Britain it would be the model for British Standard codes of practice issued in 1967 and 1979, and then, in the late 1980s, for the Part M building regulation *Access and Facilities for Disabled People.*

Tim Nugent was born in 1923 in Pittsburgh, Pennsylvania, and grew up in Milwaukee, Wisconsin. His father was partially blind and deaf, and his youngest sister was visually impaired – at the age of seven she was officially classified as being legally blind. In his early years doctors told him that he had a heart murmur, and for ten years his physical activities were restricted. In 1940 he enrolled at the University of Wisconsin at LaCrosse, aiming for a degree in health education and physical education. In 1941 he volunteered for military service, and at the military college of Tarleton State University in Texas obtained a diploma in general engineering. Active service in the American Army followed in 1944 and 1945, through northern France, Belgium and into Germany. He returned to LaCrosse to complete his BS degree in 1947, and in September 1948 joined the health services faculty of the University of Illinois in Galesburg with a view to making the development of rehabilitation education the subject of his doctoral dissertation. In 1949, with the Galesburg campus having been closed, the health services faculty was transferred to the main campus of the University in Champaign-Urbana, and he moved to work there on an experimental programme in rehabilitation education.

For rehabilitation services for handicapped students at Champaign-Urbana in 1949 there were no facilities and there was no funding. To develop the programme, Nugent had himself to do the fund-raising. A few of the university's administrators supported him. Others were sceptical; as they saw it, handicapped students involved extra costs and liabilities, and if they did graduate there was little prospect of their being able to work and pay their way. Severely disabled students, they felt, could be demoralising and distracting, and in 1951 the university administration put a quota limit on the number who could be enrolled, allowing only a small proportion of those who applied to be admitted. But steadily over the years Nugent's efforts and ideas were recognised and commended, and in 1956 he was appointed director of the university's division of rehabilitation education services and its rehabilitation education centre, and became professor of rehabilitation education.

The University of Illinois in the twin towns of Champaign and Urbana, a hundred or so miles south of Chicago, was then, and in 1997 with some 35 000 students still is, academically one of the most highly reputed universities in the United States. The handicapped students who enrolled there in the late 1940s were in the main veterans, some of them disabled on account of war injuries. The United States Veterans' Administration was the federal government agency responsible for their welfare and education, and Nugent had a contract for the services which he provided for them. Among other students were some sponsored by the Illinois Division of Vocational Rehabilitation, with whom he arranged a similar contract. With funding from these sources and from numerous other agencies who generously responded to his requests for financial assistance, Nugent was able to establish his rehabilitation centre with its purpose-designed building, its professional staff, its therapy equipment and its associated services such as transport and sports facilities. At certain other universities across America services for handicapped students were being developed, but it was Nugent's Champaign-Urbana programme which led the way and attracted most attention.

In pressing forward his rehabilitation programme at Champaign-Urbana Tim Nugent was imbued with the firm moral values of midwest America. America was a great country, the land of opportunity. To all who worked and struggled to achieve success it offered rewards. But the rewards had to be competed for – it was the duty of each American to strive for himself, not to look for welfare handouts. These were Nugent's stout beliefs and principles, and he insisted that his handicapped students must be trained to compete equally with others for the rewards that America could bring; they must learn how to manage independently, and not be obliged to look to others to assist them to do what able-bodied people could do without personal help. There should be no barriers to prevent them striving and succeeding on their own.

On the Champaign-Urbana campus there were steps and stairs for getting into and around buildings, as there were on the campuses of other American universities and in the buildings of American towns and cities where people sought to become rich and powerful. In America, as in Britain, Europe and elsewhere in the world, it was in the nature of buildings to have steps and stairs, along with narrow doors and confined lobbies and passageways. That was how buildings were: if people in wheelchairs wanted to use them they would have to be helped if they were to be able to get in at all, or else would have to resign themselves to being left out. For Tim Nugent the doctrine was inadmissible; he refused to accept what everybody else accepted, that buildings were inherently inaccessible to wheelchair users and would always remain so. Nor was it in his nature to accept that it was impossible to do what everybody else agreed could not be done. For himself and his students he was ambitious, and he was resolute. Medical specialists angered him with their discouraging dogmas. They told him that young people who were extensively paralysed and permanently chairbound as a result of neck-breaking accidents could never hope to manage independently or compete successfully with their able-bodied peers in the real world. To Tim Nugent this was an exhilarating challenge. He had a mission: he would show the medical experts that they were wrong.

Nugent demanded that his handicapped students must have a normal education, and be treated like all others. In 1949 the administrators who supported him began to arrange for the venues of classes to be changed so that, with ramps being installed at their entrances, students in wheelchairs could reach them. In 1952, with funding from private sources, he set up a bus service on the university campus, the buses being equipped with platform lifts so that students in wheelchairs could travel on them along with others. His goal was to make all the buildings on the Champaign-Urbana campus fully accessible to his wheelchair students. When in 1956 the university authorities finally agreed to officially establish him and his education rehabilitation programme, they agreed at the same time to authorise the remodelling of all the buildings on the campus. It was then that there occurred a seminal happening in the story of how, for disabled people throughout the world, the accessibility of buildings came to be regulated.

With some 200 buildings on the Champaign-Urbana campus having to be made wheelchair-accessible, an architectural brief was needed. Most importantly, there had to be design specifications for accessibility, and it was these that Tim Nugent developed. As he was to tell me, his initial design standards for matters such as the width of doors, the gradient of ramps and the size of wc compartments evolved pragmatically. But it was at Champaign-Urbana in 1956 that the world's first-ever access standard was produced.

With his design standards, Nugent checked plans for new campus buildings, along with proposals for alterations to existing buildings. He then went on to tackle the municipal authorities in the two towns of Champaign and Urbana. More ready and keen to help than the university authorities, they set up a programme for modifying all their community buildings so that they could be used independently by people in wheelchairs.

The physical therapy programme which Nugent instituted for his handicapped students at the university rehabilitation centre was punishing and demanding, even ruthless. His conviction was that he could train virtually all his students, however severe their disability, to get about independently and manage their own lives, provided they were positively motivated and keen to learn. At conference meetings, where he spoke accompanied by fast-moving slide illustrations of his students in action, the discipline was apparent: 'if you miss the bus and don't get to your lecture, too bad – you won't make the same mistake again next time'.

2.1 Tim Nugent

Handicapped students who applied for a place at the university visited the campus beforehand so that Nugent could assess their aptitudes and motivations before they were accepted. Tales about the style of the regime filtered out. One was that Nugent's standard procedure on the first day of school was to have his students bid fond parents goodbye and then tell them they could get to the dining hall under their own steam or suffer the effects of starvation. Yes and no, he said when I asked him about it in September 1994. Yes, it was vital to break the dependency bond and cut the umbilical cord; he would not have over-protective parents hanging around the campus anxiously looking to come to the aid of their son or daughter. No, his students were not told on the first day that they had to get to the dining hall on their own. At the beginning of their first term his handicapped students lived on the campus for two weeks before others arrived. The first week was the functional training week – 'they called it hell', he said. Remorselessly, students had to struggle on their own to find a way of getting on and off the bed, of dressing themselves independently, of washing and showering, of getting on and off the wc with no one to help them. 'No', they would protest each day, 'we cannot possibly do it'. 'Yes', he demanded, 'you can'. 'And they did', he told me, 'they had to persevere until they could'.

Following the rigorous training of the first week, the second was the orientation programme. Students learnt the geography of the campus, how they would travel around it, how they would be able to participate in the social life of the university and use its amenities, how they would get to their classes, and what resources – such as teaching material on tape for those who were blind – were available to them. Nugent did not automatically reject applicants who were so comprehensively disabled that they would not, in all circumstances, be able to manage without personal help. Those who in his view were properly oriented could be accepted. If help was absolutely necessary, for example with getting dressed, that was acceptable. Where it was not necessary it was forbidden. There were students who arrived on campus with powered wheelchairs which hospitals had over-prescribed. Ninety per cent of them, he told me, did not need battery-powered chairs – they could, as properly for their own benefit they should, propel themselves in manually-powered wheelchairs. The electrically-powered chairs were taken away.

A story reported to me was that Nugent told his students he had spies on the campus and in the towns of Champaign and Urbana, and that if any student was seen in a wheelchair with someone else pushing them they would be instantly dismissed. No, he said when I asked him about it, that was tongue in cheek. But among his colleagues on the staff of the university there were some who grasped what he was doing and how vital his punishing methods were. For the sake of the students concerned, they would, he said, advise him when they had observed someone in a wheelchair being pushed.

It was apparent to those such as myself who visited his rehabilitation centre and met and talked with his students that they relished the way he cajoled and bullied them. It was results that counted, and Nugent delivered them. In October 1993 in Washington DC I was introduced to a tetraplegic woman in a powered wheelchair who had a responsible full-time job, lived on her own and travelled to and from work each day on the wheelchair-accessible Metro. She had broken her neck in 1958 at the age of 17, and in 1959, unable, she said, to do more for herself than wipe her face with a flannel, she had been accepted as a first-year student at the University of Illinois. She had had to learn for herself how to manage independently, how to get herself unaided off her wheelchair and onto the wc seat. The brainwashing and the scare tactics worked – it was sink or swim. Tim Nugent was her hero – 'I could never have survived without him – I owe everything to him'.

At Champaign-Urbana during the early 1950s Nugent generated action in the locality only, his commitment being to his own personal constituency, his handicapped students. While he did not seek to operate on a national stage, word of his achievements spread, as did the exciting vision of emancipating disabled people by the elimination of architectural barriers. Among those who responded was Hugo Deffner. Disabled on account of polio, Deffner was a wheelchair user who lived 700 miles away in Oklahoma City. Principally by telephone, he communicated regularly with Tim Nugent, and with the help of his design guidelines took it on himself to run a one-man crusade aimed at encouraging the authorities in Oklahoma City to make all their public buildings wheelchair-accessible[1].

A small arm of the federal government in Washington DC, the President's Committee on Employment of the Physically Handicapped, had then (as in 1997 it still does, now as the President's Committee on Employment of People with Disabilities) a remit to promote the welfare of disabled people. Each year at its ceremonial annual meeting it honoured the person it had designated the Handicapped American of the Year. In 1957 the nominee was Hugo Deffner. Ed Leonard, assistant to the chairman of the committee, reported what happened on 23 May that year in the departmental auditorium on Washington's Constitution Avenue[2]:

> Deffner was there to receive the President's trophy as the Handicapped American of the Year. While President Eisenhower waited on the stage to make the presentation, Deffner waited outside on the sidewalk until two husky Marines could be mustered to carry his wheelchair up the entrance steps.

The incident embarrassed the President's Committee, and it was catalytic. The committee had not until then engaged itself in the issue of architectural barriers, but agreed at its next executive board meeting that national action was called for. An alliance was established with the Chicago-based national voluntary organization for disabled people, the National Society for Crippled Children and Adults, who agreed to sponsor the project. The first approach was to the Veterans' Administration, and in cooperation with them, and with advice from the local architectural society in Washington, a guide for making veterans' hospital buildings accessible to the handicapped was drafted. The vital proposition was put by the architectural society. To give the programme greater credibility and a firm steer, and recognising that formalised design standards were a familiar tool for architects, their suggestion was that there ought to be a national standard issued by the American Standards Association – now the American National Standards Institute and known as ANSI.

In May 1959 the President's Committee called a meeting at which interested individuals (among them Tim Nugent) and representatives of the sponsoring organizations agreed with ANSI officers to press ahead with the preparation of an American Standard for accessibility for the disabled. Following that, a steering committee was formed under the chairmanship of Leon Chatelain, a past president of both the American Institute of Architects and the National Society for Crippled Children and Adults. With funding from the National Society, Nugent was then commissioned to undertake a series of practical research projects on his university campus, and as secretary to the steering committee it was his job to draft a set of specifications, to be reviewed and voted upon by a full ANSI committee comprised of representatives of a host of interested organizations.

On the steering committee which supervised the preparation of the draft standard Nugent was the acknowledged expert. He, on his terms, conducted the research studies at the University of Illinois which provided the data to inform the draft specifications:

> Structured research included more than 400 physically disabled men and women as subjects. They ranged in age from 14 to 45. They ranged in height from 4ft 2in to 6ft 6in. They ranged in weight from 80 to 252lbs. They included almost every cause and manifestation of physical disability[3].

2.2 Part of the campus of the University of Illinois at Champaign-Urbana, founded in 1867. At centre is Altgeld Hall, opened in June 1897 as the first library building on the campus.

The gradient of ramps was one of the important topics on which Nugent's research focused:

> Structured research also included a special ramp which was adjustable to 62 positions of length or pitch or varying combinations of length and pitch. The ramp was of permanent construction and was constructed out of doors where varying weather conditions would prevail. Experimentation with various surfaces as to coefficient of friction or safety in both wheeling and walking was conducted. Varied subjective and objective measurements of subjects on the research ramp were made[4].

Nugent's potent influence was felt when the ANSI sectional committee was balloted on the detailed content of the draft of the proposed standard. It was also clear, or so it seemed, that, in terms of the scale of the cost penalties for building developers which could arise from the implementation of the standard, his proposed specifications were not threatening. His doctrine was that concessions ought not to be made to disabled people. If – as they should be – people with disabilities were powerfully motivated and properly trained, they would be able to cope with facilities in and around buildings that were apparently no different from those that users of public buildings in America were accustomed to finding.

Thus it was, with uncommon alacrity and unanimity and with few amendments, that the draft which Nugent presented was voted through. On 31 October 1961 it was officially issued as American Standard A117.1 *American Standard Specifications for Making Buildings and Facilities Accessible to, and Usable by, the Physically Handicapped.* Nugent had done a remarkable pioneering job. A carefully marshalled set of prescriptions based on the capabilities of a group of highly motivated, thoroughly trained, intelligent and active young people in wheelchairs on an American university campus became the model for fitting buildings to suit all disabled people.

Tim Nugent's vision of disabled people and their capabilities is reflected throughout the 1961 A117.1 American Standard, in particular in the informative footnotes that explain and illustrate the specifications. The important matter of the gradient of ramps is an instance. The finding of the research study at the University of Illinois, conducted among wheelchair users none of whom was more than 45 years old, was that 1 in 12 was manageable, and 'A ramp shall not have a slope greater than 1 foot rise in 12 feet' was the instruction that went into the 1961 A117.1[5]. From then on, 1 in 12 was the accepted prescription for virtually all the national standards and regulations that were issued around the world.

More compellingly, Nugent's vision was manifested in the specifications in section 5.6 of A117.1 for toilet rooms which would cater for wheelchair users. Earlier, in section 3, the dimensions of a standard wheelchair had been listed; the length was 42in (1070mm), the width when open was 25in (635mm) and the seat height 19½ in (495mm) – all no different from standard wheelchairs of the 1990s. Section 5.6 began as follows:

> 5.6 Toilet Rooms. It is essential that an appropriate number of toilet rooms, in accordance with the nature and use of a specific building or facility, be made accessible to, and usable by, the physically handicapped.
> 5.6.1 Toilet rooms shall have space to allow traffic of individuals in wheelchairs, in accordance with 3.1, 3.2 and 3.3.
> 5.6.2 Toilet rooms shall have at least one toilet stall that –

There I pause. In line with Nugent's treat-as-normal principles, the significance of this was that all toilet rooms must as a rule be wheelchair-accessible, not that it was sufficient for a single special facility for disabled people to be provided somewhere in the building concerned.

With metric equivalents for the feet and inches of A117.1, the specifications continued:

> 5.6.2 Toilet rooms shall have at least one toilet stall that:
> (1) Is 3 feet (915mm) wide
> (2) Is at least 4 feet 8 inches (1420mm), preferably 5 feet (1525mm), deep
> (3) Has a door (where doors are used) that is 32 inches (815mm) wide and swings out
> (4) Has handrails on each side, 33 inches (840mm) high and parallel to the floor, 1½ inches (38mm) in outside diameter, with 1½ inches clearance between rail and wall, and fastened securely at ends and centre
> (5) Has a water closet with the seat 20 inches (510mm) from the floor.

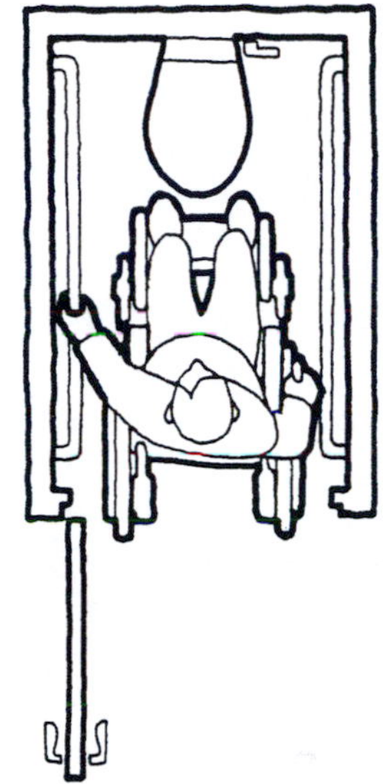

2.3 The wc compartment for disabled people advised in the 1961 American Standard

The practical effects of all this are illustrated in Figure 2.3. Drawn to scale, it shows a wc compartment with a depth of 1420mm, a wall-mounted wc whose face is at 520mm from the rear wall[7], about as close as it can be, and a user in a standard wheelchair. Clearly, the wheelchair user needs to be athletic and to have been effectively trained; there is no space to effect a lateral transfer, and he has to get on and off the wc by pushing up, grabbing one of the side rails, twisting and then dropping down.

With the wheelchair in the way, he cannot, it would seem, close the door when seated on the wc. In the course of writing this book I checked with Tim Nugent. There was, he said, never a problem – at meetings he had addressed in the 1960s he had shown slides to demonstrate how straightforward the manoeuvre was – the technique, having got onto the wc seat, was to fold the wheelchair, push it to one side and then reach to close the door. That would seem to be problematical – if, looking at Figure 2.3, we imagine the user placed on the wc seat, it is apparent that he would need to have an exceptionally long arm to reach the door and close it. I may perhaps have misinterpreted Nugent's explanations, and I do not doubt he was satisfied that his wheelchair students could be trained to cope successfully in a toilet stall designed in accord with 5.6.2. But I remain puzzled.

An interesting facet of 5.6.2 is the 'where doors are used' qualification. It was common practice for public toilets in America in the 1950s for wc compartments not to have doors, and wheelchair students on the Champaign-Urbana campus may well have not been much bothered by not having a door to close. Where there was a door, the understanding could have been that it should be self-closing, affording privacy without the door being locked, but that was not specified.

As Nugent emphasised when we talked, there was pressure from construction industry representatives, at the time the 1961 A117.1 standard was being drafted, to minimise the size of the accessible wc. But it still seems curious that the dimensions which were specified, ones which would remain unamended until 1980, came as they did.

While the toilet stall specifications for wheelchair users were peculiarly significant, they were only one component of a standard concerned with all types of disabled people. This was made clear in section 1 under the heading *Scope and Purpose*: 'This standard is concerned with non-ambulatory disabilities, semi-ambulatory disabilities, sight disabilities, hearing disabilities, disabilities of uncoordination, and ageing'. For people with hearing disabilities, the requirements were that audible warning signals should be accompanied by simultaneous visual signals, and an appropriate number of public telephones had to be suitably equipped. For blind people, there was a token requirement: 'Doors that are not intended for normal use, and that might prove dangerous if a blind person were to exit or enter by them, should be made quickly identifiable to the touch by knurling the door handle or knob'[8].

In the foreword to the 1961 A117.1 the disabled people whose characteristics and capabilities had helped inform the design prescriptions were translated into the world beyond the University of Illinois[9]:

> Approximately one out of seven people in our nation has a permanent physical disability. This segment of our population represents human resources of inestimable value and is of great economic significance to the entire nation.
>
> The most common design and construction of buildings and facilities cause problems for the physically handicapped that lessen the social and economic gains now evident in the rehabilitation of these individuals. These architectural barriers make it very difficult to project the physically handicapped into normal situations of education, recreation, and employment.

At meetings at which Tim Nugent spoke he elaborated on this theme[10]:

> Society is the origin of the problem. To return the disabled to society is the goal of rehabilitation. The biggest breakdown in the rehabilitation processes is caused by the fact that we have not properly identified the role and the responsibility of society in rehabilitation.
>
> The disabled must be projected in situations which are challenging, because potential only develops to the degree that it is challenged.
>
> Physical and architectural barriers stand in the way of total rehabilitation. They stand between the disabled and their goals. They stand between the disabled and society.
>
> Many of the disabled are afraid to venture forth because of the architectural barriers they encounter.
>
> We are basically concerned with making it possible for the great talents and resources of millions of physically disabled individuals to be put to use for the betterment of mankind by the elimination of architectural barriers.

At the October 1961 Stockholm conference I was unprepared for the explosive charge that Tim Nugent detonated. As a person with a disability I had for more than four years been a frequent user of public buildings. I encountered obstacles, but they did not worry or disturb me, and they were not, as I saw them, barriers which discriminated against me. They were simply a feature of the normal order of the built environment. It never occurred to me that anyone could be provoked and angered by them, could insist that they were universally removable, could show how that was to be done and could assure me that he was not a crackpot. Tim Nugent, it was clear, had an entirely different vision of disabled people from mine. Talking fast and animatedly at Stockholm, he had shown dozens of slides of his wheelchair students in action on the university campus at Champaign-Urbana, performing in a fashion that I had never imagined disabled people in wheelchairs could conceivably do. Remarkably, it seemed, these were the disabled people of America.

My recollection is that, aside from the exhilaration permeated by Nugent's dynamism, enthusiasm and exciting vision, I was disturbed on two counts. The first was his portrayal of the size and complexity of the constituency, of who disabled people were. We were invited to equate the proposition that one in seven of all the people in America had a permanent physical disability with the images of athletic young people in wheelchairs going about their business on the campus of the University of Illinois. Informed predictions, he said, were of increasing thousands of people paralysed each year as a result of sporting or traffic accidents. Not having met them, I had no idea that back in England there were so many paralysed people in wheelchairs; that was not the picture that I had of 'the disabled' who were to be the subject of the book I had been asked to work on. Perhaps, I thought, I had got it wrong.

The second cause for my being disturbed had to do with attitudes towards disabled people. My decent English view, inherited from my father's Norfolk family, was that disadvantaged people should be treated with concern, kindness, sympathetic understanding and compassion. Disabled people were individuals who were to be helped by dealing with their particular needs. They were not people who ought to be bunched together, treated congregately and instructed on how they should behave. Tim Nugent did not fit my way of thinking.

History is shaped by people and events, by evolutionary processes and by chance occurrences. Tim Nugent was a chance occurrence. He was a maverick, a one-off phenomenon who happened to be who he was where he was when he was. In the form he had drafted it, the 1961 A117.1 American Standard, the first-ever national design standard for making buildings accessible to disabled people, set the mould which Britain and countries elsewhere around the world would seek to emulate. It was a product based on four important premises:

1 That architectural barriers in and around buildings are a threat to disabled people, but not to able-bodied people.
2 That all disabled people can be disadvantaged by architectural barriers, and can be emancipated where they are removed.
3 That with regard to the provision of accessibility disabled people are homogeneous – their special needs can be satisfied by the application of a single package of prescriptions, by a common set of design specifications.
4 That the specifications can be precise and definitive – there are 'right' solutions.

The access standard which Tim Nugent had given to the world was a neat set of generally applicable instructions for making buildings accessible. The effect from then on was that disabled people could look at buildings or their plans and say firmly, 'yes, it's accessible', or 'no, it's not accessible'. Accessibility was good, inaccessibility was bad. Accessibility represented equal treatment and equal opportunity. Inaccessibility represented discrimination and exclusion. In later years the 1961 American Standard was to be deployed by disability activists as a vital instrument in their campaign for civil rights for disabled people. Averse as he was to special treatment, Tim Nugent was never an advocate of disability civil rights legislation. And not himself being a disabled person who fought for disability rights, he is not in America now numbered among the heroes who forced the passage of the Americans with Disabilities Act of 1990.

Had Tim Nugent never happened, a movement for the elimination of architectural barriers to disabled people might well have been fostered elsewhere by others. But had it been, and had it been differently engineered (as surely it would have been), I cannot imagine it could have made an impact on the world as colossal as that made by his legacy, the 1961 American Standard.

From 1949 until his retirement in September 1985 the management of the rehabilitation education centre at Champaign-Urbana was Tim Nugent's life's work. On two occasions when I was in America, in 1966 and 1984, he invited me to visit and stay at his home. I went with him to see the work being done at the centre, and met and talked with his staff and students. At other times over the years we met and talked at conferences in Britain, Europe and America. The last occasion when we met was in London in September 1994, when with his wife Jeanette he was on his way to Belgium for the anniversary reunion of the military unit with which he had fought 50 years earlier in the Battle of the Bulge. His home in retirement is at Champaign.

3 The welfare path that I took

From 1961 through to the early 1980s an ideological divide separated me from Tim Nugent. I describe it by saying that he was a convinced macroist whereas I was an unreformed microist. It was to communicate my own shifting stance on the business of designing for the disabled that around 1983 I invoked the terms 'macro' and 'micro' to describe the contrast between the treat-as-normal and treat-as-different starting positions. The macro doctrine is that disabled people should be treated as normal people, that they can be accommodated by normal provision in buildings, and that special provision ought not to be made for them. They are, in accord with Nugent's principles, mainstream customers. The micro doctrine is that disabled people are different, that they ought to be treated as different, and that special – and sometimes exclusive – facilities should be provided for them. They are welfare customers.

At Stockholm I was unable to comprehend or grasp the significance of the doctrinal leap that Nugent had made. To my mind, and as I later learnt to the mind of all English people imbued with the culture of social welfare, there could be only one way of treating the needs of disabled people, the microist way. When in October 1961 I set to work on the preparation of the book which was to become the first edition of *Designing for the Disabled*, it was with the presumption that disabled people ought to be treated as different people, as people with special needs for whom special provision should be made. With a microist stance which asked what architects could particularly do for disabled people, the aim was to set out recommendations for provision in buildings, which, when applied corporately or selectively, would benefit people who had a disability of one kind or another. The checklist syndrome came into play. 'What can architects do for wheelchair users?' was the leading question. Then, 'What can they do for ambulant disabled people?', followed by, 'What for blind people?', 'What for deaf people?', 'What for mentally handicapped people?', and 'What for whoever else among those who can be categorised as 'disabled'?'

From this perspective, disabled people were *them*. For the writing of the first edition of the book – and then the second and third – I perceived my brief to be the generation of advice to architects on what they could do for *them*, the disabled. I stood on the architect's ground. I did not acknowledge that I was myself a disabled person. I did not feel I had to. I was looking at the picture from my architect perspective. And the commission to publish the book came from the Royal Institute of British Architects, and what they wanted was a guidance manual telling architects what to do about *them*, the disabled.

At the Stockholm conference I had been a novice. Other participants, from Britain and other countries in Europe and elsewhere in the world, genuinely were experts in the disability field, and from then on many became valued colleagues and advisers. Two from Britain were Mr O. A. Denly, known as Denny Denly, and Lady Hamilton – Pix to her friends. Mr Denly had contracted polio while serving as a naval officer in 1945, and subsequently in his wheelchair became a hospital administrator. In 1948 he founded the Invalid Tricycle Association, a splendidly successful consumer organization which later became the Disabled Drivers Association. In 1962 he set up the Joint Committee on Mobility for the Disabled, and from 1967 to 1970 was director of Access for the Disabled, a campaigning enterprise which Lady Hamilton of the Central Council for the Disabled invited him to undertake. In Stockholm in 1961 he was excited to meet Tim Nugent, and was thrilled to learn from him how simple it was to take his wheelchair up and down escalators.

Lady Hamilton was the wife of Sir Patrick Hamilton, a baronet who was a prominent City businessman. With no children, their London home was in Cheyne Walk by the river in Chelsea. Historical family connections were represented by Nelson and Hardy, two Staffordshire Bull Terriers who roamed the house and were taken out by the chauffeur in the Bentley to be exercised. In 1955 Sir Patrick's sister had been stricken by a stroke, bringing with it chronic disability. Pix Hamilton was keen to help enable her sister-in-law to manage independently in her home, and enquired where a consultant architect skilled in designing for the disabled could be found. She was disturbed to find there was none, and her life now had a mission. In 1956 she joined the Central Council for the Care of Cripples, at that time a non-proactive agency which served as a post office for the hundreds of local voluntary agencies around the country which concerned themselves with the welfare of disabled people; it was subsequently to become the Central Council for the Disabled and is now the Royal Association for Disability and Rehabilitation. She energized its staff and brought new perspectives to its work. To fertilize her ideas she could call on the resources of the Eleanor Hamilton Trust, the family trust set up as a memorial to Sir Patrick's mother.

Through the 1960s and 1970s Lady Hamilton dominated the arena of disability and architecture, with drive and determination on one hand and philanthropy on a grand scale on the other. In 1962 she set up an exhibition 'Towards housing the disabled' at the Royal Society of Health[1] which displayed an imaginative demonstration dwelling designed by Wycliffe Noble, an architect with whom I would have close links over the years which followed. Through the Design Centre she set up a programme for evaluating product design from the viewpoint of the disabled user. In 1963 she set up the Central Council's Disabled Living Activities Group, which as the Disabled Living Foundation later became an independent organization. In 1997 I still keep in touch with her – now a widow, she lives in the family home in Cambridge.

In Stockholm in 1961 Lady Hamilton was enchanted by Tim Nugent, and was determined that his new gospel should be proclaimed in Britain. She invited him to London, cultivated the ground and arranged for him to speak at a public meeting held at the Royal Institute of British Architects on 9 October 1962[2]. From that meeting stemmed the decision to set up a British Standards Institution committee which, with myself doing the drafting, would produce a national access standard on the pattern of Nugent's A117.1; the result was the issuing in 1967 of CP96 *Access for the Disabled to Buildings*[3]. Also at Lady Hamilton's instigation, the Ministry of Housing and Local Government enlisted me to help draft an official circular *Access to Public Buildings for the Disabled*, issued jointly with the Ministry of Public Buildings and Works and the Ministry of Health in 1965[4].

The most valuable professional advice I received in the course of putting material together for the first edition of the book came from architects and sociologists in the Ministry of Housing's Research and Development Group, set up in 1959 under the direction of Cleeve Barr, the Ministry's chief architect. Sheltered housing for old people was the subject of the group's first development programme. Barbara Adams, one of the two sociologists in the group, carried out an exploratory social survey[5] to inform the brief for the group's architects, who designed and then supervised the construction of a group of flatlets in Stevenage. The architects who worked on the scheme, among them David Parkes, Peter Randall and Pat Tindale, were concerned to ensure that its planning, design and detailing would be responsive to the special needs of frail elderly people[6]. They were keen to discuss their ideas about designing for the disabled with me, and to advise me as I worked on my book.

The preparation of the first edition of *Designing for the Disabled* was a straightforward task. It was facilitated by my having only a superficial appreciation of the subject, by there not being anyone who had tackled the topic previously, by there being few people in Britain who knew much about it, and by my ignorance of the techniques of respectable scientific research. The Stockholm conference gave me a solid start and a range of valuable contacts which set me up for meetings and visits in Britain and enabled me to make an informative trip to Holland, Denmark, Sweden and Norway in 1962. It was then a matter of plagiarising the few relevant publications that I could find and giving the material a coherent structure. Maurice Goldring of the RIBA did a speedy and excellent job preparing it for the printers, and with 236 pages it was published in November 1963.

The idea that Duncan Guthrie and Gordon Ricketts had in mind when they conceived the project in 1961 was that a practising architect would spend two years learning all about the subject and, having become the acknowledged national expert on it, would be well placed to launch a specialist private practice. I had no ambition to do so, and a more attractive prospect was soon in view. The book had been well received, and Duncan Guthrie was suggesting that his fund might sponsor me to undertake further research on the topic of designing for the disabled. I knew exactly what I wanted to do.

From an academic base and in an academic fashion I had written a book about disabled people, and that was sufficient for me to be accounted an authority on the subject. In actuality I still had no idea who disabled people really were. I had gathered anecdotal impressions from rehabilitation centres, residential homes and hospitals I had visited, and also from individual disabled people to whom I had been introduced. But I did not know whether they were reliable impressions, and I suspected they were not. The urge that I had was to find out, to learn how disabled people managed in their homes, how they coped with the practical business of daily living, how mobile they were, how they travelled when they went out, what kind of public buildings they used and what problems they encountered when they did so. Was it genuinely the case that architectural barriers stood in their way? In particular I wanted to find out about wheelchair users. The image that had been fostered by Tim Nugent's vivid report of his wheelchair students cavorting on the campus of the University of Illinois was of hundreds of active young paraplegics, frustrated because architectural barriers stood in the way of their aspirations. Were they, unknown to me, out there in their thousands all around Britain? And how many of them would be found in a typical urban community?

I needed to find a town where I could conduct a survey of disabled people, the plan being that my then wife and I would move out of London and live there. To assess possible candidates I set out a list of criteria. It should be a large town, with examples of all principal types of public buildings; preferably a county borough controlling all local authority services; a town with its own outlying population catchment area; with a well-reputed architect's department, and perhaps with a university. It should be within a couple of hours or so of London by train, and it must be a congenial place to live in. Only one place fitted – it was Norwich. A meeting was arranged at the RIBA to which the city architect David Percival was invited, and he agreed to put the idea to his chief officer colleagues. On a day in early January 1964 I travelled to Norwich, and over lunch discussed what I had in mind with him, the town clerk, the city treasurer and the chief welfare officer. On the basis that the survey programme would take three years, that the project would be funded by Duncan Guthrie's Polio Research Fund and that a small office in the city hall could be allocated to me, the enterprise was put into operation. Towards the end of March 1964 my wife and I moved to Norwich.

The choice of Norwich as the venue for the project was amply vindicated. The survey, I decided, would concentrate on wheelchair users. To tackle this task I was greatly helped by George Meredith, who in 1963 had been appointed the city's chief welfare officer*. With the cooperation of his team, in particular Elizabeth Barnes, his adviser on services for physically handicapped people, he arranged for me to have the names and addresses of welfare department clients who were wheelchair users. He helped also by encouraging the regional office of the Ministry of Health to assist by letting me have the names and addresses of all the people in the district to whom Ministry wheelchairs had been issued. Local voluntary organizations were also pleased to give me the names and addresses of local people to whom they had supplied wheelchairs on loan, or who they knew had obtained chairs privately. With guidance from Roy Emerson, the recently appointed Professor of Sociology at the new University of East Anglia, I drafted and piloted my questionnaires. Armed with these, I went out to visit wheelchair users who lived in the city; without any certification papers I walked up garden paths, knocked on doors and was invited in. Wherever I went I was made welcome, and almost invariably the people I met were delighted to answer my questions and tell me about their experiences.

As well as the survey of wheelchair users I undertook a survey of disabled drivers in and around Norwich, and a study of blind people. From my explorations in Norwich, from meeting disabled people, talking to them and learning from them at first hand about how they coped with disability, how they managed at home, what obstacles were in their way when they sought to use public buildings, and the hazards that were associated with their usage of public toilets, I acquired a fund of knowledge. The capital that I acquired in Norwich served to inform all my subsequent professional work in the disability field. I had a picture of disabled people, their characteristics, their circumstances and their problems, a picture which was reliable, built up as it was on sound empirical inquiry. I had a unique resource of solid information and data, not a medley of suppositions drawn from impressions, surmises, legend and mythology.

I devised two questionnaires for the Norwich survey of wheelchair users, one on mobility and the usage of public buildings and facilities, the other on housing arrangements, home management and the activities of daily living. In the form in which they were initially drafted they reflected the preconceptions about wheelchair users that I had acquired during the two

* In 1971, with the implementation of the recommendations of the Seebohm report, Mr Meredith was to become the Director of Social Services in Norwich, and in 1974, with the restructuring of local government, the director for Norfolk county.

years I had spent producing the first edition of *Designing for the Disabled*, preconceptions derived from the images depicted by Tim Nugent and my impressions of the various people in wheelchairs that I had met. They were of the kind that I now observe are crystallised in disability mythology: that wheelchair users are chairbound and cannot walk; that many are young people who are active and are determined to cope independently; that many are paralysed as a consequence of sporting or road accidents. I recall one significant preconception. I had learnt that there were paraplegics, meaning disabled people whose lesion was relatively low down the spinal column and whose lower limbs only were paralysed, and there were tetraplegics, meaning those whose lesion was high up and whose upper as well as lower limbs were paralysed. In the false expectation that I would meet many of these disabled people in Norwich I drafted an interview response box with codes for lesions of different levels. In the event, one person only, a woman in her 20s, had been paralysed as the result of a road accident, and none on account of an accident of any other kind.

In 1964 no programmes for making public buildings accessible to disabled people had been initiated anywhere in Britain, and there was virtually no awareness of the issue. For the survey I made in Norwich I interviewed 284 wheelchair users, with a list of 28 different building types which I asked whether they had used[7]. Seventy-seven, or 27 per cent, said that in the previous 12 months they had used none at all[8]. A question which followed was which types of buildings they would like to see made easier for people in wheelchairs to use, with four choices on offer. In response 180, or 64 per cent, had no preferences, saying they were unconcerned[9]. Of the 21 building types which did score, cinemas ranked in second place with 17 votes, followed by restaurants (16), local shops (15), churches (12) and department stores (10). But way out at the top of the list with 64 votes was public toilets.

In the mid-1960s the idea of public lavatories specially designed to cater for disabled people was unheard of. The inaccessibility of public lavatories, and the frustrations, embarrassments and calamities that occurred in consequence, was the dominant theme of my conversations with wheelchair users in Norwich who were keen to go out and about. It was absolutely out on its own at the head of the agenda of practical difficulties they encountered when using public buildings. It was the issue which most urgently called for action. And it was from my interviews with severely disabled people in Norwich that the British cult of unisex toilets for disabled people stemmed. I quote from my report on the Norwich survey in the third edition of *Designing for the Disabled*[10]:

> Among severely handicapped people a regular lament was that the cultural scheme of segregated compartments in public lavatories for men and women meant that in any normal situation it was impossible for a husband to help his wife (or vice versa) to transfer from the wheelchair to the wc seat and back again. This was a job which many husbands did at home, and which they

> would readily have done in public lavatories had there been a unisex compartment. One extremely handicapped woman was always pushed out in her wheelchair and did not as a rule get out of it. Because of the conventional structure of wc compartments in public lavatories she was obliged when she went on outings from Norwich to take a stick and a tripod walking aid with her (in addition to her wheelchair) in order that she could be assisted into wc compartments on her feet. When her husband had taken his holiday earlier in the year they had made a series of day trips by train to Yarmouth, Lowestoft and Cromer. Because she could not cope independently and her husband could not help her into women's wc compartments they had to arrange for a friend (female) to take her holiday at the same time as themselves in order that she could be helped into public lavatories.

The picture that emerged from Norwich illuminated the need for special 'welfare' provision among severely disabled people who used, or sought to use, public buildings. To use buildings they needed manageable toilet facilities. Not only did they need to get their wheelchair into the wc compartment, they needed another person to help them manage, and the other person was commonly their spouse. What they wanted, and never found, was a unisex toilet facility specially designed and equipped to suit disabled people such as themselves. Arising from the evidence that I gathered, a practical initiative that I worked on in collaboration with the city's environmental health department was the adaptation of the public toilet on Castle Hill to provide what I believe was the first unisex toilet facility for disabled people in the country. As a historic monument it no longer survives; it was removed in the early 1990s when the hill was carved up to make way for the Castle Mall shopping centre.

In Britain today, 30 years later, there are thousands of unisex toilets for the disabled. Signposted at roadsides in towns and villages, they are scattered across urban and rural landscapes. In every new public building subject to the Part M building regulation there is at least one of them. In other buildings where there are public toilets they have been fitted in. In or alongside historic buildings a place has been found for them. They have proliferated. Nowhere else in the world have they been planted as densely as in Britain. They are an emblem of a caring society, of a society that is keen to help disabled people and likes to advertise how genuinely concerned it is to do so.

The specially designed and equipped unisex toilet for the disabled serves a real need, one that was unrecognised prior to my inquiries in Norwich. I refer back to the years 1961 to 1963 when I worked on the first edition of *Designing for the Disabled*. In the book I concentrated on domestic environments, and a series of diagrams indicated how wc compartments and bathrooms might be planned with space inside for a wheelchair user to transfer to and from the wc. I drew on the advice I was given by medical specialists and occupational therapists, not one of whom noted that disabled people had corresponding requirements when using public buildings. Guidance on provision for disabled people in public buildings was presented as an appendix to the book, and in drafting it I was influenced by the authoritative prescriptions in Tim Nugent's 1961 American Standard. Interestingly, my advice was, 'In public buildings where allowance is made for wheelchair users, provision for a lateral approach to the wc is not essential'[11]. Nowhere in the 1963 book was there any suggestion that in public buildings unisex facilities for disabled people were wanted.

The initiative which stemmed from the RIBA meeting addressed by Tim Nugent in October 1962 was the preparation, on the lines of the 1961 American Standard, of a British Standard code of practice on access for the disabled to buildings. During 1963 Wycliffe Noble, consultant architect to the Central Council for the Disabled, negotiated the setting up of the British Standards Institution committee which would tackle the task. Ronald Fielding, an architect who had built up his own substantial private practice, was appointed chairman of the code drafting committee, and I took on the job of drafting material for the code.

A prominent item on the agenda was the specifications for a standardised unisex toilet facility. With only theorised models to draw on and no relevant design data, the need was for an informative research exercise. We enlisted John and Lorna Angell, students at Birmingham School of Architecture, who were keen to tackle the project for their fifth year thesis, and with the cooperation of Dr Philip Nichols and his team at the Mary Marlborough Lodge rehabilitation centre at Oxford a test rig was set up with wc and wash basin and adjustable walls and grabrail positions[12]. Important functional criteria were that there should be space within the compartment for frontal transfer from wheelchair to wc seat or lateral transfer to one side, and that the wash basin should be reachable by a person seated on the wc. Beyond that a series of assumptions was made: that, subject to meeting the functional criteria, the overall size of the facility should be as small as it reasonably could be; that, in accord with the normal location of plumbing services for a row of wc compartments, the wc should be set on the rear wall opposite the entrance door; that the door should open out; and, with criteria for wheelchair users being paramount, that the wc seat should be at the same level as a typical wheelchair seat.

From the tests made with wheelchair users at Oxford the specifications were agreed for what became the CP96 unisex toilet (Figure 3.1), a facility which, with internal dimensions 1370 × 1750mm, was nearly twice as spacious as the toilet stall for wheelchair users prescribed in the 1961 American Standard. CP96: Part 1: 1967 *Access for the disabled to buildings, Part 1 General Recommendations*[13] was issued in July 1967. Aside from its being the original British standard on access for the disabled it was significant for two reasons. The first was that, by presenting specifications for a unisex toilet as the national standard for toilet provision for wheelchair users, it set accessibility controls in Britain on a firm microistic course. The second was its format, or what its format should have been. The intention was that it would be issued in two parts, the first presenting the design standards, the second the criteria for their application to different building types.

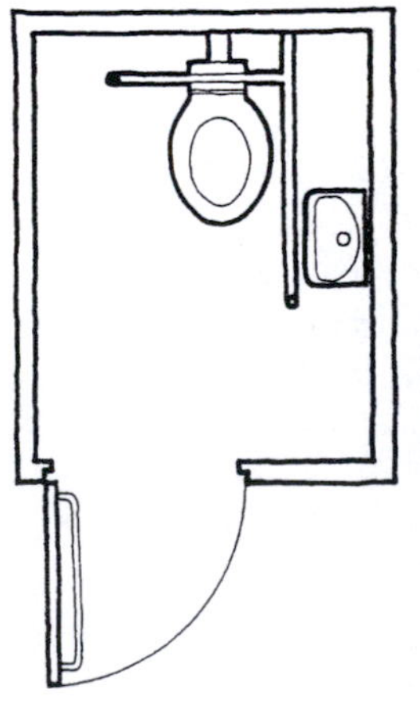

3.1 The CP96 unisex toilet

The model we worked on was the formulation I had presented in the first edition of *Designing for the Disabled*, published in November 1963, a few months before we began work on the code. Public buildings were considered in an appendix to the book, the note being that there was a lack of evidence to inform recommendations[14]. The outcome was a brief one-page introduction followed by four pages under the heading *Public buildings: Suggested provision for the Disabled*, and then two pages under the heading *Public buildings: Design specifications*. For each of 39 building types the suggested provision was summarized, with varying provision being advised for 'semi-ambulants' and wheelchair users, and similarly for visitors/customers and staff/employees; in each case there were references to the particular design specifications to be observed.

The foreword to CP96 *Part 1 General recommendations* emphasised that this was the first part only:

> The Code drafting committee is undertaking a comprehensive investigation of the provisions for specific building types and these will be issued as subsequent parts of this Code. They will be related to the disablement categories and design provisions contained in this document, and will detail the provisions which need to be made in individual building types. In the light of the investigations of building types some of the general recommendations may be modified; such modifications will be made either by the issue of amendments to Part 1 of this Code or by a revised edition.

As any who have served on British Standards Institution committees will know, the preparation of a new code of practice is a protracted and tiresome business, requiring prolonged dedication to the task from members and the secretariat. From mid-1963 when a code on access was first proposed it took four years to get the first part published. Part 2 threatened to be even more challenging and problematical. The committee felt it needed a break; it would wait for feedback on Part 1 before starting work on Part 2.

The 1963 first edition of *Designing for the Disabled* was subtitled *A Manual of Technical Information*, and that was a fair description of it. So far as it had any philosophical platform it reflected the ethos of Tim Nugent, exemplified by a paragraph in the introduction asserting that disabled people could manage independently in suitably designed buildings[15]. Norwich came up with a wealth of evidence that to my mind made Nugent's stance insupportable, most notably the findings demonstrating the lack of athleticism among wheelchair users, their dependence on others to help them use public buildings and the need that many had for unisex toilet facilities. Among the 284 wheelchair users interviewed for the Norwich survey those who came near to accordance with Nugent's prototypical model were in a tiny minority; only six were able in their wheelchairs to go out and use public buildings independently.

The second edition of the book, prepared while I was working in Norwich, was published in September 1967. In its 33-page commentary I put forward the view that the doctrine of independent management ought not to control architectural design decision-making; in that context I was critical of the 1961 American Standard, and commented on its role as an instrument in the campaign against architectural barriers[16]:

> The very considerable achievements of the campaign and the widespread attention it has received have disguised the shortcomings of the code itself and the fact that as a working tool for architects it is defective.

Itemized complaints followed, and then the salient cause of my ire:

> The toilet stalls advocated for wheelchair users are not, if given minimum standards, large enough for a wheelchair to enter. They are suitable only for relatively non-handicapped chairbound people who are capable of performing wheelchair gymnastics. People who are severely handicapped or who need personal assistance to transfer from the wheelchair are excluded. The accessibility of toilet facilities is of critical importance to disabled people, and it should be appreciated that buildings designed in conformity with the minimum standards of the American code will be unusable by those who are most handicapped.

The RIBA arranged for the second edition of the book to be published in America by McGraw Hill of New York. Leon Chatelain, the eminent American architect who had been chairman of the 1961 A117.1 committee[17], was among those who were disturbed by it. He was an honorary fellow of the Royal Institute of British Architects, and I was told that, when in London shortly after the book had been published, he called to protest personally to Gordon Ricketts; the RIBA, he said, ought not to have permitted itself to be associated with the book or my views.

Thirty years later I feel that the determinedly microistic stance I displayed in the second edition of the book was, given my comprehension of the subject at that time, justifiable. It was not until some 15 years later that I began to articulate the crucial concepts of macroism and microism, and it was understandable that in 1967, imbued as I was with the social welfare ethos of England, the way to help disabled people had to be the 'for the disabled' way. If there were people who could only use a wc when they were assisted by a wife or husband, and could not on that account engage in normal community activities, the proper response was to advocate the production of special for-the-disabled unisex toilet facilities.

I could not sympathise – or empathise – with Tim Nugent's radical vision. I recall a public argument that we had at an international conference in Oxford in 1965. We followed it, to the surprise of others who were with us, by happily going out together and spending the evening at a pub by the river. He genuinely believed that it was only because of architectural barriers that disabled people were stuck at home and were not able to go out and use public buildings. I told him about the severely handicapped people I had met in Norwich. They mattered, I insisted, and they could not possibly manage the kind of toilet facilities that were advised in A117.1. Yes, they could, he replied, they could have done so had they been properly trained.

With CP96, Britain had in 1967 an officially authorised access guidance document. Its most notable feature was its specifications for unisex toilet facilities, and, in response to calls from Lady Hamilton and others, the Ministry of Housing and Local Government agreed that a government circular on public toilet provision for the disabled would be in order. I was asked to draft its practical recommendations, and did so with help from two architect colleagues, Wycliffe Noble and Felix Walter.

Circular 33/68, *Design of Public Conveniences with Facilities for the Disabled*[18], was issued jointly by the Ministry of Housing and the Welsh Office on 24 July 1968 and distributed to all local authorities in England and Wales. With one or two marginal amplifications the practical recommendations followed precisely those of CP96. Nothing was said in the circular about suitable supplementary toilet facilities for ambulant disabled people, nor about the desirability of normal provision in a public convenience being accessible to disabled people. The principles that the circular established for a wc facility for disabled people were (1) that it should be separate from facilities for normal people; (2) that it should be special for the disabled and exclusively for the use of disabled people; (3) that it should be 'unisex'; (4) that it should come in a 'correct' standardised form; and (5) that with carefully formulated prescriptions for its planning, design and equipment it could cater equally for independent wheelchair users, assisted wheelchair users and ambulant disabled people.

Across Britain, local authorities and voluntary organizations concerned with the welfare of disabled people welcomed Circular 33/68. From 1968 on, both for municipal lavatories and public toilets in public buildings, the routine was established. To cater for disabled people, there would be a special unisex facility. For everyone else, there would be normal toilet facilities, with wc compartments planned and designed in accord with conventional custom. It was only the special unisex facility, not the normal provision, which would be subject to design prescriptions. The unisex facility, although commonly adjacent to normal provision, would be set apart, and from 1980 it was to become customary for it to be locked with a special key which would give disabled people who were keyholders access to it. On its door, and on signs in the neighbourhood indicating its whereabouts, the symbol of access would be displayed, indicating its exclusivity.

The wc facility for handicapped people advised in the 1961 American Standard was, albeit in a less commodious form, normal and integrated; in America there would as a rule be no cause to display the access symbol with its message 'Here are special toilet facilities for the disabled' – that would be superfluous. Disabled people there were treated as mainstream customers, whereas in Britain, with its CP96 facility, they were treated as welfare customers. By exposing the issue of public toilets, severely disabled people and the unmet demand for unisex toilet facilities, I had a significant role in moving Britain towards access legislation governed by the ethos of welfarism. Had I not been involved, the outcome, I am sure, would have been no different. When it came to dealing with provision for disabled people in buildings it was inevitable that Britain would go down the welfare track; when legislation was introduced, as it was in 1970 with the Chronically Sick Act, it was, unsurprisingly, welfare legislation. Interestingly, America could have taken the same course.

4 America: into the mainstream

Going back a hundred years and more before Tim Nugent arrived on the disability stage, social welfare was not an issue that the United States federal government wished to be troubled with. Following the civil war of the 1860s a small bureau was set up in the government's war department to administer welfare for war casualties, but its life was short. Some 50 years later renewed action was prompted in the aftermath of the First World War, and in 1920 a programme was established to help disabled veterans return to normal life. Placed under the control of the Federal Board for Vocational Education, its role was to promote rehabilitation and retraining for active employment. Staffed by rehabilitation counsellors, who, like other government workers, were becoming professionalised, the board, as the Office of Vocational Rehabilitation, was transferred in 1939 to the Federal Security Agency, subsequently to become the US Department of Health, Education and Welfare.

It was around 1939 that Paul Strachan, who in his early working years had been a vigorous trade union lobbyist, began to campaign for legislative action to help disabled people[1]. Following a train accident he had spent some seven years in hospital and had a spinal injury, a heart complaint and was totally deaf. In 1942 he formed the American Federation of Handicapped Persons and became its president. The idea he had conceived when in hospital in 1940 was the observance of a National Employ the Handicapped Week; to formally inaugurate it he enlisted support from congressmen who sponsored a Congressional Resolution which, having passed through the House and Senate, was signed into law by President Truman in August 1945. The first 'Week' campaign was launched in October 1945 and, prompted by Truman when the third annual proclamation for it was signed, the first meeting of the President's Committee on National Employ the Handicapped Week was held on 27 August 1947; this was later to become the President's Committee on Employment of the Handicapped and subsequently the President's Committee on Employment of People with Disabilities[2].

With the emphasis on employment opportunities, Strachan campaigned to introduce civil rights legislation for disabled people. Impressed by the terms of the British Disabled Persons Employment Act of 1944, he proposed legislation which would be applied to all companies awarded federal government contracts or grants, bringing with it a scheme for cash grants for severely disabled people who could not be rehabilitated into employment. He worked on the draft of a bill with officials in the US Department of Labor; they liked the idea of treating disabled people as a separate group (in effect a new 'union') within the workforce and giving them special rights. The Office of Vocational Rehabilitation was hostile; with their trained professional staff it was their job, they insisted, to help all people in need of special welfare services. What followed was a power battle between the Department of Labor and the Department of Health, Education and Welfare for control of vocational rehabilitation. President Truman was called in to adjudicate; his decision, influenced by a desire to restrain the increasing power of militant unionists, was that it should continue to be managed by the welfare professionals in the Department of Health, Education and Welfare. The bill that Paul Strachan had fought to introduce was lost; dismayed that the 'do-gooders' had prevailed, and no longer able to exercise any effective influence on government policy, he resigned in March 1952 from the influential committee which he had helped to create, the President's Committee on Employment of the Handicapped.

Britain has no civil rights edicts in its unwritten constitution. Nor, as in America, is the executive side of government separate from the legislature. In Britain there are three arms to the constitution, the Sovereign, the House of Lords and the House of Commons, and all citizens are subjects of the reigning sovereign – they do not, in effect, have any inherent 'rights'; such entitlements as they have are bestowed by legislation and can be taken away. With adversarial parliamentary debate there is in Britain a system of collective Cabinet responsibility, each minister appointed by the Prime Minister being accountable for the business of his compartment of government. Before a general election, each party presents its political manifesto and sets out its agenda for legislation, and to keep the legislation neat and tidy it helps greatly if it comes within the province of one minister and a single government department. Responsibilities between departments are broadly divided according to occupational spheres, and within a sphere an entrepreneurial minister or policy administrator, subject to the confines of government policy, may have substantial scope for shaping legislation in the way that he or she wishes.

Legislation which deals with people's interests across rather than within spheres is not encouraged by British Cabinet ministers or their officials. Where, in a particular sphere, the government does not move to introduce such legislation, the course open to the member of parliament as a policy entrepreneur who wants action is the medium of a private member's bill. The opportunities for success are limited; aside from being subject to the lottery of an annual ballot the government can, if it does not like a particular private member's bill, simply block it. The determined entrepreneur can, however, be emboldened and encouraged by the adversarial form of British politics; a determined single-issue pressure group can enlist powerful backing among MPs, the pressure exerted being of a force that the government of the day may not comfortably be able to resist. It was thus through private members' bills that transdepartmental legislation for disabled people came to be enacted, first by Alf Morris with what was to be the Chronically Sick and Disabled Persons Act of 1970, and then by Dafydd Wigley with the Disabled Persons Act of 1981.

In the United States there is federal legislation and state legislation, the scope of state legislation being ordained by federal statutes enacted by Congress – the Senate and the House of Representatives. State governments are jealous of their rights under the constitution, and in their domain the US President cannot interfere. Federal legislation in areas where it can be directly applied supervenes all state legislation (and also municipal regulations), although on the domestic front its scope is limited. The principal plank, set out in the American Declaration of Independence, is civil rights: 'We hold these truths to be self-evident, that all men are created equal, that they are endowed by their Creator with certain unalienable rights, that among these are life, liberty and the pursuit of happiness'.

Under civil rights legislation the federal government can exercise substantial authority over state and municipal public works and services programmes; it does this by the conditions which it applies to the awarding of federal government financial grants or loans, and in cases where programmes rely, as they frequently do, on federal funding for their realisation the control is effectively total.

Candidates for the American presidency campaign with a manifesto for legislation which, subject to the approval of Congress, they commit themselves to introducing. As chief executive of the federal government, the President appoints all senior administrators in all government departments, and they advise him about the legislation needed to put his policies into effect. On this basis, much of the legislation enacted by Congress is drafted by policy administrators accountable to the President. There is a second route by which legislation can be introduced. Any Senator or House Representative can present a bill, and with sponsorship from other congressmen can steer it through the House and the Senate so that it becomes an Act. The President can then exercise his veto, but under pressure may be obliged to sign it into law.

Tim Nugent's pioneering A117.1 American Standard for making buildings accessible to disabled people was dated 31 October 1961 when it was published, although it was not until early 1962 that it was widely distributed. It was acclaimed as news of it spread across America: Nugent's moral stance – the emancipation and enablement theme, along with the emphasis on self-help and independence – struck a vibrant national chord. The call for action was endorsed by President Kennedy in a November 1961 letter to the President of the National Society of Crippled Children and Adults: 'The acceptance and adoption of these standards now becomes the business of citizens and governmental authorities everywhere. I am sure they will rise to the challenge. . . . I can further assure you that the agencies and departments of the Federal Government that come under the jurisdiction of my office will give full support to this worthy project'[3].

In the Rehabilitation Services Administration of the US Department of Health, Education and Welfare Mary E. Switzer was the Commissioner of Vocational Rehabilitation. Following Paul Strachan's failure to get disability employment legislation 'out of welfare', all federal matters to do with disabled people were handled by the Office of Vocational Rehabilitation, and it was therefore Miss Switzer's job to energize action in response to President Kennedy's call. She did so by funding a nation-wide promotional campaign; a team of organizers appointed by her office went to each state, where, working in collaboration with the affiliate agency of the National Society for Crippled Children and Adults and the State Governor's Committee on Employment of the Handicapped, they helped set up local architectural barriers committees[4].

In 1962 the federal government had no legislation which it could invoke to enforce the implementation of the A117.1 design standards. State governments could more readily respond, and they did so swiftly and decisively. In May 1963 South Carolina, not as a rule in the vanguard of radical progress, was the first state to legislate. The South Carolina Act of 1963 required that all new public buildings sponsored by the state or any subdivision of the state must be designed with reference to A117.1, and this was recommended by the Council of State Governments as a legislative model to all states in the Union[5]. By November 1965 legislation mandating compliance with A117.1 had been passed by 21 states[6], and by July 1966 31 states had taken legislative action[7].

Mary Switzer had made it clear that architectural barriers was a welfare issue, and she looked to consolidate the authority that her office had on the federal front. An opportunity came with the passage through Congress of what was to be the Vocational Rehabilitation Act Amendments of 1965 – legislation heralded by President Johnson as presenting 'a new life for the disabled'[8]. The Act authorised federal government funding for a whole range of rehabilitation services, and into it was inserted a section authorising the Department of Health, Education and Welfare to set up a National Commission on Architectural Barriers to Rehabilitation of the Handicapped. Leon Chatelain was appointed its chairman and the executive secretariat was headed by Kathleen Arneson, Miss Switzer's deputy in the Vocational Rehabilitation Office.

Design for ALL Americans, the report of the Commission, was published in December 1967. Its principal recommendation was for the enactment of a federal law or laws which would, among other recommended duties, 'make the Department of Health, Education and Welfare responsible for the establishment and promulgation of Government-wide policies, procedures and specifications, and their enforcement, to achieve at least minimum standards of accessibility and use in public buildings'[9]. In the event, none of the recommendations made by the Commission was acted upon, and after

1967 the Department of Health, Education and Welfare, so far as legislation relating to disabled people and the accessibility of buildings was concerned, was marginalised. The reason was that Hugh Gallagher had intervened.

4.1 Hugh Gallagher

In 1952 at the age of 19, when he was an engineering student at the Massachusetts Institute of Technology at Boston, Hugh Gallagher had become permanently disabled as a result of polio. He spent two years in hospital, and from then on was always dependent on a wheelchair for mobility. In 1954, instead of resuming his MIT engineering course, he moved to Claremont McKenna College in California to study journalism and literature. In 1956 he enquired whether he might apply for a Rhodes scholarship to Oxford and was told no – he was not eligible because he was not fit in mind and body. He could, however, apply for a Marshall scholarship. He was awarded one, with a place at Trinity College Oxford. Virtually all the university's lecture rooms were inaccessible to him, as were most college amenities – there was, for example, no bath he could use. But he persevered, and in 1959 graduated with a degree in Philosophy, Politics and Economics. On his return to Washington he worked on Capitol Hill as a legislative assistant in the Senate, and in 1963 joined the office of Bob Bartlett, Democratic Senator for Alaska. He served also for a while on the staff of the White House, and in November 1965 when I first met him was developing with Senator Bartlett his ideas for the first piece of federal legislation which would deal with architectural barriers.

Gallagher had firm views on the form that legislation mandating the accessibility of public buildings should take: it ought not to be regarded as a welfare matter, and should not be the business of the welfare arm of government. Instead, in the context of civil rights, the Architectural Barriers Bill which Senator Bartlett would introduce would be mainstream legislation. It would be considered by the Senate Committee on Public Works, and the lead role in its implementation would be placed with the General Services Administration, the department responsible for the design and construction of new federal government buildings across America, along with the management, maintenance and leasing of existing buildings. Introduced in January 1967, the brief bill authorised the General Services Administrator to devise accessibility regulations for public buildings, the requirement being that federal grants and loans for the construction of public buildings should be conditional on compliance with them[10].

Mary Switzer was not pleased; architectural barriers, she insisted, was the business of the Vocational Rehabilitation Administration, and no legislation should be considered until Leon Chatelain's National Commission had reported. When Bartlett's bill was presented, she argued that the federal government lead should be taken by Vocational Rehabilitation, not by General Services. Bartlett and Gallagher were not to be dissuaded, and, with backing from disability organizations and many congressmen, Senate hearings continued through 1967. Differences surfaced on what was known as the agency turf issue; other government departments were troubled about the General Services Administration's lead implementation role, and each wanted to oversee compliance in its own sphere.

As passed by Congress in 1968, the Architectural Barriers Act required that all buildings constructed, leased or financed by the federal government should be accessible to physically disabled persons, giving them a right to use such buildings, whether as employees or as visitors on business. On account of the tensions there had been during the passage of the bill the responsibility for issuing compliance regulations was not, as sensibly it should have been, deputed to one particular government department but was split between three – Housing and Urban Development, Defense, and the General Services Administration. In consultation with the Department of Health, Education and Welfare, each was required to prescribe accessibility standards for the design, construction and alteration of buildings, structures and facilities in its domain. To work on this, the instrument they had was the 1961 A117.1, with its set of standard specifications for building features. For application conditions there was no established model on which they could draw. A firm principle had, however, been established. On the federal government front, the accessibility of buildings would be controlled by mainstream, not welfare, legislation.

The story is told later of the arguments which followed about the handling of the 1968 Architectural Barriers Act, and why it was that uniform federal accessibility standards for its implementation were not introduced until 1984, with compliance control then being the business of an independent federal government agency, the Architectural and Transportation Barriers Compliance Board. In 1997 the Architectural Barriers Act stands as the first of the three pillars of American federal government legislation which mandated rights for disabled people, the two that were to follow being the Rehabilitation Act of 1973 and the Americans with Disabilities Act of 1990. Hugh Gallagher thus has a place in history. Over the years we have kept in touch, my most recent meeting with him being in June 1994 at his home in Maryland.

5 Britain: cementing the welfare fabric

During my years in Norwich I twice visited the United States, and it was on the second occasion, a sponsored conference in May 1966 arranged by the architectural psychology department of the University of Utah, that I met Kenneth Bayes for the first time. An architect partner in Design Research Unit in London, he was undertaking research in America on therapeutic environments for mentally handicapped children. Back in Norwich a few weeks later I received a letter from Sandra Francklin, an architectural student at Sheffield University. She had been awarded a Churchill Fellowship to go to America to study environments for handicapped children. Kenneth at that time was still teaching and working in America; he was, I suggested, the person who would help her. A partnership of shared concerns and aspirations blossomed, and they married. On their return to London in 1969 they set up an organization which they called the Centre on Environment for the Handicapped. It was to be a campaigning agency, a vehicle for the promotion of independent living for mentally handicapped people, and also an advice and information service. With financial support from the Department of Health, the Hospital Centre (now the King's Fund Centre) provided them with an office. They enlisted two staff members, and in 1970 I joined as their consultant on the physical disability side.

The plan had been that I would spend not more than three years on the Norwich project, but Duncan Guthrie's Polio Research Fund generously covered the supplementary work that I undertook and my stay was extended to more than four and a half years. I still had no inclination to be a practising architect. I wished to broaden my research in the disability field, and a promising avenue was collaboration with Margot Jefferys, professor of medical sociology at Bedford College in the University of London. Our elaborate proposal was put to the Ministry of Health, who elected not to fund it. On returning to London I joined the editorial staff of the *Architects' Journal* in December 1968.

Week by week at that time, other than for special issues, the journal had a regular three-part format for its editorial material. At the front there was the news, in the middle the building study, and at the back the technical section. For the first few months I was an assistant technical editor, and then for three years the buildings editor. I handled the building study section, putting together each week, with all the commissioning, chasing and checking tasks involved, between 12 and 20 pages. The job was harassing, enjoyable and informative – I was dealing with buildings, travelling the country to see the current best of them and meet and talk with their architects.

I continued to maintain my disability interests. In February 1969 I was invited to Stockholm. The Swedish Institute for the Handicapped had it in mind that I might join them, and, while I did not wish to do that, they invited me to return later in the year to look at housing provision for disabled people around the country, review what had been achieved and what might be done, and report. I felt this was more a job for a social researcher, and suggested that Jenny Griffin of the sociological research branch in the Ministry of Housing's research and development group should undertake the task with me. This was agreed, and following two weeks of intensive travel, visits and meetings in July 1969 we submitted a report which Mrs Griffin had drafted.

On 6 November 1969 Alfred Morris drew the number one place when the result of the annual ballot for private members' bills was announced. Born in 1928, his childhood had been lived in a terraced slum in the Ancoats district of Manchester, the family being dependent for their income on national assistance and his father's war service pension. Severely handicapped by war injuries, partial blindness and chronic tuberculosis, his father had died in 1935 at the age of 44. Morris went on to gain a scholarship to Oxford University where he read modern history, first stood as a Labour Party parliamentary candidate in 1951, and in 1964 became the Member of Parliament for Manchester Wythenshawe. Services for disabled people would, he decided, be the subject of his bill, the Chronically Sick and Disabled Persons Bill. Initially it was not backed by the then government, the Labour administration headed by Harold Wilson. But two previous bills of the same kind had been blocked, and the government felt that the process was irresistible; this one, they agreed, would have to go through. It was hurriedly patched together to a tight timetable, with little enthusiasm on the part of the officials and government ministers who would have to administer it.

A crucial role in putting the bill onto the statute book was performed by Duncan Guthrie. He had become director of the Central Council for the Disabled, which he ran in tandem with the National Fund for Research into Crippling Diseases. In December 1969, with Alf Morris inundated with correspondence, the bill being constantly redrafted and time pressures mounting, Guthrie offered help with secretarial services and became in effect the manager of the enterprise. He helped organize the setting up of an ad hoc committee of members of parliament and knowledgeable outsiders, which Mr Morris chaired through the Commons stage and Lord Longford through the Lords stage. I was among those invited to join the committee. Had I at the time been engaged in disability work without distractions elsewhere I would have been a more assiduous member of it. But although the day-to-day imperatives of putting building studies together for the *Architects' Journal* could not be relinquished, I was able to attend most of the meetings.

Access was from the start a top item on the agenda for the bill, as Alf Morris later wrote in his autobiography, 'When the title of my Bill was announced, I was frequently asked what kind of improvements for the chronically sick and disabled I had in mind. It always seemed best to begin with the problems of access'[1]. The committee dealing with the bill was impressed by reports of the progress made in America on mandating the accessibility of public buildings, and, as a reference that could be cited in regulations, it was armed with CP96, the British Standard code of practice on access for the disabled to buildings issued in 1967. The prevailing view around the table was that the accessibility of buildings must, with no qualification, be a statutory requirement. On the advice of Parliamentary Counsel, government officials insisted that it could not be, and so it was that the contentious words 'in so far as it is in the circumstances both practicable and reasonable' were incorporated in each of the relevant clauses. On this topic my recollection is that I was not a dogmatist. A contribution that I made to committee discussions related to the clauses, eight in all, advocating the appointment of at least one disabled person to a series of official advisory committees. I ventured the opinion that no single disabled person could represent the interests of all disabled people. The horror at my heresy was not appeased by Frank Longford requesting that the committee should at least hear what I had to say.

The bill was rushed through, and as the Chronically Sick and Disabled Persons Act it was placed on the statute book on the day before parliament was dissolved for the general election of 1970. Through all of its 29 sections it was microistic in character. Its controlling ethos was that disabled people with their special needs should be treated as different, as a subspecies of the total population. The first section required local social services authorities to identify all the people in their area who might be regarded as disabled, keep a register of them, and inform them of the services to which they might be entitled or eligible. The following sections prescribed a wide range of special services, benefits, concessions and privileges for disabled people.

In respect of buildings and their use by disabled people, there were two important sections of the Act which needed regulations for their implementation – section 3, concerned with housing provision, and section 4, concerned with access to public buildings. Section 3 read:

> Every local authority for the purposes of Part V of the Housing Act 1957 in discharging their duty under section 91 of that Act to consider housing conditions in their district and the needs of the district with respect to the provision of further housing accommodation shall have regard to the special needs of chronically sick or disabled persons; and any proposals prepared and submitted to the Minister by the authority under that section for the provision of new houses shall distinguish any houses which the authority propose to provide which make special provision for the needs of such persons.

Section 4 read:

> Any person undertaking the provision of any building or premises to which the public are to be admitted, whether on payment or otherwise, shall, in the means of access both to and within the building or premises, and in the parking facilities and sanitary conveniences to be available (if any), make provision, in so far as it is in the circumstances both practicable and reasonable, for the needs of members of the public visiting the building or premises who are disabled.

The lay person coming across section 3 for the first time could well be puzzled by it, and be unclear precisely what in practice it is meant to achieve. By contrast, he will, when he has sorted out its convoluted terminology, be clear about the intentions of section 4 – it requires that the providers of public buildings must as a rule make them accessible to disabled people. Section 4 was a central plank of the Act, whereas section 3 was a supplementary, slotted in to cover housing. What happened was that the government moved positively and decisively to implement section 3. On section 4 it procrastinated.

The standard practice in Britain when new legislation is enacted is that the government department concerned issues an official circular advising local authorities on the interpretation of the law and how it is to be implemented. For the Chronically Sick and Disabled Persons Act a circular was issued jointly by the Department of Health and Social Security, the Department of Education and Science, the Ministry of Housing and Local Government and the Ministry of Transport in August 1970. Section 3 was well covered, with advice to housing authorities on the provision of specially designed housing suitable for wheelchair users[2]. Section 4 was not; there were a few notes regarding the interpretation of its wording, but no mention was made about how in practice its requirements were to be enforced. The circular did, however, pointedly say that the section did *not* provide grounds on which planning permission or building control approval could be withheld[3].

When the early drafts for what was to become section 4 were being considered by Alf Morris and his advisory group, the absorption was with the status of the access requirement and the unsuccessful struggle there was to prevent the insertion of the clause 'in so far as it is in the circumstances both practicable and reasonable'. In the light of the urgent haste with which the bill had to be steered through parliament, along with the lack of notice government officials had been given to prepare for it, it was predictable that the way section 4 was drafted would display shortcomings and deficiencies, but not perhaps that they would be as disconcerting as they proved to be.

The crucial flaw was that no penal sanctions for non-compliance with section 4 requirements were incorporated in the Act, the effect being that any building provider who did not wish to make his building accessible could ignore the law and do so with impunity. There were three other deficiencies. One was that no order was made to produce regulations for the enforcement of section 4. The second, most unfortunately as events were to prove, was that it was not clear which government department was to be responsible for putting section 4 requirements into operation. The third was uncertainty as to what was meant by 'any provision' – did it mean new construction only, or also – and to what extent – alterations to existing buildings?

Broadly what happened in the years that followed was that local authorities were diligent in making sure that their own buildings were designed to be fully accessible, whereas private sector developers and building owners commonly ignored the legal duty imposed on them. There were frequent and angry protests from disabled people and their organizations that the part of the Act to do with buildings had no teeth. Given that the intentions of section 4 were plain, the complaints were wholly justified. The procedure that ought to have been prescribed would have been in the form 'The Minister of Housing and Local Government shall lay regulations for meeting the requirements of Section 4'. That there was no such order in no way exonerates the government of the day; the duty of ministers and officials concerned was to see to it that the requirements of the law were enforced.

Section 4, while being the most important, was one of a bunch of five sections in the Act concerned with access provision in and around buildings. Section 7, one which underscored the microistic character of the Act, required that a 'for the disabled' notice or sign had to be displayed where any provision was made under the Act for disabled people in a building. Sections 5, 6 and 8 required certain provisions to be made for disabled people in buildings 'in so far as it is both reasonable and practicable': section 5 in respect of municipal public lavatories; section 6 in respect of public toilet facilities in premises where under the 1936 Public Health Act such facilities had to be provided; and section 8 in respect of university buildings and public sector schools. There was thus a whole package of statutory requirements waiting for regulatory controls for their enforcement. None were produced. Six years later – in October 1976, with the passing of the Chronically Sick and Disabled Persons (Amendment) Act – section 4 was amended to cover places of employment as well as public buildings. The burden of duty on the government to introduce enforcement controls increased, but prevarication persisted.

Why was it that the responsible government department, the Department of the Environment (into which the Ministry of Housing and Local Government was absorbed in late 1970), acted swiftly to implement section 3, but did nothing about section 4? The simple answer is that there was a lacuna in its organizational structure. In its administrative hierarchy, running down from commands through directorates and divisions to branches, there was a place in the department for dealing with section 3. There was no place for dealing with section 4 – there were no heads of directorates or divisions who considered it to be their responsibility to tackle it, or who were at all inclined to take it on board. No one in the Department of the Environment wanted to know about section 4. Section 3 fared better.

Translated, what the terms of section 3 of the Chronically Sick and Disabled Persons Act meant was that local authorities were told they ought to provide special housing for wheelchair users, and the government was going to keep a check on them to see that they did. For putting these intentions into practice the Department of the Environment was well placed, with three important factors being relevant. The first was that section 3 was exclusively a housing matter and did not directly concern any other government department. The second was that within the Housing Development Directorate (previously the Ministry of Housing's Research and Development Group) there were officials who properly saw it to be their duty to act on it, and advise ministers on how it should be implemented. The third was that the administrative apparatus for local authorities to deliver suitable housing for disabled people was already in place.

Within the Housing Development Directorate the head of the division which comprised architects and social researchers was Terence O'Toole. On a morning in June 1971 he telephoned me. Would I, he enquired, like to join the group to do some work on housing for the disabled? Yes, I replied, I would. Good, he said, he would fix it. It was not as simple as that. He was told by the personnel management division that he could not just phone someone outside and tell them they could come and work for the department. First he had to convince them that there was an important new task to be undertaken and a new post to be filled, and then determine what kind of skills the person who was to be appointed to the post would need to have. If that was agreed, the post would be internally advertised and there would be a trawl to discover whether anyone already working in the department might like to fill it and was fitted. Only if all that failed could there be a case, subject to an interview board, for inviting an appropriately qualified outside person to come in. The process was prolonged, and it was not until 1 May 1972 that I joined the Department of the Environment's Housing Development Directorate.

My job in Barbara Adams's sociological research branch in Mr O'Toole's division was to advise on the implementation of section 3. Had I been given the opportunity I would have preferred to work on the implementation of section 4. But I did not at all lament being given second best. The outcome was the two Housing Development Directorate Occasional Papers which I drafted. HDDOP 2/74, *Mobility housing,* was published in July 1974 and HDDOP 2/75, *Wheelchair housing,* in June 1975. In preparing the two documents I drew substantially on the evidence of my survey of the housing circumstances of wheelchair users in Norwich; it was that material, in particular the quantified data on the housing needs of disabled people in a defined population area, which prompted the idea of suitable normal housing as a preferred alternative to special wheelchair housing for the majority of disabled people.

The presumption had always been that if architects were to make provision for disabled people it must be the particular requirements of disabled people – disability criteria – which should govern design solutions. Mobility housing rejected that principle, its design criteria being governed by the parameters of normal provision, meaning the parameters of the Parker Morris standards and cost yardstick controls that were then operative for new-build public sector housing. The concomitant was that the need for wheelchair housing, for dwelling units specially designed and equipped to cater for chairbound people, was a function of the parameters of mobility housing. I did not at the time appreciate that the concept of mobility housing was revolutionary. I simply felt that in the context of housing provision for disabled people it was good common sense. It was not until some seven or eight years later that I began to realise it was a concept that could, with advantage, be applied to the design of public buildings also.

My contract was short-term; I had a letter of appointment stipulating that I would be employed by the Department of the Environment for not less than two years nor more than three. It was a four-days-a-week arrangement; one half of the remaining day would be spent as consultant to the Centre on Environment for the Handicapped, and the other on processing the third edition of *Designing for the Disabled*, work on which I had already begun. In early 1974 the personnel management division enquired when, under the terms of my contract, I was expecting to leave the department. The response from my line managers was that I would be very content to stay, and at that point, with no further ado, I was promptly established. My secure status was reinforced in May 1976 when I was awarded individual merit promotion, a condition of which was that I would retain my post so long as I continued to work in the field of my special expertise and performed competently. I stayed until I reached retirement age in 1992.

The research and development group of the Ministry of Housing had been set up to deal only with housing and housing-related issues – it was not its business to concern itself with the broad field of public building design. So far as in the Department of the Environment any controls were exercised over the design of public buildings they were handled by the Building Regulations Division, whose strict and limited remit was to administer regulations aimed at securing the health and safety of building users. Since the accessibility of buildings to disabled people was not a matter of health or safety it could not, as they pointed out, be mandated by means of building regulations. Relatedly, officials in the quite separate part of the department responsible for advice on planning legislation insisted that access for the disabled could not be a condition for granting planning permission. For seventeen years there was inertia: from July 1968 when the Ministry of Housing's circular on the design of public conveniences was issued over the signature of the assistant secretary who headed the Local Government (Miscellaneous) Division, until June 1985, when regulations for making buildings accessible were first introduced, no official advice on access for the disabled to public buildings was issued by the Department of the Environment.

In 1974, with the enactment of the Health and Safety at Work etc Act, the scope of building regulations was extended to cover welfare and convenience as well as health and safety purposes, and this permitted access-for-the-disabled controls to come within their orbit. The instrument was not, however, suited to the purpose. First, because if built environments were to be generally accessible to disabled people, the areas around and between buildings needed to be controlled as well as what happened inside a building, and the remit of Building Regulations was restricted to the structure of a building and its immediate curtilage. Second, because building regulations, with their common national rules, were relatively inflexible. The mode is appropriate for health and safety purposes, for which it is reasonable to apply standard formula prescriptions to buildings of all kinds, but not for convenience purposes, such as accessibility, which demand variable rules according to conditions and circumstances. In particular, the building regulations instrument, with its uniform prescriptions, could not deal effectively with access provision when existing buildings were being altered.

That in 1970 no legislative instrument was available for the enforcement of section 4 of the Chronically Sick Act did not excuse the government from doing nothing. It had a duty, and from inside or outside effective action could have been initiated. The activator could have been one of a number of people. In the Department of the Environment it could have been a perceptive minister appreciative of the political bonuses the issue offered. It could have been a senior administrator able to convince his ministers that positive action was required. It could have been a member of parliament who understood the legal imperatives of the issue, and who, by constant pressure through parliamentary questions and other means, could have persuaded DOE ministers to act. It could have been a legally astute disability advocate who tenaciously agitated for the law to be enforced.

In the event, no one pressed the issue. Had they done so, there would not have been the sorry saga which followed. To illustrate the character of the opportunity that was lost in 1970 I hypothesise the happenings which could have occurred:

1 The Secretary of State for the Environment would have set up an advisory committee with a brief to review all relevant issues, recommend suitable mechanisms for enforcing section 4, and report.
2 The committee would have comprised representatives of interested DOE policy and professional divisions, other interested government departments, local authority associations, the construction industry, interested professional organizations and interested consumer agencies, including those representing the interests of disabled people.
3 A delegation of the committee would have visited the United States to study American practice and procedures.

4 A subcommittee would have conducted consultations with interested bodies, for example construction industry organizations, local authority associations, disability organizations and professional bodies.

The committee's report would have followed, and its recommendations would have been:

1 That new primary legislation should be enacted for the specific purpose of regulating accessibility, for new buildings, alterations to existing buildings and the built environment around buildings.
2 That under the terms of the legislation the duty of administering access controls and enforcing them would be deputed to local authorities, who would institute procedures for the coordination of access controls, planning controls and the requirements of building regulations.
3 That to guide local authorities, architects and others the Department of the Environment would issue a comprehensive code of practice, with recommendations for application conditions as well as design standards.

The Department of the Environment was not energized to do this. From the start it was entirely content for access for the disabled to be regarded as a welfare issue, and for the Department of Health to handle it. In Britain there was no Paul Strachan and no Hugh Gallagher.

The Chronically Sick and Disabled Persons Act received Royal Assent and became law on 29 May 1970. Twenty days later a general election was held, and Edward Heath, leader of the Conservative party, became the new Prime Minister. As his Secretary of State for Social Services – and the minister who would be principally responsible for the implementation of the Chronically Sick Act – he appointed Sir Keith Joseph. Throughout his four years in the post, Sir Keith concentrated on section 1, under which local authorities were to set up registers of disabled people; on section 2, which set out the range of welfare services which local authorities were to arrange to provide for disabled people; and on section 17, which required health authorities to move young disabled people out of long-stay hospitals for the elderly – to deal with this, he obtained substantial funding from the Treasury for the construction of hospital buildings known as young chronic sick units. He did not concern himself with section 4; it was not, he felt, his business.

In October 1974 Harold Wilson returned as Prime Minister and introduced a new post into his government – that of a Minister for the Disabled, the first ever in Britain or elsewhere in the world. Alf Morris was given the job; along with regular ministerial responsibilities in the Department of Health and Social Security he had a roving commission, one which entitled him to delve into access issues. He sought advice as much from informed disabled people outside his department as from his officials within, the principal external adviser on whom he relied being Peter Large, who in 1993 for his services to disabled people was to become Sir Peter Large. Extremely severely disabled as a consequence of polio, Mr Large was spokesman on parliamentary affairs for the Disablement Income Group, and as a prominent consumer lobbyist had become actively engaged in the access field. In 1976 Mr Morris decided that to promote access policy he would set up a committee, the Silver Jubilee Committee on Improving Access for Disabled People, and he invited Mr Large to be its chairman. The Department of Health provided the secretariat and many of the 22 committee members were themselves disabled people.

The Committee was asked to consider the access difficulties encountered by disabled people and to recommend ways in which improvements could be brought about. It might have felt that at the top of its agenda should come section 4 of the Chronically Sick Act, with proposals being made for an effective and reliable procedural mechanism to enforce its requirements. Its members elected, however, to respond to the brief by running a campaign: 'we decided it was necessary to wage a campaign to increase public awareness of the problems of access and to secure from disabled people further information on their access problems'[4].

The report *Can disabled people go where you go?* was published by the Department of Health and Social Security in January 1979. It reported the achievements of the awareness campaign and also the state of play on access controls. It referred to CP96, the 1967 British Standard Code of Practice on access for the disabled, and noted, 'It is currently being revised and the Department of the Environment has said it will consider the practicability of amending building regulations when it is available'[5]. The hope was that this would be done quickly: 'We recommend', the committee report said, 'that legislation be introduced to make the access sections of the Chronically Sick and Disabled Persons Act 1970 mandatory'[6]. But no commitment was obtained from the Department of the Environment that firm action would be taken to enforce section 4 of the Act.

6 The design standards trap

In 1967, when I and my colleagues who served on the access-for-the-disabled British Standards Institution committee had produced Part 1 of CP96, no timetable was set for reconvening to work on Part 2. I was not keen to get busy again, and nor were others. In the event, the matter was taken out of our hands. The widespread response to Part 1 was that a set of design specifications was all that was needed; there was no demand for a Part 2 presenting application criteria. It was not until February 1975 that the committee met again to consider the proposal that CP96 should be updated. There was now no argument – this time the code, to be known as BS5810[1], would cover design standards only. I again worked on the preparation of the draft. Housing, we agreed, should be treated separately; with a committee comprised of many of the same members I prepared the draft of the code of practice which in 1978 was issued as BS5619, *Design of housing for the convenience of disabled people*[2].

The issue which most engaged the BS5810 committee was the design standard for the unisex toilet facility. Section 5 of the Chronically Sick Act 1970 had required that local authorities should make provision for disabled people in new public toilets, and the advice in the official circular which accompanied the Act was that technical guidance could be found in Circular 33/68, meaning unisex toilet provision in accord with the CP96 recommendations[3]. 'Get it right' had been the call from disabled people and their organizations – the specifications, they said, should be strictly adhered to. Towards the end of 1971, when CP96-type toilets began to be open for business in some quantity, complaints were persistent: CP96 had got it wrong – there was not enough space to manoeuvre a wheelchair inside the compartment, there was not enough space for a helper to assist with transfer, and the seat was much too high.

It was perhaps inevitable that we got it wrong. We were dealing with a new type of building that had never been seen before, and its development was necessarily a matter of trial and error. The principal error was that the CP96 toilet had been designed down to a standard, one that did not accommodate by any means all the customers whom it was intended to serve. But even if the recommended internal dimensions had been much more generous, complaints would still have been predictable – as we were to learn, no single standard for a unisex toilet facility could satisfy all disabled people.

An item that caused unending controversy was the height of the seat. It had seemed sensible that it should be at the same level as a wheelchair seat, and the recommended height was 505mm. The response was a chorus of complaints about having to go mountaineering.

It was evident that the size of the standard facility ought to be enlarged, and further tests with a full-size model rig were made by Dr Glyn Stanton, consultant ergonomist to the Department of Health. His findings helped inform the recommendations in the third edition of *Designing for the Disabled*, published in 1976. The preferred size wc compartment for chair-bound people had internal dimensions 2000 × 1500mm, and the design and equipment specifications that I set out in the book[4] were precisely replicated in BS5810 (Figure 6.1), and subsequently in the approved documents for the Part M building regulation issued in 1987 and 1992[5]. In 1997 the official line remains unchanged; notwithstanding an abundance of evidence demonstrating its faults, a toilet facility devised more than twenty years ago is still deemed to be 'right'.

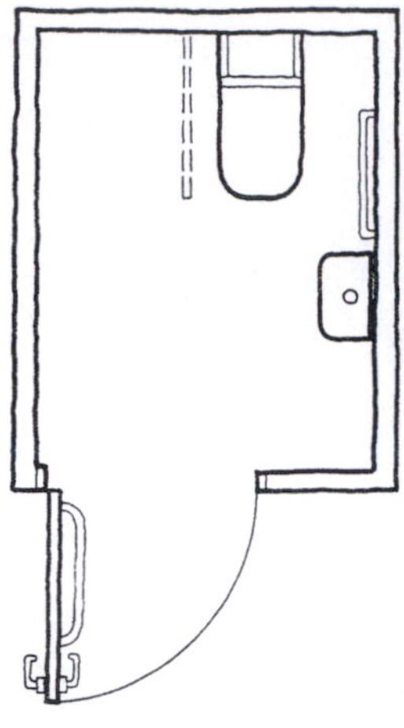

6.1 The BS5810 unisex toilet

BS5810, *Code of Practice for Access for the Disabled to Buildings*, a brief document of eleven pages, was issued in 1979. In the disability world 'BS5810' became synonymous with the BS5810 unisex toilet, and the BS5810 toilet became an icon. Drawings were checked to see that it was there. Where it was provided it was carefully examined to see that it had been got right. In public buildings it became standard practice to have one of them – as a rule one only, regardless of how many facilities there were for normal people. That, it was understood, served the needs of disabled people generally.

In Part 1 of CP96 the recommendations for toilets for disabled people had been prefaced by words such as 'where provision is made'; the assumption being that a Part 2 would indicate how many there should be where. Had we proceeded to produce a Part 2 we would not, I am sure, have advised that in any and all public buildings a single unisex facility was sufficient to cater for the needs of all disabled people. In Part 1 of CP96 one design standard was prescribed for a wc compartment for wheelchair users and another for ambulant disabled people. Part 2, had it been issued, would have advised appropriate mixes by type and size of building – advice which, in the light of experience, would have been modified in subsequent revisions of the code, both for design standards and application criteria.

When in 1987 the Part M building regulation was introduced, the advice in the associated approved document was confusing, but in essence the requirement for public buildings was that a single BS5810-type unisex toilet was sufficient[6]. In the revised 1992 approved document the guidance was yet more confusing, but for public and employment buildings what it seemed to suggest was that for visitors or customers a single unisex facility somewhere was generally all that was needed; the proviso, with multi-storey employment buildings in mind, was that a wheelchair user should not have to travel more than one storey to reach a suitable wc[7].

In Britain during the 1960s, 1970s and into the 1980s the widespread assumption in the disability arena was that all that was needed to control the provision of accessibility in buildings was a reliable set of design standards. No more was required, it was supposed, than the injunction 'The building shall be designed in compliance with the requirements of CP96' or, after 1979, 'of BS5810'. The fact that for regulating accessibility there had to be two integrated components – one the design standards, the other the application criteria – was not grasped.

In Britain, seventeen years elapsed from 1970, when accessibility legislation was enacted, to 1987, when regulations in the form of Part M were introduced for enforcing the requirements of that legislation. Through all those years I imagined that the access legislation being generated by state governments in America would all be backed by sound enforcement procedures. Since 1963, with the formulation presented in the first edition of *Designing for the Disabled*, I had considered it self-evident that for implementing accessibility there had to be two complementary processes. There had to be design standards and there had to be application conditions – there could not be one without the other. I supposed that in America this precept was followed. I was wrong. In America, as in Britain, the widespread belief was that a set of design standards was sufficient. And what I never understood until 1994 was how chaotic the whole apparatus of American building law was.

For the consistent and uniform implementation of building control measures Britain has an instrument that the United States does not have – it has national building regulations. In America the term for a building regulation is a 'code'. Codes are law and are enforceable under the police powers of state governments. Standards such as A117.1 are acceptable practices and are law only where they are incorporated by reference within a code. Matters which building code provisions can address are public health, safety and general welfare, meaning that a code can mandate accessibility. Jurisdictions for the purposes of building law are local municipalities (called cities, however small they may be) and counties. Local municipalities can have their own codes, but they are governed by state law; to limit confusion, some states impose state-wide codes.

Virtually all state and local building codes in America are adopted from one or other of three model national building codes: these are the BOCA National Building Code (that of the Building Officials and Code Administrators International); the SBCCI Standard Building Code (the Southern Building Code Congress International); and the ICBO Uniform Building Code (the International Conference of Building Officials). Some code agencies pick provisions from different model codes, and within a state different local jurisdictions may use different models. In states where state codes are generally imposed exceptions can be made, with a municipality or county being allowed to opt out and develop its own code. Each of the model codes is performance-based (meaning that compliance is judged in terms of functional effectiveness) rather than being technically prescriptive.

Broadly, therefore, codes have provisions rather than firm requirements, and in any jurisdiction the enforcement officer can waive a provision where he agrees that in the circumstances it is appropriate to do so. A final note on the indiscipline of building law in America: state governments can, under the Constitution, administer building law, but they are not obliged to do so. The odd one out is Texas, where the adoption and enforcement of codes is left to local jurisdictions and where large parts of the state are virtually unregulated[8].

With the 1961 A117.1 as their instrument, it was against this confusing scenario that state governments began from 1963 to legislate for accessibility. I have not probed how they did it; I suspect, however, that most states copied the South Carolina law which governed new construction only, and that typical terms would have been along the lines, 'New public buildings shall be accessible to handicapped people by reference to ASA 117.1'. On this basis, no attempt may have been made to prescribe application conditions, and there may not, for example, have been any definition of which kinds of buildings were to be subject to the law, in what circumstances a lift had to be installed in low-rise buildings or what toilet facilities suitable for handicapped people had to be provided where. On an ad hoc basis, the conditions would, I imagine, have been agreed between the code enforcement officer, the architect and the building developer. Inconsistency over the terms for making buildings accessible across America was therefore endemic; there were no common rules, no national guidelines were available and none of the model code organizations issued relevant guidelines to agencies that adopted their national code.

Federal buildings across America were, like other public buildings, subject to the provisions of a local code when they were newly designed or altered, and how (or whether) any access provision for disabled people was incorporated was not done with any uniformity. In the 1960s there was no mandate requiring that federal buildings, or public buildings that were federally funded, should as a matter of course be accessible, and it was this, with appropriate regulations, that the Architectural Barriers Act of 1968 was intended to remedy. There could not, however, be enforcement of the federal regulations by local code officials, since they were accountable to their local administration and did not serve the federal government; the sanction that federal officials could apply was not to grant funds until they were satisfied that there would be compliance. On this basis, there was no case for ad hoccery – the need was for firm and precise rules as to what, in any particular circumstance, had to be done.

In 1969, the year after the Architectural Barriers Act had been enacted, the General Services Administration was the first of the three designated government agencies to issue access regulations. It did so on a single piece of paper, without pausing to invite comments. For new, extended or altered buildings all that was required, with certain marginal exceptions, was conformity with the design standards of the 1961 A117.1[9]. In a similar fashion, the two other agencies – the Department of Housing and Urban Development and the Department of Defense – issued their regulations.

Awkward practical difficulties began to emerge. The 1961 A117.1 had been devised with new buildings in mind, and where state legislation and local code rules decreed that only new buildings were to be accessible it served well enough. But in the case of federally-funded buildings the works undertaken were predominantly modifications to existing buildings or alterations or additions to an existing complex of buildings; this was particularly so in the case of school and university buildings which were the concern of General Services Administration. Uniform rules that could straightforwardly be applied to new buildings on green-field sites could not be applied to alterations to existing buildings. Without agreed application criteria (known in America as scoping conditions) there were problems. Most troublesome of all was what ought to be done about buildings which were leased.

In the early 1970s Congress became increasingly aware that the intentions of the Architectural Barriers Act were not going to be realised so long as responsibility lay with three government agencies who had little enthusiasm for the task; the need was for a single federal agency to take control. A related issue was attracting attention, the need for federally-funded public transport facilities to be accessible to disabled people. In an effort to coordinate action and stimulate progress the decision was made to create an independent federal government agency, the Architectural and Transportation Barriers Compliance Board. With a broad remit, its principal task on the architectural side was to ensure that there was compliance with standards set by the General Services Administration, the Housing and Urban Development Department and the Department of Defense. The setting up of the Board, known as the Access Board, was authorised by adding on an item, section 502, to the Rehabilitation Act of 1973. It was not, however, section 502 of that Act which in later years would be recalled as having made history, but section 504.

7 America: the emergence of the disability rights movement

> No otherwise qualified individual in the United States shall, solely by reason of his handicap, be excluded from participation in, be denied the benefits of, or be subject to discrimination under any program or activity receiving Federal financial assistance.

This was the edict in section 504 of the Rehabilitation Act of 1973. Across the whole arena of public services, buildings and facilities which, in however small a part, were funded by the federal government, discrimination against disabled people was to be outlawed. The ordinance, closely replicating the wording of Lyndon Johnson's Civil Rights Act of 1964, was to become celebrated; it was the keystone on which the all-embracing non-discrimination statute, the Americans with Disabilities Act of 1990, was to be built. Earlier in the 1970s Senator Hubert Humphrey had introduced a bill for civil rights for disabled people, but its progress had been stalled[1]. Section 504 did get through, and while its mandate was to be crucial for the advancement of the disability rights movement in America, it was not engineered by consumer activists. Somewhat surreptitiously, it was presented to them by government officials.

Politically, the Rehabilitation Act of 1973 was not a strategic piece of legislation. Sponsored by the Department of Health, Education and Welfare, its practical purpose was to authorise and procure federal funding for a broad range of rehabilitation services. At hearings during the course of its passage through Congress disability agencies were consulted, among them some of the consumer-controlled advocacy groups which were beginning to emerge. Their concerns focused exclusively on the decrees which would expand the scope of federally-funded rehabilitation services, in particular those that would assist people with severe disabilities.

Within the Department of Health, Education and Welfare, officials in the Civil Rights Office headed by John Wodatch had a hand in drafting the rehabilitation bill. Their concern was that medical and welfare professionals in the Department had a narrow view of vocational rehabilitation, and that negative attitudes and discrimination on the part of employers and others were preventing disabled people from joining the mainstream of society[2]. Having worked previously on the Civil Rights Act of 1964, they were experienced in civil rights legislation and understood how effectively it could be exploited. On their own initiative they inserted section 504, with no appreciation of the impact it might subsequently have on public policies[3]. It attracted no attention; it was not debated in Congress, and among disability interest groups its importance went unrealised[4].

When the Act had been passed into law later in 1973, John Wodatch and his colleagues worked on drafts of the regulations needed to enforce section 504; to be brought into operation they would have to be approved by the Secretary for Health, Education and Welfare, and signed by him. Prior to public hearings being held on the Act's draft regulations, section 504 was brought to the attention of disability interest groups, and it was thus that consumer activists became aware of its significance. On the disability front, the person who was most actively engaged in the negotiations was Judy Heumann, from June 1974 to December 1975 a legislative aide in the office of Harrison Williams, Democratic Senator for New Jersey. On the other side, the service deliverers who would be subjected to section 504 requirements were barely consulted, and were not much involved in the drafting of the regulations[5]. John Wodatch, one of the senior legal professionals in the service of the federal government, subsequently continued to work on civil rights issues, including the Americans with Disabilities Act; in 1994 when I met and talked with him in Washington DC he was head of the Access Policy Section in the Department of Justice.

Judy Heumann was born in 1948 to a family of German-Jewish immigrants who lived in Brooklyn. At the age of 18 months she became comprehensively disabled as a consequence of polio. In New York she was deemed by the local elementary school to be a fire hazard, and for three years a teacher was sent twice a week to give her home instruction[6]. She was then sent first to a special school for handicapped children, after which she would be subject to the New York rule that at high school age children in wheelchairs must have tuition at home. Her mother successfully fought the edict, and in 1961 Judy entered a regular school. She moved on to study speech therapy at Long Island University where, on grounds apparently associated with her disability, she was refused a teaching certificate. She sued the Board of Education, and the case, following emotive press coverage, was settled out of court. In 1970 she set up a disability rights group in New York, Disabled in Action. Over the years that followed, she was politically the most prominent campaigner for civil rights for disabled people. At meetings in America and Britain, I have on a number of occasions talked with her, most recently in Washington DC in June 1994 when, having joined the Establishment as an appointee of President Clinton, she was an Assistant Secretary in the Department of Education with responsibilities for special education and rehabilitative services.

In 1973 Judy Heumann moved to Berkeley in California. The invitation to go there had come from Ed Roberts, who with other severely disabled people had launched the independent living movement for disabled people and had set up the Berkeley Center for Independent Living. He knew that

Judy, with her political flair and organizational ability, could help drive the movement. In later years at Berkeley she was to be the dominant figure in the rights movement, but her initial stay was brief. When the opportunity came in 1974 to work with Senator Williams on the central political stage on Capitol Hill, she moved back east.

Gerald Ford succeeded Richard Nixon as US president in 1974. His Secretary for Health, Education and Welfare, David Matthews, was a political appointee, and was troubled by the potential implications of section 504. In the summer of 1975 when his officials presented him with a final draft of the regulations he procrastinated, and again in March 1976 refused to sign them[7]. Pressures grew, Congress became increasingly irritated, disability lobbying groups voiced furious protests, and frustrations mounted. In November 1976 Jimmy Carter was elected next President of the United States, but yet again in January 1977, while Ford was still in office, Matthews refused to sign. Judy Heumann and the growing band of consumer activists knew they could rely on Jimmy Carter; they had campaigned for his election and he had committed himself to their cause. Heumann had by then returned to California to work with the Berkeley Center for Independent Living, and it was from there that in April 1977 the disability movement was to ignite.

In the 1960s the Berkeley campus of the University of California across the bay from San Francisco was the focus of the American countercultural revolution, of student demonstrations led by hippies and flower children, of civil rights campaigns and anti-war protests. It was the place where young political activists congregated and pressed their causes, and it was there that Ed Roberts launched what in the disability world was to become known as the independent living movement. In 1953, at the age of 14, he had been crippled by polio. More severely paralysed and immobile than Judy Heumann, he was from then on constantly dependent on a respirator machine, being able to breathe without it for a few hours at a time only. He obtained his school diploma, spent two years at a local community college and in 1962, following a struggle with university and state authorities who insisted that they could not cope with anyone who was so severely disabled, he was admitted to the University of California at Berkeley to study political science[8].

At Berkeley, unlike an increasing number of universities elsewhere, there was in the 1960s no established university programme for handicapped students and nor was there any specially designed and equipped hostel accommodation for those in wheelchairs. No one as severely handicapped as Ed Roberts, who for his care and daily living needs had always to have someone with him, had previously been a student there. For his accommodation a room was found for him at the university's student health centre, and with funding from the state rehabilitation department he employed his own care attendants. He was welcomed by other students on the campus, he made numerous friends and many volunteered to push him out and about when a paid attendant was not with him. For his daily needs he had no call on professional medical or nursing services; when personal assistance of whatever kind was required, the flexible arrangements he made with his paid attendants and volunteers served well. News of him spread, and other severely disabled students joined him at the health centre. The informal support network expanded, with many close relationships being developed between disabled students and between them and their attendants[9].

Ed Roberts completed his undergraduate degree, obtained a Master's degree in political science and began work on a doctorate. By 1967 there were twelve disabled students living at the health centre, and in 1968 the state rehabilitation department took over the management of the scheme there. The rule was that the department could only fund students who were prospectively employable, and officials became concerned that some disabled students were taking an inordinately long time to complete their courses. To threats that they might be expelled Roberts responded angrily; in the liberal culture of Berkeley it was unfair, he said, to impose strict rules on disabled students[10].

The student health centre was a secure base for incoming disabled students to develop confidence, but for long-term accommodation it was unsuitable. An alternative could have been a special-for-the-disabled student hostel. That did not appeal to Roberts and his colleagues; what they wanted, together with control of their own care attendant services, was to live in ordinary apartments in the normal community around the campus. For Ed Roberts, an exciting event was when he obtained a battery-powered electric wheelchair and found he could move around independently. The vision of independent living began to take shape[11].

In Washington DC the Department of Health, Education and Welfare administered a programme aimed at reducing the dropout rate among ethnic minority college students. Ed Roberts learnt that the scheme could also apply to disabled students, and with a federal grant he set up the Physically Disabled Students' Program (PDSP) in Berkeley in 1970. Advisers were appointed to check out available property in the area which could be adapted to accommodate severely disabled students in wheelchairs, and a pool of care attendants who could work odd hours was assembled. For the maintenance and repair of wheelchairs PDSP set up a wheelchair workshop. And to guide students through the bureaucracy which dealt with benefits and services it employed legal advisers and established an advocacy service. With nine staff and 100 student clients, PDSP was an exciting success; in Berkeley the independent living ideal had become a reality[12].

The rehabilitation office in California was more generous than many states elsewhere in the US, but it did not fund care attendants employed by disabled people who were not in college or university. This troubled Ed Roberts and his colleagues – they wanted to help all severely disabled young people to live independently. In place of PDSP, what was needed, they felt, was a more embracing enterprise – one that for all disabled people would be a social meeting ground, a resource centre, a housing agency, a care attendant provision agency, an advice bureau and a political campaigning organization. Funds were raised, spacious offices were rented, and in 1972 the consumer-controlled Berkeley Center for Independent Living was established[13].

In 1975 Jerry Brown, the new Governor of California, visited the centre. Much impressed by the consumer-led enterprise and all that it had achieved, he invited Ed Roberts to become California's Director of Rehabilitation. The thrust of the department's priorities shifted; where previously social workers had assessed severely disabled people as not being potentially employable and not therefore eligible for rehabilitation funding, Roberts, presenting himself as mentor, decreed that the bounds should be expanded, with funding going to support attendant services for all disabled people living at home. Some social work staff could not cope with the new regime and left; others welcomed the change and stayed[14]. The story of the achievements of severely disabled people who moved into ordinary houses in Berkeley to live independently, of their family backgrounds, their disabilities, their problems, their aspirations, their relationships and the remarkable network of support that they created around them was admirably reported and illustrated in the book by Raymond Lifchez (Professor of Architecture in the University of California at Berkeley) and Barbara Winslow published in 1979, *Design for Independent Living – the environment and physically disabled people*[15].

While the movement that Ed Roberts had launched was, from the start, known as the independent living movement, its thrust was always more about autonomous control than physical independence. In Roberts's view, and Judy Heumann's also, it was not demeaning to be helped if help was essential, and nor was it laudable to spend two hours doggedly performing a task independently (dressing, for example) if it could be undertaken with the help of an attendant in ten minutes. As Lifchez and Winslow noted[16], it was virtually unknown for a person in a wheelchair at Berkeley to be able to get around independently, drive a car and manage everything without help – to some members of the disabled community it was apparently amazing that there were any who could. A person in a wheelchair at Berkeley had to be someone who might wish for help, who would welcome being asked if help was needed, and who, if nothing else, would be pleased to have a friendly chat for a few minutes.

Ed Roberts at Berkeley, like Tim Nugent at Champaign-Urbana, campaigned to remove architectural barriers; in 1969 he had, with seven others in wheelchairs, attended a Berkeley city council meeting and been assured that the council planned to spend $50,000 on ramping street kerbs[17]. But he did not believe that it was only architectural barriers which stood in the way of the aspirations of disabled people. He was a disability civil rights activist, and was excited by section 504 which, in its federal services sphere, outlawed discrimination against disabled people. What he was campaigning for at Berkeley was more focused; it was a right for disabled people to be financially supported by the state, to have the cash resource to employ their own attendants, live in a home of their own and thereby avoid being placed in a welfare institution. As I learnt on the many occasions when I talked with young disabled people in America it was, understandably, a call which had massive appeal to severely handicapped people across America. On three occasions at conferences I met Ed Roberts and heard him speak; he was to die in March 1995, remembered with esteem for his driving role in America's disability rights movement.

In January 1977 Jimmy Carter was inaugurated as the thirty-ninth President of the United States. As his Secretary for Health, Education and Welfare he appointed Joseph Califano, a man who had apparently never heard of section 504. When presented with the regulations in their complete and carefully drafted form he reasonably felt that he ought to pause and consider them rather than sign them immediately. He announced that he would be conducting a review. Across America, disability activists responded with anger and fury; Carter had unequivocally committed himself to promoting the rights of disabled people, and no delay was tolerable. A national protest to be held on 5 April was organized by the American Coalition of Citizens with Disabilities; in nine cities disabled people would move into the federal administration building and occupy the offices of the Department of Health, Education and Welfare, and in Washington DC they would occupy Mr Califano's offices. Some 5000 disabled people participated in the demonstrations. In eight cities – New York, Atlanta, Philadelphia, Boston, Chicago, Dallas, Seattle and Denver – the sit-in was brief. In Mr Califano's offices it continued for 28 hours. In San Francisco, where the protest was led by Judy Heumann, it continued for 25 days[18].

Until April 1977 the majority of Americans were unaware that civil rights for disabled people was becoming a vital political issue. They knew (or many of them did) that there ought not to be architectural barriers in the way of disabled people when new public buildings were constructed, but they did not equate that with civil rights. Civil rights was about black people and, less prominently, about women. It was about equal opportunities for education and employment, and everyone knew of the struggle, following the passing of the Civil Rights Act in 1964, that the federal government had had to enforce equal education opportunities for black people in southern states.

Instantly and universally, the San Francisco sit-in changed all that. The protesters had barricaded themselves into the building, and although government officials would not allow media people in, messages got out. Each day that the demonstration continued television pictures beamed into the sitting rooms of America, presenting emotive images of a group of angry and courageous cripples occupying federal government offices and demanding their rights. Judy Heumann was the powerful orator who spoke for the group and disabled people everywhere. The Nixon administration, Americans were told, had instituted civil rights legislation for disabled people in June 1973, and neither Nixon nor Ford had acted on it. Carter had promised disabled people that they would have their rights, and now he was prevaricating. The rhetoric of the black rights movement was seized: 'We are an oppressed minority; we are the victims of discrimination; we are engaged in a struggle for emancipation'. The relentless media pressure and the force of public opinion that it generated obliged Califano to give way, and on 28 April 1977 he signed the regulations without having changed them.

8 Britain: discrimination and the force of the disability lobby

In America it did not need the 1977 San Francisco sit-in to generate the issuing of regulations to enforce section 504 of the 1973 Rehabilitation Act. Mr Califano was bound by President Carter to sign them into law, but because he did not do so immediately disability activists seized the opportunity for a sensational protest. The disability movement won a famous victory. For the first time, disabled people realised, as they had never before imagined, that they could wield astonishing power. And the San Francisco sit-in gave them a bond; in place of rival groups competing with each other they now congregately had a unity, with all engaged in a common cause. The campaign for the delivery to disabled people of comprehensive anti-discrimination civil rights legislation was firmly planted. The cries multiplied: 'Discrimination against disabled people is unlawful'; 'It must be stopped'; 'We shall fight for our rights'. The rhetoric spread to Britain. And in Britain, as in America, a principal focus of the 'we are the victims of discrimination' complaint was on the accessibility of public buildings and their usage by disabled people.

Before reporting the events in Britain which were to lead to the introduction of the Disability Discrimination Act of 1995, I bring myself into the reckoning. I wish, I say, to be treated by architects as a normal person, not as a peculiar person. I wish, when I use public buildings, to be treated as a normal person. There are, however, occasions and circumstances where the special needs that I have on account of my disability cannot be met by normal provision, where appropriate special provision is warranted, where I am a beneficiary of discrimination and I welcome it. There are also occasions when I resent the discriminatory provision expressly intended to help people such as myself, and would prefer to do without it.

Discrimination, meaning differential treatment, has two facets: it can be positive and it can be negative. In between is non-differential treatment, treatment as normal without any discrimination. Where discrimination does occur, how it is perceived is a subjective matter. What I may regard as negative discrimination, as unwelcome and irritating, another disabled person may regard as positive discrimination, as favourable and pleasing. What I may consider from my point of view to be positive discrimination that I welcome, another disabled person may regard as demeaning, patronising or condescending.

In the context of the usage of buildings by disabled people discrimination can be manifested in three forms. One is personal discrimination – the attitudes to a disabled person of individual people in and around a building, either members of the building staff or the general public. The second is institutionalised discrimination – the formal or informal rules which affect how disabled people are able to use buildings. The third is architectural discrimination – the way that physically a building treats its users differentially. I consider these forms of discrimination from the perspective of my own experiences.

Personal discrimination

In the context of public buildings in Britain and my usage of them as a disabled person over nearly 40 years, the personal discrimination score has been massively one-sided. Whether as an ambulant disabled person or a wheelchair user, the discrimination that I have encountered has almost invariably been positive. I am greeted with helpfulness, friendliness and smiling faces. When I walk with my stick across roads at uncontrolled points, motorists cheerfully stop for me. At the entrances to buildings and within them, doors are held open for me. In cafes and restaurants, people move tables and chairs for me. Building staff are courteous and frequently willing to go out of their way to help me. When I am in a wheelchair people do not talk over my head to my wife or whoever I am with; the 'Does he take sugar?' syndrome is a virtual non-happening. For each disturbing instance of perceived negative discrimination – a signal which says, 'Disabled people like you ought not to be here', 'Get out of my way' or 'You are a nuisance' – there are hundreds of pleasing instances of positive discrimination.

My impression is that the positive balance is more marked in Britain than on the continent of Europe or in North America. English people are, it seems, genuinely concerned to help people with disabilities such as myself. In a kind, considerate and decent fashion I am patronised. It is rare that the patronage – or discrimination – is condescending. I speak only for myself, of how I feel that I am treated. My experiences do not tally with the images fostered by disability rights activists, that disabled people are an oppressed minority in society, that they are victimised, and that they are subjected to widespread and unwarranted negative discrimination. I recall an evening some 15 years ago when, in my normal way, I staggered out of a club (of a reputable brand) where I had spent a sociable three hours with friends. As I walked round my car to the driver's door I did not notice the van parked behind. The policeman with his sobriety-testing equipment knocked on the window. 'I'm a cripple,' I said. 'My apologies, sir,' he smilingly replied, and returned to his van.

Over the years as I have gone about the business of using public buildings I have discerned a subtle shift in the attitudes of other people to me as a person with a disability. I became disabled in 1956 and have recorded the story of my early years as an architect with a disability. In the late 1950s disability awareness was not on the architect's agenda, or anyone else's. As a professional middle-class person I stayed in the mainstream and was treated by my peers as a normal person who happened to have a disability, not as a person who was different. With Susan Beattie, I would date the attitudinal shift to 1981, the International Year of Disabled People. The 'Year' was an event celebrated in Britain with more enthusiasm than anywhere else in the world. Choreographed by establishment agencies, it fortified cultural attitudes among the mass of British people: that disabled people were different from regular people; that they could be bunched together in a detached block; that they were sad; that they all deserved special treatment; that they all needed to be helped.

Mrs Beattie was the daughter of an architect, Donald McMorran. As an architectural historian she worked during the 1970s in the RIBA library, and it was there that from time to time we met and talked. She had become polio-disabled in adolescence, and, with both legs paralysed, relied entirely on her wheelchair for mobility. In a December 1981 feature article in *The Guardian* she wrote, 'As the International Year of the Disabled Person nears its end I have confronted as honestly as I can my own feelings about disability and the dreary image it presents'[1].

Susan Beattie had studied at the Courtauld Institute of Art, at that time the only place in England offering a BA Honours degree in the history of art; it was accessible to her because Samuel Courtauld had installed a lift in his town house for his wife and her wheelchair. She wrote of her time after graduating:

> Not once during the subsequent years of writing and research, of marriage and motherhood, of earning a living, did I come into direct contact with the vast network of voluntary and salaried workers-on-behalf-of-the-disabled who in this International Year have had such penetrating light thrown upon them. Not once, until this year, did I see myself as a Disabled Person, only as an art historian and a woman who happened to have to use a wheelchair.
>
> Much of the help I have needed has been given by countless kindly strangers who have simply done the job of lifting and gone on their way without question or privacy-intruding comment.

She wrote of the 'Aren't you people wonderful?' syndrome, and then, having mentioned the cinema manager who told her husband 'You can't bring *that* in here', she continued:

> Such occasional and not very serious attacks on individuality pale into insignificance beside the threatening shadows already cast by International Year. The cry is integration. But on all sides I see polarization. I see associations and societies for the handicapped, voluntary organizations acting on behalf of this catastrophe and that, services aimed expressly and exclusively at The Disabled and The Disadvantaged whether they want them or not.
>
> . . . I do not believe that integration will be achieved by the banding together of people with little but their infinitely varied disabilities in common and with no common pride to be taken in their very condition as other despised groups – women, black people, homosexuals – are able and right to take in theirs.

The views that Susan Beattie expressed are ones that I would endorse. She died in May 1989 and I do not know whether, had she lived longer, she would have felt her fears to have been well-founded. With me, she might not, I suspect, have been thrilled by the growing cult of disability awareness; she wished to be treated as a normal person, not as someone who was peculiar.

I cite examples of how I wish to be treated as a normal person. My right hand and arm being inoperative, I have always put my left hand out to the right hand of a person with whom I am to shake hands; I am not pleased if they, having observed my disability, deliberately stick out their left hand. At a reception when I am in a wheelchair it helps if the person I am talking to is sitting on a chair alongside. But when all around me are standing I do not want some well-meaning person to squat down on his haunches to communicate at my level. I do not wish, as certain vocal disability activists would have me do, to 'celebrate my difference'[2]. But I have never sought to 'deny' my disability – I unapologetically display it whenever I go out. And nor would I attempt to 'pass' as a regular able-bodied person.

I would be happier if the cultural mores, in Britain and elsewhere, did not insist that personal disablement is a taboo conversational topic. The most interesting feature that I display to people I have not previously met is my odd kind of disability. Small children are delightfully engaging – 'Why do you walk like that?'; 'What's wrong with your hand?'; 'Is that a magic chair?' I can explain to them, but I am never (or hardly ever) given the opportunity to do so to adult people, whose mythological assumptions about how distressingly damaged I am remain secure. I was not, for example, inclined to argue the issue on the occasion in the food court of a shopping centre when the friendly woman at the next table said, 'It makes us feel how lucky we are when we meet people like you'.

Institutionalised discrimination

I define institutionalised discrimination as the rules, relating specifically to disabled people and their use of buildings, amenities and facilities, which are set by statutory agencies, public and private companies and building management authorities. The rules may be formal or informal and their discriminatory nature may be either positive or negative. Included among them are regulatory controls governing access provision for disabled people in and around public buildings, meaning, for example, the for-the-disabled dictats of the British Part M building regulation.

I am not as a rule averse to privileged discriminatory treatment, and in my experience as a building user with a disability the benefits of positive institutionalised discrimination outweigh absolutely the constraints of the negative. I am a regular customer of shopmobility schemes which give me, at no cost, a scooter to ride around in. The orange badge on my car brings with it massive advantages which I readily exploit; on urban streets I can usually find a convenient place to park with impunity, without paying and with no fear of wheel-clamping. I welcome the reduced prices that come with being in a wheelchair on visits to Covent Garden and other theatres. I do not mind being patronised by Wandsworth Council; their decree was that registered disabled people should not have to pay to go swimming, and I know that if I were to argue the issue with the friendly staff at the Latchmere in Battersea they would feel offended.

I do not protest if, when in a wheelchair, I am moved to the front of a queue. This has happened on numerous occasions in Britain, but the most gratifying example was when I was using a wheelchair in Washington DC in October 1993. The White House is open to visitors for two hours only on most mornings, and to be assured of getting in normal people need to join the queue a couple of hours or so before opening time. In a wheelchair, the routine is to appear at the front entrance with companions, go through the security check and then be waved straight in. With my wife, my brother and his wife I was a beneficiary of the discrimination; we went in shortly before closing time on a wet Saturday morning while hundreds of people with umbrellas up were waiting hopelessly outside.

Negative institutionalised discrimination is exemplified by the restrictions on the use of public buildings by disabled people that can come with licensing controls, fire regulations and rules applied by local fire officers. As an ambulant disabled person I have always been exempt from these controls, and as a wheelchair user I have never been told that I could not use a building on account of them.

Architectural discrimination

Personal discrimination towards those with disabilities is displayed by individual people. Architectural discrimination is a very different matter. It is displayed by buildings. A public building treats its users collectively, not as separate individuals. The way that it does so (and whom it discriminates against and whom not) reflects indirectly a range of political and ideological stances. It reflects the attitudes of the architect who designed it, the client who commissioned it and whoever wrote the brief when it was being built. It also reflects the regulatory controls that governed its design and construction and affect its use. In this sense it reflects institutionalised discrimination, including, if it is a recently constructed building in Britain, the mandates of the Part M building regulation. Architectural discrimination can, like other forms of discrimination, be both negative and positive. And, perceptions of discrimination being subjective, what for other disabled people may be positive may for me be negative, and vice versa.

My reaction when, in or around a public building, I come up against a building feature which to me is negatively discriminatory may be annoyance, irritation, anger, amusement or unbothered acquiescence. Historic buildings tend to upset me less than new buildings. In London and in towns all over Britain there are large numbers of historic buildings that never were conveniently accessible to disabled people and could never be made accessible. Constructed before the days of electric lifts, they were designed by architects who worked to the design norms prevailing at the time and were not at all concerned about people with disabilities. With access regulations unheard of and discriminatory practices such as steps and stairs allowed to go unchecked, the outcomes that still stand today might not suit me, but no blame is to be attached to their architects and I do not malign them.

Architectural discrimination of a kind which annoys me is displayed by public toilet facilities. When I am using a wheelchair I do not feel I ought, every time I go out, to be obliged to take a special key with me to get to a toilet; I would like to suppose that normal public toilet provision will be wheelchair-accessible. And when I am an ambulant disabled person I do not feel that I ought to be faced by two flights of steps in the way of reaching normal toilet facilities.

The generality of building users being upright and able-bodied, I do not wish to be treated deferentially in a way which could inconvenience them, and which I would regard as condescending. As a wheelchair user, the example I cite is the height of lift controls. On the basis that lift controls should be reachable by independent wheelchair users, the recommendation in the 1987 approved document for the Part M building regulation was that they should not be higher than 1400mm, a limit reduced in the 1992 edition to 1200mm[3]. My view is that a 1200mm condition is absurd. It discriminates against me when I am an ambulant disabled person, and it is not beneficial when I am in a wheelchair. It is an extremely rare occurrence that I find myself alone in a wheelchair in a public building, and when I am I can as easily reach controls at 1500 as at 1200mm above floor level. The 1200mm condition, where it is applied, does not constitute convenient-for-all good practice; it is a manifestation of negative discrimination against the generality of building users, and of unwarranted positive discrimination in favour, supposedly, of wheelchair users.

Affirmative action and positive discrimination

In the arena of disability politics and the operations of the disability lobby, the widespread doctrine is that where there is discrimination against disabled people it has to be countered by positive discrimination, known in America as 'affirmative action'. The proposition is attractive. It seems sound. There *are* circumstances where the only effective antidote *is* positive discrimination. And if campaigning activists are to impress their constituency, they score well if they do deliver positive discrimination mandated by law. But, particularly in the field of architectural discrimination, the doctrine is flawed; what is frequently required is not special treatment but simply suitable accommodation as *normal*, with no discrimination at all. This is what I mean by affirmative action, and to illustrate it I draw on the issue of public toilet provision for women.

When using toilet facilities in public buildings – wc compartments in the case of women and wc compartments or urinals in the case of men – women typically take twice as long as men. To afford parity, the architect ought therefore to provide twice as many amenities for women as for men. In practice, he usually provides about half as many. The effect is a four to one discrimination ratio in favour of men. If the norm were equal numbers the ratio would drop to two to one, but there would still be discrimination against women. Parity would be obtained if the norm were for women to have twice as many amenities as men, and that would constitute affirmative action without discrimination.

If the norm were for architects to provide eight times as many for women as for men there would be positive discrimination in favour of women, on a scale similar to the discrimination currently exercised in favour of men.

On the principle that building regulations can be applied to building features only, the Part M regulation makes no requirements for provision for disabled people in parking areas alongside buildings. It is, however, now standard practice that selected spaces close to the building entrance are reserved for disabled people in customer parking areas to buildings such as supermarkets. It is special provision of a kind that I welcome. On the basis that it is normal integrated provision it constitutes affirmative action, but at the same time it represents positive discrimination.

To summarise. Affirmative action means, in respect of the group of building users concerned, suitable, convenient and adequate normal provision. Positive discrimination does not necessarily involve special provision, as is shown by the positive discrimination exercised in favour of men when public toilets are planned. Elsewhere, for example in the case of special for-wheelchair-users provision in theatres and other auditoria buildings where fixed seating is tiered, positive discrimination which involves special provision may simply be a matter of good practice.

The disability lobby and the Minister for Disabled People

Disabled people are the only segment of the population of Britain with a government minister specifically designated to take care of their interests. In March 1997 there is no minister for women, for children, for old people, for black people, for students, for homosexual people, for gypsies or for drug addicts. The Minister for the Disabled has a constituency of disabled people to whom it is understood that he listens and to whose concerns he responds. His role is ambivalent. He is also a member of the government, and in that regard he has to be a consensual politician. There will be occasions where government policy determinations are not compatible with the sectional interests of disabled people, and where he cannot dissociate himself from government edicts. As best he can, he has to balance his commitments.

In October 1974 Alf Morris became the first Minister for the Disabled. Mrs Thatcher, when she became Prime Minister in May 1979, retained the post and appointed Reg Prentice as her Minister for the Disabled. He was followed in January 1981 by Hugh Rossi, in June 1983 by Tony Newton, in October 1986 by John Major, in June 1987 by Nicholas Scott, in July 1994 by William Hague and in July 1995 by Alistair Burt. Having observed how they have balanced their dual commitments, my impression is that their inclination, affected perhaps by public and media focus on their 'for the disabled' duties, has been to give preponderant weight to pressure from the disability side. Other than Alf Morris, the minister with the highest profile in the disability arena was Nicholas Scott, who in 1990 made a point of changing his title from Minister for the Disabled to Minister for Disabled People. And it was Nicholas Scott who in 1994, beset with demands from disability activists (among them his daughter Victoria) for civil rights non-discrimination legislation, was most uncomfortable with his competing loyalties.

In the 1970s Alf Morris was a hero in the disability world[4]. The Chronically Sick and Disabled Persons Act was his personal achievement. It was a charter for disabled people, its edicts were sacrosanct, it was a not-to-be-disturbed monument. He saw it to be his job as Minister for the Disabled to administer the Act, including section 4. Dedicated as he was to the causes of disabled people, he was keen to develop links with organizations which promoted the welfare of disabled people and to listen to the voice of the disabled. More than anyone else, he fostered and cultivated the disability lobby.

That there is in Britain today some kind of corpus that can be called the disability lobby is not disputable. But exactly what it is and does is not easy to describe or define. I offer the following:

> The disability lobby is comprised of people who are concerned to promote what they consider to be advantageous for people with disabilities. It is a single-issue pressure group whose members view any particular topic solely from the perspective of the special needs of disabled people. It has no formalised structure and no discipline.

In Britain, as in America, the disability lobby operates on two levels, the national and the local. On the national stage its focus is on the affairs of parliament, on legislation and regulations which may directly affect people with disabilities. In the local arena it concerns itself with local issues and the needs of local disabled people. In Britain today the national disability lobby is essentially an Establishment creation, designed by politicians to suit politicians. I recall the years in the early 1970s when I served on the national executive committee of the Disablement Income Group, historically the most effective of disability lobbying organizations; our meetings were held in the Palace of Westminster (as a rule, on the Lords rather than the Commons side) at the invitation of members of parliament. Politicians, particularly constituency MPs, gain credit from being recognised as supporters of worthy causes. Responding positively to the special needs of disabled people is exceptionally meritorious, and politicians cannot go wrong on it – no one is going to stand up and tell them that promoting the interests of disabled people is not laudable. Collectively they constitute a powerful arm of the disability lobby.

I define the parliamentary lobby as members of the House of Commons and House of Lords who are instinctively inclined to back new legislation, or amendments to existing legislation, which they reckon will be widely regarded as advantageous for people with disabilities. To patronise disabled people, politicians need to have a 'voice' to which they can respond, and in the disability field they can select and cultivate useful voices, those of disabled people with whom, to their mutual benefit, they can collaborate. For the disabled people who are chosen and approved, the patronage can be seductive; there are rewards to be bestowed. Relatedly, there can be rewards for the able-bodied people who ally themselves with consumer activists and devote themselves to the cause.

The adversarial character of political debate in Britain, whereby single-issue pressure groups backed by sponsorship in parliament can exercise an immense influence on legislative decision-making, benefits the cause of consumer activists in the disability field. Among single-issue pressure groups the disability lobby would seem to be unique; it appears to be the only cause which evokes no overt hostility[5]. It is unassailable, the most potent of all parliamentary pressure groups. Within parliament the lobby has a powerful formalised body, the All Party Disablement Group. Comprising members of the Commons and Lords, it was formed in 1969 from the group of those who advised Alf Morris on the content of the bill for the Chronically Sick Act, and in late 1996 it had some 260 members.

The disability lobby is fuelled by its consumer representatives, by the people with disabilities who serve on committees to do with the affairs of disabled people, who speak at meetings, who attend national and international conferences, and who are presented by the media – by the press, on the radio or on television – as pundits who reflect the views of disabled people generally. These are leading activists, and in Britain in the context of the ideological debate on microism versus macroism, on whether people with disabilities should be treated as peculiar or as normal, their stance is significant. The disability activist is invariably a microist. He has to be, noting that here, as in the following paragraphs, 'he' means he/she. Only by presenting himself as a committed microist, as an advocate of special provision, special concessions and special benefits for disabled people, and then as a successful instrumentalist in their delivery, will he gain the applause and commendation of his constituents. In respect, for example, of new or enhanced social security benefits his stance is unexceptionable, but in the case of buildings and accessibility it has pitfalls.

The theme of this book, reflecting as it does my own personal moral and ideological views, is that architects when designing buildings can and should treat disabled people as normal. The great majority of disabled people can, I contend, be suitably accommodated by convenient normal provision of the kind obtained by expanding normal design parameters. Where that is done, there will be only a small minority of disabled people, in the main wheelchair users who are very severely disabled, who will on occasion have a genuine requirement for special provision. So in respect of access issues it may well happen that the needs of the generality of disabled people are not reliably represented by the activist.

Aside from being a microist, the consumer activist who serves as a representative of the disabled at committee tables and on the media is invariably a severely disabled person – he needs to be, both to have credibility and to demonstrate forcibly the points he is putting across. His status may be formalised. As ordained by relevant sections of the 1970 Chronically Sick and Disabled Persons Act, there are national committees on which there has to be a person who represents the interests of disabled people. Elsewhere there are 'for the disabled' organizations whose rule is that at least 50 per cent or some other proportion of their committee members have to be people with disabilities. To be appointed or elected to one of these symbolic posts, a disabled candidate has as a rule, I have observed, to have certain qualifications. Customarily, these are (i) he is not elderly; (ii) he is articulate and intelligent; (iii) he is mobile – either as an ambulant disabled person or a wheelchair user he can drive a car to get to meetings or can use public transport, or, if not able to travel independently, has a reliable partner who can regularly go with him to meetings; (iv) he is consistently able to find time to attend meetings; (v) he has a 'static' disability condition; (vi) if in employment, he works in the disability field, or has a public sector employer who allows him time off for attendance at meetings; and (vii) he is not financially impoverished.

The effect of all this is that from among the six million – or however many disabled people the activist may claim there to be in Britain – a great many are not appropriately represented; these include at one end of the spectrum the typical person whose disability is not very troublesome and at the other the person who is virtually housebound, financially insecure and has multiple disabilities.

In the early years of my professional career in the theatre of disability, before there was any disability lobby of the kind there is today, the people with disabilities who served on committees concerned with the interests of disabled people were few, and often they were polio-disabled. There are today numerous consumer representatives who are capable and effective advocates of the disability cause, but my impression is that across the board there has been a deterioration in the calibre of those who dominate the arena. In any local community there is only a small pool of disabled people who, noting qualification criteria, are prospective candidates for 'representation' service, a relevant factor being the paucity of wheelchair users in paid employment.* And on the national stage I observe how rare it is for a consumer representative to have the honesty, moral integrity and intellectual criticality which will prompt him to challenge some of the less credible doctrines which the disability lobby espouses.

Within the disability lobby a collaborator is an able-bodied person who becomes engaged in the theatre of disability and then becomes a dedicated advocate of the cause of disabled people. He (or she) is frequently a more enthusiastic evangelist than the typical consumer lobbyist, and collaborators are a vital component of the disability lobby. While there is no clear divide, the disability lobby may be seen to have two classes of membership – 'full' and 'associate'. Full members are committed-to-the-cause disability activists,

*National estimates are reported on page 176.

either people with disabilities or able-bodied collaborators; these are people whose work – either in the public or private sector, as paid employees or volunteers – is predominantly concerned with matters to do with disabled people. Associate members are people who deal only occasionally with disability-related issues, but who when they do ally themselves with the stance of disability activists. The important ones are those who are responsible for, or can influence, political decision-making, and there are occasions when members of parliament (including government or shadow ministers), quango board members and elected councillors of local authorities may be counted as associate members of the disability lobby.

Over 30 years and more I have, as participant or observer, sat at hundreds of committee tables where the force of disabled people as consumer representatives has been apparent. Predominantly these events have been national in character rather than local, as they have been on related seminar or workshop occasions. And frequently, across a wide band of topics, the same consumer activists have been present. Pulling rank is a reliable technique for controlling committee debates: 'Only disabled people know what it is like to be disabled'; 'Only disabled people can speak for the disabled'; 'Professionals patronise us'; 'We are the experts'. The exploitation of emotion and sentiment helps. It is culturally out of order to be rude to a person with a disability. Palpably false propositions asserted by consumer representatives tend to go unchallenged. The committee members representing interests inimical to those of disabled people do not wish to appear to be 'against' the disabled; they want to please and are anxious to view issues from a disability perspective. In the other direction, there is little or no reciprocity. Particularly where a deliberate decision has been made to appoint a chairman who is himself a person with a disability, the proposition that within committees dealing with the needs and concerns of disabled people there can be a balance between the interests of providers and consumers is spurious.

With crude estimates of relevant numbers I illustrate the unrepresentativeness of the activist who, at a committee table or on some other platform, purports to represent the interests of six million disabled people in Britain. As I have noted, the six million figure is based on an arbitrary measure of disability, and as an arbitrary measure it need not be disputed. My estimates, based as they are on my own impressions, are, I emphasise, simply indicative and have no secure data base.

One in a million
At any one time there are some half dozen or so politically prominent disability activists who are regularly invited by the media – radio or television – to speak on behalf of disabled people.

One in 100 000
There are some 60 national activists; these are disabled people who serve as representatives on influential national committees such as the Disabled

Persons Transport Advisory Committee, the National Disability Council (appointed by the Secretary of State for Social Security to advise him about the Disability Discrimination Act), and the management committees of leading national organizations of disabled people.

One in 10 000

There are some 600 local activists, meaning people with disabilities who are active members of local committees concerned with the special needs of disabled people.

One in 1000

There are some 6000 people with disabilities who serve as representatives on committees or at meetings of one kind or another that deal with issues of concern to disabled people.

The disability activist, as a rule a person with a severe form of disability, calls the tune. He may understand the problems caused by his own disability, but not those of others. A tendency I have observed among people with disabilities who are given a platform is to claim needs for disabled people that they do not themselves share; when asked, 'Does this matter to you?', the response is, 'No, but it matters to others'.

The disability lobby relies for its authority on the sustenance of mythology and legend. For nourishment the fertilisers include the force of suggestibility, capitalising on emotion and sentiment, the biased management of disability-related research and the selective interpretation of research findings. I define these propositions in relation to the operations of the lobby and the way that it promotes its causes. Mythology is the body of fictitious or unproven propositions which the lobby sustains and cultivates. Legend, relatedly, is popular stories whose truth has not been ascertained but which the lobby claims to be true and which it actively disseminates. The force of suggestibility derives from the constant affirmation, in a confident manner, of statements which are unproven. Sympathetic emotions and sentiments are aroused among able-bodied people by their fearful images of disability, and by the assertion or demonstration by severely disabled people of their distressing predicaments. The biased management of research is research programmes contrived in accord with politically correct premises and aimed at validating lobby prejudices. The selective interpretation of research findings means the ignoring or dismissal of results not in accord with approved mythology or established dogmas.

The dominant item in the iconography of the lobby is discrimination, the belief that disabled people are the victims of unwarranted negative discrimination in all its facets. Suggestibility is here a potent force. Able-bodied people, not themselves being people with disabilities, cannot know what it is like to be discriminated against on account of disability. It is a field where disability activists can roam unchallenged. By confident and constantly reiterated insistence that discrimination against disabled people is widespread, they can persuade and convince their audience that it genuinely is. They do not need to argue their case or seek to prove it: the force of suggestion instils blind belief and, affected by sentiment on the part of able-bodied people and political self-interest among disabled people, attracts a dedicated band of followers. Among them are many members of parliament, both in the House of Commons and the House of Lords.

As Minister for the Disabled from 1974 to 1979, Alf Morris nourished the disability lobby. In 1976 he set up the Silver Jubilee Access Committee, one of its key recommendations when it reported in early 1979 being that a successor committee should consider the issue of discrimination against disabled people. Mr Morris favoured the idea, and the Committee on Restrictions against Disabled People, to become known as CORAD, was launched in January 1979, again with Peter Large as its chairman. Later that year there was a change of government, but Reg Prentice, Mrs Thatcher's first Minister for the Disabled, decided that the committee's work should continue. Its terms of reference were 'To consider the architectural and social barriers which may result in discrimination against disabled people and prevent them from making full use of facilities available to the general public; and to make recommendations'[6].

As its report was to indicate, the committee was guided by a presumption that discrimination against disabled people was widespread, and felt that its job was to demonstrate how prevalent and disturbing it was. For this purpose a questionnaire-style letter was drafted, whose first question was 'Do you think that disabled people are discriminated against in Britain today?' Twenty thousand copies of the letter were sent out, to local authorities, disablement organizations, disabled people and other organizations and individuals. The number of responses received was 714, of which 463, or 65 per cent, agreed that yes, there was discrimination against disabled people. There were 201 replies to the question about how the situation had changed over the previous ten years, of which 185, or 92 per cent, said it had got better. On how best it was felt that discrimination against disabled people should be overcome, 61 respondents were in favour of legislation, of whom 23 did not refer to broad anti-discrimination legislation but only to the need for statutory access provision[7].

The committee attached much weight to the anecdotal reports of discrimination which it received, and these referred more frequently to access than areas such as employment and education: 'The letters we received showed clearly that disabled people perceive access difficulties as the most fundamental cause and manifestation of discrimination'[8]. To tackle access discrimination the report made eight recommendations, among them (i) access action groups should be set up to cover the country; (ii) every local authority should designate a particular person as its access officer; (iii) an English Access Committee should be established, paralleling access committees already set up in Scotland, Wales and Northern Ireland; (iv) designing for disabled people should form part of the training of all architects; and (v) legislation should be introduced to prohibit the establishment of a pedestrianised precinct or pedestrian shopping centre unless adequate parking arrangements had been made for disabled people with limited mobility range[9].

The committee's survey, relying as it did on anecdotal evidence only, presented no quantified data indicating the extent and scale of discrimination against disabled people in Britain. With nothing solid to support the claim, the note in the report was: 'We must also state that it is our firm conviction that the problems uncovered in the responses we received are only the tip of an iceberg'[10]. With the report came 42 recommendations, of which the first, and the one which would subsequently attract most attention and controversy, was that there should be legislation to make discrimination on the grounds of disability illegal. Not all the members of the committee were satisfied with the tone and content of the report prepared in their name, and three of them presented critical minority reports.

The CORAD report was issued by the Department of Health and Social Security in May 1982, and the disability lobby in parliament then began to exercise itself on energizing anti-discrimination legislation. Prior to that, in late 1980 and through 1981, the issue which most troubled the government on the disability front was the increasing pressure from the All Party Disablement Group and others for regulations which would enforce section 4 of the 1970 Chronically Sick and Disabled Persons Act. It was an issue which the Centre on Environment for the Handicapped had ventilated.

9 Britain: the pressure for regulations

At seminars which the Centre on Environment for the Handicapped held during the 1970s, the debate on how section 4 of the Chronically Sick Act ought to be enforced was sustained. Underpinning it was the presumption that enforcement mechanisms had to be developed within the bounds of currently available legislative instruments; essentially this meant Building Regulations and planning law. In connection with the work of the Silver Jubilee Access Committee, the issues involved were thoroughly ventilated on 15 March 1978 at a seminar on access to public buildings chaired by Peter Large. The consensus at the close of the meeting was that Building Regulations would be the best option for effective control[1], with access requirements being referenced to the British Standard code of practice *Access for the disabled to buildings*; in an updated version, this was to be issued in 1979 as BS5810. In the course of the seminar discussion the shortcomings of Building Regulations as a device for controlling accessibility had, however, been rehearsed: it was an inflexible instrument; it could treat new buildings but not existing buildings; it could not deal with areas around and between buildings; and so far as it could control accessibility it could do so only at the time a new building was completed, not with what might happen subsequently.

In November 1980 Dafydd Wigley, Plaid Cymru (Welsh Nationalist) MP for Caernarfon, was successful when the annual ballot took place for private members' bills. With direct experience of disability in his own family, he decided to present a bill which would augment the scope of the 1970 Chronically Sick Act and amend certain other pieces of legislation affecting the interests of disabled people. In particular he was determined to introduce measures for enforcing the requirements of section 4 and related access sections of the 1970 Act, Building Regulations being the option which he favoured.

The government did not like the idea, and on another front it was troubled by the financial burden which services for disabled people proposed in the bill might impose on local authorities. On 13 February 1981 when the bill came up for second reading in the House of Commons it prompted an objection, and the bill automatically fell. Many MPs were angry; they put down an Early Day Motion which attracted so much support that the government was obliged to give way and allow the bill to be reintroduced as the Disabled Persons (No 2) Bill. To keep it alive Mr Wigley had to make concessions, one of them being the dropping of the building regulations provision and the insertion in its place of a clause which asked local planning authorities to tell developers about the Chronically Sick Act and BS5810 when planning permission was granted.

That was not, however, the end of the matter. Making its progress through parliament at the same time was a bill which was to become the Local Government (Miscellaneous Provisions) (Scotland) Act 1981. It was a bill of the kind needed every so often to parallel English law in Scottish law, and there were MPs who thought to amend it to allow Building Regulations in Scotland to be employed to control accessibility. Worried by this and still insistent that the option was unacceptable, the government urgently set about devising an alternative access enforcement procedure to ward off the building regulations threat.

No time could be found for Mr Wigley's revived bill to be given a second reading debate in the House of Commons, and, with each stage being taken formally on the floor, it was passed to the House of Lords. It was to be debated there on 5 June, and before that an amendment reinserting the building regulations clause was put down by Lady Masham, the most prominent of the wheelchair-user activists who sat on the cross benches. With a similar amendment, the Scottish Bill was to be debated first, on 2 June, and before then the government came up with the formula it had hastily devised as a substitute for building regulations. To control access provision this relied on setting up an intervening statutory body, a procedure which the government assured Mr Wigley and his allies would guarantee the effective implementation of section 4.

Following hurried negotiations there was agreement on all sides, and the amendment which the government had concocted was incorporated into the Scottish Bill when it was debated at report stage in the House of Lords late in the evening of 2 June. With its vital amendment the bill was approved, the outcome being a statute which, when it came into force on an 'appointed day', would amend section 4 and other access sections of the Scottish version of the 1970 Chronically Sick Act. It required that any person providing a building which was to be accessible to disabled people had to make *appropriate provision*, defined as provision conforming with so much of the Code of Practice for Access for the Disabled to Buildings (BS5810) as was relevant to the case. This had to be done 'unless such body as may be prescribed by the Secretary of State is satisfied that in the circumstances it is either not practicable to make such provision or not reasonable that such provision should be made; and different bodies and different procedures may be prescribed for different classes of buildings or other premises to which this subsection applies'.

Lady Masham, noting with pleasure that she had been born and brought up in Scotland, said how delighted she was when she responded in the 2 June debate to the Scottish Minister, the Earl of Mansfield. She wondered who or what the statutory body (or bodies) might be, and how a complaints procedure might actually work. Lord Mansfield said there would be extensive consultations, and until they were concluded the appointed day for bringing the law into force could not be announced. He made a commitment: 'I do assure your Lordships that there will be no avoidable delay in working out the procedures that will apply'[2]. With the 'statutory body' amendment inserted into it, Mr Wigley's Disabled Persons Bill was debated in the House of Lords on 5 June, and, with the 'such body as may be prescribed' provision, emerged on 27 July as section 6 of the Disabled Persons Act 1981.

As a rule when new legislation is enacted the government circular presenting official advice on its interpretation and implementation follows soon after; in the case of the 1970 Act, for example, it was issued eleven weeks later. For the Disabled Persons Act of 1981 there was a delay of nine months, a happening related to section 6 not making it clear which Secretary of State would prescribe the statutory body. When eventually in April 1982 the circular was jointly issued by the Departments of Health, Environment, Education and Transport, the advice was, 'The activation of this section, the details of the procedure to be followed, and the identification of the body which would adjudicate in cases where the developer does not propose to make appropriate provision will be the subject of subsequent consultations with interested parties which are shortly to be put in hand'[3].

The decision, when it was finally made, was that the Secretary of State was the Department of the Environment's, with John Stanley being the minister who had the job of dealing with section 6. In July 1982 the Department issued a consultation paper proposing that the statutory body should be a subcommittee of the Building Regulations Advisory Committee, and that so far as developers and building providers were concerned the procedure would be self-instigated; they could complain to the body if they felt that the provision they had been asked to make was unreasonable, with no one having enforcement powers or sanctions, and without the views of consumers being taken into account[4]. Predictably, the disability lobby said this would not do. The government could not think to override the lobby and, confronted by the dilemma and with no other way out, Mr Stanley made the momentous decision; at the turn of the year he decreed that the enforcement instrument would have to be building regulations, and in February 1983 a consultation paper with proposals for control procedures was issued.

By then I was an architect member of the social research division in Directorate H(C) of the Department of the Environment's Housing Command, the Housing Development Directorate having been dismantled in accord with Mr Stanley's 'bedding-out' policy of setting professionals alongside their administrative counterparts. I had official duties within the division, and I also had a broad brief to advise others in the department on matters relating to the interests of disabled people. On that account, I communicated frequently with my building regulations colleagues, and there were many meetings when I discussed with them the form that the access regulation might take.

On 11 February 1983 the first of the private members' bills aimed at outlawing discrimination against disabled people was debated in the House of

Commons. The government would make sure that it did not proceed, and to mitigate hostility Hugh Rossi, the then Minister for the Disabled, was keen to emphasise how much the government was doing to help disabled people. He agreed, he said, with the need seen by the Committee on Restrictions against Disabled People for a national focal point on access matters, and announced his intention to consult on how an English Access Committee should be established. He saw it as being a non-statutory body with several valuable functions: it would promote and support the activities of existing local access groups; encourage the establishment of new groups and the designation of local authority access officers; provide information and help on existing legislation affecting access; and advise the government on major access problems. It would, he envisaged, comprise members with expertise from the voluntary, statutory and private sectors, and would be placed in an existing organization with experience of access matters affecting disabled people[5].

The principle was that the committee should be one on which the interests of disabled people were balanced by those of the construction industry. The Department of Health and Social Security would fund it, and to do so it would use section 64 powers, the powers of the Secretary of State for Health under section 64 of the Health Services and Public Health Act 1968 to fund national voluntary organizations which promote and deliver services of a kind that statutory health and social services authorities are authorised to provide under relevant legislation. The notion that access was a welfare issue was reinforced.

Mr Rossi's decision was to invite the Centre on Environment for the Handicapped (CEH) to provide the administrative base for the Access Committee for England, a relevant consideration being that under Miss Langton-Lockton's direction CEH was not a disability pressure group. Constitutionally the Access Committee would not be independent; technically it would be a subcommittee of CEH, the registered charitable organization. Arthur Goldthorpe, an active polio-disabled wheelchair user who before retirement had been a dental practitioner in Leeds, was invited to chair the Committee. Nineteen committee members were appointed, among them on the consumer side Peter Large and a number of other disabled people prominent in the field of disability politics. John Dobinson was appointed access director; with a professional background in social administration he was already well acquainted with access issues – he was an ambulant person with a severe physical disability, a consequence of polio in childhood. Attended by Tony Newton, the successor to Hugh Rossi as Minister for the Disabled, the inaugural meeting of the Access Committee for England was held on 23 March 1984. At that meeting, the topic which most exercised members was the Department of the Environment's consultation proposals for Part T of the Building Regulations.

National building regulations had first been introduced in England and Wales in 1976. Prior to that, local councils administered their own controls, as a rule based on model bye-laws, for the construction of buildings in accord with the health and safety requirements of the Public Health Acts of 1936 and 1961. The 1976 regulations were a substantial package of technical prescriptions specifying precisely what had to be done for compliance purposes. The proviso was that a local authority could relax a condition where appropriate, but the standard format was inflexible, and, based as it was on traditional construction methods, discouraged innovative techniques. In early 1982 the decision was made to recast the regulations. The regulatory requirements would be simplified; in place of the unwieldy collection of detailed technical prescriptions there would be a series of functional requirements, with injunctions of a kind that said, 'The building shall stand up'; 'The building shall not catch fire'; or 'The building shall not smell'. These requirements would come in Parts, and each Part would have its Approved Document. The purpose of approved documents was to present guidance on how to satisfy the regulation requirements; they would say, 'This is one way to do it, but should you wish you can do it a different way if that will be equally effective'. Compared with the old, the new procedure proved immensely sound.

The recast regulations, in eleven Parts from A to L, were to become the Building Regulations 1985. Their assembly was already well advanced in January 1983, and by then it was too late for the access regulation decreed by John Stanley to be prepared in the new form and catch up with them. Instead, it would come in three stages. As an immediate and temporary expedient it would cite BS5810 (the code of practice on access for the disabled to buildings) for deemed-to-satisfy purposes, and would come in as the fourth amendment to the 1976 Building Regulations; they were in Parts from A to S, and it would be added on as Part T. Then, when the new 1985 regulations were issued, it would, in exactly the same form as Part T, be tacked on to those regulations, as Schedule 2. Finally, when an approved document had been drafted and agreed, the 1985 regulations would be amended by statutory instrument, with the access regulation incorporated as Part M. The stage was set; Britain, it seemed, was at last beginning to catch up with America.

10 America: the advance towards the Americans with Disabilities Act

When Jimmy Carter became President of the United States of America in January 1977 the draft regulation for section 504 of the 1973 Rehabilitation Act was ready to be made effective. It was signed by Joseph Califano, Secretary of the Department of Health, Education and Welfare, on 28 April, and under the title *Nondiscrimination on Basis of Handicap – Programs and Activities Receiving or Benefiting from Federal Financial Assistance* was issued in the Federal Register of 4 May 1977. Its political significance was emphasised in background information notes[1]:

> Section 504 represents the first Federal civil rights law protecting the rights of handicapped persons . . . It establishes a mandate to end discrimination and to bring handicapped persons into the mainstream of American life.

Subpart C, Program Accessibility, was the central requirement of the regulation[2]:

> All new facilities are required to be constructed so as to be readily accessible to and usable by handicapped persons. Every existing facility need not be made physically accessible, but all recipients must ensure that programs conducted in those facilities are made accessible. While flexibility is allowed in choosing methods that in fact make programs in existing facilities accessible, structural changes in such facilities must be undertaken if no other means of assuring program accessibility is available.

The 1961 A117.1 American Standard had been reaffirmed in 1971, and in 1977 had not been amended or revised. It was the only standard that could be officially cited for section 504 purposes, and in respect both of new construction and alterations to existing buildings the advice was: 'Design, construction, or alteration of facilities in conformance with ANSI A117.1-1961 shall constitute compliance'[3]. In respect of employment practices the section 504 regulation introduced the important concept of reasonable provision. While cost was not germane to establishing discrimination, the principle was that in effecting remedies the needs of the disabled person who was an employee or job applicant should be balanced against the burden on the employer. Employers were required to make reasonable accommodation, meaning that they had to make suitable arrangements for a disabled employee unless the costs involved would cause undue hardship[4].

Encapsulated in the maxim that every American child should be able to believe that he (or she) could one day be President of the United States or become a billionaire, the principle underlying American civil rights legislation is that all Americans should, without discrimination, have equal opportunities, in particular the right of equal access to education and employment opportunities. From there on, in line with the self-help ethos of American society, each individual is out on his own; he has to compete with others, and by his own endeavours earn his way. He has no right of access to health or welfare services; those he has to pay for, subject to where, as a senior citizen, he has while in work paid his insurance dues and is eligible for Medicare, or, as an impoverished person with virtually no resources, is entitled to Medicaid.

In New York Judy Heumann, angered at the way the education system discriminated against her, had campaigned for equal opportunities for handicapped children, a campaign which, with lobbying by parents' organizations, was to result in rights legislation, the Education for All Handicapped Children Act of 1975[5]. In Berkeley, Ed Roberts and his colleagues launched the consumer-led independent living movement. Their campaign was for welfare rights, for a statutory system which would give disabled people the cash resources to employ their own care attendants and control their own lives. Section 504 would not, however, deliver any welfare rights; it was about equal rights of access to public services administered or funded by federal agencies, and it was to extend those rights to private sector services that there would be a struggle. By 1977 fifty-two independent living centres modelled on the Berkeley prototype had been set up in towns and cities across America[6]. In 1978 the Department of Health, Education and Welfare decreed that state rehabilitation offices could fund local centres in their area, and by 1987 some 300 had been established[7]. It was through them that the consumer-led rights movement became cohesive and forceful[8].

On one topic to do with discrimination and the benefits that would come with all-embracing civil rights legislation every disabled person who joined an independent living centre was a professional expert; it was architectural barriers. He or she knew about the obstacles which were encountered in and around buildings; they were real and self-evident. They were also obvious to able-bodied people; their discriminatory effects were of a character that any sensible person could comprehend. They provoked emotive images of denial, rejection, segregation and second-rate citizenship. As an issue on which to campaign for 'rights' and generate support they were unbeatable – they were immensely more appealing than arguing that people with severe disabilities should have equal employment or education rights. Public sympathy on the issue was guaranteed, and many able-bodied people, among them some in positions of power and influence, would actively collaborate, both in pressing the cause and taking practical action where they could to remove barriers. Access to public transport had its merits as a rights issue, but it was nowhere near as enticing. And little or no public sympathy, let alone positive backing, was to be gained from campaigning for people's taxes to be spent on giving disabled people cash to employ others to help them.

The emergence of the nation-wide consumer-driven disability movement which helped engineer the Americans with Disabilities Act of 1990 can be traced to two events, the opening of the Berkeley Center for Independent Living in 1972 and the incorporation of section 504 in the Rehabilitation Act of 1973. Prior to that there had been no coherent consumer force. Disability activists did not lobby for the introduction of section 504, the crucially significant first piece of pure civil rights legislation for disabled people. It had, somewhat fortuitously, been presented to them.

From April 1977, the month of the San Francisco sit-in, disabled people around America had a goal. Historically they had been denied their civil rights; now, in the limited sphere of federally-funded services, they did have rights. They could fight for more, for comprehensive civil rights on the same basis as Americans who were black people or women had fought for their rights. With regulations for the implementation of section 504 in place, the movement that was to eventuate in the passing of the Americans with Disabilities Act in 1990 became virtually unstoppable.

In 1974 the US Department of Housing and Urban Development, one of the three government agencies authorised to institute access regulations under the Architectural Barriers Act of 1968, had commissioned a programme of research for informing a revision of the 1961 A117.1 American Standard and extending it to include residential environments. Ed Steinfeld, a research architect at the University of Syracuse, conducted the programme and, with Tim Nugent as his chairman, was appointed secretary to the American National Standards Institute committee. The new standard was issued in 1980. It did not, as it might have done, tackle the vexing issue of application criteria; instead, in line with the 1961 precedent, it limited itself to the specification of design standards and left the job of establishing application conditions to enforcement agencies.

With design standards for housing facilities incorporated, the 1980 A117.1 was more comprehensive than its 1961 predecessor – it had 68 pages in place of 11. It benefited from the accumulated knowledge and experience of dealing with access issues over nearly 20 years, and it was more carefully drafted. It would seem, nonetheless, that the committee was satisfied that the 1961 A117.1 had prescribed specifications which were essentially right. The 1 in 12 ramp gradient remained. So also did the narrow toilet stall for wheelchair users, although it was now presented as the alternative, not the 'standard' wc compartment, and the front-to-back internal dimension had become minimum 66in (1675mm) rather than 56in[9]. The new standard facility, shown in Figure 10.1, was designed to permit wheelchair access and lateral transfer; its minimum internal dimensions were 1420 × 1525mm – slightly less spacious than the 1967 CP96 toilet, which in Britain had been

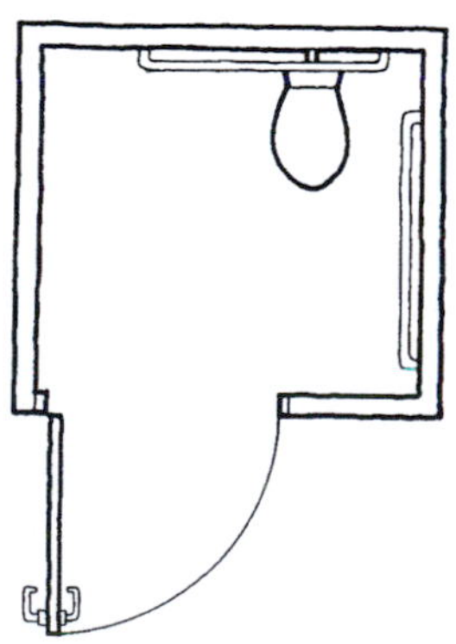

10.1 The 1980 A117.1 accessible toilet stall

rejected because of its inadequate space and replaced in 1979 by the BS5810 toilet*.

An important feature of the 1980 A117.1 was the extended list of definitions, in which 'accessible' now had a place: 'describes a site, building, facility or portion thereof that complies with this standard and that can be approached, entered and used by physically disabled people'. The concept of the 'accessible route' was also introduced; this was a principle which had from early years been grasped by practitioners – the rule that if buildings were overall to be usable by people in wheelchairs there had to be a convenient approach to at least one accessible entrance, from where there had to be a level or suitably ramped route to all parts of the building that a wheelchair user might need to reach. The definition of an accessible route was: 'a continuous unobstructed path connecting all accessible elements and spaces in a building or facility that can be negotiated by a severely disabled person using a wheelchair and that is also safe for and usable by people with other disabilities'[10].

This, more than any particular design standard, served to reinforce the paramountcy of the independent wheelchair user in the arena of accessibility politics, and it was from then on to be a key feature of accessibility codes and standards. The presumption was that an accessible route for independent wheelchair users could automatically take care of the access needs of all other disabled people; where, for example, a lift was available to move wheelchair users from one floor to another, it was unnecessary for stairs serving the same vertical circulation function to have handrails for the benefit of ambulant disabled people[11].

The field on which disability activists were to campaign most effectively for all-embracing civil rights legislation was architectural barriers. On this, there was work to be done. The framework for mandating rules for making buildings accessible was still only half-made. The 1980 A117.1 presented the design specifications. But the other and equally essential part – national application conditions – had yet to be produced. They needed to be, and for meeting the requirements of section 504 and the Architectural Barriers Act of 1968, it was the Architectural and Transportation Barriers Compliance Board (the Access Board) which would battle for the rigorous conditions that would satisfy the demands of disability activists.

Back in 1973, concerned that the Architectural Barriers Act was not being treated seriously, Congress had asked the United States General Accounting Office to investigate what in practice the General Services Administration had so far achieved. The report, when it was received in July 1975, was described by one House Representative as 'a horror story of agency inaction and confusion which I find hard to believe'; it was 'a shocking commentary on our system of values that more has not been done to make public

* Comparative data are in Appendix 4, page 379. The 1980 A117.1 accessible toilet stall was retained as the advised standard when A117.1 was revised in 1986, and in 1991, still unchanged, became the standard for toilet accessibility to meet the requirements of the Americans with Disabilities Act.

buildings accessible to the physically handicapped'[12]. From then on, Congress was increasingly disinclined to suppose that the General Services Administration, along with the two other agencies asked to produce regulations, would generate the action that was needed.

The brief given to the Access Board when it was first set up in 1973 was to coordinate and encourage efforts to implement the requirement of the 1968 Architectural Barriers Act that all federal and federally-funded buildings should be accessible to disabled people. As initially instituted the board had eight members, the heads (or their delegated officers) of the government departments or agencies who were principally interested*. An executive director was appointed and then staff members, among them people with disabilities. The board at first had no mechanism for heeding the voice of disability interests; this was remedied in 1974 by an amendment to the 1973 Rehabilitation Act which authorised the appointment of a consumer advisory panel.

On the Access Board each federal agency member sought to protect the particular interests of his own agency and press its concerns. There was virtually no cooperation, let alone any coordinated drive. The board was frustrated, and when its director reported that it was unable to develop an effective independent role, Congress decided that it must be restructured[13]. Using an Amendments Bill, Congress decreed in 1978 that the board would have, alongside its nine agency members, eleven public members appointed by the President, at least five of whom would be people with disabilities. At the same time, having become increasingly irritated by the failure of the four designated agencies** to cooperate on the production of regulations for the implementation of the Architectural Barriers Act, it asked the Access Board to issue minimum guidelines and requirements for accessible design. This was a crucial mandate, one that the board was to exploit. The idea was that there would be collaboration all round, but the board saw itself as having a brief to duplicate independently the work that the four agencies had been asked to undertake. Its staff set about their task with determination.

President Carter was unhappy about the provisions made under the bill and unsure that it was right for public members to be in a majority on the board; he would have preferred an equal vote[14]. He could not change the law, but for nearly a year he dithered before appointing public members. Without a quorum the board could not meet, and the staff worked uninterruptedly on the preparation of access guidelines and requirements. Eventually, in December 1979, Carter appointed the public members. Nine of the eleven were people with disabilities, six of them being wheelchair

* These were Transportation; Labor; Interior; Health, Education and Welfare (HEW); Defense (DOD); Housing and Urban Development (HUD); the General Services Administration (GSA); and the Veterans Administration. In 1976 they were joined by the US Postal Service. In 1980 HEW was divided into the Department of Education and the Department of Health and Human Services, both of whom had a place on the board.

** The GSA, HUD and DOD had in 1976 been joined by the US Postal Service.

users[15]. Power shifted immediately. The board was now a disability pressure group, and its public member activists proceeded to stifle the federal agency representatives by preventing those who were not agency heads from having voting powers. Time was pressing. So long as Jimmy Carter was President, the public members, with a disabled person as chairman, could press ahead. The threat was that in January 1981 Ronald Reagan would be the new President and would seek to emasculate the Access Board.

On the design standards side, the presumption had been that A117.1 was inviolable, adopted in toto as it had been by hundreds of building code agencies around the country[16]. On the application conditions side, there was no established precedent. In February 1980 the board issued a notice of intent to undertake rule-making for minimum guidelines and requirements[17]. The notice posed questions, among them the awkward matter of how accessibility standards were to be applied to leased buildings.

Under the terms of federal government legislation in America, Congress (the legislative arm of government) can authorise a government agency to introduce statutory regulations, and there is then technically nothing that the President or other agents of the executive arm of government can do to prevent the agency setting what rules it wishes. The Access Board, with its activist staff now backed by most of the public members, could therefore seek to impose design standards and application conditions on any terms that its members determined. In August 1980, following its February notice of intent, it issued a detailed set of proposed rules for its Minimum Guidelines and Requirements for Accessible Design[18]. Some but by no means all of the design standards were in accord with A117.1 and those that were not were more demanding[19]; the board also included additional material to explain the standards. But predictably it was not the standards but the proposed application conditions which provoked the feud that followed.

At issue was the accessibility of federal buildings which were constructed, altered or leased with the help of federal funds. New construction was not the problem; under the terms of the Access Board's proposed requirements new buildings on green-field sites could as a rule be designed without any significant cost penalties. The controversy focused on existing buildings which were to be altered or leased. Broadly what had been happening across America up to that time was that state or local access law covered new buildings only, and where it did extend to building alterations there did not have to be strict compliance with A117.1 standards – suitable provision was agreed on an ad hoc basis. Under its new militant chairman Mason Rose (who had ousted Max Cleland, the moderate chairman appointed by President Carter) the Access Board now proposed that any existing building which was to be altered or leased would, with whatever restructuring might be necessary, have to be brought into line with the strict requirements applicable to new buildings[20].

On the controversial issue of leased buildings the board sought the advice of the Department of Justice, whose view was that, under the terms of the

Architectural Barriers Act as amended, the board was entitled to mandate the accessibility of leased buildings when leases were arranged or renewed. The Carter administration, concerned about the implications, asked the board to delay the issuing of the final rules. Mason Rose replied that, as an independent agency, the board was not obliged to obey White House instructions[21]. With its public members controlling its decisions, it defied the federal agencies and refused to modify its proposed rules. It moved swiftly, realising that the Reagan administration when it took office would seek to thwart its intentions. On 16 January its final rules were officially published[22]. The date for compliance with them was immediate, with no period for phasing them in. The US Postal Service announced that it would not observe the board's requirements and would follow instead its own, less stringent rules.

On 20 January 1981 Ronald Reagan became the fortieth President of the United States. Deregulation and curbs on extravagant public expenditure were his policy themes. His Vice-President, George Bush, headed a task force on regulatory relief. Principal targets were section 504 and the Architectural Barriers Act, a major concern being the considerable expenditure that the Access Board's minimum guidelines threatened to generate. The task force recommended that the board be eliminated and its duties transferred to the General Services Administration; 1 October 1981 was the date set for abolition.

Threatened with extinction, the Access Board was prepared to compromise. Its guidelines, its chairman now contended, were a 'living tool' - they were constantly under review and could be changed. He suggested issuing an advance notice soliciting comments on how they might be improved. For the federal agencies, this was not good enough. At the May meeting of the board the US Postal Service representative proposed that the guidelines issued less than four months earlier should be annulled.* The chairman ruled the motion out of order. One of the public members then defected to the federal agency side. This shifted the balance of the board, and at the July meeting the proposal for the guidelines to be revised was defeated, and a motion to annul them passed.

Mason Rose, the chairman of the board, was not going to give in easily; the annulment order must be challenged. Out in the country there was a hidden army of disabled people whose troops he and his backers could enlist. Comments on the order were invited, and with the help of a suitably phrased draft protest, more than a thousand were received from disabled people and their organizations. Members of Congress reacted sympathetically; for Senator Alan Cranston, Reagan's determination to destroy the Access Board was 'a blatant example of this administration's lack of concern for the requirements of laws designed to guarantee basic civil rights for this significant segment of our citizenry'[23].

At the September 1981 meeting of the board Mason Rose reported that 93 per cent of the comments received favoured retention of the guidelines. But the pressure to conciliate had become immense. Rose had been talking with

* American terms are 'rescinded' and 'rescission'.

C. Boyden Gray of Vice-President Bush's office, who indicated that a way out of the predicament might be found. The compromise agreed at the December meeting of the board was that the annulment move would not go ahead, and that the board would amend its existing rules in a form that the administration could accept. This was facilitated by a climb-down, whereby the board agreed that existing leased buildings would not be regulated; the contrived device was that there was a legal dispute which the courts were expected to resolve and on which the board would express no opinion[24]. The board also agreed that its design standards should generally be brought into line with the 1980 A117.1, and that some of the more stringent application conditions should be modified. At the May 1982 meeting the proposed revisions were unanimously agreed. On 4 August 1982 the Access Board's suitably revised version of its *Minimum Guidelines and Requirements for Accessible Design* was officially published in the Federal Register[25].

In the meantime, the four standards-setting government agencies (the General Services Administration, the Department of Housing and Urban Development, the Department of Defense and the US Postal Service) continued to work on their uniform guidelines, and as the *Uniform Federal Accessibility Standards* these were issued in August 1984[26]. In no important respects were its application requirements significantly less onerous than those of the Access Board's minimum guidelines. Two very similar accessibility standards were thus in place, but for federal and federally-funded buildings the Uniform Federal Standard became the officially approved standard, and in 1984 it was only these buildings which under civil rights legislation, meaning section 504 of the 1973 Rehabilitation Act, had to be accessible to disabled people. Prospectively, however, the Access Board could look forward to the day when all-embracing civil rights legislation for disabled people would be enacted, and for private sector buildings its minimum guidelines would then prescribe accessibility requirements.

The turbulent years were over: the Access Board had survived and it could view the outcome with much satisfaction. The only significant issue on which it had been obliged to give way was on the accessibility of existing leased buildings, and that was a minor impediment; under the terms of the Uniform Federal Standard accessibility was required when a lease was arranged for any building that had not previously been leased for federal purposes, or when an existing lease was renewed. When any leased building was altered or extended, it had to be made accessible on the same basis as buildings that were owned.

In the form in which it emerged, the Uniform Federal Accessibility Standard was substantially more demanding – and therefore favourable to disability interest groups – than the federal agencies would have wished to settle for at the start, or would themselves have put in place had they elected in 1968 to work together positively. Disability activists and their supporters could be well pleased with it, the first officially authorised national standard that mandated application conditions as well as design standards. The ultimate goal they now had in sight was comprehensive civil rights legislation.

11 Britain: the turmoil on the way from Part T to Part M

On statutory accessibility controls, the position in 1984 was that America had surged ahead while Britain lagged way behind. The decision had been made in early 1983 that building regulations would be the instrument for enforcing national controls, but in the preceding 12 years no preparatory development work had been undertaken; the only official material that was available was BS5810 *Access for the disabled to buildings*, an 11-page document with an inadequate set of design standards.

The first stage of the legislative process for enforcing access requirements would be the Part T regulation, Part T being an add-on to the 1976 Building Regulations. It would be provisional, serving only until the new-style building regulations were brought into operation in 1985, an effect of which, a year or two later, would be to bring in a new access regulation, Part M. For the quick delivery of Part T, BS5810 would be cited; compliance with its design recommendations would be deemed to satisfy the requirements of the regulation. BS5810 dealt only, however, with design standards; it did not cover application conditions, and predictably it was application conditions which would provoke argument and controversy. Although ultimately it was Part M that mattered, the application conditions of Part T would anticipate the scope of Part M, and a vital issue was therefore the scope of Part T.

The proposed Part T regulation represented a radical departure from established practice. From A to S, all the other regulations had been instituted under the health and safety remit decreed by the 1936 and 1961 Public Health Acts. Part T was different; it was coming in under the welfare and convenience remit authorised by the 1974 Health and Safety at Work etc. Act. It was of particular concern to one segment of the building user population – disabled people, whose interests were represented by disability organizations. These were not on the Department of the Environment's list of organizations consulted on matters to do with building regulations, and an ad hoc list had to be compiled which predictably had gaps. As a result, two consultation rounds on Part T were completed without a number of interested disability organizations having learnt of it[1].

The first proposal for the new Part T went out for consultation in February 1983, with comments requested by the end of March; its provisional conditions were that new public and employment buildings would be required to be accessible only if they were above a certain size, and that alterations or extensions to existing buildings would not be covered. The response to it was critical, so that when in October 1983 the second round followed, the size condition for new buildings was dropped, and certain alterations and extensions were to be covered. But at the same time there was a new and unexpected proposal, one that would severely restrict the scope of the Part T regulation; it was that in the case of new construction only single-storey buildings, meaning buildings consisting of a ground storey only, would be required to be accessible – new multi-storey buildings would not be covered.

The rationale was that BS5810, the British Standard Code of Practice on which Part T would depend, specified design standards only for *access* for the disabled; there was no related code of practice which prescribed suitable provision for *egress* for the disabled, and without an egress code there had to be constraints on Part T's scope. The relevant statute was section 24 of the 1984 Building Act, formerly section 59 of the 1936 Public Health Act; it required that where plans of a building were submitted to a local authority for approval in accord with building regulations:

> the authority shall reject the plans unless they show that the building, or, as the case may be, the building as extended, will be provided with such means of ingress and egress and passages or gangways as the authority, after consultation with the fire authority, deem satisfactory, regard being had to the purposes for which the building is intended to be, or is, used and the number of persons likely to resort to it at any one time.

The Department of the Environment officials who had seized on this apparent impediment to the scope of the proposed Part T did not, it would seem, seek to review and debate the implications of it, or to explore whether it might after all be feasible to introduce a Part T which would mandate access provision on all floors of new multi-storey buildings without prejudicing section 24 requirements. Their preoccupation was with the lift dilemma. For access to the upper floors of multi-storey buildings, people in wheelchairs could go up in passenger lifts. But since lifts could not be used as a means of escape they would not, in the event of a fire, be able to come down in them. The principle underlying evacuation procedures was that everyone in a building would be able to escape unaided by using protected fire escape stairways. Wheelchair users could not do that. Part T would therefore need to have a ground-floor-only rule, a situation which could not be remedied until an appropriate code on egress for the disabled had been issued by the British Standards Institution.

Back in 1970, access for the disabled to public buildings had been mandated by section 4 of the Chronically Sick and Disabled Persons Act. Had the Department of the Environment been encouraged at that time to act positively to implement section 4 the issue of egress as well as access would surely have been addressed, and the problems it presented would have been resolved. For a start, the idea that people should be allowed into multi-storey buildings only if they could walk downstairs to get out could have been challenged. In hospital buildings it was not assumed that when the alarm sounded all the patients would jump out of bed; the design principle was horizontal compartmentation, with those in an area where a fire occurred being moved to a protected area nearby. Reasonably therefore the same principle could be applied to wheelchair users in public buildings; they could move (or be moved) to a place of refuge from where they could be assisted to a place of safety, if need be by being carried out by rescue service officers.

What would also have been realised had section 4 been tackled in the early 1970s was that accessibility controls could not rely only on building regulations, and nor could they depend on a code of practice issued by the British Standards Institution. By 1983, when the government was obliged by force of circumstances to opt for building regulations for the enforcement of section 4, BS5810 was firmly established as an icon in the disability world. It was taken for granted that it had to be the instrument on which control mechanisms would be built, and when the egress hitch occurred the understandable assumption was that the British Standards Institution would have to back it up with a complementary egress code.

Following the October 1983 consultation on their proposed Part T regulation linked to BS5810, the Department of the Environment felt satisfied, by March 1984, that appropriate procedures had been conducted, and were drafting a statutory instrument which would be the Fourth Amendment of the 1976 Building Regulations; this, the Part T regulation, would require that only single-storey buildings had to be accessible to disabled people. On 23 March 1984 the newly established Access Committee for England held its first meeting. The Department of the Environment's recently issued consultation proposals for Part T of the Building Regulations was on the committee's agenda, and when it was discussed several members expressed dismay that the long-awaited access regulation would cover single-storey buildings only. Rather than take it as a fait accompli they wanted it stopped. With that in view, the plan, to be guided by John Dobinson, was that the regulation should be prayed against.

Building Regulations in Britain are secondary legislation, made in the form of statutory instruments. For England and Wales, the Secretary of State for the Environment and the Secretary of State for Wales have joint powers to make building regulations under the controlling primary legislation, the Building Act of 1984. Scottish building regulations are made by the Secretary of State for Scotland under Scottish legislation. A statutory instrument is first *made*; it is then (a few days later) *laid before parliament*; and then, on an appointed day (usually some months later), it *comes into operation*. Since appropriate consultation procedures will have preceded the making of a regulation, the process is usually unimpeded. But for a period of three weeks following the laying of a statutory instrument for a new regulation, members of parliament may *pray against* it; if any do so, it has to be withdrawn or the matter debated in parliament.

The Access Committee's vital link was with the All Party Disablement Group. The Group asked Ian Gow (who had succeeded John Stanley as the Minister for Housing and Construction) to explain the proposals, and a meeting was arranged with him and his building regulations officials in early April. The Group was not satisfied and, impressed by the representations they had received from the Access Committee, decided that if the statutory instrument were laid they would pray against it. On 22 May 1984 Jack Ashley and John Hannam, the chairman and secretary of the Group, wrote to *The Times* to explain why: 'Disability organizations do not accept that means of access should be dependent on means of escape. . . . they have always maintained that egress is a question of management'. Unless access to all floors of buildings was regulated, buildings would continue, they said, to be built with design features that prevented access to those floors, and the letter went on:

> The regulations would be a retrograde step based on an assumption that disabled people are not given access above the ground floor unless specific egress conditions are applied. The consequential implications are very obviously discriminatory. Disability organizations feel they have little to lose by not accepting the regulations. Their acceptance would be yet another step in the history of compromise, delay and pussyfooting. This has proved fruitless in the past and they are now saying loud and clear that it must end.

Faced with the threat, Mr Gow felt he had no option, and announced that he would not proceed with the regulation[2]. The onus was then on his officials to find some way out of the predicament. In the event, they did; a means of retrieving Part T was discovered by invoking parts of British Standard 5588 *Fire precautions in the design and construction of buildings*, which had already been issued. These were Parts 2 and 3; Part 2 was the code of practice for shops, and Part 3 the code for office buildings[3]. Both included notes on the management of means of escape for disabled people; this, it was felt, allowed access to all floors of shop and office buildings to be regulated by Part T, and on that basis the Access Committee was content for it to go ahead. For all multi-storey public buildings not covered by Part T, it was agreed that a part of BS5588 would be prepared to deal with means of escape for disabled people, one which would eventually be issued as Part 8.

The statutory instrument for the Part T regulation in its revised form was made by the Secretary of State on 22 March 1985, laid on 2 April 1985, and came into operation on 1 August 1985. Item T2, *Provision of facilities for disabled people*, decreed that the regulation applied to (a) office and shop buildings; (b) single-storey factory buildings; (c) single-storey school buildings; and (d) 'other single-storey buildings if they are buildings to which the public are to be admitted, whether on payment or otherwise'. Enforcement relied on BS5810. Other than for school buildings, for which the Department of Education's Design Note 18 *Access for Disabled People to Educational Buildings* was applicable, the advice under item T3 was that the requirements of regulation T2 would be deemed to be satisfied by compliance with the design recommendations in clauses 6.2 to 8.4.4 of BS5810:1979.

With regard to multi-storey office and shop buildings, nothing was said under T3 to the effect that egress requirements would be satisfied by reference to relevant recommendations in Parts 2 and 3 of BS5588. This may (I do not know) have been because there were not in those Parts any recommendations for suitable physical provision for egress for disabled people; there was not, for example, a recommendation that suitable refuges should be provided by escape stairs to assist the evacuation of wheelchair users. The form and content of the Part T regulation did not demonstrate the validity of the restrictive determination, that without an all-embracing egress code there could not be an access-to-all-floors-of-all-buildings regulation. Had debate on the issue been permitted, it might have been found, as in America, that the only building provision which warranted a mention was refuge spaces. In the form in which they were needed – large enough for wheelchair placement – the provision of refuges was simply good practice; it was not provision of a kind that had to be made specially for disabled people.

It was not until 1992 that regulations were introduced which did cover all floors of all public buildings. Had there not been procrastination in 1983 the seven-year wait could have been avoided; a Part T regulation covering access to all floors of public buildings could have been produced in 1984 without reference to any egress code of practice issued by the British Standards Institution. The relevant factor was that the Part T requirements presented in 1985 included items not covered by BS5810, for example wheelchair spaces in auditoria buildings, and they could have included design and application conditions for places of refuge for means of escape purposes. Had information been sought about American procedures, this means of resolving the problem might have been identified.

The initial American Standard, the 1961 A117.1, had specified design standards for access provision only, and through the 1960s and 1970s this had not inhibited state governments from mandating accessibility throughout multi-storey buildings. The 1980 revision of A117.1 did cover egress provision; the terms of the relevant specification and supporting advice[4] were:

> A reasonable number, but always at least one, of accessible routes serving any accessible space or element shall also serve as a means of egress for emergencies or connect to an accessible place of refuge. Such accessible routes and places of refuge shall comply with the requirements of the administrative authority having jurisdiction.
>
> In buildings where physically handicapped people are regularly employed or are residents, an emergency management plan for their evacuation also plays an essential role in fire safety.

America, in other words, did not make a meal of egress provision. Three factors were pertinent. First, America was bold where Britain was cautious. America, the land of opportunities and civil rights, had a vision: from the start, from the day that the 1961 A117.1 was launched, it was determined that its buildings could and should be made comprehensively accessible to disabled people. Second, America was spirited where Britain was niggardly; it had an idealistic commitment to the cause which defied meanness. Third,

America was dedicated to integration where Britain was drawn to segregation and discrimination. In America disabled people might have special needs, but they could be treated as normal people. In Britain the doctrine was that disabled people were not normal people: they were disadvantaged people whose special needs had to be dealt with by making special provision for them; in the event of an emergency they would not be able to get out of buildings in the same way as normal people, and it was proper to discriminate against them.

The enforcement of access controls under Part T was a temporary arrangement; for long-term purposes, what mattered would be the terms of the proposed new Part M regulation. The introduction of Part T was nonetheless a notable happening in history. For the first time in England and Wales access provision in buildings would be regulated under legislation. To celebrate the event, a national conference 'Implementing Accessibility' was arranged by the Access Committee for England and held on 26 March 1985. It was chaired by Stephen Byrne, President of the Royal Town Planning Institute, and among those who spoke was Tony Newton, Minister for the Disabled. The keynote speech was delivered by Patrick Jenkin. As Secretary of State for the Environment, he was pleased to announce the introduction in England and Wales of statutory controls for implementing accessibility. He had previously been Secretary of State for Social Services, and during his time in that post the International Year of Disabled People had been held. The government was determined to maintain the impetus that the Year had created, and in the Environment department Mr Jenkin had, he said, new and challenging opportunities to help disabled people[5].

Behind the new regulations there were, Mr Jenkin emphasised, three important precepts, the key words for which were *enablement, normalisation* and *collaboration*. Enablement meant giving disabled people the opportunity to contribute, to make choices, to seek new horizons, to realise their potential; it was a precept that should guide those who design, construct and manage public buildings. To create accessible environments which would help disabled people there had to be collaboration – from planners, developers, architects, building control officers, building managers and fire officers, along with representatives of the disabled.

On the second precept, normalisation, Mr Jenkin wanted a revolutionary shift in attitudes to disabled people; in particular, he wanted architects to shift their attitudes[6]:

> To put my message across, I am going to use two horrid words, micro and macro.
>
> Micro, meaning a focus on individual needs and individual remedies, is the traditional way that we have treated disabled people. It has served us well, and Britain has an excellent record for its concern for disabled people, and for the comprehensiveness of its services and benefits.
>
> But ought we constantly to treat disabled people as a special group, as disadvantaged people with special problems, who need special attention and special amenities and special gadgetry?

> Entrenched attitudes, particularly sincere and caring attitudes, are not easy to shift. It isn't a comfortable shift to make. But can we try? Can we go macro? Isn't the best way, wherever we can, to make all our buildings accessible to everyone – so that they cater, as a matter of course, equally for those who are disabled as well as for those who are able-bodied?

With the coming into force on 1 August 1985 of the Building Regulations 1985, the Part T access regulation became Schedule 2, *Facilities for disabled people*; Schedule 1 comprised Parts A to L – the new recast regulations. Schedule 2 had been anticipated as 'the breakthrough we all wanted'[7], but it was no breakthrough – it was identical to Part T, in a new guise. The real breakthrough that was looked for would come, it was hoped, with the new Part M building regulation, a revolutionary access regulation that would, in response to Patrick Jenkin's normalisation precept, be formulated on macro principles. That, however, was not to be.

The story of the progress from Patrick Jenkin's vision in March 1985 to the production of the Approved Document for the new Part M regulation in November 1987 was a story of relapse: of reverting from idealism back to expedient pragmatism, and of continuing to push one step at a time along a faulty route rather than leaping boldly in a new direction. There are three strands to the story, running in parallel with each other. One is about the Access Committee for England and the line taken by disability lobbyists, another about the way the Part M regulation was handled, and the third, which I cover first, about myself and my advocacy of macroism.

A feature of the third edition of *Designing for the Disabled* as I wrote it during the early 1970s much troubled me; it was that the book displayed no firm ideological stance. On a secure ethical foundation it ought to have presented a coherent methodology of designing for the disabled, and it did not. The most constructively critical review of the book was published in *Design for Special Needs*, the journal of the Centre on Environment for the Handicapped[8]; it was written by Frank Duffy, who in later years, from 1993 to 1995, was to be President of the Royal Institute of British Architects. I quote extracts:

> My criticism starts where the book stops. One of the many traps architects have fallen into in the last twenty years in this country has been to overvalue technical information. Another mistaken characteristic of design methodology in the same period has been a tendency to seek and magnify the abnormal: the severe problem, the prison, the total institutions, the handicapped: half of the explanation is compassion: the other half, I think, an implicit fear that it is only in stressful circumstances that design data becomes entirely relevant.
>
> In *Designing for the Disabled*, the technical data are presented entirely separately from the commentary. There is a contradiction here. The commentary is intelligent and sensitive to a point where it begins to dither. The beautifully argued, but in the end unresolved, discussion of the balance between independence and dependence in the lives of the handicapped is one example of this. . . . all this sensitive, if rather hazy and in the end inconclusive heart-searching, co-exists with technical data marshalled with a precision rarely

> equalled... Is this precision entirely possible in such an apparently cloudy context?
>
> The second tendency – the implicit belief that it is the abnormal which is the generator of design solutions – is, of course, exaggerated firstly by the very particular condition of the disabled and secondly by the very format of the design data which highlights special requirements. This is entirely justifiable except that it tends to make us forget whatever designing for the disabled has in common with designing for anyone.
>
> Perhaps the fourth edition of this admirable book will resolve the gap between the commentary and the information and so contribute as much to design methodology as to the disabled.

For some twelve years following the publication of the third edition of *Designing for the Disabled* I had little inclination to prepare a fourth edition, for two reasons. First, I had no wish to indulge in the prolonged chore of revising the book in the same encyclopaedic format as the third edition. Second, and more importantly, I had no clear vision of the political ideology that ought to inform the design guidance presented to architects. It was only when I began to articulate the concept of macroism as a new paradigm for designing for the disabled that I was encouraged to feel there was a task I wanted to tackle.

As it was first set up by Kenneth Bayes in 1969 the Centre on the Environment for the Handicapped campaigned to promote independent living in the community for mentally handicapped people. The policy theme was normalisation, a theme maintained by the two directors who followed, George Miles and Jean Symons. Sarah Langton-Lockton, who took over in April 1979, was determined that the Centre should not be a disability pressure group; it must be non-aligned. In its role as an information and advice centre, and as a forum for debate on issues relating to disabled people and their environments, it should seek impartially to serve all those who looked to it – disabled people, disability organizations, building developers, architects, planners, occupational therapists, local authority administrators and others. At the same time as not being an overtly political agency, it needed, however, to have a policy platform. Broadly, its aim was to promote the shaping of environments which for handicapped people would be enabling, which gave them opportunities to contribute to and participate in the normal life of society. Essentially, normalisation was still the dominant theme.

But how, in terms of the practicalities of buildings, was normalisation to be interpreted? In discussions I had with Miss Langton-Lockton, normality was a concept that troubled us. Could we say that disabled people were normal people? Clearly, in respect of their physical characteristics, they were not normal people. They were different people, and that meant – did it not? - that they ought to be treated as different people. We needed to resolve the matter.

It was in 1980 that at meetings and conferences where I spoke I began to talk about microenvironmental and macroenvironmental. The homes where disabled people lived were microenvironmental; they could be specially designed or adapted to meet the special needs of a particular disabled person. Public buildings were macroenvironmental; they could not be 'special', and they had to accommodate their users collectively, including those who were disabled. In 1983 I was invited to present a paper at the annual meeting of the American Environmental Design Research Association, held that year at Lincoln, Nebraska. It was an opportunity to clarify my thinking, its title being *The ideology of designing for the disabled – some thoughts on cultural influences in the United States and Britain on design formulations and their moral and ethical bases*[9]. I drew on the contrast between the self-help culture of America and the social welfare culture of Britain: the historical and established British culture for helping disabled people was microenvironmental – whether for employment, education, housing or transport, remedial action was concentrated on individual disabled people, or identifiable groups of disabled people. In America, energised by Tim Nugent's 1961 American Standard, a macroenvironmental breakthrough had occurred; it was, I noted, a revolution which only America could have activated.

Back in England when I talked at meetings, my line was that America was macroist while Britain was microist. Only by taking the macro route could disabled people be treated as normal people. Britain, I suggested, should follow American practice. 'Oh no', was the reaction from wheelchair users who had been to America – the small-size toilets for the disabled in America were inaccessible, and if that was good macroism in practice the idea was indefensible. That macroistic toilets in America were not as spacious as they might be did not, I said, affect the principle. Toilets were, however, the issue which would constantly bug the debate.

Where I became confused was with the supposition that macro and micro were mutually exclusive, that there had to be a choice, that artefacts (building features, for example) had to be either macro or micro. In a sense that was admissible: micro is special provision for the disabled, and macro is normal provision which accommodates disabled people. What I did not adequately comprehend was the significance of degrees of macroism.

My simplistic and muddled stance was exemplified by the paper I read when I was invited to give a memorial lecture in Belfast in October 1985[10]. Implying polarities, it was entitled *Macro or micro – how should we treat disabled people?* Having discussed provision in public buildings I went on to talk about housing, and the initiative launched by the Prince of Wales Advisory Group on Disability and the National House-Building Council to promote the concept of visitability housing. I concluded by saying that macroism was about having a downstairs loo in two-storey houses. The proposition was one I felt at the time was apt, but I had not then refined the concept of macroism in the context of building design. Not to have a downstairs loo in a two-storey house does not constitute microism. In a small house a single loo upstairs is normal provision, and as such it is macro, in that it caters for disabled people who can get up and down the stairs without difficulty. A downstairs loo, however small it may be, is much more macroistic. If it is large enough for a person in a wheelchair to enter, use, turn around in and exit, it will be yet more macroistic. Macroism, in other words, is about extending the parameters of normal provision.

With my absorption with artefacts and whether they were macro or micro, what I did not initially realise was that the issue of macroism versus microism was thoroughly political. Micro provision on its own – for example, the special unisex facility in an otherwise inaccessible public toilet – displayed microistic for-the-disabled societal attitudes. Embracing macro provision displayed macroistic for-everyone societal attitudes. By focusing on attitudes in his plea for normalisation as a precept for implementing accessibility, Patrick Jenkin was wholly right when he spoke at the March 1985 conference.

In 1985 I was satisfied that, in the context of designing for the disabled, the virtues of macroism as a controlling ideology were unarguable. What was not so straightforward, with the concept not at that time having been operationally articulated, was how the precepts of macroism were to be translated into practice for the purpose of instituting the proposed Part M building regulation. But not having begun to think about the intricacies of the matter, that did not trouble me. Sarah Langton-Lockton was keen for CEH to adopt macroism as its governing policy plank, and her chairman and management committee members agreed. With the establishment, under CEH's auspices, of the Access Committee for England in March 1984, the access director, John Dobinson, also backed the macro policy line, and agreed that it should inform the work of the Committee[11].

Within the Department of the Environment none of us was comfortable with the usage of the terms 'macro' and 'macroism' for our purposes, and we spent many weeks, including an intensive afternoon workshop discussion, seeking some alternative and more friendly word that could communicate the concept. The nearest analogy was 'universality'. But that did not have the same connotations, and we remained stuck with 'macro' and 'micro'. As Patrick Jenkin had said, they were horrid words.

Circular 33/68, the Department of the Environment's advice to local authorities on special public toilets for disabled people, had been issued in 1968, and through the mid-1970s there were frequent calls for it to be updated. In 1978 I worked on a draft revision of it, and to discuss the draft, and with it the whole issue of public toilet facilities for disabled people, a seminar arranged by CEH was held on 4 October 1978[12]. The topic that most engaged participants was vandalism and how to prevent it. Local authorities could not afford to employ attendants at all their public conveniences, and the regular practice was that they were unsupervised. Particularly in urban locations, the unisex toilet for the disabled was an attractive target for young people who relished causing destruction and wreckage. Rails had been ripped from walls, basins had been smashed and doors had been set alight. Remedial work was expensive, repairs could not be completed before there was more damage, and toilets for the disabled had had to be kept locked.

Four authorities represented at the seminar had instituted a key scheme to help local disabled people, with keys being issued on request to people on their disabled register. The idea of a national key scheme was debated, and although its potential disadvantages were recognised there was agreement that a meeting should be held to consider the proposal. It took place at the offices of the Royal Association for Disability and Rehabilitation (RADAR) on 21 August 1979 and the scheme was then set up, with the national key being manufactured by the sanitaryware company Nicholls and Clarke and distributed through RADAR. The key scheme prospered, but Circular 33/68 never was revised. The lack of official enthusiasm for it was endorsed by the policy edict of Mrs Thatcher's incoming government in 1979, which was that central government ought not to instruct local authorities on how they should deal with matters such as the provision of public lavatories which they could just as well handle themselves.

11.1a

During the 1980s, aside from the controversy surrounding the terms of the Part M building regulation, the debate on the ideology of macroism versus microism focused principally on the planning and design of public toilets. It was most spirited during 1987, affected first by an article 'Is the unisex loo ideologically sound'?, which I wrote for the April 1987 issue of the CEH journal *Design for Special Needs*[13], and then by a follow-up seminar two months later. The event which prompted the article was a visit I made in July 1986 to the public toilets at Cartgate, on the A303 London to Exeter road between Ilchester and Ilminster. On trunk roads frequently used by holidaymakers the Department of Transport was at that time planning a series of rest areas, each with picnic tables and a public toilet, and Cartgate was the first. A wheelchair-using member of the Access Committee, travelling regularly as she did between Exeter and London, had learnt of the scheme and had stopped off to inspect the facility. The disabled toilet, she reported, was not exemplary – it had not been correctly planned and equipped in accord with BS5810. Encouraged by her, I called in to look at it on a journey from Plymouth back to London a few weeks later. It was a brick building (Figure 11.1a) with normal male and female amenities on either side, each approached by a single high step (Figure 11.1b). Tucked in on the female side was the special disabled facility (Figure 11.1c), approached by a ramp. The door was locked, and above it was a large notice:

11.1b

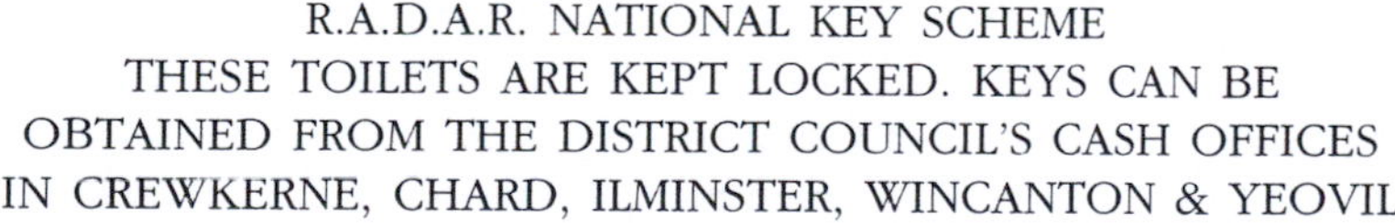

R.A.D.A.R. NATIONAL KEY SCHEME
THESE TOILETS ARE KEPT LOCKED. KEYS CAN BE
OBTAINED FROM THE DISTRICT COUNCIL'S CASH OFFICES
IN CREWKERNE, CHARD, ILMINSTER, WINCANTON & YEOVIL

Thoughts occurred to me. Did South Somerset District Council imagine that a wheelchair user arriving on an urgent mission without a RADAR key would be encouraged to journey seven miles down the road to Ilminster, find the cash office (assuming they arrived on a weekday during working hours), purchase a key, and then travel back again? Yes, given that the site

11.1c

11.1 The public toilet on the A303

was unsupervised, it was necessary for the disabled toilet with its array of grabrails and gadgetry to be kept locked; that could have been anticipated. So why, to help all those wheelchair users and other severely disabled people who would arrive without a key, could not the approach to the normal male and female facilities have been level or suitably ramped rather than having a high step? And at the same time, why could not one of the wc cubicles on each side have been sufficiently large to accommodate a wheelchair user and helper, even if vandal-prone equipment had to be omitted?

The Cartgate toilet facility was microism epitomised. Later that year I chanced unexpectedly on public toilets that I felt exemplified macroism in practice; they were in Coronation Gardens by the sea at West Kirby in the Wirral. Without a special for-the-disabled unisex toilet, normal male and female amenities were approached on the level behind a screen which afforded privacy. On the female side were three wc cubicles, one of which was planned and equipped for wheelchair users. On the male side the only wc cubicle was similarly large and accessible.

At the June 1987 seminar on public lavatory provision I illustrated my macroism-is-better-than-microism theme with slides of the Cartgate and West Kirby facilities. Alan Lacey of the Wirral's department of environmental protection spoke, with illustrations, about his council's preference for macro-style public toilet facilities[14]. A critical view of macroism, supported by other wheelchair users among the participants who spoke, was put by Arthur Goldthorpe, chairman of the Access Committee for England; he reported the inaccessible for-the-disabled toilet facilities he had found in America, and asked whether macroism might destroy the freedom of disabled people to move around the country with confidence and destroy the twenty years of steady improvements to sanitary facilities in Britain[15].

In 1987 I still imagined there had to be a choice between macro and micro, that particular building features had to be one or the other. As I realise now, there never was a problem. Macroism and microism are not mutually exclusive: when, for example, public toilets are planned, there is no reason why wheelchair-accessible macro facilities should not be incorporated in normal male and female areas, with a separate micro unisex facility being provided alongside. The macro principle, that, when a building is designed the interests of the disabled people who are to be its users will be best served by extending the parameters of normal provision, is, as I see it, logical and simple. It ought, it might be supposed, to be a straightforward matter to communicate it to others, to people of normal or above-average intelligence. The reality is that it is not. At meetings, conferences, and in journal articles that I have written, I have for years been attempting to explain what it means, almost always without success. The dominant reason is that the generality of English people are inherently incapable of imagining that there can be any means of treating disabled people other than in a microist fashion. The English are so conditioned by the culture of social welfare, manifested, for example, in the edicts of the 1970 Chronically Sick and Disabled Persons Act, that they can only think of disabled people in terms of individuals or groups of individuals, of people with particular problems, difficulties and disadvantages. In absolute form, the images and ethos are most entrenched among disability organizations and their campaigning activists.

I record an anecdote as an example of the comprehension barrier. The Queen Elizabeth II conference centre in Westminster had been the venue for a national conference on disability issues, attended by large numbers of wheelchair users. The few special unisex toilets in the building could not satisfy the demand, and the normal facilities were not wheelchair-accessible. I discussed the issue with a prominent disability activist, a leading member of the Access Committee for England; the fault, I said, was a lack of convenient macro provision. No, he insisted, what there should have been was much more micro. There was no meeting of minds.

At the root of the barrier is an apparently insurmountable obstacle: the radical leap that is required in attitude of mind. The leap is from thinking top-down, the microist way, to thinking bottom-up, the macroist way. In the example just cited, the disability activist could only think top-down: some disabled people need special unisex toilets; special unisex toilets suit all disabled people; all disabled people need special unisex toilets. Where the item under consideration does not have a special for-the-disabled ingredient the thinking is related: automatic doors at supermarkets are good for the disabled; automatic doors are good for everyone; what is good for the disabled is good for everyone. That perspective is microistic; the macroistic view is that what is good for everyone is good for the disabled.

Top-down microist thinking, of thinking of the disabled only in terms of individuals with particular problems, difficulties and disadvantages, is pervasive, and amenable to the force of suggestibility. It can be reinforced by oft-repeated claims, allegations and complaints put out by disability activists and their collaborators. Disability activists have a vested interest in fertilizing the cult of microism. And collaborators, among them some with impressive records in business or public service, have a habit of discarding their criticality, and sometimes even their common sense, when they engage in the arena of disability politics. Fallacies, to their mind, become facts: that it is technically possible to make any existing building wheelchair-accessible, for example; that knobbly bubbles on pavings at street crossings genuinely help blind people; that wheelchair-accessible London taxis really are convenient for everyone. Against the volume of prejudiced microistic thinking, the field for the propagation of macroism is not well seeded.

The initial 1983 proposals for the Part T regulation had been drafted impartially by the Department of the Environment – there were no preliminary soundings which afforded more prominence to the views of any one outside organization more than another. But following the 'pray against' threat in May 1984, the Access Committee for England was acknowledged as the dominant agency with whom from then on there had to be negotiations, and what was to be crucial was that the Committee was controlled by disability activists of a microist persuasion.

I worked in a research division of the housing command of the Department of the Environment, and advised on matters relating to building regulations only when asked to do so by colleagues in the Building Regulations Division. The arrangement was that I spent a nominal half day each week as adviser to CEH, and in that connection I had a useful role; it was helpful for my building regulations colleagues to have a neutral outside agency as a forum for debate on the formulation of access regulations, and the seminars which CEH held with representatives of disability organizations, the construction industry and professional and local authority interests served that purpose well. Through the Centre I had close links with the Access Committee, and had frequent discussions with Sarah Langton-Lockton and John Dobinson on the form of the proposed regulations, discussions to which colleagues in the Department of the Environment's Building Regulations Division contributed from time to time.

In September 1985 Kenneth Baker replaced Patrick Jenkin as Secretary of State for the Environment. Affected by the admissible view that a policy adopted by one Secretary of State did not necessarily bind his successors, the official policy line shifted. It reverted back to for-the-disabled microism. The rationale was that the Department of the Environment was obliged to institute access regulations only in order to enforce the requirements of section 4 of the 1970 Chronically Sick Act; they therefore came under the welfare (not the convenience) remit of Building Regulations, and they must be specifically for the disabled.

It was on this basis that the draft approved document for the proposed Part M regulation was put out to consultation in September 1986. On behalf of the Access Committee, John Dobinson negotiated its terms with Department of the Environment officials[16]. Compromises were in order. An important item was the cut-off point for lift provision in multi-storey buildings. This was measured in terms of floor areas, and John Dobinson asked that the areas initially proposed should be reduced; when this was agreed, he felt that the revised draft for the approved document should be accepted. Arthur Goldthorpe, chairman of the Access Committee, backed him; on the 'one step at a time' principle, he favoured acceptance of the first stage of the Part M regulation in its microistic form. At its May 1987 meeting the Access Committee agreed that Part M should go ahead on the terms negotiated with the Department of the Environment.

A rift was provoked between CEH and the Access Committee for England. Constitutionally the Access Committee was not an independent organization – technically it was a subcommittee of CEH. Hugh Spencely, the then chairman of CEH, and members of his management committee asserted that CEH had a macro policy, that it had been endorsed by John Dobinson, and that agreement to go ahead with a microistic Part M should not have been conceded. Arthur Goldthorpe was not to be persuaded; the Access Committee, he claimed, could and should, under its terms of reference, operate independently. The scene was set for a feud that persisted. In November 1987 the approved document for Part M was issued, and in the following month the new Part M regulation came into effect. At its January 1988 meeting the Access Committee, pressed by its disability activists, voted overwhelmingly in favour of abandoning macroism and adopting instead a micro policy. By then, affected by a health problem which had troubled him through much of 1987, John Dobinson had resigned as access director.

The 1987 Part M regulation, like the 1985 Part T regulation, applied to new multi-storey buildings only where they happened to be office or shop buildings. And, notwithstanding Patrick Jenkin's urging of macroism, it was still informed by the ethos of welfarism. But on the access-to-buildings front, Britain, it seemed, was catching up with America. It was, however, to be another five years before Part M, in a new version, would cover all new multi-storey buildings. And before then, with its Americans with Disabilities Act of 1990, America would again have leapt ahead.

12 The Americans with Disabilities Act

In America the Architectural Barriers Act had been passed in 1968. It then took 16 years, to 1984 when the Uniform Federal Accessibility Standard was issued, to produce the guidance needed to explain how the law was to be implemented. The Rehabilitation Act had been passed in 1973; after that it took four years for regulations to be issued on the operation of its vital civil rights mandate, section 504.

With the enforcement of the Architectural Barriers Act and section 504, one corner of the civil rights battlefield had been conquered – the sector which was federal government territory. With that sector now occupied, the disability movement had troops in place to launch its broad campaign across two other sectors. One was the remainder of the public sector, the buildings, services and facilities that were administered and developed by state governments and local municipalities without federal funding. The other, the private and commercial sector, was the biggest prize, and in 1984 it seemed that it would involve a prolonged struggle to take it. Private business interest groups could not be expected to yield readily. In the case of black people and women, all that private businesses had been obliged to do under the 1964 Civil Rights Act was to change their practices. There had not as a rule been any cost penalties, and never any harsh ones. Rights for disabled people, with buildings of all kinds having to be made accessible, was a different matter.

With varying conditions, numerous state governments and local municipalities had already issued building codes requiring that private sector buildings such as offices and shops must be made accessible when they were newly constructed or altered[1]. As private businesses had learnt, the costs involved could be onerous. If proposed civil rights legislation were now to indicate that private businesses were to be subjected to demands similar to those applied to federal buildings, there could be an uproar. Given what had happened with the Architectural Barriers Act, a protracted, arduous and acrimonious struggle was predictable. But in the event, with the terms of the bill having been negotiated and compromises agreed, the Americans with Disabilities Act of 1990 sailed through Congress. A crucial factor was that President Bush had been converted.

Back in 1981, the brief that George Bush as Vice-President had been given by Ronald Reagan was deregulatory relief. A principal target was the provisions which disability interest groups had secured under the Rehabilitation Act of 1973, in particular those of section 504. When hearings were held on the form that deregulation might take, there was a chorus of protest from the by now well-orchestrated disability lobby. Some 40 000 cards and letters were sent to the White House[2]. Bush agreed to negotiate his plans with disability groups; with his legal adviser and close associate Boyden Gray he met with leading activist Evan Kemp, a legal professional whose disability was a form of muscular dystrophy. Disabled people, Kemp told Bush, wanted independence; they wanted to get out of the welfare system and into jobs; they did not need a paternalistic government to help them – they wanted to help themselves[3]. Bush was impressed. In March 1983 he announced that the section 504 regulations and education rules would stay as they were. The lesson he had learnt was that it was politically injudicious to tangle with the disability lobby – it was better to join them.

Within the Reagan administration there were senior officials who favoured the enactment of civil rights legislation for disabled people. In 1986 the National Council on the Handicapped (now the National Council on Disability), an independent government agency whose members were appointed by the President, issued its report *Toward Independence*[4]. The existing limited patchwork of protections for disabled people was, it said, inadequate; what was needed was comprehensive civil rights legislation. In 1988 it followed this with *On the Threshold of Independence*[5]. The legislation would be called The Americans with Disabilities Act, and a draft for it was prepared by Robert Burgdorf, a polio-disabled person who was the Council's legal specialist.

Evan Kemp and Boyden Gray became close friends, and from Kemp in his bulky electric wheelchair Gray learned at first hand about the discriminatory effects of inaccessible buildings. He became convinced that comprehensive civil rights legislation was needed, and he helped convince Bush. In August 1988 when he accepted nomination as the Republican party's presidential candidate, Bush pledged, 'I'm going to do whatever it takes to make sure the disabled are included in the mainstream'[6]. He became a dedicated advocate of civil rights legislation, and many disabled people who at presidential elections traditionally voted for the Democratic candidate switched to vote for him.

All was in place in January 1989 when George Bush was inaugurated as the forty-first President of the United States. The Americans with Disabilities Bill had been revised in a form that made it more acceptable to small business interests. The important modifications were to the proposed application conditions for accessible private sector buildings, both new construction and alterations or extensions to existing buildings; these were set out in new draft guidelines prepared by the Access Board for attachment to the legislation.

In May 1989 the revised bill was introduced for Congress to consider. In June Attorney General Dick Thornburgh testified that it had the full support of the Bush administration; with backing from all sides of Congress, it was clear from the start that its passage into law would not be obstructed. Committee hearings on the bill continued through 1989 and into 1990. Small business interest groups complained that the provisions were vague and potentially costly, but the opposition that had been predicted was muted. Disability activist groups continued to hold rallies and demonstrations, but no more pressure was needed. When the few remaining contentious issues had been settled by negotiation the bill was put to final votes; on 12 July 1990 in the House of Representatives it was passed by 377 to 28, and on 13 July in the Senate by 91 to 6. On 26 July, at a celebratory gathering on the White House lawn, it was signed into law by President Bush. He enthused; the Americans with Disabilities Act would ensure, he said, 'that people with disabilities are given the basic guarantees for which they have worked so long and so hard. Independence, freedom of choice, control of their lives, the opportunity to blend fully and equally into the right mosaic of the American mainstream ... let the shameful wall of exclusion finally come tumbling down'[7].

In Britain when new legislation is introduced the government department responsible for its implementation issues an advisory official circular to agencies concerned; in the case of legislation relating to services for disabled people these are principally health and local authorities. The drafting of any circular is undertaken by civil servants; they do not as a rule consult outside on the form the advice should take, and their aim is to complete the task with the minimum of delay. Guidance is presented in the circular about the interpretation of the law, but statements about precisely what it might mean tend to be avoided; the understanding is that where the interpretation of the law is disputed there can be recourse to the courts and they will settle the matter. Official circulars tend as a rule to be brief; the one accompanying the Chronically Sick and Disabled Persons Act 1970 comprised seven pages, and that for the Disabled Persons Act 1981 four pages.

Procedures for the introduction and presentation of federal government legislation in America are remarkably different. According to its character and scope, a bill is considered by appropriate standing committees of the Senate and the House of Representatives who conduct public hearings. Rule-making follows when the bill has been passed into law, with the final rules being issued by the Secretary of the government department concerned; in the case of the Americans with Disabilities Act this was the Attorney General, the head of the Department of Justice.

In the course of its passage through Congress the bill for the Americans with Disabilities Act was considered by one Senate committee and five committees of the House of Representatives. It was presented in five parts, called Titles; those with provisions for making public buildings accessible to disabled people being Title II, *Public Services and Transportation*, and Title III, *Public Accommodations*. For the purposes of Title II, state and local governments were *public entities*, and their civic buildings, schools, colleges and universities had to be accessible; where their existing buildings and facilities could not be made fully accessible there had to be programme accessibility. For the purposes of Title III, a *private entity* was any individual or entity (other than a public entity) which owned or administered a place of public accommodation. For Title III the Access Board had been instructed to draft accessibility rules which would be referenced in the Act. In January 1991 the Board issued an update of its 1982 Guidelines, the new version[8] being consistent with the 1986 A117.1 American Standard.

At Congress committee hearings, and then in the course of rule-making, the Access Board's draft was considered, with negotiations focusing predominantly on the proposed application conditions[9]. The Department of Justice had overall responsibility for the implementation of the Americans with Disabilities Act, and for Titles II and III it issued notices of proposed rule-making on 22 and 28 February 1991. Comment period followed; when it closed two months later 2718 comments had been received on the two rules, with 222 more coming shortly after. To encourage public participation in the development of the rules the Department held four public hearings during March, at Dallas, Washington DC, San Francisco and Chicago. At these hearings 329 people testified and 1567 pages of testimony were compiled. The comments that the Department received, 75 per cent of which came from disabled people or disability interest groups, occupied six feet of shelf space and contained more than 10 000 pages. All were read and analysed.

The Attorney General was authorised to prescribe regulations, and as final rules these were issued by the Department of Justice and published in the Federal Register of 26 July 1991. Part III, *Nondiscrimination on the Basis of Disability by Public Accommodations and in Commercial Facilities*, is the rule for the implementation of Title III, and as published it incorporated as Appendix A the approved final version of the *Americans with Disabilities Act Accessibility Guidelines*, known in America as ADAAG and referred to here as the Accessibility Guidelines.

For compliance with the accessibility provisions of the Act, a private entity had to satisfy relevant requirements of the Accessibility Guidelines. A public entity could choose between the Accessibility Guidelines and UFAS – the Uniform Federal Accessibility Standards. The proviso if it chose the Accessibility Guidelines was that it was not given the elevator exemption, the rule whereby for private entities it was not mandatory for certain two-storey buildings to have a lift. In practice, virtually all public entities use the Uniform Federal Standard – there are marginal differences only between it and the Accessibility Guidelines.

The Accessibility Guidelines occupy 87 pages of the 26 July 1991 United States Federal Register, the commentary on the Title III rules a further 61 pages and the commentary on the Title II rules another 30 pages. Viewed from a British perspective, the Accessibility Guidelines and the Department of Justice's commentary are astonishingly impressive. The commentary reports the background to the Act and the ideology which informed it, the purpose and application of the Title III rule and its relationship to other laws, the evaluation of advice that came from public hearings and public comments, the reasons for the determinations which were made, the precise definition of all the terms used, and the intentions, scope and practicalities of the Accessibility Guidelines requirements. All this it does with impeccable argument, informative explanations, sound logic and great clarity; nothing is overlooked.

Under the Americans with Disabilities Act a private entity is a public accommodation, one which for legal purposes has to be associated with a person; the Act prohibits discrimination by any person who owns, leases (or leases to), or operates a place of public accommodation. A place of public accommodation is a facility operated by a private entity whose operations affect commerce and which comes within at least one of 12 specified categories of types of public buildings*. A private home can be covered as a place of public accommodation to the extent that it is used as a facility that would fall within one of the 12 categories. If a professional office of (for example) a dentist, doctor or psychologist is located in a private home, the portion of the home dedicated to office use (including the approach to it) would be considered a place of public accommodation[10].

The ideology of the Americans with Disabilities Act was macroistic, and in this context the advice regarding integrated settings was particularly significant. The Department of Justice commentary reads[12]:

> The ADA recognizes that the provision of goods and services in an integrated manner is a fundamental tenet of nondiscrimination on the basis of disability. Providing segregated accommodations and services relegates persons with disabilities to the status of second-class citizens.
>
> Sections 36.203(b) and (c) make clear that individuals with disabilities cannot be denied the opportunity to participate in programs that are not separate or different. This is an important and overarching principle of the Americans with Disabilities Act. Separate, special, or different programs that are designed to provide a benefit to persons with disabilities cannot be used to restrict the participation of persons with disabilities in general, integrated settings.

* These are[11]:

1 Places of *lodging*, eg hotels.
2 Establishments serving *food or drink*, eg restaurants and bars.
3 Places of *exhibition or entertainment*, eg cinemas, theatres, concert halls, stadia.
4 Places of *public gathering*, eg auditoria, convention centres, lecture halls.
5 *Sales or rental* establishments, eg shops, stores, shopping centres.
6 *Service* establishments, eg laudromats, dry-cleaners, banks, hairdressers, travel agents, petrol stations, accountants' or lawyers' premises, pharmacies, insurance offices, doctors' or dentists' surgeries, health centres, hospitals.
7 Public *transportation* terminals and stations, eg private company bus stations. Private company air transportation facilities are excluded, but commercial facilities within air terminals are places of public accommodation.
8 Places of public *display* or collection, eg museums, libraries, galleries.
9 Places of *recreation*, eg parks, zoos, amusement parks.
10 Places of *education*, eg private sector schools and further education establishments.
11 *Social service* centre establishments, eg daycare centres, facilities for elderly people.
12 Places of *exercise or recreation*, eg gymnasia, health spas, bowling alleys, golf courses.

A facet of adherence to the non-segregation rule is that unisex toilet facilities are not positively encouraged in America. In public buildings in America the rule is that there are separate toilet rooms for men and women; that is considered right, proper and normal, and if therefore accessible facilities are to be provided for disabled people the correct practice is for them to be separate for men and women. In conversation in America I have been told that disabled veterans were particularly adamant that under the Americans with Disabilities Act the separation rule must be retained. And, going back in years earlier, a relevant anecdote was reported to me when I was in Seattle in 1983. A federal government agency had taken over the tenancy of an office building originally designed in accord with the Washington State building code, and it needed modifications. The requirement was for an increase in the number of toilet stalls for general use, and it was felt that the logical way for this to be done was to insert more standard stalls in the altered existing toilet rooms by removing the wheelchair-accessible stalls, and then to have a separate unisex facility nearby. A woman employed by the agency who was a wheelchair user protested; she was entitled, she said, to non-discriminatory provision, and her civil rights would be violated if she were obliged to use a unisex facility. There are currently (in early 1997) no plans to incorporate requirements for unisex toilets in the Accessibility Guidelines. For toilet areas with separate male and female facilities, the ADA requirement is for an accessible toilet stall of the type prescribed in the 1980 A117.1 and shown in Figure 10.1 on page 79.

The reachability of controls is an item covered by the Accessibility Guidelines. Where they might be used by members of the general public, building fittings and equipment such as telephones, lift controls, thermostats, light switches, door locks and window latches must be placed so that they can be reached by independent wheelchair users. The maximum height condition prescribed in the 1991 Guidelines was 54in (1370mm)[13]. This troubled The Little People of America, the national organization of people of short stature; it subsequently undertook an inquiry among its members, the finding being that some 25 per cent could not reach an object higher than 48in even when standing next to it[14]. Representations and negotiations followed, the outcome, in early 1996, being a decision by the review committees of the American National Standards Institute and the Accessibility Guidelines to reduce the decreed maximum height reach from 54in to 48in (1200mm)[15].

By the ideology that governs the ADA, independence is not a negotiable commodity. The issue is illustrated by programme accessibility, the requirement that, in an existing public building which cannot be made fully accessible, services needed by any disabled person must be provided in accessible areas. For the delivery of such services, carrying a person up or down steps is forbidden; the Department of Justice commentary on the Title II rules reads[16]:

> The Department (of Justice) wishes to clarify that, consistent with longstanding interpretation of section 504, carrying an individual with a disability is considered an ineffective and therefore an unacceptable method for achieving program accessibility.
>
> Carrying will be permitted only in manifestly exceptional cases, and only if all personnel who are permitted to participate in carrying an individual with a disability are formally instructed on the safest and least humiliating means of carrying.

The freedom that American citizens have under the Constitution to worship how they wish, and along with it the autonomy that religious organizations have to conduct their affairs without interference from the state, is manifested in the ruling that 'religious entities' are exempted from the requirements of the Americans with Disabilities Act. If, for example, a church operates a daycare centre, a nursing home, a private school, or a diocesan school system, the buildings concerned would not be subject to any accessibility requirements.

Under the terms of the Americans with Disabilities Act it is discriminatory – and therefore unlawful – to design and construct new buildings that are not readily accessible to and usable by individuals with disabilities. Where the design and construction of a new building complies wholly with the Accessibility Guidelines or the Uniform Federal Standard, the provider of that building is afforded immunity under the law; a disabled person who, for whatever reason, finds that the building is inaccessible cannot claim that his rights have been violated.

To take account of the interests of small private businesses, an exception is made to the readily accessible requirement for certain new private entity buildings. This is the elevator exemption. Other than for buildings which would incorporate a shopping centre, a shopping mall or the professional office of a healthcare provider, an elevator is not required in new small buildings that have less than three storeys or less than 3000 sq ft on each storey. On this basis, for example, a new two-storey office building with 20 000 sq ft on each floor does not have to have an elevator, and nor does a new five-storey office building with 2800 sq ft on each floor. Where a building does not have an elevator the rule is, however, that within a storey all floors have to be accessible, including to disabled people using wheelchairs. A narrow exception to the 'readily accessible' rule is also allowed where a private entity can, in a particular case, demonstrate that accessibility in strict accord with the rules is impracticable owing to the peculiar character of the terrain.

Under Title III of the Americans with Disabilities Act existing buildings which are places of public accommodation must be made accessible if that is readily achievable, meaning that the necessary works are easily accomplishable and can be carried out without much difficulty or expense*. Where

* The commentary to the Title III rule lists 21 examples of barrier removals that might be readily achievable; these include installing ramps; making kerb cuts in sidewalks and entrances; repositioning shelves; adding raised markings on elevator control buttons; repositioning the paper towel dispenser in a bathroom; and installing an accessible paper cup dispenser at an existing inaccessible water fountain.

barrier removal is not readily achievable, a public accommodation has to make its services available through alternative methods if that is readily achievable, for example by relocating activities to accessible locations, by bringing the service to a disabled person waiting at the door, or by providing home delivery. In an existing public restaurant it is acceptable for selected areas to be accessible. In existing buildings toilets which are inaccessible do not, unless they are altered, have to be made accessible.

For Title II public buildings the readily achievable rule is inapplicable, since services and programmes must be accessible. An example cited in the ADA *Technical Assistance Manual* is[17]:

> D, a defendant in a civil suit, has a respiratory condition that prevents her from climbing steps. Civil suits are routinely heard in a courtroom on the second floor of the courthouse. The courthouse has no elevator or other means of access to the second floor. The public entity must relocate the proceedings to an accessible ground floor courtroom or take alternative steps, including moving the proceedings to another building, in order to allow D to participate in the civil suit.

When an existing place of public accommodation is structurally altered, the alterations must be made in a manner that provides access. Where compliance with requirements for new construction is technically infeasible, meaning that structural, physical or site constraints prevent the accomplishment of full accessibility, accessibility must be provided to the maximum extent feasible.

When alterations are made to a *primary function area*, there has, to the maximum extent feasible, to be an unobstructed path of travel connecting the building entrance and the altered area. A primary function area is one where a major activity takes place; it includes both customer services areas and work areas in places of public accommodation, and all offices and work areas in commercial facilities. A difference between an accessible route in new construction and a path of travel in an altered building is that on a path of travel the provision of a platform lift for wheelchair users is acceptable where appropriate.

In an existing building where alterations are made to a primary function area on an inaccessible storey, the installation of an elevator is not required where (a) it would be technically infeasible; (b) the building is of a type that, if it were new construction, would be entitled to the elevator exemption; or (c) the cost would be disproportionate to the cost of the overall alteration. The definition of disproportionality is that the cost of providing an accessible path of travel exceeds 20 per cent of the cost of the alteration to the primary function area; other costs which may count as costs to provide an accessible path of travel include those associated with making the entrance to the building accessible or making toilet facilities accessible.

In respect of alterations to existing buildings, the Accessibility Guidelines rules do not discriminate between *alterations*, ie changes to a building or facility, and *additions*, ie where there is an increase in the gross floor area of a building. All of an addition has to be accessible, and where access to it is only through the existing building the entrance to the building has to be made accessible if it is not already.

The readily achievable rule is applicable to alterations to historic buildings, but is not operable where access works would threaten or destroy the historic significance of a building. In a public entity historic building there has to be programme accessibility. Noting that in America the first floor means the ground floor, an illustration is as follows[18]:

> Installing an elevator in a historic house museum to provide access to the second floor would destroy architectural features of historic significance on the first floor. Providing an audio-visual display of the contents of the upstairs rooms in an accessible location on the first floor would be an alternative way of achieving program accessibility.

Under Title III of the Americans with Disabilities Act, work areas in newly constructed buildings must be reachable, meaning that employees with disabilities can get to and from such areas, but individual work stations do not have to be accessible – they do not, for example, need to have space for wheelchair manoeuvre or shelves at low level. Only areas used exclusively by employees are 'work areas' for the purposes of the Act; in a hotel, for example, the hotel kitchen must be reachable, but there is not a requirement that all guestrooms must be reachable by a disabled person who works as a cleaner.

Under Title I of the Act employers with 15 or more employees are required to make *reasonable accommodation* to enable people with disabilities to enter or remain in the workforce, unless the necessary action would involve undue hardship (meaning significant difficulty or expense) to the employer. An employer is *not* required to make existing buildings or facilities accessible until a particular applicant or employee with a particular kind of disability needs to be accommodated. In this regard, the Title III 'readily achievable' rule for making existing buildings accessible does not apply to work areas in such buildings.

The Accessibility Guidelines requirements for special provisions for people with hearing impairments are for assistive listening devices. Where public telephones are provided within a building, not less than one in four must have a volume control, and where there are more than four in one location at least one must be a text telephone for deaf people. In assembly areas, assistive listening devices, for example an induction loop or infra-red facility, must be provided. In new hotels, one guestroom in 25 (one in 50 in large hotels) must be equipped with an auxiliary visual alarm and a volume control telephone with an electrical outlet to facilitate the use of a text telephone.

In America the campaign call of disability activists in their urging of civil rights legislation was 'Jobs, not welfare'. In Britain it is 'Rights, not charity'.

In this context, it would seem that in America the concepts of welfare and charity are interchangeable. The authors of *Complying with the Americans with Disabilities Act* quote Robert Burgdorf, author of the first draft of the Act. What the Americans with Disabilities Act represents, he says, is 'a shift in the way our society thinks about and relates to people with disabilities: a shift away from government charity, paternalistic helpfulness, support of dependency, and segregated services for a group considered unfortunate victims; and toward equality, integration, jobs, independence, and most importantly – *rights* for all of us individuals with disabilities[19]. The authors of the book, who had traced the history of the disability rights movement to the day in 1964 when Hugh Gallagher in his wheelchair wanted to conduct research at the Library of Congress, went on to say, 'Gallagher and 43 million other individuals with disabilities have new and expanded rights and new opportunities that provide for economic and personal independence unparalleled elsewhere in the world'[20].

Relatedly, Joseph P. Shapiro, journalist author of *No Pity – People with Disabilities Forging a New Civil Rights Movement*, an account of the personalities and activities of the movement, wrote, 'Passage of the ADA was an earthshaking event for disabled people. It signalled a radical transformation in the way they saw themselves – as a minority that now had rights to challenge its exclusion. But it was an odd victory; as radical as the ADA's passage would be for disabled people, nondisabled Americans still had little understanding that this group now demanded rights, not pity'[21].

From a British perspective, the response to these assessments has to be in 'Yes, but' terms. Yes, the Americans with Disabilities Act was a landmark in history. Yes, it was a magnificent American enterprise. Yes, it has enhanced employment opportunities for Americans with disabilities. Yes, it has served to help make public buildings all across America more readily accessible to disabled people than those in any other country in the world. Yes, the prospect of universally accessible public transport throughout America is one that no other country can yet realistically envisage. Yes, all this could never have been achieved had the disability rights movement, with consumer activists in the lead, not spread across the country.

Yes, the Americans with Disabilities Act is undoubtedly serving to counter the widespread attitudinal discrimination to which Americans with disabilities have historically been subjected. I begin here to draw comparisons. I have noted already my own personal experience, as an English person with a severe disability, of the abundance of positive discrimination that has come my way, and the paucity of negative discrimination. My hypothesis is that in America discrimination against people with disabilities has been of a different order from that in Britain, the reasons being socio-cultural. The materialistic and competitive self-help culture of America has always been more uncomfortable for disabled people to live with than the social welfare culture of Britain. I began this account of the process of legislation in America with the story of Paul Strachan and his failed ambition to bring to

America an equivalent of the British Disabled Persons Act of 1944. The quota scheme instituted under that Act has run its course, but over the years many thousands of disabled people have been able to obtain gainful and dignifying employment that without the Act they would have been denied. Elsewhere, employers in Britain have always, I suspect, been more supportive of their disabled employees than those in America. Whatever the benefits to young disabled Americans of vocational rehabilitation services may have been, my suspicion is that far more frequently disabled people in America had reasonable cause to complain about employment discrimination than their peers in Britain. It could well be that the Americans with Disabilities Act is now serving to narrow the gap or – quite possibly – to turn it in favour of America.

So yes, in respect of equal opportunities for employment – one of the two pillars of civil rights along with education – the Americans with Disabilities Act scores, and scores convincingly. It scores also on equal access to public buildings and public transport, matters on which, as I discuss later, no related legislation in Britain could ever hope to yield equivalent results. So where are the 'buts'?

The campaign which culminated in the passing of the Americans with Disabilities Act was partial. The 'jobs, not welfare' emphasis was politically necessary; George Bush would not happily have stood up and committed himself to instituting nationwide welfare rights for disabled people as part of a civil rights package. And 'jobs, not welfare' was a winning ticket, one that the leading consumer campaigners were not ill at ease with. They were young, articulate, active and determined disabled people, many of them, as Shapiro reported, people who had experienced employment or education discrimination and who wanted to 'get out of welfare'.

'Rights, not pity' is superficially appealing, and I imagine there are few disabled people who, any more than I do, relish being pitied. But excoriating pity does not mean relinquishing compassion. And if disabled people who, on account of disadvantaging personal circumstances and the gross severity of their disability, have no means of helping themselves 'out of welfare', they do, by any civilized norms, deserve compassion. They also deserve welfare support, whether it be called welfare or charity, and never mind whether it be dispensed by the state or by some benevolent voluntary agency.

When the American Constitution was drafted there was no mention of welfare rights – from the start, the absolute rule for personal health and welfare services was that it was the duty of each American and his family to look after themselves, and if professional healthcare was needed they had to find cash to pay for it. That principle remains. The Americans with Disabilities Act gives disabled people no welfare or health rights. But among the 43 million – or however many disabled people there are reckoned to be in America – there must be large numbers of severely handicapped people for whom employment rights are an irrelevance, and who I suspect would, had they ever been given the option, have much more welcomed health and welfare rights than the whole apparatus of the Americans with

Disabilities Act. These were people who were not represented by the activists who campaigned for the Act. And the welfare rights issue that had launched the independent living movement – the demand for state funding for severely handicapped people to employ their own care attendants – was nowhere on the agenda.

Across America, severely disabled people who cannot work and cannot afford health insurance continue to be sidelined. Handicapped children whose parents have been able to afford only limited insurance can be denied the healthcare that they urgently need. Where there is impoverishment and hence eligibility for Medicaid, the health and welfare services that can be provided may be distressingly inadequate. For disabled people in America who are struggling to survive, the Americans with Disabilities Act offers no relief.

For Tim Nugent's students in the 1950s, personal independence was about being able to propel a wheelchair manually and unaided. By 1990 electric wheelchairs had become a common means of mobility for disabled people, giving personal independence to many who were too severely disabled to propel a manual wheelchair. The prospect that the Americans with Disabilities Act gave them, if it was not already reality, was driving out from home, travelling by accessible public transport and getting to their destinations unaided. Many of the young activists who campaigned for the Act were, I suspect, users of electric wheelchairs. But, for disabled people in America who were dependent on state welfare, an electric wheelchair was beyond their limited financial resources. The husband who was obliged to stay at home to care for his handicapped wife might find it difficult or impossible to retain paid employment, but the state gave him no support. In the chorus of self-congratulation with which America greeted the Act the uncomfortable reality tended perhaps to be ignored – for many severely handicapped people it was decent and affordable health and welfare services that were most urgently needed, not rights of the kind granted by the Americans with Disabilities Act.

13 Britain: the Part M building regulation

In Britain the Part M building regulation was brought into operation in two stages. The first, Part M of Schedule 1 of the Building Regulations 1985, came into force in December 1987. At that time the British Standards Institution was still working on the code of practice on egress for the disabled which would complement the BS5810 access code, and, as with the 1985 Part T regulation, this meant that offices and shops were the only multi-storey buildings for which comprehensive access requirements could be mandated. By comparison with the 1985 Part T, the coverage of the 1987 Part M was, however, extended. Whereas for new construction other than offices and shops Part T regulated single-storey buildings only, the 1987 Part M required that the principal entrance storey of all new multi-storey public buildings should be accessible.

The concept of 'relevant premises' was introduced. For any building subject to the Part M regulation there were three regulatory requirements, M2, M3 and M4; M1 contained definitions only. M3 and M4 were 'where appropriate' supplementary requirements relating to sanitary conveniences (M3) and audience or spectator seating (M4). For all buildings, M2, *Means of access*, was the principal functional requirement that had to be met to satisfy the law; it read, 'Reasonable provision shall be made to enable disabled people to gain access to the relevant premises, and to those parts of the relevant premises to which it is reasonable to provide access'. In the associated Approved Document, disabled people were defined as 'people with a physical impairment which limits their ability to walk and people who need to use a wheelchair for mobility'.

The rejection of Patrick Jenkin's let's-go-macro exhortation, with Part M being informed instead by for-the-disabled micro principles under a welfare remit, was confirmed in the foreword to the approved document for the 1987 regulation:

> The Chronically Sick and Disabled Persons Act 1970 (as amended in 1976) imposes a duty on building providers to make provision for access and sanitary conveniences for disabled people in so far as it is in the circumstances both practicable and reasonable. The 1970 Act, however, does not contain enforcement powers and building regulations have taken over the responsibility of ensuring that suitable provision is made.

No agency had previously had the responsibility, and it was not therefore 'taken over'. Although section 4 of the 1970 Act remained in place, it did not have to be cited in aid – the welfare and convenience remit authorised by section 1 of the Building Act 1984 could have been enlisted. The 1970 Act did, however, afford a licence to go micro. The foreword continued, 'The underlying philosophy in introducing access regulations is that as far as reasonable the built environment should be as accessible to disabled people as it is to able-bodied people. Buildings that are so accessible are even more conveniently used by the general public'[1]. The inference was apparent – disabled people were not felt to be members of the general public.

On 21 January 1988 the Centre on Environment for the Handicapped held a seminar, Can the Part M Approved Document be made to work?'[2] The event was reported in the *Architects' Journal* of 27 January under the heading 'Difficult entry for Part M'. The opening speaker was Tony Field of the Department of the Environment's Building Regulations Division, and the report read:

> Tony Field looked shell-shocked after a day of defending Approved Document Part M against its critics. He conceded that some of the criticisms of the document were just. If he had not made that admission he would never have escaped from the seminar alive. The consensus was that the document was confused and confusing. The audience wanted explanations or blood.

Among the complaints were that the Approved Document was chaotic; it was ambiguous and illogical; its advice on hotel bedrooms was arrant nonsense; its definition of disabled people was too restrictive; its diagrams were ill thought-out; its technical deficiencies, ambiguities, inconsistencies and perversities would make it difficult for developers, architects and building control officers to deliver accessible buildings; it should have been much more comprehensive[3]. The narrow definition of disabled people was criticised, the widespread view being that if the regulation could not be about access for everyone, it ought at least to cover people with sensory impairments, not only those with mobility impairments. There were complaints about the technical propriety of the requirements. 'Where', 'what' and 'how' were prescribed, but 'why' was not explained. How, it was asked, would building control officers be able to evaluate the suitability of solutions different from those advised in the Approved Document? A year later, in a journal article headed 'Unhappy Birthday, Part M', Stewart McGough, access officer for the London borough of Brent, wrote, 'To the practised eye, the AD is seen to be extremely flawed, compromised in its effectiveness by anomalies, loopholes and dubious perspective'[4].

The opportunity to improve the 1987 Part M regulation would come when, following the issuing of the code of practice on egress for the disabled, Part

M was extended to cover all new multi-storey buildings. In 1988 the British Standards Institution issued BS5588 *Fire precautions in the design and construction of buildings, Code of practice for means of escape for disabled people,* and in October 1990 the Department of the Environment went out to consultation with a draft Approved Document for what was to become the 1992 Part M regulation, *Access and facilities for disabled people.* To consider its proposals, the Centre for Accessible Environments (as the Centre on Environment for the Handicapped had become) arranged a seminar on 14 December 1990.

Tony Field was again the opening speaker. The Department, he said, had commissioned a study of how the 1987 Approved Document was working in practice, and what improvements needed to be made to it; this had been undertaken by outside consultants, who had interviewed developers, architects, builders, building control officers, access officers and representatives of organizations such as the Centre for Accessible Environments and the Access Committee for England. In December 1990 the report of the study had not been published, and nor was it subsequently. At the seminar Mr Field reported that its principal finding was that the overwhelming majority of those interviewed thought that Part M and its approved document had made a valuable contribution to access for the disabled[5]. In the course of the inquiry a number of issues had, he noted, been identified which needed to be addressed, and those interviewed had made many suggestions on how the approved document might be improved.

Mr Field indicated that some of the report's suggestions were radical, but the Department felt it would be a mistake to introduce major fundamental changes to the approved document while the industry was still becoming familiar with the current guidance[6]. Changes that were, however, incorporated in the draft for the proposed new Part M included access requirements applicable to all storeys in new non-domestic buildings and also self-contained extensions to existing buildings, and new provisions to help people with impaired sight or impaired hearing. The last was perceived as a successful outcome of lobbying pressure; one of the draft recommendations was for tactile floor surfaces, on which no one at the December 1990 seminar had the temerity to point out that they could be worthless.

The second stage Part M regulation came into force in June 1992. Buildings were now regulated rather than relevant premises, and extensions to existing buildings were covered as well as new construction, provided that the extension included a ground storey. The M2 regulation requirement was now 'Reasonable provision shall be made for disabled people to gain access to and to use the building'. That it came, as in 1987, in the terms 'reasonable provision shall be made', not 'access shall be provided' (or some equally positive and absolute mandate) reflected the uncertain position in which Britain stood by comparison with America.

For the Americans with Disabilities Act, access prescriptions, set out in the *Americans with Disabilities Act Accessibility Guidelines,* were based on precise operational definitions of access and accessibility, and for alterations to existing buildings as well as provision in new buildings, 'access' meant access for independent wheelchair users. As a policy construct that was viable in America, and it came in a form which was solid enough to support the doctrine of 'rights'. In Britain the Part M building regulation was a pragmatic and shaky response to political concerns, practical conditions and prevailing circumstances. Along with all that, it was constrained by two other factors: one the operational principle governing building regulations as a package, the other the doctrine of microism.

The operational principle is that a building ought, in its design and construction, to meet a series of basic functional requirements, with there being appropriate technical means of satisfying each requirement. The approved documents issued by the Department of the Environment in support of each part of the regulations present guidance on how this can be done; each says, in effect, 'here is one way of doing it', while acknowledging that alternative ways may be equally appropriate. The 1992 Part M Approved Document advises, like others[7]:

> There is no obligation to adopt any particular solution contained in an Approved Document if you prefer to meet the relevant requirement in some other way. However, should a contravention of a requirement be alleged then, if you have followed the guidance in the relevant Approved Documents, that will be evidence tending to show that you have complied with the Regulations. If you have not followed the guidance then that will be evidence tending to show that you have not complied. It will then be for you to demonstrate by other means that you have satisfied the requirement.

Non-compliance with building regulations being a criminal offence, this might be construed more as a threat than a warning.

With regard to buildings subject to Part M, the building regulations compliance inspector is as a rule a local authority building control officer, a professional with accumulated expertise on building construction techniques. In the case of the regulations which say, for example, 'the building will stand up' (Part A); 'the building will not leak' (Part C); or 'the building will not smell' (Parts F, G and H) he may well have the technical knowledge to responsibly agree or disagree with the architect who puts forward a solution different from that in the relevant Approved Document. But for Part M, with its edict 'the building will be reasonably easy for disabled people to get into and use', he could be out of his depth: he may only be satisfied where the architect has rigorously and conscientiously followed precisely the one-way guidance in the Part M Approved Document.

The building control officer is not helped by being given no advice about what the broad conceptual parameters of reasonable provision are officially held to be. He may be left feeling that the overall provision prescribed in the approved document constitutes reasonable provision in all circumstances, regardless, for example, of particular provision being unwanted by any disabled person who might use the building concerned, that it could be inappropriate or the cost of making it out of all proportion to its possible usefulness. The advice in the 1987 Part M approved document and again in 1992 might have been that the requirement to make reasonable provision for disabled people could on occasion (for example, where the building concerned was of a type which no disabled person could reasonably be expected to use) be interpreted as meaning that no special for-the-disabled provision need be made; no advice of that kind was, however, given.

14 The European scene

In Britain, as in other member countries of the European Union, national laws are subordinate to European legislation. In association with the Council of the European Union, the European Parliament issues Directives – these prescribe European requirements with which each member state must harmonise its own legislation and regulations. Notionally therefore there could be an access directive, issued perhaps with an annex presenting design standards for accessibility, with whose principles the British Part M building regulation would be obliged to conform. It is in this context that the development of the *European Manual for an Accessible Built Environment*[1] is reported. A brief note on the Council of Europe comes first. With a broader membership of nations than the European Union, the Council of Europe can press policy issues by passing resolutions, and over the years it has passed resolutions on access for the disabled, to do with housing, public buildings and recreational facilities. But these resolutions, unlike European Union directives, are not legally binding and can be ignored.

The European Commission's Directorate of Social and Economic Affairs, within which is the Bureau for Action in Favour of Disabled People, has responsibility for matters of concern to disabled people. During the 1970s and into the 1980s I regularly attended meetings on housing and independent living arranged by the bureau in Brussels and Luxembourg, and at those meetings the idea that there should be an access directive was regularly pressed. It was felt it could be advantageous if across Europe there were common standards, for example, for the accessibility of hotel guest-rooms and toilets in public buildings, and it was with this in view that the *European Manual* was generated.

A major conference, Access to Public Buildings and Facilities, was held in Utrecht in early October 1987. Sponsored by the European Commission, the event was organized by the Stichting Nederlandse Gehandicaptenraad, in English terms the Dutch Council of the Disabled. Attended by some 180 delegates from across Europe, the important resolution passed at its close was that the European Commission should set up as soon as possible a committee which would draw up a European document on access based on the existing rules, directives and research in the various member states[2].

There were good reasons for the Commission to look to the Netherlands for the management of this task. Exemplified by the regularly updated design manual *Geboden Toegang* ('Access demanded!')[3], a substantial corpus of relevant expertise had been built up over the years, and the Dutch were accustomed to presenting their material in English. Significantly also, the Dutch Government was interested. It was in the process of accomplishing the change that Britain had effected in the 1970s, of ending the responsibility that local municipalities had for regulating building controls, and instituting national building regulations instead. The regulations would be concerned with health, safety and access, and their drafting could be informed by work on a European manual; it was on this account that the major share of funding for the project came from the Dutch Government.

The Commission negotiated the setting up of the project with the Dutch Council for the Disabled and the Dutch Government's Central Coordinating Committee for the Promotion of Accessibility for the Disabled (CCPT), a unit in the Ministry of Welfare led by an architect, Roy van Hek. The contract for the production of the manual was placed with EGM, an architectural and planning consultancy in Dordrecht; Maarten Wijk of EGM was to be the principal author of the manual. In the policy lead was Maarten van Ditmarsch of the Dutch Council; he was the philosopher, keen to ensure that the manual would be based on sound ideological principles. I had for some years often met and talked with him about macro and micro, and it was the macro concept – which he termed *integral accessibility* or the *extended scope* (and which in America was called *universal design*) – that would be the governing precept of the manual. The *integrated* approach he compared to two other design approaches to accessibility, both, in my terms, microistic; the *individual* approach, represented, for example, by house adaptations specifically geared to meet the needs of a particular disabled person, and the *categorical* approach, meaning special provision for a distinct group of disabled people, represented, for example, by special housing for wheelchair users, special unisex toilets for the disabled, or tactile pavings for blind people.

At the November 1990 international conference at which the manual was officially launched the Dutch promoters of its prospects as an operational model for Europe did not assist their cause. Attended by some 120 delegates, myself among them, the conference was held over three days at Hoensbroek near Maastricht. The launch being an important event which had been long awaited, we imagined that at the start of the conference we would have copies of the manual, that its Dutch authors would report how, in association with the European Commission, it had been tackled, explain its philosophy, its contents and its recommendations, and indicate how a European directive might enforce accessibility requirements based on it. Conference delegates would, we supposed, spend much of the three days examining it, debating its content and considering its implications. We were disappointed. Protocol, we were told, prevented this happening. On the final morning, the first copy of the manual was to be ceremonially presented to Princess (formerly Queen) Juliana, who would fly in by helicopter. She must be the first to see it, and the first two days were to be spent filling in time on group meetings, outings and social events. On the last day, as we were leaving, each of us was given a copy of the manual to take home.

In its first edition form the *European Manual for an Accessible Built Environment* comprised 123 pages in a ring binder. Its guidance on buildings related to new construction, and as well as public buildings and housing it dealt with outdoor environments and public transport facilities. It came in two parts: Part A presented functional principles and Part B the design standards for integral accessibility, illustrating the 'extended scope'. Application conditions were not prescribed; the note was that these would be for each country to determine according to local circumstances, the understanding being that the 'extended scope' design standard for each building feature would be the norm, applied generally.

In the manual the design standards for integral accessibility reflected its Dutch authorship. The Netherlands being a prosperous country, its normal provision norms were more extended than those in less advanced countries, ones where there might not be the capability for adopting them in 'extended scope' form. One example was the integral accessible standard for toilet facilities, another was the 850mm design standard for the clear opening width of doors.

Predictably, it was in respect of toilet facilities that the practical interpretation of the concept of integral accessibility would be most problematical. The advice in the manual was that in public buildings there should, on every floor where there was more than one wc compartment, be an integrally accessible toilet, in conjunction with 'moderately' accessible toilets (Figure 14.1). The Dutch authors of the manual were here perhaps pushing the concept of integral accessibility too far: was it not the moderately accessible toilets that were integral, and was not the 'integrally accessible' facility really special provision for wheelchair users, and therefore 'categorical'?

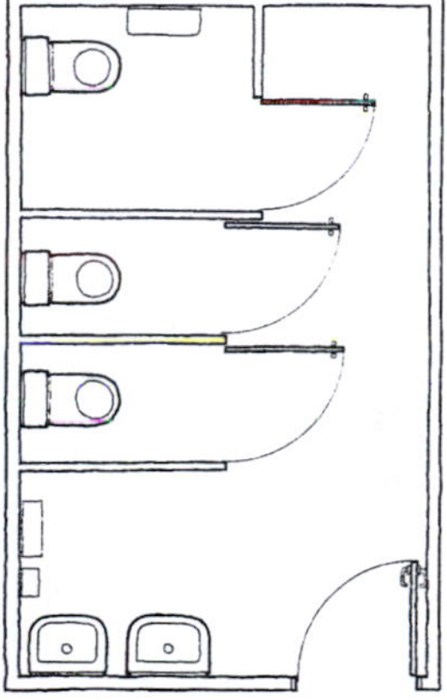

14.1 The toilet provision advised in the *European Manual.* The wc facility at the top is termed integrally accessible, the two in the middle moderately accessible

Nine days after the launch of the manual on 14 November 1990, Maarten van Ditmarsch and Maarten Wijk were in Britain. They spoke at a conference on the development of access regulations arranged by the Centre for Accessible Environments, and then participated in a discussion meeting at the Department of the Environment. By that time the draft content of the 1992 Part M building regulation, all in the same mode as the 1987 regulation, was irrevocably set. The *European Manual* was irrelevant: Britain would continue to go down the for-the-disabled micro track.

The production of the *European Manual* was none the less a notable happening in the story of the evolution of accessibility controls. It was the first concerted effort to go macro, to switch the groundrules for accessibility from 'for the disabled' to 'for everyone'. Maarten van Ditmarsch, Roy van Hek and Maarten Wijk understood the nature of their leap, and although at meetings where they spoke it was by no means everyone who grasped its implications, their access-for-everyone message got through. Where they faltered was by considering specific design standards from a microist 'what suits the disabled is good for everyone' perspective, rather than the macroist 'what suits everyone is good for the disabled' angle. In the process they sought to move the boundary of the 'extended scope' beyond where it could be reasonably pressed.

The November 1990 *European Manual* was a 'first draft', and following the Hoensbroek meeting a supervisory committee of access practitioners from around Europe was formed to advise on how it should be revised. At the first follow-up meeting, held in The Hague in October 1992, the view was that Part A, the functional principles, was agreeable, but Part B, the design standards, was not. The extended scope principle was accepted, but the interpretation of the integral accessibility concept posed difficulties. Standards for integral accessibility ought, it was felt, to be flexible, affording compatibility with the design standards applied in different countries. For toilet provision, the 'moderate accessibility' option was abandoned.

In March 1993 the CCPT presented a revised draft version of Part A, now called *Guiding Principles*[4]. This was followed in March 1995 by the *European Manual for Accessibility, Draft Revision 1*[5], with a revised Part B, *Examples of Accessible Facilities.* The recommendations for toilet facilities now prescribed an 'integral accessible' toilet only, one which was even larger than before*. Whether labelled 'integral' or not, it could not be perceived as being normal for everyone. Affected by the confusion which can emanate from the intervention of a committee with diverse voices, the *European Manual* had regressed; it had been driven into a microist position similar to that of the approved document for the British Part M building regulation.

The principle that across Europe there should be common design standards for integral accessibility, and with it the prospect of a prescriptive European Directive, was now compromised. Whether it was on account of that or not, the Dutch authors of the *European Manual* decided that Part B of the Manual, the design standards section, should, with the next revision, be dropped. In early 1995 Marjan van Zuylen succeeded Roy van Hek as Secretary General of CCPT, and under her direction a radically amended version of the *European Manual* was issued for consultation in November 1995. It was now called *European Concept for Accessibility*[6], and the preface read:

> The shortening of the original document by no means implies that the examples to which everyone contributed so enthusiastically will now be filed away for good. On the contrary, at a later stage we will still want to publish a European book of good practice, in order to show what kind of beautiful solutions can be devised to create an environment which does not impose any restrictions. We feel, however, that the process of standardisation and harmonisation of the regulations should not be delayed by the need to reach agreement on the content of the book of good practice.

To debate the new proposal, a conference, *European Approaches to Accessibility*, was held at Doorn near Utrecht early in March 1996. At the

* For this and comparisons with other design standards, see Appendix 4, page 379.

conference, a policy statement was agreed by members of the steering group which had for five years been advising the Dutch initiators of the enterprise. Placed at the start of the report which followed[7], it read:

> The European Concept for Accessibility is a result of a request from the European Commission, made in 1987. The Concept is based on the universal design principles. These principles apply to the design of buildings, infrastructure, building and consumer products.
>
> 1. The objective is the provision of environments which are convenient, safe and enjoyable to use by everyone, including people with disabilities.
> 2. The universal design principles reject the division of the human population into able-bodied and disabled people.
> 3. Universal design includes supplementary provisions where appropriate.

The statement was commended by Sarah Langton-Lockton, writing in *Access by Design*[8]:

> The breakthrough is provided by Principle 3, which contains a subtle but important nuance which has hitherto eluded definitions of universal design.
>
> The concept of universal design as it has evolved in America is concerned to extend the parameters of what is provided as the norm and to exclude as few building users as possible. The tail-enders who are excluded, however, who are still defined as having 'special needs', will still be subject to special provision, but there is no accommodation for this within the concept of universal design.
>
> The European Universal Design Principles embrace supplementary provision as an integral part of the concept, ensuring that the needs of all users of buildings are met by a considered balance of 'for everyone' and supplementary provision. A bonus is that the balance can be variously achieved, according to the type and use of the building. Conceptually this is an important advance.

The next conference, one that I did not attend, was held in Barcelona in November 1996. At this conference the principles of the European concept were confirmed, and it was agreed that a working group would prepare a further revision of the document. The *European Concept for Accessibility* – displaying in effect the same concept as that which informs the proposals I put forward in this book for reformulating accessibility controls in Britain – could eventually be endorsed by the European Parliament, with member states of the European Union being advised to apply its principles. As I see it, a directive could not, however, be based on it.

15 Britain: the Disability Discrimination Act

Britain's Disability Discrimination Act, placed on the statute book on 8 November 1995, was modelled on the Americans with Disabilities Act. With the regulations in place which would be needed to enforce its requirements, it would be unlawful to discriminate against disabled people in connection with employment and the provision of goods, facilities and services, and, like the Americans with Disabilities Act, it incorporated conditions relating to the accessibility of buildings. It was legislation which would be grievance-led. Confronted by a building he could not use but which could have been made accessible, a disabled person would be able to demand of the building owner that he rectify the situation, and take him to court if need be.

The Disability Discrimination Act was an unusual piece of legislation. It was a government bill backed by all political parties, and when given its third readings in the Commons and Lords it went through unopposed – no member of parliament voted against it. But it was legislation of a kind that the government (under Margaret Thatcher and then John Major) had previously been determined must never go through. It had been preceded by a series of private members' bills aimed at outlawing discrimination against disabled people, all of which the government had, until 1995, contrived to block. But in 1995 continued resistance was unsustainable. The government was obliged to concede. It was no longer able to stifle the force of the disability lobby in parliament, a contributory cause of its impotence being the handicap it had given itself of having a Minister for Disabled People.

In early 1979, as reported in Chapter 8, Alf Morris, the first Minister for the Disabled, had set up the Committee on Restrictions against Disabled People (CORAD). He appointed Peter Large, the consumer activist whose views and capabilities he respected, to be its chairman, and the majority of its members were people who were disabled or had experience of disability in their families. The Committee obtained no evidence to substantiate their presumption that discrimination against disabled people was widespread, but that did not deter them; their principal recommendation was that legislation should be introduced which would make discrimination on the grounds of disability illegal.

Following the publication of the CORAD report in May 1982, pressure in parliament for anti-discrimination legislation was fostered by the All Party Disablement Group. Jack Ashley, the Labour MP for Stoke-on-Trent South who in 1967 at age 34 had become totally deaf following a medical operation which went calamitously wrong, was chairman of the Group, and John Hannam, Conservative MP for Exeter, was secretary. In July 1975 they appointed Peter Mitchell (who had previously worked for Alf Morris) as their research assistant; initially he was funded by Duncan Guthrie's Action for the Crippled Child research fund, and then from April 1979 by RADAR – the Royal Association for Disability and Rehabilitation headed by George Wilson. The arrangement Mr Wilson made was that he would be employed as RADAR's research and policy officer, while at the same time being research assistant to Ashley and Hannam and serving as adviser and administrative secretary to the All Party Group. It was Mitchell, a Cambridge classicist with a powerful intellect, who was to pioneer the drafting of anti-discrimination legislation and help steer the work of the All Party Disablement Group[1].

Jack Ashley was the first to act in response to CORAD's urging of anti-discrimination legislation; on 6 July 1982 he presented his Disablement (Prohibition of Unjustifiable Discrimination) Bill as a Ten Minute Rule Bill. This is a bill which has not been drafted, is explained for ten minutes by its sponsor and needs a further bill, one that is formally introduced, if it is to progress towards legislation. In November that year Donald Stewart, Scottish Nationalist MP for the Western Isles, was successful in the private members' ballot; his bill had the same title, and it was Peter Mitchell who helped him draft it. Its operational mechanism for tackling unjustifiable discrimination against disabled people, and helping complainants take cases through the courts, was to be a regulatory commission which would be an arm of the Equal Opportunities Commission, the government agency with duties under the Sex Discrimination Act of 1975.

A bill receives its first reading when it is presented, and its second reading when it is voted through following a debate in parliament. For Donald Stewart's bill, the second reading debate was held on 11 February 1983. Discounting those who intervened, 16 members made speeches: 11 of them, including Jack Ashley, John Hannam and Alf Morris, commended the bill, and five, including Minister for the Disabled Hugh Rossi, did not. Mr Rossi's 50-minute speech came halfway through the debate. He spoke first of how rewarding his job was, and of the many people he had met who were dedicated to giving support to disabled people: 'Everywhere that I have gone I have found . . . overwhelming goodwill for disabled people'. So it might, he felt, be considered a little curious that the House should be discussing discrimination *against* the disabled[2]:

> Discrimination . . . generally means to the man in the street treating someone wrongfully because he or she belongs to an identifiable group or minority of people towards whom there is deliberate unfairness or dislike, antipathy or even hostility in the community. Surely that cannot be said of the disabled as a minority within our society.

There was, Mr Rossi conceded, much thoughtlessness and ignorance of the problems and needs of the disabled. Referring to buildings and transport, and then to employers who were unaware how reliable disabled employees could be, he asked whether these were matters which were more for education, enlightenment and example, rather than for punitive legislation imposing the risk of court proceedings against those whose failure was not yet to have understood.

The idea that legislation was the best way to solve the problems which beset disabled people drew heavily, Mr Rossi said, on the CORAD report. Referring to the evidence which CORAD had collected, he expressed unease about the conclusions which had been reached. Some 20 000 detailed questionnaires had been sent out, and only about 40 of the 700 who responded specifically favoured the kind of legislation now being considered. The bill, he said, rested essentially on 40 advocates of law out of 20 000[3]. Aside from the CORAD member who had submitted a minority report challenging the Committee's conclusions, Mr Rossi reported that he had subsequently received representations from two other members who were critical of the way the survey had been conducted and how its findings had been interpreted[4]. He noted also that RADAR had planned a conference in the autumn of 1982 to discuss the CORAD report; although it had been widely publicised, the response to it had been so poor that it had had to be cancelled[5]. He concluded his speech by acknowledging that while disabled people still faced serious problems, much could be done through education and persuasion, that people should be judged by their abilities rather than their disabilities, and that the cornerstone of government policy was, and would continue to be, the promotion of integration and participation.

The line advanced by those who supported the bill was that the widespread discrimination to which disabled people were clearly subjected could only be effectively countered by legislation, that the bill must have its second reading, and that such shortcomings as there were in its terms and wording could, with appropriate amendments, be resolved in Committee.

Ivan Lawrence, Conservative MP for Burton-on-Trent*, made the closing speech on behalf of the government. He opened by saying that he had the highest regard for Donald Stewart, but he wished that the bill had not been introduced and he resented being put in the false position of having to oppose a bill for the disabled. After a brief exchange with Dennis Skinner (who had interjected, 'You're rotten to the core – we'll let the people in Burton know'), he continued[6]:

> Surely we owe some responsibility to the people who sent us here not to put bad law on to the statute book just because that would be warm-hearted and a nice magnanimous gesture, or because we are frightened that if we do not we shall lose the votes or the support of the disabled.

* Here, as elsewhere, individuals cited are given the title they had at the relevant time. In 1992 Ivan Lawrence became Sir Ivan Lawrence. Relatedly, Hugh Rossi became Sir Hugh Rossi later in 1983, Patrick Jenkin became Lord Jenkin in 1987, John Stanley became Sir John Stanley in 1988, Jack Ashley became Lord Ashley in 1992, John Hannam became Sir John Hannam in 1992, and Nicholas Scott became Sir Nicholas Scott in 1994.

And shortly after[7]:

> Hon. Gentlemen know well that the predominant feeling in the minds of a large proportion of hon. members who go into the Lobby will be 'We have not read the Bill. We do not know whether the Bill is any good, and we do not know whether the Bill makes sense or nonsense or whether it is practical, but it will look good if we are seen going into the Lobby on behalf of the disabled'.

Hugh Rossi and Ivan Lawrence had done all that they could to discredit the bill and encourage MPs to vote against it. But, as was customary with Friday morning private members' bills, there had been no government whip, and members of parliament had a free vote. When the Division was called, the vote was unanimous – 77 members were in favour of the bill being given a second reading and none against. None of those who had spoken against it voted. The bill had not, however, received the necessary 100 votes for it to make progress, and it automatically fell.

Four months later, following the June 1983 general election, Mr Rossi was succeeded as Minister for the Disabled by Tony Newton. The ballot for the next round of private members' bills came soon after, and this time it was Robert Wareing, Labour MP for Liverpool West Derby, who took up the banner of anti-discrimination legislation, with provisions similar to Donald Stewart's in a bill which would amend the Chronically Sick and Disabled Persons Act of 1970. On 18 November 1983, the day of its second reading debate, the government had summoned its troops to Friday morning duty, and by 210 votes to 164 the bill was stopped in its tracks. Having given notice that it could impose discipline if need be, the government felt better equipped to block any similar private member's bill which might subsequently be introduced*.

In the course of his 11 February 1983 endeavours to counter support for Mr Stewart's bill, Mr Rossi had remarked on the lack of evidence indicating that discrimination was widespread, and had issued an invitation[8]:

> If any responsible organization or right hon. or hon. Member writes to me on behalf of a disabled person with evidence that he or she has suffered discrimination on the ground of disability, I shall pursue the case with the utmost vigour. My colleagues in other Departments will give me their full support. In that way not only will it be possible to have the matter put right for the individual, but a body of evidence will build up to show positively the extent of discrimination and the nature and form that it takes.

Sackloads of complaints were not forthcoming. Five years later, a written parliamentary question was put to the Secretary of State for Social Services asking him how many cases of discrimination against disabled people had been referred to his Department in each of the past four years. Nicholas

* In 1986 a private member's bill introduced by Tom Clarke passed into legislation; it was concerned with services for disabled people, not with discrimination.

Scott, the then Minister for the Disabled, replied on 8 March 1988: in 1984 there had been *three* complaints of alleged discrimination, in 1985 *two*, in 1986 *none*, and in 1987 *four*. In addition, two complaints had so far been received in 1988[9].

For the disability lobby, material evidence which contradicted established dogma was out of order, and within and outside parliament the pressure for legislation which would outlaw discrimination against disabled people continued unabated. In November 1991, as he had in November 1969, Alf Morris drew a high position in the ballot for private members' bills, and he now called his bill the Civil Rights (Disabled Persons) Bill. With its thirteen sections and a schedule, it was more elaborate than the Stewart and Wareing bills, and when he opened the second reading debate on 31 January 1992 Mr Morris warmly thanked Peter Mitchell for his help in drafting the bill[10]. It was modelled substantially on the Americans with Disabilities Act, with a part which dealt with the provision of goods, facilities and services and covered discrimination caused by the inaccessibility of public buildings. To advise the Secretary of State and undertake investigations aimed at enforcing the bill's requirements there would be a body named the Disablement Commission; this would have between eight and 15 members, at least three-quarters of whom were to be disabled people or the representatives of disabled people.

To prevent the bill proceeding, the Government did not on this occasion employ its whips to exercise discipline. From what was to occur, it seemed that it had decided instead that the bill should be talked out – if, during a Friday second reading debate, a member of parliament was still speaking at 2.30pm and refused to give way, the debate would be adjourned and the bill would fall. Robert Hayward, Conservative MP for Kingswood Avon, began speaking at 2.16pm. Three minutes later he was asked whether he was talking the bill out. No, he said, he was not[11]. He went on to tell the House that seven years earlier he had been diagnosed as having multiple sclerosis; he was therefore more conscious than others of the problems faced by disabled people, and he said that his experiences had led him to the conclusion that the bill was inappropriate. At 2.30pm he was still speaking and did not give way. Stopped in its tracks, the bill was dead. Members who had supported it were furious, and five days later Mr Hayward was obliged to return and apologise to the House for misleading it[12]. For consumer activists outside he became the number one target for vilification, and they were not at all dismayed when he lost his Kingswood seat to the Labour candidate in the general election held two months later.

From 1990 there was one group of activists which pressed the cause of civil rights for the disabled by way of direct action rather than dialogue with government. It was to become known as DAN, the Direct Action Network, and its protests and demonstrations were patterned on militant activism in America. The pioneering essay in civil disobedience was on the market square in Chesterfield in November 1989: protesting against the local authority's proposed pedestrianisation scheme, a band of militant activists sat down on the square, shouted their slogans, waved their banners and obstructed the traffic[13]. Subsequent DAN demonstrations were regularly aimed at inaccessible public transport; much relishing the commotions which they caused, and always looking for media attention (which they invariably got), a band of militant activists travelled to venues where they could disrupt traffic, chain themselves to buses or trains or otherwise generate mayhem.

In June 1993 consumer activists were interested to learn that Robert Hayward was back in business. Robert Adley, the Conservative MP who in 1992 held his seat at Christchurch in Dorset with a 23 015 majority, had died, and Hayward had been nominated to contest the by-election. The DAN apparatus moved into action, and on a day before the election seventy angry activists descended on the town. Their determination was to disrupt Hayward's campaign; throughout the day they hounded him, and wherever he went he could not escape them. The election result came on 29 July: Hayward had lost to the Liberal Democrat candidate by 16 433 votes. A DAN spokesman commented: 'We feel we had a big impact on the voters and showed what can be achieved through direct action'[14]. Members of parliament got the message – the prudent line on anti-discrimination legislation was not to tangle with the disability lobby.

In November 1993 Roger Berry, the Labour MP who had taken the Kingswood seat from Robert Hayward, was successful in the private members' ballot and introduced a Civil Rights (Disabled Persons) Bill which replicated Alf Morris's 1992 bill. It was scheduled to be debated on Friday 11 March 1994, and, fortified by the publicity they were obtaining and the political impact they could make, disability organizations held a mass rally outside and inside the Palace of Westminster on Wednesday 9 March. Estimates of the number who came to lobby their members of parliament ranged from upwards of 1000[15] to around 2000[16]. DAN activists were prominent among them.

Members of parliament knew which side it would be to their benefit to be on. In the course of the 11 March debate 31 members made speeches or intervened, and of these only one, Michael Stern, Conservative member for Bristol North West, spoke forthrightly against the bill. His particular concern was for the owners of small boarding houses; faced with a legal obligation to make their premises accessible, they could never, he said, cover the investment cost[17]. Shortly before, Simon Coombs, Conservative member for Swindon, had reported that the English Tourist Board had said that billions of pounds were being lost to tourist attractions because of the lack of access[18]. Provisions for making polling stations accessible were in Roger Berry's bill; on this, Sir John Hannam said that the sad fact remained that 60 per cent of all polling stations were inaccessible to disabled people[19]. His assertion went unchallenged, as had Mr Coombs's.

A significant name was noted by Alf Morris when he spoke during the debate. Referring to MPs who had already spoken in support of the bill, he said, 'I am sure they and many others on both sides of the House will join me in paying warm tribute to the immense help that we all receive from Vicky Scott, of the All-Party Disablement Group, than whom no one has done more to promote the Bill'[20]. He knew, as did others, that Victoria Scott was the daughter of Nicholas Scott.

In 1976 Nicholas Scott had separated from his first wife Elizabeth, and she then married Lord Walston, a wealthy landowner, prominent anti-apartheid campaigner and formerly, in the 1960s, a minister in Harold Wilson's Labour government. His daughter Victoria's political attitudes were much influenced by her stepfather, and in early 1991, as an activist who backed the cause of civil rights legislation for disabled people, she was appointed research assistant to the All Party Disablement Group and policy officer to RADAR.

Whatever he may have felt about his daughter's doings, Nicholas Scott would have realised on 11 March 1994 that he had an intractable dilemma; one that stemmed from the ministerial post which he held. As Minister for Disabled People (and also Minister for Social Security), he was a member of the government; he had to abide by decreed government policy, and his duty was to prevent the bill going through. But in his role as Minister for Disabled People he had to listen to the voice of the disabled – and also to the voices of the members of parliament (among them some on the Conservative side) who spoke in favour of the bill – and the message they gave him was that he must permit the bill to go through. His stance, he said, was one of benevolent neutrality[21]. He could not afford the opprobrium he would attract if he were to allow the bill to be talked out, and he was obliged to let it go to a division. Predictably, the outcome was unanimity. By 231 votes to none the bill was given its second reading.

The bill then went into committee, with the opportunity for government-inspired amendments to be put down which would obstruct its progress. Government amendments were not, however, put down until the bill returned to the House of Commons at report stage on 6 May, and it then came with 82 amendments in the names of five Conservative members of parliament. Without time for them all to be considered, the bill was stifled. In the debate Mr Scott talked for more than an hour, and when challenged, denied that he had asked Parliamentary Counsel to draft amendments to kill the bill[22]. Subsequently, in an apologetic statement to the House of Commons on 10 May, he confessed that he had[23]. Media journalists were then excited to discover the role that his daughter Victoria had played in events. When interviewed, she criticised her father for betraying the cause to which she felt he ought to have been committed. She was not averse to letting the media know how angry she was; the honourable thing, she felt, would be for him to resign[24]. Reportedly she said 'I am a disability activist, not a blonde bimbo'[25]. With the media and public opinion on her side, her stance was applauded.

In early 1994, even before the embarrassing debacle over the Roger Berry bill, the government was preparing to capitulate – it would have to concede that resistance could no longer be maintained. Predictably, the November

1994 ballot for private members' bills would result in another member of parliament coming up with a ready-made bill replicating the blocked Berry bill, and to counter the threat the government would need to introduce an alternative piece of legislation of its own; it would be a bill which, with enough compromises, expediencies and concessions, would be sufficiently attractive for parliament to see it through, rather than a rival and more disconcerting private member's civil rights bill. Nicholas Scott set about the task; in May 1994 he announced that there would be extensive consultations on a range of measures for combating discrimination against disabled people, and in July he issued a consultation document, one which put forward proposals for legislative and other government action relating to access to goods and services, financial services, building regulations, and the establishment of an official advisory body on disability[26].

Access to goods and services was a troublesome issue. To make existing public buildings accessible, disability lobbyists in Britain were insistent that disabled people should have a right equivalent to that of the 'readily achievable' condition of the Americans with Disabilities Act – an existing building had to be made accessible if the necessary works were easily accomplishable and could be carried out without much difficulty or expense[27]. Roger Berry's 1993 bill had incorporated an apposite clause: a building owner could be charged with unlawful discrimination against a disabled person if he failed to remove architectural barriers which were in the way of his providing services to that disabled person, provided that the removal of those barriers was practicable and would not impose undue hardship on him. Factors to be considered in determining what would constitute undue hardship would include the nature and cost of the actions in question and the overall financial resources of the provider body concerned.

Viewed from the government's position, the demerit of this was that, with no objective quantifiable criteria, there could be much scope for vexatious complaints, unreasonable demands and potentially extravagant litigation. In his July 1994 consultation paper on the possible terms of government-sponsored disability discrimination legislation, Nicholas Scott indulged in a somewhat confused discussion before declaring that building owners should *not* be required to make their premises accessible: 'It is not', he said, 'the government's intention to impose unrealistic burdens on business', and then, with Roger Berry's bill in mind, 'It is very important that those providing goods and services should not be required to carry out modifications to existing premises, as would have been the case if the Civil Rights (Disabled Persons) Bill had been enacted'[28].

A day or two after the document had been issued, William Hague replaced Nicholas Scott as Minister for Disabled People. Promoted to the rank of Minister of State at the age of 33, he was keen to make his mark, and the challenging task he faced was to present a government-sponsored anti-discrimination bill which he could successfully steer through parliament. In a statement to the House of Commons on 24 November 1994 he announced his intention to introduce a bill which would go further than Mr Scott's consultation paper had indicated. Before he had it ready, the private member's bill which the government had anticipated had made its appearance.

It was Harry Barnes, Labour MP for North East Derbyshire, who had been successful in the ballot, and on 14 December 1994 his Civil Rights (Disabled Persons) Bill was printed. Its provisions for making existing buildings accessible to disabled people were the same as those in Roger Berry's bill which Nicholas Scott had criticised. In addition, there were six clauses aimed at making polling stations accessible. The most significant proposals were, however, for the establishment of a Disability Rights Commission. With a disabled chairman and deputy chairman, and at least three-quarters of its members being disabled people or representatives of disabled people, the Commission was to have investigative and enforcement powers, among them powers to provide legal and financial assistance to disabled people to help them claim their non-discrimination rights.

Presented on 12 January 1995, Mr Hague's government bill contained six parts: Part I prescribed the meaning of 'disability' and 'disabled person'; Part II dealt with employment discrimination; Part III concerned the right of access to goods, facilities and services; Part IV provided for the establishment of a National Disability Council; and Parts V and VI contained supplemental and miscellaneous provisions. Parliament was thus faced with two bills having a similar purpose, and the Speaker, Betty Boothroyd, needed to make a ruling; she had to determine whether or not they were incompatible – whether their provisions were different or substantially the same. She ruled that the two bills were different, and it was the government's bill which was given a second reading debate first, on 24 January. The Labour party, which favoured the Harry Barnes bill, opposed it. Its principal complaint was that the National Disability Council proposed by the government would, with an advisory role only, be toothless; it would not, like the Disability Rights Commission, have any investigative or enforcement powers.

The government could rely on its majority in parliament, and when the House divided its bill was given its second reading by 307 votes to 280. The Barnes bill followed when it had its second reading debate on 10 February. To the government it was immaterial whether it was voted through or not; if it went into committee it could be crippled by being encumbered with government amendments. The Conservative MPs who opposed it abstained from voting, and with the backing of the Labour party it was given its second reading by 175 votes to none. It went into committee and ran out of time when, with its amendments, it returned to the House of Commons at report stage on 14 July.

The focus was then on the government's Disability Discrimination Bill. When it was being drafted Mr Hague's concern was that it would have to satisfy the disability lobby, and in September 1994 he had travelled to Washington, his purpose being to see and learn how the Americans with Disabilities Act was working in practice, and meet and talk with prominent politicians and officials who had helped guide it through Congress. What he wanted, we may suppose, was ideas for making the bill he was preparing look like the Americans with Disabilities Act – in particular, ideas for doing something positive about making existing public buildings accessible.

A Command Paper, *Ending discrimination against disabled people*, accompanied the government's Disability Discrimination Bill when it was printed on 12 January 1995. What was revealed was that on the vital access issue the government had changed its mind; it had decided that Britain could, after all, attempt to emulate the Americans with Disabilities Act. Part III of the bill, with provisions on which there had been no consultation, set out the duties of building owners and providers. Where his premises were inaccessible to disabled people, but where it was reasonable that they should be and the cost did not exceed an amount prescribed by associated regulations, a building owner had, at his own expense, to make them accessible. If he did not, the threat was that he could be charged with discrimination against disabled people and taken to court.

The Government's change of heart was explained in the Command Paper: 'In the light of the responses to the consultation document, it is clear that disabled people and others would like to see faster progress towards an accessible environment than would be possible through the operation of the Building Regulations alone. The Government supports these aspirations . . . '[29] The phrase 'through the operation of the Building Regulations alone' reflected the government's awareness of the restricted scope of building regulations; since regulations were applicable only when work was to be carried out, there could be no duty under building regulations to improve access for its own sake, and this was a problem which would remain even were Part M to be extended to cover structural alterations to existing buildings.

As the bill progressed, the pressure from the parliamentary disability lobby and activists outside was to extend its scope; 'we want more', they demanded. They urged a Disability Rights Commission in place of the weaker National Disability Council, and on that they failed. But they successfully obtained new provisions relating to education and transport, among the latter being a provision for regulations to be introduced which could require all licensed taxis to be wheelchair-accessible at some future date. On the access-to-buildings front, they did not press any significant changes. Absorbed as they were with grasping more elsewhere, they accepted the government's line that after the bill had been enacted workable regulations would be introduced which would effectively enforce access provisions. On 8 November 1995 the Disability Discrimination Act was passed into law. At that time procedures for its implementation were not yet in place, as they had been in America when the Americans with Disabilities Act was introduced.

Until 1995, the principle which guided British legislation to do with the accessibility of buildings was that provision should be service-led. Through planning controls and the Part M building regulation, enforcement powers were vested with local authorities. The Disability Discrimination Act discarded that principle. Like the Americans with Disabilities Act, its enforcement would be grievance-led. Under the Act a disabled person who alleges that his rights have been violated will have to find someone or some organization he can sue. In the case of alleged discrimination caused by the inaccessibility of a building, the person he sues has therefore to be the provider of the building, not the architect (should he happen to be still alive) who was instrumental in making the building inaccessible.

If and when regulations for the enforcement of the access to buildings provisions of the Disability Discrimination Act are introduced, the complainant will be able to claim that he has been unlawfully discriminated against by the provider of a building where, for the service that he requires, he has to be able to get into and around the building, where the building is not accessible to him, where it is reasonable that it should be made accessible to him, and where the provider had made no effort to make it accessible to him. He will be able to pursue the matter by taking his claim to a court (in the case of England and Wales, a county court); should his complaint be upheld, the court could require the building provider to make the building accessible to him, and the damages he might receive for being the victim of unlawful discrimination could include compensation for injury to his feelings.

Part III of the Disability Discrimination Act deals with discrimination to do with the delivery of goods, facilities and services, with provisions to do with the accessibility of buildings being set out in section 21 of Part III. Prior to that, section 20 defines discrimination for Part III purposes and section 19 lists examples of services to which section 21 will apply when, at some future date, it is fully implemented; these include access to and use of any place which members of the public are permitted to enter; accommodation in a hotel, boarding house or other similar establishment; and facilities for entertainment, recreation or refreshment. Broadly, the coverage corresponds to what the Americans with Disabilities Act calls 'public accommodations'.

Looking at Part III from a personal perspective, I find it devious. On the meaning of discrimination, section 20(1) reads: 'For the purposes of section 19, a provider of services discriminates against a disabled person if – (a) for a reason which relates to the disabled person's disability, he treats him less favourably than he treats or would treat others . . . ; and (b) he cannot show that the treatment in question is justified'. With regard to item (a), I consider my own experiences as a person with a severe disability when I use buildings such as shops, restaurants, hotels, theatres, railway stations and airport terminals. The record is unequivocal. Where there is any differential treatment (which commonly there is not), it is invariably in my favour. Help is given to get me in through the door; if I am in a wheelchair I am helped to get over a step or up a ramp; and I am courteously asked whether I need anything special done on account of my disability. Should I need any special treatment, I ask; the response is usually most considerate, and practically always willingly offered. Where my needs cannot be accommodated on the same basis as other members of the public, for example in respect of provision in en-suite bathrooms in hotel rooms, I am not, in terms of personal attitudes, treated less favourably by the management.

It is not, however, personal attitudes which will matter for the purposes of satisfying the law of Part III of the Disability Discrimination Act. The building owner's attitude to me may be unexceptionable, but he will still have transgressed the law if he has not happened to do practical things he might have done to make his building easier for me to use, and because he has not done those things he can be held to have treated me less favourably than other members of the public. Section 21 sets out what he has to do to avoid offending me, with subsections (1) and (2) being of most relevance. They read as follows:

> (1) Where a provider of services has a practice, policy or procedure which makes it impossible or unreasonably difficult for disabled persons to make use of a service which he provides, or is prepared to provide, to other members of the public, it is his duty to take such steps as it is reasonable, in all the circumstances of the case, for him to have to take in order to change that practice, policy or procedure so that it no longer has that effect.
>
> (2) Where a physical feature (for example, one arising from the design or construction of a building or the approach or access to premises) makes it impossible or unreasonably difficult for disabled persons to make use of such a service, it is the duty of the provider of that service to take such steps as it is reasonable, in all the circumstances of the case, for him to have to take in order to:
> (a) remove the feature;
> (b) alter it so that it no longer has that effect;
> (c) provide a reasonable means of avoiding the feature; or
> (d) provide a reasonable alternative method of making the service in question available to disabled persons.

Were subsection 2 of section 21 of the Disability Discrimination Act ever to be brought into operation, it could in practice be difficult to determine what should or should not for its purposes be deemed to constitute an unacceptable physical feature of a building. To illustrate the matter, I consider a classic feature of the urban environment in Britain, the single step at the entrance to a small high street shop. For wheelchair users, and sometimes for ambulant disabled people also, it manifests inaccessibility. With reference to myself, my disability and the ordinance of the Act, I hypothesise a scenario:

> As an ambulant disabled person I go to the shop. I cannot get in because there is a high step and no rail I can grab to pull myself up and over. I summon the manager: 'My rights are violated; I cannot get in because there is no grab rail; you must fix a rail or I shall take you to court'. He obliges.
>
> At the same shop a few weeks later I am in a wheelchair. I summon the manager: 'My rights are violated; I cannot get in because there is a step in the way; you must provide a ramp or I shall take you to court'. He obliges.
>
> Two months later I return, again in a wheelchair. The ramp is steep, and at the top of it there is no platform in front of the door. I summon the manager: 'My rights are violated; I cannot get in because I cannot get up this ramp; you must remove it and then reconstruct it'. 'No', he says, 'I can't do that; it's not practicable'.

> Four weeks later I am back again, this time as an ambulant disabled person. I can get up the ramp and into the shop, but when I move to go out the ramp is too steep for me to negotiate it safely and without great difficulty. I summon the manager: 'My rights are violated; this ramp makes it impossible for me to use your shop; when there was a step and a rail I could do so; you must remove the ramp – it doesn't suit anyone, and for disabled people it would be better to have a single step'. 'No', comes the reply, 'I can't do that – I'm told that ramps are what disabled people want'.

The single step at the entrance to small shops is indigenous to the English high street. American towns do not, or only rarely, have urban high streets with a packed row of shops on the English pattern. Where in America shops, restaurants and other small buildings do have a single step, it is often practicable, owing to the spaciousness of American streets, to adjust the level of the sidewalk to afford convenient wheelchair access in accord with the requirements of the Americans with Disabilities Act Accessibility Guidelines. In America the single step issue did not prejudice the viability of applying uniform rules for alterations to existing buildings, ones which, based on wheelchair user criteria, were the same as those for new buildings.

In Britain there cannot be uniform rules for making alterations to existing buildings, and there cannot therefore be an access standard, one which precisely defines what accessibility means for the purposes of law enforcement. Without an access standard, section 21(2) will be inequitable. Under related provisions in section 25 any disabled person could make a complaint – be it responsible, frivolous, vexatious or with an eye to compensation for injured feelings – and demand that the building provider should remedy the matter. The predicament facing any building owner concerned to avoid being accused of discriminatory practices would be that he would not know what he would need to do to stay on the right side of the law.

The lack of preparatory planning behind Britain's legislation for countering discrimination against disabled people contrasted with the immense amount of preliminary work which preceded the introduction of the Americans with Disabilities Act. On 26 July 1991, exactly 12 months after the ADA was signed into law by President Bush, the US Department of Justice issued a comprehensive package of final rules for its implementation, with relevant Federal Register documents running into hundreds of pages. Through to 26 July 2020, the date by which it was planned that all subway stations would have been retrofitted, the enforcement of the law was to be phased. The regulatory prescriptions for its operation were already available, with those for accessibility requirements being drawn directly on the guidance issued in 1982 by the US Access Board.

By comparison, and in particular in respect of Part III, Britain's Disability Discrimination Act would be brought into operation in a piecemeal rather than a coordinated fashion. For the series of regulations needed to enforce the provisions of Part III there would be codes of practice, and on the preparation of these the Secretary of State for Social Security would be advised by the National Disability Council, the statutory body he would appoint under the terms of Part VI of the Act. As provided for in Schedule 5 to the

Act, at least half its members were to be disabled persons, persons who had had a disability or who were the parents or guardians of disabled persons, the implication being that the Council is an authorised disability lobbying agency. When it was first set up in January 1996, ten of its 18 appointed members were disabled people or the parents or guardians of a disabled person. No member of the Council was an architect or otherwise directly involved in the business of the construction industry.

As proposed in consultation papers issued in March 1996[30], the government's plan was for Part III to be implemented in four stages. The first stage covered the provisions relating to the refusal by a service provider to provide a service to a disabled person, or to provide it less favourably than to other members of the public. On this there was no cause for delay. A draft code of practice was presented with the March 1996 papers, and, with comments on it taken into account, it was issued in July 1996[31], with 2 December 1996 stipulated as the date for its enforcement. On the same date, the employment provisions in Part II were brought into operation[32]; among other matters, these were concerned with the accessibility of a building in which a disabled person might be working or wish to work, but in respect of them there was no need for there to be a defined measure of accessibility, as eventually there would be for section 21 in Part III.

The second stage, to be implemented in 1998, would cover the provisions in Part III relating to the policies, practices or procedures which service providers would have to change so that disabled people could more easily make use of a service; for example, allowing blind people to bring guide dogs into restaurants[33].

The third stage would cover the duty that, according to circumstances, a service provider would have to provide some auxiliary aid or service (such as the provision of information on audio tape or of a sign language interpreter) to a disabled user of a service; the plan was that this would be implemented in the year 2000[34].

The fourth stage, acknowledged as the one it might be most difficult to implement, would cover section 21(2), the duty which, according to circumstances, a building provider would have to alter or modify his premises to suit the needs of a disabled person. The Government's view, with the idea that an access standard should be produced, was that building providers should be given a long lead-in time to prepare for what they might have to do, and the date suggested for implementation was the year 2005[35].

16 America and Britain: the faultlines of accessibility controls

With the Part M building regulation dominating the show, and no regulations for the enforcement of the access-to-buildings provisions of Part III of the Disability Discrimination Act as yet in sight, *Reasonable Provision* could be the title of the picture of accessibility controls in Britain in 1996. The corresponding American picture could be called *Access Rights*. Both pictures display selectivity and discrimination, and – more noticeably in the British version – messy patches and empty spaces. Both depict only people with disabilities, not everyone. Outside the frame, others, such as pushchair users, may be presented as supporting actors. But they remain outside. It is only people with disabilities who are entitled to a place inside.

The original picture from which both the current British and American versions owe their derivation was painted by Tim Nugent. When he presented the first American Standard in 1961, his stance was ambivalent. As an idealist he was a macroist. He asked that disabled people should, without discrimination and with no special rights or privileges, be treated in the same way as others, as normal and not as different people. But in pressing his cause, in particular the interests of his wheelchair students, he was obliged to adopt a microist line. He presented and publicised his standards as *for the disabled*, and in promoting them he emphasised the benefits they would bring to disabled people. With its title *American Standard Specifications for Making Buildings and Facilities Accessible to, and Usable by, the Physically Handicapped*, his 1961 A117.1 was perceived as a design standard which was special for disabled people.

In his stance as a macroist, Nugent worked from the bottom up; the parameters of normal provision had to be expanded in order for people with disabilities to be included as normal people. And, in accord with the tenets of macroism, a line had to be drawn. Wheelchair users who by Nugent's criteria were correctly oriented and could be trained to manage independently were accommodated. Those who were not could be disregarded and excluded. Thus it was that design standards based on the characteristics and capabilities of the independent wheelchair user ordered national rules for buildings which were to be accessible and would not discriminate against disabled people.

The instrument which Nugent had crafted in 1961 was adopted in the late 1970s by American disability activists who were campaigning for their civil rights. Inaccessible buildings, they claimed, manifested unwarranted discrimination against disabled people, and the elimination of architectural barriers became the central feature of their campaign, a campaign that was to lead to the enactment in 1990 of the Americans with Disabilities Act. With the Act came the regulations, *The Americans with Disabilities Act Accessibility Guidelines*, modelled on the 1961 American Standard. On account of the accommodation limits of correct 'accessible' provision, the Americans with Disabilities Act was inevitably discriminatory; instances where discrimination was implicitly acknowledged as legitimate included discrimination against (a) disabled people with a need to be helped by someone of the opposite sex when using a public toilet; (b) disabled people with a need to have someone else to assist them to get on or off a wc seat; and (c) wheelchair users without the ability to propel their wheelchair up a ramp with a 1 in 12 gradient.

The proposition underlying the Americans with Disabilities Act Accessibility Guidelines is that accessible provision for independent wheelchair users will afford accessibility for all other disabled people. The effects of this can be discriminatory, an example being the inconvenience caused to ambulant disabled people where, with 'accessibility' being provided by an elevator elsewhere in the building, steps and stairs do not have to be suitable for them. Discrimination may similarly occur where paramountcy is afforded to the supposed needs of the independent wheelchair user to the disadvantage of ambulant disabled people, an example being the incorporation of a steep ramp in place of a single step when a building is altered.

Swimming pools are an interesting case. Access for ambulant disabled people could have been facilitated had there been a requirement for suitable steps with a handrail. But that would not have constituted accessibility. The advice in *The Americans with Disabilities Act Technical Assistance Manual* was:

> A swimming pool complex must comply fully with ADAAG in the parking facilities, route to the facility door, entrance to the facility, locker rooms, showers, common areas, and route to the pool. However, ADAAG does not contain technical standards for access to the pool itself. Thus, the owner cannot be found in violation of ADAAG for failure to install a lift or other means of access into the pool[1].

Most notably it is, however, in respect of toilet facilities and severely handicapped people in wheelchairs that discrimination is implicitly admissible under the terms of the Americans with Disabilities Act. For new construction, an 'accessible' wc compartment can have dimensions 1420 × 1525mm, and for alteration work where that standard is not feasible, a smaller facility, with dimensions 915 × 1675mm or 1220 × 1675mm[2], can count as being accessible. Compared with the BS5810/Part M unisex toilet, the internal areas of these three are respectively 28, 49 and 32 per cent less spacious*, and the wheelchair manoeuvring space within them even more markedly less.

More significantly perhaps than any other feature of the Americans with Disabilities Act, the 'accessible' toilet defines the people with disabilities who in America have 'rights'. In Britain, disability activists, calling as they have done for civil rights legislation on the American model, have imagined that all disabled people in America genuinely do have comprehensive access rights under the Americans with Disabilities Act; they are not, in my experience, usually aware that in America spacious unisex toilets are virtually nowhere to be found, and that people with severe disabilities have no 'right' to accessible and usable toilet facilities.

In the early 1960s I helped set the pattern for accessibility controls in Britain. On the strategy there was no debate; in 1963 my colleagues and I were agreed that Britain should follow the line which Tim Nugent had laid out for America, and so it was that the first British Access Standard, CP96 of 1967, came with national rules. That precept was always secure, and when section 4 of the 1970 Chronically Sick Act eventually came to be enforced, it was building regulations with their national rules which would be the legislative instrument.

Where we intended in the 1960s to take Britain on a different course was in having CP96 prescribe application conditions as well as design standards; an aim that was not then realised and was abandoned when BS5810 was drafted in the late 1970s. The important departure we did make from Nugent's model was to set the British Standard firmly on a microistic welfare base. Among the consequential effects of going down the welfare track were (a) accessibility controls influenced by welfare legislation; (b) national rules based on a welfare model; (c) an absorption with special provision for disabled people, in particular the provision in public toilets of unisex facilities; (d) the authority afforded to a welfare minister, the Minister for the Disabled, to concern himself with access issues; (e) a national access committee, the Access Committee for England, whose chairman was appointed by the Minister for the Disabled and whose work was funded by the Department of Health; and (f) in 1995, the authority given to the Secretary of State for Social Security to make regulations for alterations to existing buildings under the terms of the Disability Discrimination Act.

'Reasonable provision shall be made for disabled people' was the requirement of the Part M building regulation, both in 1987 and 1992. More assertively in the 1992 regulation, when people with hearing or sight impairments were brought within the definition of 'disabled people', the policy perspective was microistic. The Access Committee for England had been identified as the primary disability agency to whose views there must be deference when the terms of the approved document for Part M were being

* For comparative data see Appendix 4, page 379.

considered, and whose advice must be respected*. As a disability pressure group it viewed every issue from a microistic 'for the disabled' viewpoint. It was dominated by activists who were people with severe disabilities – those towards the tail end of the disability spectrum, people for whom special 'for the disabled' provision could more commonly be needed than by the generality of disabled people whose needs could be accommodated by suitable normal provision. Their view was reflected in the terms of the provisions advised in the approved documents for Part M: in effect, what was held to constitute 'reasonable provision' did not mean provision which by commonsense criteria was reasonable; instead it meant practically any special provision for disabled people which it was feasible to incorporate into buildings.

The microistic policy reflected in the Part M building regulation involves working from the top down, not the bottom up; it means focusing on the particular needs of severely disabled people and making special provision for them, so that separate provision for the disabled is tacked on to normal provision for the generality of building users. Without a seamless join, an effect of working top down is that comprehensive accessibility is not assured – vital gaps can be left unfilled, with resultant discrimination against many disabled people and other building users. The dangers inherent in this concept of designing for the disabled are illustrated by what happened at Liverpool Street Station.

Historically the London terminus of the Great Eastern Railway, Liverpool Street Station used to be two disconnected stations alongside each other, one opened in 1874, the other in 1894. Plans for its reconstruction as an entirely new station were announced in 1975, work on site began in 1985, and completion, at a cost of some £120 million came in 1991[4] As a reconstructed rather than a new building (and also as a British Rail station building), it was technically not subject to the 1987 Part M building regulation *Access for disabled people*. But, as reported at a Centre on Environment for the Handicapped seminar held in May 1989[5], care was taken by the architects to ensure that it was designed in conformity with Part M requirements.

In the new building as in the old, the concourse and train platforms are at a level some 5 metres below that of the two main streets from which the

*In 1997 the Access Committee for England remains in being. The feud which had developed in 1987 between it and its parent body, the Centre for Accessible Environments, persisted[3], and in January 1993 Nicholas Scott, the then Minister for Disabled People, announced that on a temporary basis it would be placed with the Royal Association for Disability and Rehabilitation (RADAR). In July 1995 the three government departments with whom it was involved, Social Security, Health, and Environment, decided that its work and future should be reviewed. In June 1996, Minister for Disabled People Alistair Burt, concerned perhaps to avoid upsetting the disability lobby, announced that it would continue to be government-funded for a further two years and would stay with RADAR. In future its post-holders would not, however, be ministerial appointments, and it would no longer be authorised to advise ministers and government departments on access policy issues – that would be the job of the National Disability Council.

16.1 The concourse at Liverpool Street Station. The war memorial is to the right. The ticket office is below the information board, to the right

station is reached, Bishopsgate and Liverpool Street. To facilitate access for ambulant disabled people, wheelchair users, those with infants in pushchairs and those encumbered with heavy baggage, two or three spacious passenger lifts might have been provided. But the initial view was that a lift was not essential – the idea was that those in wheelchairs could, along with others, transfer from the street to the concourse level by journeying round the building and come in via the ramp at the far Broadgate end of the complex[6]. During the course of the project the idea was dropped, and a small special for-the-disabled lift was incorporated. At the upper level, its door is discreetly inserted in the bottom corner of the retained monumental Great Eastern Railway war memorial (Figure 16.2). At the lower level, the lift opens on one side into the booking hall, and on the other into a corner of the approach to the underground station.

On the same level as the station concourse (Figure 16.1) are the train platforms, the taxi rank and, with one exception, principal amenities such as the booking hall, shops and refreshment facilities. The exception is the public toilets, which alone are below the concourse and can be reached only by way of two steep flights of stairs (Figures 16.3, 16.5). Technically this does not contravene the Part M requirement that reasonable provision must be made for disabled people, since for compliance purposes it is only necessary for there to be special 'for the disabled' toilet facilities. These are located behind a door in the corner of the ticket hall; with a 'Private Staff Only' injunction, the door displays the access symbol, with a notice advising that a key to the toilets within can be obtained from station staff.

The key is the RADAR key, the Royal Association for Disability and Rehabilitation being responsible for the management of the National Key

16.2 The for-the-disabled lift which goes down to the ticket office

16.3 The approach to the public toilets

16.4 The notice reads: Customers with special needs
Facilities for customers who experience difficulty with stairs; alternative facilities are available in the ticket office area
A baby changing room is also available
Please contact reception for key (RADAR) or ticket office staff if reception is closed

16.5 The stairs to the toilets

Scheme for disabled people. British Rail has adopted the scheme, and at all its stations which have a special for-the-disabled toilet the facility is kept locked. Only a tiny proportion of all disabled people, something of the order of 1 in 200, regularly carry a RADAR key with them[7]. The other 99 per cent or so may, or may not, find that normal public toilets are conveniently accessible when they need to use them at British Rail stations.

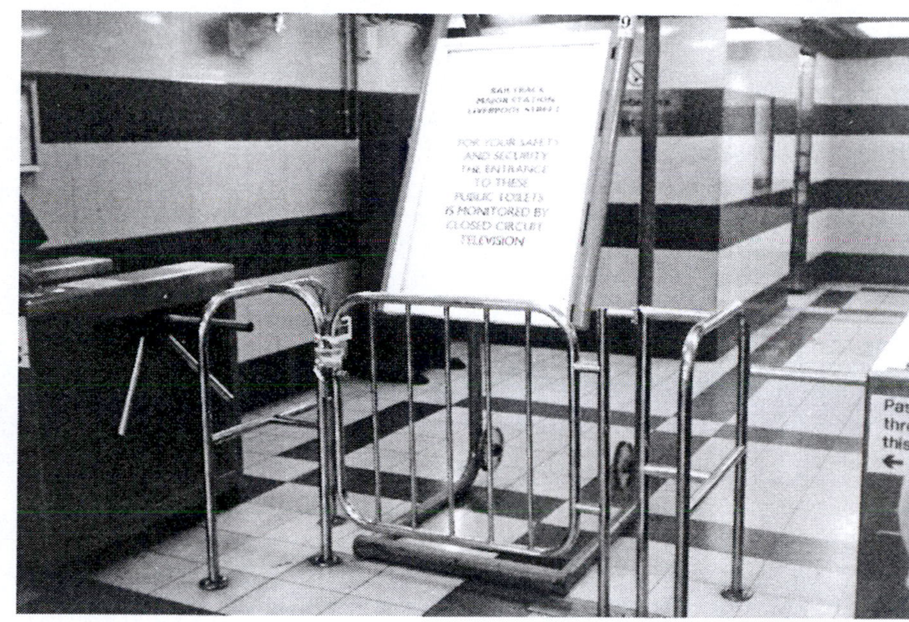

16.6 The pay-to-pass-through barrier at the foot of the stairs

At Liverpool Street Station the public toilets are below the concourse, down 22 steps (Figure 16.5). With 300mm treads and 180mm risers, they are not comfortably graded. They have to be tackled by all those who need to use the public toilets, by people with disabilities, by elderly people, by people with infants in pushchairs, by small children, and by people carrying heavy baggage. There is an escalator to bring customers back up, but not one to take them down.

Down at the bottom, the male and female toilet facilities are reached by squeezing through a coin-operated barrier (Figure 16.6). Inside, the wc cubicles are of the conventional small oblong brand, and, both for men and women, all of the same size. With internal dimensions of 1640 × 850mm, they are marginally bigger than typical wc cubicles elsewhere, but, in line with universal practice in Britain, their doors open in and pushchair access is precluded. The mother with an infant in a pushchair faces a choice. If it is she who needs to use the toilet, she can leave the infant, the pushchair and the baggage outside, or struggle to get the lot in. If it is the infant who is demanding, she can leave the pushchair outside, or somehow get it and the baggage in, and, encumbered as she will be in the confined space, help the infant as best she can to perform.

In line with conventional architectural practice, men are treated much more generously than women in terms of the number of toilet amenities provided for them. On the men's side under the concourse at Liverpool Street Station there are 49 toilet appliances for men (18 wc cubicles and 31 urinals); on the women's side there are 20 wc cubicles. If anyone has to wait in a queue, it will be women.

The faultlines in the system which Britain currently has in place for controlling the accessibility of buildings are exemplified at Liverpool Street Station, and, with a view to there being a new system which would rectify them, questions are raised. Ought the current 1992 Part M Approved Document to be discarded? If a Part M building regulation is to be retained, what form should it take? Ought it to regulate access for everyone, not just disabled people? For access purposes, ought planning and building controls to be combined? Ought new primary legislation to be introduced to cover the whole arena of accessibility controls? If so, how would the battery of controls be best administered? What ought to be done about the provisions in the Disability Discrimination Act to do with the accessibility of existing buildings?

Discussion on all this is deferred until Part 3, in which I put forward proposals as to how in Britain accessibility controls might sensibly be reformulated. Before then, the need is for material which will inform the debate, and this comes in Part 2, under the heading *Architectural disablement.*

Part 2

Architectural disablement

17 Architects and the architectural model of disability

From 1951 to 1954 at Cambridge and then from 1954 to 1956 at the Bartlett in London, my years as an architectural student came and passed while I was still a normal able-bodied person. During that time I was never presented with any prescriptive model of the building user for whom I would, were I to keep on course for the goal at which my training was aimed, eventually be designing buildings. At Cambridge in October 1951 the first exercise we were given to tackle on our drawing boards in the studio was to design a knocker to go on the entrance door of a nunnery. From then on, for buildings large and small, we were set a series of design problems; designing buildings was what we had to learn how to do. In between stints at the drawing board we were lectured on the mechanics of building construction and the history of architecture.

Among the books we read was Le Corbusier's *The Modulor*; the physical capabilities of his modular man, a six-foot high Englishman, were reflected in a grid of proportions which he claimed to be the key to the harmonious resolution of all design problems[1]. But when they were teaching us about design, none of our tutors asked us to think methodically about the people who would be the users of our buildings – what, for different types of buildings, their characteristics might be, and how their needs might vary.

From design textbooks, the weekly technical journals, glossy architectural magazines and other people's drawings we picked up the conventions of accommodating the users of buildings. We evidently got the right idea; I do not recall any occasion when one of my tutors, examining my efforts on the drawing board, said, 'That stairway is too steep', 'How are you going to get a pushchair through that lobby?', or 'What about access for the disabled?' Informed criticism was more frequently offered when the subject was domestic housing, but where it was public buildings the practicalities of how users would cope did not feature on the agenda. What we unconsciously learnt was that the building user (so far as we had one in mind, which we did not) was some kind of amorphous corporate organism. The effect was a bunch of confused and variable rules. In public buildings stairways were broader and less steep than they were in domestic houses, and passageways were wider and doors were bigger. In all types of buildings wc compartments were the same small size. The building user was not an entity.

My estimations of the performance of architects as building designers rely principally on experiential evidence – on the brief period I spent as a practitioner, on my instructive years with the *Architects' Journal*, on the many links I have had with practising architects over 40 years, and on my observations when looking at buildings or using them. There are architects who design buildings which treat their users sensitively, and in the course of the design process are keen to consult the kind of people their buildings will serve. But they are not as a rule imbued with a zealous mission to serve humanity; whether in the private or public sector they aim simply, to the best of their ability and to whatever pressures they may be subject, to do a good, conscientious and efficient professional job.

Architects who are ambitious and determined to make their mark in the world are eager to have the acclamation of their peers. When designing buildings they tend to have two priorities. The first is to produce a building which is aesthetically stunning. The second is to display technical cleverness. In third place – or lower than that – is making the building convenient for the people who will use it. A job that I had as buildings editor of the *Architects' Journal* was to commission photographers. Among those who looked to me for work were architectural photographers who wanted only to produce beautifully composed representations of the building with all its aesthetic and technical refinements, and with no disturbing people in view. As a rule, it was one of them whom the architect concerned preferred me to commission.

The architect of a prestigious public building may look to achieve sculpturally engaging spaces and vistas. Varying floor levels can assist, and to connect them flights of stairs are more appealing than ramps. And, where a firm political statement is in order, an imposing flight of steps at the entrance to a building serves well. Architects like to be free to design their buildings how they wish. They recognise, however, that mandatory health and safety regulations are appropriate, and what they then want is to be told what they have to do to comply with them. They welcomed the new-style building regulations introduced in England and Wales in 1985, with for each part an Approved Document telling them how they could satisfy the functional requirements of the regulations.

My impression has been that architects in Britain were generally happy to take on board the Part M building regulation *Access for disabled people* when it was introduced in 1987. They were willing to believe that historically they had been guilty, that they had discriminated against disabled people by keeping them out of their buildings. In the spirit of welfare for the disadvantaged they became concerned about disabled people – they wanted to help them, and now they could do so. They wanted to be told exactly what they had to do, and they welcomed the Part M Approved Documents. They liked the ethos that Part M reflected – the idea that disabled people were different, that they had special needs, and that suitable provision for them could be tacked on to whatever kind of building they were working on without unduly disturbing their design concept.

The teaching of designing for the disabled in architectural schools

From the early 1960s requests for advice frequently came to me from architectural students who were engaged on a project to design some kind of special building for handicapped people. That was, and remained, the way that tutors in architectural schools handled the issue of designing for the disabled – handicapped people were a special needs, not a mainstream, issue. The matter of what was, or was not, being done in architectural schools to teach students about designing for the disabled was one which surfaced regularly at disability meetings and seminars during the 1970s and beyond. One of the 42 recommendations made in February 1982 by CORAD, the committee on restrictions against disabled people set up by Alf Morris as Minister for the Disabled, was that designing for disabled people should form part of the training of all architects[2]. This could not be mandated since each architectural school in Britain sets its own curriculum and, while being subject to certification inspections, cannot be instructed by the Board of Architectural Education on precisely what is taught and how.

In an attempt to tackle the issue, two of my colleagues whose practices specialised in buildings for the disabled, Wycliffe Noble and John Penton, separately launched initiatives; they set out to visit architectural schools (of which there are some 36 in Britain) and encourage their tutors to establish designing for the disabled as a standard feature of student teaching. Their efforts failed to prosper, my understanding being that tutors in architectural schools tended to say 'Keep out', or words to that effect. Only where a head of school was personally interested in the topic was there a sympathetic response. On the two occasions that this happened, and a working relationship was then established with the Centre on Environment for the Handicapped, the emphasis was still very much on the disabled people as different, as people with special needs.

The lack of concern among tutors in architectural schools for teaching students about disabled people as building users is illustrated by my own experiences. In the arena of disability and architectural design, my name has been recognised since 1961. During the 35 years that have followed, only four architectural schools have invited me to talk to their students about designing for the disabled and my work.

The social versus the medical version of disability

Architectural disability, the topic explored throughout this book, is a version of the social model of disability. This brings the disability lobby back into the discussion, since among the consumer activists who orchestrate the disability lobby in Britain and lead what is known as the disability movement, the social model of disability is perceived as the guiding light. Mike Oliver, now (in January 1997) Professor of Disability Studies at the University of Greenwich, was the first commentator to articulate and define the social model, in a paper published in March 1982[3]. Prior to that, as the social interpretation of disability, the concept had been presented by Vic Finkelstein: he is now the Senior Lecturer on Disability Studies in the Open

University's School of Health and Social Welfare, and has for twenty years been revered in the disability world as a guru of the disability rights movement.

Finkelstein's early years were spent in South Africa, where in 1954 at the age of 15 he broke his neck while attempting to master the sport of pole-vaulting. He spent a year in rehabilitation at Stoke Mandeville Hospital in Buckinghamshire, and then returned home. He associated himself with the African National Congress, became a militant protester against the evils of apartheid, and, in his wheelchair, was imprisoned for ten months. As a refugee, he was back in Britain in 1968. In London he developed with Paul Hunt his thinking on the social oppression of disabled people. Hunt, who through the 1960s I had come to know well, was a brilliant and provocative commentator on the disability scene – crippled by muscular dystrophy, he had for 14 years prior to his marriage in 1970 lived in a residential institution for disabled people. Together they formed a militant campaigning group, the Union of the Physically Impaired Against Segregation. Its seminal document, *Fundamental Principles of Disability*, was published in 1976, and in it Vic Finkelstein wrote[4]:

> In our view, it is society which disables physically impaired people. Disability is something imposed on top of our impairments by the way we are unnecessarily isolated and excluded from full participation in society. Disabled people are therefore an oppressed group in society. . . . We define disability as the disadvantage or restriction of activity caused by a contemporary social organisation which takes no or little account of people who have physical impairments.

This prompts an examination of the distinction between the social and medical models of disability, or, as I term them, the social and medical versions. As defined by the World Health Organization and employed for the purposes of the national survey of disability in Great Britain undertaken during the late 1980s by the Office of Population Censuses and Surveys (OPCS), the medical version involves three concepts, 'impairment', 'disability' and 'handicap'. But to define it, only impairment and disability matter. An *impairment* is any loss or abnormality of psychological, physiological or anatomical structure or function. Resulting from an impairment, a *disability* is any restriction or lack of ability to perform an activity within the range considered normal for a human being. By the medical version of disability, disabled people are thus individuals who are disabled because there are things they cannot do owing to having non-operative bits of their bodies or bodily systems.

By the social version of disability, disabled people are those who are disabled on account of social barriers, by societal institutions which exclude them, and by the apparatus of architectural and other impediments which place them at a disadvantage. Disability commentators have, however, habitually applied it only to people with medical impairments, and by doing so have fostered a false interpretation of it. It is not the case that the medical version can somehow be exchanged for the social version of disability; the two are quite different concepts, with socially disabled people making up a very different population from medically disabled people. To illustrate the matter, any brand of the social version of disability could be invoked, for example employment disability, educational disability or transport disability. Better than any other, the architectural version of disability does, however, exemplify the issues involved.

There is not a straight correlation between medical disability and architectural disability; there are medically disabled people who are no more vulnerable to architectural disability than normal able-bodied people are. Architectural disability is not, as medical disability is, a bodily condition which people possess and always carry with them. In the form of architectural disablement it is manifested only in particular environmental circumstances, ones where there is an encounter with a building impediment. The people it affects are not therefore a discrete population, and they cannot be scored and counted as being 'disabled' in the same way as medically disabled people can be. And, as with other forms of social disability, architectural disability is not exclusive to medically disabled people.

For any building user, the incidence of architectural disablement is associated with the frequency of public buildings usage. In the case of any medically disabled person, the determinants of building usage include the effects of disabling impairments, and also factors such as personal financial means, the availability of travel by car, and having a partner who can help tackle architectural impediments. I use public buildings frequently, and in consequence I often happen to be architecturally disabled. Such happenings are, however, as they are for others, simply a function of the interaction of medical impairments (in my case all physical) and the character of architectural obstacles.

Architectural disability – the false premise

In the 1950s on the Champaign-Urbana campus of the University of Illinois, Tim Nugent engineered the removal of the architectural barriers which stood in the way of the rehabilitation of his handicapped students. He followed that with his seminal accomplishment, the drafting of the 1961 American National Standard which prescribed detailed specifications for making buildings accessible to disabled people. From then on, the proposition which informed the numerous access standards and codes of practice issued around the world was that it was only people with disabilities who were architecturally disabled when using buildings – normal able-bodied people were not. Taking the notion on board, commentators in the architectural arena then put forward a related proposition, that architects designed buildings which were convenient for normal able-bodied people but not others, and that was the reason why buildings were not convenient for disabled people to use.

Architects do *not* design buildings which are convenient for normal able-bodied people to use. They work to the precepts of what I call the organic muddle paradigm, which brings with it design conventions such as the provision of twice as many toilet amenities for men as for women, and wc compartments which are too small for anyone to use comfortably. Able-bodied people can be architecturally disabled on the same basis as people with medical disabilities. Architectural disability is, in effect, synonymous with architectural discrimination, the principle being that a building user can be discriminated against on account of a building feature that is *disabling*, whereas he would not have been had the architect, as he might have done, incorporated an *enabling* feature instead.

The inadmissibility of the conventional designing-for-the-disabled position – that architects should concern themselves only with people who are medically disabled – is demonstrated most forcibly by the comparison between the blind person and the pushchair user. The blind person has a medical disability, which is that he cannot see. He is socially handicapped by his blindness. When he is using public buildings, the impediments he comes up against are multifarious. But only occasionally will he, on my terms, be architecturally disabled, since the architect cannot as a rule moderate the social effects which building impediments have on him, or can do so only very marginally. By contrast, the mother (or father, or whoever it may be) who uses buildings with an infant in a pushchair can frequently be architecturally disabled, by features such as steps and stairs, heavy doors, narrow doors, confined lobbies and inaccessible wc compartments. The impediments are the same as those that confront the wheelchair user, and they can be similarly disabling. And as with the wheelchair user, the architectural discrimination to which the pushchair user is subjected could be largely avoided.

Architectural disablement and enablement

By taking enabling action, the architect can be a preventative therapist; he can prevent people being disabled when they use buildings. For people with medical disabilities, his job is to avoid medical disability being compounded by architectural disability, and for those without, to ensure that architectural disablement does not occur. With regard to buildings of all kinds, the definition of architectural disablement which I offer is as follows:

> An architecturally disabled person is a person who, when using or seeking to use a building, is confronted by an impediment which would not have been there, or would not have been so irksome, had the architect who designed the building done so in a way which was responsive to his or her particular needs.

The complementary concept is architectural enablement, for which I offer the following:

> An architecturally enabled person is a person who, when using a building, is able to do so on account of a building feature or features without which he would not have been able to use that building, or to do so conveniently.

Architectural disability in public buildings is most commonly caused by two sorts of impediments. One is *steps or stairs* where there could have been level access. The other is *confined space* where the space provided could have been more generous. Among people with medical disabilities it is those with a locomotor disability – ambulant disabled people and wheelchair users – who are most vulnerable to disablement when using public buildings, and whom the architect, as enabler, can most effectively help.

The status of special for-the-disabled buildings

In terms of the scope the architect has to help his building users there is an important distinction between public buildings and special buildings for disabled people. When architects design special for-the-disabled buildings, the opportunities they have to create therapeutic environments can be extensive. In special buildings for blind people there can be tactile cues on floor, wall or door surfaces that will help those who have no sight to locate where they are and find their way around the building and outside it. For those whose sight is less impaired, floor and wall surfaces can incorporate colour differences whose meaning is understood, or particular colours can identify particular building features. In nursing homes for people with dementia similar cues can assist orientation and warn of hazards. In residential buildings for deaf people the fenestration of neighbouring dwelling units can be angled to facilitate sign language communication. In residential homes and workshops for mentally handicapped people graphical devices can assist usage of the building and its facilities.

In special buildings such as these the architect as designer can respond sensitively to the particular needs of the kind of disabled people who will use them, with a vocabulary of therapeutic interventions appropriate to the type of building concerned. Public buildings are quite different. They are normal buildings which serve the needs of normal people. They are for the generality of the population, not an odd segment of it. And the location-specific, function-specific and user-specific therapeutic devices which can be designed into special for-the-disabled buildings cannot be applied to them.

The top-down measure of medical disability

There can be no clear distinction between people who, by the medical version of disability, are disabled and those who are not. Among all the people in a population, the degree of disability displayed is a continuum, running from the bottom end of the spectrum, where there is virtually no disability, to the top end, where there is extremely severe disability; this is illustrated in Figure 17.1a, where people who are not disabled are represented by the clear segment at the foot of the column, and those with disabilities by the tinted segment above it.

As is exemplified by the measure adopted by the OPCS for the national study of disability undertaken in Britain in the late 1980s, the measurement of disability for any particular purpose is drawn at some point on the way down from the top. According to the definition of disability a threshold level is set, above which people are deemed to be disabled and below which they are not. Figure 17.1b illustrates the effect where the definition describes

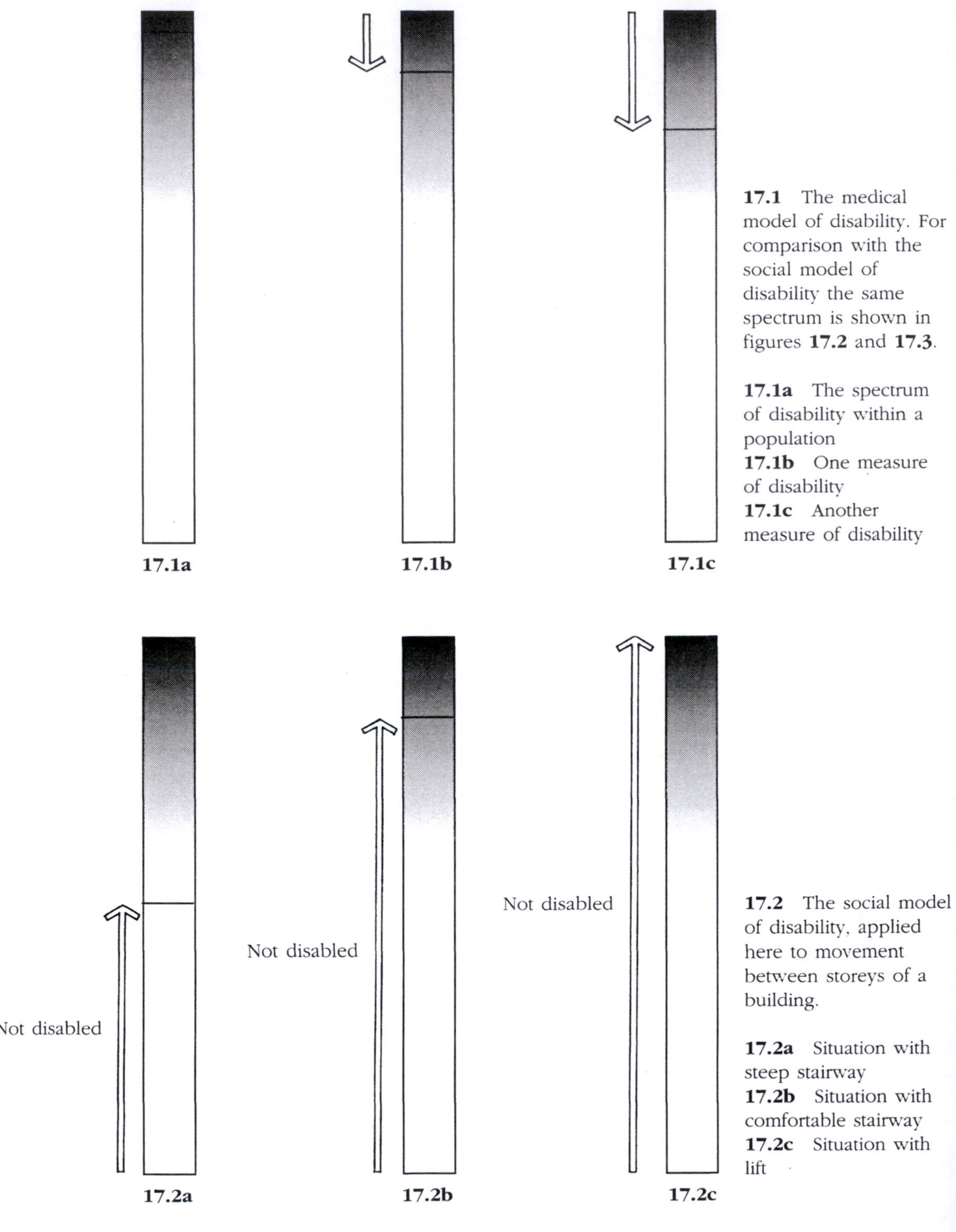

17.1 The medical model of disability. For comparison with the social model of disability the same spectrum is shown in figures **17.2** and **17.3**.

17.1a The spectrum of disability within a population
17.1b One measure of disability
17.1c Another measure of disability

17.2 The social model of disability, applied here to movement between storeys of a building.

17.2a Situation with steep stairway
17.2b Situation with comfortable stairway
17.2c Situation with lift

only people with relatively severe disabilities, and Figure 17.1c where it covers people with minor as well as more severe disabilities.

For virtually all disability-related purposes the top-down rule is applied. According to how severely disabled they are, people in Britain with disabilities may be eligible for a range of benefits. Examples are the Disability Living Allowance and, on the services side, the Disabled Persons Railcard and, for car parking, the Orange Badge. The principle behind the delivery of these benefits and services is that compensatory special provision ought to be made for disabled people on account of their disability. There have to be rules governing entitlement to them, and a cut-off has to be applied at some point down from the top end of the spectrum.

Architectural disability – the bottom-up measure

The provision made by architects for their building users brings into the reckoning an important axiom, one that is valid across the board of service provision. It is that the need for special provision is a function of the parameters of normal provision. Where the normal provision that is made in a building is of a kind that meets the special needs of all disabled people, the people with disabilities who use that normal provision will not be architecturally disabled. Where normal provision is not so accommodating, the people who are not architecturally disabled will be those who are not inconvenienced by it, whereas those who are inconvenienced – and may not be able to manage – will be architecturally disabled. To help disabled people, the architect will extend the accommodation parameters of normal provision. In doing so, he works from the bottom up, not the top down.

To illustrate the matter, I consider the issue of vertical circulation within a building. Where, to get from one floor to another, there is a steep stairway with winders and no handrail, it will be only fit able-bodied people who are not architecturally disabled, the effect here being shown in Figure 17.2a. Where there is a gently graded stairway with handrails, many people with disabilities will not be architecturally disabled, as shown in Figure 17.2b. Where there is a lift, with people in wheelchairs being conveniently accommodated as well as all other disabled people, there will not be any who are architecturally disabled, the effect being shown in Figure 17.2c.

The architect who is a macroist – who, when designing a building, observes the treat-as-normal design principle – does not incorporate special provision for disabled people where suitable normal provision will serve. His aim is to extend the parameters of normal provision as far as they can reasonably go. Normal provision is integrative, and what the architect should appreciate is that, in line with the precepts which govern the Americans with Disabilities Act, he has a moral duty to offer the integration option, to respond positively to the aspirations of disabled people who say:

> I want to be treated like everyone else; I want to feel that I belong in the mainstream; when I go out for the day with my family or friends I want to be able to use public buildings in just the same way as they do; when I'm at the

> building where I work I want to be able to get around and use it just like my office colleagues; I want to be accepted, not excluded; I don't want to be made to feel odd or peculiar.

Product design – the demerits of top-down

Among all the professional people concerned with the delivery of services used by disabled people, the architect has a privileged status. He can always apply the bottom-up integration rule, whether he is planning new buildings or altering existing ones. Others, for example housing managers, educationalists, transport operators, occupational therapists and social workers, can be obliged to recognise from the start that special services may have to be provided for their disabled clients, and that to cater for them they need to work from the top down. Similarly in the field of product design, special aids and equipment for disabled people are devised top-down rather than bottom-up. The special needs of disabled people are not, however, by any means always best accommodated by targeting them specifically.

Through my early years as a person with a disability, well-meaning friends used to tell me how I could be helped by the gadgets they had heard about – the Nelson knife for example, a knife/fork for one-handed people. I rejected that and all the rest of the for-the-disabled gadgetry that I came across, exceptions being the knob on the car steering wheel and the elastic shoelaces which I used before slipper shoes became sartorially respectable. After I moved professionally into the field of designing for the disabled it was not uncommon for budding product designers to seek my advice – they had ideas for suitable-for-the-disabled products which they imagined might have a large market, perhaps a mass market. I do not recall any that made a breakthrough.

Looking at the product design field from my personal perspective, I note that the innovative products which have been of greatest practical benefit to me as a severely disabled person have all been ones which were, I believe, developed on the bottom-up principle and aimed at the regular mainstream market, not at a specialist disability market. I list five. One, the remote-control television operator. Two, the standard car with off-the-peg features such as automatic drive, central door-locking, electronic windows and power-assisted steering. Three, the personal computer. Four, the microwave cooker. Five, the mobile telephone. The first three of these are products which I use almost every day, and I compare them with what was available in 1957 when I emerged from hospital as a chronically disabled person; their de-disabilizing effects have, I observe, been phenomenal.

Welfare provision – the deficits of working top-down

In looking to set controls for the accessibility of buildings Britain went down the welfare track. It wanted special provision to be made for disabled people, a policy line that consumer activists were keen to press. In accord with the welfare ethic, the strategy was top-down, not bottom-up. At the same time the principle was that there had to be 'right' solutions. For toilet provision for disabled people, the right solution was a carefully prescribed special unisex toilet. With it, the deficits of working top-down were exposed.

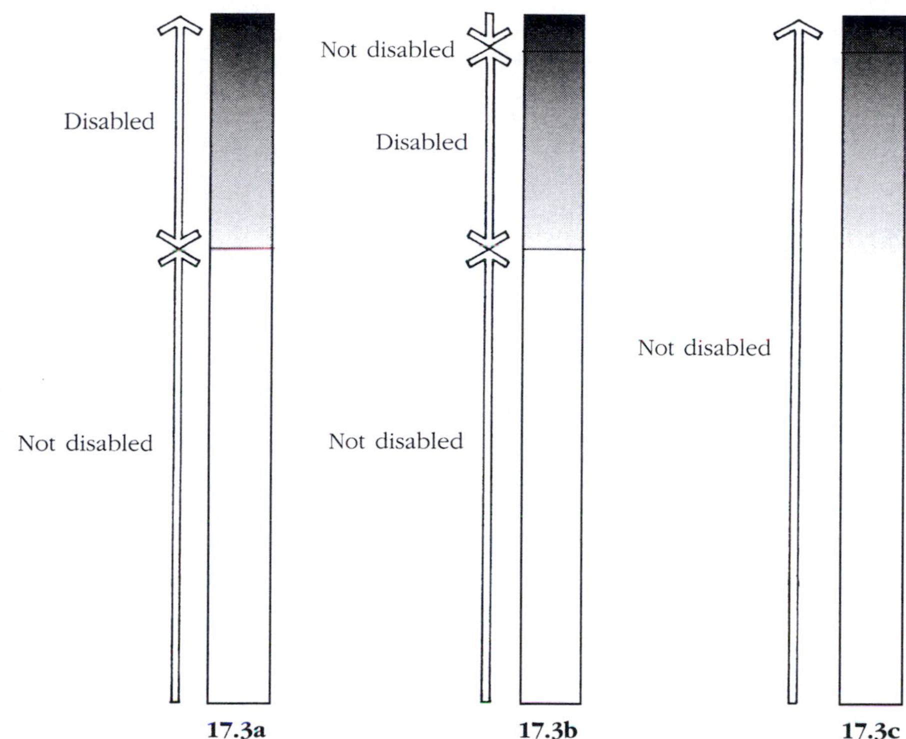

17.3 The architectural model of disability, applied here to the users of public toilet facilities

17.3a Normal toilets reached by stairs
17.3b Normal toilets reached by stairs, supplemented by special unisex facility with level access
17.3c Normal toilets with level access which include wheelchair-accessible toilets, supplemented by special unisex facility

The effect of incorporating only special unisex provision can, as demonstrated by Liverpool Street Station, be to discriminate against disabled people who could have used suitable normal facilities had they been provided.

With no seamless join between normal provision and special provision, some disabled people and certain other building users can be left unsupported in the middle. In the field of welfare benefits where help for the disabled is given top-down, an unfilled gap can be unavoidable – there are disabled people who are not entitled to the Disability Living Allowance but could cope financially if they had it, and some who are not eligible for an orange badge on their car and could much more easily manage if they had one. But architects can macroistically work bottom-up, and by doing so can close the gap.

Public toilet facilities illustrate the principle. Figure 17.3a shows what happens where a public toilet, one with conventional small wc compartments, is accessible only by way of stairs. Figure 17.3b shows what happens where, as at Liverpool Street Station, provision of the kind in Figure 17.3a is supplemented by a special unisex facility, one which is readily accessible only to those few people with disabilities who carry the special key with them. Figure 17.3c shows the effects of extending the accommodation parameters of normal toilet provision. Here, with level access, there are normal male and female facilities which are wheelchair-accessible and are convenient for virtually everyone. The only people who will not be suited by them will be those whose special needs can only be met by a suitable unisex facility, and where this is added no one (or virtually no one) will be architecturally disabled.

Questions are raised. Who, given the way that buildings have customarily been designed, are the people who as building users are losing out? Who would be accommodated were it the norm for design parameters to be extended, not only for public toilets but for all features of buildings? Who really needs special provision because normal provision cannot be geared to accommodate them? What are the real numbers?

18 Building users - the real numbers

In everyday usage 'the population' means the total population – the population of a town, city or country. For the survey of the prevalence of disability undertaken by the Office of Population Censuses and Surveys (OPCS) in the late 1980s, the population surveyed was that of Great Britain, at that time just over 55 million. While its composition has changed since then, its profile by age and sex remains much the same. Children aged 15 or under account for some 20 per cent of the population, adults between the ages of 16 and 64 for 64 per cent, and people aged 65 or over for 16 per cent. Among younger people there is a balance between males and females, but in the older age groups women predominate – of all those aged 65 or over there are half as many women again as men.

In response to the question 'How many disabled people are there?', a claim commonly made is that there are some 6 million, or about 10 per cent of the total population. The figure is loosely drawn from the estimate that, by the OPCS measure of disability, some 14 per cent of all adults (the total population less children aged 15 or under) are people who have a disability. Properly the claim ought to be that some 10 per cent of the total population are people who have an OPCS-type disability. But disability, as noted earlier, is a continuum, and the number of people who are reckoned to be disabled is determined by the point on the continuum at which the measure is taken; on this account it would be as fair to claim that 5 or 20 per cent of the total population are disabled people as that 10 per cent are. But 10 per cent (or thereabouts) came out of the OPCS survey, and for the sake of discussion 10 per cent serves as well as any other figure.

The uneven spread of disabled people

Fallacies come with the trick of extension. If 10 per cent of the total population are disabled people, it may be supposed that 10 per cent of the users of any public building have to be disabled people; this logic, as I have observed at meetings, appeals to disability activists keen to promote their cause. The inferences are false; it is not the case that all disabled people (meaning all OPCS-type disabled people) use all kinds of public buildings, are uniformly spread around, and that for different building types the ratio of their numbers to those of non-disabled building users is constant. The only type of building which all disabled people use is housing, either private dwelling units or communal establishments such as nursing homes or residential homes for old people. Of the estimated 6.2 million adult people in Great Britain reckoned by the OPCS to have a disability, 422 000, or 7 per cent, were people living in communal establishments[1]. Of all adult disabled people, an estimated 47 per cent were aged 75 or over, and 70 per cent were aged 60 or over. Of all adults aged between 16 and 59, an estimated 6 per cent were reckoned to be disabled; for those aged 60 or over, the estimate was 37 per cent, and for those aged 75 or over, 83 per cent.

While the great preponderance of people with disabilities are elderly, a very much smaller proportion of the users of public buildings are. Without needing to draw on such relevant population data as are available, broad estimates can be made for particular types of buildings. Hotels are used significantly more by middle-aged adult people, less by children and elderly people. Pubs are used hardly at all by children and are used more by middle-aged adults than by elderly people. Cinemas and theatres are used more by middle-aged adults than by children or elderly people; so are museums, art galleries, concert halls, railway stations and airport terminals. Sports stadia, while being more used by children than cinemas or theatres, are generally used more by middle-aged adults, less by elderly people. Swimming pools are used substantially more by children, relatively less by middle-aged adults and considerably less by elderly people. Supermarkets are used significantly more by infant children accompanied by parents than other building types, and generally more by middle-aged adults than by elderly people. Department stores are used more by middle-aged adults, less by children and elderly people. Local shops are possibly used as much by elderly people as by middle-aged adults and children; so perhaps are churches. Employment buildings such as offices and factories are a different matter; the people who work in them are middle-aged adults, not children or elderly people.

The inference of all this is clear: the fact that some 10 per cent of the total population are deemed to be disabled by the OPCS measure does not mean that 10 per cent of the users of all types of buildings are disabled people. The profile of the total population is not an indicator of the profile of the users of particular public and employment building types, or of the proportion of disabled people to be found among them. Nor is it reasonable to assume that among all the users of public buildings (as distinct from the users of individual building types) the proportion of disabled people corresponds with the proportion in the total population.

Architecturally disabled people

In considering the population of building users with regard to architectural disability, the focus is on people whom the architect can enable, those whose proneness to architectural disablement he can, according to circumstances, remove or minimise. In this connection, disablement associated with the height factor is noted first, for example the reach limitations of wheelchair users and people of short stature with regard to the height of supermarket display shelves, the needs of people with rheumatoid arthritis with regard to the height of wc fixtures, and the problems of small children with regard to the height of wash basins. Here, architectural disability is commonly of a kind that the architect can only alleviate in certain circumstances, for example where the building is special for a particular group or where a range of choice can be provided.

As has been noted, there are two principal causes of architectural disability which the architect can, as a general rule, effectively prevent. They are first, steps or stairs in the way of moving around, and second, inadequate space rather than comfortable space, for example in respect of the width of doors, the dimensions of lobbies and the size of wc compartments. On this basis, there are three groups of building users who are most vulnerable to architectural disability and whom the architect can most particularly help – ambulant disabled people, wheelchair users and pushchair users.

For the architect who designs a particular public building, for example a supermarket, a hotel, a theatre or a swimming pool, it is the composition of the user population of that building which matters, not the composition of the total population or the population of building users generally. The information which would help him would be a picture of the profile of the users of the building on a typical day, with an indication of the proportion among them of ambulant disabled people, pushchair users and wheelchair users. I move on to report how, starting with an interest in pedestrianisation, it happened that my professional work in the field of designing for the disabled generated such information.

Pedestrianisation

London Street in Norwich was pedestrianised in 1967. It was the exemplar for others that followed, and urban shopping centres in Britain were increasingly pedestrianised during the 1970s and on into the 1980s and 1990s. As the trend developed, there were certain disabled people for whom it signalled a threat, and at Centre on Environment for the Handicapped seminars, other meetings and in disability motoring journals they expressed their hostility to the pedestrianisation process[2]. With orange badges on their cars, these were disabled people accustomed to driving into urban high streets and parking directly outside any venue that they wished to visit. Their complaint was that pedestrianisation schemes could deprive them of their 'rights', and must be resisted. If and when they were introduced, concessions must be made; disabled people should be permitted to drive into them at designated times, and if not, there must be perimeter parking spaces reserved for orange badge holders, the rule they suggested being that no venue should be more than 50 metres from a parking space[3].

As the Department of Transport advised[4], there needed to be a balance between competing considerations. My own impression – admittedly with no evidence to back it – was that pedestrianisation schemes were positively attractive and beneficial for the great majority of disabled people who went out shopping. The protesters were, in the main, disabled people who were young and active, who drove their own cars and who were not impoverished. They did not represent the views of the generality of disabled people, and perhaps were being unduly selfish. It would be informative, I felt, if I were to carry out a survey to explore the issue, starting perhaps in Europe, where pedestrianised town centres were at that time more common than in England.

Wheelchair counts in European and English towns

For a holiday in the summer of 1986 I arranged with a friend to spend two and a half weeks in August travelling around Europe, looking at towns in Belgium, Holland, Luxembourg, Germany, Switzerland and France. I prepared a pro forma to score the disabled-access convenience rating of each town, to test whether there was a relationship between town convenience and the number of disabled people – wheelchair users and blind people – seen on the streets. The convenience rating plan failed, and in almost all the towns we went to there were no blind people to be seen at all. The intriguing outcome was the wheelchair scores. With typically about two hours spent in each town, 11 of the 27 that we visited scored none, and for 15 of the remaining 16 the highest score was four. The exception was Trier in West Germany, a splendidly restored historic town which had at its centre an uncommonly attractive pedestrianised shopping street. On a Thursday afternoon it scored 21 wheelchair users. To learn whether there was some particular explanation for the phenomenon I checked with the local tourist office – the answer was that there was not.

Back in England I continued the game, and it was soon evident that wheelchair users were much thicker on the ground than in Europe. I kept version one of the game – counting wheelchair users only – going until October 1989. Discounting Trier, I had by then accumulated 61 counts from 48 European towns*; with French and Italian towns producing modal scores of zero, the cumulative wheelchair score was 60, an average of 1.0. In England, excluding central London where there were three zero scores, 33 counts from 29 towns produced a cumulative wheelchair score of 289, giving an average of 8.8.

Why was it that the typical English town displayed so many more wheelchair users than its counterpart in Europe? The finding, it seemed, dented an important assumption, one on which across the world the campaign for accessible environments is promoted. It is that accessibility is a determinant of behaviour, that if buildings or towns are not wheelchair-accessible, people in wheelchairs are not able to go there, and that if they are, they will. In terms of topography, the typical European town that I visited was, if anything, more wheelchair-manageable than the typical English town – not by any means was it much less accessible. In England the scores suggested

* The towns and their scores are listed in Appendix 1, page 365.

a relationship between spacious covered shopping centres and busy wheelchair activity, examples being Peterborough (with a wheelchair score of 31) and Telford (25). In two towns – Barnsley (23) and Doncaster (28) – the availability of wheelchair-accessible scheduled bus services clearly had an effect. Beyond that, both in towns in England and those in Europe, there was no discernible environmental factor which appeared to be positively correlated with wheelchair activity.

Shopping centre users

I refined the rules of the game as it progressed. For systematic comparability between towns the routine was a one-hour counting time, and I took to counting stick users and blind people as well as wheelchair users. I then began keeping a check on the number of pushchair users. The important next step was to consider comparisons in terms not of absolute numbers but as proportions of total shopping centre populations, a concern being to test whether the relative prevalence of wheelchair users appeared to be related to any particular accessibility factors. As the process evolved, the routine became 30-minute counts, with six categories of shopping centre users being identified who could be distinguished and counted simply by observation. Five of these were (1) wheelchair users; (2) stick or crutch users; (3) blind people; (4) single pushchair/pram users; and (5) double pushchair users. The sixth was everybody else – adults and children who appeared to be able-bodied and whom I termed 'regular' people. The first count that I made on this basis was in Redditch in August 1989.

The new version of the game became an absorbing occupation. Whenever there was 30 minutes to spare in places where we went shopping in and around London, and in towns that were visited on weekend outings or in the course of official Department of the Environment business, I took out my clipboard and sat and counted people. There were occasions, I admit, when my wife Becky felt that my absorption had become an obsession.

I had not anticipated how valuable the accumulating fund of data was to be. The straight recording of observations of people in a population is the most impeccable of empirical research techniques; the methodology was unsophisticated, but a sound principle is that the cruder the data which informs hypotheses, the more reliable will be the validation of those hypotheses. The vital feature of my population counts was one that I had not recognised when they began as a pastime – it was that they displayed a picture of the by-the-day profile of the population of the users of public buildings.

The sanitary provision research project

During the last three years that I was with the Department of the Environment much of my time was spent on the research project *Sanitary provision for people with special needs*. Its purpose was to generate empirical data which could inform a revision of Part M building regulation requirements for sanitary facilities in new buildings, although in the event the

Approved Document for the 1992 Part M was issued before the complete report on the project was published.

It was around 1985 that I had first mooted the idea of a national survey of the sanitary provision needs of disabled people. Had the methodology been considered then, I could perhaps have advised national population surveys, involving first a postal questionnaire of a random sample of households, and then, for those with people with disabilities, an intensive interview survey. By early 1989 when the signal for the project to go ahead was given, a more attractive and economic option for targeting the population concerned was in view: it was a survey of populations of shopping centre users, the presumption being that their composition reflected that of the population of the users of public buildings generally*.

The pattern of counts

During the period that the brief for the project was being formulated and the contract arranged, I refined the procedures for the counting I was doing in a series of shopping centres around England. In different towns, proportions of people in the six subgroups identifiable by observation were variable, but a broad pattern emerged. Some 96 per cent of the users of shopping centres were regular people, rather more than 3 per cent were pushchair users (either single or double), and less than 1 per cent were people who were apparently disabled – stick or crutch users, wheelchair users or blind people.

The picture was not as I had supposed it would be. I knew from my 1960s research in Norwich how few active wheelchair users there were, and, affected by the notion that 10 per cent of the total population were disabled people, I had imagined that among overtly disabled people the great majority would be stick users. Had I been asked, I might have guessed that they accounted for as many as 3 or 4 per cent of all shopping centre users, and that there were perhaps ten times as many of them as there were wheelchair users. So it was a surprise to find that the actual figure for stick/crutch users was around half of 1 per cent – one person in 200 – and, relatedly, that they numbered only about twice as many as wheelchair users. Blind people, meaning those who when they go out carry a white stick or a white cane or are accompanied by a guide dog, were of particular interest. By September 1990, 54 half-hour counts had been made in 34 different locations in England[5]. The aggregate number of people counted was then just under 115 000, and of these only 11 – ie 1 in 10 000 or 0.01 per cent – were blind people.

The research programme

With a remit which covered pushchair users as well as people with disabilities, the contract for the sanitary provision research project was placed with British Market Research Bureau Ltd in February 1990. The objective was to

* The validity of the methodology is discussed in Appendix 2, page 366.

produce national estimates of the proportion of building users who had special needs when using (or attempting to use) public toilets, along with information on the kind of provision that would be required to meet those needs; this was to be done in respect both of individual public building types and public buildings generally, and also in respect of workplaces where disabled people with special toilet facility needs might be employed.

The selection of locations for the public buildings survey was affected by the 'would use' factor. There were commentators who supposed that disabled people could not use buildings which were not accessible, but would use them if they were accessible, and, relatedly, that they would not go to towns whose shopping areas were not conveniently accessible. So had the survey locations all been on hilly terrain, the reasonable complaint would have been that, particularly in respect of wheelchair usage, the findings were unreliable and unrepresentative. A deliberate decision was therefore made to select four towns which had uncommonly good accessibility characteristics, and in the event they virtually chose themselves – they were Carlisle, Eastbourne, Hereford and Peterborough.

The survey data which would inform the findings would come from two sources: one from population counts carried out nationally and in the four towns, the other from interviews with people intercepted at random in the shopping centres of the four towns; because young children could not be interviewed, the survey would be of the adult population only. Representative samples would be obtained for each of the six population subgroups, with questions being asked which would identify those who had special needs when using public toilets. The 'special needs' proportion in each subgroup would then be related to the subgroup proportions found from counts in shopping centres nationally, giving an estimate of the proportion of the total population of building users with a need for special provision in public toilets. Some of the more important findings are reported in this chapter, with supplementary notes and the bulk of relevant statistical material being placed in Appendix 2.

Defining 'special needs'

A basic project requirement was an operational definition of 'special needs', whereby in the context of the usage of public toilet facilities people with special needs could be separated from those without. It would need to be generally applicable, and the defining characteristic would need to be a simple one which could be readily grasped by interviewees when questions were put to them. The principle would be self-assessment – in response to interviewers' questions subjects would make personal judgements, and according to their answers they would be categorised as either with or without a need for special provision when using public toilets.

It is axiomatic, in whatever context, that the need for special provision is a function of the parameters of normal provision. What then constitutes normal public toilet provision, provision of a kind which is typically found? With regard to architectural disablement it has, I suggest, two significant features. One is that public toilet facilities are commonly approached by steps or stairs. The other is that wc compartments are small, with the space within them being very restricted. Normal able-bodied people are not as a rule troubled by these conditions – they do not have a no-steps need and they do not consider they have an extra-space need. They feel no cause to complain – their view is that public toilets are simply as they are, and there is no reason to expect them to be found other than as they are. Other users tend, it seems, to share their view and do not complain. But many of these 'other' users could, in practice, be inconvenienced by having steps in the way of getting to toilets or inadequate space within wc compartments. Many pushchair users, for example, might prefer there not to be steps and would wish that wc compartments were more spacious. So would those wheelchair users who would like to be able to use normal toilet facilities. Similarly, ambulant disabled people, those with sticks or crutches, would prefer not to be obliged to negotiate steps or stairs. And so perhaps would blind people.

The reasonable expectation when the interview survey was being planned was that pushchair users and wheelchair users would be the toilet users who presented themselves as having an extra-space need. These extra-space needs toilet users would predictably also be no-steps needs people. Presuming that the no-steps needs population encompassed all those with an extra-space need, the controlling criterion of special need could therefore be in terms of the steps or stairs obstacle, and on this basis the question put at interviews with regular people, stick/crutch users, wheelchair users and blind people was:

> If you are trying to use a public toilet, how important is it for you to have level access, so that you don't need to use steps or stairs to get there?

For pushchair users the question was the same, qualified by 'when you have the pushchair with you, and there's just you and your child'. The options for a response to the question were 'essential', 'important', 'not very important' and 'not at all important'.

When interviewed, the great majority of pushchair users, wheelchair users, blind people and (to a lesser extent) stick/crutch users said 'essential' or 'important', and for analysis purposes all these were classified as 'special needs' people. For regular people who said 'essential' or 'important', the follow-up question was, 'Is that because of a disability or health problem of some kind?' If the response was positive, they were asked to describe their disability or health problem and as 'regular disabled people' were classified as special-needs people.

The prevalence of regular disabled people

Professional interviewers employed by British Market Research Bureau began work on location in Carlisle, Eastbourne, Hereford and Peterborough in the fourth week of July 1990. All interviews were conducted on site, except that wheelchair users, for whom the questionnaire was lengthier, were interviewed at home after contact had been made on site. It was not long before results emerged which were remarkable. They had to do with regular people, the walking-about people in shopping centres who were not stick or crutch users.

In the course of counting people in shopping centres I had observed regular people who apparently had a disability, but there seemed to be few of them – virtually all regular adult people were, I thought, normal able-bodied people. The impression supported the proposition that there could be a close correspondence between the shopping centre 'disabled' population and the population described by the OPCS as people with a locomotor disability. Of OPCS locomotor-disabled people, 10 per cent were wheelchair users and 44 per cent were people who used walking aids such as a stick or crutches. The remaining 46 per cent were, I imagined, people whose mobility was not much affected by their disability, and not all of them, I assumed, would assess themselves as 'disabled' by the project definition. So I guessed that among all regular people a relatively insignificant number, perhaps about 1 per cent, would be found to be 'regular disabled' people. On this basis, the project brief asked for a sample of 200 regular people only, enough for data comparisons on public buildings usage to be made with wheelchair users and stick/crutch users.

The message from British Market Research Bureau in early August was that among the first batch of regular people who had been interviewed the proportion who assessed themselves as 'disabled', meaning those who responded 'essential' or 'important' to the question about the need for level access to public toilets, was not 1 per cent – it was around 12 per cent. At that rate, regular disabled people would be a much larger 'special needs' group than any of the others. The decision was made to increase the interview sample of regular people from 200 to around 2000, the final tally being 1954. Of these, 240, or 12.3 per cent, were classed as regular disabled people, the principal causes of disability being arthritis, heart and lung impairments and lower limb impairments[6]. With separate data tabulations being produced for regular disabled people and regular able-bodied people, there were, for analysis purposes, seven subgroups of the building user population – regular able-bodied people, regular disabled people, single pushchair users, double pushchair users, stick/crutch users, wheelchair users and blind people.

Interviewees' ratings of the importance of level access to toilets

In respect of their usage of public buildings and toilets in them, the presumption was that the people in each subgroup randomly selected for interview would be nationally representative. When asked how important it was to them personally that public toilets should have level access, they had no objective criteria against which judgements could be made. They made subjective judgements, and both within and between user subgroups different practical experiences and different personal concerns would have influenced their responses. For analysis purposes, the findings set out in Table A3.1 on page 374 are taken at their face value. With a score of 10 assigned to each respondent who said 'essential', 5 to those who said 'important', 2 to those who said 'not very important' and 0 to those who said 'not at all

Table 18.1 Access to public toilets: the architectural disability league

1	double pushchair users	8.5
2	wheelchair users	8.2
3	single pushchair users	7.8
4	blind people	7.4
5	regular disabled people	6.4
6	stick/crutch users	6.0

important', the ranking by mean rating of the user subgroups (other than regular able-bodied people) is shown in Table 18.1.

In this architectural disability league double pushchair users come out ahead of wheelchair users, with single pushchair users not far behind. Two factors are relevant. The first is that people with infants in pushchairs can be immensely inconvenienced by being obliged to use steps or stairs to get to public toilets; in particular, those with very young infants can be – all the 28 single pushchair users with an infant less than 12 months old said 'essential' or 'important' in response to the level access need question[7]. The second is that only a minority of wheelchair users are chairbound; there are some who can get out of their wheelchair and walk up or down stairs. Figure 18.1 illustrates how wheelchair users interviewed in the course of the survey responded when asked to describe their usual ability to walk.

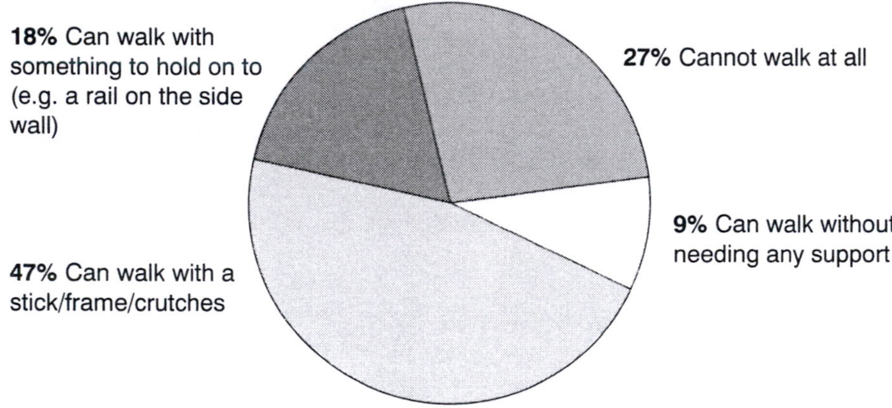

18.1 Wheelchair users' ability to walk

With estimates drawn from national population count data, Figure 18.2 shows the proportion of the total national population of adult building users who, on a typical day, were in the subgroup categories*; blind people, whose percentage figure was 0.22, are not identified.

* Notes on how these were calculated are in Appendix 2.

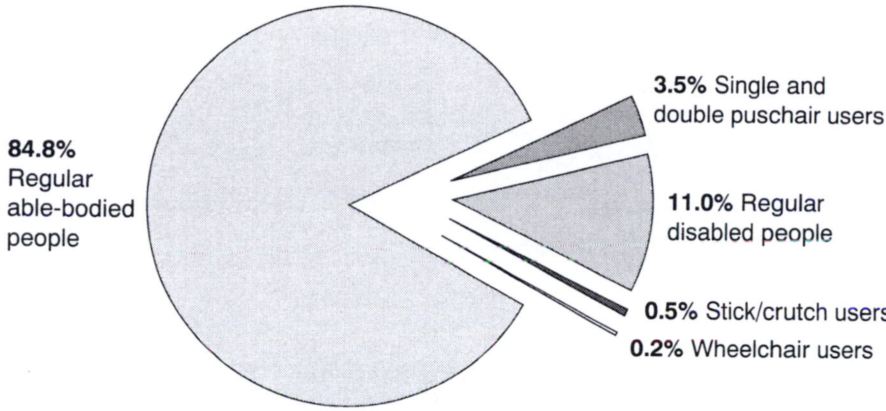

18.2 The distribution of adult users of public buildings on a typical day

Regular able-bodied people with special needs

Eleven per cent of the regular able-bodied people who were interviewed – people who, by definition, were not people with disabilities – said that their need for level access to public toilets was essential or important. The reasons given by some two-thirds of them were in terms such as 'more convenient'/'easier to use'/'save climbing up steps'/'better for other people'[8]. The remainder, 76 people, said the reason was that they were elderly, were pregnant, or had children with them, and it was these people, 4.4 per cent of the regular able-bodied people who were interviewed, who were categorised as having a genuine special need for level access. Three-quarters of them said the reason was 'having children with me/us'.

Unlike people in other special-needs subgroups, regular able-bodied people with special needs do not have a distinct corporate characteristic, nor are they all people with an attribute which consistently gives them a special need. 'Having children with me/us' – what might be termed 'children hassle' – constitutes a legitimate reason for having a special need, but the degree of need is variable, associated, for example, with the number of children in train and their behaviour at any particular time. It is not a concept amenable to objective or precise definition. But pushchair users had been given special-needs status, and it was unreasonable to disregard people with children hassle, or those who said the reason was pregnancy or old age. Taking them into account, the overall estimates which resulted were:

- 19 per cent of the total by-the-day population of adult building users generally were people with a special need for level access to public toilets, meaning that they were putative architecturally disabled people.
- 11.7 per cent were medically disabled people. Of these, 94 per cent were regular disabled people, 4.1 per cent were stick/crutch users, 1.7 per cent were wheelchair users and 0.2 per cent were blind people.

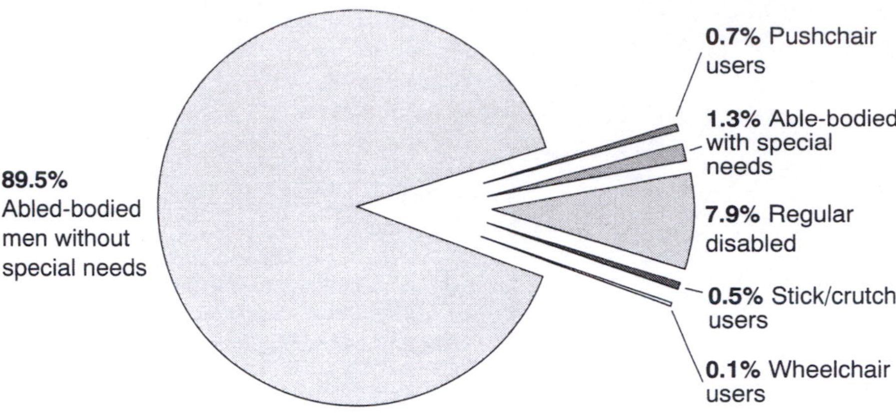

18.3a Men

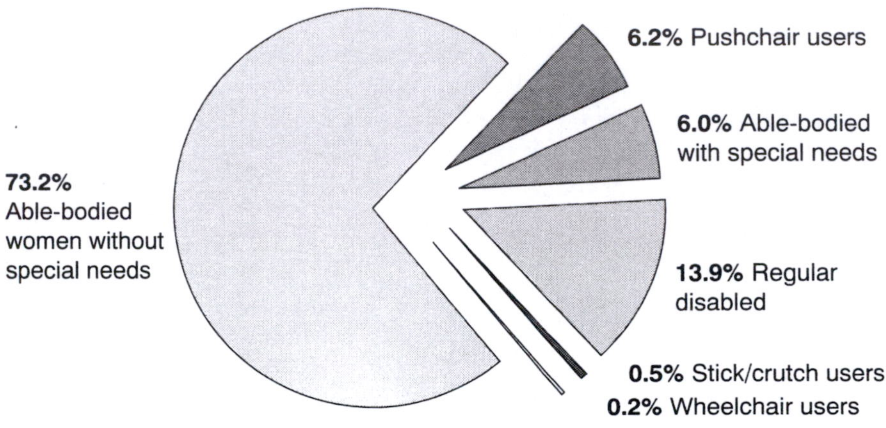

18.3b Women

18.3 Estimated distribution of adult male and female building/toilet users on a typical day

Among putative architecturally disabled people women were relatively much more numerous than men[9]. Those who used buildings with infants in pushchairs were predominantly women, as were those who said they had to cope with children hassle, and pregnancy came into the reckoning. On the medical disability side, it was predictable, owing to the correlation between disability and age, that the sanitary provision survey findings would show that among elderly people there were more disabled women than men. What was not predictable was that there would also be more among younger people; of all regular people aged between 16 and 64, the finding was that 8.2 per cent of women were people with disabilities, compared with 5.0 per cent of men[10]. Of the disability causes for a claimed need for level access, arthritis was cited by twice as many women as men[11].

The contrast between the prevalence of men and women among those who can be regarded as putative architecturally disabled people is shown by the estimate drawn from the survey data that 27 per cent of adult women had a special need for level access to public toilets, compared with 10 per cent of men[12]. For the male and female adult populations of building/toilet users, estimated subgroup proportions (other than for blind people, who for both men and women were 0.02 per cent) are shown in Figures 18.3a and b.

Individual public building types

In the course of the sanitary provision project interviewees were asked which of 13 types of public buildings they had used during the previous 12 months: for eleven of these, the results are set out in Table A2.3 on page 369, with Table A2.4 on page 370 showing the estimated proportions of the users of each type of building on a typical day. The data show that disabled people – and pushchair users also – tend to use most types of public buildings in relatively smaller proportions than regular able-bodied people; for an 'average' public building, the estimated proportion of all by-the-day users who were disabled people was 7.4 per cent, compared with 11.7 per cent of all shopping centre users.

Pushchair users visited cinemas or theatres hardly at all, but scored highly on swimming pool usage. Few blind people had been to cinemas/theatres, museums/art galleries or swimming pools/leisure centres. For all public building types, Table A2.4 shows that the great majority of users who were people with disabilities were regular disabled people; in an average public building, the estimated proportion was 92 per cent. Pushchair users were shown to be some 23 times as numerous as wheelchair users in this average building.

Attitudes to amenities and facilities in the four towns

Carlisle, Eastbourne, Hereford and Peterborough were selected as project survey locations on the basis that they rated highly as towns which were conveniently accessible to disabled people. To check whether it was felt that they were, eight propositions were put to interviewees, with attitude responses on a scale from 'agree strongly' to 'disagree strongly'. As shown in Appendix 2 on page 370, 'The pedestrianisation of the streets here makes it easier to get around' gained top place, followed by 'It is an attractive town to visit' and 'It is easy to get around here'. At the bottom was 'The toilet facilities here are good'.

Independent wheelchair users

The 174 wheelchair users interviewed in the shopping centres of the four towns were not asked whether they were getting around independently, a factor being the impracticability of devising an appropriate definition of independence. Would it mean that they had travelled independently from home, were getting around the town independently, were moving around the covered shopping centre independently, or were using certain shops independently? Instead, having been asked which buildings they used, the question put to them was, 'When you are going out and about, visiting these kinds of places, do you always go with someone else, or sometimes with someone else, sometimes by yourself, or always by yourself?' In response, 79 per cent said they always went out with someone else, 20 per cent said they sometimes went out with someone else and sometimes on their own, and 1 per cent (two people) said they always went out on their own[13].

Interviewees who said they could use buildings on their own were asked which types of buildings they had used independently. Expressed as a proportion of all wheelchair users in the sample who had used one or other type of building (independently or not) during the previous 12 months, the building types where numbers of 'could-use-independently' wheelchair users were highest were department stores/supermarkets and railway stations; the lowest were museums/art galleries, cinemas/theatres and airport terminals[14]. Particular questions were asked about hotels[15]. Of the 174 wheelchair users in the sample, 45 had stayed in a hotel, 42 of whom had taken their wheelchair with them. Of the 42, 26, or 62 per cent, needed to take the wheelchair into an en-suite bathroom. Three of these 26 people had stayed in a hotel on their own.

Architecturally and medically disabled people - the comparison between populations

For the purposes of the project, building users were defined as the people who visited a shopping centre and used particular types of public buildings on a typical day. In the context of architectural design decision making that was sensible; what architects who design buildings most usefully need to know is what the profile of their building users looks like on a typical day. The population of by-the-day building users is not, however, the same as that of all building users, defined, for example, as all those who use buildings during the course of a year. The matter is of relevance to comparisons between populations, for example between the size and make-up of the total population of people with disabilities and that of the population of disabled people who use buildings.

The early expectation had been that there would be a correspondence between the adult population of locomotor-disabled people as defined by OPCS and the project population of people with disabilities having a need for level access to toilets. That was dashed when regular people were interviewed, but it was of interest to learn how the two populations compared. With regard to the project population, the methodology of the process is reported in Appendix 2, with the by-the-year compared with the by-the-day results shown in Table A2.5 on page 372.

The OPCS survey finding was that an estimated 9.9 per cent of the adult population of Great Britain in the mid-1980s were locomotor-disabled people, of whom an estimated 10 per cent were wheelchair users and a further 44 per cent walking aid users, or, in terms of proportions of the total population, 0.99 per cent and 4.36 per cent[16]. Correspondingly, the sanitary provision project findings for by-the-year shopping centre visitors were 0.26 per cent and 0.48 per cent. The inferences to be drawn are that some 74

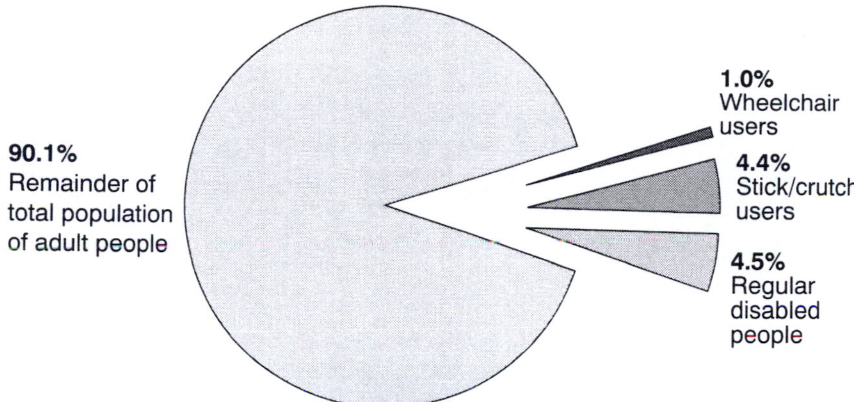

18.4a Medically disabled people with a locomotor disability

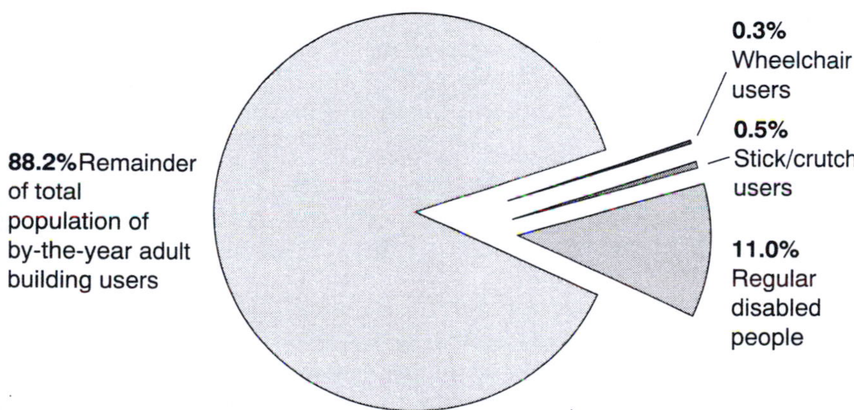

18.4b Architecturally disabled people with a locomotor disability

18.4 The comparison between medically and architecturally disabled people

per cent of wheelchair users are not building users (as defined by the shopping centre usage measure) and something approaching 90 per cent of stick/crutch users.

Comparative data on the prevalence of blind people also come from the OPCS survey report and, more informatively, from the report *Blind and Partially Sighted Adults in Britain* commissioned by the Royal National Institute for the Blind and published in 1991[17]. Relevant data in the two reports suggest that among the total adult population about three people in 1000 (0.30 per cent) are blind people who use a white stick or cane or who have a guide dog. The corresponding sanitary provision project estimate was that 0.021 per cent of by-the-year building users were blind people[18], suggesting that some 93 per cent of blind people with a mobility aid are not shopping centre users.

The notion that only 1 in 4 wheelchair users, 1 in 10 stick/crutch users and 1 in 14 blind people go out and visit a shopping centre during the course of a year is difficult to accept and, as discussed in the project report, there is a whole series of provisos to be made about the reliability of the data and its interpretation[19]. The evidence of population counts does, however, remain secure: in an 'average' shopping centre on an average day, only about seven in 1000 of all the people there are wheelchair users, stick/crutch users or blind people.

'Where have they all gone to?' is the pertinent question, and the reports of the two surveys suggested that the principal reason why many disabled people were apparently not to be found in shopping centres was the severity of their medical disabilities, emphasising their disabilit*ies*, not their disabilit*y*. Discussion around this issue is in Appendix 2 on page 372. From the evidence of all relevant data a firm conclusion can be drawn; it is that it is inadmissible to suppose that the profile of the total population of people with disabilities is reflected in that of those who use public buildings – the two populations are quite different. On the basis of OPCS and sanitary provision project data, the comparison shown in Figures 18.4a and b is between people who by the OPCS measure have a locomotor disability and those building users who have a locomotor disability *and* are vulnerable to architectural disability.

Wheelchair users in open employment

The employment buildings part of the Department of the Environment research project on sanitary provision for people with special needs was conducted in parallel with the public buildings inquiry. The purpose being to inform future revisions of the Part M building regulation, the focus was on people in employment with a need for special toilet facilities such as provision of the BS5810 kind – the type advised in the Part M Approved Document for people with disabilities. The aim was to estimate the prevalence of the population with this need, described as lateral space need, and ascertain in which areas of what kind of buildings the need was most likely to occur. The target group was thus wheelchair users, the aim being to interview a representative sample of 100 or so wheelchair users who were in open employment – working either as paid employees or volunteers in the kind of buildings covered by the Part M regulation. Those whose workplace was their own home or a local authority sheltered workshop would be excluded.

The survey was to be conducted in a sufficient number of district council areas to give a sample of 100 subjects. In each area the aim would be to identify all wheelchair users living in that area who were in open employment, so that, assuming representativeness, the national prevalence of people with a lateral space need in toilets in employment buildings could be estimated. No registers were kept by local authorities or any other agencies of wheelchair users in open employment, and no previous survey had presented data giving any indication of what their prevalence might be, of how many there might be in a population catchment of, say, 100 000. The district council areas of Carlisle, Eastbourne, Hereford and Peterborough, the four towns which were fieldwork locations for the public buildings inquiry, would be surveyed, and, with an aggregate population approaching 400 000, the surmise was that the required 100 could be found there. But there was not confidence that they would be, and Thamesdown (Swindon) and The Wrekin (Telford) were added; this gave a total catchment of more than 680 000.

The task of gathering the names and addresses of wheelchair users in employment was not as daunting as the lay outsider might have supposed. Wheelchair users, on account of mutual associations, common healthcare links and common social and community needs and interests, are a fraternity of club members. One knows another, and another knows others. This, known in the trade as 'snowballing', was the chosen survey method. In each of the district council areas the contractor (British Market Research Bureau) employed a local project liaison officer, either a person with a disability or someone active in the local disability field. Each project officer worked intensively to identify all local wheelchair employees, through personal links, local voluntary organizations, major local employers, and press and radio publicity. To increase the size of the representative sample, wheelchair users who worked in a district but lived outside it were included.

The outcome of rigorous searches in all six areas was less than 70 successful interviews, and to obtain more a seventh area was added. This was Ipswich and three adjoining district councils in Suffolk – Babergh, Mid Suffolk and Suffolk Coastal. With ten district council areas the effect was to bring the population catchment up to 1 082 000, and the final outcome was interviews with 94 wheelchair users who were in employment. By cause of disability their profile was quite different from that of the public buildings sample of 174 wheelchair users. Thirty-eight per cent of wheelchair users in employment had been disabled from birth, compared with 14 per cent of public building users, and 23 per cent said they were paraplegic/tetraplegic, compared with 10 per cent[20].

Seventy-seven of the 94 wheelchair users in employment who were interviewed lived in the population catchment districts. Of these, 52 were doing paid work and 25 voluntary work. Eight of the 77 did not use their wheelchair when at work. Information on the type of work done was obtained for 41 of the 45 who were in paid employment and used their wheelchair at work. Of these, 32 were doing clerical or office-type work, 26 of them in administration or office buildings. Of the remaining nine, six worked in industrial buildings, and three as teaching staff in education buildings.

Given the thoroughness of the search, the reasonable assumption was that virtually all the wheelchair users who were targeted were found. One who was not was later discovered, and one or two of the few people who did not wish to be interviewed could have qualified. For the purposes of prevalence estimates, the assumption was that 53 (rather than 45) people who lived in the ten districts were in paid employment and used a wheelchair at their workplace. Drawing on national employment statistics and assuming representativeness, the estimates that emerged[21] were:

- for every 100 000 people in paid employment in England there were 11 wheelchair users.
- for every 100 000 people employed in office-type buildings there were 18.
- for every 100 000 people employed in other workplaces there were 5.

No statistical reliability can be claimed for these figures. Given that three of the survey locations (Peterborough, Swindon and Telford) were towns which it might be supposed were able to offer unusually attractive job opportunities for wheelchair users, the actual proportions of wheelchair users in employment in the national population could be less.

The findings of the national survey of disabled people undertaken by OPCS indicated that about 1 per cent of the total adult population were wheelchair users. On this basis, there might in all have been some 10 000 wheelchair users living in the employment survey districts, with the estimated 53 who were in paid employment and used their wheelchair at the workplace representing 1 in 200 of all wheelchair users. How many of the others might have been in paid employment had suitable opportunities been available for them was not an issue that the inquiry examined. An indicator which it was felt could be relevant was the proportion of those who were doing voluntary work, and when interviewed, said they were looking for paid work; if it was a large proportion, the hypothesis was that a factor impeding their aspirations could be inaccessible buildings and inaccessible toilets. Twenty-nine people in the sample of 94 wheelchair users in employment were doing voluntary work, and of these only one person, a paraplegic man, said he was actively looking for paid employment.

The likelihood that nationally the number of wheelchair users in open employment will decrease in coming years is discussed in the project report[22]. There is nothing to suggest an increase, and in this connection a relevant note is that when I surveyed wheelchair users in Norwich in the mid-1960s, 11 of the 284 who were interviewed, representing one in 26, were in open employment[23]. Five of the 11 were polio-disabled people.

19 Public toilets – the issues encapsulated

Women are obliged to queue where men do not. It happens in theatres, cinemas, department stores, motorway service stations and public parks: the queue that women are in is at the public toilets. No research programme is needed to demonstrate the inequity; everyone knows that it happens. Men do not mind about it. And nor, it seems, do women; they do not stridently protest that here is shocking discrimination and injustice; they are patient, they tolerate it, and they say that understandably it happens because women take longer. Women do indeed take longer – relevant research suggests that on average they take twice as long[1]. So there is a practical remedy – instead of providing (as it is supposed they do) roughly the same number of amenities for women as for men, architects when they design buildings should as a rule give women twice as many.

The issue interested me in the course of the sanitary provision project – it was pertinent in the context of accessibility and discrimination, and it had not previously, to my knowledge, been systematically investigated. In typical public buildings, were women normally provided with about the same number as men, in which case men were twice as well catered for, or what kind of ratio was there? The evidence I needed could be obtained simply by going in and counting, a procedure that involved a partnership. My wife Becky was my partner and we launched our explorations at a motorway service station on the way home from north Wales after Christmas in 1991. Most of the subsequent inspections were made in public buildings in London, and from the results that emerged a selection is presented in Table 19.1. A fuller list of the venues we visited is in the article 'The queue starts here: a raw deal for women', which my wife wrote for the January/April 1992 issue of the journal *Access by Design*[2].

The table is not representative of all public toilet venues, but the findings are indicative. Among those listed, only Harrods has more amenities for women than for men. Of the 36 others visited, only three, all department stores, also had more. In a public building where usage by men and women is equivalent, rough parity (meaning that women will be no more likely to be obliged to queue than men) is obtained by having twice as many amenities for women as for men. In buildings where there is twice as much usage by women as by men, such as may happen in department stores, parity requires that women have four times as many amenities.

There is a range of reasons why this form of architectural discrimination against women is universal. For a start, architects apparently do not think. When they plan toilet facilities in new buildings, a common practice, it would seem, is to map out two approximately equal areas of space on plan drawings, allocating one to men and the other to women. Urinals occupy much less space than wc compartments, the effect when the areas are filled being more amenities for men than women. Women, not being regular visitors to men's toilets, do not realise that men get a much better deal. The briefs to which architects work when designing buildings typically incorporate no relevant instructions. The discrimination that is rife in public buildings goes unchallenged.

As my wife and I were to learn, building managers commonly have no idea how remarkable the scale of discrimination displayed on their premises genuinely is. The published report of our survey was taken up by press and radio journalists; when the management staff of some of the more delinquent buildings were telephoned the response was disbelief, followed in one case by a check and a denial (which was unproven) of the accuracy of the figures.

The configuration of typical wc compartments

The discrepancy between the quantity of amenities that men and women are given is one side of a disturbing picture. The other is the size and configuration of typical wc compartments in public buildings. I cite for illustration the happening reported by Jeffrey Bernard on the occasion of his being invited to open new lavatories at the *Coach and Horses* pub in Soho[3]:

> I'm glad to say that the Ladies is being made larger. The last time I was called to it was to rescue a very fat woman who had passed out in there. Getting her out was damned nigh impossible since she was wedged firmly between the lavatory itself and the door which opens inwards.

Irrespective of whether they be fat or pass out, women are for three reasons more commonly disabled than men by the constricted size and awkward configuration of a typical wc compartment in a public lavatory. The first is that the clothes they wear are more prone to contamination as they struggle to get round the in-opening door – 'sweeping the seat', as my wife says. The second is that they always have to sit down or squat, which involves the adjustment of clothing (and sometimes taking off an overcoat) in a confined space. The third is that a sanitary waste disposal bin placed to one side of the wc restricts the manoeuvring space available.

Wc compartments in public toilets in Britain (and also in America and European countries) are never – or hardly ever – spacious, meaning comfortably spacious. In the course of the survey my wife and I made in late 1991 and early 1992 I measured the dimensions of male wc compartments; while I did not venture into female territory, my wife's reports confirmed that the size and configuration of corresponding female wc compartments was invariably similar. The findings indicated that the

Table 19.1 Public toilet facilities for men and women in public buildings
Other than for the RIBA building (inspected in September 1996) the data below are for buildings and their facilities as they were in April 1992. The figures for wcs exclude unisex toilet facilities for disabled people. All the buildings listed are in London other than the motorway service stations.

	Men		**Women**	**Ratio**
	Urinals and wcs	*Urinals/wcs*	*wcs*	*Men:women*
Theatres, concert halls				
National Theatre				
serving Olivier and Lyttleton Theatres	**64**	53/11	**28**	
serving refreshment facilities	**12**	10/2	**6**	
serving Cottesloe Theatre	**7**	6/1	**2**	
all facilities	**83**	69/14	**36**	2.3 : 1
Barbican Centre				
in basement, serving concert hall and theatre	**43**	37/6	**22**	2.0 : 1
Royal Festival Hall				
all facilities	**64**	45/19	**28**	2.3 : 1
Museums, art galleries				
British Museum				
all facilities excluding those in special exhibition areas	**41**	25/16	**19**	2.2 : 1
National Gallery				
all facilities	**33**	24/9	**24**	1.4 : 1
Department stores				
Harrods				
all facilities	**55**	33/23	**60**	0.9 : 1
Selfridges				
all facilities	**51**	28/23	**42**	1.2 : 1
Hotels				
Langham Hilton, Portland Place				
basement facilities	**23**	17/6	**12**	1.9 : 1
Copthorne Tara, Kensington				
facilities serving first floor conference suite	**31**	24/7	**7**	4.4 : 1
Railway stations				
Euston				
concourse facilities	**42**	27/15	**20**	2.1 : 1
Liverpool Street				
concourse facilities	**49**	31/18	**20**	2.5 : 1
Motorway service stations				
Membury, M4 westbound				
concourse facilities	**16**	10/6	**12**	1.3 : 1
Scratchwood, M1				
concourse facilities	**21**	14/7	**14**	1.5 : 1
Other buildings				
Royal Institute of British Architects				
basement facilities	**9**	6/3	**3**	3.0 : 1

average-size wc compartment in a public building had an internal depth of 1472mm, a width of 825mm and an in-opening door giving a clear opening width of 634mm. Figure 19.1a shows that it is uncomfortably small – manoeuvring space inside is tight, restricted as it is by the swing of the in-opening door. Were it, as shown in Figure 19.1b, to have an out-opening door, it would be much more convenient to use, in particular by those with infants in pushchairs.

The survey covered 409 male wc compartments, of which 404 had in-opening doors; one of the five out-opening doors was in Harrods department store and the other four at the Science Museum in South Kensington. It also confirmed the lack of consideration for women with infants in pushchairs who use toilets in public buildings. In only one venue, Harrods, were there women's toilets – six of the sixty in the store – which were pushchair-accessible. In none of the venues were any of the wc compartments for men large enough to get a pushchair into. The position may, however, have changed since 1992, the time when the information in Table 19.1 was obtained.

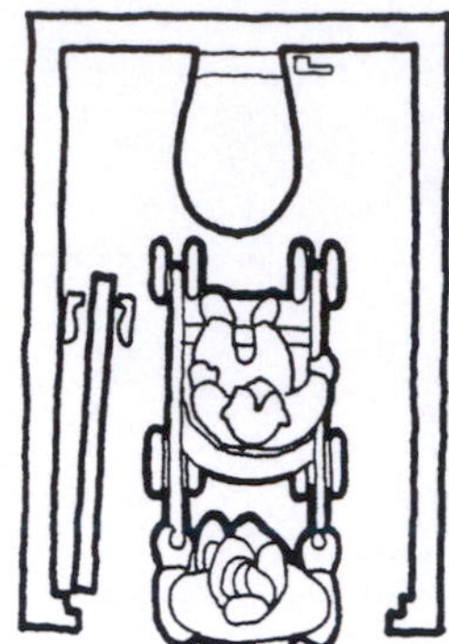

19.1a

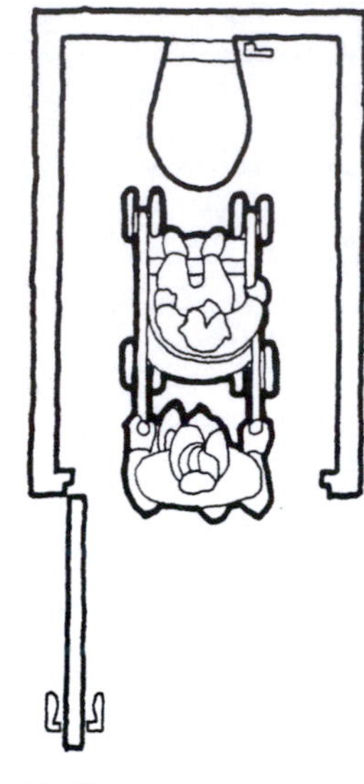

19.1b

Interviewing for the sanitary provision project

For the sanitary provision research project, each interviewer was asked to obtain interviews with a certain number of people in each of the subgroup categories – regular people, single pushchair users, double pushchair users, stick/crutch users, wheelchair users and blind people. When introducing themselves, interviewers said they were conducting a survey about the design and planning of toilets in public buildings for the Department of the Environment, and would like to ask the person they were speaking to about how he or she managed in public toilets as a wheelchair user, someone with a small child in a pushchair, a blind person, etc. The report after the first few days was that the interviewers were thrilled. With their clipboards, they were accustomed to a stream of polite (or not so polite) rejections. But not on this occasion; many of those who were intercepted were keen to help – yes, they said, they would be delighted to sit down and answer questions for a few minutes. Those who were most enthusiastic were pushchair users.

Pushchair users

When interviewed, pushchair users were asked about the need for level access to public toilets; as noted earlier, they were adamant about its importance. For the questions which followed, they were shown photographs; the first, similar to that shown in Figure 19.2, of a toilet facility layout where it was not possible to get a pushchair through the lobby leading to the wc compartments. With an infant in a pushchair (or two in a double pushchair), they were asked what they would do. If it was they, not the child, who wanted to use the toilet, would they leave the child outside in the pushchair? Or, if either they or the child wanted to use the toilet, would they (a) leave the pushchair outside; (b) fold the pushchair and carry it and the child into the wc compartment; or (c) give up and go somewhere else?

19.2

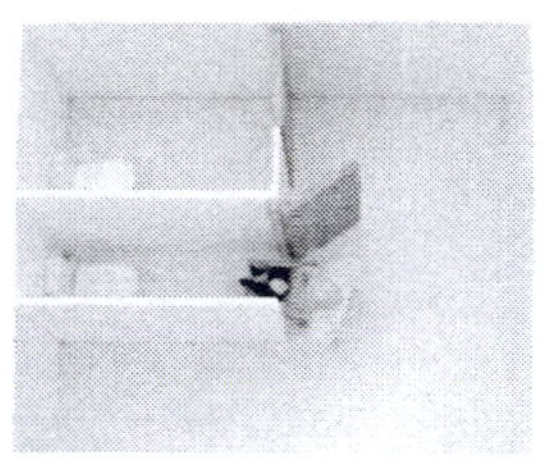

19.3a

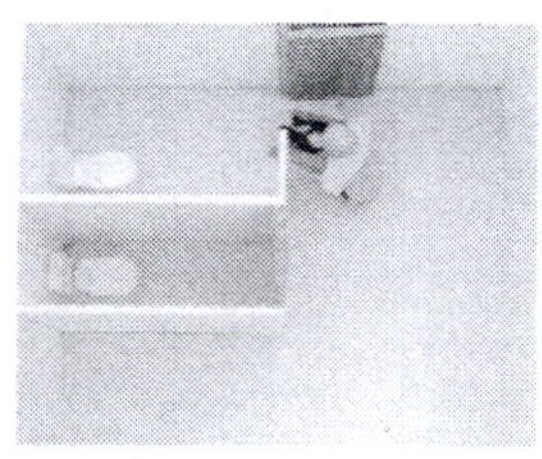

19.3b

Where it was the respondent, not the child, who needed to use the toilet, fewer than one in ten were prepared to leave the child/children outside in the pushchair. Usually it was a matter of leaving the pushchair outside and taking the child or children in. Understandably, it was those with double pushchairs who had more of a predicament; of the 49 who were interviewed, 13 said they would not go or find somewhere else if they needed to use the toilet, and five would go elsewhere if one of the children needed to do so. The results are reported more fully in Table A3.4 on page 376.

The second photograph showed an arrangement where two wc compartments were pushchair-accessible, one with just enough space for a pushchair (Figure 19.3a), the other with lateral space by the wc and ample room for pushchair manoeuvre (Figure 19.3b). When asked how important it was that a pushchair-accessible wc compartment should have the extra space, nine out of ten of those interviewed felt it to be essential or important. Relevant data are found in Table A3.5 on page 377.

Ambulant disabled people

Pushchair users were not asked about the need for grabrails in wc compartments, but ambulant disabled people were. The issue is an item which features in what-to-do-for-the-disabled checklists – when the question 'What can we do for ambulant disabled people?' is asked, a ready answer is that grabrails to the side of a wc are useful. The provision is endorsed in the 1992 Part M Approved Document: in buildings where all floors do not have to be reached by a lift, the recommendation is that there should, on a storey to which the only access is by a stairway, be at least one wc compartment for ambulant disabled people, one which has horizontal and vertical grabrails to both side walls[4].

The question put to ambulant disabled and blind people interviewed in the course of the sanitary provision research project was 'If you are using a toilet, how useful is it for you if there are special rails for you to hold on to?' From an analysis of relevant data, the indication was that some 14 per cent of all ambulant disabled people, meaning stick/crutch users, blind people and regular disabled people, found that grabrails in wc compartments were useful, an interesting note being that a larger proportion of blind people than stick/crutch users considered them very useful or quite useful[5]. But with regard to the planning and design of public toilet facilities generally, the findings clearly demonstrated that among ambulant disabled people the need for grabrails in wc compartments was marginal by comparison with the need for level access.

Wheelchair users

The examination of the project findings now moves on to focus on wheelchair users and their need for special toilet provision. Broad generalizations are made first:

- Virtually all ambulant disabled people, ie stick/crutch users, regular disabled people and blind people, need level access to public toilets.

- Virtually all pushchair users need level access and, within a wc compartment, lateral space to the side of the wc.
- Virtually all wheelchair users need level access, and most need lateral space.

The qualifying note for wheelchair users needs explaining. The 174 wheelchair users who were interviewed in the course of the sanitary provision research project were shown three models, and also cards with diagrammatic representations of wc compartment layouts, transfer positions and grabrails they might use. Seventy-four probing questions were asked about how they managed, and from an analysis of their responses an eight-way categorization of their needs was made[6]. In summary, 44 per cent could manage separate-sex toilet facilities where there was level access, access through the approach lobby and access to wc compartments, but *not* space within the compartment for lateral transfer. The other 56 per cent did need lateral space or, for other reasons, a unisex facility.

The project findings suggested that, among wheelchair users who go to shopping centres, some 45 per cent of women and 67 per cent of men would be suited by normal wc compartments with lateral space of a kind convenient for pushchair users, for example as shown in Figure 19.5. The reasonableness of making normal toilet facilities wheelchair-accessible is reinforced by the current inaccessibility to many wheelchair users of the hundreds of unisex toilets around the country that are kept constantly locked; of the project sample of 174 wheelchair users, there were 46 (or 26 per cent) who said they had a key for them.

Unisex provision

Unisex toilets are needed by wheelchair users who depend on someone else to help them manage when they use public toilets, and whose helper is someone of the opposite gender, usually the wife of a man or the husband of a woman. The need that a wheelchair user has to be helped by someone else is due to their disability, but it can also be due in part to the character of the wc compartment being used in terms of its size, configuration and equipment. Relevant findings of the sanitary provision research project indicated that some 50 per cent of all wheelchair users could always manage on their own, a further 25 per cent could manage on their own if the wc compartment was convenient, and 25 per cent always needed to be helped. Of those who always or sometimes had to be helped, 36 per cent were always helped by a person of the same gender, 38 per cent were sometimes helped by a person of the opposite gender and 27 per cent were always helped by a person of the opposite gender[7].

When they need to use a public toilet, wheelchair users who have to be helped by a person of the opposite gender may find that no unisex facility is available. The woman wheelchair user may then need to be taken into the male side, and the man into the female side. Thirteen of the 108 women who were interviewed and 23 of the 66 men said this had sometimes happened to them. In response to the question 'Have there been embarrassments for you when you have done this?', three women and eleven men said there had; the lesser prevalence of embarrassment among women may be attributable to a tendency for women to be taken into the women's side by their husband. The 56 wheelchair users who usually or always needed help were asked whether, if there was not a unisex facility but there was instead a BS5810-type toilet on both the men's and women's sides, that would be convenient for them. Seventy per cent said it would be[8].

The BS5810 toilet

The specifications for the planning and design of the unisex toilet facility which was to become the BS5810 toilet were set out in the third edition of *Designing for the Disabled*, published in 1976[9]. In 1979, the year that British Standard Code of Practice 5810 was issued, the BS5810 toilet became established as the 'right' design standard, and from then on the call which went out from disabled people and their organizations was 'Get it right!' Not by any means was it always got precisely right, but across Britain it sprouted in its thousands. By 1990, wheelchair users who were interviewed in the course of the sanitary provision research project could be shown a detailed model of the BS5810 toilet and asked, 'Have you ever used a toilet like this?'; 86 per cent – 150 of the 174 who were questioned – said they had.

In 1979 the form that the BS5810 toilet took seemed sensible, whereas in 1997 I recognise its many shortcomings. While the idea that it could be right for every disabled person was always absurd, it was a proposition that many people concerned with toilet facilities for the disabled were keen to take on board. For disability activists it became an icon; if disabled people were to have rights, a right they should be entitled to was the availability of a BS5810-type wc compartment.

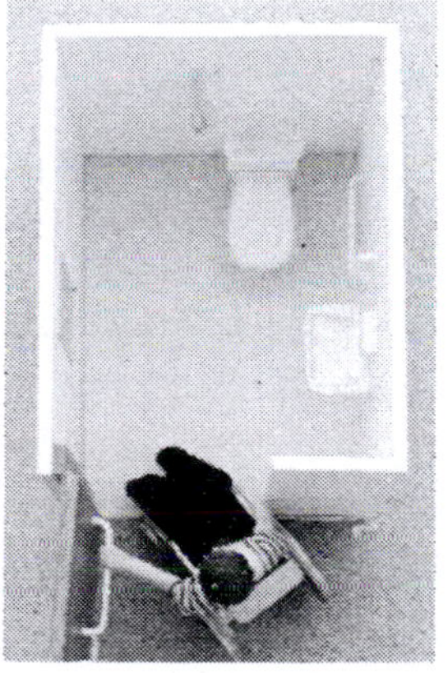

19.4a

A premise which governed my thinking about the layout of the facility was that the drainage infrastructure would be at the rear end, and, as with normal wc compartments, its long dimension would be its depth; this was set at 2000mm, with the width being 1500mm. The unavoidable consequence, with the wc in a corner off the far back side, was that the space for wheelchair manoeuvre was inefficiently distributed; it was difficult, if not impossible, for a wheelchair to be turned around inside. That was considered acceptable; a wheelchair user could drive in forwards and out backwards, and it was not felt necessary that he should be able, like normal ambulant people, to conveniently turn around. A related effect of the space layout was that the wheelchair user who had driven through the door would be unable to turn the chair so that he could readily reach back and close the door (Figures 19.4a and b).

Had the idea occurred to me, I would have recognised that, rather than having the short side at the rear, the BS5810 toilet would have been much more suitable for its purposes had it been turned on its side, as shown in Figures 19.5a and b. Where incorporated in a single-sex situation it could then, with its 1500mm depth, be aligned with adjoining normal wc compartments, and for detached unisex provision the side layout would also have

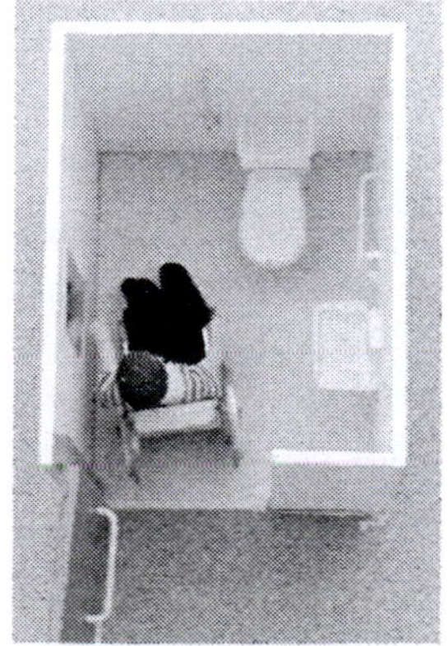

19.4b

afforded more wheelchair manoeuvring space than the officially advised configuration.

With the wc off the side rather than the rear wall (Figure 19.6), wheelchair manoeuvring would be even more markedly facilitated. There is space for the wheelchair to turn, and for the user to position the chair in order to reach and close the door. And for an assistant who is manoeuvring the chair and helping the wheelchair user transfer to and from the wc, the space available makes management easier.

Another error in the BS5810 design standard was the 500mm dimension from the centre line of the wc to the side wall. The thinking was that an attendant helping with transfer might need to get into the back corner. The space is too tight for that to be done comfortably, and a major demerit was that the important side horizontal rail was too far away from the wc for it to serve efficiently for pushing-up purposes; to do so, the dimension needs to be between about 350 and 400mm. A related error was the prescribed 750mm dimension from the rear wall to the face of the wc. The idea was that for lateral transfer the wheelchair needed to be parallel to the wc with the two seats alongside each other, and, given the large main wheels at the rear, that could only be done by projecting the wc forwards. This small advantage was far outweighed by the penalties; aside from the construction problems, an effect was to significantly reduce vital wheelchair manoeuvring space within the compartment.

An established rule for wheelchair-accessible wc compartments is that the entrance door opens out, the understanding being that if the door opens in, the wheelchair, when inside, will obstruct the closing of the door. The premise is valid, for example, in respect of the confined BS5810 wc compartment. But it is not where there is sufficient unobstructed floor space, as there would be if the internal dimensions were 2200 × 1700mm (Figures 19.7a and b). Particularly where the wheelchair user has to be helped by someone else, the added space makes for more comfortable management, as is shown by the comparison between the 2200 × 1700mm version (Figure 19.8a) and the 2000 × 1500mm BS5810 (Figure 19.8b).

19.5a

19.5b

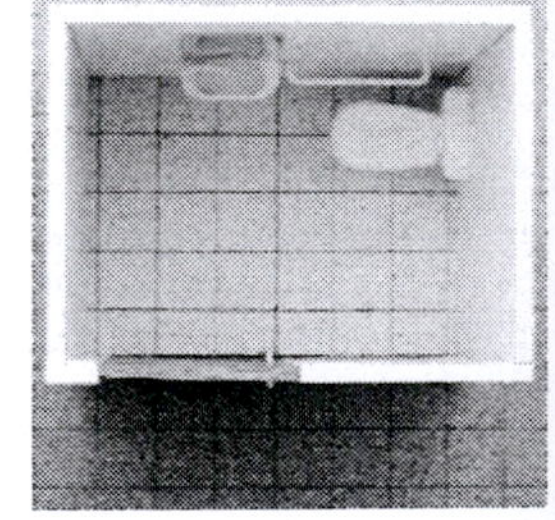

19.6

Grabrails in wc compartments

As the accompanying illustrations show, the BS5810 toilet has five grabrails to help users transfer to and from the wc. Relevant findings of the sanitary provision project indicated that grabrails were more often used for transfer on than for transfer off the wc, with the side horizontal rail being by far the most useful (shown in Table A3.6 on page 377). Wheelchair users in employment were found to have less need for grabrails than those who used toilets in public buildings, for whom the drop-down side rail could often be useful. Interpretation of the data suggests that in special BS5810-type toilets for disabled people three rails are important: the side horizontal fixed rail, the drop-down rail and the vertical rail on the side wall. In normal toilets where there is lateral space to the side of the wc, the provision of a side horizontal rail only could be appropriate.

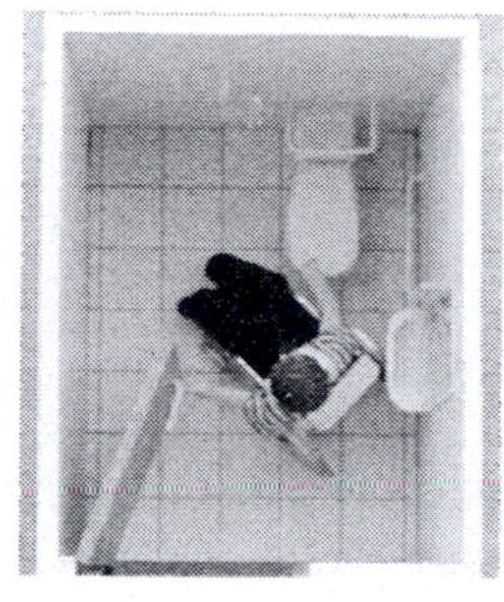

19.7a

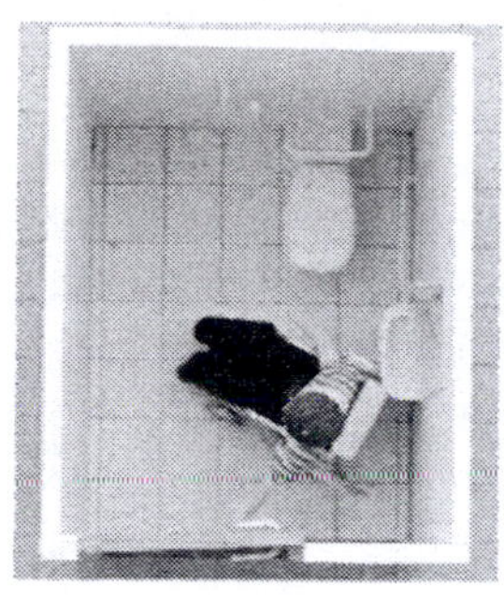

19.7b

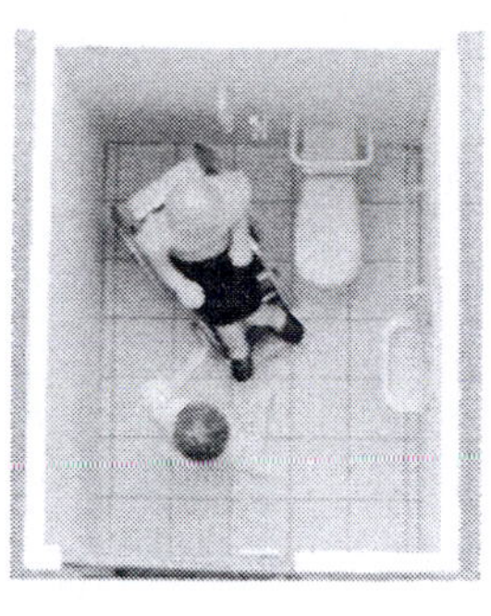

19.8a

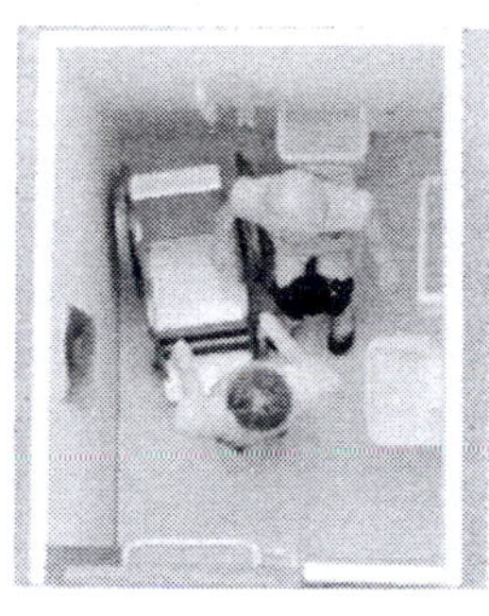

19.8b

The peninsular layout compared with BS5810

BS5810-type unisex toilets usually come singly, a consequence being that there is allowance for lateral wheelchair transfer from one side only. Most wheelchair users when using a wc do not, however, transfer laterally; of the 174 who were interviewed for the sanitary provision research project, 45 (or 26 per cent) said that they did and Table A3.7 on page 377 summarizes their abilities and preferences. An estimated 8 per cent of all wheelchair users who take their wheelchair into public toilets could be unable to transfer to the wc owing to one-way-only lateral transfer provision.

The alternative to the transfer-one-side-only BS5810-type unisex toilet is a peninsular layout (Figures 19.9a–c). Aside from permitting transfer from either side, its advantages are its more generous space for wheelchair manoeuvre, and with it space for two people to assist with transfer where a wheelchair user is weighty and cannot be handled by one person only. It also more readily enables a helper standing in front of the wheelchair to grasp the disabled person around the waist, pull him (or her) up to a standing position, swivel him on his feet and lower him onto the wc seat. Its disadvantages are that the wash basin cannot be reached by a person seated on the wc, and a drop-down rail is not as secure for pushing up against as a wall-fixed rail.

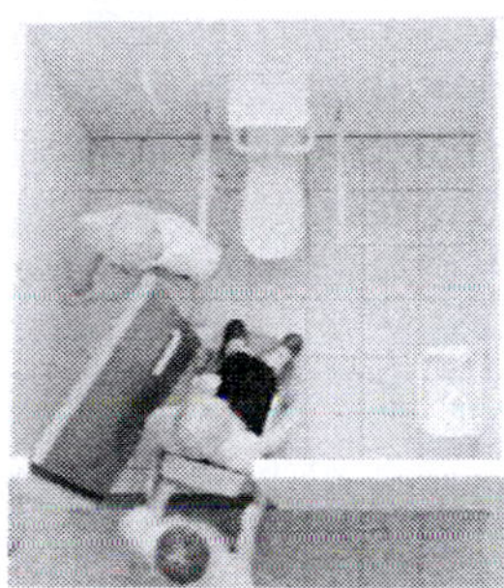

19.9a

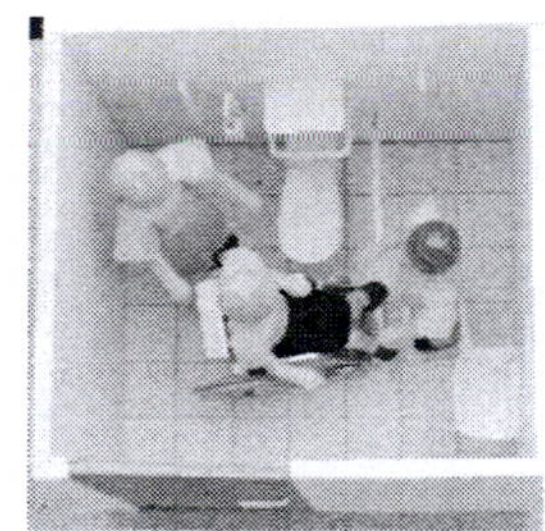

19.9b

When in a new public toilet there is to be one unisex facility only, the peninsular layout, with its either-side option and catering as it does for severely handicapped people not suited by the BS5810 toilet, might seem on balance to have the advantage. That is the line which in recent years a number of local authorities in Britain have taken when new municipal public toilets have been planned[10]; the example shown in Figure 19.10 is at Portsmouth. The findings of the sanitary provision project showed, however, that among wheelchair users as a whole there was a distinct preference for the BS5810-type layout*. The desirability of there being a shelf for the placement of personal equipment etc in special toilets for disabled people was also mentioned; as noted in Appendix 3 (page 378), this is particularly useful for people with ileostomies.

19.9c

* See Appendix 3, page 378.

Normal toilets in public buildings: the need for provision for people with special needs

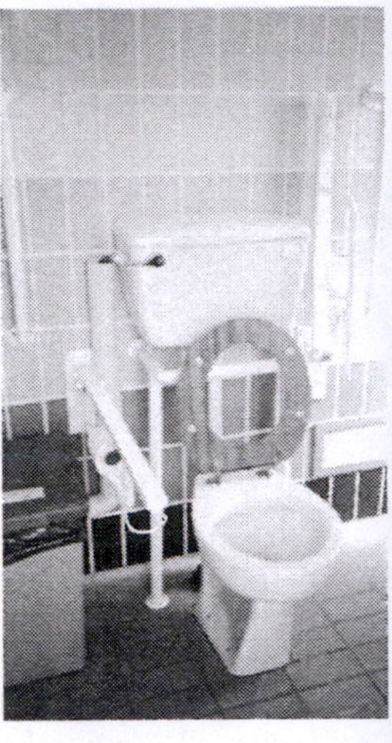

19.10

At present when toilet facilities are incorporated in new public buildings the standard practice is for there to be a BS5810-type unisex facility for disabled people in compliance with Part M requirements. Elsewhere it is unusual for any wcs to be designed to suit people with disabilities or others with special needs; whether for men or women, normal wcs customarily come in a row of small and narrow compartments with in-opening doors – provision of a kind which barely suits anyone well.

The scale of the prevalence of people who have special needs when using public toilets, and hence the need for normal facilities to meet those needs, was demonstrated by the findings of the sanitary provision research project, both for general and particular purposes. For the particular building types about which questions were asked, interview data permitted estimates to be made of the proportions of toilet users who had special needs, either for level access to toilets, or, within wc compartments, lateral space by the wc. Expressed as percentages of all adult male and female toilet users of the respective buildings on a typical day, the findings are listed in Table A3.2 on page 375. Doctors' surgeries was the building type where the estimated prevalence of users with special needs was greatest; among public building types, the highest proportions were for department stores/supermarkets, cafes/restaurants and swimming pools/leisure centres.

The distribution of male and female usage

Estimates were made from an analysis of the project data of the ratio of male to female adult users of public toilets in the buildings concerned, with results which are set out in Table A3.3 on page 376. For parity of provision between men and women, the findings suggested that in department stores/supermarkets there should be three times as many toilet amenities for women as for men, and in cafes/restaurants two and a half times as many.

The planning of normal wc compartments to cater for people with special needs

With regard to suitable normal provision for people with special needs, Figure 19.3a showed a relatively narrow wc compartment which could cater for single pushchair users if it had an out-opening door. The model was built to 1:25 scale; the wc compartment is 800 × 2000mm internally, the dimension from the wall to the front face of the wc is 700mm, and the clear opening width of the door is 720mm. As Figure 19.11 shows, it is too tight for comfortable use by independent wheelchair users, although manageable by those who can stand to transfer. Interestingly, it is 23 per cent more spacious than the toilet stall for wheelchair users advised in the 1961 American Standard.

19.11

The internal dimensions of the lateral-space compartment shown in Figure 19.3b are 1400 × 2000mm; as Figure 19.12 shows, it is suitable for independent wheelchair users. With a wider door, giving a clear opening width of 820mm or more in place of 720mm, it would, as well as suiting single pushchair users, be convenient for users of double pushchairs of the buggy type.

The wc compartment shown in Figure 19.13 has internal dimensions 1400 × 1500mm and an out-opening door giving a clear opening width of 930mm, making it suitable for double pushchair users as well as most independent wheelchair users.

19.12

The height of the wc seat

It was not practicable in the course of the sanitary project survey to test the wc seat height which suited each wheelchair user, and the question asked of wheelchair users was whether when they used toilets they usually found the wc seat too low, about right, or too high, for which the responses were respectively 37 per cent, 48 per cent and 9 per cent[11]. In normal wc compartments for able-bodied people, the rim of the wc bowl is typically at about 400mm above floor level[12]. The BS5810 specification is 450mm, and in special toilets for disabled people this would seem to be appropriate.

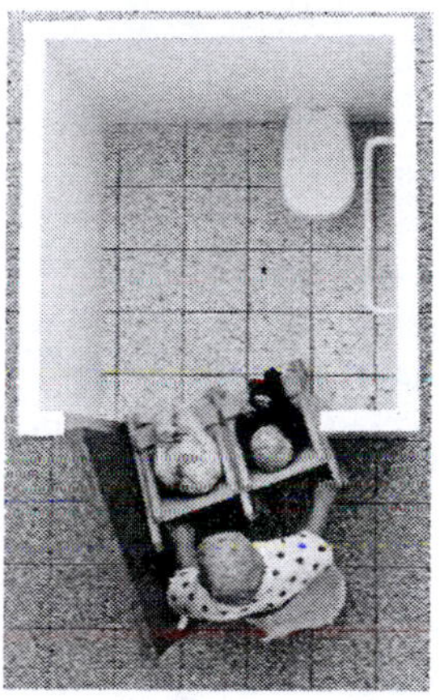

19.13

Urinals

In recent years, the trend in Britain has been for urinal bowls to be placed in men's cloakrooms rather than traditional stalls. The merit of bowls is that they look nicer than stalls, but for meeting the needs of their users they commonly have deficits. There is no level at which a urinal bowl may be fixed so that it will be convenient for all users; if, for example, it is placed at a level which suits adult men of below average height it will not suit tall men, and nor will it suit small boys.

In public toilets in Britain it is customary for there to be a row of urinal bowls at the same level, with, on occasion, an odd one placed at a somewhat lower level. The average rim height of at-the-same-level bowls is about 630mm[13], which is convenient for men of average height or taller, but not for short men or small boys. The average rim height of odd ones alongside is about 510mm[14], which is convenient for short men but can be unmanageable for small boys.

With regard to suitable height levels for urinal bowls in public buildings, the issues involved are discussed in Appendix 6, the disappointing note being that the kind of research data needed to inform reliable design guidance seems not to be available. From such relevant data as can be found, a list is presented in Table A6.3 on page 387 of preferred bowl rim heights for different users; while it has no assured credibility, the inferences to be drawn from it are that the standard height of urinal bowl rims for adult users ought to be of the order of 550mm rather than 630mm, with related provision for small boys being down at around 300mm rather than up at 510mm. A simple and economic research project could provide much-needed information on this topic.

In the context of extending the accommodation parameters of normal provision in buildings, the straightforward solution has to be stall urinals. Preferably they should not be on a platform; where there is a platform the concerns of ambulant disabled people come into the reckoning, and the step to it should desirably be not higher than 150mm.

The height of wash-hand basins

As with the height for fixing urinal bowls, the height at which wash-hand basins are placed in public buildings displays the workings of the organic muddle paradigm: the set of loose conventions which traditionally have governed architectural design decision-making. Whereas the urinal bowl is commonly too high for its users, the wash basin is too low; typically its rim is placed at about 820mm above floor level[15], a height which suits short people and children of around the age of 12 or 13, but not able-bodied people of average or above-average height; Figure 19.14 shows a man of average height (1755mm) and a basin rim at 820mm. For a wash basin to be convenient for a standing person, its front rim should be about 150mm below elbow level; relevant data for different users are set out in Table A6.4 on page 387.

19.14 The typical low-level washbasin, not ideal for a standing user

For wash basins in public cloakrooms there is not the same cause for varying fixing levels as there is for urinal bowls. Bearing in mind the extension of the accommodation parameters of normal provision, a rim height of around 820mm, while being too low for the comfort of able-bodied people, has the merit of taking care of the needs of most children. It is also about as suitable as can be in women's powder rooms, where users may be either seated or standing. In cloakrooms in employment buildings and staff-only areas of public buildings where all users are likely to be standing adult people, basin rim heights of around 900mm are appropriate. The particular problems of wheelchair users as wash basin users are considered in Appendix 6 on page 387.

Wash basins in wc compartments

Within wc compartments in public toilets in Britain it is not standard practice for there to be a wash-hand basin. But the BS5810 unisex toilet facility, being self-contained, needed to have one. For disabled people as against normal able-bodied people it could be more desirable to have a basin within a wc compartment, but only for disability-related practical reasons. As is implied by the Mant and Muir Gray report*, a sensible rule for the prevention of health hazards would be to require there to be a wash-hand basin within every wc compartment in any public toilet facility.

In the context of toilet provision for disabled people, the findings of the sanitary provision project showed that women felt it to be more inconvenient than men not to have a wash basin within the wc compartment[16]. The discrimination exercised against women when public toilets are planned is relevant here; the common outcome is for men to be better catered for because urinals occupy less space than wc compartments. With the function they perform at urinals men may be less bothered about washing their hands than when they have used the wc for the sitting-down function, and perhaps

* See Appendix 5, page 381.

in their role as commissioners of buildings, architects or brief-writers they have set the cultural rule, that it is not necessary to have a wash basin inside every wc compartment.

Lobbies to public toilets

In public buildings where public toilets are provided, it is common practice for there to be approach lobbies. Off a public circulation area there is a door which says 'Gentlemen' and another which says 'Ladies', and through that door there is an enclosed lobby. Or else there is a notice saying 'Toilets', with a door giving access to a lobby in which there are 'Gentlemen' and 'Ladies' doors, and beyond each of those doors another lobby. Particularly for wheelchair users and pushchair users, such lobbies can be architecturally disabling.

The typical public toilet user may suppose that the enclosed lobbies are there because they are necessary on account of regulations to do with protection against health hazards. But, as is shown by an examination of relevant regulatory controls*, that is not the case. Only in respect of toilet facilities immediately adjacent to restaurants, cafes or other food-eating places is there a statutory requirement for a lobby or space separation by other means. Elsewhere, in all other public buildings, enclosed lobbies are not called for. Where they are to be found, thoughtlessness may be a factor. When toilet facilities in public buildings are planned, it seems that architects tend automatically to show enclosed approach lobbies on their drawings, regardless of there being no regulatory requirement for them.

With regard to accessibility provision in both new and existing buildings, the matter is of major significance. In new public buildings it would be beneficial for all users were it to become standard practice for public toilets to have screened open lobbies rather than doors. Relatedly, in existing buildings there is much scope for alterations aimed at improving accessibility. With or without the provisions of the Disability Discrimination Act in mind, building owners and managers would be sensibly advised to check their public toilets and remove superfluous lobby doors.

* See Appendix 5, page 381.

20 Sensorily impaired people

The discussion on the character, prevalence, causes and effects of architectural disablement now moves on to consider the status of sensorily impaired people, meaning people with sight or hearing impairments. From a political and then from a personal perspective, the approach to the subject is first briefly examined.

On the political front, the material in the previous two chapters has indicated that women and pushchair users can be more prone to architectural disability than many medically disabled people. Legislative controls in Britain – the Part M building regulation and the provisions of Part III of the Disability Discrimination Act – do not protect them. The law is partial – it is focused exclusively on medically disabled people, including those with sensory impairments, but not others whose concerns it might equally be addressing. And because the architectural discrimination which affects women and pushchair users might well be more prevalent, more troublesome in degree and more readily removable by appropriate interventions than that which affects sensorily impaired people, the law is yet more biased.

On the personal front, I have, through all the previous chapters of this book, drawn extensively on autobiography, on my associations with the evolution of accessibility controls in Britain, on my links with people and events in America, on research projects I have handled, and on my own attitudes and experiences as a person with a severe physical disability. And the chapter which follows, on my experiences as a building user, is wholly autobiographical. The point I make is that while on occasion I have certain sight and hearing problems, I am neither blind nor deaf, and cannot from personal experience report the nature of the architectural discrimination which blind and deaf people may encounter. It is in respect of my experiences as an ambulant disabled person and a wheelchair user that my account may correspond with those of other locomotor-disabled people, and it is only if it can be shown that the kind of discrimination experienced by sensorily impaired people is not of the same order, and is not so remediable, that my report might have broad practical relevance. To test this proposition, the need is for a full and thorough analysis of the character and scale of architectural discrimination which can trouble blind and deaf people, an examination of the kind of provision which could counter it, and an assessment of the practical effectiveness of such provision.

The item which prompts most attention is tactile pavings as an information or warning device for blind people, and in the context of the entire debate it is extremely significant. Across Britain, the belief that tactile pavings are of value to blind people is near-universal, for disability activists it is an article of absolute faith, and much national and local endeavour and vast sums of public money have been invested in it. It is not a belief that I share, and if it is to be dispelled the argument has to be near incontrovertible; it needs to look at the background to the tactile pavings programme in Britain, have regard to relevant research material on the mobility of blind people, record the terms of a succession of official guidance documents, report the sequence of associated research and development programmes and examine the findings of their reports. The narrative would be disturbed were all this to be catalogued in this chapter, and supporting material, including an account of the series of practical projects commissioned by the Department of Transport, is therefore presented separately – it comes in Appendices 8 and 9, on pages 390 to 396.

The 'equal weight' tenet

The disability activist's supposition is that architects can help people with all types of disabilities, that all can be substantially helped, and that any disabled person can be helped as much as another. The notion affects the way that access audits – mechanisms for evaluating the overall accessibility of existing buildings – tend to be conducted; with a checklist of relevant items, each disability group is given equal weight. That is not, however, what happens when new buildings are designed or existing ones altered. It is always wheelchair users who get most attention, and a common complaint from disability commentators is that people with sensory impairments get nothing like their fair share. In considering the politics and practicalities of the issues involved, I focus on visually impaired people in the discussion which follows; brief notes on hearing-impaired people come at the close of the chapter.

Definitions

For its national survey of disability in Great Britain the Office of Population Censuses and Surveys (OPCS) drew on the medical version of disability. This, described also as the individual model of disability, is disability which is caused by an individual's physical, mental or sensory impairments. The OPCS study categorised those with a visual impairment as having a *seeing disability*, and by the measure which was applied the finding was that 24 per cent of all disabled adults had a seeing disability[1], or 3 per cent of the total population; analyses of the findings did not distinguish between blind people and those who were not blind but whose sight was impaired.

In the context of the use of buildings there are many people (myself, for example, with regard to the legibility of labels to lift controls) who have a seeing problem which would not, by the OPCS measure, constitute a 'seeing disability', and, as noted earlier, the medical version of disability is out of place in the field of architectural disablement – national figures of registered blind or partially sighted people are, for example, misleading and irrelevant. With regard to architectural disability caused by seeing problems, the important distinction to be made is between those who rely on their sight when using buildings and those who, being blind, do not. The terms I adopt are 'sight-impaired' and 'blind', for which the definitions – ones that relate to activities which are performed without there being entire dependence on assistance from an accompanying partner – are as follows:

- *Sight-impaired people* are people with a visual impairment who, when they use buildings, rely entirely or predominantly on their ability to see.
- *Blind people* are people who, when they use buildings, rely entirely or predominantly on senses other than sight, ie touch, hearing, smell and taste.

Sight-impaired people

I start by considering sight-impaired people and their special needs. The building features listed below are ones which could be included in a checklist; some would also help blind people, but the list excludes features which would be helpful for blind people only.

- Suitable lighting – in any part of a building, adequate lighting and the avoidance of glare.
- The identification of stair nosings.
- The identification of the position of fully-glazed doors by means of an imposed panel, a distinctive strip of colour or other visible device.
- Readily comprehensible graphic symbols, for example a clear distinction between male and female toilet facility symbols.
- Legible printed information, for example on signage, display boards and captions to exhibits.
- Colour codes for lift controls, for example red for the alarm, yellow for re-opening a closing door and green for the ground floor level.
- Legible labels to lift controls.
- 'Correct' positioning of water taps – on wash-hand basins, etc. the hot tap to the left, the cold to the right.
- Protecting guard rails to exposed floor surface drops etc.
- Audible announcements in lifts.
- Audible announcements generally, for fire warning and other purposes.

The comparison with criteria for normal able-bodied people

A comparable 'What can we do for?' checklist could be produced for other OPCS types of disability, such as reaching and stretching, dexterity, hearing, continence, behaviour, intellectual functioning (covering people with what are now known as learning disabilities) and consciousness (covering epileptic people). Asking 'What in particular can we do for?' is an informative game. The question not usually asked is 'In particular for by comparison with whom?' If it is, and the person being asked is pressed, the answer might be 'By comparison with normal able-bodied people'. The follow-up question could be 'Well, but what do architects do for normal able-bodied people?'

Had Le Corbusier, pleased as he seemed to be with his discovery that a six-foot-tall Englishman was the key to the harmonious resolution of all architectural design problems[2], produced an information manual setting out what the correct solution was for every building feature, and had every architect then followed his instructions, the question would perhaps have had a clear answer. But he did not, and nor has anyone else, and the organic muddle paradigm, with no definitive prescriptions, continues to control architectural design decision-making. It has no concrete substance and no consistent parameters, and with no distinct entity anything can be built around it. The rules that Tim Nugent helped devise for the 1961 American Standard were placed on top of it, and so were the rules for the British Part M building regulation. Relatedly, it was practicable to place over it any prescriptions which were considered appropriate for people with one type of disability or another.

The 1987 Part M regulation dealt only with people with a locomotor disability. It was criticised by disability activists who felt that it ought to cover all disabled people, and with its 1992 revision its scope was extended to include people with impaired hearing or sight. Requirements which were considered particularly useful for hearing or sight-impaired people had to be incorporated, one for sight-impaired people, not in the list above, being that out-opening doors should not cause an obstruction on a path running along the face of a building[3]. This illustrates the point – an effect of the organic muddle paradigm having no rules is that a whole range of interventions can be prescribed as being particularly beneficial for people with disabilities, whether or not the need for them is peculiar to disabled people.

'Normal people' norms

To further the discussion, the hypothesised assumption is that instead of the 'for the disabled' Part M regulation there were a 'for normal people' regulation. The characteristics and capabilities of normal able-bodied people would govern its design standards and prescriptions, among them a requirement that normal wc compartments should be sufficiently spacious for normal able-bodied women to manage comfortably, and another that the distribution of toilet facilities should not be biased in favour of men. The convenience of normal able-bodied people being the criterion, most, if not all, of the features listed on the opposite page as being beneficial for sight-impaired people would be included; they are all, it may be observed, features for which the need among building users is general, not peculiar to sight-impaired people.

Two queries are raised. One is whether sight-impaired people have any particular needs that other building users do not have. The other is which building users, on account of their having characteristics or capabilities different from those of normal able-bodied people, would *not* be suitably accommodated by provision based on what might be called the convenient-for-normal-able-bodied-people paradigm, and for whom different or supplementary provision would be required. Dealing with the second question first, the answer is that there would be a sizeable congregation of them. The principal factors are ones that have been noted previously – steps and space.

The 'no stairs to public toilets' measure

Normal unencumbered able-bodied people, subject to their not having to get to the top of a multi-storey building which does not have a lift, are not at all inconvenienced by being obliged to use steps or stairs, and, by the rules of the convenient-for-normal-able-bodied-people paradigm, steps and stairs without handrails would be permissible. For separating these able-bodied people from those who would be inconvenienced, an appropriate measure has already been offered – it is that the people who would be inconvenienced (or, meaning the same thing, architecturally disabled) would be those with a valid reason for considering it essential or important that there should be no steps or stairs in the way of getting to a public toilet they might wish to use. As the findings of the sanitary provision project showed, these include wheelchair users, ambulant disabled people, blind people, pushchair users, people subject to children hassle, pregnant women and people encumbered with heavy luggage. With regard to the space factor, the findings also showed that wheelchair users and pushchair users would be particularly helped by having more space in wc compartments than would be needed for the convenience of normal able-bodied people, and also more space in enclosed lobbies to cloakrooms. Elsewhere, the findings indicated that wheelchair users and blind people would be helped by having grabrails in wc compartments.

Colour contrasts

What has not yet been established is whether sight-impaired people have any particular needs that other building users do not have, in which regard the advice commonly put forward in for-the-disabled design guidance manuals is that in and around public buildings colour contrasts can be valuable. In considering whether they genuinely are, and how they might be prescribed by an architect, the need first is to understand the difference between colour, hue and tone. Colours such as red, green and blue possess a hue and are chromatic colours, whereas black and white do not and are non-chromatic. Colours are distinguished from each other by their hues, but hues of the same tone do not contrast. The tone of a colour is changed by adding black or white to it, and effective colour contrasts are between distinct shades of black and white. A colour photograph of a building shows colour differences, whereas the same picture in black and white does not – it shows tonal contrasts, invariably affected by light and shade. When seen against bright sunshine, a solid sheeted floor surface such as coloured terrazzo appears white where the sun reflects off it, and black where an obstacle obstructs the sun and no light is reflected.

Stair nosings

Within buildings tonal contrasts are employed to identify the nosings of steps and stairs. This is done, for example, by imposing across the stair a nosing strip of a different material from the stair tread, meaning that when light is reflected there will be a tonal contrast. Or a thin contrasting strip may be set into the tread an inch or so behind its face – if the tread is inherently dark in tone, the strip will be white, and if light, black. Or, in the case of stone steps, the nose of the tread may be painted white or yellow, the relevant note being that yellow has a much lighter tonal hue than other colours[4].

Where, either within or outside a public building, the nosings of steps and stairs are not distinguished, the unobservant building user will be most at risk when he is set to go down stairs in circumstances where lighting is from a single light source, the steps have sharp noses, and the treads are of uniform tone, whether they be of brick, stone, timber or other material. Looking from above, the treads, as they follow each other down, may be indistinguishable from each other. An equivalent hazard does not occur when the user is set to ascend the stair, since the treads and risers as he looks at them will have a different tone when light is reflected off them.

Of all the normal features that the architect designs into a building it is steps and stairs that pose the most common threat to the safety of the user and where interventions are of most obvious value, either as hazard warning indicators or stability or mobility aids. Handrails to stairs serve primarily as mobility aids, but in certain circumstances they can usefully augment colour-contrasted stair nosings as hazard warning indicators, particularly, for example, where the level of the floor changes within a storey of a building and there are one or two steps only.

Colour differences

Colour-contrasted stair nosings serve as hazard warning indicators, and there is no place else in buildings, other than means-of-escape signage, where it is standard practice for colour contrasts to be introduced for safety purposes. Colour differences, on the other hand, can be applied by the architect for a range of purposes. Aesthetic reasons are the most usual, notably, for example, the multi-coloured patterned terrazzo or ceramic floor tiles which enliven buildings such as shopping malls, department stores, prestige office buildings and hospitals.

A problem of concern to sight-impaired people is raised here – one that cannot be resolved. The reasonable hypothesis is that unaccompanied sight-impaired people can be disconcertingly confused by multi-coloured patterned floors which give them the impression that they are approaching steps when they are not, the hazard being that they will stumble. The query then is whether the assumed interests of sight-impaired people should prevail over those of other building users, and whether there can be any formula for identifying particularly hazardous patterns which ought to be proscribed. The answer has to be negative. Aside from the impracticality of specifying proscriptions, the unbeatable hazard on a floor is sunshine-delineated shafts of light and shade, which to sight-impaired people might seem to be steps.

One of the propositions behind the idea that colour contrasts in and around buildings can assist sight-impaired people is that different colours can effectively define adjacent building features. Here it is colour differences, not colour contrasts, that are being called into aid; a notional example of the doctrine is that within a room the door face is green, the door frame is purple, the wall is yellow, the carpet on the floor is pink and that, to orient the enquirer who enters the room, the desk behind which the receptionist will be found is orange. The concomitant of all this is that for the plan to succeed the colours that meet each other should desirably be discordant – not a feature that the architect, who for aesthetic reasons is looking to achieve harmony, will find congenial.

Special buildings

The discussion so far has focused on public buildings. Special buildings for blind or near-blind people are a quite different matter. Here the residents (or students, trainees or employees) can be trained to pick up informative cues which the architect has inserted. There is no research data indicating which devices could be particularly helpful, but among those that might be are, for example, doors to residents' rooms in differing colours, floor texture changes (for example from carpet to vinyl tile) which serve as locational cues, along with wall surface texture changes, handrails with configuration changes and small knobs fixed to the underside of handrails on stairs or along walls. Around the building there can be tactile floor surfaces to warn of an approaching hazard or identify travel route junctions, and, in the vicinity of the building, tactile pavings on street pavements to indicate safe crossing places. The feature of these interventions is that there is a vocabulary, meaning that the coded messages which they transmit are ones that will be understood by people who have learnt the language. As noted on page 153, the same cannot be done in public buildings.

Blind people

In Britain in the late 1970s local access groups began to be set up in towns across the country, usually as a subcommittee of the local for-the-disabled voluntary organization. To inform the tasks they undertook, such as checking proposals for new public buildings, they relied on the advice of their consumer representatives, among whom there could be two or three wheelchair users, an ambulant disabled person, a deaf person and a blind person. In these groups, and also in national committees concerned with access issues, the blind representative had a privileged status. Blindness, aside from having a special aura, had a distinct set of accessibility referents, and others around a committee table tended to treat their blind colleague with exceptional deference. Not themselves being blind, they had emotionally charged images of what blindness would entail, and, relatedly, an anxiety to help blind people by identifying what might, in practice, be done to help them.

An associated factor was status rivalry. When accessibility issues are discussed in the context of any particular building or access-related issue, it is predictably provision for wheelchair users which heads the agenda. Both blind and non-blind consumer representatives may feel that blind people deserve to be given equal attention, and will be gratified if ways can be found to shift the balance. There is an urge to identify interventions which can be presented as beneficial for blind people, however marginal their practical value might be, and then to press that they should be mandated.

In line with the checklist procedure for each type of disability, the focus is always on provision for which the need is special – in this case, special for blind people, and peculiar to them. So non-special items which can help blind people – such as the avoidance wherever possible of an obligation to use steps or stairs, the provision of handrails to steps or stairs and the fixing of grabrails in wc compartments – are disregarded because they are bespoke elsewhere. There is a search for ideas. One commonly put forward is that braille labels can be fixed alongside building features to tell blind people where they are or what to do.

Braille labels

The proposition that information presented in braille can assist blind people who use public buildings is manifested most notably in lifts where braille button labels are attached alongside controls. The intervention is one that would potentially benefit relatively few blind people: the findings of the Royal National Institute for the Blind survey of blind and partially sighted adults in Britain undertaken in 1986–7 indicate that only about 3 per cent of registerable blind or partially-sighted people can read braille, and some 8 per cent of all registered blind people[5].

The alternative that would seem to be preferable is embossed symbols; either embossed markings on lift control buttons or raised symbols alongside controls and on the wall outside the lift. But when decisions are made it is not always good practice that governs them. For those who press for special treatment for blind people, among them activists who are able-bodied people, the great merit that braille button labels have is that they more loudly shout 'Look – we have done this to help blind people!'

Braille buttons are special for blind people who can manage independently. As with wheelchair users when 'What can we do for?' checklists are devised, the focus is on blind people who can get around on their own in suitable environments. In line with the equal-status principle, all positive interventions are considered, however trivial they might be. And numbers are irrelevant; as I have observed, people who serve on access committees do not want to know about numbers. There are, they say, blind people out there who can be helped in the same way as other disabled people, and they are, they claim, numerous.

The prevalence of blind people among building users

I also used to suppose that blind people were frequently to be found among building users. They are noticeable. 'There is a blind person', one says to oneself when someone walking along a street is observed carrying a white stick or cane or being led by a guide dog. The more they are noted, the greater the impression becomes that blind people are not uncommon. It was not until I started counting them that I came to realise how rare they actually were.

The process, as I noted earlier, began in European towns which I visited, and was subsequently systematised when counts were made in shopping centres in towns in England. Applying the 'with an aid' definition and drawing on the evidence of counts which I and others made during the years 1989 to 1993, the resultant estimate was that among shopping centre users in a typical town on a typical day only about one person in 5000 is someone who is blind*.

Population definitions need to be clarified here. In the context of architectural disability I define blind people as those who, when using buildings, rely entirely or predominantly on senses other than sight, and relevant research data (Appendix 8, page 390) indicates a close correlation between this and the use of a 'for the blind' mobility aid. There is no correspondence between the population of blind people who, by my definition, are building users and the total population of 'with an aid' blind people, and nor is there any correspondence with the 'registered blind' population: here we are back with the distinction between social and medical measures of disability.

Looking at the usage by blind people of particular public building types, the findings of the Department of the Environment's sanitary provision research project indicated that most types were used in much the same proportions as they were by others, the exceptions being cinemas/theatres, museums/art galleries and swimming pools/leisure centres (Appendix 2, Table A2.3, page 369). Interestingly, the pedestrianisation of the centres of the four towns which were project locations was felt, by the blind people who were interviewed, to make it much easier for them to get around (Appendix 2, page 371).

Mobility and touch contact

Arising from the project findings, the estimate was that about one in two of the blind people who visit shopping centres are able on occasion to travel independently, either to get to buildings or within them when they reach them. For getting around within buildings, in particular for the usage of public toilets, associated findings (Appendix 8, page 390), suggest that blind people who can manage independently rely substantially on direct physical touch contact.

In respect of mobility in the external environment the picture is different, as shown by the findings of two surveys made in the 1960s[6]. Among blind people able to travel independently in unknown places, physical touch contact was not found to be a primary source of information for mobility purposes (Appendix 8, page 391). And with regard to the princi-

*Relevant data are reported in Appendix 2: Table A2.1, page 367; Table A2.2, page 368; Table A2.5, page 372.

pal hazards which independent blind people encountered when travelling outdoors (Appendix 8, page 391), it would seem that there was not as a rule any practical means by which secure protection against them could have been effected. It is in this connection that the use of tactile pavings as an information and warning device for blind street users is now considered.

'Knobbly bubbles'

All across Britain there are knobbly bubbles on pavings at street crossings. On either side of crossings, and often in the middle as well, they protrude from concrete paving slabs, sometimes pink in colour, sometimes buff, sometimes grey. From my own experiences of walking over them, watching others do so and talking with people about them, there are impressions: they could be ankle-twisting for women with high-heeled shoes; they could cause pain to people with arthritis who slip on them; they could rattle a child's pushchair; they could skew the wheels of a wheelchair, bringing it to an abrupt halt; they could be disconcerting for a blind person's guide dog walking across them.

I hypothesise an anecdotal scenario. A person – a woman perhaps – imagines they must be there to prevent people slipping. But she is unsure, and to find out she telephones the local council. 'Ah', she is informed, 'they are helpful for blind people'. 'Are they? – what a good idea!' She is satisfied, and pleased to learn that the council is concerned to help blind people. Another enquirer may not be impressed: 'I'm sorry, but I don't understand – in what way *are* they helpful for blind people?' The council officer, one who is not in the technical department concerned, is uncertain: 'I think they're there to tell blind people it's a safe place to cross'. The woman is perplexed: 'But often they're in places where there are no traffic lights or zebra stripes – they're not safe places for blind people to cross'. 'Well', comes the reply, 'perhaps they tell blind people that it's not a safe place to cross'.

Kerb ramps

At Norwich in the mid-1960s I advised on the setting up of an innovatory programme for ramping kerbs at street intersections, the idea at the start being to develop routes for wheelchair users to travel from their homes to city centre shops and back again, and also to and from the local social club for handicapped people. It was a pragmatic programme without any strict specifications for the works – the city engineer's department simply went out and ramped the kerbs at locations which were on the list. Subsequently, in towns around Britain kerb-ramping for wheelchair users became a busy enterprise. Initially it was standard practice for there to be a low upstand at the intersection with the road surface to assist rainwater drainage, and in CP96, the 1967 British Standard code of practice on access for the disabled to buildings, an upstand an inch high was shown in the diagram presenting a suitable method for blending pavement and roadway surfaces[7].

As ramped kerbs with low upstands became standard practice around the country, angry complaints came in from wheelchair users. They reported that any upstand, however low, could skew the wheels of their wheelchairs, and only a flush join was acceptable. From the early 1970s, the advice put out by disability organizations and others was that surfaces must be blended to meet flush with each other, and in BS5810, the revised access code issued in 1979, a suitable example was shown[8].

The conflict – blind people versus wheelchair users

The Department of Transport, the government department responsible for advising local authority highways departments on how they should perform their duties, became actively engaged in the issue from the beginning of the 1980s. A disability unit had been established within the department in 1980, and through it disabled people and their organizations advised on transport-related matters. The complaint came from blind people – flush kerb ramps for wheelchair users posed a dangerous threat. Mobility training for white cane users and guide dog owners emphasised the vital importance of kerb upstands – they were the demarcation line that had to be located before an unguided blind person could cross a road. Without the upstand, blind people could walk unknowingly out into a busy traffic street. A resolution of the problem was needed.

The American solution

In America the issue had already been addressed. Where practicable, the solution was to separate the provision for wheelchair users from that for blind people. At street intersections there were kerb upstands on the direct route for pedestrians, meaning that blind people, along with other pedestrians, waited on the kerb at controlled crossings, and at uncontrolled crossings paused to check that the road was clear. To the side of the main crossing a ramp was inserted which, with its base flush with the road surface, was convenient for wheelchair users and also pushchair users (Figure 20.1).

The missed opportunity

With their diverse character, the footways of British streets are not as amenable as those in America to standard treatment. An official instruction prescribing American-style channel ramps might, however, have been issued when the differing requirements of blind people and wheelchair users were first recognised. Such action could have been taken during the 1970s, and it could still have been taken in 1981 when the Disabled Persons Act came into force with its section 1 requirement that local highway authorities must have regard to the needs of disabled and blind people when ramps were provided between carriageways and footways. The response could have been to follow American practice, but that was not the course taken. The assumption was that for the kerb ramp problem there ought to be a single solution which would be convenient for everyone – blind people and wheelchair users included – and the idea which emerged was that knobbly

20.1 Pedestrian crossing in Seattle

bubbles on pavings could warn blind people that a ramped kerb did not have an upstand. The examples shown in Figure 20.2 are in Battersea Square, close to where I live.

The tenets of the disability lobby

Over the 35 years that my work has been associated with the interests of disabled people, I have, as mentioned earlier, been a regular observer of the disability lobby in action. Congregately it is a powerful body. Again, as I have noted earlier*, it relies for its force on the sustenance of legend and mythology. It is concerned to maintain that force, and it wishes that research should be conducted on the basis that its preconceived ideas are right. The classic example was the programme conducted in the years 1979 to 1981 by the Committee on Restrictions against Disabled People*. It was the positive hypothesis, the supposition that disabled people really were subjected to widespread and unjustifiable hostile discrimination, that CORAD was keen to prove. In doing so, it disregarded a basic axiom of sound scientific research: that inquiries should never be predicated on validating positive hypotheses, they ought always to be aimed at disproving negative hypotheses, meaning, in the CORAD case, disproving the hypothesis that discrimination against disabled people was *not* widespread.

The tactile pavings presumptions

Preconceptions came with the setting up in Britain of the tactile pavings programme. The starting presumption was that tactile pavings genuinely

* See page 70.

20.2a

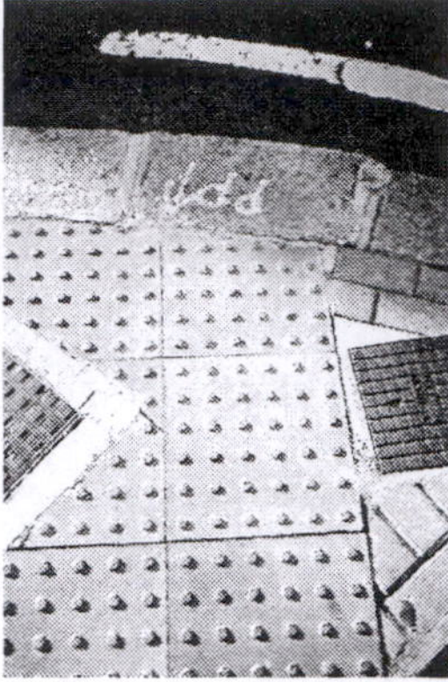

20.2b

20.2c

20.2 Pedestrian crossings in Battersea

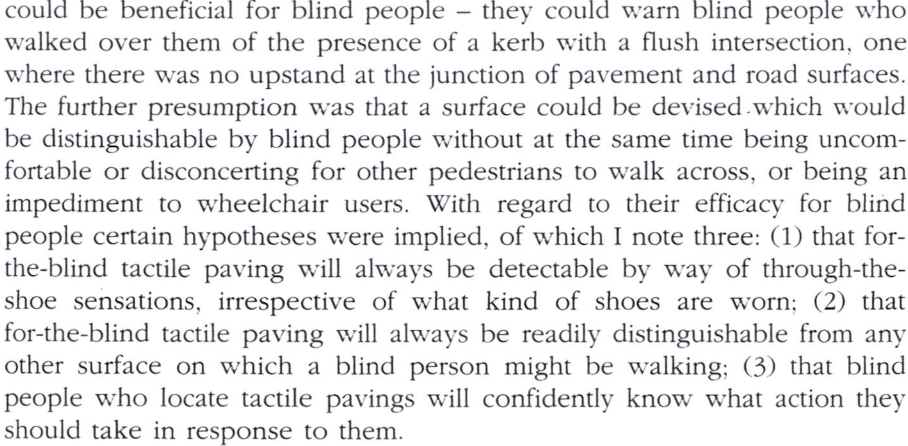

could be beneficial for blind people – they could warn blind people who walked over them of the presence of a kerb with a flush intersection, one where there was no upstand at the junction of pavement and road surfaces. The further presumption was that a surface could be devised which would be distinguishable by blind people without at the same time being uncomfortable or disconcerting for other pedestrians to walk across, or being an impediment to wheelchair users. With regard to their efficacy for blind people certain hypotheses were implied, of which I note three: (1) that for-the-blind tactile paving will always be detectable by way of through-the-shoe sensations, irrespective of what kind of shoes are worn; (2) that for-the-blind tactile paving will always be readily distinguishable from any other surface on which a blind person might be walking; (3) that blind people who locate tactile pavings will confidently know what action they should take in response to them.

It was not only in Britain that the idea that tactile pavings could help blind people was fostered, and I report what happened in the Netherlands and America.

Gouda

In 1981 the European Commission in Brussels launched an initiative; in a suitable European town it would sponsor a practical project aimed at demonstrating how, in typical urban environments, accessibility for people with disabilities could be greatly improved by making modifications to buildings and spaces between buildings. The town selected was Gouda in Holland,

and a report on how the programme was to be developed was issued in August 1982. Among the works to be undertaken provision for blind people featured prominently. Pedestrian routes from outer areas to the town centre were identified, along with principal travel routes within the central area. On these routes, continuous lines of corrugated tactile pavings were laid, with variants to indicate junctions and street crossing points.

The Gouda demonstration project was completed in early 1986, and an illustrated report on the provisions made was issued by The Netherlands Department of Transport and Public Works and the City of Gouda in May 1986[9]. The plan was that after two or three years a comprehensive evaluation would be made of the practical value of all its component features, with a report of the findings being issued. To see what had been done I spent two days in the town in August 1986; I saw two blind people while I was there, introduced myself and talked with them. The first, a man with a white stick who was with his wife, was critical of the pavings scheme. Wholly blind, he had for years walked round the town on his own, but the people who devised the project had not, he said, consulted him or other blind people he knew; it was all useless. The second, also wholly blind, was a Canadian tourist with a white cane. What did he reckon to it all, I asked. 'How interesting', he said, 'I had no idea it was all there'.

In May 1989 I was in Holland again, and arranged to meet municipal officials who had worked on the Gouda project and were assessing the results of it all. The tactile pavings project, they said, had been a complete failure, and corrugated tiles were not being replaced when street works were undertaken. No report on the results was to be issued. In June 1993 I was in Gouda again. Only a few remnants of the tactile paving routes were still to be seen.

America

At pedestrian crossings in towns and cities around America it is standard practice for kerb upstands to be retained at direct crossing points, meaning there is no cause for British-style tactile pavings to be incorporated at those locations. In America this has not, however, silenced the advocacy of tactile floor surfaces as an aid for blind people. Detectable warnings for blind people are a 'rights' item; the advice in the 1991 Americans with Disabilities Act Accessibility Guidelines[10] being that detectable warnings on walking surfaces could be in the form of truncated domes.

In America there are two national organizations for blind people. One, the American Council of the Blind, backed tactile surfaces as a valid aid: 'We absolutely believe that they're necessary'[11]. The other, the American Foundation for the Blind, did not; its leading members felt that in and around buildings blind people ought to be treated as normal people, with no concessions or special provision made for them[12]. Peggy Pinder, the Foundation's vice-president, was their spokesperson: 'We believe that once people get to looking at this they're going to find that women in high heels, little kids learning to walk, people who use wheelchairs, people who have cerebral palsy and can't lift their feet, all these people are going to have a hell of a time with this stuff put into the sidewalk'[13]. She also maintained that truncated domes on floor surfaces were of no value to blind people. The Accessibility Guidelines requirements, the Foundation insisted, must be suspended, and in support of its cause it enlisted the International Mass Retail Association, who petitioned the Access Board: 'Compliance with these provisions may pose a significant safety risk to persons with and without disabilities, create a potentially hazardous situation, and could lead to fatalities'[14].

The Architectural and Transportation Barriers Compliance Board felt obliged to concede; at its November 1992 meeting it voted to suspend the detectable warning requirements until January 1995, when the position would be reviewed in the light of relevant new research evidence[15]. The research, in the main studies directed by Dr Billie Louise Bentzen of the Department of Psychology in Boston College at Chestnut Hill in Massachusetts[16], was completed in November 1994. On detectable warnings at kerb ramps, the findings showed that blind and sight-impaired people used a combination of cues to detect and cross intersections. Although detectable warnings helped such people locate and identify kerb ramps and provided a useful cue, the findings suggested that detectable warnings were redundant at most intersections, and that other technologies could be as effective and less costly. The case for tactile pavings was thus unproven, and in the light of the Access Board's continuing review of the provisions in the Americans with Disabilities Act Accessibility Guidelines, the suspension of the requirements for detectable warnings was extended until July 1998[17].

The test which could be made in Britain

In Britain a series of inquiries and research projects to do with tactile pavings has been commissioned by the Department of Transport over the years since 1981; these are recorded in Appendix 9 with summaries of the findings of published reports. But as yet (early 1997) no research programme has been undertaken to evaluate the practical value for blind people of the tactile pavings laid at street crossings around the country.

A simple and economic project conducted by a market research organization could, I suggest, be informative. Taking a representative sample of street crossings where they are to be found – say, fifty or so of the many thousands that there are – interviewers with clipboards could go out and wait for unaccompanied blind people to come along. They might do so unavailingly for hours, if not for ever, but when rewarded they would observe the action taken by a blind person who walked onto the paving slabs, and then intercept him (or her) and ask questions about their utility. The questions would be designed to elicit the subject's impressions of the usefulness of tactile pavings on known routes he travelled regularly versus those on routes with which he was not familiar. In between times the interviewer's time could be occupied by keeping a count of the number of non-blind pedestrians who passed by, with a random selection of them being approached and asked what their own opinions of tactile pavings were. As a supplementary, video recordings could be made at locations where tactile pavings had been laid, a purpose being to check how frequently blind people travelling independently were found to be using them.

The disability lobby

The spread of tactile pavings across the streets of Britain has been, and is, a remarkable phenomenon. More than any other single item in the inventory of devices aimed at making the built environment more accessible and manageable for disabled people, it manifests the potent influence at national and local levels of the disability lobby. At national level the lobby is aided by a statutory advisory committee, the Disabled Persons Transport Advisory Committee. Set up under section 125 of the Transport Act 1985, with not fewer than half its members having to be people with disabilities, its remit is to advise the Secretary of State for Transport on all the matters he deals with which are of concern to disabled people. As recorded in its annual reports[18], the Committee has, since its inception, firmly backed the tactile pavings programme. So also has the Royal National Institute for the Blind, whose staff have regularly cooperated with the Department of Transport's disability unit, now known as the mobility unit.

At local level the lobby is aided by local access groups and the backing they receive from local authority officials and members. My impression here is that it is collaborators – the able-bodied people who are access officers, who serve on access committees or who are relevant decision-makers – who are often most fervent in their faith in the virtues of tactile pavings. The blind person who represents the interests of blind people on a local committee will predictably oblige; his or her role is to identify the special things that can be done to help visually handicapped people, and he or she will commonly be keen to advocate tactile pavings and encourage the laying of them around the streets of the district. From the various meetings I have attended and conversations I have had with politically active blind people, my impression is that it is unusual for such a person to deny the efficacy of tactile pavings, or to acknowledge how troublesome they might be for other pedestrians and then offer the view that blind people who press for more of them are being unduly selfish and inconsiderate.

The force of suggestibility helped promote the tactile pavings programme. People like to believe that what they are told is helpful for disabled people really is helpful. They imagine that knobbly bubble pavings really do benefit blind people: the evidence is all around them; everyone is doing it and so obviously it must be a good thing to do; it *can't* be wrong. I recall a meeting about tactile pavings that I attended in April 1994. Arranged by the social services department of a London borough with invited speakers, there were 100 or so participants. Some 70 organizations were represented, among them more than 40 local authorities. In the course of the discussion no one queried the value of knobbly bubble pavings. That was assumed. The concern was to 'get it right'; a major worry was that many local authorities were not laying the pavings precisely in accord with official instructions. Buff pavings (indicating an uncontrolled crossing) were being laid at controlled crossings, where they ought to be pink. It would need only one error, it was suggested, for a blind person to make a mistake, to be disconcerted and confused, and to no longer have the confidence to go out on his own.

Tactile pavings in buildings

In March 1996 the Department of Transport issued a consultation document on the scope there might be for applying different tactile paving surfaces for different purposes[19]. One of these was a 'corduroy' surface, to be used to warn of hazards such as steps or stairs. When in 1992 the Part M building regulation was revised, with an extended mandate which covered people with impaired hearing or sight, the advice was that corduroy pavings should be laid at the top of a stepped approach to a building. But as the related diagram in the approved document showed[20], it is customary for there to be handrails to steps and landings on an approach to a building, and as an information and warning cue for blind people I would submit that these serve better than any tactile floor surface. The syndrome again observable here is the desire to demonstrate that something supposedly helpful is being done for blind people, never mind how worthless it might be.

Tactile pavings at pedestrian crossings

The seven different purposes for which the Department of Transport has suggested that distinctive tactile surfaces might be laid are listed in Appendix 9 (page 396); at the time this is written, March 1997, it is not yet known whether the entire programme is to be activated.

On tactile pavings at pedestrian crossings, official guidance was first issued by the Department of Transport in October 1986 in Disability Unit Circular 1/86[21], and then refined in May 1992 with the issuing of Circular 1/91[22]; this remains operative in 1997. As the Appendix 9 account of relevant research studies commissioned by the Department of Transport indicates, no substantive evidence has been obtained in support of the positive hypothesis that tactile pavings genuinely do help blind people, whereas the negative hypothesis, that they do not, has scored better. While there has thus been no confirmation that public money spent on tactile pavings is not money wasted, local authorities have not been deterred – they have responded enthusiastically to official guidance, with their endeavours being encouraged by the Audit Commission.

Set up in 1983, the Audit Commission for England and Wales has responsibility for the external audit of local authorities. With its duty being to ensure that public funds are used economically, effectively and efficiently, its aim is to promote value for money in the services provided by local authorities. Since 1992 it has directed them to report their performance on delivering certain services[23], one added to the list in 1993 being the percentage of pedestrian crossings (meaning controlled crossings and zebra crossings) which incorporate facilities for disabled people. For a crossing to qualify, all the approaches to it must have dropped or flush kerbs *and* tactile surfaces.

For the year 1994/95, the scores reported by local highway authorities (county councils, metropolitan district councils and London borough councils) were published in 1996[24]. The two authorities with the lowest proportion of crossings equipped with tactile pavings were Bexley (0.0 per cent) and Kensington and Chelsea (0.5 per cent). The top scorers were Brent, West Sussex and South Tyneside, each claiming 100 per cent. Among all English authorities the mean score was 51 per cent, an amount which will predictably have risen when the next set of returns is published later in 1997.

People with hearing impairments

The person who cannot hear at all and is able to understand people to whom he is talking only by reading their lips is assisted where the light is bright. When a public building is being designed, the kind of instruction which deaf people might therefore wish for would be, 'Adequate light should be provided for deaf people'. In practice, this cannot be delivered by the architect in compliance with any preset formula prescription. Architects can insert windows into buildings, and they can prescribe a sufficient number of suitable lighting appliances and where they are to be placed. But they cannot decree how much light there is in a room at any particular time; that depends on sunshine, the weather and the time of day, and on the people who happen to turn the lights on or off.

People who are hard of hearing but not deaf can, in their usage of public buildings, be assisted by audio-amplification systems. These can be beneficial in concert halls, theatres, cinemas and churches; in meeting rooms and lecture theatres; and in ticket offices and at counters (as in banks and post offices) where a glazed security screen separates the customer from the service deliverer. The systems are currently of two kinds. One, for people with a suitable hearing aid only, is the induction loop system, whereby a signal from a microphone is passed to an amplifier which directs a current through a loop (normally round the walls of a room), so generating a magnetic field whereby the signal is converted into familiar sound when picked up by the listener's hearing aid. The other, the infra-red system, translates microphone signals into radiated invisible light which is demodulated and converted into familiar sound when picked up by a stethoscope worn by the listener.

The induction loop is the more commonly used of the two systems, but it has drawbacks. It cannot suppress interfering background noise, and sound may spill over beyond the loop, meaning that confidential discussions can be picked up outside meeting rooms. Relatedly, the sounds of conversations in different rooms in a building which are loop-equipped may overlap. Particularly in large auditoria buildings, it may be technically impossible to install a system which works satisfactorily. In any room or building for which a loop system is specified, a proficient and expert specialist will need to be employed to plan and install it. It is not a feature that the architect can properly be asked to provide and deliver.

The infra-red system is technically much more reliable than the loop system. But it is not the architect's job in any building to see that it is introduced. The stethoscopes which have to be worn can only be provided by the building management, and in any particular building it will be for the building owner or manager to set the system up. Regarding audio-amplification systems, the advice in the 1992 Part M Approved Document[25] is that it is for the building owner to decide which system better suits the layout and use of the building and to plan accordingly.

For deaf people, visual alarm systems feature on the 'What can we do for?' checklist. In America, the Americans with Disabilities Act requires visual alarms for deaf people in new hotels or existing hotels when reconstructed; one guestroom in every 25 has to be equipped with a visual alarm appliance, with a signal visible in all parts of the unit[26]. In Britain, having regard to the character of British hotels and the infrequency of occasions on which deaf or near-deaf people are on their own when staying in hotels, the sensible routine might be for deaf people to ensure on arrival that the hotel management knows of their whereabouts should there be a fire incident, and to have a suitable notice to hang on the door outside their room.

In June 1995 a disability journal[27] reported that a Welsh disability group was calling on the government to change 'potentially lethal' building regulations. Backed by the British Deaf Association, they wanted the Part M regulation amended so that visual fire alarms were fitted in all buildings, and they complained, 'The regulations only require sound alarms to be fitted. This is not good enough. Unless visual alarms are fitted, how do deaf people know there is a fire? Hearing people are protected, but deaf people are not. This is blatant discrimination'.

21 My experiences as a building user

I report in this chapter my experiences as a building user and the encounters that I have had over the years with impediments in and around buildings. Three reasons are pertinent. First, because I can responsibly vouch for my own experiences, whereas I cannot for those of others. Second, because specific illustrations based on actuality have more authenticity than loose generalizations of a kind that may be influenced by presumptions, preconceptions, legend or mythology. Third, because I have appropriate qualifications – I have been an ambulant disabled person and a wheelchair user as well as, historically, a regular able-bodied person. By the terms of the definitions set by the Office of Population Censuses and Surveys, I am, as well as being a person with a locomotor disability, a person with a reaching and stretching and also a dexterity disability.

I bring into the discussion my experiences in America as well as those in Britain. Aside from three trips to Canada and one to Colombia in South America I have been to America, meaning the United States, on seven occasions. With four extended visits, I have travelled from Vermont and Massachusetts in the north east to California in the south west, and from Washington State in the north west to Florida in the south east. On four occasions I went in and came out as an ambulant disabled person. On one I went in as an ambulant disabled person and eight days later came out as a wheelchair user; that was in 1981 when, with an airline ticket to Japan and on around the world, I stopped off in Minneapolis for half a day and broke a leg while visiting an accessible housing scheme. On the sixth occasion, in October 1993, I went in and came out as a wheelchair user, having broken my leg in London ten weeks earlier. On the seventh, in May–June 1994 when my wife and I spent two weeks in and around Washington DC, I was ambulant disabled rather than chairbound, but we took my wheelchair with us and used it frequently when going out to meetings or visiting museums, art galleries and historic buildings.

Hazards

In recent years I have normally been an ambulant disabled person. The eight or so periods during which I have regularly needed to use a wheelchair have usually been for two or three months at a time, with the longest stint, in 1990, lasting six months. When I have been obliged to be a wheelchair user (rather than its being more convenient) it has been on account of a leg fracture, usually caused by my weak right knee crumpling while walking. A particular feature of the built environment, a level floor which unpredictably runs into an unnoticeable downward ramp, can trigger the crumpling of the knee. What happens is that I put my right foot forward, supposing that it will land on the level. Instead it does not; it suddenly dips, causes the knee to unlock, and me to fall on top of the leg, which cracks under my weight.

I cite two incidents. One was in a hotel in Yorkshire which was a model refurbishment of a historic industrial building. With a dark carpet on the floor, an opening had been created between two separate parts of the old building whose floor levels were not quite aligned. The other was in a celebrated London department store. The opening separated two functionally different sectors of the store, with the non-alignment of the floors caused by the different surfaces that had been laid. I am disinclined to look for someone else to blame when I injure myself in this way, and I have always found abhorrent the idea that I ought, in American fashion, to grasp every opportunity to sue and obtain legal redress. Had I taken either of these two cases to court I could not responsibly have stood up and said that the architect or the building manager had been negligent. In a range of circumstances there necessarily have to be marginal changes in the level of floor surfaces within buildings. They cannot all be subjected to the 'there ought to be a colour contrast warning' edict, even if, which is not the case, that could be reliable. I simply have the misfortune, on account of the unique and peculiar way that the polio virus damaged me, that I happen to be a great deal more vulnerable to inconspicuous floor level changes than other building users. Outside my home I have since 1990 regularly worn a brace over my right knee, an effect of the stiff leg being that the knee muscles I use to climb stairs have become weaker. As a result of the series of fractures, the right leg is now more than an inch shorter than the left, to compensate for which the right shoe has to be raised each time a new pair of shoes is bought.

Wheelchair manoeuvre

When I am a wheelchair user I can as a rule propel my own wheelchair within buildings, but elsewhere I need to be pushed. During the years that I worked in the Marsham Street offices of the Department of the Environment I could, as a wheelchair user, move around the building independently. In public buildings I can be an independent wheelchair user, but when someone is with me I am usually pushed. The character and effects of the impediments that I encounter when using buildings vary significantly, according to whether I am being pushed by someone else or am on my own and propelling myself. Broadly, impediments are less troublesome when I have another person with me – the height of lift controls is academic, the fact that books in libraries and goods on shelves in supermarkets may be beyond my reach does not bother me, and getting through doors is facilitated when they are opened by someone else. But, on the other hand, there are impediments that are more easily tackled when I propel myself.

The companion who steers my wheelchair can only push or pull it – it is, in effect, a cumbersome cart. The thrust on the handles passes to the main rear wheels, and the castor wheels in front are undirected. The main wheels perform conjunctively – neither one of them can be controlled independent of the other. A regular obstacle is raised thresholds at doors. I am not able to tilt the wheelchair on its rear wheels in order to ride over thresholds, and when my wheelchair is pushed against even a low upstand its castor wheels automatically skew. The same problem occurs in streets where a ramped kerb has a low upstand. The orchestration is very different inside buildings where I can propel the wheelchair myself. I have a sensitive and responsive instrument. It swivels and turns; its castor wheels can be held on course; skewing tendencies can be countered; it can be precisely directed; and it can, forwards or in reverse, be steered neatly around sharp corners. The benefits of self-propulsion are most apparent in confined spaces. It is easier to turn in a narrow cloakroom lobby, to move into or out of a lift, to get into position at a restaurant table or to manoeuvre inside a wc compartment. If someone else necessarily had to do the steering, more clear space would be needed.

Scooters

I use a battery-powered scooter when I am the customer of a shopmobility scheme, where, in a location linked to a shopping centre, wheelchairs, powered chairs and scooters are available on loan to disabled people. I prefer a scooter to a powered wheelchair for two reasons – it is much easier to manoeuvre and is less cumbersome. A scooter neutralizes many of the impediments, both architectural and non-architectural, which can disable me as a building user. I can safely, with ease and in comfort, move around independently, and uneven floor surfaces, kerb ramps and inclines are not obstacles in my way.

The merits of motor cars

Much of the travelling that I undertake is done by driving my car, with the proportion increasing over the years as my disability has become more handicapping. Were I obliged constantly to rely on public transport for getting around, or always on someone else to drive the car, I would, relatively, be immensely handicapped, or, put in another way, be far more frequently subject to transport disability. With the car always readily available outside the front door to take me where I wish, I can drive off and choose which buildings to go to. Because I can be selective, inaccessible buildings can as a rule be avoided. Independent of the car but associated with it, the mammoth benefit afforded by my disability is the orange badge that I can display on the windscreen. Parking in certain areas of central London can, I acknowledge, pose problems, but with the badge in place when I park there is no threat of finding, on my return, that the car has been towed away or has a clamp on one of its wheels. Aided by the badge

I have much less difficulty reaching the buildings in London that I think to visit than those who need to rely on public transport or who do not have an orange badge. The privilege that came with my disability during the years that I worked at Marsham Street for the Department of the Environment was a pass to use the underground car park. It took me some twelve minutes to reach the office each morning.

Taxis

The London black taxicab, whether allegedly wheelchair-accessible or not, is a means of transport that I avoid unless there is absolutely no alternative. In my disability years when I was maximally mobile it was always awkward and uncomfortable to get in and out of it, and today it has become intolerably inaccessible. Its impediments are its high floor, the lack of any grabrails that I can use to pull myself in by, and the deep recess to its rear seat. No competent designer, I suspect, could produce a vehicle for use as a taxi which for me could be more unmanageable. The contrast is with a normal saloon car. To get in on either the driver or passenger side, I drop onto the seat and then pull my legs in. To get out, I push off with my left hand on the seat or backrest. When my right leg is in plaster following a fracture, I can get in by dropping through the open offside rear door onto the seat, and lift myself out by pushing against the driver's seat backrest.

When I have travelled away from home without my car, for example to go to an airport, I have usually called a minicab company which brings me an accessible saloon car. Problems have been presented when I have to get home from a place where black cabs only can be hired. Relatedly, when I have to travel out of London by train I have been troubled by what I call the Manchester syndrome, meaning that at my destination all the taxis are inaccessible. On two occasions in recent years an effect of this has been that I have travelled by car to meetings outside London, instead of going by train as I would have wished. There have been some six occasions when, as a wheelchair user, I have hired a wheelchair-accessible London taxi to get home. That there are such taxis is then welcome, although I always feel insecure, sitting as I do in a wobbly wheelchair that is facing backwards.

Buses

The last time I travelled on a London bus was in 1983. I doubt there will ever be another time, since I could not now get myself onto the platform to get in. Nor might I feel confident that I would get to a seat before the bus lurched on starting and tipped me over. Historically there was never a scheduled bus service on the street outside my home in Battersea, but now there is – a small bus that travels between Clapham Junction and Victoria. Were it one day to present itself in low-floor format – on the pattern of new buses designed to be friendly for disabled passengers – I very much doubt that I would be encouraged to use it. It could not compete with my private car in terms of convenience.

Trains

On some ten occasions when I have been a wheelchair user I have travelled on my own by train in England. The staff at railway stations have never failed me – they have always been helpful, courteous and efficient. Similarly they have been when I have travelled as an accompanied wheelchair user or an ambulant disabled person. It has helped that I have usually started the journey from a London terminus, with time to board the train and get settled. It is inconceivable that I would now ever, for example, have cause to go down the road in Battersea and take a train from Clapham Junction. As an ambulant disabled person I continue on occasion to use trains when I travel, although not as frequently as I did before retirement. Where platforms are low, I need a push from behind to get up the first step into a coach, and a rail to pull up against.

The last time I travelled on an underground train in London was, I think, in 1981. A merit that the London underground shares with other subway systems is that its vehicles have floors at or about the same level as station platforms. But that is no compensation for the inaccessibility of its stations, and I doubt that I shall ever again travel by it. The comparison in my experience is with the Washington DC metro, which was planned and designed to be wheelchair-accessible throughout. With myself as a wheelchair user we travelled on it in October 1993, when my brother did the pushing, and in June 1994, when my wife did. With lifts which were always working giving direct access from streets to platforms, the only obstacle – for my wife more troublesome than for my brother – was getting the loaded wheelchair into train carriages. Floors are at the same level, but necessarily there is a gap at the threshold, and castor wheels tended to skew in it. Had I been an athletic independent wheelchair user capable of tilting the chair on its propelling wheels, the castor wheels could have been raised off the floor, and access would have been easier.

Air travel

In recent years when I have travelled by air I have always been pushed in a wheelchair through airport terminal buildings. As a rule, the wheelchair has not been my own. Travel distances within terminal buildings are often extended, and when I am an ambulant disabled person I welcome the wheelchair porterage service. With it come personal attention services that I appreciate. As a genuine wheelchair user I have, either on my own, with my wife or with colleagues attending disability meetings, used airport terminal buildings in England and eight other countries. For friendliness, an unpatronising readiness to help and sensible practical assistance, the staff at airports in Britain are, in my experience, unrivalled – the service at Heathrow, my wife says, is 'magic'.

Historically, access to aircraft was up the steps of a portable stairway, and at times during the 1980s when I was wheelchair-dependent for mobility there were occasions when I had to be carried up and down by airport staff, not always with enthusiasm. With the general availability in airport terminals of ramped access tunnel passageways, that does not now happen.

There is here a pleasing example of bottom-up macroism in practice – a building feature developed for the convenience of normal people which happens at the same time to be very beneficial for those in wheelchairs.

Street environments and pedestrianisation

When I go out, the accessibility of buildings is not guaranteed for me by the elimination of architectural barriers or the availability of a place to park my car. The crucial factor is the state of the weather. When street and pavement surfaces are icy after rain or snow, I cannot sensibly risk walking on them, and I can be prevented from reaching buildings I would otherwise use. Both as an ambulant disabled person and a wheelchair user, the pedestrianisation of shopping areas in English towns in recent years – and with it the development of associated covered shopping malls – has for me been a boon. When out on shopping expeditions with my wife I can move around in safety and comfort, with virtually no impediments along the way.

The contrast is with the traditional high street, with its row of shops either side of a busy, noisy and fume-ridden traffic route. In large and small towns many such streets can still be found, and for disabled people such as myself they are not user-friendly. The impediments that, as an ambulant disabled person or as a wheelchair user, I may encounter include narrow and congested pavements with lighting poles and other items of street equipment which get in the way; uneven, warped and cracked paving slabs; paved and tarmac surfaces where contractors' work associated with below-ground services has left uneven strips or patches; steep cambers that pull the wheelchair off course or upset my balance when walking; and kerb ramps.

Pavements and kerbs

Tactile pavings with concrete bubbles have now been laid at thousands of street crossings in Britain. I do not like them; whether as an ambulant disabled person or a wheelchair user, I would be more comfortable without them. Subject to that, my impression is that the construction of kerb ramps in England has markedly improved in recent years. But the English are still not good at producing kerb ramps which can be comfortably negotiated by people in wheelchairs, whether self-propelled or pushed. Too often the English kerb ramp is steeply graded, has a wheelchair-skewing camber, is jaggedly finished and has a castor wheel-stopping and occupant-lurching upstand at the point where it meets the road surface. The road surface alongside commonly has a steeply shelving camber which leaves a pit for the wheelchair to get stuck into, a receptacle for rainwater puddles and, as an added obstacle, there may be a drainage cover whose apertures are slots for castor wheels. The perils of kerb ramps are most acute when I am being pushed down a ramp in my wheelchair by someone who is unacquainted with the hazards. Where trouble threatens I can, if there is time, shout 'Hey, stop!' or I can trust in survival. By good fortune I have only once been tipped bodily out of my wheelchair into the roadway.

When I am an ambulant disabled person the English kerb ramp can be an impediment. The mechanics of my disability mean that I cannot securely walk forwards down a steep ramp; instead I go down crab-wise with my left leg leading. Where the ramp is very steep, I avoid it and step directly off the kerb.

The comparison is with America, where standardized moulded concrete channel ramps are set into sidewalks. Wide enough for a wheelchair or pushchair, the ramp meets flush with the road surface. The character of the urban infrastructure in America helps greatly: with rectangular grid road planning, wide sidewalks, service covers set back, street furniture set out of the way and standardised kerb upstand heights, there are as a rule far fewer impediments in the way of procuring satisfactory kerb ramps than there are in England. When pushing me in a wheelchair in America, my wife did, however, find that the gradient of kerb ramps was frequently too steep for comfort and, as in England, uneven paving slabs could be troublesome.

External floor surfaces

When I am in a wheelchair, either being pushed or not, there is only one external floor surface that an architect may have prescribed which I find to be an absolute obstacle. It is coverings of loose gravel, fortunately a surface that I rarely encounter. Cobbles, stone or concrete setts where they have been carefully laid are less upsetting, although my wife finds bumpy cobbles troublesome when she is pushing. Nor, when I am an ambulant disabled person, are cobble surfaces unduly irritating, even where the cobbles are historic and come in diverse shapes and contours. The advantage that cobbles have over paving slabs is that the hazard they present is immediately discernible; when I meet them, I take more care to see where I am putting my feet than when walking on pavements whose slabs appear to be even when they are not. Rainwater on external floor surfaces, particularly in conjunction with fallen autumn leaves, can trouble me. Other than terrazzo or marble, the surface I find most threatening when it is wet is smooth brick setts.

Steps, stairs and ramps

Steps, stairs and ramps can present me with a number of impediments when I use buildings, and I summarize here how I manage when I am an ambulant disabled person:

- I am always more secure when going *up* stairs or a ramp than when coming down.
- Where there is a choice between steps and a ramp I prefer the ramp for going up and the steps for coming down, provided there is a handrail.
- I can go up a steep ramp that does not have a handrail; when coming down a steep ramp a handrail is helpful.
- When I am going up or down two or more steps a handrail is essential.

- To go up a single high step I need a handrail, or a side wall against which I can brace myself.

I have had numerous falls on steps or stairs over the years, some of them startling. In the early years, when tissues were resilient and I could fall relaxedly, I was able to fall without seriously hurting myself, including one occasion when I fell forwards down half a dozen icy concrete steps, and another when, going up a straight flight staircase from ground to first floor, I fell backwards from near the top. On only one occasion has a fall on stairs caused a fracture, and that was twenty years ago. I know now that if I fall when going down stairs or a ramp I could damage myself severely – falling when going up is less perilous.

Handrails

For myself as an ambulant disabled person a handrail to a flight of stairs or a steep ramp can, according to circumstance, serve one or more of four remedial functions: (1) it can simply be a stabilizer – it helps me to maintain my balance as I go up or down; (2) it can enable me to retain my balance, when without it I would find it difficult or impossible to maintain my balance; (3) it can be a locomotory aid – it can assist me to raise my legs from one step to another when ascending, or lower them when descending; and (4) it can be a damage-limitation device, in that if I stumble and cannot retain my balance I may, when I fall, be able to grasp it and limit the injury I cause myself.

When I was maximally mobile – from around 1964 to 1978 – I did not use a stick and could cope with all but the steepest steps without a handrail. Since 1978, according to the state of my disability and the configuration of the steps that I am attempting to negotiate, the availability of a handrail has become crucial. On steeply graded steps, where risers are more than about 170mm and treads less than about 260mm, I need a handrail which I can grasp to pull up on when ascending, and hold to retain my balance when descending. On gently graded steps, where risers are less than about 140mm and treads more than about 370mm, I need only a stabilizer – a rail or balustrade that I can put my hand on to maintain balance but which I do not need to grip or press on.

In and around public buildings I come across balustrades and rails with a variety of configurations. External steps may have a stone balustrade with no rail. Internal stairs usually have a rail on both sides, but it is frequently not a rail which I can comfortably grasp. Of the ten handrail configurations in Figure 21.1, H1 is the most suitable for me and H10 the least. Broadly, H1 to H4 are convenient, H5 to H7 are quite convenient and H8 to H10 not convenient. For H5 and H6, the thumb is on the side to the right.

Where one rail only is provided to the side of a stairway, there is no level above the line of the stair nosings where it may be fixed which will be ideal for me. This is not because I am peculiar. A rail which effectively serves the business of coming down will be at a higher level than that for the business of going up, and the universal custom is that the rail is fixed

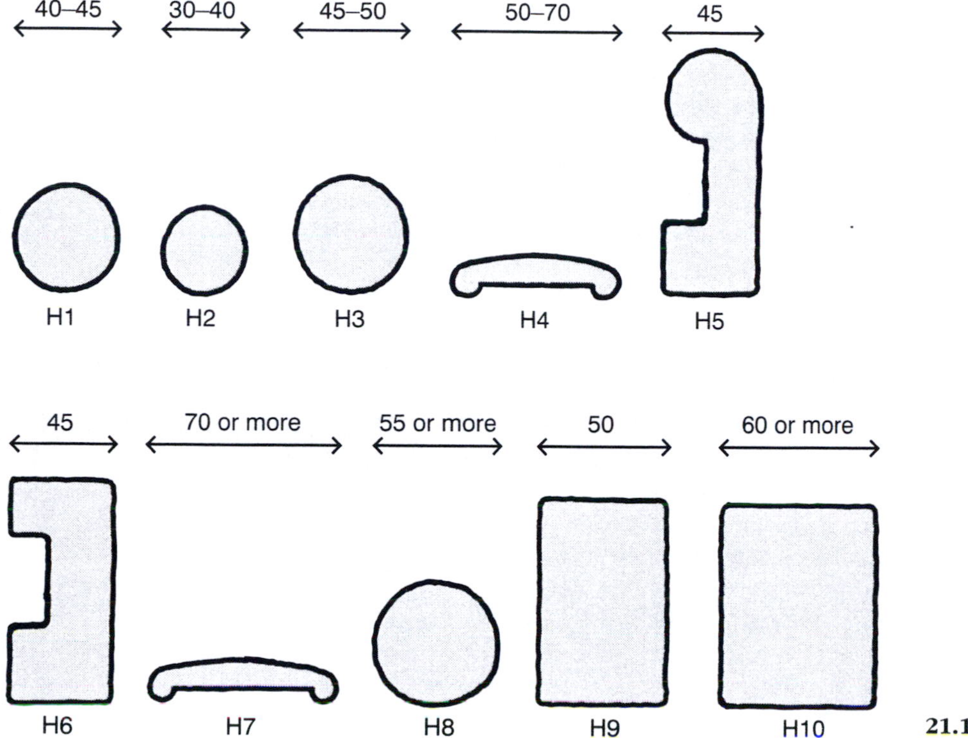

21.1

at a convenient level to assist stair-climbing, not stair-descending. For my retention-of-balance and damage-limitation functional requirements I estimate that the stair-descending rail needs to be at about 1300mm above the line of the nosings, compared with the 900mm for stair-climbing.

The lack of a convenient handrail when I am descending a stairway is significant only in respect of steeply graded stairs, not gently graded stairs where the risk of losing my balance or falling is very much less. As I have noted, I use only my left hand to grasp a handrail. This does not mean that when coming down a steep stairway I prefer to use a rail on the left. Where it is on the left I have to put my left arm forward to hold it, and at the point where it is grasped it is much too low for either retention-of-balance or damage-limitation functions. A rail on the right serves much better. With my left leg leading I descend sideways (or backwards if the stairs are very steep) and can grasp the rail at a point which is much higher and therefore functionally a great deal more suitable.

When I am going up stairs, a handrail at 900mm above the line of the nosings (as advised in the Part M Approved Document[1]) is convenient. If there is no rail on the left, a rail on the right, while being functionally much less suitable, is substantially better than no rail at all. On stairs whose gradient is shallow a leftside rail has a balance-retention function, on stairs which are somewhat steeper it is used for pushing up, and on very steep stairs it is used for pulling up, aided by pressing the lower arm against the rail.

At the head of a flight of stairs, an extension of the lefthand rail some 300mm beyond the nosing of the top step is very important (Figure 21.2a). In this connection, it is more often in other people's homes than public buildings that I encounter problems; where the stairway is steep and the wall turns at the line of the top step, as shown by the broken line in Figure 21.2a and the plan drawing at Figure 21.2b, the handrail (if there is one) finishes short, and where the wall turns I have nothing to press my hand against in order to push myself up and over the top two steps. In either public or domestic buildings, steep and narrow winders make stairways completely unmanageable.

21.2a

At the foot of a flight of stairs, an extension of a normal 900mm-high rail in front of the nosing of the bottom step is of little value; at the bottom step the handrail is a damage-limitation device and my hand, needing to be kept high for body balance, is behind the step riser. The idea I have heard mooted is that an extension of the rail can help blind people to locate the position of the stairs they are about to ascend. I am sceptical; it is not an item mentioned in the Royal National Institute for the Blind's design manual, *Building Sight*[2].

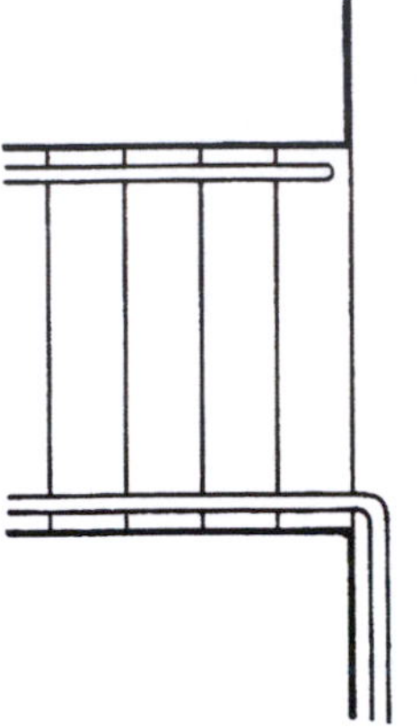

21.2b

The configuration of steps and stairs

In 1997, using my stick as a leg-raising and balance-retaining aid, I can manage a single low step (not higher than about 140mm) that does not have a handrail. As with roadside kerbs, it is a matter of pressing the stick down at a point some way ahead of the step (Figure 21.3a), placing my right leg on the step and then swinging the left leg up and landing it well in front of the right leg so that my balance is retained (Figure 21.3b). This cannot

21.3a

21.3b

21.4

be done where there are two consecutive steps. Where, without a handrail to either left or right, there is a wall surface to the left against which I can brace myself, I can get myself up two or more steps (Figure 21.4). Where there is not, I am confronted by an absolute impediment.

When I am being pushed in a wheelchair a single step does not present the same obstacle as two consecutive steps. My companion presses the foot tipping lever down, tilts the chair and pushes the wheelchair over the step. How high the step can be depends on how strong the pusher is – my wife cannot comfortably manage more than about 130mm.

Consecutive gently graded steps are less tiresome than steep steps. The four steps between the entrance door and the lift at my home have risers 130mm high and treads 395mm deep, and a strong able-bodied man can get me in my wheelchair up or down them without too much strain. I have on occasion been carried up and down a storey-high flight of steps in my wheelchair.

The norm in public buildings is for stairs to be less steeply graded than those in new domestic housing. In houses with a typical floor to floor height of 2600mm and a stairway with 13 steps, the riser height of 200mm is too steep for me to manage without a handrail to both sides. In public buildings I prefer stairways to have solid risers and straight treads. But where a stairway is comfortably graded and has a convenient handrail to both sides, the presence of open risers or splayed treads does not trouble me. Confined spiral staircases can be impossible to manage.

Ramps

When going up or down ramps as an ambulant disabled person I use my stick in my left hand as a balance-retaining aid. Going up a ramp, because there is less risk of tipping over, is a great deal easier than coming down. Except where a ramp is steep – with a gradient more than about 1 in 8 – a handrail does not help me. Where there is a going-down choice between steps with a handrail and a ramp steeper than about 1 in 15, I prefer the steps. Where the going-up choice is between steps and a ramp, I prefer the ramp.

When I am propelling myself in a wheelchair and am on my own I cannot get up any ramp, meaning a surface with an incline, and can get down ramps only where they are relatively short and not steeper than about 1 in 15. The limits are associated with the unusual way that I propel my wheelchair, using the left hand and left foot; on any ramp the chair tends to skew to the right. When I am being pushed, the limits depend on who is doing the pushing – my wife finds it uncomfortable if the gradient is more than about 1 in 15 going up, or 1 in 18 coming down.

On an extended straight ramp where a level platform has been incorporated, I can be disconcerted when I am an ambulant disabled person. Either going up or down, the effect of the platform can be destabilizing if I fail to notice it. Whether I am walking or being pushed in a wheelchair, it is only on long ramps – of the order of 30 metres or more – that I consider a level platform to be helpful. Where platforms have been inserted at intervals along a straight ramp whose total length is no more than about 25 metres, I would have preferred them not to have been there, and to have had instead a continuous ramp to a lesser and more manageable gradient.

Entrances to buildings

Other than where doors open automatically, entrances to public buildings tend not, in my experience, to be free of impediments. The principal irritant is spring-loaded self-closing doors. When I am on my own as an ambulant disabled person I can have difficulty getting through such doors; when I am in a wheelchair on my own someone has to be there to open the door for me; and when I am being pushed by someone else it needs a third person to hold the door open and let us through.

When, as an ambulant disabled person, I am obliged to use a revolving door, I do so with trepidation. The small conventional quadrant-style revolving door is a menace. I wait until there appears to be no one approaching from the other side who is going to barge through at speed and let a door leaf hit me from behind while I am inside. Once inside, there is not enough space for me to manoeuvre comfortably, and I am aware that if I am caught in the rear or otherwise lose my balance I will, in the awkwardly confined space, land in a shattered heap. I need to have a partner in the following quadrant who restrains the revolution of the doors. I am little happier with the large merry-go-round doors which in recent years have been installed at the entrances to shopping malls and other public buildings. They remorselessly chase me when I get inside, and I do not trust them. Commonly, but not always, a revolving door is accompanied by an alternative normal side-hung door which (if it is not locked, which too often it seems to be) I can safely use. But only a straight-sliding (not a launch-out-and hit-me) automatic opening door is, on my terms, barrier-free.

Single steps at shop entrances

In shopping streets a common practice is for internal floor levels of shops to be some four to ten inches above the level of the adjacent pavement, with a single step to each shop and the entrance door set at the face of the step. When I need to use such shops there is an impediment in my way, whether I am ambulant disabled or a wheelchair user. To negotiate a single high step when I am an ambulant disabled person I need, in order to pull myself up and over, to have a side wall against which I can brace myself or a suitably placed rail which I can grasp with my left hand. Were there to be a short vertical rail on the front wall in line with the face of the step I would not be helped; a rail, if it is to serve my purpose, must be fixed some 500 to 700mm beyond the face of the step. The illustrative analogy here is the standard London taxi which has a variety of grabrails but not one that I can use to pull myself in. At single-step shops an absolute impediment occurs when the in-opening door has been opened and there is nothing solid for me to push or pull against so that I can get in. When I am in a wheelchair this impediment is relatively less troublesome; with the door held open I can, if the step is not too high, be pushed up and over it.

I consider a related shop entrance arrangement. The entrance door is set back from the shop façade, with a single-step platform in front of it. This as a rule is not difficult to manage, whether I am ambulant disabled or in a wheelchair. Where the trouble occurs is when some well-meaning body, imagining that he is assisting the cause of access for the disabled, has arranged for the platform to be removed and a ramp put in its place. Either way I lose. If I am an ambulant disabled person I can get up the ramp well enough. But when I leave the shop it may be perilously steep to walk down. If I am in a wheelchair the paramount rule for wheelchair access has been broken. To get through any door comfortably in a wheelchair, either in self-propelled or being-pushed mode, there has to be a level platform in front of the door. If instead there is a steep ramp there is a problem, exacerbated when it comes to getting out of the shop and descending the ramp, either forwards or backwards.

Entrance lobbies

Two-door entrance lobbies to buildings are not as a rule an impediment when I am ambulant. In a wheelchair they can be, particularly where manoeuvring space is restricted and a turn is involved. Those that I find most troublesome tend to be in small ground-floor restaurants. But with a willing waiter to help hump the wheelchair to and fro, a third person to hold the door open, and the removal, if necessary, of the projecting leg-rest, I have always been able to get through.

My perceptions of 'accessible' building entrances

As a wheelchair user, I have my own assessments as to what constitutes an 'accessible' entrance to a public building. Provision made at an entrance to a building may happen to be in accord with advice set out in some official design guidance manual – and is therefore technically deemed by others to constitute accessibility – but that does not mean I have to agree that it suits me. To my mind the only building entrances that are properly wheelchair-accessible are those which are principal entrances for visitors, where there is a level approach, and where, either self-propelled or pushed, it is a simple matter to pass through the entrance and into the main body of the building.

I do not regard as 'accessible' a building whose main entrance is some two metres or so above the adjoining street level, and where an extended open-to-the-elements ramp has been built in compliance with official guidance. Nor do I consider spiral ramps, ones which can cause the wheelchair to veer off course, to be 'accessible'. I do not regard a long hike round to a goods entrance at the back of the building as giving me proper accessibility, and nor do I consider that a special platform lift, either usable independently or for the operation of which someone inside the building has to be found, to be a decent way of getting into a building. In short, I wish, as a wheelchair user, to be treated as a normal person and with dignity. I acknowledge, however, that a contrivance which permits me to get into a building without my having to be carried in bodily in my wheelchair is better than nothing.

Circulation within buildings

Within public buildings the space in circulation areas and passageways does not as a rule present problems. In department stores, away from primary circulation routes, the space between and around merchandise displays, particularly portable clothes racks, can be too tight for wheelchair manoeuvre. And china displays can be at risk when I am driving a scooter.

Problems can come where a change of floor level in an existing building involves two or three steps, and a removable ramp has been placed over the steps to help wheelchair users. When I am an ambulant disabled person the ramp can be too steep for me to walk down comfortably, and the space left on the sides too narrow for me to use the steps (Figure 21.5). Where there is sufficient space, or where a fixed ramp has been provided alongside the steps, I am handicapped if there is no handrail to the steps.

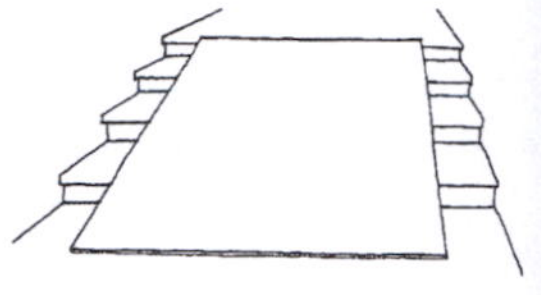

21.5

Floor surfaces

When I am pushing myself around in my wheelchair within a building, carpeting can be tiresome. The smoother the floor surface is, the better – the ideal is polished marble. Similarly, when my wife is pushing me, a carpet, particularly one with a deep soft pile, makes for heavy going. As an ambulant disabled person, I am always aware that I may trip and fall. If I do so on a solid surface, be it concrete, quarry tile, terrazzo or whatever, I injure myself. On carpet I do not, or nothing like as severely.

Doors inside buildings

Within public buildings, self-closing doors are not usually as heavily spring-loaded as those at building entrances. They are not therefore such an impediment in my way, although it less often happens that there is someone at hand to hold them open for me when I am on my own in my wheelchair. The really troublesome double doors are those that swing one way only and where a single leaf, when open, is not wide enough to get a wheelchair through. I cannot easily, as some wheelchair users do, strike my wheelchair against the doorplate of a door and push through it. Within buildings, the double doors that I prefer, fire controls permitting, are those that swing both ways – the technique is to push the left-hand leaf slightly open, and then to pull the right-hand leaf across in front of my wheelchair.

As a rule, I am unconcerned whether a door has a lever or a knob handle. In public buildings the matter is commonly irrelevant, the norm being that in public areas a towards-opening door has a D handle and an away-opening door a pushplate. Where a spring-loaded door has to be pulled or pushed open by turning the latch handle, I find it marginally easier if it is a lever rather than a knob.

When I am in a wheelchair, the opening of in-opening single doors is facilitated where there is clear wall space to the side of the door handle. It is preferable if it is of the order of 800mm, as shown in Figure 21.6a; where it is only 300mm wide (as advised in some design codes) the manoeuvre is much more awkward (Figure 21.6b). Where there is no space to the side

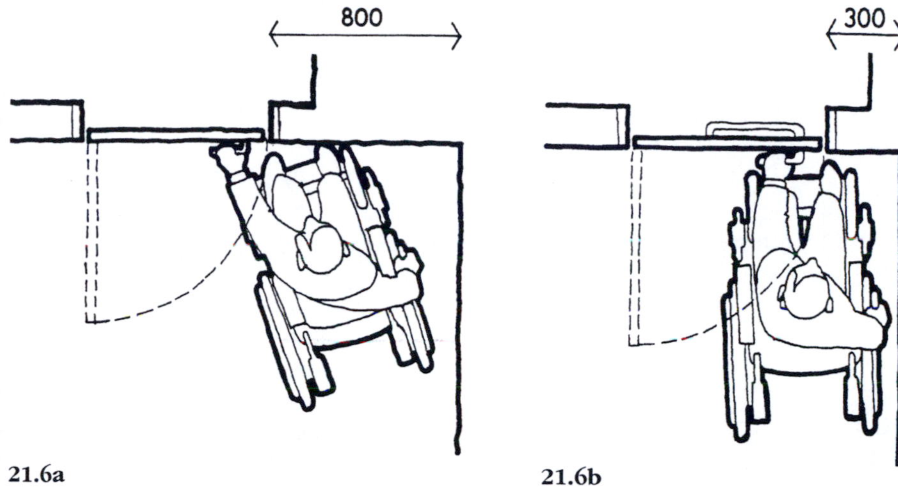

21.6a **21.6b**

(as, for example, when I open the entrance door to my flat from the inside) I am, however, able to reach out with my left arm, turn the latch, pull the door open, reverse the wheelchair and pass through.

Door hazards

A feature of my disability condition is that I can be destabilized when standing or moving – it needs only a small prod from in front to tip me over backwards. In any public building I am at risk when I approach a door that opens towards me – the hazard is that an unseen person on the other side will open it sharply and bang it into me. This has occurred on numerous occasions, but because I am careful I have always stayed upright. By being careful I mean that I set myself in a secure walking or standing position so that I will not be pushed over; this is a circumstance, like walking across cobbles, where a hazard is minimized if one is alert to it. To guard against hazards, the customary advice is that doors should have glazed panels. This may serve well enough in straight passage circulation areas. Elsewhere people will approach doors from one side or the other and will not see a person approaching on the other side; in such circumstances, glazed panels are of limited value.

For reasons discussed earlier, I advocate out-opening doors to wc compartments in public toilets. The notion that such doors could, when opened, be a fearsome hazard to people happening to be passing outside can be dismissed. As architects would realise if they were to check typical toilet plan drawings, passing-outside-the-door traffic is usually a non-event.

Lifts

Lift technology having much improved in recent years, I am not now worried that a bumpy landing might unbalance me, and a handrail in the lift car is superfluous. There is still a regular need to check, when the lift has stopped, that its floor is precisely aligned with the threshold – on a few occasions when it has not done so I have tripped and fallen over the upstand.

When as an ambulant disabled person I am using a lift in a public building, the impediment that I regularly encounter is not related to my polio-caused disability but to my visual impairment. I wear spectacles for reading and office work, but not when I am outside or moving around buildings. On entering a lift I frequently find that I am disabled. The basic information I must be able to read in order to use the lift is illegible. The numbers and letters for the activator buttons are small, indistinct, uniformly colour-uncontrasted, or, where marginally incised in the same neutral tone as the panel face, are obscure. I have to dig in my pocket, extract my spectacle case, open it, get the spectacles out and put them on my nose. Or, if there is not time to do all that, I stab a button and trust that I have hit the right one. On occasion I am additionally insulted. To demonstrate how genuinely concerned he is to help handicapped people, the well-meaning person responsible for signage in the lift has planted braille indicators for the benefit of the one lift user in 100 000 or so who is blind, unaccompanied, can locate the controls and knows how to read braille.

When I am using a lift in a public building an impediment I regularly encounter as a wheelchair user is that there is not enough room to turn around inside. Admittedly a common obstacle is the other people who are occupying the lift, but it is rare in Britain – by contrast with America where spacious lifts seem to be the norm – to come across a lift that is large enough to turn a standard wheelchair around, let alone a scooter. Where a lift is small, my preferred manoeuvre is to reverse my wheelchair in and propel it out forwards. If I have to reverse out I cannot see where I am going. The hazard, potentially more alarming when I am driving a scooter, is that someone else's feet will be in the way as I move out. It is in recently constructed multi-storey shopping centres in Britain, heavily pushchair-populated as they are, that I am most irritated by the inadequate size of lifts.

The location of lift controls

In lifts of all shapes and sizes, there is no single position for the location of controls that assuredly will suit me when I am in a wheelchair. When I am on my own and there is no one to help – a situation which rarely occurs in public buildings – I can usually find a way of getting at the controls, and it matters not whether they are low down at around 1200mm or high up at around 1600mm. As I noted earlier with regard to discrimination (page 63), I do not applaud the practice of placing lift controls at low level to suit wheelchair users. Nor, relatedly, do I like to see lift controls arrayed horizontally; a lift goes up and down, not sideways, and it is simple common sense for controls to be arranged vertically. In circumstances where it is reasonable for special provision to be made for independent wheelchairs, there could be a horizontal set of controls to supplement the normal vertical set.

I note a disabling feature of lift controls which is unrelated to my disability. Inside a lift, it can happen that, as the doors begin to close, a person on the outside is seen attempting to reach the lift and get inside. There is an urgent search for the door-open button, but before it is found the doors are shut. The relevant issue is good manners in the design of buildings and their facilities. A door shut in someone's face is a discourtesy, one that might commonly be avoided were it standard practice for lift manufacturers to identify the door-open button clearly, for example by placing it on a distinctive yellow panel. The safety factor is also relevant; such provision could reduce the risk of someone such as myself being knocked over by a fast-closing lift door.

Historically accustomed as I have been to quietude inside lifts in public buildings, I confess that I can be irritated by the intrusive disembodied voice which now insists on telling me which way the lift is going and where it has got to. But I recognise that the performance can be helpful for building users generally, not only blind and sight-impaired people.

Escalators

During my maximally mobile years I regularly used escalators in public buildings, both for going up and coming down. I only once had a fall, a backwards fall on an up-moving escalator which caused consternation in the vicinity but did not damage me. There came a time when I would use down-moving escalators only where the level sector at the top was relatively extended before the steps formed, giving me time to secure my balance. Today I would never attempt to use a down-moving escalator, but I can comfortably manage those that are up-moving.

Toilet facilities

A common starting impediment in the way of my using toilets in public buildings is a steep flight of stairs without a convenient handrail. Where there is no such barrier, the obstacles which may follow will not as a rule be troublesome, the reason being associated with the business that I am undertaking. The sitting-down function is almost invariably accomplished at home. On more than ninety-five occasions in a hundred it is only the standing-up elimination function that I perform in public toilets. Urinal bowls are no problem, and nor are stalls that have level access. Stall urinals on a high platform can be difficult for me to manage. Wc compartments are, however, always available as an alternative. With regard to facilities when we travel on long journeys by car, I have, as a man, the advantage that I can use a convenient open-air venue by the roadside. When I am a wheelchair user, I can take a urine bottle with me.

For the sitting-down function, a normal wc compartment in a public toilet facility in Britain is not manageable when I am a wheelchair user because of the in-opening door. I am unconcerned whether the wc in a toilet that I use is corbel or pedestal. I do not like a very low seat and nor, for straight functional reasons, do I like a high seat. The seat height that I prefer is in the range 420 to 450mm. A typical wc, principally on account of its in-opening door and the restricted space that it gives me, can also be awkward to use when I am an ambulant disabled person, particularly where it is narrow and has a low seat. The higher the seat, the easier the manoeuvre. When I push off a low seat, I need space to the side to swivel and swing my right leg round; a wc compartment narrower than 750mm in conjunction with a seat height lower than 380mm can be uncomfortably difficult to manage and impossible where it has no cistern whose top surface I can press on in order to push up.

When I am a wheelchair user and an unlocked for-the-disabled unisex facility is available I can, if need be, use it for the standing-up function. With my wheelchair placed in front of the wc bowl (a manoeuvre which can be difficult to accomplish inside a typical BS5810-type wc compartment owing to the need to shunt) I push up and stand with my weight on one leg. But the procedure is a good deal more troublesome than using a bowl urinal. I prefer therefore to use adjacent normal male toilet facilities where they are wheelchair-accessible. The customary finding is that they are not, on account of the impossibility of getting the wheelchair through the confined approach lobby with its two doors.

Special for-the-disabled toilet facilities

As a wheelchair user I have observed the contrast between the accessibility of normal public toilet facilities in America and Britain. In America the universal practice is for provision for disabled people to be incorporated as normal in every public facility, and I find that the standard arrangement, small though it may be, is convenient for me. In Britain, with its normal facilities not being wheelchair-accessible, I feel I am discriminated against. The standard special for-the-disabled product is the BS5810-type toilet, often kept locked and accessible only with a RADAR key. There are three reasons why I do not as a rule take my key with me when I use public buildings. First, because it is bulky – its length is 99mm and its width 49mm. Second, because I do not like its image – the idea that toilets suitable for disabled people have to be kept locked and that their use should be restricted to authorised club members. Third, because I prefer to use normal and not special toilet facilities, and do not wish to be obliged to use a special for-the-disabled unisex toilet; in this connection, I recognise that as a man I can afford to be more obstinate than a woman could be.

The BS5810-type toilet

I report my experiences of using BS5810-type toilets as an independent wheelchair user and a scooter user. The first impediment is the out-opening door. I can drive forwards through it, but having done so it is virtually impossible to close it behind me if I am in a wheelchair, and absolutely impossible if I am using a scooter. Once inside, there is not enough space to turn my wheelchair and nowhere near enough to turn a scooter. Where the facility has been designed precisely in accord with BS5810 specifications the important horizontal side rail is set too far from the wc for me to use it as an aid for pushing up to a standing position; the matter is not, however, critical since I can push with my left hand on the wc seat to raise myself to a standing position. Where the rail is close enough, it suits me at the recommended height of 250mm above the wc seat. On account of the nature of the muscle weaknesses in my legs I cannot raise myself from a seated to a standing position by grasping a vertical rail and pulling up. Where a diagonal rail has been fixed it suits me not at all; it serves neither for pushing up nor pulling up.

An irritating feature that I seem to find too often in BS5810-type toilets is a wc seat that, when raised, does not hold in the upright position, a common cause being that the rear horizontal rail has been set too far forwards. As I have noted, my wc business is virtually always performed standing up, and, one-handed as I am, I cannot at the same time hold the seat out of the way. I like, as in a BS5810-type toilet, to have a wash-hand basin within reach when I am seated on the wc, though it is no more necessary in a wheelchair-accessible toilet than any other. Where the flush handle to the wc is placed is not a matter which troubles me.

Hotels

In my experience – and, I suspect, that of many other severely disabled people – hotels have a unique and special status among all public building types with regard to their accessibility. The reason is that other public buildings serve *visiting* purposes only; they are places which disabled people need to get into and around, use customer services and use the public toilets where they are provided. Hotels, as places to stay in for a night or more, serve *living* as well as visiting purposes.

The livability factor

In public buildings where visitability is the only concern, the impediments that I encounter may be troublesome but are not usually intolerable. There are theatres in London that I cannot use when I am in a wheelchair; some are listed historic buildings which cannot be made accessible, and I accept that they are out of bounds. My wife and I can go to other theatres which are wheelchair-accessible. A department store that I am in when I am driving a shopmobility scooter may have areas that are barred on account of steps, but other shops and stores are wholly accessible. When I am ambulant disabled and we are on holiday and looking for a bar or restaurant, we may reject the first that we see because the toilets are not accessible. Other places will be more convenient.

Hotels, on account of the livability factor, are a different matter. Except when we know that a hotel we have booked really is accessible, we travel hopefully. When I am in a wheelchair I need, when I stay at hotels, to be able to manage independently in the bedroom and bathroom. We may have checked in advance and been told that we shall have an accessible room with an accessible bathroom, but when we arrive we may find we do not. As a rule, we have no alternative – there is nowhere else to go to.

Back in 1961 when my work in the field of designing for the disabled began, no one in the world, I believe, had incorporated any specially designed and equipped guestrooms for disabled people in a hotel serving business people or tourists. The idea was developed in America during the late 1960s and early 1970s, and spread to Europe, initially to Sweden and then to Britain in the late 1970s. During the 1980s when I travelled as an ambulant disabled person on professional business, the reasonable expectation was that hotels where I would be staying would have a lift, and if on occasion they did not, I would be able without difficulty to manage the stairs. I did not ask for a 'special for the disabled' room.

Today when I travel, either as an ambulant disabled person or as a wheelchair user, I prefer to be assured that the hotel is disabled-accessible. Since 1989, whether on professional business or on holiday, I have on most occasions travelled with my wife. We check through guidebooks, select a hotel rated disabled-accessible, telephone to make a reservation and are assured that all will be well. In Britain, and when on holiday in Europe, we are frequently disappointed.

Britain and France: the different brands

I distinguish four brands of hotel to be found in Britain and France:

1 The elderly hotel on different levels which has been extended, adapted and uprated, and which never did – and never could – provide convenient accommodation for people in wheelchairs.
2 A similar, though perhaps less elderly, hotel where the management, aware that suitable provision for disabled visitors is a marketing plus, has identified one or more rooms the approach to which can be ramped, and whose bathrooms can be given a wider door and dressed up with grabrails.
3 A long-established hotel whose principal public rooms are wheelchair-accessible and to which has been added a ground floor extension incorporating purpose-designed rooms for disabled visitors, or where there is a lift to accessible rooms which have been refurbished.
4 A hotel recently built by one of the management chains to a standard house style, with one or more 'special for the disabled' guestrooms incorporated.

Our experience is that even hotels of the first brand can claim in guidebooks that they have facilities for the handicapped. Hotels of the second brand can be annoying. An allegedly accessible guestroom may have been contrived, but at the same time wheelchair access to public rooms may be barred by steps or stairs or, when I am an ambulant disabled person, by steps or stairs without handrails. Variants of this brand are hotels where there is a detached single-storey building with special rooms for the disabled in the grounds of the hotel, usually involving a hazardous walk when I am ambulant disabled, or, when I am in a wheelchair, an awkward push to the main building, made more uncomfortable if it is raining. Hotels of the third brand, to be found in our experience more often in France than in England, are those that tend to suit us best. Hotels in England of the fourth brand can make us angry.

In England there seems to be a common pattern to hotels of the fourth brand. Commissioned by one or other of the major hotel companies, they have been designed by their architects on the basis of a structural grid and a common shell size for all guestrooms. 'Special for the disabled' rooms are laid out and equipped within the same space constraints as 'regular' rooms; either they were designed for the purpose when the hotel was built, or at some stage existing rooms were restructured. The outcome, compared with regular rooms, is that for-the-disabled rooms have a larger bathroom and a smaller bedroom area. This upsets the bed layout. Without enough space around a large double bed or twin freestanding beds, the solution is either two single beds, one of which is stuck tightly against a side wall, or one single bed along with a settee that has a pull-out mattress. A single bed, it seems, is what hotel companies suppose any disabled person wants to have.

In respect of relatively new major-company hotels in England, my wife and I have learnt from experience that when I am in a wheelchair we are often as well suited by regular rooms as by those that are 'for the disabled'. The main entrance door is always wide enough, and the bedroom area, because it is larger, is more conveniently manageable. The only important requirement is to be able to get the wheelchair through the bathroom door.

America

The contrast is with what happens in America. The norm for a hotel in America is a recently constructed fully accessible multi-storey building, with motels having ground floor rooms which are wheelchair-accessible. In 1993, with myself in a wheelchair, we spent a week in Washington and then a week travelling through Virginia and North Carolina. Only one of the hotels at which we stayed had blemishes. Built before the days of special provision, space in its adapted room was too tight for comfort, and to get to the breakfast room there were steps. Elsewhere there was comprehensive wheelchair accessibility. Set against the confined bedroom space in typical British or French hotels, the guestrooms in recently built American hotels are expansive. With an en-suite bathroom the norm for a regular room is two double beds; for a 'handicapped' room within the same overall area the bathroom is larger and the bedroom has a single king-size bed. That suited my wife and myself very well.

In the hotel where we stayed at Rockville outside Washington we had a 'handicapped' room (Figure 21.7), whose shell size, 3.81 × 8.33m, was the same as that of regular rooms alongside. The comparison is with British practice, illustrated by for-the-disabled guestrooms in some hotels, for example, as shown in Figure 21.8, where within a shell size of 3.6 × 6.0m there is a single freestanding bed and a settee with a pull-out mattress[3]. The accessible room layout advised in the approved document to the Part M building regulation (Figure 21.9), showing two single beds, one being against a side wall, is also within a shell size of 3.6 × 6.0m[4].

A hotel guestroom of the kind shown in Figure 21.8 caters well for independent wheelchair users who do not have a spouse with them. But

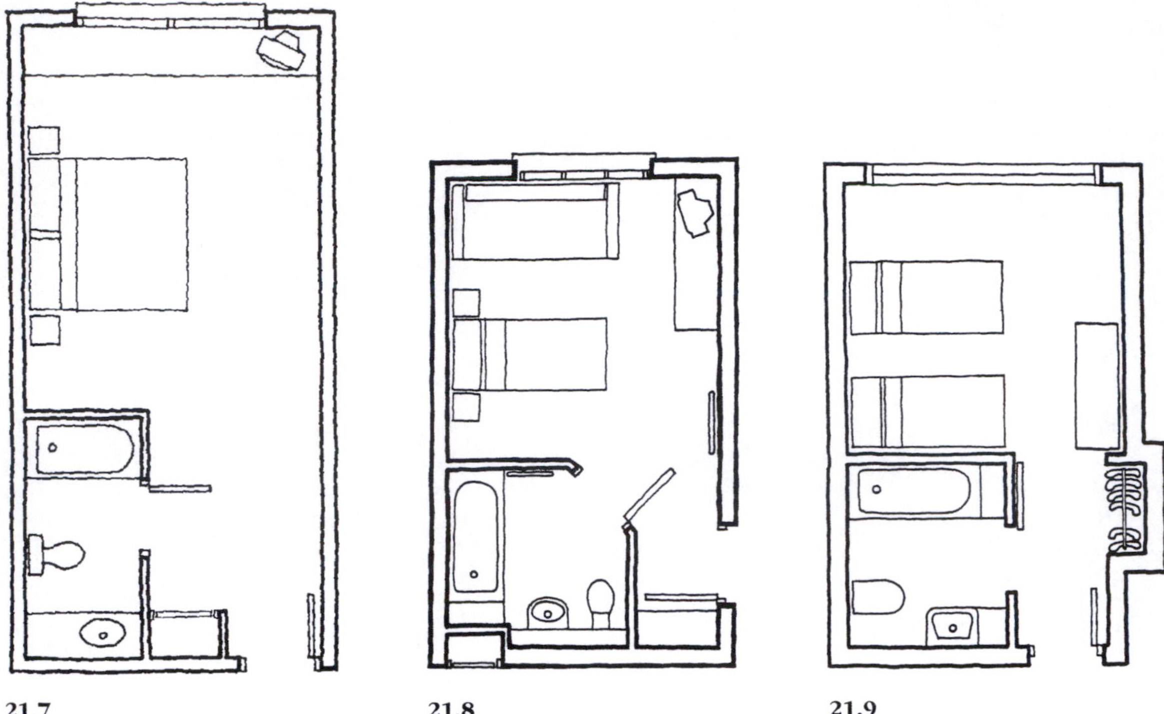

21.7 **21.8** **21.9**

when I am in a wheelchair it does not suit my wife and I, and nor does any other for-the-disabled guestroom which has a shell size of 3.6 × 6.0m. Its overall area, $21.6m^2$, does not afford convenience; by comparison, the Rockville room, with an area of $31.7m^2$, is 47 per cent larger.

Personal hygiene facilities in hotel guestrooms

During my maximally mobile years I could, when staying at hotels in Britain and Europe, manage any bath that I happened to come across. Using the side rim (not a grabrail where one was fitted, because it was invariably too high, or inconveniently located) I could push myself up from a reclining to a standing position. In the following phase, which lasted some 12 years, I could still do so, but only – and this was vital – if on the floor of the bath I had a suction mat that I could grip with my feet.

It is uncommon in hotels in England for a suction mat to be provided in bathrooms, and often for none to be found when requested. That bath users might be at risk of destabilisation is, however, acknowledged. On the bottom of the bath there is commonly a patch of dimples, a gesture described in promotional literature as a non-slip surface. For other bath users they may have some merit, but for me they are worthless – there is no way that anyone can produce an ordinary bath with a surface that is comfortable to lie on, is easy to clean and which will at the same time prevent me slipping when I attempt to get out.

Following the August 1993 fracture I could no longer push myself off the bottom of the bath we have at home, or any other bath. At hotels the only option is now a shower. I prefer it to be associated with the bath, not in a compartment on its own. Where it is on its own there is nothing that the architect can do by way of providing a tip-up seat, a variable-height shower appliance, grabrails or whatever which will make it a more attractive facility for me than a suitable shower allied with a bath. With a portable seat across the bath and a hand-held shower, I can sit down, reach for the shower and spray myself. With a suction mat on the floor of the bath, I can push up, stand and use the shower in a fixed position. I can half-fill the bath with hot water and wash myself with soap and flannel – being one-handed, I cannot soap myself while using a hand-held shower. A feature we occasionally find in 'for the disabled' hotel bathrooms in England is a platform at the head end of the bath; it is not of any use to me, though it may be for others. Also on occasion we find that the wc has a very high seat, which I do not need and my wife does not like.

The sculptured freestanding wash basin fixture often still in place in English hotel bathrooms I regard as an impediment not because I am disabled, but because it does not cater for the need, which only a desktop basin will serve, of setting out all the personal artefacts of bathroom usage. In special for-the-disabled hotel bathrooms where the controlling consideration has been provision suitable for wheelchair users, a feature we have sometimes found has been a wash-hand basin set at lower than normal level. For my wife, who spends more time at the basin than I do, it can be uncomfortable and back-aching. I do not like it because it does not suit her, and also because when I am in a wheelchair I can comfortably manage a basin at normal level, one with the rim at around 820mm above floor level.

Hotels: conference and leisure facilities

Hotels have frequently been the venue for conferences and meetings on disability topics that I have attended over the years. In Britain there are few that serve well when there are numerous delegates in wheelchairs, and even fewer that do so economically for disabled people who pay their own way. Where hotel conferences are arranged by disability organizations and a substantial number of wheelchair users attend, there are two predictable occurrences. One is that the bedroom accommodation in the hotel suitable for wheelchair users will be insufficient. The other is that between conference sessions the public toilet provision accessible to wheelchair users will not satisfy the demand.

As an ambulant disabled person I have on occasion used hotel swimming pools in Britain and America, but not as often as I would have wished. As a rule they are of the rectangular tank variety, with ladder access only. It is rare to find one with comfortably graded steps and a convenient handrail I can use to get into it. I would wish also to sit in the jacuzzi now commonly provided alongside the pool, but nowhere yet in Britain have I found one I can manage.

Other building types

Pubs, bars, cafes and restaurants

Subject to a step at the entrance, the drinking and eating areas of a typical English pub are commonly disabled-accessible. Not so the public toilets: they may be downstairs in the basement, out through a yard at the back or, if on the level, unreachable with a wheelchair. In France and other European countries there are bars around the town square. Outside if not inside, the tables for eating and drinking have a level approach. But the toilets commonly do not; on occasion in French towns we have needed to check their location before deciding which bar to patronise.

At cafes and restaurants where chairs and tables are not fixed and which are busy when we arrive (or leave) it commonly happens when I am in a wheelchair that there is an upheaval of other customers and their chairs. This is invariably done with great good humour. My wife and I are not regular customers at fast-food establishments such as McDonalds. A merit of any McDonalds is, however, that it will assuredly have a disabled-accessible toilet.

Shops and shopmobility

As a disabled person I have benefited in recent years from the widespread development of covered shopping malls. The shops within them are not obstructed by ice or snow, and getting into them does not as a rule involve struggling with heavy spring-loaded entrance doors. And more excitingly, I have benefited from shopmobility schemes, of which there are now (1997) about 150 across Britain. Both when I am ambulant and non-ambulant, but more significantly when I am a non-ambulant wheelchair user, shopmobility is liberating and life-enhancing, and a blessing for my wife. It is a struggle for her to push my wheelchair when it is heavily loaded with me in it, and lifting it in and out of the car boot is always potentially back-damaging. The scheme we have used most often is the one at Kingston-on-Thames, located on the top level of a carpark near the town centre. I telephone beforehand to book a scooter. When we arrive, it is brought to the car, I push out of my seat, stand and swivel on one leg, and transfer into it. I push the throttle and off we go, down the lift to the covered shopping mall, through the streets and around the market. My wife is unencumbered because the scooter has a large basket into which coats, umbrellas and the goods we have purchased can be thrust.

Elsewhere I have been a shopmobility customer in some twenty-five other towns in England and Wales. I note Wales because Cardiff has been particularly rewarding, with its extensive pedestrianised area in the city centre, its excellent shopping facilities, its Victorian covered market and its historic arcades.

Supermarkets

Until the late 1980s it was customary for aisles and most of the check-out points to be just wide enough for shopping trolleys to pass through. One or two check-out positions were given a wider passageway, signposted with the access symbol and labelled 'for wheelchair users'. Pleasingly the standard practice for new supermarkets now seems to be for all check-out points to be wheelchair-accessible, and for aisles throughout supermarkets to be much more spacious than they once were.

Banks

When I returned to London from Norwich in 1969 I needed to transfer my bank account. The Midland Bank nearest to the Architectural Press in Queen Anne's Gate was in Victoria Street. It was new and functional, with a forbidding security screen across the counter. Down the road I looked at the bank in the Central Hall building opposite Westminster Abbey. It was grand, with a stone staircase, a patterned quarry tile floor and no security screen. I liked it. A few months later, the obligatory security screen was installed and then, more sadly, the floor was covered in carpet. But twenty-seven years later my account is still there. As an ambulant disabled person, I continue to climb the stairs to get there.

Known technically as ATMs (Automatic Telling Machines), help-yourself cashpoints outside and inside banks do not present problems when I am a wheelchair user. In street environments I cannot manage my wheelchair independently and am always accompanied. That does not mean that I always ask my partner to fetch money for me, but when I am out in the car with my wife and we stop outside a bank it is simpler if she gets out to operate the machine.

Theatres and cinemas

Over the years that I have been a disabled person my visits to theatres have invariably been with a companion, in recent years always my wife. In terms of building impediments, the same considerations that affect our visits to theatres apply when we go to a cinema, a concert, the opera or a ballet. I report first my experiences as an ambulant disabled person when using theatres.

For three reasons we always ask for stalls seats. The first is access within the theatre to the auditorium; there are usually fewer steps to negotiate on the way to stalls than circle seats, and while, in many London theatres, there are stairs on the route to the auditorium, there is always a handrail to both sides of them. The second and more important reason is the configuration of seating. I wear a brace on my right leg, and space is needed for the leg to be comfortable. In stalls seats there is normally space for my foot below the seat in front (Figure 21.10a), whereas in tiered circle seats my foot is wedged against the back of the seat in front (Figure 21.10b). It helps if my seat is at the end of a row with an aisle on the side to the right, and, whether in stalls or circle seats, I can find it difficult to push up to let others pass in front of me. The third reason is that tiered circle seats may be approached by steep steps with no handrail to either side; with a supporting shoulder in front of me I can get down, but I may not be able to get up.

When I am a wheelchair user, the special provision may be in the form of a wheelchair pen, the demerit of which is that I may be detached from

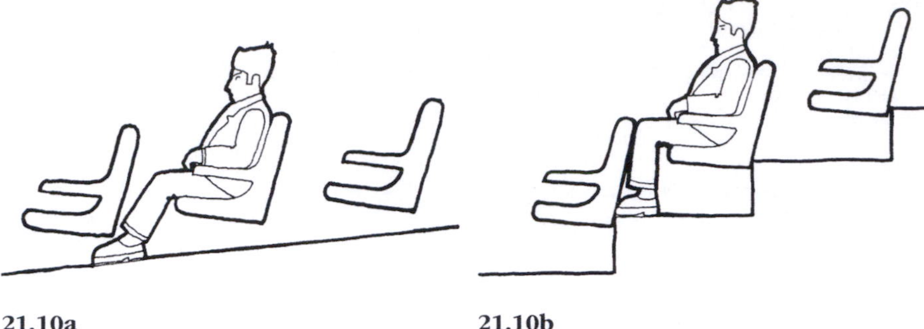

21.10a **21.10b**

my wife. My related experiences in America have been pleasing. On two occasions with myself in a wheelchair, my wife and I have been to shows in a tiered auditorium. On both, access for wheelchair users was by lift to the top of the auditorium, and we sat together.

As a disabled person I have never had cause to use back-stage facilities in theatre buildings. At conferences in lecture halls or theatre-type buildings there have been occasions when I have, in a wheelchair, had to be carried up the steps to reach the stage. I prefer this to finding that a hazardously steep temporary ramp has been specially constructed.

With cinemas we are not normally restricted to a single venue. When a new film is released, the choice of which cinema we go to is determined principally by car parking convenience; in this regard, new multiplex cinemas in shopping centres or out-of-town locations are attractive. Neither as an ambulant disabled person nor as a wheelchair user am I much concerned that certain central London cinemas are effectively out of bounds.

Art galleries

When as a wheelchair user I go to art galleries, the discrimination to which I can be subjected is not of a brand that the architect – or anyone else – can mitigate. Pictures are properly hung at the eye level of standing people, and if the gallery is crowded there are, as there are not when I am ambulant, bodies blocking the view. In many public galleries a valuable service is the availability of loan wheelchairs, and an interesting problem occurs when the chair is not one I can propel myself. Does the person who is doing the pushing decide which pictures we should look at and for how long, or do I? Compromises are in order.

Public swimming pools

In Norwich during the late 1960s my regular Sunday morning occupation was to ferry handicapped people to the Aylsham Road swimming pool for the once-a-week special session organized by the local swimming club for the handicapped, and to go swimming myself. Aside from being enjoyable, swimming was a good means of keeping the bits of me on which I relied for mobility in operational order. On my return to London in 1969 I did not join any swimming club for the handicapped. My Sunday morning outings, with two small sons who were delighted to go along with me, were to normal public sessions at swimming pools in and around London. In the early 1970s waves and beaches were unheard of; swimming pools were rectangular tanks, with vertical ladders for getting in and out. I was able then to climb the ladders, but there came a time when, with legs weakened by fractures, I could no longer do so.

The pleasing happening came in 1983. Down the road from my flat in Battersea the Victorian bathhouse on the Latchmere Road had been demolished and a new leisure centre, designed in Wandsworth borough architect's department, had been built in its place. Inside was a splendid new swimming pool which could not have been bettered had it been specifically designed to suit me. I reported the building in a 1987 issue of *Design for Special Needs*[5]. The pool has a shelving beach which, graded at 1 in 13 for compatibility with the action of the wave machine, I can comfortably walk down with support from the conveniently placed side rail. On the male changing side there is a special for-the-disabled toilet and changing room which I never use; aside from being overtly discriminatory, it is small and does not have a changing bench. I prefer the communal changing area which has long seat benches of the kind that I need when dressing; I could not, for example, manage in a dressing cubicle having a small tip-up seat as advised in the 1992 Part M approved document[6]. The communal showering area has a level access floor laid to a fall; it suits me as well as would any 'special for the disabled' shower compartment such as that advised in the approved document[7].

Sports stadia

Through the late 1970s when my two sons were addicted to football I travelled regularly with them to football league and cup games around London. I was then more mobile than I am now, though there were occasions when the steep concrete steps to reach our seats on high terraces were difficult to manage. As a disabled spectator I recall not being able to see the action when the fans in front of me, excited by what was happening, rose in unison from their seats. I have not been to a football stadium since 1983, or a sports stadium of any other kind.

Court buildings

In October 1988, when I happened to be a wheelchair user, I was summoned to attend a coroner's court, having witnessed a fatal road accident some weeks earlier. The courtroom was on the upper level of an old building, with a steep dogleg staircase leading to it. Two policemen carried my wheelchair with me in it up the stairs, and two hours later down the stairs. The toilet outside the courtroom was not wheelchair-accessible, but I had no urge to use it while I was there.

The doctor and dentist

My general practitioner holds his surgeries in a single-storey purpose-designed health centre which, although I have used it only as an ambulant disabled person, is entirely wheelchair-accessible. My dentist used to have a first-floor consulting room, approached from the waiting room on the ground floor by two flights of stairs. His premises were in a terrace of listed historic buildings and, with steps at the entrance, the building could not be made wheelchair-accessible. Through the years I went to see him there I was, on all occasions, an ambulant disabled person. In September 1996 he transferred his surgery to a building with level access at the entrance and a lift to his consulting room.

Polling stations

I have never been a wheelchair user when I have voted at the polling station in Battersea. With one low step the building is, however, wheelchair-accessible. Were I more severely handicapped I would ask for a postal vote; I do not regard the physical accessibility of polling stations as an important matter.

Historic houses, churches and monuments

The historic built heritage of Britain and Europe affords pleasures that America cannot equal. In my schooldays in Derbyshire I bicycled out at weekends to see towns, villages, churches and historic houses. When I became disabled the pleasures were undiminished, and in the early years there was little that could defeat me. I recall a day some 15 years ago when I climbed the steep spiral stairs to the turrets of Conway Castle. A crunch point came in June 1989 when much of the papal palace at Avignon proved to be a no-go area. In 1995 I continue with my wife to enjoy visiting castles, churches, cathedrals and historic houses, but the scope of my explorations is limited. I shall not again, for example, climb the stairs to the chapter house in Wells Cathedral. And in country houses that we visit I shall often find myself keeping to the ground floor.

On occasion I go to churches to participate in services of worship, and some five or six times a year I go to a church because a relative or friend is being married, or because someone I have known has died. On more frequent occasions I visit churches because I like looking at them. The medieval churches of England normally present no access problems, and nor do many cathedrals. The test is scooter-accessibility when I am a shopmobility customer. The cathedrals at Hereford and Norwich have proved top-scorers, and Winchester would have done had the platform lift to the retrochoir been in working order.

My local church, St Mary's by the river in Battersea, is not medieval. Built in the 1770s, it is one of the most delightful Georgian churches in London. The portico has Tuscan columns, and to reach its podium there are three steps on one side, five in front. At the door is a single step, and then two steps to the lobby, where stairs to the side go up to the gallery. To reach the floor of the nave there are then seven steps, with handrails to both sides. There is no way that suitable access for wheelchair users could be incorporated without spoiling the building. Nor would I wish any such attempt to be made; if need be, I would prefer, like other wheelchair users who attend services there, to be carried up the steps.

America does not have such a wealth of history as Britain and Europe. There are attractive old towns and villages in New England, down the east coast and in other scattered locations. Elsewhere there are isolated historic buildings, few of them dating back more than two hundred years. Making those that the public can visit accessible to disabled people is high on the agenda for securing the non-discrimination edict of the Americans with Disabilities Act.

In June 1994, with myself in a wheelchair, we visited Mount Vernon, George Washington's farmstead in Virginia. So far as could be, it had been made accessible, meaning accessible to vigorous independent wheelchair users. From the car park to the house was an extended trek, much of it over loose gravel. At the entrance to the house a removable ramp involving an awkward turn had been inserted, with obtrusive rails. I suspected what was coming when we had passed through the ground floor rooms. At the foot of the stairs to the upper floor the attendant was beaming when she saw me. The prize she had was a pack of photographs showing me what the upstairs rooms looked like. For the purposes of removing discrimination under the terms of the Americans with Disabilities Act the practice, as noted earlier, constitutes 'alternative accessibility'. Disabled people in America may applaud it, as might many in England. To my mind, it is akin to going into a restaurant which is not wheelchair-accessible and being told that there are colour pictures of the food on offer.

I welcome the determined efforts made in recent years by English Heritage and other agencies to improve the accessibility of historic buildings and monuments. It is, however, patently absurd to imagine they might all be made accessible to disabled people such as myself, and I do not like to see splendid historic buildings damaged by excrescences engineered in the cause of access for the disabled. I ally myself with the views of Quentin Crewe, a writer, traveller and occasional colleague at disability events, who for some fifty years has been chairbound on account of muscular dystrophy. In a letter to *The Times*[8] responding to a news item about the threats to historic buildings posed by the Disability Discrimination Bill, he wrote:

> It is preposterous, selfish and philistine for disabled people to argue that historic sites such as Hadrian's Wall, churches and other buildings should be defaced in order to give them access. Why can they not accept that there are places that they will never reach, just as blind people have to accept there are things they will never see?
>
> I will never walk up Snowdon. This does not mean it should be bulldozed flat to accommodate me. There is so much to enjoy in life; why whinge about the few things one cannot do? The notion of suing for distress because one cannot get somewhere is simply pathetic.
>
> Some American friends recently asked me to stay with them in one of London's leading hotels. The access was appalling. "Can't you sue?" my friends asked. "No, thank God", I said, "I can look after myself".

Independence

In recounting my experiences when using buildings I have frequently mentioned occasions and circumstances where I have not, on account of my disability, been able to manage independently. Not being able to do so is, for me, simply a fact of life. I could no more walk up Snowdon than Quentin Crewe. It is better, as he says, to relish the pleasures of life than complain resentfully about what cannot be done.

The first American Standard, drafted by Tim Nugent, was issued in 1961, and since then design for independence has been the doctrine which around the world has governed guidance material to do with designing for the disabled. It is enshrined in the Americans with Disabilities Act: the carrying of a person in a wheelchair so that he can use a building is out of order – if it is unavoidable, it can only be done by someone who has been 'formally instructed on the safest and least humiliating means of carrying'. In recent years the 'humiliation' theme has spread to Britain; I have been at meetings where consumer activists have insisted that being carried up steps is humiliating. Personally, I do not feel that it is, any more than I feel humiliated when I have to be pushed up a ramp.

Designing for the disabled ought to be about designing for independence and designing for dependency. That does not mean that architects should deliberately design for dependency where independence can be granted; where the approach to a building can be level, it should be level, not up a ramp with a gradient of 1 in 12. Back in the 1960s I rejected Nugent's doctrines, and, with the advocacy of unisex toilets for the disabled, helped steer Britain down the welfare path. The strategy had pitfalls, but a feature of the unisex toilet was that it signalled the importance of catering for dependent as well as independent disabled people. It was right to cater for a person who had to be lifted – or carried – in order to get onto the wc. The lesson is clear. In line with the ethos of macroism, the aim in every possible circumstance must be provision which enables people with disabilities to manage independently, conveniently and normally. But where there has to be dependency, where help has to come from someone else, that also must be accommodated. Having to be carried may not be dignified. But it should not be outlawed.

Getting out of buildings

In the account of my experiences as a building user and elsewhere in this narrative I have noted the risks and hazards to which I am exposed when I use buildings. Much more than the typical able-bodied person who uses public buildings, I am, owing to the character of my disability, prone to life-threatening situations. With regard to disabled people such as myself, the line regularly taken by commentators is that particular consideration should be given to egress provision when buildings are designed or altered. On this issue, I earlier expressed the view (page 89) that appropriate arrangements for the generality of building users, involving the provision of suitable refuges on escape routes in multi-storey buildings, would cater for people with disabilities, with there not as a rule being any cause for architects to do more.

Some commentators reckon that because disabled people can be particularly at risk when they use buildings, society owes it to them to ensure that they are given special protection against mortality, with constraints being exercised (for example, through the agency of licensing controls) on what properly, for their own sakes, they should be permitted to do[9]. To my mind, this attitude is patronising and misguided, and to explain the matter I cite what I wrote in the third edition of *Designing for the Disabled*[10]:

> There has not, to my knowledge, been any study made of comparative attitudes to death among disabled and able-bodied people. . . . The impression is, however, that people with severe disabilities are in general not at all as neurotic about dying as able-bodied people are. For all people there is the possibility that death is imminent, but it is a possibility which is generally ignored. Among many disabled people, either because of poor prognosis or proneness to injury, it is a possibility which cannot be ignored. The response is to make the most of the days that remain. It is important to be able to carry on doing the things that are fulfilling, to go to work, to carry on studying, to see shows at the theatre, to hear music at the concert hall, to keep up with the latest films at the cinema.

The precept which informed the commentary was that the purpose of living was to make the most of being alive, and the purpose of buildings was to enhance the business of living. I went on:

> Every time that old or handicapped people are the victims of a building fire there is massive publicity. There are demands for yet more stringent controls. For those who administer fire regulations the easy way out is always to say 'Yes, we must impose more controls because we are bothered about people dying'. The more difficult alternative is to say 'No,' we shall not, because we are concerned about people living'.

My hypothesis is that if, notionally, all the users of buildings were people with disabilities, statutory health and safety controls would be less constraining than those which in 1997 come with current legislative controls. The balance, I suggest, might be somewhat redressed were accessibility controls always to come with the positive aim of making buildings more convenient for everyone to use.

Part 3

Britain: how accessibility controls might be reformulated

22 Why Britain can't be like America

On what should be done in Britain to make buildings and the built environment accessible, disability activists have a ready answer – Britain should do what America has done. 'Look at America', they say, 'look at the Americans with Disabilities Act'. 'It is civil rights legislation which protects disabled people against discrimination'. 'In America public buildings and public transport are all accessible because of civil rights'. 'They could be in Britain too if disabled people had their rights'.

The rhetoric may seem persuasive, but is the logic sound? Could what America has been able to achieve be replicated in Britain? To assess the matter, I rely substantially on my own observations and experiences, drawing in particular on the two weeks that I spent in America in October 1993. Together with my wife, my brother and my sister-in-law, the visit had been arranged in February 1993, its purpose being to inform the writing of this book. By August a series of meetings and visits had been fixed, and it was then that I broke my leg again and became dependent on my wheelchair for mobility. In the expectation that America would be comprehensively wheelchair-accessible we decided to go ahead, though with a schedule cut from three weeks to two.

Our confidence in America was not misplaced. From the hotel in the Rockville district of Maryland where I stayed with my brother for the first week, we travelled into Washington by the wheelchair-accessible Metro. At the Metro stations all the wheelchair lifts were working. The hotels that we booked in Virginia and North Carolina during the second week (when the four of us were together) all had special rooms for the handicapped. All the buildings where meetings were arranged were wheelchair-accessible, as were all the museums, art galleries and tourist venues we went to. With the exception of a bookshop in an old building in Georgetown that had two steps at the entrance, all the shops we visited were wheelchair-accessible. And where a comfort station was sought, other than at a takeaway in a small town in North Carolina, we found an American-style accessible toilet that I could get into and manage comfortably.

Along the way America put obstacles in our way, notably heavy self-closing doors. But the contrast with accessibility in Britain was unmistakable. The operation in reverse would be fraught. No American spending two weeks in Britain on business or as a tourist could hope, if dependent on a wheelchair for mobility, to get through the course without colossal hassles. He would be disenchanted were he to suppose that Britain might be as accessible as America – in the way of his using or attempting to use public buildings in Britain, either as a wheelchair user or ambulant disabled person, he would find a large number of obstacles. On the accessibility of America versus Britain, the score is that there is no contest. On why there is not there are two major factors – politics and practicalities.

The politics of the issue

In both Britain and America the political goal is to make the built environment comprehensively accessible to people with disabilities. Four conditions affect the realisation of this objective: popular will; practicability; economic wealth and suitable operational mechanisms. In respect of all four, America has the advantage. Before proceeding, there is a query about the objective. Why is it that the aim is to make the built environment accessible to people with disabilities, not to everyone? The answer, going back in history to Tim Nugent, is that America set the agenda, and Britain bought it.

In both Britain and America the popular will is that buildings ought to be made accessible to disabled people. The difference is in the character of the will. America has a self-help culture, fortified by civil rights legislation which insists that all Americans must have equal rights to opportunities for helping themselves to become self-sufficient and materially prosperous. Britain has a social welfare culture backed by welfare legislation. At the head of its welfare apparatus is its national health service and national insurance. Below are a range of legislative provisions designed to ensure that disadvantaged people, among them those with disabilities, are supported. In looking to make the built environment accessible, America and Britain see disabled people and their needs from diverse perspectives. America, with a moral tone articulated by Tim Nugent, sees the virtues of self-help; the disabled people whom it wishes to help are those who, given the opportunity, can help themselves. Britain sees the virtues of communal responsibility and social justice; it is anxious to help disabled people who may not be able to help themselves, as well as those who can.

The British ethos of social welfare is laudable, but for helping disabled people when buildings are designed it has pitfalls. The British – and I generalise – cannot understand that. The popular will is a welfare will, and in terms of the practicalities of accessible provision it produces different results from those energised by the American self-help will. In the business of creating genuinely accessible environments, America operates from a firm ideological base, whereas Britain does not.

The scope of this book is limited to the work of architects and the design of buildings. Transport facilities and equipment are beyond its remit, but they are covered by the Americans with Disabilities Act, the aim over the next thirty-five years being that all public bus and railway services in America are to be made entirely accessible to people in wheelchairs. The programme is hugely expensive; from both public and private purses it will demand massive funding. America perhaps has the wealth to see it through, whereas a similar programme in Britain would, on financial grounds alone be prohibitive. Dealing with the built environment is also expensive, but less so. In the way that America is tackling the matter, the cost, it might seem, is not unduly troublesome. Were Britain to be similarly committed, the financial resources required would be far more burdensome. And even if Britain had the requisite wealth, practicalities would stand in the way of its ever accomplishing what America has been able to achieve.

American towns

Britain cannot ever hope to make its towns as conveniently accessible to disabled people as those in America. Nor can other countries in Europe. The character of urban environments is the reason, with history and space being major factors. American towns, as I have observed from my travels, tend to be uniform in character. Without identifying a specific example, and excluding large cities from the reckoning, a typical American town is describable. Planted on flat land, it is spaciously laid out on a straight grid plan, with broad avenues crossing each other. Its buildings, predominantly of recent construction, are placed in blocks. When it was first built in the age of the railway, its commerce was concentrated in a sector known as downtown. With the coming of the motor car its character changed, and commerce moved away from the centre of the town.

As redundant buildings were demolished, parking lots were inserted among the downtown buildings that survived. Out beyond the old residential quarters new commercial buildings were constructed. In ribbon developments spreading out and away from the town came shopping plazas, retail outlets and fast-food restaurants. Almost invariably they were single-storey structures, and alongside them were extensive parking lots. Back in downtown the old town hotel lost business; it was outdated and it decayed. To serve the businessmen who travelled by car, new multi-storey hotels were built on the boulevards that ringed the town. They had comfortable rooms with en-suite bathrooms, along with conference and leisure facilities. Further out came the motels.

In pleasant estates with spacious plots, modern detached houses were built, usually with garaging for two cars. The wage-earner could drive to work from them, and the family could go to the local supermarket, drugstore, DIY store, fast-food restaurant, school and church. The town centre, which was once a place for people to walk around in and meet their friends, no longer was; it had become a place to be avoided. The close-knit urban fabric had gone. The people who lived out in the nice suburbs did not go out walking. They took their cars, and at their destinations they needed to be able to park the car, preferably directly alongside the building they wanted to use. Out-of-town buildings had become utilities where transactions were conducted.

Going back to the 1950s and earlier, the rule was that commercial buildings in an American town must always have parking spaces alongside; without them they would not flourish. They must be convenient for their customers – they must be easy to get into and around. An effect was that they suited people with disabilities, provided of course that disabled people, like others, had a car to get to them. In terms of the accessibility of the buildings, nine-tenths of what was needed was already there. Even had there been no barrier-free movement and no Americans with Disabilities Act, the buildings of American towns would have served disabled people well.

Newark-on-Trent

The typical English town has evolved over many centuries. It is compact, it has a central commercial core and a cobweb layout of streets reaching out to the surrounding villages and towns. Within an English county there is more variety in the character of towns and villages than is found across the whole of America. Without the uniformity characteristic, there is not a typical English town in the sense that there is a typical American town. To inform the comparison, I draw for illustration on the example of Newark-on-Trent, the town where I was born.

Newark is a market and manufacturing town in the East Midlands, with a population approaching 25 000. Built on a Roman road, the Fosse Way, it grew in Saxon times as a market trading place. Its principal historic buildings are its Norman castle by the river and its huge fifteenth-century parish church. Around the spacious market square, one of the finest in England, are old town houses with upper storeys over arcades with shops, a magnificent eighteenth-century town hall, historic public houses, the former town hotel and more recent commercial buildings; beyond it are shopping streets and alleys dating from early medieval times. On the cobbled square the stalls are set up for the three-times-a-week market, at its busiest on Saturdays when local people throng into the town, not only to do their shopping but to have an enjoyable day out, to go to a pub for a drink or a cafe for a meal, and to meet and talk with friends and acquaintances. Many of them walk from their homes, pushing their infant children in their pushchairs. Others come in by bus or in cars. The centre of the town is pedestrianised, and, with limited parking space nearby, those who do not arrive early may have a long walk from the place they find to park their car. That does not deter them.

I speculate about the typical wheelchair user in Newark, for whom a merit of the town is that its centre is on flat terrain. He or she will come in with a husband or wife who will push them around among the market stalls and enjoy the town with them. When they need a break for refreshment they have to be selective – many of the pubs, cafes and restaurants are not easily wheelchair-accessible, and toilets within them can be up or down steep stairs. That does not trouble them unduly, since choices will still be available. What is important is that they are sharing in the life of the town; they are celebrating their belongingness, as members of a cohesive social community.

Newark happens to be a fortunate town. In the early 1960s it resisted pressures, on alleged grounds of health, safety and convenience, to move its traditional open-air market off the uncomfortable cobbles into a planned purpose-designed and suitably sanitised covered hall. Since then the town

22.1 Newark-on Trent, the market place and Town Hall

has been sensitively treated by concerned conservationists, and is now a much more delightful place than it was in the years of my childhood. By no means all other English towns have equivalent assets. There are new towns without the heritage of history. There are towns built on hills which are not easy for disabled people to get around in. But the common feature of all English market towns is that they are not places whose buildings are simply utility destinations; they are places to visit, to walk around in and to meet friends.

Europe

Often more markedly than in England, the European town is also a closely-knit community, sometimes on a hill with the buildings in its historic core packed densely together. In France the once-a-week street market is the focus of social activity for the town and its hinterland. In Italy the evening passegiata brings the people of the town together. In the towns of Europe cafes and bars have their tables and chairs set out in the square or the street outside. As in England, the towns of Europe were made for people to walk around in, not for motor cars.

Car travel and accessibility

In America the accessibility of the built environment to disabled people (and everyone else) is governed by a quite different set of parameters from those that apply in Britain and Europe. The important factor is the motor car and the effects it has on planning and design standards for accessibility.

When the first American Standard was drafted, the presumption was that for reaching buildings accessibility meant being able to get to the entrance to a building from the nearby place where the car would be parked. The American model was followed when standards for accessibility were developed in Britain. But public and commercial buildings in English towns did not always have adjacent car parking facilities. People with disabilities displaying an orange badge on their car could as a rule park on the road outside them, but with town centres becoming pedestrianised the picture changed. The idea that limits might be set, for example that no building should be further than, say, 50 metres from a disabled parking space or bus stop[1], was never a viable proposition. In America, reachability is not as a rule a vital access factor, assuming travel by car. For disabled people in Britain it can be, although there is no substantive data indicating that it significantly affects the usage of buildings. As evidenced by survey findings (Appendix 2, page 371), the pedestrianisation of town centres has clearly been beneficial for the generality of disabled people.

Pubs in England are scattered around town centres, local neighbourhoods and villages out in the country. So, similarly, are bars in France and other European countries. In America such bars as are devoted only to social drinking are usually found in town centres. The more interesting comparison relates to eating venues. In America restaurants and fast-food outlets are generally found on the outskirts of towns, in recently built single-storey structures with ample parking space for their customers. In England the car-travelling we-need-it-fast clientele is increasingly catered for on out-of-town main roads, but cafes and restaurants are concentrated in town centres. There, particularly in elderly buildings, the restaurant may be upstairs, down in the basement or otherwise not have level access, and the toilets are often not at the same level.

Hotels and workplaces

In the case of hotel buildings (ignoring bed-and-breakfast lodging houses) the accessibility contrast between America and Britain and Europe is remarkable. In America there are single-storey or low-rise motels, and multi-storey hotels managed by the big national companies. Those that were built before the era of mandatory access provision for the disabled did not as a rule present any technical difficulty bringing them into line. That could not happen in Britain or Europe, where hotels new and old come in diverse shapes and sizes; they are often in elderly, sometimes historic, buildings, and there is no uniformity about them.

A feature of Newark and other towns in England is that many of the buildings where local people may be employed on office-type work – the kind of employment that people with disabilities are most commonly seeking – are relatively elderly buildings in and around the town centre, often ones which are not comprehensively accessible. In America, where in comparable towns most office-type buildings are of recent construction and are commonly fully accessible, it would seem that the problem barely occurs. Similarly in America it is easier for disability organizations to find suitable buildings for their workforce, or for conferences attended by wheelchair users and other disabled people.

Existing buildings in America

The requirement under the Americans with Disabilities Act is that existing public buildings must be made accessible where that is readily achievable. By 'accessible' is meant the same standard of accessibility as has to be obtained with new construction, meaning provision which caters for independent wheelchair users. By the wheelchair-through-the-front-door measure an abundance of public buildings in America already demonstrated compliance before the era of accessibility controls, and for many of the operators of those buildings the cost of effecting complete accessibility for wheelchair users was relatively trivial.

Historic buildings

In the typical American town there are few historic buildings, and perhaps none that warrant listing under the US National Historic Preservation Act. In England, with historic buildings being defined as those which are listed by English Heritage as buildings of special architectural or historic interest, the picture is very different. All buildings built before 1700 and which survive in anything like their original condition are listed, and so are most of those built between 1700 and 1840[2]. Those built after about 1840 are listed only if they are of definite quality and character. In all, there are some 500 000 individual buildings which are listed. Some 6000 are Grade I, some 18 000 Grade II starred, and the remainder Grade II. In Newark-on-Trent, for example, there are 368 listed buildings – four Grade I, 11 Grade II starred and 353 Grade II[3]. Listing impacts directly on the potential scope there might be for alterations aimed at improving accessibility – the owner of a listed building must apply to the local planning authority for listed building consent if he wishes to demolish it, or alter or extend it in a way that affects its character.

In Britain there are disability activists who assert that it is technically possible to make any existing building accessible, and genuinely suppose that what they say is true. There are, I agree, clever ways of using equipment such as platform lifts, but while such provision may be technically acceptable by reference to design guidance manuals it does not give what I would regard as proper accessibility. And there are, in any event, thousands of existing public buildings which cannot by any means be made accessible to independent wheelchair users. They are not all listed historic buildings, although it is historic buildings which most readily come to mind. Archetypal examples are on-the-street London terraces where there are four or five steps to building entrances, such as doctors' and dentists' premises in Harley Street or Wimpole Street, or offices and institutes in South Kensington, Bloomsbury or Mayfair. It needs only a few minutes driving around London – or cities elsewhere in Britain – to demonstrate convincingly that not every building can be made accessible to wheelchair users.

23 Accessibility controls: the position in early 1997

In the business of attempting to make the built environment fully accessible to disabled people, Britain, I say, cannot do what America has been able to do. But disability lobbyists have insisted that it can and should. They have embraced American doctrinalism and pressed its axioms. I recite the litany. Disabled people, they say, have rights. Among those rights they have a right of access to public buildings, and that includes wheelchair users – a building is not accessible if its wheelchair users cannot get into and use it independently. As the Americans with Disabilities Act has shown, firm prescriptions can, the lobbyist says, be ordained by law; there are right – meaning correct – solutions which can be universally applied. What suits disabled people, he says, suits everyone; suitable provision for disabled people should be a paramount consideration when new buildings are designed or existing buildings altered. Virtually any existing public building can, he submits, be made accessible to disabled people – on technical grounds there are no excuses.

My impression, as I have noted before, is that among disability activists who serve on local access groups and other committees which deal with access issues, it is the able-bodied collaborators who are most prone to rigid doctrinalism rather than those who are themselves people with disabilities. It is they who are most determined that polling stations should be wholly accessible, that tactile pavings must be laid for blind people, and that to suit wheelchair users lift controls should be down at low level. When the design of a new building subject to the Part M regulation is under consideration they demand strict conditions, and, relatedly, they press for rigorous requirements when existing buildings are altered.

Building control and its national rules

The current Part M building regulation covers new buildings and certain existing buildings which can, when they are altered, be treated as though they were new buildings. Like other regulations, it mandates national requirements. That building regulations orthodoxly prescribe uniform national requirements has always been perceived by disability activists to be a vital asset, not a troublesome constraint. From the day in October 1962 when Tim Nugent spoke to a public meeting at the Royal Institute of British Architects the principle of national rules for access for the disabled has been unchallenged dogma in the disability arena. America had a national set of design specifications which could be cited in legislation, and Britain must do the same – the British Standards Institution would issue a code of practice on access for the disabled, and emanating from it there could be national controls. I thought then, and so did others, that this was the right and proper way forward.

In 1962 there was no national disability lobby and no campaigning for rights for the disabled, and nor was there in America. Tim Nugent might not have been delighted had he known that his American Standard with its uniform rules for accessibility would help trigger the movement that was to lead to the Americans with Disabilities Act of 1990. And in Britain the disability lobby's crusade for American-style civil rights would have been less advantageously equipped had there not been a Part M building regulation with uniform national prescriptions.

The 'reasonable provision' requirement

The discriminatory effects of conforming with the design guidance set out in the Part M Approved Document have already been examined. In Britain, as in America, discrimination follows from imposing uniform rules, and, as demonstrated at Liverpool Street Station, it is exacerbated by the welfare ethos which imbues Part M. The Part M requirement is that reasonable provision has to be made for disabled people. Patently and undeniably, the public toilets at Liverpool Street Station do not manifest reasonable provision for disabled people. And nor in countless other buildings has the application of Part M requirements served to eliminate discrimination against disabled people, or discrimination against women and pushchair users.

Recognising that there are places such as Liverpool Street Station where locked-up unisex toilet facilities for disabled people may be warranted, reasonable provision for disabled people can involve a combination of suitable special and normal provision. For toilets, as for many other building features, there cannot be singular 'right' solutions, and, with different provision being appropriate according to circumstances, the logical effect of a 'reasonable provision' edict is a variety of outcomes. The compliance goal is variable, and without a definitive common goal the 'here is one way to do it' instructive guidance set out in the current Part M Approved Document is falsely based.

The Secretary of State for the Environment is responsible for the law of building regulations, meaning that in the context of Part M it is his duty to determine what reasonable provision for disabled people ought to mean. He is advised by the Building Regulations Advisory Committee (who in turn are advised by the Department's officials), and the current Secretary of State's predecessors were presumably assured that the guidance in the 1987 and 1992 Approved Documents genuinely did constitute reasonable provision. Officially the principle is sustained, with the 1992 Approved Document continuing to be operative in 1997. Nor is the notion challenged; out on the ground, architects and local authority officers want to be told precisely what they have to do to keep within the law, and they like instructions which come in an ostensibly authoritative guidance document with the insignia of the Crown on its cover. Disability activists like what they have got, and want more of it. And the generality of observers believe that the government ought to do more to help disabled people, that architects ought to do more, and it is right that regulations should prescribe what has to be done to make buildings accessible to disabled people.

The advice in the 1992 Part M Approved Document, as in others, is that anyone who wishes to meet the regulatory requirements in some way other than the 'one way' set out in the Approved Document is entitled to do so. The Part M regulatory requirements are all ones which say, 'Reasonable provision shall be made' (see Appendix 11, page 398), and in the official manual to the Building Regulations the advice was, 'You can choose whether or not to use the Approved Documents or you can follow some or parts of them. You are obliged only to meet the requirements of the Regulations'[1]. In any particular case subject to Part M it is thus for the architect, in association with his developer, to propose how the 'reasonable provision' requirement is to be met, and to satisfy the local authority that his proposals are appropriate. Relatedly, there is no bar to using a procedure other than that advised in the 1992 Part M Approved Document, and in Chapter 25 I indicate the form that a new procedure for meeting the requirements of the current Part M building regulation might sensibly take. Before that, I look at the problems associated with improving the accessibility of existing buildings, and, relatedly, the ramifications of the Disability Discrimination Act of 1995.

Alterations to existing buildings

The architect when designing a new building starts with a clean sheet, with no significant practical constraints in the way of incorporating such provision for accessibility as he is asked to make. With existing buildings he does not work from scratch; he is treating a building that at some time in the past was designed by another architect. Much more in Britain than in America, its built form presents constraints, frequently of a kind which make it impossible for him to alter it to provide the same degree of accessibility as he could with a new building. If his brief is simply to improve its accessibility (rather than work to some dogmatic formula), he has, pragmatically, to do the best he can.

In recent years when alterations have been made to existing public buildings to help disabled people, they have, in the great majority of cases, been undertaken voluntarily. Public bodies have been diligent in doing what they can to enhance the accessibility of their public buildings, much more so than is indicated by the picture of the performance of local authorities presented in Audit Commission reports*. And commercial organizations have often acted positively; there must, for example, be many hundreds of hotels and pubs where unisex toilet facilities for disabled people have been voluntarily installed by their managements, and also many hundreds (or perhaps thousands) where access provision has been made for wheelchair users. The response to the disability activist who doubts the effectiveness of voluntarism

* See Appendix 10, page 397.

in Britain is that he should compare the score with what is done, for example, in France or Italy.

Most local authorities and other public agencies have a good record in respect of buildings of their own where disabled people might be employed. As a rule, the larger the building the more practicable it is to achieve wheelchair accessibility, and in many recently constructed existing buildings it is relatively easy to obtain. In historic buildings, particularly historic town halls, there can be considerable problems. The most interesting examples are in the north of England, where imposing town halls came with manufacturing prosperity in the Victorian era. In Manchester and Rochdale, both with magnificent Grade 1 listed town halls designed by Alfred Waterhouse, it was, I understand, disabled employees who urged accessibility action. At Rochdale the porte-cochère (under which carriages dropped their passengers at the stepped main entrance) had its floor raised to align it with the floor inside. At Manchester something like £2 million has been spent in recent years on improving the accessibility of the town hall buildings[2].

Where the principal concern has been to serve disabled people as visitors, it is at major museum buildings, such as the Ashmolean in Oxford and the National Portrait Gallery in London[3], that substantial works have been undertaken to improve accessibility. Equivalent interventions have not been needed for the medieval cathedrals of England, which were made accessible (or near enough) when they were first built. It is prestigious Victorian civic buildings which can present the most challenging accessibility problems, where there are political demands to achieve accessibility, where the ingenuity of the architect can be most taxed, and where costs can be considerable. For buildings such as these, there cannot be common rules for implementing accessibility.

The idea of extending Part M to cover alterations

Through the late 1980s and into the 1990s the Department of the Environment's aim was to find a way of regulating alterations to existing public and employment buildings. The Part M building regulation as it was first introduced in 1987 did not cover all new public buildings, and at meetings at which they spoke officials from the Department of the Environment's Building Regulations Division indicated the strategy; the 1987 regulation would be replaced by a new regulation covering all new public buildings (as happened in 1992), and this would be followed by a further Part M regulation dealing with alterations to existing buildings[4]. In March 1992 the Department commissioned Stephen Thorpe, an architect whose practice specialised in building for disabled people, to recommend options for amending Part M to include alterations, with proposals on how the matter should be tackled[5]. At a Centre for Accessible Environments seminar at which he spoke in March 1993, Mr Thorpe said the hope was that there would be a consultation paper on the subject before the end of that year[6]. In the event, there was no consultation paper, and nor was any report of the study issued. The inference was that the Department had not after all been able to find a means of employing Part M to control the accessibility of existing buildings when they were altered, and, assuming there to have been adherence to the line that uniform national prescriptions had to be applicable, that was understandable.

The enlistment of planning controls

The 1992 Part M building regulation stayed in place, with the only existing buildings which it covered being those which, when altered, could be treated as though they were new buildings. All others remained untouched by building control legislation in respect of access provision, an effect being that disability activists increasingly sought to employ planning controls in the cause of engineering access provision when existing buildings were altered. The important instrument they enlisted was local authority development plans.

Under section 13 of the Town and Country Planning Act 1990 local planning authorities have a duty to prepare development plans; in these plans each authority sets out its local plan policies, and these are of dominant relevance when applications for planning permission are considered. It did not take long for local authority access officers, access groups and keen-to-help-the-disabled members of local authority planning committees to recognise that they had been given an opportunity they could exploit. Aided by the advice in Planning Policy Guidance Note 1[7] that where access for the disabled was a material planning consideration it had to be taken into account, the way was open for local authorities to pronounce in their development plans that access for the disabled must be a paramount planning consideration. They were helped by the Access Committee for England, which in 1993, in association with the Royal Town Planning Institute, issued a comprehensive guidance document *Access policies for local plans*[8]. Prior to that, many local authorities, among them Richmond upon Thames, had, however, already drafted their plan policies.

Richmond upon Thames policy

The unitary development plan which Richmond London Borough Council prepared went out to consultation as the deposit draft plan in March 1992. In it the policy statements relating to public buildings and access for the disabled[9] were:

> Applications for the development, change of use, alteration or extension of buildings open to the public and buildings used for employment, educational or recreational purposes, will be required where practicable and reasonable to provide full access for people with disabilities, as both customers and employees.
>
> . . . BS5810 sets out the minimum standards with which access provision should comply. Developers will be encouraged to design to higher standards and these will be set out in design guidelines with which applicants will be expected to comply.
>
> The Council will require a high standard of design in all new and altered shop-fronts. When considering proposals, the Council will have special regard to the following matters: . . . Shop doorways must incorporate suitably designed access for people with restricted mobility, and equipment such as cash dispensing machines should be at a height suitable for wheelchair users.

23.1a and b
65 Sheen Road, Richmond

In Richmond, as elsewhere, a principal means by which access provision could be secured under planning law was when applications were made for permission for changing the use of buildings. The condition would be that 'full' access must be provided, or, if not, that existing access provision must be improved. A case which exercised Richmond Council during 1993 and 1994 was 65 Sheen Road.

The Sheen Road case

Some half a mile east of Richmond town centre, on the busy main traffic route to Wandsworth and south-east London, 65 Sheen Road was a small shop in a conservation area. There was a first floor flat above the shop, and underneath a cellar basement lit by pavement lights. The owner wished to use the ground floor and basement as a cold sandwich bar, and the alterations he proposed, which included a door recess to give separate access to the first floor flat, involved an application for changing the use from shop to mixed use. The existing shop entrance had a single step off a pavement which at that point was 840mm wide, narrowing a little further along to 520mm; without the floor level of the shop being lowered it was therefore technically impossible to obtain wheelchair accessibility. To make the basement usable, the floor of the shop needed, however, to be raised, an effect being two steps at the entrance rather than one.

Planning permission was refused by Richmond Council, one of the grounds being that suitable access for disabled people was not provided, contrary to the policy declared in the deposit draft unitary development plan. The architect employed by the building owner appealed against the decision, and, in accord with statutory practice, a planning inspector appointed by the Secretary of State for the Environment was asked to inspect the premises, take account in his report of all relevant considerations and determine whether or not the appeal should be allowed. His decision was that it should be[10]. Richmond Council then appealed to the High Court against the Secretary of State's decision.

The 'access' practicalities were not in dispute. Wheelchair access could not be provided, and, with parking absolutely prohibited outside the shop, such other disabled people as might be looking to buy a sandwich would negotiate the narrow pavement at their peril, get up two steps and open a door. Richmond Council might have let the matter rest, recognising, whether or not the planning inspector had done his job properly, that the sensible outcome would be to allow the works proposed by the building owner and his architect to go ahead. On that basis, the interests of disabled people would, however, have been disregarded.

It was only on technical grounds that the council could appeal against the planning inspector's decision, and its contention was that the inspector had not in his report given due consideration to the access-for-the-disabled policy statements in the draft development plan. The High Court judge felt that the inspector had not; his judgment was in favour of Richmond Council[11]. The case was remitted to the Department of the Environment, and the appointed planning inspector reversed his predecessor's decision. With no planning permission for redevelopment, the premises were put on the market in early 1994 and when the photographs shown in Figures 23.1a and b were taken in October 1996 they still were. I review the case again later, but before then I consider the ramifications of the Disability Discrimination Act of 1995.

24 The problems posed by the Disability Discrimination Act

The purpose of the Disability Discrimination Act is to outlaw discrimination against disabled people, those who in this book are termed medically disabled people. Part III of the Act is concerned with discrimination relating to the provision of goods, facilities and services, and within it, in section 21, there are provisions regarding the accessibility of buildings. Section 21 is to be implemented in four stages, with the fourth stage, the one which will cover adjustments to buildings, being planned to come into effect in the year 2005. The relevant provisions are in subsection 2, referred to from now on as section 21(2); their precise terms have been set out previously, on page 133.

What, in effect, section 21(2) says to a person with a disability is, 'If you come across a building which you find not to be conveniently accessible, but which you reckon should and could be made accessible to you and other disabled people, you can charge the person who owns the building with discrimination against you, take him to court, ask him to reconstruct the building, and then insist that he compensates you for the hurt he has done to your feelings'.

This replicated the terms of the Americans with Disabilities Act. But behind the introduction of the two pieces of legislation there was a vital difference. America had taken steps to ensure that the providers of buildings would know what they had to do to protect themselves against unreasonable charges of discrimination, whereas Britain had not. The American device was the Americans with Disabilities Act access standard, whereby a building owner would be immunized against charges of discrimination in respect of any of his buildings which conformed with it. The access standard was therefore central to the implementation of the American Act, a factor which aided its viability for the purpose being that the generality of pre-existing public buildings across America could be brought into line with the standard without undue difficulty or burdensome expense.

Britain had no such access standard, and on account of the character of its existing buildings it would not, had it had one, have been able to employ it as effectively as America could. But the government needed to find a way of implementing the intentions of section 21(2), and, supposing perhaps that Britain actually could do what America had done, it proposed the production of an access standard. Before reporting the terms of the proposal, I clarify what is meant by an access standard.

Access standards and an access standard

The distinction to be made is between what is technically meant by 'access standards' and 'an access standard'. *Access standards* are the design standards prescribed for features of buildings, ones which, when associated with regulations, are commonly governed by criteria for wheelchair users. They generally include, for example, standards for the width of doors, the gradient of ramps and the internal dimensions of lifts. *An access standard* is the corporate package which represents accessibility, one which incorporates all the individual design standards and, for whatever type of building may be under consideration, relevant application conditions, or, as they are called in America, scoping conditions.

For an access standard to be serviceable for disability rights purposes it has to be coherent, precise and definitive, and its constituent design standards have to be uniform standards which are universally applicable. The pioneering exemplar, the first American Standard, came in 1961, before the era of 'rights'; on the application conditions side it was weak, and years of argument followed before, in 1984, the US Access Board issued the guidelines from which the access standard supporting the Americans with Disabilities Act of 1990 was directly developed. In Britain, CP96 of 1967 was not an access standard, though it would have become one had its second part been issued. BS5810 of 1979, which presented design standards only, was not an access standard. The Part M Approved Document (whether of 1987 or 1992) may be classed as an access standard, but because its mandate is 'reasonable provision shall be made' rather than 'access shall be provided', it is not serviceable for the purposes of civil rights legislation.

The idea of an access standard for the Disability Discrimination Act

In March 1996, four months after the Disability Discrimination Act had been placed on the statute book, the National Disability Council and the Minister for Disabled People issued a consultation package presenting the government's proposals on how the rights of access to goods, facilities and services might be implemented[1]. A paper in it discussed how buildings might be deemed not to be discriminatory for the purposes of the Act, a suggestion being that such buildings as had been designed in compliance with Part M requirements would be deemed to satisfy the test of reasonableness for section 21(2) purposes. For all other existing buildings (with the very limited exception of those for which extension works were to be undertaken) Part M was not, however, applicable; on this account, the paper said, building regulations would not suit, and it continued[2]:

> Another approach might be to work with a new access standard (possibly one prepared by the British Standards Institution (BSI)). When a business received certification that it had achieved the access standard, it could be confident that it provided an acceptable degree of accessibility for people with disabilities.
>
> Equally, disabled people could be confident that the business premises would be reasonably accessible to them. The standard could, therefore, provide reliability to all concerned. . . . To provide the required degree of certainty, the

> Government would regulate to deem achievement of the standard to meet the Act's requirements to remove physical barriers. Meeting the standard would be entirely voluntary. . . . For those businesses who chose to do so, and for their disabled customers, there could be considerable advantages in the resulting certainty of compliance.

Presented plausibly and with no intimation that it came with any drawbacks, this access standard proposition could be expected to appeal to all concerned – to disability organizations, disabled people, building owners and managers, architects and others. From the government's viewpoint, it would help that its handling would be passed to the British Standards Institution, who would appoint a committee to prepare the standard, with a series of research projects being undertaken to inform its drafting[3]. Since the plan was that the section 21(2) building adjustments provisions would not be brought into effect until the year 2005, time was not pressing.

The disabled people who in 1996 were members of the National Disability Council perhaps had a simplistic view of what an access standard meant. They may have felt, as disabled commentators had done back in 1968 when Part 1 of CP96 had been issued, that it was only design standards that really mattered, and on that basis they might have supposed that all that was wanted for section 21(2) purposes was an update of BS5810, one which would present right (meaning correct) design standards for making existing buildings accessible.

The idea that, congregately for all disabled people, there can be universally right design standards for accessibility has always been attractive, both to disabled people and practising architects. But it was never an idea which was soundly based. People with disabilities are a disparate collection of people who come in a great variety of shapes and sizes, with a quantity of different characteristics, capabilities and aptitudes. There is no way that a singular set of design standards for building features will satisfy them all. A pertinent matter is the planning and design of wc compartments – a glance at relevant illustrations and diagrams on pages 181 to 187 and 323 to 325 of this book confirms that there cannot be a single 'right' solution for all disabled people. Elsewhere – bringing alterations to existing buildings into the picture as well as newly constructed ones – how can there, for example, be a universally right standard for the weight of spring-loaded doors, for the gradient of ramps, for the configuration of steps, for the height of wash basins or for the positioning of lift controls?

Against the odds, the BSI could come up with a genuine access standard, one that sets design standards and also, for existing buildings of all shapes and sizes, application conditions. Against the odds, because it is not practicable to devise application conditions capable of covering each and every situation that might occur. Consider, for example, situations where the answer might be installing an automatic-opening door in place of hinged doors, putting a platform lift over steps, providing a ground floor wc in a cafe or restaurant to supplement inaccessible basement facilities, installing a passenger lift in a building where previously there was none, or (with reference to the problematical scenario described on page 133), incorporating a ramp in place of a step at a shop entrance. How could there be standardised application conditions for these?

There are, it has to be admitted, flaws in the access standard idea, and I note a related issue. In the event that some sort of access standard were to be produced, who would regularly inspect all the existing buildings in the country to assess whether or not they complied with the standard? Would this be the job of local authorities, or would the Department of Social Security employ an army of inspectors? And would the Treasury be content to produce the necessary funds?

Finally, as demonstrated by the operation of the Americans with Disabilities Act access standard, the employment of an access standard for the purpose of delivering rights to people with disabilities cannot but be discriminatory. With an access standard there have to be cut-off points, with people who are not accommodated within them, in the main those with severely handicapping disability conditions, being excluded.

The idea of a certification system

The discussion around the concept of an access standard has been a diversion. Irrespective of all else, there is a fundamental reason why national prescriptions, whether in the form of an access standard, access guidelines or official documentation of any other brand, cannot serve to enforce section 21(2) of the Disability Discrimination Act. It is to be found in the wording of section 21(2): the legal duty of a building provider, it says, is to take such steps as it is reasonable, in all the circumstances of the case, to take in order that a physical feature of his building does not make it difficult or impossible for disabled people to use a service which he provides*.

Clearly and incontrovertibly, what it is reasonable to do in all the circumstances of any particular case can only be determined on the spot, at local level. It follows that for the implementation of section 21(2) there will need to be local control procedures, ones which, if found to be practicable, might perhaps be administered by local authorities. Were local authorities to take on this task they would not be responsible, as they are in the case of building regulations, for enforcing the law. The American-style principle behind the Disability Discrimination Act is that its enforcement is grievance-led: a disabled person has to allege unlawful discrimination, and if he goes to court and the judgment is in his favour, the building provider has to take such remedial and compensatory action as the court requires.

The law, it may be observed, would be biased were the building provider to have no means of protecting himself against its potential penalties. In America his counterpart is able to protect himself by having his building comply with the requirements of the Americans with Disabilities Act access standard. When he has done that, he knows that his building is not discriminatory. In Britain, given local control procedures, a comparable certification system could notionally be set up. The certificate that a building provider

* For the precise terms see page 133.

would receive would say, in effect, that his premises were not discriminatory because he had taken all such steps as he reasonably could to fulfil his legal duty under the terms of the Disability Discrimination Act.

The current position

Through 1996 and into 1997 building owners and managers have become increasingly aware of the threat posed to them by the Disability Discrimination Act. 'What do we have to do?' they have been asking, 'Tell us what we have to do'. Neither the government, nor anyone else, can tell them what they have to do, but the line which the government has been fostering is that building owners should make advance preparations; they could usefully, for example, commission access audits of their buildings, learn from professional experts what features of their buildings might be most vulnerable to discrimination charges, and what they might possibly do to protect themselves[4].

Ultimately, building providers will only be securely protected by procedures which result in the award of an official certificate, one which says, 'These premises meet the requirements of the Disability Discrimination Act'. Nothing less will serve. As any building manager whose building has been the subject of an access audit will know, there can be countless features of his building which warrant a warning, with, in many instances (for example, those where the complaint is of a lack of the colour contrasts which could remove discrimination against sight-impaired people), no indication of what remedial measures might be effective. And, as any architect who has gone around a building with a disability activist will know, there is no way that any building can be designed which wholly satisfies a critical examiner; faults will always be found.

Local authority test procedures

At this point I speculate, the hypothesis being that a national certification system could be set up, with local authorities being charged with the duty of checking building premises all around the country to test their compliance with the law. It would predictably be a daunting and costly enterprise.

Prior to launching the venture, no local authority would know how many premises in their area they might be asked to inspect. Some might think in terms of 200, others 500 and some 1000 or more. For each of the premises they inspected, matters they might need to record could include:

1. The nature of the service provided in the premises by the building provider.
2. The physical character and physical features of the premises.
3. The financial status of the building provider, the commercial prospects of his business, and how financial considerations might affect the reasonability of such action as might be proposed.
4. The interests of people with disabilities who use or might wish to use the premises.

5 The form of such building adjustments as might be proposed, the cost of them and the benefits they might afford to people with disabilities.

For all inspection purposes there would, I assume, be a local authority inspector and a disability rights inspector. In each local authority area local organizations of or for disabled people would nominate approved disability rights inspectors. With a brief to consider relevant matters from the viewpoint of disabled people, the role of the disability rights inspector would be to attend all meetings relating to a particular case, advise on the form that building adjustments might take, and engage in negotiations on the terms of conditions for the award of a certificate.

With regard to the measures needing to be taken for the award of a certificate, cases which a local authority would deal with would come into one or other of five categories:

1 No building adjustments required.
2 Ad hoc adjustments required; for example, the fixing of handrails, the rehanging of wc compartment doors to open out or the removal of a superfluous lobby door.
3 Relatively straightforward adjustments required; for example, the fitting of hold-open catches to doors in circulation areas, the installation of a stairlift on a straight stair, the ramping of a single step or the installation of automatic-opening doors.
4 Less straightforward adjustments required; for example, the reconstruction of existing toilet facilities, the installation of a platform lift or the provision of ramps alongside steps in circulation areas.
5 Major alteration works required; for example, the complete reconstruction of the entrance to the building, the relocation of toilet facilities or the installation of a lift serving upper floors.

In many cases it could be appropriate for adjustment works to be phased, with relatively straightforward works being undertaken initially and more major alteration works following later should circumstances permit. With this strategy line in mind, and noting that the circumstances relating to any premises might change after a first certificate had been awarded, the standard practice might be for certificates to be valid for a limited period only. For all premises that had a certificate the local authority would make a further inspection some months before the expiry date, and in the light of the assessment determine whether or not a new certificate should be awarded. For those where the decision was negative, the procedures would be worked through again.

The issue of 'rights'

Altogether, this is not a credible proposition; given that the whole operation would be prohibitively extravagant, both in terms of manpower and costs, the government would surely reject the idea. But with no other available means of implementing and enforcing section 21(2), it would have a dilemma, and it might then be encouraged to take a critical look at the purpose of the Disability Discrimination Act and, in particular, the purpose of section 21(2).

The story of how the Disability Discrimination Act came to arrive on the statute book was reported in the first part of this narrative. It was not driven there by sound commonsensical or good utilitarian aspirations, but simply for craven political reasons, because the government had to find a way of extricating itself from the hole it had been thrust into. At issue was rights for the disabled; on the model of American civil rights legislation a succession of private members' bills had been presented, and the time had come when the government, besieged on all sides by the disability lobby in parliament, could no longer block the process. To restore its authority, it produced its own legislation to give rights to disabled people.

The right which would be afforded to disabled people under section 21(2) of the Disability Discrimination Act in conjunction with section 25 (which covers enforcement remedies) would be a curious right. It would not be a right to use public buildings. Self-evidently, the government could not deliver that right, since there are many thousands of existing buildings in Britain which could never be made accessible, assuming that 'accessible' would be interpreted as having to make suitable provision for wheelchair users. In place of that, the right which disabled people would have under the Disability Discrimination Act would be a right to complain, and only in respect of some particular building which they complained about, and where their complaint was upheld in court, would remedial action follow.

Had the government not been pressed to introduce 'rights for the disabled' legislation on the American model, and within it provisions to do with the accessibility of existing public buildings, it might perhaps have got around to tackling the matter in a quite different way. So should it in the next year or two be obliged, as I suspect it could be, to recognise that section 21(2) is inoperable, it could be looking to find a way of tackling what it might have claimed was in fact the real purpose of section 21(2): to make existing buildings more accessible to disabled people. How – if at all – a suitable mechanism for doing this might be devised is considered subsequently, but I first look at how accessibility controls for new buildings might sensibly be reformulated.

25 The reformulation of controls for new buildings

The prospect that I have in view is the introduction of comprehensive new legislation for controlling the accessibility of the built environment in Britain. It would relate to all building users, not just disabled people, and it would cover both new buildings and alterations to existing buildings. In England one government department only, the Department of the Environment, would be responsible for its administration and implementation. In this book the title which it is given is the Built Environment (Accessibility) Act and in the discussion which follows I refer to it as the Accessibility Act.

The advent of independent approved inspectors

Under the Accessibility Act planning and building control operations would be merged, both for new buildings and alterations to existing ones; by this I mean that for any particular case there would be only one set of accessibility requirements, not one set of conditions from the planning side and another from the building control side. I regard this principle as essential, but it raises awkward problems regarding the implementation of accessibility controls in the field of public buildings, ones that have become potentially more troublesome in the light of recent changes to administrative mechanisms.

Prior to January 1997 it was only local authorities who in the public buildings arena were responsible for enforcing the law of Building Regulations. Had that position remained, and had there been no possibility that it might change, the merging of planning and building control functions for accessibility purposes might not have been unduly difficult. The authority responsible for planning control would always be the same as that responsible for building control, and coordination of the two functions would have been relatively straightforward. But this was not an arrangement which would last into perpetuity, the reason being the arrival on the building control front of corporate and independent approved inspectors.

Sections 16 and 17 of the Building Act 1984 permit the Secretary of State for the Environment to designate bodies other than local authorities to supervise building control and issue certificates of compliance with building regulations. Other than for the National House-Building Council in respect of housing developments, the power was unused until late 1996. It was then that the Secretary of State appointed new inspectors for buildings other than in housing; in the first batch, in business from 1 January 1997, there were five corporate approved inspectors (in the main, small companies), and 27 independent approved inspectors. With others who will be appointed in future, I refer to them collectively as independent inspectors.

Behind the innovation there were political and practical reasons, the government's thinking being that this was a field where there should be competition, and competition would make local authority agencies more efficient. An effect would be that local authorities would have no control at all over schemes handled by independent inspectors; they would not, for example, have any say in the conditions to be imposed for meeting Part M requirements.

The shift could gather pace over the next few years, with an increasing amount of building control work being handled by independent inspectors and correspondingly less by local authorities. In consequence, there will, steadily, be fewer opportunities for coordinating planning and building control operations under one roof. Where they are separated, the local authority might point to its development plan and seek to impose stringent planning conditions for accessibility purposes, and although the independent inspector could be asked to take account of them, the only duty he will have will be to assure himself that there is compliance with the law of Building Regulations.

The proposed Part Z building regulation

For building regulations other than Part M, the broad rule currently is that conditions may be applied to the building, its structure and provision within it, but not to spaces outside the building – those are the business of planning control. With Part M the parameters are expanded; as the 1992 Approved Document indicates, conditions may be applied to approach routes from the edge of the site, leaving car parking areas as the only external provision directly associated with the use of the building by disabled people that is not covered by Part M. Parking provision, whether outside or within buildings, is clearly a planning matter, but there would seem to be no good reason why it should not, like approaches and access to the building, be covered by Building Regulations as well as by planning law.

The Accessibility Act would bring with it a revised Part M regulation, though to avoid confusion with the current Part M it is referred to here and elsewhere as the Part Z building regulation. It could, I suggest, have a single requirement which would read as follows:

> Z1 Reasonable provision shall be made to facilitate the usage of the building and associated spaces around it by such people as might use or wish to use the building, including people with disabilities.

The phrase 'including people with disabilities' is incorporated to emphasise that attention must be given to the needs of disabled people, but since the mandate has a 'for everyone' remit it is not necessary to define exactly who people with disabilities are. The Z1 requirement, like Part M, will cover new buildings and alterations which can be treated as new buildings, but my thinking is that the Part Z regulation could, in addition, cover certain other types of alterations to existing buildings; the means by which this might be achieved is discussed in the next chapter.

With a view to formulating a strategy for controlling accessibility under the terms of the Accessibility Act I rehearse relevant considerations; they are: (a) the status of independent inspectors; (b) their detachment from local authorities; (c) the increasing number of cases where the administration of planning and building control is separated; and (d), for any particular case, the desirability of having only one set of accessibility requirements for both planning and building control purposes.

In the light of this there is, in my view, only one tenable option: it is that all accessibility control measures should be concentrated on the building control side. The role of planning control would be curtailed; the standard line being that for any building under consideration the granting of planning permission would be subject to accessibility provision being in accord with the requirements of the new-style Part M building regulation. In this connection, I review the interpretation of relevant planning guidance issued by the Department of the Environment.

The terms of planning conditions to do with accessibility

In a revised form, Planning Policy Guidance Note 1 *General Policy and Principles* was issued by the Department of the Environment in February 1997. By comparison with the 1992 guidance which it replaced, it modified the line which local planning authorities were asked to take when considering planning permissions in the context of access provision for the disabled. It no longer said that detailed attention should not be given to matters such as the specifications for steps, ramps and doors; instead, the advice was, 'The internal layout of buildings is *not normally* (my italics) material to the consideration of planning permission'[1]. With the italics again being mine, it continued:

> When a new building is proposed, or when planning permission is required for the alteration or change of use of an existing building, the developer and local planning authority should consider the needs of disabled people at an early stage in the design process. They should be flexible and imaginative in seeking solutions, taking account of the particular circumstances of each case. Resolving problems by negotiation will always be preferable, but *where appropriate the planning authority may impose conditions requiring access provision for people with disabilities.* Such conditions should fulfil the tests set out in Circular 11/95.

Department of the Environment Circular 11/95, *The Use of Conditions in Planning Permissions*, was a revision of a circular issued in 1985. Planning conditions, it said, should be clearly seen to be fair, reasonable and practicable[2]. When granting planning permission subject to conditions, local authorities would have to state their reasons for the conditions[3], and a reason such as 'to comply with the policies of the Council' would not suggest proper justification[4]. The advice was that before a condition could be imposed the policy tests which it had to satisfy were that it was (a) necessary; (b) relevant to planning; (c) relevant to the development to be permitted; (d) enforceable; (e) precise; and (f) reasonable in all other respects[5]. On access provision its advice was that where there was a clear planning need it might be appropriate to impose a condition to ensure adequate access for disabled people[6]. For this purpose, a model condition was presented[7]:

> Before the development hereby permitted is commenced a scheme indicating the provision to be made for disabled people to gain access to ( ) shall have been submitted and approved by the local planning authority. The agreed scheme shall be implemented before the development hereby permitted is brought into use.

The inference here is apparent. A scheme which the developer does not agree with cannot be imposed; he must, following negotiations, reach agreement with the local authority on what should be done. The resolution of problems has to be the rule, with the local authority not being entitled to dictate conditions unilaterally. Properly, the advice in the planning guidance note ought to have been 'Problems must always be resolved by negotiation'. To my mind, the principle is sound; if, for a particular building, planning conditions relating to access provision are to be imposed they have to be reasonable, and should the local authority seek to impose a condition which the developer can demonstrate is unreasonable, that would be good reason for rejecting it.

In the chapter which follows, on alterations to existing buildings, I consider the practical implications of the matter with reference to the case of 65 Sheen Road in Richmond. Staying now with new buildings, I note that for the purposes of the Accessibility Act the Z1 requirement, like the Part M requirements, says, 'Reasonable provision shall be made'. Planning conditions also have to be reasonable. At least in respect of new buildings, there ought not in any particular case to be occasion for specific requirements to be imposed by way of planning law which are at odds with those imposed by way of building control law. For relevant building development for which planning permission is sought, it would be appropriate for approval to come from the planning authority with the condition 'Planning permission is granted, subject to accessibility provision being in compliance with the requirements of the Part Z building regulation'.

The Annex A document, entitled *The Proposed Built Environment (Accessibility) Act: Draft Model for Authorised Guidance Document*, is, in effect, a draft Approved Document for Part Z. In practice, it would not need to come with new legislation; as a building regulation, it could be brought into effect under the terms of section 1 of the Building Act 1984. But I continue to refer to Part Z as being under the terms of the Accessibility Act; it would be one item (although the most significant) in the Act's inventory, and alongside it there could be a range of matters for whose operation new powers could be required.

For presentational reasons also, it would be helpful to have new legislation. Without it, a new Part M building regulation (which is what I assume Part Z would be) would, I fear, continue to be regarded as a 'for the disabled' regulation. With the Accessibility Act, with its emphasis on access provision for everyone, that would not occur; the provisions in the Act regarding Part Z would be widely understood to be an integral piece of new legislation, not a modification of some pre-existing statute.

The management of Part M conditions

Prior to the advent of independent inspectors, local authorities had the field of building control, and with it the management of the Part M regulation, to themselves. Because they had responsibility for compliance certification they could, and often did, take the lead on Part M. For any new development in their areas it was their job to impose conditions – ones that, with few inhibitions being put in their way by the Part M approved document, they could claim constituted reasonable provision. To advise them, they commonly had an access officer and a local access group, and for the consistent application of Part M in their areas some issued their own guidance documents.

Broadly, local authorities could tell architects 'These are our conditions for Part M, and you will observe them'. They did not encourage architects to take the lead and say 'For this building, this is what we propose in order to meet Part M requirements, and we think you will agree'. For buildings in their areas which from now on are handled by independent inspectors, control will be out of the hands of local authorities, and for such buildings the administrative procedure may well be turned around. Citing, for example, supermarket companies, department store chains, hotel groups and building societies, management boards will recognise the benefits of employing independent inspectors, looking as a rule to work always with the same inspector. For all their new buildings there will then be consistent Part M conditions, and, equally importantly, their architects will be in the lead – they will present their own proposals to the inspector, and negotiations will be on the basis of them.

Annex A and Part Z

The Annex A document in this book was in final draft form before I knew that corporate inspectors would be appearing on the building control stage. The guidance in it is geared to serving the purposes of the proposed Accessibility Act and its Part Z regulatory requirement, but is at the same time designed to serve for meeting current Part M requirements. It represents the new paradigm, and the character of its departure from the form of the 1992 Part M approved document has already been indicated.

The precept is that, for any proposed new building, reasonable provision for disabled people cannot be prescribed nationally; it can only be determined locally in the light of all relevant circumstances. It follows that the architect, in alliance with his building developer, should set the terms for negotiating Part M conditions, or, as they are called for the purposes of the proposed Accessibility Act, Part Z conditions. For any building subject to the Part M/Part Z building regulation there would, I suggest, be strategic and tactical conditions for meeting requirements. The strategic conditions would be core conditions, and the standard core condition, applicable as a rule to all new buildings, would be that all public areas of the building, or zones of such areas, should be accessible without there being a need to negotiate steps or stairs to get to them. This, and such other core conditions as would be appropriate, would be mutually agreed at the start by the architect, the developer and the enforcement agency, the last either the local authority or an independent inspector.

The tactical conditions would be for the various elements and features of the building concerned, and for these there would be menus of condition options of the kind set out in section 6 of the Annex A document. From the door menu the architect could, for example, opt for an automatic-opening door at the principal entrance, from the lift menu a lift large enough for a wheelchair to be turned inside, and from the sanitary facilities menu wc compartments for all users which would be wheelchair-accessible. Having regard to relevant circumstances, the condition selected from a menu would, as a rule, be the one which best served to extend the accommodation parameters of normal provision. The architect, having agreed the proposed conditions with the building developer, would present them as a package to the enforcement agency for approval. The agency would then agree them in toto, or negotiate amendments to them with the architect and the developer. A politically interesting feature of the whole procedure is that the menu system means that uniform design standards are out of order – uncritical dogmatism gives way to constructive pragmatism. And with Part Z there would no longer be an exclusive preoccupation with the special needs of medically disabled people.

For the purpose of meeting the Part Z (or Part M) reasonable provision requirement, a significant aspect of the new system is the distinction that is made between public and staff-only areas of buildings, the guiding principle being that public areas should, as a matter of course, be wheelchair-accessible whereas staff-only areas need not be. I comment on the reasonability of this and then, with reference to the content of Annex A, move on to discuss how discrimination against women should be tackled when public toilet facilities are provided in new buildings, how the European Union's Directive on lift controls should be interpreted, and how the problems associated with guestrooms in hotel buildings should be handled.

Public and staff areas of buildings: the core condition

For new buildings to be used by members of the public, the standard core condition for meeting Part Z requirements would be that all public areas of the building, or zones of them, should be accessible without a need to negotiate steps or stairs. On the reasonableness of making this a general rule, the findings of the Department of the Environment's sanitary provision research project are relevant. The estimate drawn from project data was that among the users of an 'average' public building some 114 of every 1000 adult visitors were people who would be classed as having a level access need, meaning a need for level access to toilet facilities[8]. At 11.4 per cent of all adults, there is here a significant proportion of all building users – more than enough to confirm that, as a matter of course, it is reasonable to require that all public zones of new public buildings should have level access.

In any building where the no-steps-in-the-way precept is applied, it will normally be feasible for people with disabilities to be employed in the building. And in the case of any new speculatively developed multi-storey office building, all work areas and staff amenities can as a rule be planned to be wheelchair-accessible. With public buildings and the people who might work in them, the issue for debate is whether certain staff areas could reasonably have access by way of steps or stairs; such areas include, for example, storage rooms, staff offices, staff canteens, staff sitting rooms, kitchen and food preparation areas, work spaces in factory buildings, projection rooms to conference facilities, translation booths, and residential facilities for staff in buildings such as hotels.

Disabled people who work in buildings

Among people with disabilities who work in buildings the majority are ambulant disabled people, and the question raised is whether among the staff employed in buildings generally, or particular types of buildings, ambulant disabled people with a locomotor impairment are so numerous as to make it reasonable to require that all staff areas should have level access, meaning no-steps access from the building entrance.

With regard to the Part Z (or Part M) 'reasonable provision' mandate, the premise here is that criteria for staff and their provision are not the same as those for the public and theirs. In public areas of buildings, basic provision for functional activities (such as getting to a toilet and using it) is reasonable, and so also, with a view to better serving members of the public, is provision which enhances the comfort and convenience of building users. In staff areas – and in public areas where staff work – suitable provision for staff to perform their employment duties and use staff amenities is reasonable, but there is not, as there is in public areas, a reasonable requirement for added comfort. Bearing in mind this distinction, relevant findings of the sanitary provision project are considered; they come from the report of the public buildings study, since only wheelchair users were surveyed for the employment buildings inquiry.

The number of regular people, meaning walking-about adult people who were not in another category, who were interviewed for the public buildings survey was 1954, and of these 240 – or 12.3 per cent – were classed as regular disabled people; this was because, on account of a disability, they responded 'essential' or 'important' to the question 'If you are trying to use a public toilet, how important is it for you to have level access so that you don't need to use steps or stairs to get there?' In interpreting this finding for the purpose of determining what would constitute reasonable access provision in public areas of buildings, the presumption is that both the 'essentials' and the 'importants' have a justifiable need for level access to public amenities and facilities.

In the case of staff employed in buildings, the presumption is that only the 'essentials' have a justifiable need for level access to staff-only areas of buildings. The extrapolation of the public buildings survey data to the sphere of staff needs in places of employment cannot be reliable, but the exercise is interesting. The number of regular people aged between 16 and 54 who were questioned was 1179, and of these 11 were 'essentials', or 0.9 per cent. For those aged between 16 and 64, the corresponding figures were 1451 and 22, or 1.5 per cent[9].

The prevalence of wheelchair users in open employment was a topic explored in the course of the sanitary provision research project. The estimates drawn from the findings were that for every 100 000 people in paid employment in England there were 11 wheelchair users: for every 100 000 who worked in office-type buildings there were 18, and for every 100 000 in other workplaces there were 5*. Related data suggested that there was no reason to suppose that the number of wheelchair users in paid employment might increase in future years.

Practical inferences

For practical purposes these findings are interpreted as follows. In new public buildings it is reasonable to require that all public zones should have level access. In new multi-storey employment buildings (as a rule, office-type buildings) it is reasonable to require that all floors should have level access. In new low-rise office-type buildings it is reasonable to require that the ground floor should have level access, but not upper floors. In other new buildings which are places of employment it is *not* reasonable to require that areas used exclusively by staff should have level access. With regard to sanitary facilities, the paucity of wheelchair users in paid employment, along with the sanitary project finding that they tended not to be severely handicapped[10], suggests that in staff-only cloakrooms in administrative buildings it could be reasonable for there to be a wheelchair-accessible wc compartment in each toilet area, but not that it should be a unisex facility.

In certain buildings there are areas which are not distinctly either 'public' or 'staff'. Examples are dressing rooms and associated facilities for stage performers in theatres, changing rooms for players in sports buildings, and members-only bars, lounges and other facilities in club buildings. The consideration is whether provision should be made for wheelchair users, and, if so, what rules should apply. For dressing rooms etc in theatres, the 'at least one' rule would normally be appropriate. In sports buildings where wheelchair users could be players, it would be reasonable to require that changing facilities should generally be wheelchair-accessible. In others, for

* See page 176.

example buildings for specific sports such as football, rugby football, hockey, rowing and ice hockey, stairs to changing facilities would be acceptable. In club buildings, if not all areas, at least parts of all zones used by members should be wheelchair-accessible. Overall, however, there is no need for preordained formulas; as sections 5 and 6 of Annex A demonstrate, appropriate determinations can be made for whatever particular building happens to be under consideration.

Staff-only provision

On access issues and accessibility controls, the theme of this book has been the desirability of shifting the balance; of moving away from an exclusive preoccupation with the special needs of medically disabled people, and towards instead an equal concern (admittedly with a focus on public toilets, but in the access arena it is public toilets which matter most) for women and, in particular, mothers with infants in pushchairs. Disability doctrinalism, of the kind which insists that wheelchair access to all staff areas of all buildings ought to be provided, that lift controls must be at low level for the benefit of wheelchair users and that tactile pavings are essential for blind people, deserves, in my view, to be countered.

For buildings with which they would be dealing under the terms of the Part Z regulation (or the current Part M regulation), local authorities could seek to invoke the banner of equal opportunities. Wheelchair users, they might submit, should have the same employment opportunities as able-bodied people, and they could press for all staff areas of new buildings to be wheelchair-accessible. With regard to buildings of their own – many of which would be administration buildings – they could make that a firm condition. Similarly, national agencies of a quango type might do the same. If, for example, their determination in respect of a new conference building was that all translation booths must be wheelchair-accessible, that would be their prerogative. Where local authorities would not, however, be entitled under a reasonable provision mandate to impose dogmatic conditions for staff-only areas would be in respect of new commercial and industrial buildings such as restaurants, hotels, supermarkets and factory buildings.

Sanitary facilities

With regard to sanitary provision in any building subject to the Part Z building regulation, architects will need to think when they interpret the guidance in the Annex A document. For toilet facilities in any building or part of a building, the provision that is suitable will be specific to locations and sectors, and to the character – often difficult to predict – of toilet users and their needs. Among considerations which may need to be taken into account are: (1) the number of toilet facilities to be provided; (2) the proportionate distribution of facilities for women versus men; (3) the differences between 'public' and 'staff' requirements; (4) accommodation for infants and pushchair users, particularly in female sectors; (5) mixes of wc compartment types in normal male and female sectors; (6) the scope for all disabled users to be catered for by normal provision; (7) the type of provision where unisex provision for disabled people is required; (8) the matter of small boys and suitable urinal provision; and (9) the avoidance of awkward cloakroom lobbies.

Elsewhere in the catalogue of conditions for making buildings accessible under the new system, it will as a rule be feasible for architects to produce 'right' solutions, meaning solutions that are right and proper in the circumstances of the case. In respect of toilet facilities in public or employment buildings this will not so easily be achieved; however well the architect understands the Annex A procedures and however much careful thinking he does, it will be rare that he is able to say confidently, 'Yes, I have got it right'. With a building being constructed speculatively, the profile and characteristics of the people who will use it will not be known. And where the brief is for a particular type of building with a predetermined usage, it could be that the nature of the building's usage will change during the course of construction, or will change subsequently when taken over by a new owner.

The conventional male/female separation

Flexibility is a commodity which the architect may be asked to incorporate when he designs a new building. Partition walls can be removed, new partitions inserted, allowance can be made for the function of spaces and individual rooms to change, and new technology may bring changes to services installations. But toilet provision, with its confined space and fixed services infrastructure, is often peculiarly inflexible. The convention that men and women must have separate facilities is constraining; a substantial measure of flexibility would, it may be noted, be obtained were it the norm for all toilet provision to be 'unisex', as in domestic housing, aircraft and railway trains. For reasons that my wife reports, the idea ought to be rejected: 'Why is it', she asks, 'that men aim so inaccurately, sprinkle their smelly urine elsewhere than in the receptacle provided, leave the lid up and never wash their hands?' In consequence, the established separation convention informs relevant guidance in the Annex A document.

Tackling discrimination against women

Under new legislation and regulations an important objective would be to remove, so far as possible, the discrimination exercised against women. Invariably it seems to be women who find themselves obliged to queue when using public toilets, not men. Theoretically, there would be no queues if architects were always to incorporate a sufficient quantity of amenities to meet women's needs. But I doubt whether for any public building type there can be a reliable formula for predicting what the maximum demand might be, and how many amenities would be appropriate. Should the proposed new control system become operative it will, however, be possible to set conditions, both for the overall quantity of toilet amenities to be provided and the ratio of male to female provision.

For the architect who designs a new building, catering adequately for men presents no problems. Suitable provision comes with economy, the economy with which urinals can be inserted. Where usage is light, there can, in a small toilet area, be a single wc compartment and two or three urinals; where it is heavier and the area bigger, there can be, say, four wcs and 12 urinals. Should the overall space allocated for women be similar, women will only get two wc compartments in the first case and perhaps seven in the second. The effect, with women getting half as many and taking twice as long, is that men are four times better provided for. And women, being much more likely to have infants in pushchairs with them, will be further penalised when, in line with standard practice, the wc compartments are small and have in-opening doors.

In the light of this analysis, architectural planning and design strategy ought, I suggest, to be predicated on the needs of women. The architect who plans toilet facilities in buildings should, in respect of each toilet area, start by considering suitable provision on the women's side: how many wcs will be appropriate; how many should have out-opening doors and be pushchair-accessible; ought at least one to be wheelchair-accessible; should there be a baby-changing facility? With the brief for women's provision being determined and its overall area provisionally calculated, what goes in on the men's side will be ancillary. The means by which Part Z conditions should be applied to sanitary facilities in new buildings is illustrated in the examples of notional building types in section 5 of the Annex A document, in conjunction with the associated menus in section 6.7.

Lift controls

In June 1995 the European Parliament and the Council of the European Union issued Directive 95/16 on the approximation of the laws of the Member States relating to lifts[11]. One of the essential requirements was clause 1.6.1, which read, 'The controls of lifts intended for use by unaccompanied disabled persons must be designed and located accordingly'. This recalls my earlier comments on architectural discrimination and lift controls*, in particular the discrimination caused by compliance with the advice in the 1992 Part M approved document that no controls should be higher than 1200mm above floor level. Is this what the European Directive had in mind, or how is clause 1.6.1 to be interpreted?

The circumstance considered first is a lift which has a single batch of controls arranged vertically. Research findings indicate that among wheelchair users it is paraplegic people who most commonly use buildings independently[12], and relevant data presented in Appendix 6 (page 384) suggest that the majority of them would not be unduly incommoded by needing to reach controls at, say, 1450mm above floor level. Of independent wheelchair users who could potentially be incommoded, meaning those who might find themselves alone in a lift, some would be able to operate controls within the Part M approved range of 900 to 1200mm, but others would not. Among the latter would be some disabled people in powered wheelchairs and scooters, often people with such severe upper limb impairments that reaching to activate lift controls independently would never be practicable.

European Directive requirement 1.6.1 did not, we may assume, presuppose macro principles for the accommodation of unaccompanied disabled persons; like other European Union documents incorporating references to disabled people, the premise would have been that unaccompanied disabled persons were building users with a need for special provision. Lift controls intended for them could therefore be assumed to be different from lift controls intended for normal able-bodied people. Was requirement 1.6.1 therefore inapplicable in respect of lift controls intended for use by normal people?

The menu system for meeting Part Z requirements comes with options rather than singular definitive prescriptions. Where, in a lift which has a single batch of controls arranged vertically, maximum height options include, for example, 1600mm, 1500mm and 1400mm, and with a low limit of, say, 1100mm, the provision made ought not to inconvenience any users of the lift concerned – macro provision will serve. In circumstances where there is felt to be good cause for making special micro provision for independent wheelchair users, a supplementary batch of lift controls arranged horizontally could be incorporated.

Hotels

In the context of accessibility provision, the special status of hotels among buildings used by members of the public was discussed in Chapter 21, the pertinent issue being that hotels serve livability as well as visitability purposes. For the 'visitability' areas of hotels – such as restaurants, bars, public toilets and customer amenities such as swimming pools – accessibility considerations are no different from those for related public building types. The complications come with the livability areas, specifically hotel guestrooms and how they should be planned, designed and equipped to cater for people with disabilities.

In new hotel buildings in Britain the prevailing practice is for there to be a standard shell size for hotel guestrooms, typically of the order of 6.0 metres deep by 3.6 metres wide. With the spaciousness and functional convenience of the bed/sitting/working area being a major consideration, an effect of the constraints of the shell size is that the en-suite bathroom, geared as it is to meeting the needs of non-disabled people, is economically planned. With the space inside it being restricted and the door to it usually being narrow, it is out of bounds to wheelchair users. So special rooms have to be provided if wheelchair users are to be accommodated.

The strategy would shift with the introduction of a 'for everyone' Part Z building regulation. In line with the extended parameters tenet, it would be reasonable to require that in any multi-storey hotel building all guestrooms should have no-steps accessibility and wide entrance doors, and similarly the ground floor guestrooms in a low-rise hotel building without a lift. With reference to Figure 18.1 on page 168, this would suggest that perhaps 50 per cent of all the wheelchair users who might stay in a hotel could be accommodated in normal rather than special guestrooms.

Disabled people: bathroom provision in hotel guestrooms

Short of every guestroom in a new hotel building being convenient for all wheelchair users, there would be a residual need for special guestrooms for people with disabilities, with the focus of questions needing to be answered being on the planning and design of the en-suite bathrooms and the facilities and equipment in them. Assuming wheelchair access through the bathroom door, these questions could include the following.

Is space to drive in forwards and reverse out sufficient, or should there be comfortable space to turn the wheelchair around inside? Would a shower suit all disabled people, without there having to be a bath also? Or, assuming transfer from the wheelchair to an across-the-bath portable seat, would a shower over the bath be convenient? Should there be a platform at the head end of the bath to facilitate transfer into the bath? If there is a separate shower area, should it be unobstructed at floor level? Should there be unobstructed space to one side of the wc to permit lateral transfer from a wheelchair? Should there be an overhead hoist to carry a severely disabled person from the bed area through to a position in the bathroom to be lowered into the bath or onto the wc? Should the wash basin be particularly suitable for management by a person seated in a wheelchair? Should bath and basin taps have lever handles? Should special provision for the disabled user of the bathroom be the paramount consideration, without regard to the concerns of the able-bodied person, perhaps a wife or husband, who could be sharing the guestroom and the use of the bathroom?

With the menu system in play for setting conditions for meeting Part Z (or current Part M) building regulation requirements, a whole range of hotel bathroom options could theoretically be set out diagrammatically, in the same way as is done for wc compartment options in the Annex A document. Even if that were sensible, it would not be practicable, and for controlling guestroom/bathroom accessibility provision in new hotel buildings a more manageable tactic is called for.

The line adopted in Annex A (page 328) is to have three broad options. The first, GR1, is a guestroom which can be entered in a wheelchair, where there may or may not be convenient wheelchair turning space in the bed area, and where the bathroom is not wheelchair-accessible. The second, GR2, is where there is turning space in the bed area, and the bathroom is wheelchair-accessible, though on the basis that the wheelchair user enters forwards and reverses out. The third, GR3, is where there is space in the bathroom for a wheelchair to be turned around.

For building control purposes, it is predictable that the employment of independent inspectors will become standard practice among national hotel companies, with no local authority control and Part Z (or current Part M) conditions being agreed between the developer, the architect and the independent inspector. For any particular case, the character of the proposed hotel development will affect the form of appropriate – and reasonable – conditions, with conditions being variable for different types of developments. Taking the three menu options as a starting base, an initial consideration will be conditions for the distribution of the guestrooms; they might be a mix of GR1 and GR2, a mix of GR1 and GR3, or a mix of GR1, GR2 and GR3.

For hotel developments subject to local authority building control the principle would be the same, with the developer and the architect formulating the provisional conditions and then negotiating them with the local authority. Procedures are illustrated by the two notional examples of hotel developments in section 5 of Annex A, referenced to the menu options in section 6.

Continuing to deal with Part M

The proposals I put forward as to how accessibility controls for new buildings might sensibly be reformulated are hypothetical; they would be realised only if the government were, at some future date, to be persuaded not to reject the thesis I present in this book, and then inclined to take on board my ideas for new legislation and a remodelled Part M building regulation. More likely than not, however, the government would not proceed in that fashion; it might instead decide to do nothing, or else look for a different track to go down.

In the meantime, and perhaps indefinitely, the current Part M regulation will remain in place. The approved document which goes with it, currently the 1992 edition, could be withdrawn or revised. But whether or not it is, the Annex A document could be employed by architects as guidance on how to meet Part M requirements. Relatedly, it could be used by building inspectors in the business of setting Part M conditions. While some of them might welcome the Annex A document, others would, I imagine, have preferred to stick with the 1992 Approved Document. They will, should architects elect to adopt Annex A, need to retrain themselves in operational procedures for Part M cases. In the process they will become steadily more knowledgeable about accessibility issues, and, while continuing to deal with new-build cases only, will be better equipped should the day come when building alterations are also subject to statutory control.

26 Alterations to existing buildings

There are, in my view, three important reasons why, if it can possibly be done, there should be a statutory mechanism which would permit accessibility provision to be regulated when material alterations are made to existing buildings.

First, on account of the Disability Discrimination Act. Should the government be obliged to acknowledge that section 21(2) cannot be made to work, there will be a political imperative to assure disability lobbyists that a viable and effective means of implementing the underlying intentions of section 21(2) – to make existing public buildings more conveniently accessible to disabled people – can and will be brought into operation.

Second, for the public interest. Undeniably it is in the public interest that new public buildings are designed so that they are conveniently usable by people with disabilities and other building users with special needs, and correspondingly it would be in the public interest were it standard practice for the accessibility of existing public buildings to be improved when alterations were made to them.

Third, on account of planning control issues. For controlling the accessibility of new buildings, the procedure that has been proposed is that such planning matters as have to do with accessibility could in future be covered by building control, with it being standard practice for planning approval to be subject to accessibility provision being in compliance with the requirements of the Part Z building regulation. The same factors as prompted the advocacy of this line for new buildings apply to building alterations which are subject to planning control, and it would therefore be appropriate for the proposed Accessibility Act to come with regulations (either Building Regulations or some other form of regulatory control) which would prescribe what action would need to be taken when such alterations were made.

The scope for regulation

There are two kinds of buildings with which we are concerned. One is a building where material alterations are already proposed. The other is simply a building which is in use, one whose owner has no intention of doing more than keeping it in good repair. Clearly, the first kind of building offers more favourable opportunities for intervention on the accessibility front, subject, as it would be, to building control approval.

The regulatory requirement might be in the form 'Reasonable accessibility provision shall be made when alterations are made to the building'. Reservations about this are that there cannot be national prescriptions and all alteration works aimed at improving accessibility necessarily have to be handled pragmatically. A related consideration is that, of all the alterations of one kind or another that are made to buildings, most have nothing at all to do with accessibility provision.

I continue, however, to pursue the idea that, under the terms of the proposed Accessibility Act, building regulations could be employed to mandate accessibility when existing buildings are altered. There might be a Z2 regulation to complement the Z1 regulation, and the scope of it would be selective; in respect of any case for which building control approval was sought, it would apply only to such alteration works as would be deemed to have an accessibility ingredient. With the regulation being applicable only to accessibility provisions covered by the works, not to accessibility provision elsewhere in the building, relevant works might include alterations to (a) any public entrance to the building; (b) any toilets used by visiting members of the public; (c) circulation areas and public amenity areas within a storey; and (d) vertical circulation provision involving the installation of a passenger lift, platform lift or stairlift.

The circumstances for the application of a Z2 regulation would be carefully prescribed, and initially my thinking was that its requirement might have read as follows:

> Z2. Where a material alteration is made which affects accessibility provision within or around the building, such provision as it is reasonable in all the circumstances of the case to make shall be made to facilitate the usage of the building by such people as might use the building.

Given, however, that 'all the circumstances of the case' would include the financial status of the building owner and the potential effects of the work on his business, there is, in effect, no substantive difference between this Z2 and the proposed Z1 regulation for new buildings. Nor, as I see it, is there any good reason why the Z1 regulation should not in relevant circumstances be employed to mandate alterations to existing buildings. Its requirement is repeated:

> Z1 Reasonable provision shall be made to facilitate the usage of the building and associated spaces around it by such people as might use or wish to use the building, including people with disabilities.

The proposed terms of the application of Z1 to relevant alterations to existing buildings are set out in section 2.1 of the Annex A document on page 295. As a rule, its activation would be triggered by a building owner who proposed to make alterations to a building and was doing so voluntarily. A non-voluntary circumstance could be in respect of a building for which planning permission was required for a change of use, and for illustration I refer to the case reported earlier, that of the shop in Sheen Road in Richmond upon Thames.

Under the terms of the Accessibility Act and associated guidance issued by the Department of the Environment, the terms of approval for the use of 65 Sheen Road to be changed would have been, 'Planning permission is granted, subject to accessibility provision being made which meets the requirements of the Part Z building regulation'. Those involved in the process would have been the developer, the architect, the local authority building control officer and, since the building was in a conservation area, the planning department's conservation officer. The upper floor being a dwelling, the provision of access to it would not have been subject to Part Z. Access to the ground floor shop would have been, and to meet the Z1 requirement the condition could have been that the two steps would be suitably graded with, perhaps, a suitable handrail being fixed. The negotiations would not have been complicated.

To cover cases such as this, Building Regulation 3(2), which defines what is meant by a 'material' alteration, would need to be amended, with an additional item which would be in the form, 'An alteration is material for the purposes of these regulations if the work is carried out in order to meet the requirements of a planning permission condition'.

Part Z procedures

Should the Accessibility Act with its Part Z building regulation be brought into effect, an architect or building surveyor commissioned by a building owner would normally know whether alterations he was proposing to make to a building would be subject to the Z1 regulation. Where they would be, he would present drawings and specifications of his proposed provisional conditions for meeting the Z1 requirement to the building inspector, either a local authority building control officer or an independent approved inspector. It would then be the duty of the inspector to decide whether the proposed provisional conditions would be suitable without being amended, or to apply different conditions, ones that could be more stringent than the building owner had had in mind.

Among all Z1 building alteration cases it could quite often happen that the inspector's view of what would constitute reasonable accessibility would be somewhat different from the building owner's view. The need in such cases would be to negotiate a mutually agreeable solution, one where the inspector did not feel obliged to impose a condition which the building owner, perhaps having regard to the costs involved, felt to be unwarranted on grounds of reasonableness. Across the board, such disagreements might more often surface when the building inspector happened to be a local authority building control officer, and in this context the character of works likely to be handled by independent inspectors is a relevant factor.

The status of independent inspectors

National companies in the business of managing, for example, department stores and hotels could advantageously employ an independent inspector for building regulations purposes. The prime consideration could be the operation of the Part B regulation, a merit of having an independent inspector being consistency in the application of conditions for means of escape in case of fire. Relatedly, there would be consistency in the application of current Part M conditions for new-build work, and prospectively for building alteration works which would be regulated with the introduction of a Part Z regulation.

A national department store or hotel company would already be experienced in making suitable provision for customers with disabilities, with an appreciation of what appropriately ought to be done where. For a certain type of hotel building a company might, for example, have a strategy of building extensions in which guestrooms would cater for the generality of guests, with rooms in the main building being enlarged and adapted to suit those with disabilities. With the company's independent building inspector becoming an integral member of the planning team, such building works as would be subject to Part Z could be considered within the strategy frame, not necessarily as self-contained items.

As well as department stores and hotels, building types which for regulatory purposes could commonly be handled by independent inspectors could include supermarkets, banks, roadside service stations, building society premises, fast-food restaurants, pubs, insurance company office buildings, airport terminals, railway stations, bookshops and wine merchants. For all these, there could be standardised design practices for new construction and building alterations, drawn from design guidance in Annex A, for meeting Part Z requirements; this would help towards negotiating suitable building control conditions without hassle.

Writing as I do in March 1997, when as yet only a small number of independent approved inspectors have been appointed, all this is speculative. My guess is, however, that the administration of building regulations, in the past the exclusive domain of local authorities, will increasingly become the business of independent inspectors. And looking to the future and the operation of Part Z, the troublesome building alteration cases – those where the building owner and the building inspector find themselves disagreeing over what reasonable provision should be held to mean – will most likely be ones where a local authority has the building control function.

Extensions and material alterations

For building works subject to Part Z, the principle will be that extensions to existing buildings, along with reconstruction behind a preserved façade or inside a retained structural frame, will be treated in the same way as new buildings. In conjunction with the important core condition – that there should be no-steps access to public areas or zones of them – the building feature conditions applied to them will not as a rule be different from those appropriate to new buildings.

Building alterations that are not treated like new buildings will range from the entire refurbishment of a multi-storey office building to virtually nil-cost ad hoc alterations such as refixing a handrail or changing a door handle. Clearly, the refixing of a handrail ought not to be a matter for which the owner of a building has to seek permission from a building inspector, and on its own it is not. The reason is that it is not, in effect, a structural alteration, and is not for the purposes of building regulations defined as a material alteration. Relatedly, other ad hoc alterations, for example the rehanging of a wc compartment door to open out, the removal of a superfluous door in a cloakroom lobby or the fixing of hold-open catches to doors in passageways, would not on their own require building control approval.

The proviso to this would be that where the building concerned was listed, and where the alterations proposed could affect the character of the building, listed building consent would be required[1]. In such cases the building owner would consult the local authority's conservation officer, who, assuming he was content with what was proposed, would advise the authority to agree to give formal consent. Should consent be refused, the building owner could, if he wished, appeal to the Secretary of State for the Environment.

The platform for Part Z

Were the government to opt for a Part Z regulation under the terms of new legislation, it would, predictably, be widely publicised. Assuming that the unworkability of section 21(2) of the Disability Discrimination Act had been acknowledged, it would be presented as an effective means of implementing the intentions of that Act. In early 1997, with the 'serving the public' part of section 21 having been brought into force, a government advertising campaign is being targeted at service providers, with building providers being encouraged to anticipate the legal duties they will have when section 21(2) comes into operation, as the government supposes that it will do. Viewed from another angle, a platform is being built for the arrival of a Part Z building regulation covering alterations to existing buildings.

Conditions and guidelines

In the case of substantial building alteration works, for example the reconstruction of the main entrance to a building, the relocation of toilet facilities or general refurbishment, the menu system could be employed to set building feature conditions for Part Z purposes. For reasons noted in section 4.3 of Annex A, it would in certain circumstances be permissible for less stringent conditions to be applied than would be appropriate for new buildings.

If a Part Z building regulation were to be introduced, there would be cause for monitoring the operation of building alteration cases, with the Department of the Environment perhaps selecting a number of independent inspectors and local authority agencies with whom it would liaise regularly and look to for advice on guidance which might be issued regarding operational procedures. One that could be appropriate when building control approval was sought would be for information requested on application forms to include (1) the estimated total cost of the works to be contracted; (2) the estimated cost of the works directly aimed at improving accessibility; and (3) the rateable value of the premises concerned. Such information could be of relevance in the event of disagreements surfacing in the course of the negotiation process. For illustration, I hypothesise four instances where conditions might be disputed:

- At the main entrance to a shop building the steps are to be made more manageable, but wheelchair access will still be by way of a service entrance at the back of the building. The inspector asks for a platform lift at the main entrance.
- On three steps on a circulation route in a museum building the building owner proposes a stairlift. The inspector advises structural alterations whereby a suitable ramp would be provided in a diversion to one side of the steps.
- The downstairs wc facilities in a pub are to remain, although with access to them improved. The inspector requires a supplementary unisex facility at ground level.
- A three-storey building without a lift is to be extensively modified and refurbished by an entertainment company to provide bars, lounges and disco facilities. A lift is not proposed, but the inspector requires that one should be incorporated.

In cases such as these, and others like or unlike them, the financial circumstances of the building owner/developer and his business expectations would be relevant when considering reasonable accessibility provision. While the rateable value of the premises and the cost of proposed alteration works could have a bearing on negotiations for compliance with the Z1 requirement, I doubt that any cost formula related to them could ever be generally appropriate as a means of assessing what might or might not be reasonable. Each and any Z1 building alteration case would need to be handled pragmatically, the aim always being to achieve mutual agreement following negotiations. An outcome of the monitoring process could, however, be that circumstances would be identified where formulas might indicate reasonable cost parameters, for example the percentage of additional expenditure above estimates that building owners could reasonably be expected to carry.

The Part Z challenge to building inspectors

Around the country there would, I imagine, be many local authority building control officers, and some independent inspectors as well, for whom the prospect of a Part Z building regulation would be unattractive. Building inspectors are construction industry specialists; they are skilled in handling the technicalities of building regulations such as come with current Parts A to L, but Part M can be foxing. With Part M as it now stands, many, I suspect, would wish to stay with the current Approved Document and the scope that it gives for applying conditions precisely in line with its national prescriptions. With a Part Z regulation, most dauntingly in respect of controlling building alterations, they would need to learn new skills. The path to Part Z would, however, be made easier for them if from now on (from when this book is published) it were to become regular practice for Part M new-build cases to be dealt with in the manner set out in Annex A, with strategic core conditions in conjunction with tactical building feature conditions drawn from menus.

With Annex A procedures there are clear reasonable provision parameters for new buildings – the no-steps core condition and the extended parameters rule for building features. For any particular new building, the conditions set by a local authority would therefore probably be little different from those set by an independent inspector. For building alterations works, variable as they are, there are no common guiding parameters, an effect in any particular case being that the conditions set by one inspector could be quite different from those set by another. And across the board it might also happen that the conditions set by local authorities for Part Z building alterations could generally be different in character and degree from those set by independent inspectors.

The independent inspector is an independent agent. In dealing with any Part Z building alteration case, the responsibility he will have for interpreting the law and applying it will be to himself, not to anyone else. The conditions he sets will be ones that he has negotiated with the building owner and the architect, and while their views will have influenced him, his decisions will, we may suppose, have been made without prejudice.

The local authority inspector is not an independent agent. The local authority is the building control agency, and in setting conditions for Part Z cases the inspector properly defers to such policy edicts as the local authority has adopted for dealing with matters to do with public buildings and disabled people. The stance of able-bodied collaborators, in particular those who are members of the council, may come into the reckoning. For able-bodied collaborators, disabled people are 'them', not 'us', and as a rule anything they can arrange to be specially done to help them, the disabled, will be perceived as being laudable.

With regard to the bullet points noted above, it could be that a local authority inspector might be more inclined to impose the particularly demanding condition – the one that the building owner would not have wanted – than an independent inspector. I do not contend that one would necessarily be right and the other wrong, since subjective judgements would inform decision-making in all Part Z building alteration cases. But it could be that a building owner contemplating Part Z alteration work might help himself were he to employ an independent inspector.

For a related reason, it could in any event be advantageous for a building owner thinking to undertake accessibility alterations to employ an independent inspector. The key to the successful working of the Part Z regulation will be collaboration between building providers and building inspectors. With a view to realising ideas he may already have had about improving the accessibility of his building, a building owner might contact an independent inspector and ask him to come round and look at his building. Together they could discuss what might best be done in the light of the building owner's ideas and the amount of costs he would be willing to carry. The independent inspector's view could, however, be that the already existing access provision was satisfactory, and potentially expensive works were unwarranted. In that case the inspector, being a freelance consultant, could charge a fee for his services and both would be content. Alternatively, with informal agreement on the kind of works needing to be done to meet Part Z requirements, the inspector would ask the building owner to put in an application for Part Z approval, along with appropriate drawings and specifications. The work would go ahead harmoniously.

A local authority inspector would not be in a position to offer such a friendly service. First, because local authorities can only charge fees when building works are undertaken, and their inspectors could be reluctant to give a building owner informal advice when the outcome could be no action. Second, because the local authority inspector, not being a free agent, would not be able to make on-the-spot determinations of what ought or ought not to be done.

Determinations

Referring back to the four bullet points, I hypothesise a situation where a building owner had used the local authority service and where the outcome was implacable disagreement. As a last resort, the building owner, insistent that the local authority's conditions were unreasonable, could request the Secretary of State for the Environment to make a determination, meaning a determination of whether or not the proposals that he (the building owner) had put forward would be deemed to satisfy the Z1 requirement.

While technically this recourse would be available under the law, my view is that it could never be sensible for it to be invoked. With advice being given to him by his officials, the Secretary of State's duty is to determine whether, in all the circumstances of a case, the applicant's proposals satisfy the statutory requirement, not whether they comply with the guidance in an approved document. Predictably more so than for current Part M determinations for new buildings, the making of Part Z building alterations determinations would be informed by subjective judgements. Consideration of all relevant circumstances would always be a problematical business, the effect in any particular case being that the Secretary of State could not confidently assure himself that the decision he would make would be soundly based.

The assumption at this point is that, had the building owner employed an independent inspector in the first place, there would have been mutual agreement on exactly what ought to be done. The circumstance we are considering is, however, one where he did not and is disputing a local authority inspector's ruling on Part Z conditions. What then, if a request for a determination is to be avoided, should the building owner do, short of not undertaking any alteration works or defying the ruling and doing them his way?* The answer, I suggest, would be that he would employ an

*Should the determination find in favour of the inspectorate agency's ruling, the building developer cannot appeal against it. He cannot himself take the matter to court; if he is determined to construct his building in defiance of the ruling, he will do so knowing that under section 36 of the Building Act 1984 the local authority may by legal notice require him to pull down or remove the work, and that only then, if the authority persists, will he be able to argue the matter in court.

independent inspector and repeat the negotiation process. Since pragmatism and subjective judgements would be operative, it would not, in my view, be admissible for the law to bar him from taking that course. And if his first independent inspector were to take the same line as the local authority, he could, presumably, try again with another.

Summarizing the scenario

In presenting this speculative scenario, there are, I suspect, points where my understandings are misguided, and about which an informed commentator could have disabused me. I would not, however, suppose that the nature of my misapprehensions is such as to destroy the whole idea of regulating building alterations by way of a Part Z-type regulation. This could, I believe, be a viable way forward, and, in the light of all relevant political and practical considerations, the only sensible way.

Buildings in use and the Disability Discrimination Act

A Part Z regulation under which accessibility provision could be mandated when existing buildings were altered could do a great deal to compensate for the unworkability of section 21(2) of the Disability Discrimination Act. The generality of people with disabilities would not, I imagine, be at all troubled by not having a right to walk into a building and tell its owner that it unlawfully discriminated against them. They could tackle the matter more diplomatically; in the case of a building which they found difficult to manage and for which they had ideas on how its accessibility might be improved, the line open to them would be to talk to the owner (or manager) about the kind of alterations which might be made, and, on more occasions than not, he would be sympathetic and ready to listen.

How many such building providers would be recalcitrant and remain determined, despite the introduction of a Part Z regulation and sustained pressure to implement the intentions of the Disability Discrimination Act, to do nothing would be a topic which could, when the time came, be the subject of a research inquiry. My guess is that relatively few would be found. And even if disability activists were still to insist that they must be brought to book, I doubt they would obtain the crucial support they would need from the disability lobby in parliament.

Hypothesising that I could be wrong, I would not suppose that any legislation could be devised which would satisfy them. Assuming that any mandatory statute would be a non-starter, some kind of permissive legislation would have to serve, and I offer the following for consideration:

> In respect of an existing building in its area used by members of the public, a local authority may, with a view to alterations being made to improve the accessibility of that building, require the owner of that building to consider proposals for such alterations as might be appropriate.

The purpose here would be to encourage the building owner to consider suitable proposals and then undertake alterations which would be subject to the Part Z building regulation. But I would not suppose that local authority associations would welcome the idea, or advise the government that their member authorities would be pleased to take on the administrative burdens that the legislation could entail. Were the problem of what to do about buildings in use to have to be faced, it could be, however, that someone else will come up with a more effective and generally acceptable legislative proposition.

With section 21 of the Disability Discrimination Act remaining in place, the first three stages of action for its implementation would be unaffected – those relating to services provided directly to disabled people; the changes to a building provider's policies, practices and procedures; and the provision of auxiliary aids. Only the fourth, the one relating to the adjustment of building features, would not survive. Without it, there could be some disabled people who would lament not being able to go into a building and confront its owner with the threat, 'Your building is discriminatory, it's illegal, and if you don't do something about it I'll sue you'. But their numbers, I guess, would be tiny.

27 The Annex A document and thoughts on further research

Explanations are in order on the form and content of Annex A. I refer variously in this book to 'Annex A', 'the Annex A document' and 'Annex A material'. Annex A is the material which comes under the heading *The Proposed Built Environment (Accessibility) Act: Draft Model for Authorised Guidance Document*, and this comprises the Annex A document. Elsewhere in this book there is material which supports the Annex A document, and it is this related material, together with the whole of Annex A, which is Annex A material. An effect of this is that the Annex A document is not self-contained – for interpreting its content and advice, reference has to be made to a variety of other pieces in this book, notably in the Appendices and Parts 2 and 3 of the narrative.

In effect, the Annex A document is a draft approved document for a new Part M building regulation (called Part Z) which would come with the proposed Accessibility Act. The terms of the Part Z regulatory requirement and its scope are set out in section 2. The means by which Part Z would be applied are detailed in sections 3, 4, 5 and 6; the form of the design guidelines is discussed in section 3 and that of the control mechanisms in section 4. Practical guidance on how design conditions would be applied in order to meet regulatory requirements comes in sections 5 and 6. For building features, the principle is that relevant conditions are drawn from menus: to explain how this is done, section 5 presents eight notional examples of new buildings with appropriate conditions listed for each; these conditions are referenced to the menus in section 6. Ancillary material is in sections 7 to 11.

The Annex A document is not a corporate enterprise. Like the rest of this book, it reflects my personal understandings of the issues it deals with, and, associatedly, it reflects my personal biases and prejudices. No one elsewhere has, to my knowledge, produced and published a document on lines similar to it, meaning, it would seem, that I could claim it to be my intellectual property. Be that so or not, it is copyright material, and, other than for review or comment purposes, anyone who wishes to incorporate pieces of it in documentation which could be given public circulation will need to request permission from the publisher of this book. Practising architects who are attracted by it, and wish to adopt it when working on building schemes subject to the current Part M building regulation, will, I trust, find that it works well. They will discover gaps and faults in it, but a merit of the menu system is its flexibility – any architect who employs it can insert his own proposed conditions and test their viability.

The premise on which Annex A is presented is that the Department of the Environment might acknowledge that the for-the-disabled exclusivity of the current Part M regulation ought to be discarded and a for-everyone regulation substituted for it, along with a new Approved Document. That might not happen: those concerned could instead elect to do nothing and leave the current Part M approved document in place. But were they to decide that a for-everyone regulation was wanted and that Annex A with its Part Z regulation was a sound model for it, a new approved document would have to be drafted and put out to consultation. It could then be better presented than my temporary expedient, and, with further research studies having been undertaken, better informed.

Future research inquiries to do with designing for the disabled ought, I suggest, to have either a 'buildings' or a 'users' perspective. On the buildings side, both for new buildings and alterations to existing ones, particular types of buildings could be examined, with inquiries being conducted in cooperation with practising architects. With a view to amending or amplifying menu options for building features, such building types could include hotels, schools, hospitals, courts and police stations, and – with particular regard to seating provision for wheelchair users – theatres, cinemas and sports stadia.

On the users' side, the sanitary provision project methodology, of random intercepts and then interviews in shopping centres, could be employed to gather information on particular building usage topics from (for example) samples of wheelchair users and pushchair users. With regard to wheelchair users, a study of the status of personal independence could be valuable. The main focus would be on wheelchair users who regularly go out on their own and use public buildings independently. With reference to matters such as getting up ramps, getting through doors, reaching lift controls and doing the shopping in supermarkets, the importance of independence – of not being obliged to ask others to help – would be explored.

A survey of pushchair users could be informative, not only because it would yield information about pushchair usage in buildings. Mothers who were interviewed could be asked about baby-changing and baby-feeding facilities in buildings, about the planning and design of such facilities and the equipment in them, and in which types of buildings they ought to be provided. Mothers – and fathers – could be asked about the problems of assisting infant children to use typical wc facilities, and about helping small boys to use urinal facilities. In respect of pushchair accessibility to public toilet facilities, information could be obtained about the types of buildings where, for security as well as practical reasons, full access for loaded pushchairs was most important.

While empirical research studies such as these could yield useful data, informative anecdotal evidence on the lines of the Chapter 21 report of my usage of buildings could also help. The experiences of others could differ markedly from my own, and in the context of producing reliable design guidance reports of them could have a moderating effect. Systematic, detailed and comprehensive reports – or ones which focused on particular issues of concern to their authors – could come, for example, from pushchair users and others who have small children with them when they use buildings, from independent wheelchair users, from wheelchair users wholly dependent on assistance from others when using buildings, from ambulant disabled people, from people with sight impairments, from blind people and from deaf people.

Annexes and Appendices

Annex A

The Proposed Built Environment (Accessibility) Act: Draft Model for Authorised Guidance Document

Contents

1 Introduction

A series of assumptions have governed the form and content of this document, the important one being that at some future date the UK government will introduce new primary legislation and associated new regulations for controlling the accessibility of the built environment. The following are among related assumptions:

1 The new statute will be called the Built Environment (Accessibility) Act, known as the Accessibility Act.
2 The purpose of the Act will be to promote architectural action which enhances the accessibility of the built environment for all building users.
3 The principal instrument employed to further the aims of the Act will be Building Regulations.
4 New regulations mandating accessibility provision in public and employment buildings will replace the current Part M building regulation, the new regulation being described in this document as the Part Z regulation.
5 The Part Z regulation, with requirements being in the form 'reasonable provision shall be made', will cover new buildings and material alterations to existing buildings which affect the accessibility of the building concerned.
6 For meeting Part Z requirements there will be local control procedures.
7 With the introduction of the Part Z regulation, planning and building control functions will be merged in respect of accessibility provision in public and employment buildings. For any particular building subject to Part Z, a planning condition could be in the terms, 'Planning permission is granted, subject to there being accessibility provision which meets the requirements of the Part Z building regulation'.

The document is presented in the style of an official Department of the Environment Approved Document. The practical guidance contained in it is not comprehensive; in respect of a variety of items reference is made to material elsewhere in this book.

2 The Part Z building regulation

2.1 The requirements of the regulation

Requirement	*Application*
Z1 Reasonable provision shall be made to facilitate the usage of the building and associated spaces around it by such people as might use or wish to use the building, including people with disabilities.	1 The requirement applies to: (a) a newly constructed building; (b) the extension to an existing building where the extension includes a ground storey; (c) a reconstructed building where the formerly existing building has been substantially demolished to leave only external walls; (d) a reconstructed building where the formerly existing building has been substantially demolished to leave only the structural frame; (e) material alterations which affect the accessibility of the building, such material alterations to include alterations to: (i) an entrance to the building; (ii) circulation areas within the building, including vertical circulation provision which involves the installation of a passenger lift, platform lift or stairlift; (iii) amenity areas within the building used by visiting members of the public; (iv) sanitary facilities within the building. 2 The requirement does not apply to: (a) a dwelling, or the common parts of a building which are intended for the exclusive use of two or more dwellings; (b) any part of a building which is used solely to enable the building or any service or fitting in the building to be inspected, maintained or repaired.

2.2 The interface with other parts of the Building Regulations

The provisions made to meet the Part Z requirement will complement, not duplicate or conflict with, those prescribed under other parts of the Building Regulations. Parts A to K come under the health and safety remit of the regulations, Part Z under the welfare and convenience remit. On where the divide between the two remits should lie there are grey areas, most notably in respect of provisions under Part B *Fire safety*, which covers means of escape; Part G *Hygiene*, which covers sanitary conveniences; and Part K *Stairs, ramps and guards*, which includes handrails. In this document, items which are covered include:

- the 'convenience' gradient of stairs and ramps (as distinct from the 'safety' gradient)

- the location, height level and configuration of handrails (as distinct from guard rails and balustrades)
- the location of toilet facilities
- the proportionate distribution of male/female toilet facilities
- the size and configuration of wc compartments

Relatedly, items which are not covered, implying an understanding that they are or will be covered by Building Regulations other than Part Z, include:

- the location and dimensional specifications of refuge spaces
- guards to protect against drops at the edge of an internal or external floor surface
- special fire hazard warning signals for blind and deaf people

3 The terms of the Guidance

3.1 The threshold for the prescription of Part Z conditions

The premise which informs this document is that disabled people are normal people, the principle underlying its design guidance being that virtually all the needs which people with disabilities have when they use buildings can be catered for by normal 'for everyone' provision. There will be occasions when special arrangements have to be made for them, when special provision is needed to supplement normal provision, but this will be the exception rather than the rule. For the purposes of presenting the guidelines in this document there needs, however, to be a demarcation line, a dividing line between the status of design conditions which are appropriately applied in order to meet the requirements of Part Z and those which could be very reasonable requirements but which it would be inappropriate to prescribe as Part Z conditions.

The controlling design precept for facilitating the usage of buildings is the extension of the parameters of normal provision, and the threshold is defined with reference to it. The building users who will most particularly be helped by an extension of the parameters of normal provision will be those who will be people with disabilities or others with special needs; they will not, in other words, be normal able-bodied people. There is then an assumption that there are tenets of good design practice, ones which, when observed by the architect, will make buildings convenient for normal able-bodied people to use. These good practice tenets are applied on behalf of all building users; they are not 'special need' items.

The matter is illustrated with regard to the concerns of sensorily impaired people. Their needs are considered in Chapter 20, with a list of building features which could be on a 'what can we do for?' checklist for sight-impaired people (page 192). None of the items is one for which the need is peculiar to sight-impaired people; all are ones which would benefit everyone, including normal able-bodied people. Generally, they represent good practice. The criterion for Part Z provision emerges: building features which ought, simply as a matter of good practice, to be incorporated in all such buildings as might be used exclusively by normal able-bodied people do not warrant coverage in the design guidance in this document. These include:

- suitable lighting
- appropriate internal and external floor surfaces
- the clear identification of stair nosings

- the clear identification of glazed doors and other glazed surfaces
- appropriate door and window furniture
- fenestration which does not produce uncomfortable glare
- appropriate protection against floor surface drops
- legible signage
- sanitary equipment which is functionally convenient to use

In short, the criterion for the prescription of items for Part Z purposes is that they are building features which do not have to be provided for the convenience of normal able-bodied people, but which ought, where appropriate, to be provided for the convenience of people who are *not* normal able-bodied people.

3.2 The reasonable provision mandate

'Reasonable provision shall be made to facilitate the usage of the building by such people as might use or wish to use the building, including people with disabilities' is the Part Z requirement. *To facilitate* is the purpose; it implies enhanced convenience – provision which, in a suitable and appropriate way, accommodates as near as can be all the prospective users of the building. But the provision has to be *reasonable* for the purpose; for any building feature or features subject to the requirement it means provision of such a character, amount, size, configuration etc as in the light of all relevant circumstances is *appropriate* for the relevant purpose, and is not irrational, absurd or ridiculous.

For any new building subject to Part Z, or an existing building which, when altered, is treated as though it were a new building, the overall reasonable provision made will be the aggregate of the appropriate provisions made for the building as a whole and component features of it. There is a strategic objective, to procure suitable overall provision, and tactical objectives, to procure suitable component provision. For other buildings which are altered, it will be only the alterations that are subject to Part Z, not the building as a whole. While there may be a strategic objective, for example to enable independent wheelchair users to gain access to the building, the focus will be on component provision, for example the entrance component of the building. It is in respect of the component features of a building, particularly where alterations are made to them, that there may be a need for special provision.

3.3 Special provision: tests of reasonableness

Building users other than normal able-bodied people, for example small children, pushchair users and wheelchair users, may have needs which are 'special' because they are distinct from those of normal able-bodied people. That certain building users have special needs does not as a rule mean that they need special provision, but where in the designing of a building special provision is proposed of a kind intended to benefit a particular segment of the population of the users of the building, its reasonableness for Part Z purposes will be subject to four tests:

1 That there is substantive data or secure prima facie evidence confirming that the provision will be of *genuine value* to the building users concerned.
2 That the special provision *does not inconvenience other users* of the building. This applies other than where the advantages it will have for its intended beneficiaries will outweigh the disadvantages caused to others, taking into account the prospective proportion of such beneficiaries among all users of the building and the value of the provision for them.

3 That the special provision *is warranted*: as a rule, it will not be warranted if the need which it is intended to serve could just as well or better have been served by suitable normal provision.
4 That the *cost* of the special provision *is not unduly disproportionate* to the scale of need there might be for it.

3.4 Zones of public areas of buildings

The core condition which as a rule it will be reasonable to apply to new buildings is that all public areas of the building concerned, or zones of such areas, should be accessible without there being a need to negotiate steps or stairs. The reasonability of this rule, along with why it ought not, as a standard condition, to be applied to staff-only areas of buildings, is discussed in Chapter 25 (page 269). On what constitutes 'public areas', the American concept of 'public accommodations' is helpful (book page 104). The offices of public and commercial organizations are, for example, places of public accommodation where they provide services which members of the public may use; on this basis it would be reasonable, for example, to require that in any multi-storey office building all floors should be accessible without a need to negotiate steps or stairs.

The 'zones' qualification comes into play where, in the circumstances of the case concerned, it would not be practicable for all public areas to have no-steps accessibility, or not reasonable. The following are examples in respect of which it would be reasonable to apply the no-steps condition selectively, either as a core condition or a building feature condition:

1 Only the ground floor guestrooms in new low-budget hotels of two or three storeys, assuming near-equal numbers on each floor.
2 Only the ground floor in two or three-storey office-type buildings where all services in that building for visiting members of the public could be provided on the ground floor.
3 Areas having tiered seating, for example in sports stadia, theatres, concert halls and lecture and meeting rooms. In such cases, the condition applied would normally relate to the areas or number of seating spaces suitable for wheelchair users.
4 Customer seating areas in, for example, hotel lounges, restaurants, cafes and bars. Where and as appropriate, a condition would prescribe the proportion which could be on stepped platforms or in recesses.
5 Viewing areas for exhibitions or displays in circumstances where it could be reasonable for secondary viewing areas such as platforms or walkway galleries to be approached by steps or stairs.

4 The control system

4.1 The three stages of accessibility controls

For new buildings, the conditions for meeting Part Z requirements will usually be exercised in three stages – the strategic core conditions at stage 1, provisional planning and design conditions for building features at stage 2, and refined or amended planning and design conditions at stage 3. For building alterations one stage only, the equivalent of new buildings stage 2, will commonly serve.

The procedures for new buildings are explained with reference to (1) the stage 2 pro forma on the opposite page; (2) the examples of the application of conditions to eight types of buildings in section 5; and (3) the menus for conditions in section 6. As a rule the developer or his architect will communicate first with an officer in the local authority's planning department, who will confirm that the no-steps core condition is applicable, and advise also of core conditions applicable to parking provision and approaches to the building. The planning officer's advice will then be ratified by the building control officer, either a local authority officer or an independent inspector.

With the plan drawings he would be preparing, the architect, using the stage 2 pro forma, would draft the building feature conditions which could be appropriate, and submit his proposals to the building control agency for consideration. At this stage the proposed conditions might be in coded form, referenced to relevant condition options in the menus in section 6. Stage 2 conditions, being subject to review or further consideration at stage 3, would be provisional.

The setting of Part Z conditions: stage 2 pro forma

Proposed development:

Core conditions

Approach routes	
Provision within the building	

Building feature conditions

Approaches to the building	
Car parking provision	
Entrances	
Internal circulation features	
Sanitary facilities	
Other provisions	
Staff-only areas	

4.2 The menu system

The section 5 examples of the application of Part Z conditions and the menus in section 6 illustrate the working of stages 2 and 3 condition-setting procedures. For various features of public buildings the menus present condition options; ones which, it is emphasised, are not exhaustive. For reference purposes, these options are numbered, from 1.1 in section 6.1 to 11.10 in section 6.11; they are either functionally described or specify type options. The type options, with codes such as CP2, ES1 or HR3, refer to diagrams. The diagrams, while usually being precisely dimensioned, are indicative; the rule is that type options say, for example, CP1 or equivalent, ES1 or equivalent, or HR3 or equivalent. Table An4.1 lists the codes for relevant building features and where the associated diagrams are placed.

Table An4.1 Coded type options for building features

	Feature	*Diagrams, page numbers*
CC	changing cubicles	329
CL	cloakroom entrance lobbies	320
CP	car parking provisions	308–9
DL	lobbies at building entrances and in circulation areas within buildings	314
ES	external steps	311
GR	hotel guestrooms	328
HR	handrails	311
IS	stairways within buildings	316
LP	passenger lift dimensions	317
MR	mirrors	327
TS	fixed seating in theatres, etc.	319
UR	urinals	327
WC	Wc compartments	323–6

At stage 2, the stage at which proposed building feature conditions are presented to the building control officer for consideration, the core conditions will be confirmed. The building control officer will then notify the local authority planning department that Part Z requirements are to be met, and the planning authority will confirm that planning permission is granted.

The building feature conditions, while being firmly indicative of the conditions to be applied in order to meet Part Z requirements, will be provisional at stage 2. At stage 3 they will be confirmed, either by their being unaltered from stage 2 or with amendments and refinements having been made to certain of them; at that stage building control approval will be granted.

For wc facilities, the standard practice will be for conditions to be refined at stage 3. At stage 2 broad agreement will have been reached about the kind of wc provision which will be required in each location where there are toilet facilities, and numbers (often provisional) are prescribed for types coded as WC1, WC2, WC3, etc. These relate to the size of the wc compartments concerned, and at stage 3 the specifications for the layout and equipment are amplified and the codes are WC1A, WC1B, etc.

In the case of a public building which has areas used only by staff employed in the building, the provision to be made in staff-only areas will as a rule be subject to a staff-only package condition, with terms as indicated in 6.11.

With the 'as agreed' conditions having been noted, there will, at stage 3, be a complete record of agreed conditions against which a check could be made when the building is completed.

4.3 Building alterations

The principle which comes with the menu system for determining accessibility conditions is that there are not 'right' solutions which are generally applicable. In any particular case, an appropriate (and reasonable) building feature condition has to be within an acceptable range of measures, the premise being that there is a cut-off point above which the provision is acceptable, and below which it is not. When designing a new building, the architect ought as a rule to be able to satisfy whatever accessibility conditions he is asked to comply with, and building feature conditions for new buildings can therefore be stringent, with a high cut-off point for acceptable accessibility.

For building alterations which are subject to Part Z requirements, the building feature conditions appropriate for new buildings should be prescribed where they are reasonable and practicable, but where they are not the threshold for cut-off points may reasonably be lower; any provision which expands accommodation parameters is better than doing nothing, even though the outcome may not display what, by conventional access-for-the-disabled norms, constitutes accessibility. It follows that for building alterations the conditions may be to a less demanding standard than is acceptable for new buildings, and in the menus in section 6 examples of these are indicated separately under relevant headings. In section 6.2, for example, the condition options 2.1 to 2.16 are applicable to new buildings and to alterations where appropriate, and options 2.17 to 2.27 are for alterations to existing buildings only.

Where for an existing building the alteration works proposed are selective and limited, four items might be on the priority list:

1 The fixing of handrails by steps or stairs.
2 The rehanging of wc compartment doors to open out.
3 The removal of superfluous doors in cloakroom lobbies.
4 The provision of hold-open catches for doors in passageways.

5 Building types: notional examples of the application of Part Z conditions

The eight examples presented in this section are purely illustrative.

5.1 The conference hotel

Location: On the edge of a large city. Undulating terrain.
Accommodation: 150 guestrooms in multi-storey block. Restaurants, bars and lounges at ground level. Conference rooms at first floor level. Leisure centre with swimming pool in linked single-storey block with visitor entrance and hotel guest approach from main block. Car parking on site.

The conference hotel, continued

Stage 1 core conditions

Approach routes: Level to main entrance from parking spaces close to building; suitably ramped from elsewhere. To other entrances, suitably ramped approaches.
Provision within the building: All public zones in main building to have level approach from main entrance, and in leisure centre from visitor entrance. Link from main building to leisure centre to be suitably ramped. All guestrooms to be reachable by visitors in wheelchairs; to be as type GR2, with some as type GR3.

	Stage 2 building feature conditions	Stage 3 amendments
Approaches to entrances	All routes level or ramped, max. ramp gradient 1:15. Level from designated car parking spaces. Cover at main entrance.	
Car parking	6 designated spaces: 2 as CP1, 4 as CP2. Other spaces as CP3.	10 designated spaces: 4 as CP1, 6 as CP2
Entrances	**Main entrance:** Outer and inner automatic doors, min. c.o.w. 1500mm. **Entrance from car park:** Automatic doors, min. c.o.w. 1200mm.	
Circulation features	**Passageways:** Min. 2000mm wide, hold-open catches to all doors. Link from hotel to leisure centre ramped, gradient 1:18. **Doors:** All min. c.o.w. 820mm. **Lifts:** 4 as LP1, controls max. 1500mm a.f.l. **Stairways:** To first floor as IS1, others as IS2.	link gradient 1:16
Sanitary facilities	**Ground floor** (females 12 wcs) Lobby, access as CL2. *Male side*: 3 wcs, 2 as WC3, 1 as WC6. 5 urinals as UR1. *Female side*: 12 wcs, 11 as WC4, 1 as WC6. Baby-change facility. *Unisex facility*: 1 as WC9. **Conference floor:** (females 18 wcs) Lobbies, access as CL1. *Male side*: 4 wcs, 3 as WC3, 1 as WC7. 8 urinals as UR4. *Female side*: 18 wcs, 17 as WC2, 1 as WC7. **Leisure centre** (females 4 wcs) Lobby access as CL2. *Male side*: 1 wc as WC6, 1 urinal as UR3, 1 as UR4. *Female side*: 4 wcs, 3 as WC1, 1 as WC6.	WC3s as WC3A WC4s as WC4A WC3s as WC3A, WC7 as WC7A WC2s as WC2A, WC7 as WC7A WC1s as WC1A
Other provisions	**Lounges:** Public seating area: not more than 20% on stepped platform. **Bars:** Public seating area: not more than 40% on stepped platform. **Guestrooms and guestsuites:** 2 rooms as GR3, others as GR2. **Swimming pool:** Stepped access as IS1. **Conference rooms:** Audio-amplification system.	14% 26% 4 rooms as GR3, others as GR2 management to arrange
Staff-only areas	SO1 package.	

5.2 The tourist hotel

Location: Off a motorway. Sloping terrain.
Accommodation: In two separate blocks. Restaurant off road at foot of site. Hotel at higher level with 40 guestrooms in two-storey block with common entrance. Visitor parking areas near both blocks.

Stage 1 core conditions

Approach routes: To the *restaurant block*, suitably ramped from visitor parking area and public road. To the *hotel block*, suitably ramped from visitor parking area. The direct pedestrian route from the restaurant to the hotel block to be suitably stepped.
Provision within the building: *Restaurant block*: Level access from entrance to all public zones. *Hotel block*: Level access from building entrance to all guestrooms at ground level; special provision for wheelchair users to be negotiated; stairway from ground to first floor to be suitably graded.

Restaurant block

	Stage 2 building feature conditions	**Stage 3 amendments**
Approaches to entrances	Pedestrian route from designated parking spaces to be level or suitably ramped, max. ramp gradient 1:15.	
Car parking	2 designated spaces as CP2.	
Entrances	Single door, min. c.o.w. 850mm, no enclosed lobby.	
Circulation features	Level access from entrance to all public areas.	
Sanitary facilities	Single lobby giving access to 2 wcs; 1 as WC5 for males, 1 as WC5 for females.	Lobby as agreed WC5 as WC5C
Staff-only areas	SO1 package.	

Hotel block

	Stage 2 building feature conditions	**Stage 3 amendments**
Approaches to entrances	Pedestrian route from designated parking spaces to be level or suitably ramped, max. ramp gradient 1:15. Steps on pedestrian routes from restaurant to hotel to be as ES1.	Handrails as HR3
Car parking	2 designated spaces as CP2.	
Entrances	Single door, min. c.o.w. 820mm, no enclosed lobby.	c.o.w. 840mm
Circulation features	Level access from entrance to all ground floor rooms, and on first floor from head of stairs to all rooms. Passageways min. 1800mm wide, to have hold-open catches to all doors. Stairs to first floor as IS2.	
Other provisions	Regular guestrooms as GR1. 2 for-the-disabled guestrooms on ground floor as GR2.	Special guestrooms as agreed
Staff-only areas	SO1 package.	

5.3 The supermarket

Location: In a new estate at the edge of a town. Level terrain.
Accommodation: Retail space 5000m^2 and associated storage space at ground level. Staff offices and canteen at mezzanine level.

Stage 1 core conditions

Approach routes: All routes to main entrance to have level access. Developer's proposals for parking provision for customers with disabilities or those with infant children to be agreed.
Provision within the building: All public areas to have level access from building entrance.

	Stage 2 building feature conditions	Stage 3 amendments
Approaches to entrances	Level approach to main entrance from all parking areas.	
Car parking	20 designated spaces; 6 as CP1, 6 as CP2, 8 as CP3. Other parking spaces as CP3.	26 designated spaces; 8 as CP1, 6 as CP2, 12 as CP3
Entrances	Automatic opening doors, min. c.o.w. 1800mm.	
Circulation features	Level access to all public areas.	
Sanitary facilities	(females 5 wcs) Common lobby. *Male side*: 1 wc as WC6; 3 urinals as UR1. *Female side*: 4 wcs as WC1, 1 as WC6. Baby-change facility.	Lobby as agreed WC1s as WC1A
Other provisions	Check-out aisles min. 750mm wide; provision for customers with double pushchairs and large wheelchairs to be arranged.	As agreed
Staff-only areas	Stairs to mezzanine floor as IS2. Other provisions as SO1 package.	

5.4 The department store

Location: In new shopping centre under development.
Accommodation: Retail premises on three floors, each floor 1200m^2. Principal vertical circulation via escalators. Restaurant and public toilets to be on third floor, toilets to be supervised. (Public toilets in shopping mall are to have unisex facility as WC9.)

Stage 1 core conditions

Provision within the building: All public areas to have level access.

	Stage 2 building feature conditions	Stage 3 amendments
Entrances	Public entrance to have open access during opening hours.	
Circulation features	Level access to all public areas. Stairs as IS1. Escalators. 2 lifts as LP1.	Lifts with voice announcements
Sanitary facilities	(females 16 wcs) *Male side*: Lobby as CL1. 3 wcs; 2 as WC2, 1 as WC5. 5 urinals as UR1. *Female side*: Lobby as CL1. 16 wcs; 13 as WC1, 2 as WC4, 1 as WC5. *Unisex toilet*: As WC8. Baby-change facility.	WC2s as WC2A. WC5 as WC5A WC1s as WC2A, WC4s as WC4A, WC5 as WC5C WC8 as WC8B
Staff-only areas	SO1 package.	

5.5 The large office building

Location: Close to city centre. Level terrain.
Accommodation: Six-storey block, 800m^2 on each floor. Single tenancy. Limited parking space on site.

Stage 1 core conditions

Approach routes: All routes to main and rear entrances to have level approach.
Provision within the building: All areas of all floors to have level access. 3 lifts. Toilets on all floors.

	Stage 2 building feature conditions	Stage 3 amendments
Approaches to entrances	Level approach to main entrance from all parking areas.	
Car parking	No special provision.	
Entrances	Main entrance, automatic opening door, min. c.o.w. 1200mm.	
Circulation features	Level access to all areas. All doors to offices, meeting rooms, etc. c.o.w. min. 800mm. 3 lifts as LP3; controls max. 1600mm a.f.l. Stairways as IS2.	3 lifts as agreed
Sanitary facilities	Male and female provision on all floors. Lobbies type CL1. In each sector 1 wc as WC6, others as WC1.	WC1s as WC1A. Other provision as agreed
Other provisions	Audio-amplification system for meeting rooms to be provided.	Infra-red system to be provided by tenant

5.6 The small office building

Location: Infill site near centre of small town. Level terrain.
Accommodation: Proposal submitted by private architects for offices for own use. Accommodation on two floors, each 300m². Parking space on site.

Stage 1 core conditions

Approach routes: Approaches to main entrance from parking spaces and public road to be level.
Provision within the building: All areas on ground floor to have level access from building entrance. Stairway from ground to first floor to be suitably graded. Toilet facilities to be provided on both floors.

	Stage 2 building feature conditions	Stage 3 amendments
Approaches to entrances	Level approach to main entrance from all parking areas.	
Entrances	Main entrance door min. c.o.w. 850mm.	
Circulation features	Level access to all ground floor areas from entrance, and from head of stairs to all areas at first floor level. All doors to offices, meeting rooms, etc. c.o.w. min. 800mm. Stairway to first floor as IS2.	
Sanitary facilities	Male and female provision on both floors. Lobbies as CL2. In each sector 1 wc to be as WC5; other provision to be agreed with architect.	WC5 as WC5C Other provision as agreed

5.7 The local community centre

Location: In large village. Slightly sloping terrain.
Accommodation: Single storey. Hall with stage. Meeting rooms. Meal preparation facilities. Parking space on site.

Stage 1 core conditions

Approach routes: From nearby parking spaces, to be level; from public road, to be suitably ramped.
Provision within the building: All public zones to have level access from building entrance. Access to stage to be suitably stepped, with alternative ramped access.

	Stage 2 building feature conditions	Stage 3 amendments
Approaches to entrances	All pedestrian routes between public road, parking areas and building entrances to be level or ramped, max. ramp gradient 1:15; from nearby parking spaces to main entrance to be level.	
Car parking	No special provision.	
Entrances	**Main entrance:** Double door, each leaf having c.o.w. min. 700mm. Lobby as DL1. **Side entrance:** Single door, c.o.w. min. 820mm.	
Circulation features	All areas other than stage to have level access from main entrance. Doors to all zones to have c.o.w. min 800mm.	
Sanitary facilities	(females 6 wcs) *Male side*: Lobby as CL2. 1 wc as WC7, 4 urinals as UR1. *Female side*: Lobby as CL2. 6 wcs; 5 as WC4, 1 as WC7.	WC7 as WC7B WC4s as WC4B, WC7 as WC7A
Other provisions	*Stage*: Stepped access as IS3. Ramped access max. gradient 1:12. *Hall*: Induction loop audio-amplification system.	Ramp gradient 1:8

5.8 The public toilets

Location: In recreational theme park. Level terrain immediately around building. No adjacent parking.
Accommodation: Provision to cater for crowds on busy days.

Stage 1 core conditions

Approach routes: Level approach to all entrances.
Provision within the building: Level access to all public areas. Single main entrance with unisex toilet and baby-change facility in entrance area. Normal toilet facilities to be suitable for disabled users.

	Stage 2 building feature conditions	Stage 3 amendments
Approaches to entrances	Level pathway 3m wide around building.	
Entrances	Main entrance and entrances to male/female sectors screened as CL1.	
Circulation features	All areas level access.	
Sanitary facilities	*Male side*: 6 wcs; 5 as WC2, 1 as WC7. 8 urinals as UR1. *Female side*: 20 wcs; 17 as WC1, 2 as WC5, 1 as WC7. *Unisex toilet*: 1 as WC9. Baby-change facility.	WC2s as WC2A, WC7 as WC7B WC1s as WC1A, WC5s as WC5A, WC7 as WC7A, WC9, 2800 × 2200mm

6 Menus for the setting of Part Z conditions

6.1 Car parking provision

Conditions for parking provision in and around buildings may cover the number, configuration and dimensions of (a) normal parking spaces for staff and visitors; and (b) designated spaces for disabled people, visitors with infant children or other visitors or staff with special parking needs.

With each case being unique and different types of spaces being appropriate for different users, no common rules can be applied. In the case of buildings such as supermarkets, shopping malls, hotels and railway stations, designated spaces for disabled people or other special-needs users may be in order, with conditions for numbers and types being negotiated. A standard practice is for spaces to be designated for the use of disabled people, a consideration being space for wheelchair users to transfer in and out of their vehicles. Normally the need is for lateral space, the occasional need being for transfer through the rear of the vehicle via a tail-lift or portable ramp; these needs are catered for by spaces of type CP1 or CP2.

6.1.1 Parking provision outside buildings

1.1 N designated parking spaces to be provided for customers

1.2 N designated parking spaces to be provided for staff

1.3 N designated parking spaces to be as type CP1 or equivalent

1.4 N designated parking spaces to be as type CP2 or equivalent

1.5 N designated parking spaces to be as type CP3 or equivalent

1.6 Non-designated parking spaces to be as type CP3 or equivalent

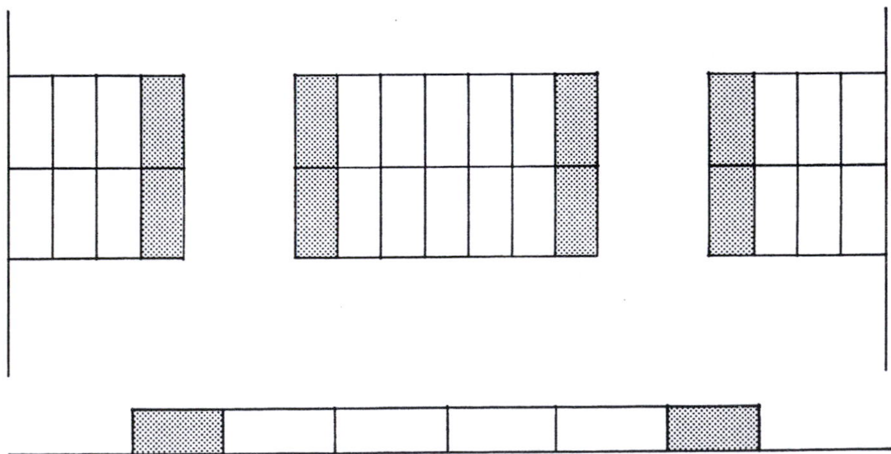

CP1 Type CP1 is an open-on-two-sides space at the end of a row of bays. Alternatively, it could be placed laterally alongside a kerb.

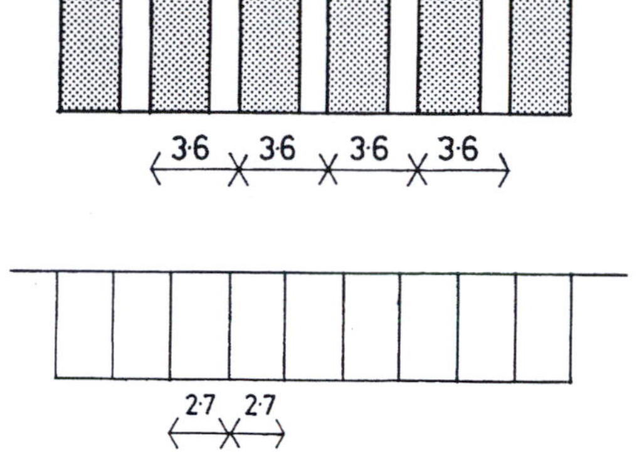

CP2 With an aisle to the side 1.2 m wide for wheelchair approach, type CP2 is for spaces in wide bays alongside each other

CP3 Type CP3 would serve ambulant disabled people, pushchair users whose needs would be catered for by spaces 2.7 m wide, ie slightly wider than the conventional 2.4 m width of parking bays.

6.1.2 Parking provision within buildings

1.7 | Access to public/staff areas in the building from parking areas within the building to be level, suitably ramped or via a lift |

Where condition 1.7 is applied, it may, where appropriate, be in conjunction with any of conditions 1.1 to 1.6.

6.2 Approaches to buildings

The approach to a building is defined as the route or routes taken by pedestrians to the face of the building's entrance doors from (a) the adjacent public footway; (b) a point on the edge of the site curtilage, or (c) car parking spaces on the site.

For new buildings on level terrain, condition 2.1 should be applied. On level approach surfaces, the fall for rainwater drainage purposes should not exceed 1:40.

For new buildings on sloping terrain, condition 2.3 should be applied as a matter of course and condition 2.2 wherever practicable. In the case of buildings with a single on-street entrance (as a rule, shop-type buildings), condition 2.4 should be applied. Where a building has two or more on-street entrances, condition 2.4 should be applied to the principal entrance. Where other entrances need to be stepped, condition 2.14 should be applied to entrances used by visitors to the building.

Some wheelchair users can propel themselves independently only on level ground, not where there is an incline, and where for a new building, there has to be a ramp it should be with the condition that it is not steeper than 1:15. Reasons for setting 1:15 as the defining gradient are:

- It is an operationally suitable compromise. In respect of any individual new building subject to the Part Z regulation, it should be practicable, whatever the constraints of the terrain, for strategic approach routes to have ramps graded no steeper than 1:15.
- For downward travel, 1:15 is not so steep as to be uncomfortable for an independent wheelchair user or an ambulant disabled person to negotiate, whereas a steeper ramp may be.
- For upward travel, 1:15 is not so steep as to be uncomfortable for a capable unassisted wheelchair user, a person pushing someone in a wheelchair, an ambulant disabled person or a person pushing a child/children in a pushchair to manage.

- A 1:15 gradient is not so steep as to warrant a handrail as an aid for an ambulant disabled person – a steeper ramp should have a handrail.
- A 1:15 gradient is not so steep as for there to be a need for a supplementary or alternative stepped approach for ambulant disabled people.

Where practicable, a 1:18 condition should be applied. For downward travel, a ramp graded at 1:15 can make it difficult for an assistant to restrain a loaded wheelchair.

No condition options are listed for handrails to ramps or kerbs at the edge of exposed ramps; where there is a drop to the side of a ramp, the presumption is that suitable guards will be incorporated, either as a matter of good practice or to meet the requirements of Building Regulation K.

For relevant notes on kerb ramps, external floor surfaces and steps, stairs and ramps, see book Chapter 21, page 215.

6.2.1 New buildings: level approaches to building entrances

2.1 All approaches to all entrances to the building to be level

2.2 Approaches from designated parking spaces to the main entrance to the building to be level

2.3 Approach to the main entrance to the building from the setting-down point for visitors' cars and taxis to be level

2.4 Entrance at point ⊗. to be level with adjacent public footway

2.5 Embedded heating system to be laid to surface at point ⊕

6.2.2 New buildings: ramped approaches to building entrances

2.6 Approach routes to all entrances to the building to be not steeper than 1:18 [1:15]

2.7 Approach route from point ⊗ to entrance ⊕ to be not steeper than 1:15

Condition 2.7 is applicable where a level or near-level approach is practicable on some parts of the site but not all.

2.8 Embedded heating system to be laid to ramp at point ⊗

6.2.3 New buildings: level platforms

2.9 At the head of any ramped or stepped approach, the floor in front of the entrance to be level, the unobstructed area to be minimum 1500 × 1500mm

Condition 2.9 is standard for space in front of entrance doors.

2.10 Level platform length 2400mm to be provided on ramp at point ⊗

Condition 2.10 is applicable where a ramped approach to a building entrance is extended; it should be applied where the ramped travel distance is 25 metres or more. For related commentary see Chapter 21, page 219.

6.2.4 Rain cover at main entrance

2.11 The setting-down point for visitors' cars and taxis at the main entrance to be covered

6.2.5 Kerb ramps

2.12 | Kerb to be suitably ramped at point ⊗ |

For new buildings there will not usually be cause to apply condition 2.12. Outside the entrances to supermarkets, hotels etc the boundaries between pedestrian routes and vehicle areas may be distinguished by differing floor treatment, avoiding the need for differing floor levels.

6.2.6 New buildings: stepped approaches to building entrances

2.13 | Stepped approach at entrance ⊗ to be as type ES1 [ES2] [ES3] or equivalent |

2.14 | Stepped approach at entrance ⊗ to be as type ES4 [ES5] or equivalent |

Condition 2.13 is applicable in the case of a new building where not all public entrances can have a level approach or be suitably ramped. Condition 2.14 may be applied to entrances used only by staff employed in the building. For related guidance on the configuration of steps and stairs, see section 9, page 336.

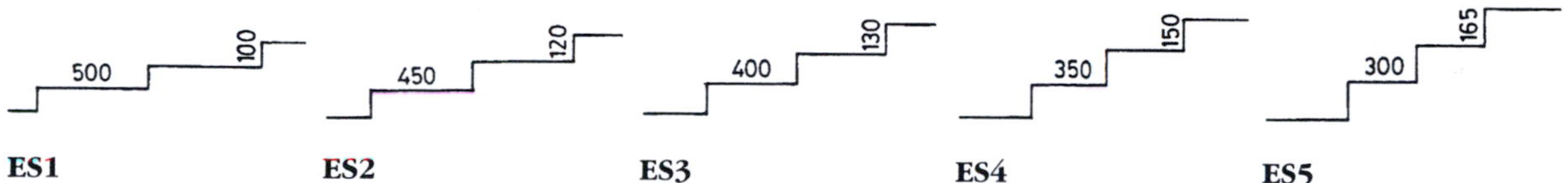

6.2.7 Handrails to stepped approaches to buildings

2.15 | Handrail to be provided to both sides of stepped approach at entrance ⊗, as type [HR1] [HR2] [HR3] [HR4] or equivalent |

2.16 | Central handrail to be provided to stepped approach at entrance ⊗, as type [HR3] [HR4] or equivalent |

For related commentary on the configuration of handrails see Chapter 21, page 217.

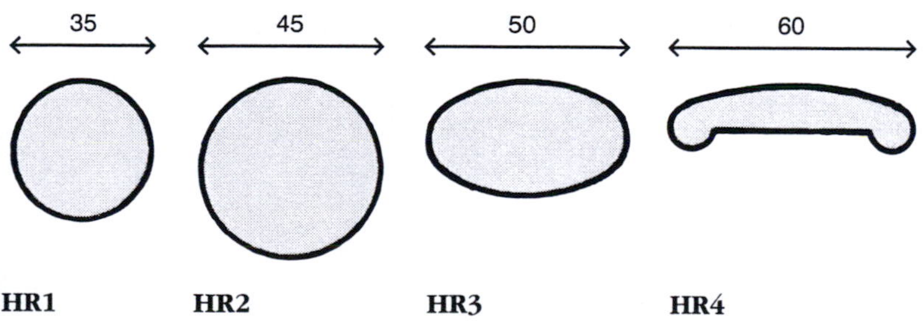

6.2.8 Existing buildings: handrails to stepped entrances

2.17 | Handrail(s) to be provided over steps at location ⊗ |

Condition 2.17 is applicable to any existing steps/stairs where there is no existing handrail, a rail on one side only or an existing unsuitable rail.

6.2.9 Existing buildings: ramped approaches to building entrances

2.18 | New ramped approach route from point ⊗ to entrance ⊕ to be not steeper than 1:15 |

2.19 | New ramped approach route from point ⊗ to entrance ⊕ to be not steeper than 1:12 |

Condition 2.18 may be applied for the replacement of an existing stepped approach. Condition 2.19 assumes an existing approach with steps where the terrain does not permit a 1:15 ramped approach but where a 1:12 ramp can be laid to supplement the steps.

2.20 | Handrail(s) to be provided to ramp at location ⊗ |

Condition 2.20 is applicable where the ramp gradient is steeper than 1:15.

2.21 | Level platform with a depth in front of the entrance door of 1500mm [1200mm] [1000mm] to be provided at head of ramp at point ⊗ |

Condition 2.21 should be applied as a matter of course where a ramp replaces existing steps. Where a ramp is new and does not replace steps, condition 2.9 should be applied.

2.22 | Suitable ramp to be provided in place of single step at location ⊗ |

2.23 | Suitable ramp to be provided in place of two steps at location ⊗ |

Condition 2.22 or 2.23 could be applicable in a range of circumstances. The broad rule is that either condition will be appropriate where the resultant ramp will not be steeper than 1:12. Where the ramp is steeper than 1:12 the advisability of substituting a ramp for one or two steps will depend on the gradient and length of the ramp and the particular circumstances of the case; on this matter there can be no reliable guidelines.

Condition 2.21 should be applied where 2.22 or 2.23 is applied. Only in exceptional circumstances (for which there cannot be reliable guidelines) should a single step on the line of the face of the entrance door to an existing building be replaced by a ramp whose head is at the line of the door without there being a level platform.

For related notes with regard to shop entrances, see book Chapter 15, page 133; Chapter 21, page 220; Chapter 23, page 255.

6.2.10 Existing buildings: stepped approach with ramp

2.24 | Stepped approach as type ES3 [ES4] [ES5] to be incorporated at location ⊗ to supplement existing ramp |

Condition 2.24 is applicable where the existing approach to a building entrance is by way of a ramp having a gradient steeper than 1:15 and where it is practicable to install steps alongside which are suitable for ambulant disabled people.

6.2.11 Existing buildings: ramped approach with steps

2.25 | Ramp to be provided at point ⊗, to be not steeper than [1:10] [1:8] [1:6] |

2.26 | Level platform 1500 × 1500mm [1200 × 1200mm] to be provided at point ⊗ |

Condition 2.25 is applicable where an existing stepped entrance to a building is to be retained as the normal approach route, where space is not available for a conveniently graded ramp, but where a short steep ramp can be installed alongside or nearby.

Where an existing entrance to a building is stepped and the proposal is for a ramp to be placed alongside the steps, the preferred outcome is a ramp gradient not steeper than 1:12 with a platform not less than 1500mm deep at its head. Where this is not achievable, a ramped approach steeper than 1:12 may be appropriate for the benefit of wheelchair users.

An important consideration is that the ramp should not compromise the suitability of the steps for ambulant disabled people, as it may do by restricting the width of the steps or precluding the provision of a suitable handrail. Where the steps are convenient for ambulant disabled people and where, at the head of the adjoining ramp, there is a level platform of the order of 1200 × 1200mm, the ramp gradient should preferably be not steeper than 1:8 and should never exceed 1:6. A steeper gradient, however short the length of the ramp may be, is hazardous and unacceptable.

Where provision is made in accord with condition 2.25, the understanding will be that any wheelchair user who uses the ramp will be assisted by a strong able-bodied helper.

6.2.12 Existing buildings: platform lift at approach to building entrance

2.27 | Platform lift for wheelchair users to be provided at point ⊗ |

Condition 2.27 should be applied only where there is no other practicable means of altering the approach to an existing building in order to provide wheelchair accessibility. At approaches to buildings, the installation of a stairlift over existing steps should not be regarded as an acceptable alternative to the provision of a wheelchair platform lift.

6.3 Entrances to buildings

6.3.1 Thresholds at entrance doors

3.1 | Thresholds at all entrance doors to be flush |

6.3.2 Entrance doors: automatic-opening doors

3.2 | The main entrance at point ⊗ to have an automatic-opening door, clear opening width [1200mm] [1500mm] |

6.3.3 Entrance doors: side-hung doors

3.3 | The main entrance [the entrance at point ⊗] to have a double door [double doors], each leaf clear opening width 700mm or equivalent |

3.4 | The main entrance [the entrance at point ⊗] to have a double door [double doors], each leaf clear opening width 820mm or equivalent |

3.5 | The main entrance [the entrance at point ⊗] to have a single door, clear opening width 820mm or equivalent |

For commentary on the clear opening width of doors, see section 8, page 333.

6.3.4 Revolving doors at building entrances

3.6 | Side-hung door, clear opening width 820mm or equivalent, to be provided alongside revolving door at entrance at point ⊗ |

For relevant notes, see book Chapter 21, page 220.

6.3.5 Entrance lobbies

Condition 3.7 may be applied to lobbies on circulation routes within buildings as well as to entrance lobbies.

3.7 The entrance lobby at point ⊗ to be as type [DL1] [DL2] or equivalent

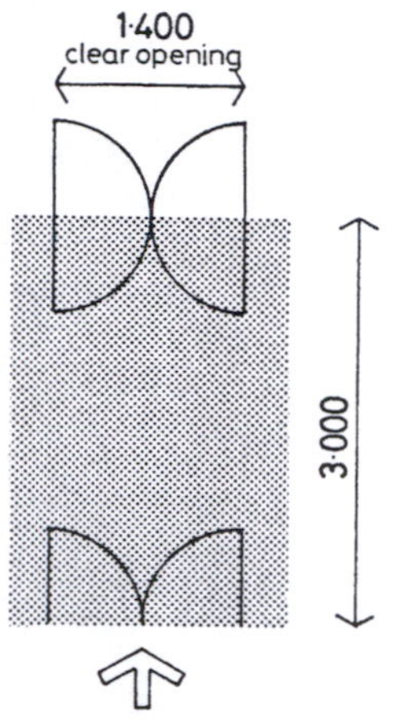

DL1
Lobby with each doorleaf giving clear opening width of 700mm

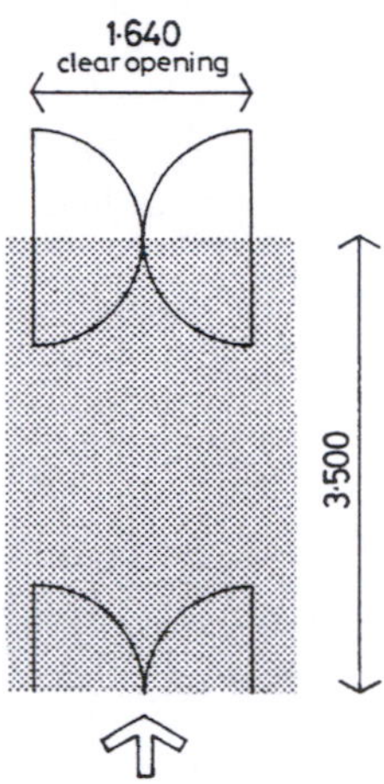

DL2
Lobby with each doorleaf giving clear opening width of 820mm

With both doorleaves being opened, types DLI and DL2 permit access for all users. With one doorleaf open, type DL1 permits access for single pushchair users and some wheelchair users, and type DL2 for all wheelchair users, double pushchair users and scooter users.

3.8 The entrance lobby at point ⊗ to be as type [DL3] [DL4] [DL5] [DL6] or equivalent

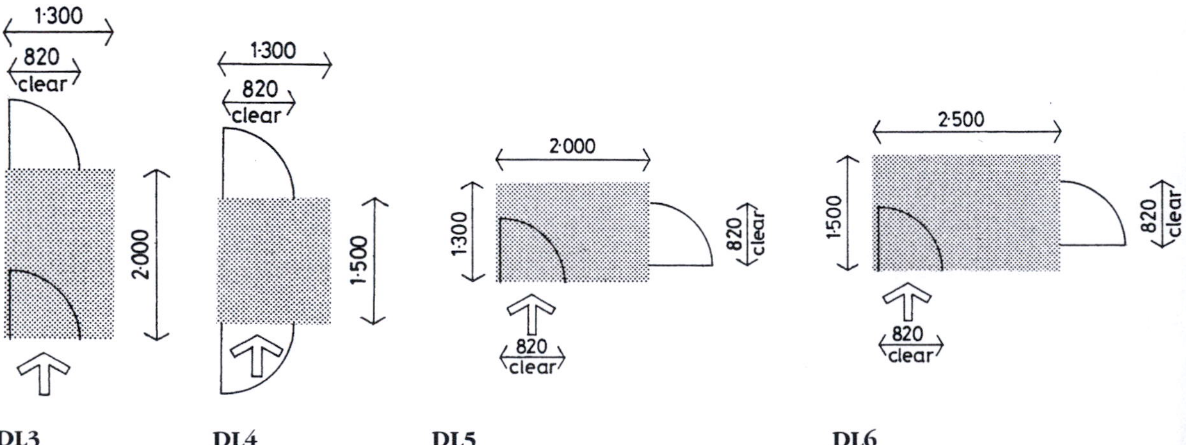

DL3 **DL4** **DL5** **DL6**

Types DL3, DL4 and DL6 permit access for all users, including wheelchair and scooter users. Type DL5 permits access for wheelchair users but not scooter users.

6.4 Circulation features within buildings

6.4.1 New buildings: floor level consistency

4.1 On all storeys within the building, all floors to be at the same level

4.2 On all storeys, all public areas to be at the same level

4.3 Zones in all public areas of the building to be at the same level as the main entrance or a lift floor

Where there is a floor level change on a main circulation route within a storey, a condition such as 4.4, 4.5 or 4.6 will be applied, with 4.1, 4.2 or 4.3 being qualified. For notes on the application of condition 4.3 see section 3.4.

6.4.2 New buildings: floor level changes on circulation routes

4.4 Ramped surface at point ⊗ to be not steeper than 1:18

4.5 Ramped surface at point ⊗ to be not steeper than 1:15

4.6 Ramped surface at point ⊗ to be not steeper than 1:12

Condition 4.4 is preferred, with 4.5 being acceptable. Condition 4.6 is applicable only where suitable steps are also available.

6.4.3 Existing buildings: stepped floor level changes on circulation routes

4.7 Handrail(s) to be provided to steps at point ⊗

Condition 4.7 should be applied where there are two or more steps without a handrail on a circulation route within a building.

6.4.4 Existing buildings: ramps in lieu of steps on circulation routes

4.8 Ramped surface at point ⊗ to be not steeper than 1:15

4.9 Ramped surface at point ⊗ to be not steeper than 1:12, with suitable handrail(s)

Condition 4.8 is preferred, but in an existing building where a ramp replaces steps on a circulation route a gradient not steeper than 1:12 may be appropriate, as against maximum 1:15 for new buildings.

6.4.5 Existing buildings: ramps alongside steps on circulation routes

4.10 Steps at point ⊗ to be retained, with ramp alongside

Where a ramp is proposed, the steps should be retained where the ramp gradient will be 1:12 or steeper.

4.11 Steps at point ⊗ to be replaced by new steps as type IS3 or equivalent

Condition 4.9 is applicable where new steps are needed in conjunction with ramp alongside. For IS3 diagram, see 6.4.5, page 316.

4.12 Ramped surface at point ⊗ to be not steeper than [1:10] [1:8] [1:6]

Condition 4.12 is applicable in association with 4.10 or 4.11. For relevant notes see commentary to condition 2.25.

6.4.6 Existing buildings: platform lifts and stairlifts within buildings

4.13 | Wheelchair platform lift to be provided at point ⊗ |

4.14 | Stairlift to be installed over stairs at point ⊗ |

Condition 4.14 should not be regarded as a satisfactory alternative to 4.13, and should be applied only in circumstances where condition 4.13 is not a practicable option.

6.4.7 Doors and passageways

4.15 | Passageways to be not less than [1800mm] [2100mm] [2400mm] wide |

For relevant notes on space considerations, see section 8, page 334.

4.16 | Double doors on internal circulation routes to have hold-open catches |

4.17 | Double doors in passageway at location ⊗ to have hold-open catches |

4.18 | Doors at points ⊗ and ⊗ to open automatically |

4.19 | Lobbies on circulation routes to be as type [DL1] [DL3] or equivalent |

4.20 | Doors to public rooms, meeting rooms, etc. to give clear opening width 820mm or equivalent |

4.21 | Doors to Ø and Ø rooms to give clear opening width 770mm or equivalent |

Notes relating to conditions 4.20 and 4.21 are in section 8, page 333–5. For doors to wc compartments see pages 323–6.

6.4.8 New buildings: stairways between storeys

4.22 | Stairway at point ⊗ to be as type IS1 or equivalent |

4.23 | Stairway at point ⊗ to be as type IS2 or equivalent |

4.24 | Stairway at point ⊗ to be as type IS3 or equivalent |

Condition 4.22 is preferred for main public-usage stairways in public buildings. 4.23 is appropriate for less busy stairways in public areas of buildings. 4.24 is suitable for stairways in staff-only areas of buildings.

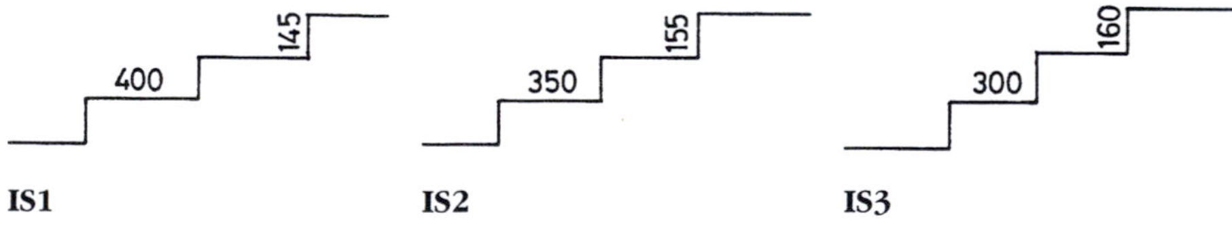

4.25 | Suitable handrails to be provided to both sides of all stairways |

4.26 | Handrail at head of stairs at point ⊗ to have horizontal extension 300mm |

For agreed locations, condition 4.26 will be applied at control stage 3. For relevant notes see book Chapter 21, page 218.

6.4.9 Existing buildings: stairways between storeys

4.27 | Handrail(s) to be provided to stairs at point ⊗

Standard condition where existing steps/stairs are without handrails.

4.28 | Additional handrail at approx 1300mm above the line of nosings to be provided at point ⊗

Condition 4.28 may be applied to an existing steep stairway as an aid for disabled people when going down. For relevant notes see book Chapter 21, page 217.

6.4.10 New buildings: lifts

4.29 | N lifts to be provided at location ⊗

4.30 | Lift(s) at location ⊗ to be as type [LP1] [LP2] [LP3] or equivalent

The dimensions shown are internal wall-to-wall dimensions.

Lift type LP1 affords access for wheelchairs, scooters and single or double pushchairs, and permits a wheelchair or pushchair to be turned within the lift. Type LP2 affords access for wheelchairs, scooters and single or double pushchairs, and permits a single pushchair to be turned within the lift. Type LP3 affords access for wheelchairs and single pushchairs. For dimensions of mobility equipment, see section 7, page 331.

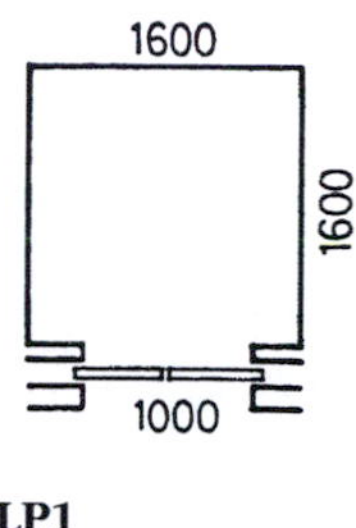

LP1

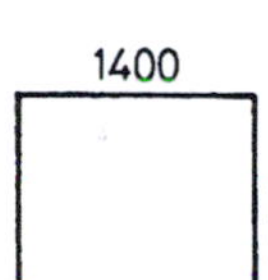

LP2

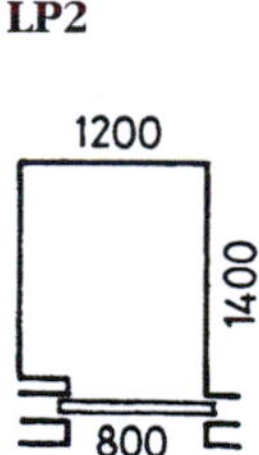

LP3

4.31 | Lift controls to be between 1200 and 1500mm above floor level

4.32 | Lift controls to be between 1100 and 1600mm above floor level

4.33 | Supplementary line of lift controls to be arranged horizontally at 1200mm above floor level

Condition 4.31 is preferred where there is a single batch of vertically arranged controls, with condition 4.32 being applicable where 4.31 does not conveniently accommodate the number of control items to be incorporated on the panel. Condition 4.33 is applicable where special provision is made for independent wheelchair users. For relevant notes, see book Chapter 24, page 274 and Chapter 8, page 63. For notes on height criteria, see book Appendix 6, page 384.

4.34 | The lift(s) to be equipped with synchronised voice announcements

Condition 4.34 is applicable where appropriate.

6.4.11 Existing buildings: lifts

4.35 | Lift to be installed at location ⊗

Condition 4.35 is applicable in an existing multi-storey building which does not have a lift and where there is a suitable place to install one. Where the space available is too confined for an LP3-type lift, a small lift, with no rules for its minimum dimensions, is better than none.

6.5 Access to platforms, stages, etc.

6.5.1 Platforms/wells within a storey

The standard core condition that zones of all public areas must have no-steps access, in conjunction with condition 4.3, will mean that parts of all public seating areas in cafes, restaurants, bars, hotel lounges, etc. will, with level access, be wheelchair-accessible. The proportion, if any, which it may be reasonable to be approached by way of steps or a ramp will vary according to circumstances.

5.1	About [20%] [30%] [40%] of the seating area for customers at location ⊗ to be on a platform

5.2	About [20%] [30%] [40%] of the seating area for customers at location ⊗ to be in a recessed well

Condition 5.1 or 5.2 would be applied at control stage 2, with a check of the precise amount being made at control stage 3.

5.3	Steps to platform/well at point ⊗ to be as type IS3 or equivalent

Condition 5.3 does not involve an associated handrail requirement. For IS3 diagram see 6.4.5.

5.4	The platform/well at location ⊗ to have a ramped approach at point ⊕, gradient not steeper than 1:15

5.5	The platform/well at location ⊗ to have a ramped approach at point ⊕, gradient not steeper than 1:11

Condition 5.4 is applicable where the approach is ramped and there is no alternative stepped approach; it applies also in new buildings where there is a stepped approach and a ramped approach is provided to cater for wheelchair and pushchair users. Condition 5.5 is applicable in existing buildings where there is a stepped approach and a supplementary ramped approach is provided to cater for wheelchair and pushchair users.

6.5.2 Theatre stages

Stages for performers in theatres, etc. are not public areas for core condition purposes.

5.6	Steps giving access to the stage from the auditorium to be as type IS3 or equivalent

Condition 5.6 is applicable whether or not there is also a ramped approach to the stage.

5.7	The stage to have a ramped approach not steeper than 1:12

5.8	The stage to have a ramped approach not steeper than 1:8 [1:6]

Condition 5.7 is preferred to 5.8. Provided a stepped approach is also available, a ramp catering for wheelchair users may be graded as steeply as 1:6.

5.9	Wheelchair platform lift to be installed to give access to the stage

In new buildings, the need for a wheelchair platform lift to be installed should be avoided. In existing buildings, the provision may be appropriate.

6.6 Seating in theatres, etc.

Suitable provision may need to be made for wheelchair users in buildings such as cinemas, theatres, concert halls, lecture theatres and sports stadia where seating is tiered. No general rules are applicable for the amount of such provision that should be made in any particular case, or of the ratio of seating spaces for wheelchair users to the total number of seats provided; with a core condition such as 'suitable provision to be made for wheelchair users', the number and type of spaces will be a matter for negotiation among the parties concerned.

6.1 Space at location ⊗ to be available for N wheelchair users

With this condition wheelchair spaces are undesignated; they are in an accessible area which happens to be suitable for the placement of wheelchairs.

6.2 Spaces for people seated in wheelchairs to have plan dimensions 800 × 1200mm or equivalent

6.3 N spaces for wheelchair users to be provided at point ⊗

6.4 N seats at point ⊗ to be removable to provide N spaces for wheelchair users

Designated spaces for wheelchair users will usually be placed alongside fixed seating available for accompanying partners. For guidance on approach spaces see section 8, page 333.

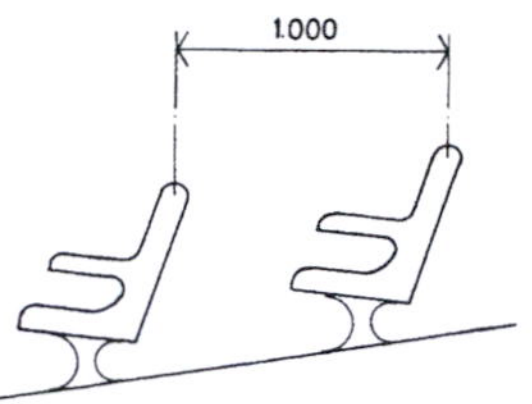

TS1

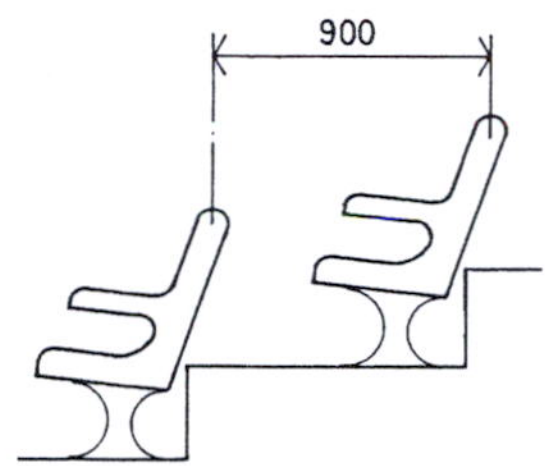

TS2

6.5 Planning of seating at location ⊗ to be as type TS1 or equivalent

6.6 Planning of seating at location ⊗ to be as type TS2 or equivalent

The dimensions shown in TS1 and TS2 will be variable according to circumstances. For relevant commentary and explanatory diagrams, see book Chapter 21, page 233.

6.7 Stairs to tiered seating at location ⊗ to have goings minimum [270mm], rises maximum [260mm]

6.8 Suitable handrails to be provided to stairs to tiered seating at location ⊗

Precise specifications for conditions 6.7 and 6.8 will be subject to negotiation.

6.7 Sanitary facilities

6.7.1 Sanitary facilities: procedures for the application of controls

As indicated by the sequences of coded instructions for toilet facilities in the examples of new buildings in section 5, the setting of conditions for reasonable sanitary provision in buildings can be problematical. For any building or part of a building, the conditions to be applied have to be specific to locations and sectors, and to the character – often difficult to predict – of toilet users and their needs. Among considerations which may need to be taken into account are:

- The distribution of toilet facilities by location
- The scope for all disabled users to be catered for by normal provision
- The differences between 'public' and 'staff' requirements
- The proportionate distribution of amenities for women versus men
- The avoidance of awkwardly planned cloakroom lobbies
- Mixes of wc compartment types in normal male and female sectors
- In wc compartments, the advisability of wash-hand facilities as a matter of course
- Accommodation for infants and pushchair users, particularly in female sectors
- Urinal provision for small boys
- Baby-change facilities and provision for nursing mothers
- The type of provision where unisex provision for disabled people is required

Conditions for the location of toilet facilities could be stage 1 core conditions. At control stage 2 a primary consideration would be the distribution of male/female facilities in toilet areas, and in this connection architects are advised to determine first the number of wc compartments to be provided for women; the reasons for this are explained in book Chapter 25 (page 273). The procedure which may be used on stage 2 pro formas under the sanitary facilities head is to start with 'females N wcs', as shown in section 5 examples such as 5.1.

Much more than for other building features, the details of layout, dimensional and equipment specifications of sanitary facilities have to be carefully prescribed and correctly implemented if the convenience of users is, so far as it can be, to be assured. On the basis of provisional stage 2 conditions the architect would refine his proposals; the precise terms of all conditions being agreed at stage 3.

6.7.2 Sanitary facilities: location of provision

7.1 Toilet facilities for males and females to be provided on all floors of the building

7.2 Toilet facilities for males and females to be provided at location ⊗

7.3 Toilet facilities for visiting members of the public to be provided on the ground floor

6.7.3 Distribution of male/female toilet facilities

7.4 Toilets at location ⊗ to have N wc compartments for women

7.5 At location ⊗ the ratio of female to male toilet facilities to be of the order of [3 to 1] [2 to 1] [3 to 2] [1 to 1] [2 to 3] [1 to 2]

With regard to condition 7.5, see book Appendix 3 (page 376) for relevant data for different building types.

6.7.4 Cloakroom lobbies: new buildings

7.6 Cloakroom lobby at location ⊗ to be as type CL1 or equivalent

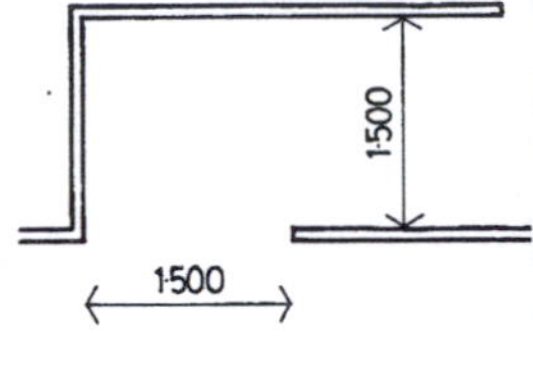

CL1

Condition 7.6 should be applied wherever practicable and appropriate.

7.7 Cloakroom lobby at location ⊗ to be as type CL2 or equivalent

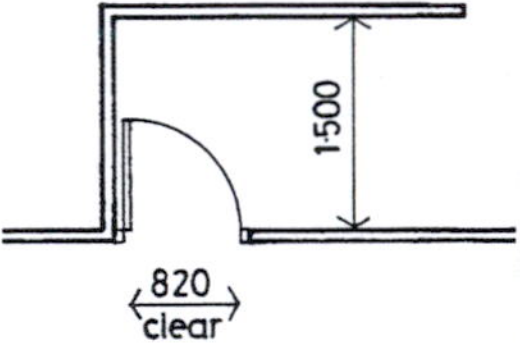

CL2

Condition 7.7 is advised where 7.6 is not feasible.

7.8 Cloakroom lobby at location ⊗ to be as type [CL3] [CL4] [CL5] or equivalent

Condition 7.8 is appropriate only where a cloakroom lobby must have two doors to satisfy regulatory requirements. Type CL3 is as DL3, CL4 as DL5 and CL5 as DL6; for diagrams see 6.3.5.

6.7.5 Cloakroom lobbies: alterations in existing buildings

7.9 The inner door to the cloakroom lobby at location ⊗ to be removed

7.10 Screened open lobby to replace enclosed lobby at location ⊗

For related notes, see book Chapter 19, page 189 and Appendix 5, page 381.

6.7.6 Terms of conditions for types of wc compartments

The menu options in the material which follows are in the terms, 'wc compartment(s) to be as type WC1 or equivalent'. Each type such as WC1 has common overall dimensions, with variants for the layout, door width etc being shown in WC1A, WC1B, etc. As indicated in section 5, a relevant condition at stage 2 is, for example, 'as type WC1', meaning a wc compartment which, if not precisely as WC1, is equivalent to it.

For normal toilet provision, seven type options are presented:

WC1	850 × 1500mm	wc only: out-opening door
WC2	850 × 1500mm	wc only: in-opening door
WC3	1000 × 1500mm	wc and wash basin: in-opening door
WC4	1000 × 1500mm	wc and wash basin: out-opening door
WC5	1200 × 1500mm	wc and wash basin: out-opening door
WC6	1500 × 1500mm	wc with/without wash basin: out-opening door
WC7	2000 × 1500mm	wc and wash basin: in- or out-opening door

For special unisex provision, two type options are presented:

WC8	1700 × 2200mm	BS5810 layout
WC9	2500 × 2000mm	peninsular layout

Each of types WC1 to WC9 has certain accommodation parameters. With planning and design variations which afford equivalent provision being in order, it is not essential that the plan layouts and dimensions indicated in relevant diagrams are followed precisely.

In all diagrams, the dimension from the wall against which the wc is fixed to the front face of the wc bowl is shown as 520mm. For related comment, see book Chapter 19, page 184.

Fixtures and fittings

For wc fixtures and fittings other than those shown in relevant diagrams, the application of good practice design criteria is assumed. Such items include, for example, (a) the location of hooks for hanging clothes; (b) the type of wash-hand basin or wash-hand facility; (c) the position of the soap dispenser; (d) the position of the paper towel dispenser or hand drier; (e) the position of the mirror; (f) the position of the toilet paper holder; (g) the position of the flushing handle to the wc; and (h) the location of a facility for the disposal of used sanitary towels in women's toilets. In any particular case where a local authority considers it important that an item of this kind be prescribed to meet Part M regulation requirements, the matter should be discussed with the architect and a suitable condition agreed for application at stage 3. Data of relevance to height criteria for certain listed items is in book Appendix 6, page 383.

Door closers

Doors to wc compartments should not have spring-loaded closers. In particular, special wcs for disabled people must not be placed in locations where there could be a Part B (means of escape) requirement for a spring-loaded closer; such provision could make it impossible for a wheelchair user who had got in to get out.

6.7.7 Wcs: single compartment provision

In locations where there is one toilet facility only for both sexes, or one facility only for males and one for females, the provision advised to cater for varying needs is as type WC5.

Such provision may be appropriate (a) in buildings where staff facilities may be used by visiting members of the public; (b) in small buildings such as petrol service stations; and (c) in subsidiary locations in buildings such as department stores, restaurants, hotels, leisure centres and museums where alternative facilities are available in principal public toilet locations.

6.7.8 Wcs: provision in normal male/female sectors

Where two or more wc compartments are to be provided in the male/female sectors of normal public toilet facilities, a mix of types may be appropriate in order to cater for people with special needs. As indicated by the public building examples in section 5, an appropriate mix is affected by the type of building, the characteristics of toilet users and whether or not a special unisex toilet is also available.

To cater for pushchair users, there need not be a mix; all wc compartments could be as type WC1. Alternatively, there could be a mix of WC4 and WC2.

To cater for wheelchair users as well as pushchair users in normal male/female toilet sectors, one wc compartment could be as type WC6 or WC7, with others as type WC1 or WC2.

Where a special unisex facility is allied with normal facilities a WC5 (which caters for independent wheelchair users) could be provided in normal sectors.

Unlike a unisex facility (WC8 or WC9) which is kept locked or is supervised, a WC6 or WC7 may be unprotected. In part on this account WC6 and WC7 have a single horizontal grabrail only; for data of relevance to the placing of grabrails, see book Chapter 19, page 184 and book Appendix 3, Table A3.6, page 377.

Where there is to be a wash-hand basin in all wc compartments in normal sectors, WC3 is advised, or WC4 where provision is made for pushchair users.

In buildings such as airport terminals or railway stations where toilet users may be carrying bulky luggage, a WC3 or WC4 serves better than a WC1 or WC2.

6.7.9 Wcs: unisex provision

A unisex toilet facility, where provided, should be accessible to disabled people using manual wheelchairs (either self-propelled or pushed), 3 or 4-wheel powered scooters or 4-wheel powered wheelchairs.

Where allied with normal toilet facilities which do not incorporate a WC5, WC6 or WC7, a layout as type WC8 may be appropriate. To facilitate usage by independent wheelchair users it has an in-opening door.

Where there is a WC5, WC6 or WC7 in normal sectors, a peninsular layout as type WC9 may be appropriate.

For the convenience of all users both WC8 and WC9 have a shelf; as noted in book Appendix 3 (page 378) this is important for people with ileostomies.

As noted in the commentary in book Chapter 19 (page 185) on unisex provision, user needs and the BS5810 versus the peninsular layout, it is principally severely handicapped people who prefer a type WC9 to a type WC8, and a positive need for a type WC9 tends to be most marked among those who need two personal helpers in order to transfer to or from a wc. The need such people may have to use a public toilet may come when a day out is taken, rather than an hour or so away from home. A WC9 may thus be appropriate for public toilets at day-out venues relevant locations being, for example, on seaside promenades, in theme parks, in major department stores or at motorway service stations. In the generality of public buildings where there is cause for having a unisex toilet (noting, for example, that fathers with small daughters might use it where available), a WC8 may be appropriate. Among wheelchair users a facility as type WC8 is more frequently preferred than a WC9 (book Appendix 3, Table A3.8, page 378).

6.7.10 Scooter users

For non-ambulant independent scooter users who need to turn through 180° within a wc facility, only a type WC9 will be suitable. As a general rule, it may be assumed that scooter users are able to walk, and can leave the scooter outside when they need to use a wc.

6.7.11 WC1: 850 × 1500mm

7.11 | wc compartment(s) to be as type WC1 or equivalent |

WC1A is suitable for in-row wcs in female sectors where provision for single pushchair users is a consideration. Where there is clear space in front of the door of the order of 1500mm deep, it affords, with the door being left open, access for wheelchair users able to stand and use the wc as a urinal. The placing of the wc at 350mm from the side wall allows space on the open side for the placing of sanitary bins in female facilities.

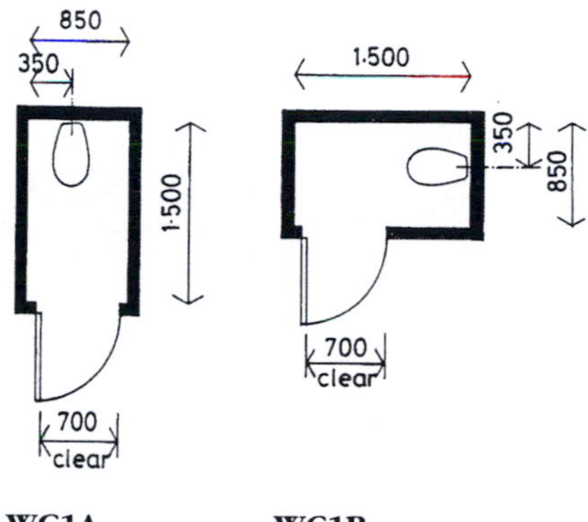

WC1A **WC1B**

6.7.12 WC2: 850 × 1500mm

7.12 | wc compartment(s) to be as type WC2 or equivalent |

WC2A is suitable for in-row male or female wcs where pushchair access is not a consideration. For wcs of type WC2, an internal dimension of 1800 rather than 1500mm is desirable.

6.7.13 WC3: 1000 × 1500mm

7.13 | wc compartment(s) to be as type WC3 or equivalent |

WC3A is advised for in-row wcs having a wash hand facility where pushchair access is not a consideration. For wcs of type WC3, an internal dimension of 1800 rather than 1500mm is desirable.

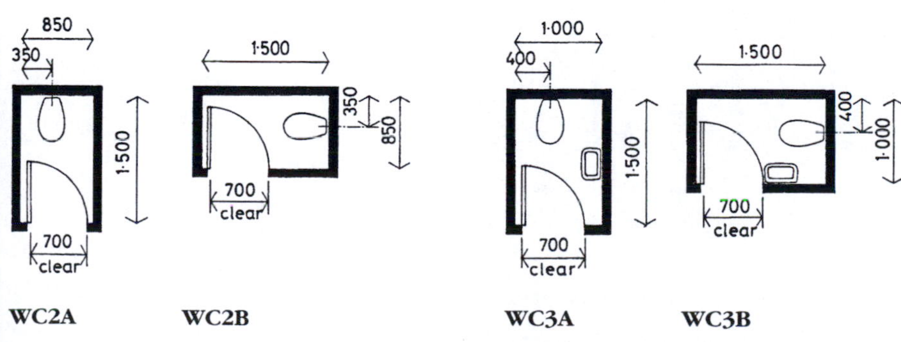

WC2A **WC2B** **WC3A** **WC3B**

6.7.14 WC4: 1000 × 1500mm

7.14 | wc compartment(s) to be as type WC4 or equivalent |

WC4A is advised for in-row provision giving access for single and double pushchairs. With the door being left open, it affords access for wheelchair users able to stand and use the wc as a urinal. WC4B gives more convenient space for the placement of pushchairs, and in suitable locations is preferred to WC4A.

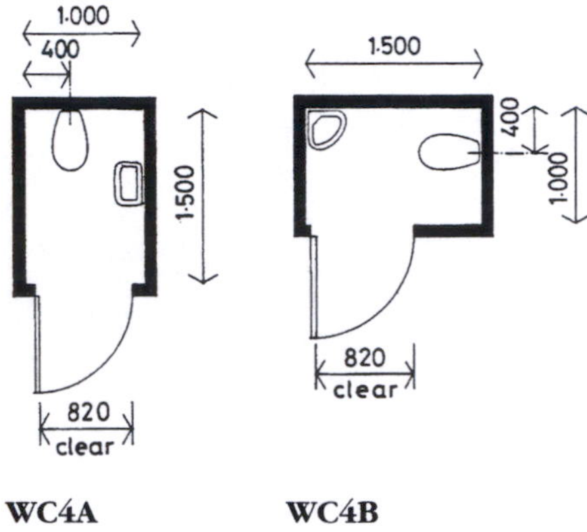

WC4A **WC4B**

6.7.15 WC5: 1200 × 1500mm

7.15 | wc compartment(s) to be as type WC5 or equivalent |

WC5A, WC5B and WC5C accommodate ambulant disabled people, single and double pushchair users. They can also cater for independent wheelchair users who might reverse in and then transfer laterally.

Wash basins are advised in WC5 facilities, but where a WC5A is placed in a row alongside wcs such as WC2A and wash basins are in the adjacent cloakroom area the wash basin could be omitted.

In WC5 facilities (and also WC6 and WC7) the side horizontal rail should be placed as shown in the diagram to WC8.

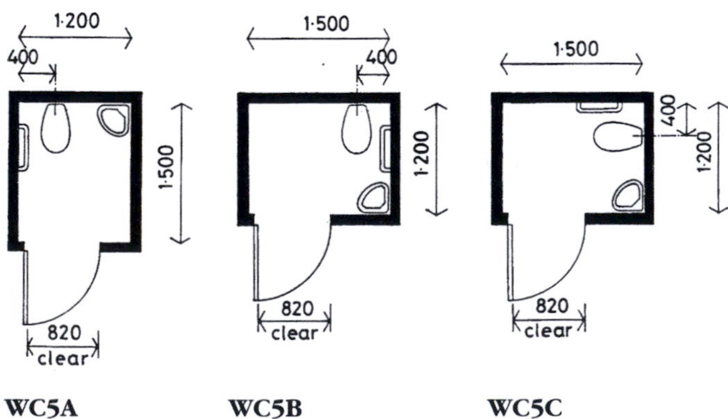

WC5A **WC5B** **WC5C**

6.7.16 WC6: 1500 × 1500mm

7.16 wc compartment(s) to be as type WC6 or equivalent

WC6 is suitable for ambulant disabled people, single and double pushchair users and most wheelchair users.

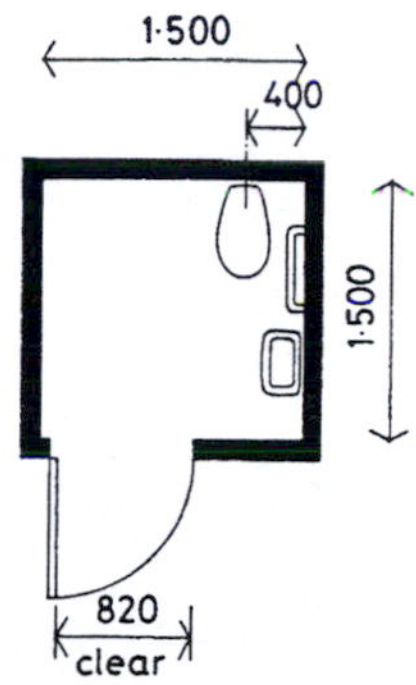

WC6

6.7.17 WC7: 1500 × 2000mm

7.17 wc compartment(s) to be as type WC7 or equivalent

Both WC7A and WC7B are suitable for single and double pushchair users, ambulant disabled people and most wheelchair users. With its in-opening door, WC7B makes it easier for an independent wheelchair user to enter, close the door, manoeuvre and reverse into position by the wc than WC7A with its out-opening door. The dimension from the side wall to the centre line of the wc in WC7B is 350mm rather than 400mm, giving slightly more space for wheelchair manoeuvre while keeping the rail in a position which can be used for pushing up. For related commentary and illustrations see Chapter 19, page 184.

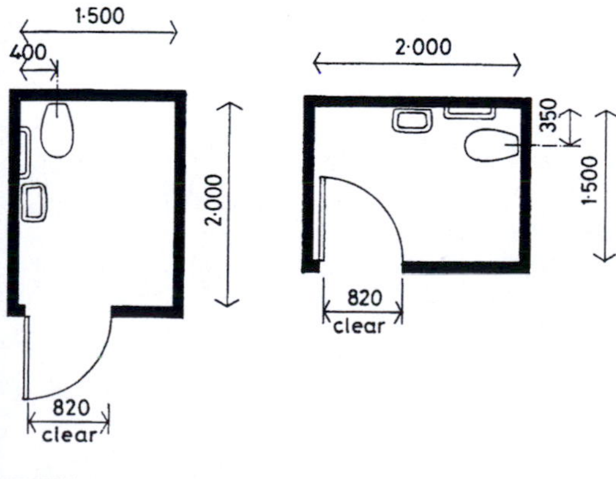

WC7A **WC7B**

6.7.18 WC8: 1700 × 2200mm

7.18 | A unisex toilet to be provided, as type WC8 or equivalent |

For wheelchair manoeuvring, WC8B is preferred to WC8A. For related commentary and illustrations see Chapter 19, page 184.

The grabrails advised for WC8 are as recommended in the 1992 Part M Approved Document for a BS5810-type toilet, except that the horizontal rail immediately behind the wc is omitted. The two vertical rails, length 600mm, should be at 800 to 1400mm above floor level. The drop-down rail should be at 250mm above the level of the wc bowl, ie at 700mm above floor level where the wc bowl is at 450mm, and should extend 200mm in front of the face of the wc bowl. For related commentary and information see Chapter 19, page 184, and Table A3.6 in Appendix 3, page 377.

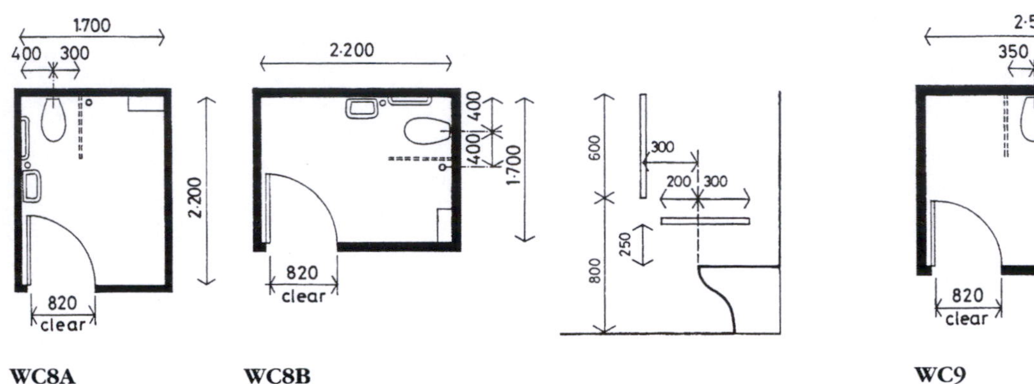

WC8A **WC8B** **WC9**

6.7.19 WC9: 2500 × 2000mm

7.19 | A unisex toilet to be provided, as type WC9 or equivalent |

For a WC9, the internal dimensions should be not less than 2500 × 2000mm. To give more comfortable space for wheelchair turning and manoeuvre, an area of the order of 2500 × 2500mm is preferred. The wash basin may be placed on the side wall.

For commentary and illustrations on WC9 and comparisons with WC8 see Chapter 19, page 185 and Appendix 3, page 377. The model shown in Figures 19.9a–c on page 185 has an internal width of 2200 mm and a depth of 2000 mm

6.7.20 The height of wc seats

For the purposes of conditions, the height of wc seats is the height above floor level of the top face of the wc bowl (not the drop-down seat).

7.20 | The height of wc seats at location ⊗ to be within the range 380 to 420mm |

7.21 | The height of wc seats at location ⊗ to be within the range 410 to 450mm |

7.22 | The height of wc seats at location ⊗ to be approx. 450mm |

Condition 7.20 is advised where the provision concerned is not designed to cater for people with disabilities; 7.21 where it will cater for the generality of toilet users, including people with disabilities, and 7.22 where it is special for disabled people, for example as type WC8 or WC9. For comments see Chapter 19, page 187.

6.7.21 Urinals

7.23 | Urinals at location ⊗ to be as type UR1 or equivalent |

A urinal as type UR1 is the preferred condition to cater for small boys, ambulant disabled people and wheelchair users who can stand.

7.24 | Urinals at location ⊗ to be as type UR2 or equivalent |

7.25 | Urinal bowls at location ⊗ to be as type UR3 or equivalent |

7.26 | One urinal bowl at location ⊗ to be as type UR4 or equivalent |

For data of relevance to user needs and the height of bowl urinals see Chapter 19, page 187 and book Appendix 6, page 387.

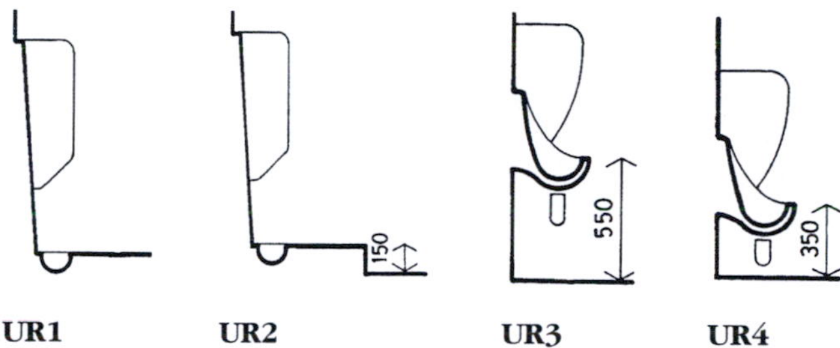

UR1 **UR2** **UR3** **UR4**

6.7.22 Wash-hand basins

7.27 | Wash basins at location ⊗ to have rims at 820mm above floor level |

7.28 | Wash basins at location ⊗ to have rims at 900mm above floor level |

For notes and data of relevance to user needs and the height of wash-hand basins see Chapter 19, page 188 and book Appendix 6, page 387. In cloakrooms in the generality of public buildings, wash basins with rims at approx. 820mm are advised. In staff-only areas of buildings and locations where all users will be adults, rims at 900mm are preferred.

6.7.23 Mirrors

7.29 | Mirror at location ⊗ to be as type [MR1] [MR2] [MR3] or equivalent |

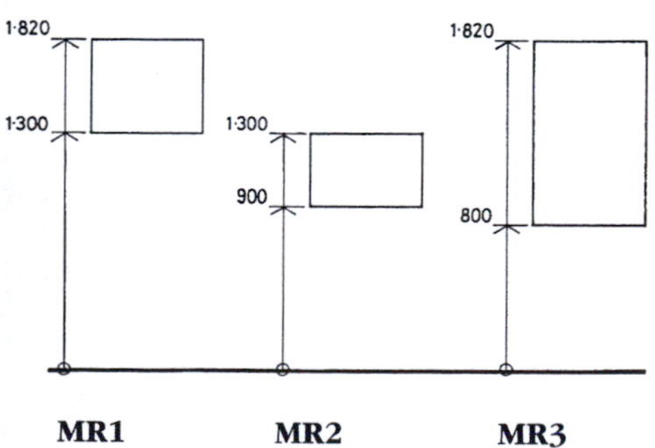

MR1 **MR2** **MR3**

For data of relevance to user needs and the height of mirrors, see book Appendix 6, page 386. For standing adult people, a mirror as type MR1 is appropriate; for seated people MR2; and for all users MR3.

6.8 Hotels

The condition options presented here relate to the planning and design of hotel guestrooms, the understanding being that other accessibility considerations in hotel buildings would be covered by conditions drawn from other parts of section 6.

Commentary on hotel guestrooms is in book Chapter 21, page 227. With regard to the condition options and the plan diagrams for GR2 and GR3, attention is drawn to the commentary in book Chapter 25, page 275.

6.8.1 Hotel guestrooms

8.1 All guestrooms to have level access

Condition 8.1 is standard for new multi-storey hotel buildings, as a rule meaning that all guestrooms should be at the same level as the main entrance to the hotel or the floor level served by lifts.

8.2 All guestrooms on the ground floor of the building to have level access

Condition 8.2 is standard for two- or three-storey hotel buildings with no lifts.

8.3 All guestrooms to be as type GR1 or equivalent

Type GR1 could be a standard hotel guestroom. Its only 'accessibility' provision is an entrance door which is conveniently wide for customers with bulky luggage, eg as condition 4.20. The door permits wheelchair access to the room, and GR1 is suitable for wheelchair users who are able to walk short distances; on this basis, the bathroom does not have to be wheelchair-accessible, and wheelchair turning space does not have to be provided in the bed area.

In the type GR1 bathroom, a shower may be substituted for a bath. In hotels where standard guestrooms have a shower cubicle and no bath, condition 8.3 would mean the provision of a shower.

8.4 Guestrooms at location ⊗ to be as type GR2 or equivalent

Type GR2 is a guestroom which could be standard provision where circumstances permit. Although as standard provision it would not be specially equipped for guests with disabilities, it would be suitable for most wheelchair users; it allows space (circle

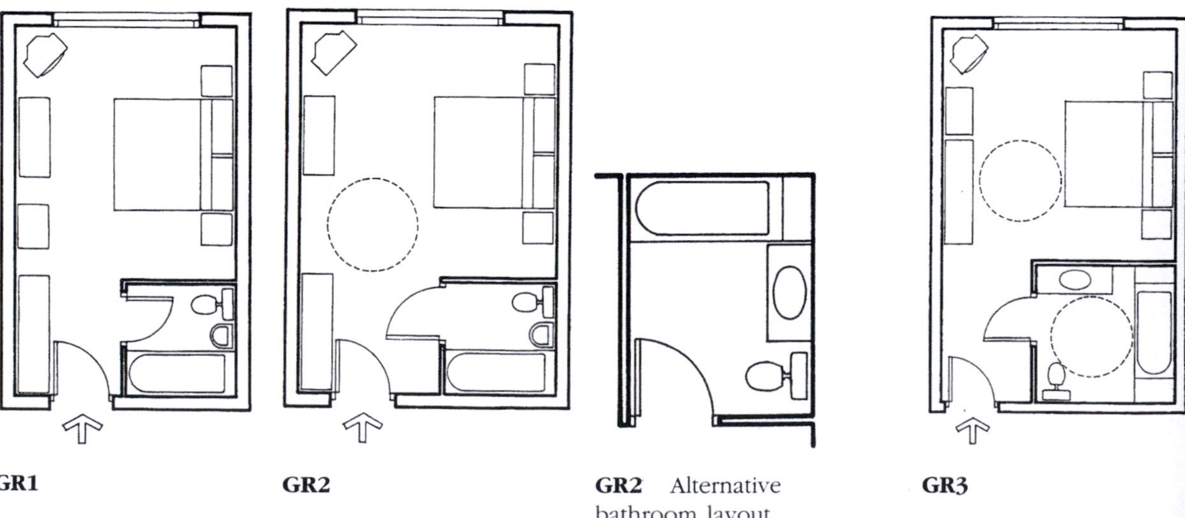

GR1 **GR2** **GR2** Alternative bathroom layout **GR3**

diameter 1500 mm) for turning a wheelchair in the bed area and access to the bathroom on the basis of entering in and reversing out. The plan diagram shows an out-opening door to the bathroom; the alternative bathroom layout shown alongside has an in-opening door with sufficient internal space for a wheelchair user to close the door.

As for GR1, a shower cubicle may be substituted for a bath in GR2 bathrooms.

In hotels where standard guestrooms are as type GR1, special guestrooms for disabled people could be as type GR2; in cases where a shower (not a bath) was the standard arrangement for GR1 rooms, the shower facility in the special guestrooms would have level access.

8.5 | Guestrooms at location ⊗ to be as type GR3 or equivalent |

A GR3 guestroom is one where within the bathroom there is space for a wheelchair to be turned around. Where provided, this will be a special for-the-disabled facility, for which the details of design and equipment will be negotiated at stage 3 of the control process.

As for GR1, a shower cubicle may be substituted for a bath in GR3 bathrooms.

6.9 Swimming pools etc

For user provisions in swimming pools in new leisure centres, hotels and related buildings, other type options than those presented here may be appropriate.

6.9.1 Swimming pools

9.1 | The pool to have stepped access at point ⊗, steps as IS1 or equivalent, with central handrail or handrail to both sides |

9.2 | Suitable support rail(s) to be provided at point ⊗ |

Condition 9.2 could be applied to assist access to pools with beaches by ambulant disabled people.

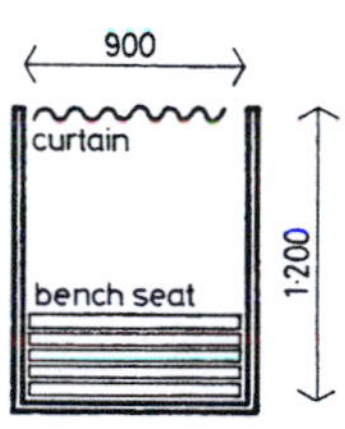

CC1

6.9.2 Changing rooms

9.3 | Changing cubicles to be as type CC1 or equivalent |

9.4 | N changing cubicles at point ⊗ to be as type CC2 or equivalent |

Type CC1 may be appropriate for curtained cubicles for normal able-bodied people, and type CC2 where provision is made for families or wheelchair users. For wheelchair users to transfer laterally, the bench seat in a changing cubicle should be open at one end, as shown in Figure CC2.

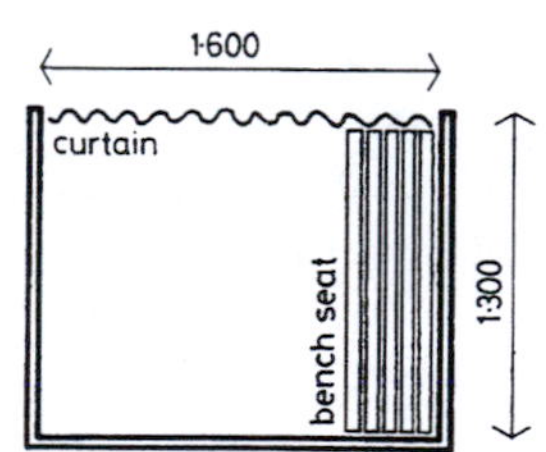

CC2

6.9.3 Shower rooms

9.5 | Shower rooms to have level access from approach area |

9.6 | Shower controls to be at a height above floor level within the range 1300 to 1500mm |

6.10 Fixtures and fittings

Information relating to height criteria for building fixtures and fittings is in book Appendix 6, page 383. For different types of building users, data on reach heights are in Table A6.1, page 384.

6.10.1 Controls for the operation of building services equipment, dispensing machines, etc.

Discussion on the height and layout of lift controls is in book Chapter 8, page 63, Chapter 21, page 224 and Chapter 25, page 274.

10.1 Controls for [purpose] to be not higher than [1600mm] [1400mm] or lower than [1000mm] [300mm] [100mm] above floor level

For condition 10.1, the heights prescribed will vary according to the type of equipment concerned, and for which building users the controls are to be reachable – whether for standing adult people only, standing adults and children or standing people and independent wheelchair users.

6.10.2 Storage and display shelves

10.2 Storage or display shelves at point ⊗ to be not higher than [1800mm] [1600mm] above floor level

6.11 Staff-only provision

Other than in certain office-type buildings, staff-only areas of buildings need not have level access. For relevant commentary, see book Chapter 18, page 173 and Chapter 25, page 269.

11.1 Provisions in staff-only areas to be as package SO1

For staff-only areas of buildings, appropriate building feature provisions may be prescribed as a package. SO1 is the standard package where all staff will be ambulant disabled people; the conditions to be applied will be 11.2 to 11.7 inclusive.

11.2 Approach to staff entrance to be level, or stepped as type ES4 or equivalent

11.3 Staff entrance door to give a clear opening width of 820mm

11.4 Doors to rooms in staff-only areas to give a clear opening width of 770mm

11.5 Stairways to be as type IS3 or equivalent, with handrails as type HR1 or equivalent

11.6 Passageways to be not less than 1500mm wide

11.7 In staff cloakrooms wc compartments to be as type WC1 or equivalent; wash basins to have rim at 900mm above floor level

In the case of a building where variants to these conditions or ones supplementary to them are applied to meet Part Z requirements, relevant prescriptions will be incorporated on the stage 2 pro forma.

11.8 Provisions in staff-only areas to be as package SO2

SO2 is the standard package where all staff-only areas have no-steps access and where wheelchair users may be employed; the conditions to be applied will be 11.3, 11.4, 11.6, 11.9 and 11.10. Variants of these and supplementary conditions may be applied where appropriate.

11.9 Approach to staff entrance to be level

11.10 In staff cloakrooms one wc compartment to be as type WC5 or equivalent; others to be as type WC1 or equivalent

7 Mobility equipment: pushchairs, wheelchairs and scooters

'Convenient for wheelchair users' and 'convenient for pushchair users' are terms which commonly occur in the comments on section 6 menus. Most frequently they relate to spaces in buildings, and space criteria for the users of pushchairs, wheelchairs and scooters are examined in section 8. The dimensions of the equipment concerned and the models employed for the purposes of presenting design guidance are reported here.

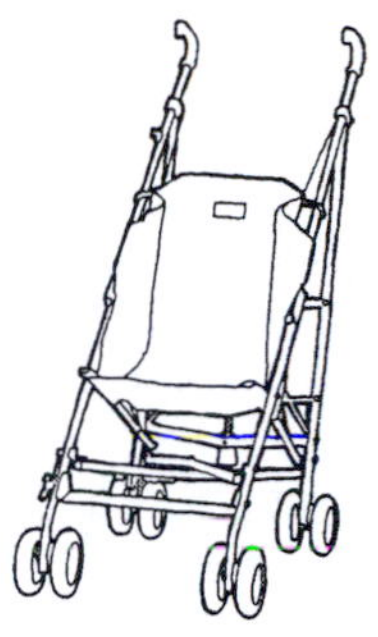

An7.1 Single buggy: length 840mm, width 435mm

7.1 Pushchairs

The length and width dimensions of child pushchairs, both single and double, are very variable; there is not, as there is in the case of self-propelled wheelchairs, a standard model for informing design criteria.

Elsewhere in this book the term 'pushchair' is used generically, and for Annex A guidance purposes the single and double buggies shown in Figures An7.1 and An7.2 are the models for single pushchair users and side-by-side double pushchair users.

For the purposes of this section, the distinction is made between a 'buggy' and a 'pushchair'. A buggy (or, as it is called in America, a 'stroller') is a vehicle in which infants sit up. A pushchair, a vehicle catering principally for small babies and infants up to the age of 12 months or so, serves 'lie-down' as well as 'sit-up' purposes. In shopping centres and in and around public buildings, buggies are found more frequently than pushchairs. A relevant factor is transportation by car or public transport; the advantage that a buggy has, particularly with regard to travel by bus, is that it is lightweight and compact when folded.

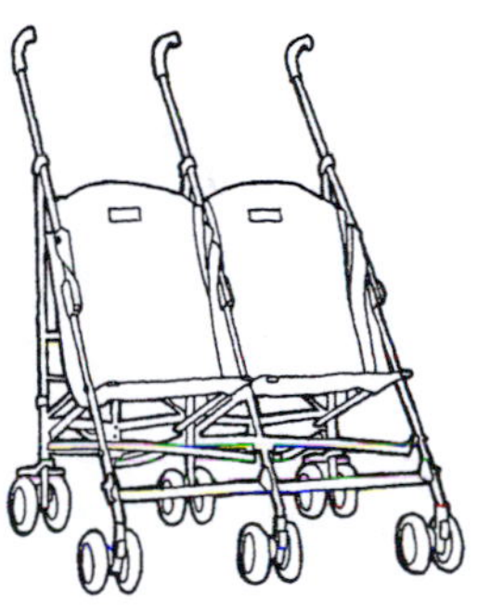

An7.2 Double buggy: length 840mm, width 740mm

The pushchair, bringing with it degrees of luxury, occupies more space than a buggy and is much less compact when folded. A typical single pushchair is shown in Figure An7.3. The side-by-side double pushchair shown in Figure An7.4 can be set so that the beds are raised to a horizontal position.

The model of a fore-and-aft double pushchair shown in Figure An7.5 is one which may be set so that two infants face each other or both may face forwards.

The principal constraint being the width of doors, a two-seat fore-and-aft pushchair is more easily manoeuvred around buildings than a side-by-side pushchair. But it is not the case that on account of the characteristics of buildings fore-and-afts could

An7.3 Single pushchair: length 1060mm, width 560mm

An7.4 Double side-by-side pushchair: length 860mm, width 950mm

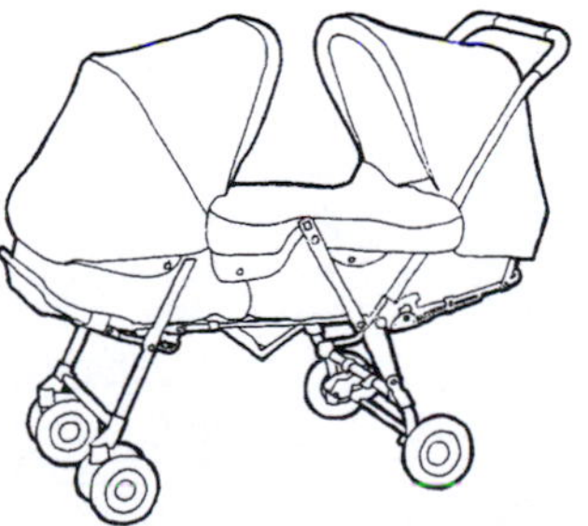

An7.5a and b Fore-and-aft double pushchair: length 1210mm, width 550mm

become more common than side-by-sides. The reason is that double buggies (as against double pushchairs) come only in side-by-side form; they cannot be fore-and-aft owing to the need for compactness when folded.

On singles versus doubles, the estimate drawn from relevant research (book Table A2.5, page 372) is that among the users of shopping centres on a typical day there are some 26 single pushchair/buggy users for each double pushchair/buggy user. No reliable data are available on numbers of side-by-side as against fore-and-aft doubles, the only relevant note being that in the sample of 49 double pushchair users drawn for the DOE sanitary provision survey there were 40 side-by-sides and 9 fore-and-afts.

With regard to pushchairs and the usage of buildings, the accessibility of toilets is a prime consideration. The pertinent note, given that babies are usually the occupants of lie-down pushchairs, is that where the prospective user of a toilet is the infant concerned rather than the pushchair pusher, the pushchair involved will usually be a buggy.

7.2 Wheelchairs

A standard self-propelled wheelchair is illustrated in Figure An7.6a and shown on plan in Figure An7.6b. It is the model for wheelchairs used for Annex A guidance purposes, but some 25 per cent of wheelchair users who are users of public buildings have a wheelchair which is longer than 1100mm, in the main those in a type of wheelchair which has to be pushed rather than being self-propelled. Most wheelchairs are between 600 and 650mm wide, with few being wider than 700mm. As Figure An7.7 shows, a typical 4-wheel powered chair does not occupy significantly more space than a manually propelled wheelchair.

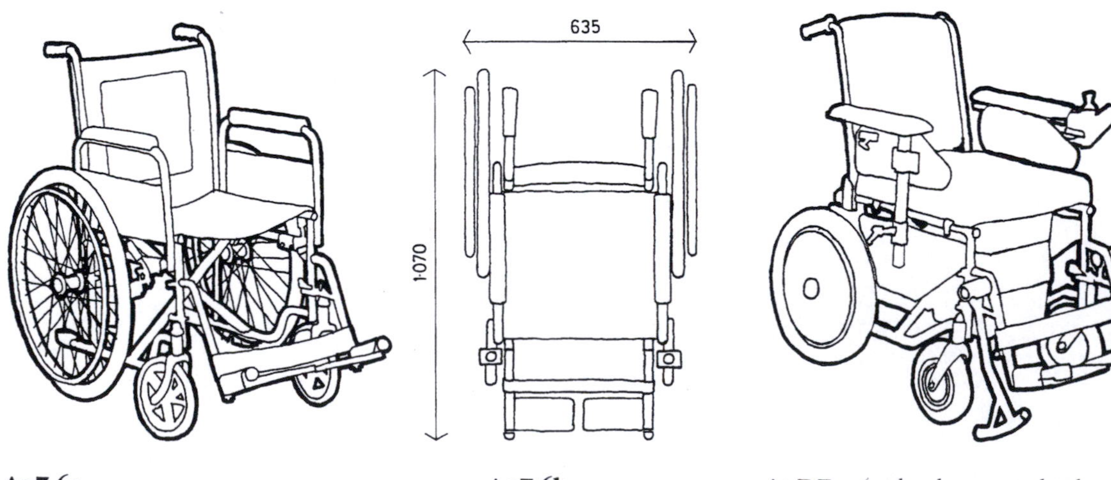

An7.6a

An7.6b

An7.7 4-wheel powered wheelchair: length 1110mm, width 650mm

7.3 Scooters

The 3-wheel scooter illustrated in Figure An7.8 is the model for space criteria in section 8 for scooter users. Four-wheel scooters are generally slightly longer, of the order of 1220mm, but not wider. The large 3-wheel scooter shown in Figure An7.9 has a length of 1430mm with an extended chassis.

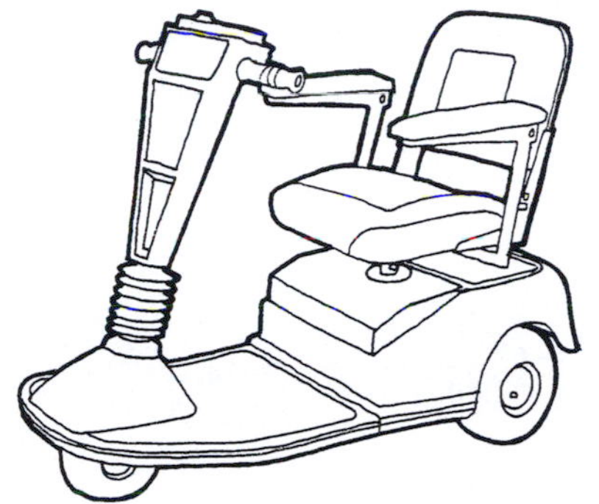

An7.8 Small 3-wheel scooter: length 1190mm, width 610mm

An7.9 Large 3-wheel scooter: length 1360mm, width 640mm

8 Criteria for spaces in buildings

8.1 Unidirectional movements

For adequate space on straight-through routes, such as direct travel through a door opening or through a check-out point in a supermarket, a clear space 650mm wide accommodates ambulant people and single pushchair users, 750mm accommodates wheelchair users and 850mm accommodates double buggy users (Figure An8.1).

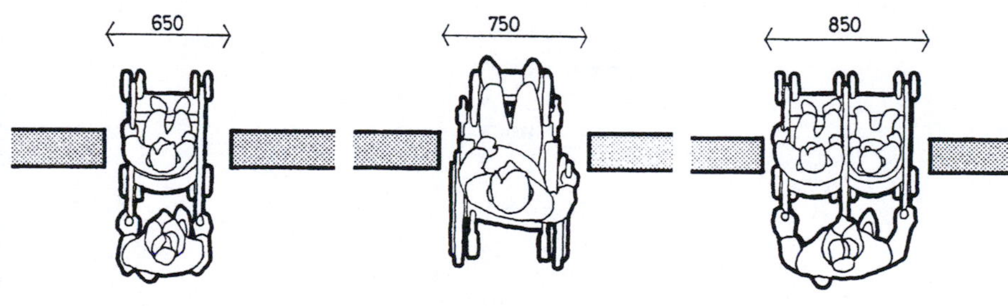

An8.1a **An8.1b** **An8.1c**

8.2 Door widths

As with design specifications for other building features, there is no universally correct prescription for the width of doors for accessibility purposes; the width that is appropriate being variable according to circumstances.

For wheelchair users (and also scooter and pushchair users), the important door dimension is the clear opening width (Figure An8.2). A standard internal timber-framed door has a clear opening width which is approximately 45mm less than the width of the doorleaf, and a fire-rated door 60mm less.

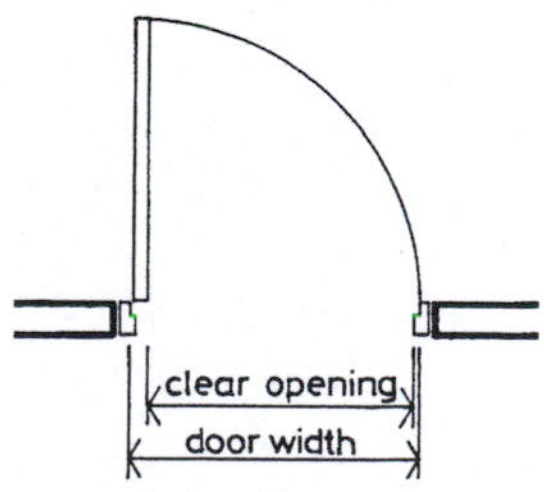

Figure An8.2

For guidance in this section and elsewhere in this document three measures are adopted for the clear opening width of doors: 700mm, 770mm and 820mm. For the purposes of Z1 regulation conditions for building features, the application of the 700mm dimension is limited to certain types of wc compartments. The 770mm dimension is related to standard internal doors which come with 900mm doorsets; where wheelchair users are to be accommodated this standard is reasonable for domestic purposes, but in public buildings a more generous base measure is reasonable, having regard, for example, to the interests of the users of double pushchairs. On this basis, the 820mm measure is the advised Z1 condition for external and internal doors in public buildings, other than where wheelchair or pushchair accessibility is not a consideration, when the 770mm measure may be appropriate.

As a rough guide, the 'giving a clear opening width of 820mm or equivalent' condition in section 6 menus should be interpreted as providing a clear width of not less than 810mm. But in line with the extended parameters precept, the 'or equivalent' should preferably be interpreted generously. For double-buggy type pushchairs having a width of approximately 740mm, a clear opening of 810 or 820mm is adequate, but a much wider opening is appropriate if side-by-side pushchairs like the 950mm wide example shown in Figure An7.4 are to be catered for.

8.3 Turns through doors

The space that a wheelchair user (or any other building user) needs to turn through a door is a function of the opening width of the door and the space available for approaching the door. Table An8.1 presents relevant data; for respective users, comfortable turning space will be afforded by the application of B and C space measures in conjunction with associated A measures for door openings.

In-and-out movements

In-and-out movements by wheelchair and pushchair users, usually where in-movement is forward and out-movement reverse, relate, for example, to wc compartments, passenger lifts and wheelchair seating spaces in theatres, etc.

The C measures in Table An8.1 assume a situation where, for example, a pushchair or wheelchair user makes a reverse exit from a wc compartment, a 3-point turn is needed to move off to leave the toilet area, and there is a wall to the non-exit side; the C measures in the table relate to the non-exit side.

Turns from passageways

The assumed design standard for passageways in public buildings is a width of 1800mm, and 1800mm measures are therefore included in the B column of Table An8.1.

As indicated by the Table An8.1 data, all users can be accommodated by passageways 1500mm wide in association with doors giving a clear opening width of 820mm. The assumption here is that doors do not open out into the passageway.

8.4 Turns in enclosed spaces

Where a wheelchair is to be turned within an enclosed space, for example a wc compartment or a lift, the broad rule is that suitable provision will be made where a circle diameter 1500mm will not be obstructed when placed on a plan drawing (Figure An8.3).

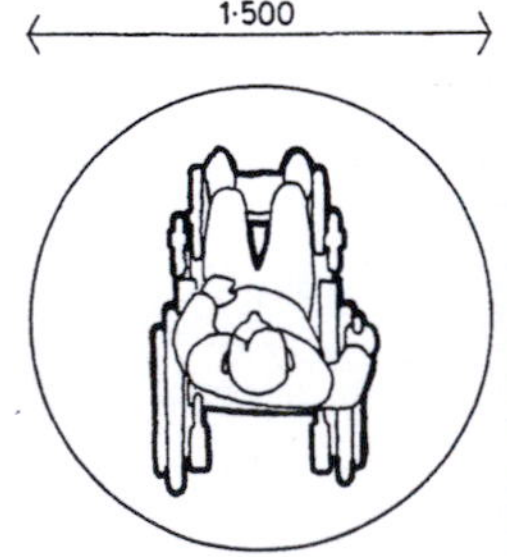

An8.3 Space for a wheelchair to be turned through 180°

In practice, an independent wheelchair user can accomplish a 3-point turn through 180° in a T-junction area in which a 1500mm circle would be obstructed, as shown in Figure An8.4. The plan diagram corresponds with the space requirements indicated in Table An8.1 for an independent wheelchair user, ie an opening 820mm wide, a 1200mm dimension in front of it and a 700mm dimension to the sides.

As relevant data in Table An8.1 indicate, more space is required for wheelchair turning when the person in the wheelchair is pushed by an attendant than when the wheelchair is manoeuvred independently. For relevant commentary see Chapter 21, page 210.

It is less easy for a 3-point 180° turn to be made in a scooter. For a continuous forward turn to be made, the unobstructed circle should have a diameter not less than 2000mm, and preferably 2500mm.

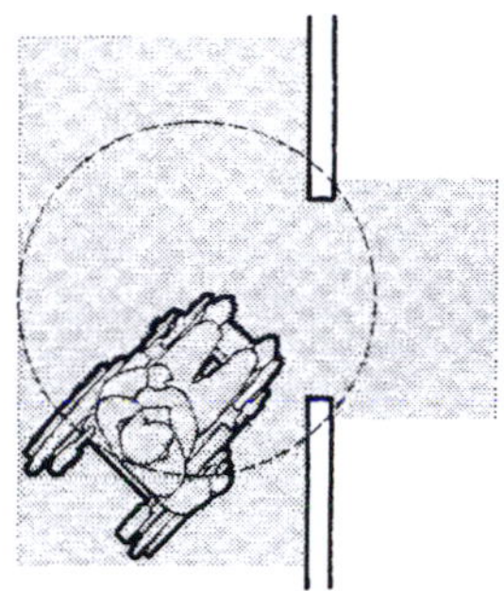

An8.4 Space for an independent wheelchair user to make a 3-point turn

Table An8.1

	Clear opening width of door (**A**) mm	Clear approach space in front of door (**B**) mm	Clear approach space to side of door (**C**) mm
Single buggy/pushchair user	700	1000	150
User of fore-and-aft double pushchair	700	1500	300
	700	1800	150
User of standard wheelchair, self-propelled	770	1300	650
	820	1200	700
	820	1800	150
User of standard wheelchair, pushed/pulled by attendant	770	1500	800
	820	1500	800
	820	1800	150
User of large wheelchair, pushed/pulled by attendant	820	1500	900
	820	1800	300
Double buggy user	820	1200	300
	820	1800	150
Scooter user	820	1500	1000
	820	1800	500

9 Steps and stairs

Matters to do with the configuration of steps and stairs are discussed in book Appendix 7, page 388. With regard to extended parameter standards, the design standards that are predicated are:

For the users of public buildings, including people with disabilities:
For external steps, rises should not be more than 140mm and goings not less than 400mm.
For internal stairs, rises should not be more than 160mm and goings not less than 300mm.

For areas of buildings used by staff only:
For external steps, rises should not be more than 150mm and goings not less than 350mm.
For internal stairs, rises should not be more than 170mm and goings not less than 300mm.

In buildings where there are special considerations relating to public areas, for example in auditoria or sports stadia where public seating is tiered, steeper stairs may be appropriate.

Table An9.1 indicates appropriate going/rise relationships for different circumstances. The figures in the table are purely indicative; it is not, for example, suggested that goings should necessarily be to one or other of the dimensions listed.

Table An9.1 Suggested configurations of stair rises and goings

		Goings (mm)	Rises (mm)
Public users of public buildings	external steps	400	125–140
		450	115–135
		500	100–125
	internal stairs	300	155–160
		350	140–160
		400	130–150
Users of staff-only areas of buildings	external steps	300	150–170
		350	130–160
		400	125–150
	internal stairs	300	150–170
		350	145–160

Annex B
Housing

1 Introduction

For accessibility control purposes, new housing cannot be treated in the same way as public buildings, most importantly because livability comes into the reckoning as well as visitability. With regard to housing provision, disabled people have on the one hand a need for a dwelling that is convenient to live in, and on the other for houses which are convenient to visit, those of their relatives, friends and neighbours. Over the years the focus of the debate on how housing should be made accessible has, however, been predominantly on livability, not visitability.

For local authority housing in Britain the concept of mobility housing was introduced in 1974, the principle being that, wherever reasonable and practicable, new housing should be convenient for the generality of disabled people to live in. To cater for those confined to wheelchairs for their mobility, special wheelchair housing was provided. Public sector housing – new social housing for rent – is now provided by housing associations, to design standards set by the Housing Corporation. Criteria for accessibility are set by the Corporation, although the important item, the provision of an entrance level wc, only applies to dwelling units for five or more persons. In January 1995 the Department of the Environment consulted on proposals for a Part M housing regulation, with draft regulatory requirements and a draft Approved Document with provisions which, if brought into operation, would be applicable both to new public and new private sector housing. The proposals were severely criticised by the House Builders Federation (HBF), and, although at the time this is written (March 1997) there has been pressure for the matter to be expedited, revised proposals for a Part M housing regulation have yet to be presented.

My expectation is that there will, eventually, be a Part M housing regulation. How it might evolve is a matter for speculation. With the Housing Corporation's accessibility controls being operative for new public sector housing, my view is that it should be geared to dealing with private sector housing, and the conditions which I suggest might come with it are discussed in section 6, along with my thinking on how they would be administered. The material has been prepared with regard to procedures currently operative in England; it does not take account of those applied in Scotland and Wales.

As a person with a severe physical disability, I report my own experiences as a user of houses. The observation I make is that there is no way at all whereby the housing environment in Britain could ever be made anywhere near as accessible to myself and similarly disabled people as the public buildings environment.

2 The concept of accessible housing

When it was first introduced in 1987 the Part M building regulation covered only new public and employment buildings, and at that time the Department of the Environment had no plans for it to be extended to cover new housing. The Access Committee for England had not raised the issue; with regard to the terms of the brief it had been given by the Minister for the Disabled in 1984*, the understanding was that it restricted itself to access issues to do with the public environment and did not concern itself with domestic housing. In October 1989, following the period during which the Committee had been placed in abeyance, the position changed. In its reconstituted form the Access Committee was given new terms of reference, with housing now being specifically included within its remit. It set up a housing working party whose work was to be guided by Sabrina Aaronovitch, the Committee's then policy officer. On the agenda was the idea of pressing for the Part M building regulation to be extended to cover new housing.

For making public buildings accessible the 1987 Part M regulation had proved effective, and the Access Committee's working party agreed that a housing regulation should be modelled on it; with a 'reasonable provision' requirement, the provisions needed to make new housing accessible to disabled people would be set out in the form of prescriptions for 'right' solutions. At meetings and through correspondence, the Access Committee put its ideas to Department of the Environment officials, government ministers and members of the parliamentary All Party Disablement Group. During 1991, the idea that a Part M housing regulation ought to be introduced appealed increasingly to the Department of the Environment. In parliament there was growing pressure for disabled civil rights legislation to be enacted: on matters to do with disabled people government ministers were keen to display good intentions, and bringing forward a Part M housing regulation could compensate for the non-appearance of the promised regulation for alterations to existing public buildings. In February 1992 Tim Yeo, the then Minister for Housing, noted, when he responded to a parliamentary question that building regulations did not yet extend to requirements for disabled people in new housing, and said, 'My Department is currently assessing the scope and timing of such an extension, which it hopes to implement next year'[1].

In September 1992 the Access Committee published its strategy document *Building Homes for Successive Generations – Criteria for Accessible General Housing*[2]. The criteria came in three categories, 'core', 'desirable' and 'optional', and of these the core criteria were the 'essentials' – they were recommendations which the Access Committee proposed should be mandated by a Part M regulation, and are listed in Table B.1. As the table shows, the criteria were geared to meeting the special housing needs of wheelchair users.

For public buildings, accessibility means visitability – provision which enables people with disabilities to visit public buildings, to get into them and make use of the service or services which they provide. Accessible housing is a different matter – it implies livability as well as visitability. Livability means being able to get into the dwelling, move around inside it, open and close doors, operate heating and lighting controls, get things in and out of storage spaces, prepare meals in the kitchen, do the washing up, do the clothes-washing, use the wc, take a bath or a shower, get into and out of bed, and keep the home clean. The inventory is extensive. Visitability is less onerous – it means being able to get into the dwelling and its living rooms, and get to and use a wc.

* See page 75.

Table B.1 The Access Committee for England's essential criteria for accessible general housing

1 Entrances to dwellings should, wherever possible, have a level or gently sloped approach.
2 Where dwellings (usually flats) are accessed by lifts, the lifts should be accessible to wheelchair users.
3 Entrances to dwellings should have flush thresholds and a minimum clear opening door width of 800mm.
4 Internal doorsets should have a minimum clear opening width of 750mm.
5 Circulation spaces at entrance level (eg halls and corridors) should have a minimum width of 900mm, and allowances should be made so that wheelchair users can turn into rooms and corridors.
6 There should be a wc and a living room at entrance level.
7 The entrance level wc should allow for access by a wheelchair user who has sufficient mobility to make either a front, diagonal or lateral transfer to the wc unaided.
8 For dwellings on more than one storey or level, a staircase should be designed to allow for possible future installation of a stairlift.

My experiences as a housing user

In Chapter 21 of this book I reported my experiences as a user of public buildings, normally as an ambulant disabled person and sometimes as a wheelchair user, and I now do the same as a user of houses. My disability being severe, I could not sensibly now live in a two-storey house, and I choose therefore to live in a flat whose rooms are all at the same level. In my ambulant disabled mode it suits me and my wife well, although it is smaller than we would wish. In my wheelchair-using mode it is less satisfactory – inside the communal entrance there are four steps to get to the lift, and within the flat the door to the bathroom is too narrow for a wheelchair to pass through. We do not, however, think to move into a wheelchair-accessible flat elsewhere. We like the flat with the view across the river, we have many good friends nearby, we have a willing porter and neighbours whom we can call on when help is needed, and outside in Battersea Square there are attractive amenities, including a general store and six restaurants.

Of all the houses I use, the flat that I live in is one among many. Others are other people's houses – the homes of friends and relatives that I visit. The crucial consideration is then visitability. For brief visits, it is a matter of getting inside and then to a living room for sitting and talking. For visits which come with an invitation to have a meal, the vital matter is the accessibility of a wc. Should there not be one at entrance level I can be distressingly disabled (meaning architecturally disabled), although on occasion an outside garden can be called into aid. For visits involving staying for a day or more in a friend's house where bathroom and bedrooms are upstairs I have generally found it possible, even if difficult, to manage the stairs. Desirably this will be an up in the evening and down in the morning exercise only; through the day it is important that there is a downstairs wc.

When I have been chairbound rather than an ambulant disabled person, visiting other people's homes has necessarily been more difficult, and on occasion I have needed to be carried up steps to front doors. In my ambulant disabled mode I can think of only one friend whose house has proved inaccessible on account of a steep flight of steps to the entrance door. I can, however, be troubled by the height of the step or steps facing me at the front doors of typical houses. But across the board of my agenda for visitability no other feature of other people's houses comes near in importance to the downstairs wc – it matters not how small it is so long as it is there.

The 'accessibility' score

My judgements of the livability and visitability ratings of houses are related to my own brand of physical disability. For other people, they will vary. For the fit able-bodied person, even the most 'inaccessible' house may be manageable; whether for living or visiting purposes, it will not be troublesome that there are steps or stairs to the entrance, or that within the house the wc is upstairs. For the severely disabled person, the house that he lives in may be convenient, but on the visiting front other people's houses may all, or practically all, be inaccessible. Theoretically, the livability and visitability population quotients of any particular house or flat could be measured. Were it, for example, the case that every two- or three-storey family house in Britain had an entrance level wc, overall visitability ratings would be substantially higher than they currently are.

Among all the houses I have visited as a wheelchair user, it has been only the homes of other wheelchair users which I have found to be wholly convenient. As an ambulant disabled person more have scored well, but they have been nowhere near a majority. In this connection the findings of the 1991 English House Condition Survey are relevant. The accessibility of housing for disabled people was examined, with a dwelling being deemed accessible if it had no more than two steps to the floor which provided kitchen, wc and bathroom facilities and at least two other rooms. By this measure, one which did not equate with provision suitable for wheelchair users, only just over a quarter of the housing stock qualified as 'accessible', the dwellings concerned being principally bungalows and flats with lifts[3].

Were I still to be around thirty years from now, I doubt that the record would be much better. Unlike existing public buildings, existing houses are not regularly replaced, and commonly there is little or no scope for upgrading them to improve their accessibility. The houses that notionally I would visit in thirty years' time would (if not the same ones) be much like the houses I visit today – there would be steps up to the entrance, and frequently there would not be a ground floor wc. The new houses being built would predominantly still be two-storey boxes, with stairways, often perhaps having awkward winders, which I would not be able to manage.

The comparison is with public buildings. Had access for the disabled never become a prominent political issue and had there never been a Part M building regulation, I would probably have still been able to use many public buildings without undue difficulty, either as an ambulant disabled person or a wheelchair user. That it did become an issue and that there have since 1985 been statutory access controls has, however, been immensely beneficial to me. There are still buildings which I cannot use, but often – as in the case of cafes, restaurants, cinemas and theatres – there are alternatives which are accessible.

If, as may be contended, the purpose of accessibility controls is to create wholly accessible environments, it is an objective which in the public sphere can, near enough, be secured. In the domestic sphere it cannot be, the simple reason being that English people like to live in two-storey houses. With a stairway in the way of getting to the upstairs rooms, the two-storey house is not, at least for livability purposes, fully accessible to wheelchair users. In a particular house it may be that a stairlift could be placed over the stairs, or there could be a convenient place for installing a through-floor lift which could carry a person seated in a wheelchair. But such devices could not make a two-storey house as convenient for a non-ambulant wheelchair user to live in as a suitably designed single-storey unit. So the story of efforts in recent years to procure suitable housing for disabled people to live in or visit has been a story of nibbles at the edges, not of interventions across the board. It has been a story of good intentions and commendable initiatives, with laudable efforts being more notable in the public than the private sector of the field.

3 Mobility and wheelchair housing

In October 1961 a seminal event occurred in the history of public sector housing in Britain – the publication of the report *Homes for today and tomorrow*[4]. Sir Parker Morris was the chairman of the committee appointed by the Minister of Housing to produce the report, the brief being to consider the standards of design and equipment applicable to family dwellings, and to make recommendations. From the day the report was published, the standards which came with it were known as Parker Morris standards.

The provision of new public sector housing in 1961 was not directly controlled by central government. Instead, under relevant legislation – most importantly the Housing Act of 1957 – local authorities had broad housing powers, and it was their job to determine how best the housing needs of people living in their districts should be met. The houses they built were subsidised; on an open-ended demand-led basis the Exchequer (the Treasury) contributed two-thirds of the capital costs. There was thus cause for the government to be concerned that it obtained value for its money, although the matter was not one which the Parker Morris Committee was specifically asked to consider.

Prior to 1961, local authority housing standards were derived from the recommendations of a 1944 government-appointed committee and were framed largely in terms of minimum room sizes. The Parker Morris report dropped that practice, and, with recommended standards for amenities within dwellings, opted instead for overall minimum floor areas according to the number of bed-spaces and the type of dwelling concerned; the space standards are listed in Table B.2[5]. With the standards officially approved, the Ministry of Housing developed an elaborate cost control system for housing built in line with them. For individual dwellings there would be cost allowances, and for any new housing development there would be cost yardsticks which would set overall cost limits and determine the amount of subsidy which the local authority concerned would receive from the Exchequer. With the apparatus in place, there were established design norms for new public sector housing, an effect being that the parameters of normal provision were clearly defined by Parker Morris space and amenity standards

The Parker Morris report made no mention at all of disabled people or how new housing might be designed to cater for them. In 1961 disabled people were not on the agenda; the first task I was given when I began work on the first edition of *Designing for the Disabled* in October 1961 was to go to Sweden, to a conference where I would learn about the pioneering work being done in Scandinavia on housing for the disabled, in particular about the planning and design of kitchens and bathrooms for wheelchair users. From 1962, affected by Lady Hamilton's endeavours*, local housing authorities increasingly set about providing special housing for the disabled, and that meant wheelchair housing. Many of the wheelchair units designed in the 1960s were lavish. They were not subject to Parker Morris space

* See page 20.

standards, no official advice on how they should be designed had been issued, and under the Ministry's cost control system there were no prescribed cost allowances for them. Architects could make them as spacious and generously equipped as they wished; for cost subsidy purposes, the arrangement was that they would attract an ad hoc allowance, with standard Ministry practice being that the allowance would be for whatever the additional cost happened to be.

The genesis of mobility housing

Section 3 of the 1970 Chronically Sick and Disabled Persons Act required local authorities to concern themselves with the special housing needs of disabled people, and it was owing to it that I joined the Department of the Environment in 1972 to work on the drafting of official design standards for housing for the disabled*. The understanding was that to meet the housing needs of disabled people dwelling units should be specially designed to suit people confined to wheelchairs, with kitchens and bathrooms equipped for wheelchair management. On that basis, local authorities were already building special housing in some quantity, and by 1972 housing managers were reporting that it was not as easy as they had supposed it would be to allocate tenancies to people in wheelchairs who matched the stereotype. Had there not been a section 3 the Department would, I imagine, have in any event devised standards for wheelchair housing – the open-ended ad hoc system could not have been sustained indefinitely. There might not, however, have been mobility housing.

Housing Development Directorate Occasional Paper 2/74 *Mobility housing*[6] was issued by the Department of the Environment in July 1974, followed in June 1975 by HDDOP 2/75 *Wheelchair housing*[7]. Wheelchair housing was special housing for disabled people, whereas conceptually mobility housing was not – it was general needs housing designed to meet the needs of most disabled people, including wheelchair users who were not chairbound. It was a manifestation of macroism in practice, the principle that in designing buildings which are to cater for people with disabilities the starting premise should be that they are normal and not different people.

The scope of mobility housing

From the findings of the survey I had made in Norwich during the 1960s, the impression I gained was that what the great majority of disabled people needed was not special housing but simply conveniently designed ordinary housing. The established benchmark for normal family housing was Parker Morris space and amenity standards, and the query, applying the bottom-up rule, was how far disabled people could be accommodated within their parameters.

The first consideration was the constraints of steps and stairs: with ambulant disabled people and wheelchair users in mind two-storey housing appeared to be ruled out, meaning that potentially suitable dwelling types were ground floor flats, lift-accessible flats and single-storey houses with a level approach to the entrance. The next, with wheelchair users in mind, was circulation space constraints. On account of the cost limits there could not be as much manoeuvring space as there would be in special wheelchair housing. Doorsets to principal rooms could be 900mm, giving a clear opening width of 775mm, but for passageways the prescribed minimum width could not be pressed beyond 900mm – a condition which, although tight, would be manageable by people in small wheelchairs. The door to the bathroom/wc was a problem. An analysis of typical floor layouts indicated that a

* See page 38.

Table B.2 Wheelchair housing: Department of the Environment space standards (1975) compared with Parker Morris standards

	Bed-spaces per dwelling	Parker Morris space standard* m²	Wheelchair housing space standard* m²	% increase
Single-storey houses**	1	30	35.5	18.3
	2	44.5	49.5	11.2
	3	57	63	10.5
	4	67	73	9.0
	5	75.5	86	13.9
	6	84	94.5	12.5
Two-storey houses	4	72†	n/a	
	5	82†	91	11.0
	6	92.5	101.5	9.7
	7	108	113	4.6

*Overall floor area: minimum net space, excluding general storage space. For 4-, 5- and 6-person houses, the Parker Morris space standard for general storage was 4.5m²; for corresponding flats, it was 3.5m².
**For flats, Parker Morris space standards for 4-, 5- and 6-person units were respectively 70m², 79m² and 86.5m²; for wheelchair housing, space standards for flats were the same as for houses.
†For semi-detached or end-of-terrace houses; for centre-terrace 4- and 5-person two-storey houses, the space standards were respectively 74.5m² and 85m².

requirement for a 900mm doorset could involve significant cost penalties, and a wheelchair-accessible bathroom/wc had to be ruled out.

The outcome was the setting of three important conditions for meeting the mobility housing standard. They were (1) that the entrance to the dwelling should be accessible to people in wheelchairs; (2) that the principal living room, the kitchen and at least one bedroom should be accessible to wheelchair users other than the completely chairbound; and (3) that the bathroom and wc should be at entrance level, although not necessarily wheelchair-accessible. A subsequent amendment to the standard was that two-storey housing could be classed as mobility housing on a similar basis, provided there was a wc at entrance level and a straight flight staircase suitable for the installation of a stairlift giving access to the bathroom and bedrooms upstairs. Relevant research and statistical data[8] suggested that some 98 per cent of disabled people in Britain (among them the majority of those who were wheelchair users) could be conveniently accommodated in housing designed to mobility standard.

Space standards for wheelchair housing (Table B.2) were necessarily more generous; to be wheelchair-accessible, rooms needed to have 900mm doorsets with passageways not less than 1200mm wide, and within living rooms, kitchens, bathrooms/wcs and at least one bedroom there had to be space for wheelchair manoeuvre. Two-storey houses could be wheelchair housing if a bathroom/wc and a bedroom were at ground level. Houses and flats built by local authorities to these standards attracted an additional cost allowance on top of the allowance for corresponding Parker Morris units; in 1975 the amounts ranged from £650 to £1,250 according to dwelling type.

Based on an analysis of public sector housing construction data for 1972, the estimate made in 1974 was that some 25 per cent of all new public sector dwellings might be designed to mobility housing standard[9]. As statistical returns published by the Department of the Environment would show, this amount was never approached; the highest proportion achieved was 7.8 per cent in 1979[10], with the reasons, it would seem, being more to do with practicalities rather than a reluctance to take the idea of mobility housing on board.

Although not on the scale of the 1960s, it was still the practice in 1972 for a significant number of local authority dwelling units to be in the form of flats with lift access. These were units which could readily be designed to mobility standard, but after 1972 it was rare for them to be built. Without them, only ground floor flats and houses with a ground floor wc could qualify, and the 1972 analysis probably over-estimated the number of these which would be on suitable terrain; the mobility housing requirement was that a dwelling entrance should have a ramped or level approach and a flush threshold, the threshold to be not higher than 25mm to either side and the ramped approach not steeper than 1 in 12.

The more limiting condition was the need in two-storey houses for a downstairs wc, and it was here that cost allowances tied to Parker Morris standards were constraining; only for 5- or 6-person, not those for 3- or 4-person two-storey houses or maisonettes, were two wcs required to meet Parker Morris standards. For housing built to mobility standard there was an additional cost allowance, but it related only to the flush threshold, and in 1975 was set at £50.

4 The Housing Corporation and housing associations

In the mid-1970s Parker Morris standards for public sector housing seemed to be a permanent fixture; no one supposed that they could be abandoned, but it was in April 1982 that they were. Mrs Thatcher had become Prime Minister in 1979, and, with her vision of a home-owning democracy, her policy edict was that council houses should be sold to their tenants, with local authorities being discouraged from building more of them. John Stanley was her Housing Minister; he pushed right-to-buy legislation through parliament and dismantled the whole apparatus of Parker Morris standards and their associated cost controls.

The determination of Mrs Thatcher's administration to curb the role of local housing authorities did not signal the end of new-build public sector housing. In place of local authorities the government would favour charitable housing associations, with Exchequer funding for their new housing schemes being channelled through the Housing Corporation, the government agency set up in 1964 to promote the development of renting and co-ownership housing schemes by registered housing associations.

Initially, as allowed for by the 1974 Housing Act, virtually the entire capital cost of new housing association schemes was covered by central government by way of Housing Association Grant (HAG), a practice which was to end with the enactment of the 1988 Housing Act. Under that Act private sector finance was instituted for housing association schemes. For their development costs, housing associations were able to borrow money from banks or building societies to supplement HAG, and new avenues were open to them. They could buy existing housing units and renovate them, and they could buy new housing being constructed by private sector developers. For their own new schemes, they bought land and were in the design-and-build business. The houses they built could be all for rent, with development costs being recovered from the rents they would charge. Or they could work in partnership with a private sector housebuilder, in which case the outcome could be a mix of three brands of dwelling: houses for rent, shared ownership (with the householder paying the association part rent and part purchase cost), and houses for sale to private purchasers. The cost of housing for rent continued to be subsidised by HAG, with grant rates varying across the country.

Provision for disabled people

Following the abolition of Parker Morris standards, the Housing Corporation issued guidance on amenity standards for housing association schemes, first in its *Design and Contract and Contract Criteria*, from 1989 in *Design and Contracting Requirements*, and from 1993 in *Scheme Development Standards*. With its remit to produce social housing, and in particular housing for people with special needs, the Corporation encouraged the building of mobility-type and wheelchair-type housing. Historically, the scope of mobility housing for meeting the housing needs of disabled people had been a function of the application of Parker Morris space standards, and so long as they remained in place it was practicable for normal housing to be suitable for many wheelchair users to live in. But when they were dropped and space standards began to slip, the scope necessarily diminished – the less generous the space in circulation areas and habitable rooms in a dwelling, the less convenient it would be for wheelchair users to manage.

Under the mixed funding procedures which came with the 1988 Act, the costs of mobility-type houses were subsumed into the basic cost criteria for new dwellings. For wheelchair housing additional cost allowances were available, and housing associations continued to build wheelchair units in line with the guidance set out in HDDOP 2/75. Some six or so national housing associations specialised in the provision of housing suitable for disabled people; of these the most prominent was the Habinteg Housing Association. In 1989 Habinteg issued the first edition of its *Design Guide*[11], which for housing associations became the authoritative design guide and technical manual for special provision for wheelchair users in integrated social housing schemes.

The Housing Corporation's welfare ethos

When local authorities were in the housebuilding business they provided community housing, whereas the Housing Corporation now provides social housing. In accord with current (1997) government policy, subsidised new housing (meaning housing funded with the help of Housing Association Grant) goes to people in most need of it, in particular people who have special needs. In this regard, the Corporation has issued guidance on housing for visually impaired people[12] and elderly people[13], and for special housing for wheelchair users amenity standards are prescribed in the Corporation's *Scheme Development Standards*[14].

In effect, social housing means welfare housing. Historically – at least in the years after the Second World War – local authorities did not regard their new housing as welfare housing. But as a consequence of welfare legislation, the Chronically Sick and Disabled Persons Act of 1970, they were encouraged to build special housing for wheelchair users. In this connection, it could be that local authorities, had they retained all the housing powers they once had, would not now be building wheelchair housing – they would be building adaptable housing. Britain would have followed Dutch practice.

Adaptable housing

In the Netherlands during the 1970s and early 1980s specially planned and equipped units for wheelchair users were built, but, as in Britain, the independent wheelchair users for whom they were intended were not readily found. And the units, as a rule distinct and separate from others, became stigmatised. The policy decision was to drop special housing, and, for the accommodation of disabled people with special needs, to develop adaptable housing as a feature of general needs housing provision. As a rule, adaptable units were flats in low-rise blocks; space standards (which were more generous than in Britain) were not raised, but units were planned to be adaptable to suit a tenant who was a wheelchair user, and provision was made to incorporate a lift if needed[15].

In America the concept of adaptable housing was introduced in the 1980 edition of the American Standard A117.1. The design standards were amplified to include standards for adaptable kitchens, bathrooms, showers, etc and dwelling units would be classed as 'accessible' where they complied with the standards and associated A117.1 conditions. Domestic housing is not covered by the Americans with Disabilities Act, but under the provisions of the US Federal Government's Fair Housing Amendments Act of 1988 adaptable housing units have to be provided in new housing developments which incorporate buildings where there are four or more dwelling units under one roof[16].

On account of the two-storey small-box character of its normal housing, Britain would probably not have tended to apply Dutch or American design practices for adaptable housing. Had the Department of the Environment continued, however, to have a professional Housing Development Directorate, I imagine that ways would have been found of setting appropriate design standards for adaptable housing in the form of single-storey houses, ground floor flats or lift-access flats.

The Housing Corporation's Scheme Development Standards

In September 1992 the Access Committee for England published its strategy document *Building Homes for Successive Generations – Criteria for Accessible General Housing*. At that time the Housing Corporation was drafting the first version of its *Scheme Development Standards*, the corporate package of amenity standards which housing associations would be asked to apply in order to obtain grants for their schemes. Section 1.3 of the Corporation's scheme development standards, first published in October 1993 and then revised in August 1995, is called *Accessibility*[17]; the criteria for it, set out in Table B.3, correspond with the Access Committee's criteria for accessible general housing (Table B.1).

For housing that is to be suitable for disabled people to live in or visit, there is, as has already been noted, one dwelling amenity which matters way above all others – the entrance level wc. In the Access Committee's essential criteria for accessible general housing it was an item which was unqualified – houses which were to be accessible had to have an entrance level wc. But in the Housing Corporation's criteria for accessibility it is a requirement which for two-storey houses applies only to dwellings for five persons or more. Two-storey houses for three or four persons do not need to have an entrance level wc.

There are a number of features in the Housing Corporation's list which could be deemed to be essential for people wholly dependent on a wheelchair for mobility, but not for other disabled people. With reference to Table B.3 I note four of them: (c) a level or gently sloped approach to the dwelling; (f) a level standing area outside the front door; (g) a flush threshold; and (j) passageways giving wheelchair access at entrance level. Noting item (c), an effect, in my view, was to mislay priorities. For approaches to new public buildings the no-steps condition can always be satisfied, but not for new housing. Houses are relatively small buildings; they sit on the plot of land where they are placed, and where the land slopes there may have to be steps between the place where a car is parked and the front entrance. Such

Table B.3 The Housing Corporation's criteria for accessibility
The items listed below are the essential items for the test of compliance with the Housing Corporation's requirement that external and internal environments should provide access for user groups and visitors with limited mobility.

(a)	Entrance path gateways provide min. 850mm clear opening?
(b)	Dropped kerbs provided where main paths meet roads and drives?
(c)	Dwelling approaches level or gently sloped?
(d)	Lifts, where provided, to be sized for wheelchair access?
(e)	Main paths min. 900mm wide with firm, even surface?
(f)	Level standing area outside front door at threshold level?
(g)	Dwelling entrance has flush (max. 15mm upstand) threshold?
(h)	Dwelling entrance provides 775mm min. clear opening?
(i)	Internal doorways provide 750mm min. clear opening?
(j)	Passageway widths provide wheelchair access at entrance level?
(k)	Staircase suitable for future stairlift provision?
(l)	Entrance level wc and basin provided (5 person units and above)?

dwellings will not be accessible to unassisted wheelchair users, but they will, if the steps are suitably graded and have a handrail, be conveniently accessible for ambulant disabled people. An appropriately drafted where-there-are-steps condition could have been on the Corporation's checklist; without it, uphill (or downhill) dwelling entrances may continue to come with uncomfortably high steps, both on the approach and at the door threshold. On the accessibility priority list, the entrance level wc surely comes in at number 1; as to which should be number 2 there can be arguments, but a strong contender could be suitably graded steps to the dwelling entrance where steps are unavoidable.

Lifetime Homes

Minimum overall space standards – the prime safeguard for maintaining quality standards for new housing – had been lost to housing associations when Parker Morris standards were abandoned in 1982. Amenity standards had to suffice from then on, and understandably there was a tendency to minimise as far as possible the space needed to accommodate the amenities. Against that background, consumer interest groups in the housing field campaigned for the enhancement of housing standards, their efforts being focused on promoting the concept of Lifetime Homes.

In 1989 the Helen Hamlyn Trust launched its Lifetime Homes project, the lead on its promotion being taken by Andrew Rowe, the Conservative MP for Mid Kent in Kent[18]. The initiative was forwarded from 1992 by Richard Best, the director of the Joseph Rowntree Foundation, and, with 16 design criteria being set (Table B.4), the concept was described in a 1993 publicity brochure[19]:

> Lifetime Homes are designed to meet the needs of their occupiers throughout their lifetime. The design features help parents with young children as much as grandparents who come to stay. The homes can cope with life events such as the teenager breaking a leg and being in a wheelchair for a few weeks. They can be visited by everyone, young or old, able-bodied or disabled. The homes are easy to adapt if a member of the household becomes disabled or frailer in old age.

Table B.4 Lifetime Homes criteria

Access

1 Where car-parking is adjacent to the home, it should be capable of enlargement to obtain 3.3 metres width.
2 The distance from the car-parking space to the home should be kept to a minimum and should be level or gently sloping.
3 The approach to all entrances should be level or gently sloping.
4 All entrances should be illuminated and have level access over the threshold, and the main entrance should be covered.
5 Where homes are reached by a lift, it should be wheelchair-accessible.

Inside the home

6 The width of the doorways and hallways should accord with the Access Committee for England's standards.
7 There should be space for the turning of wheelchairs in kitchens, dining areas and sitting rooms and adequate circulation space for wheelchair users elsewhere.
8 The sitting-room (or family room) should be at entrance level.
9 In houses of two or more storeys, there should be space on the ground floor that could be used as a convenient bed space.
10 There should be a downstairs toilet which should be wheelchair-accessible, with drainage and service provision enabling a shower to be fitted at any time.
11 Walls in bathrooms and toilets should be capable of taking adaptations such as handrails.
12 The design should incorporate provision for a future stairlift and a suitably identified space for potential installation of a house lift (through-the-floor lift) from the ground to the first floor, for example to a bedroom next to the bathroom.
13 The bath/bedroom ceiling should be strong enough, or capable of being made strong enough, to support a hoist at a later date. Within the bath/bedroom wall provision should be made for a future floor to ceiling door, to connect the two rooms by a hoist.
14 The bathroom layout should be designed to incorporate ease of access, probably from a side approach, to the bath and wc. The wash basins should also be accessible.

Fixtures and fittings

15 Living room window glazing should begin at 800mm or lower, and windows should be easy to open/operate.
16 Switches, sockets and service controls should be at a height usable by all (ie between 600mm and 1200mm from the floor).

Lifetime Homes, with the important condition that a space should be identified for a through-the-floor lift from the ground to the first floor (item 13 in Table B.4), presented the potential for general needs housing to be adaptable to meet the overall living needs of wheelchair users, and as a regular feature of housing new-build schemes they could substantially enhance the scope for normal housing to accommodate the great majority of people with any kind of disability. The concept appealed to housing associations, for some of whom it was to become standard practice. But it did not appeal to private sector housebuilders – for them the idea of a 'lifetime' home was anathema. Their new low-cost housing was aimed at first-time buyers, who, when they could upgrade, moved on to better houses (preferably, again built speculatively) and sold their first house to a new first-time buyer. Housebuilders felt that 'lifetime' homes would not help the marketing process, and the House Builders Federation did not favour the concept[20].

In 1997, with the Joseph Rowntree Foundation continuing to promote it busily, the Lifetime Homes initiative is prospering on the public sector side. An informative guidance document, *Designing Lifetime Homes*, has been published[21], with diagrammatic illustrations indicating how the 16 criteria can be met and a series of examples of Lifetime Homes plans.

5 Private sector housing and planning guidance

Through the 1970s the prevailing housing policy view was that it was local authorities and housing associations who should be in the business of providing suitable housing for disabled people to live in. The idea that private sector housebuilders could contribute never surfaced: speculative developers operated in a competitive market, and for commercial reasons they could not be expected to concern themselves with special housing for disabled people – their standard product was two-storey family housing of a kind which was not convenient for disabled people to live in. It was not until the concept of visitability emerged – the idea that ordinary housing ought to be designed so that disabled people could go visiting – that it was realised that private sector housebuilders could make a valuable contribution to meeting the housing needs of disabled people.

The International Year of Disabled People was held in 1981. When it was over, it was widely felt that the impetus it had generated should be maintained, and the Prince of Wales was encouraged to respond. In early 1983 he set up an advisory group, the Prince of Wales' Advisory Group on Disability, and I was one of those invited to join his team. Our role as advisers was to identify new initiatives which he could sponsor and help promote, and housing for disabled people was one of the topics on the agenda.

On 12 February 1985 the Prince of Wales hosted a lunch meeting at Kensington Palace, among those attending being Ian Gow, the then Minister for Housing, and a number of prominent housebuilders. Papers sent out in advance had set the scene; the idea of visitability housing had evolved from mobility housing, its basic requirements being that the dwelling entrance should be accessible, the principal sitting room should be reachable in a wheelchair, and there should be a wc at entrance level. Nancy Robertson, the polio-disabled director of the advisory group, exemplified the issue when she spoke at the meeting. When her son was small she had held parties for his friends, and when their parents came to collect them she met and talked with them. But when her son went to parties for his friends she was left outside.

Among the housebuilders at the meeting Sir Lawrie Barratt was keen to cooperate; he was, he said, launching his new 'Premier' collection of houses for sale, he would arrange for modifications to be made to them in accord with visitability principles, and he invited the Prince of Wales to come to Bracknell to see them when they were completed. In September 1985 the Prince of Wales was at Bracknell for the opening ceremony; while the results were not all as we had hoped – in particular, the dwelling entrances and thresholds were not conveniently manageable by wheelchair users – the visitability idea was prospering. The National House-Building Council (NHBC) had in the meantime agreed to take the lead role on the promotion of visitability housing, and subsequently, in 1987, launched a national awards scheme; housebuilders would submit schemes demonstrating good visitability practice, and at an annual event held over three years from 1989 the Prince of Wales presented awards to the winners. Affected by the recession in the housebuilding industry, the awards scheme was deferred in 1991 and was not subsequently revived.

In the course of the awards scheme there was never a suggestion that the accessibility of private sector housing should be statutorily regulated – with exhortation, encouragement, awards and royal patronage, the trust was that the incorporation of visitability features in new housing was an idea that would take hold among housebuilders and become standard practice. But despite the mammoth effort put into the enterprise by the NHBC, it did not – the venture prospered hardly at all. Housebuilders were not willing to change their ways. When surveys associated with the project were made[22], all who had a downstairs wc in their homes agreed that yes, a downstairs wc was essential. But first-time buyers at whom low-cost new houses were aimed commonly preferred to have a spacious living room and a well-equipped kitchen, never mind that the only wc would be in the bathroom upstairs. Detached houses conventionally came with steps at the front door, housebuilders always put the steps in, and potential purchasers liked to have the steps – they did not want a level entrance. A survey made subsequently on a housing estate in York[23] confirmed the attractiveness of steps at dwelling entrances. It found that even occupants who were unsteady on their feet or who used a wheelchair did not want a ramped front entrance, although ramped access at the rear was more acceptable; ramps were perceived as highly visible and unwelcome indicators of vulnerability and disability.

For its awards scheme the NHBC had issued guidance on visitability provision[24], and subsequently drafted a voluntary code of practice presenting guidance on how new private sector housing could be made accessible to disabled people. When the proposed Part M housing regulation was announced, its decision was to delay the issuing of the code of practice until it was known what the Part M regulation would require.

The threshold issue

Following the completion of the demonstration houses built at Bracknell, Barratts funded a practical project to assess the visitability features of the houses; through the Centre on Environment for the Handicapped (CEH) the project was managed by Shirley Comrie-Smith (an architect with Phippen Randall and Parkes), workshop meetings with disabled people testing the provision were held at Bracknell, and the project was reported[25]. The feature of the demonstration houses which provoked by far the most concern was the thresholds – these were a mix, with upstands ranging from about 15 to 50mm.

The configuration of thresholds at dwelling entrance doors which will not impede wheelchair users has always been a problematical issue. On the basis that the entrances to public buildings never have an upstanding threshold, it might be supposed that there is no reason why houses should not. In practice, there are various reasons why not, and an upstanding threshold has to be virtually obligatory for dwellings with entrances at ground level – a consideration confirmed by the Housing Corporation's compliance test being not for absolute flushness, but for a maximum 15mm upstand (Table B.3).

By comparison with a normal chunky timber threshold, a low upstanding threshold facilitates wheelchair access but can still impede it, particularly where the person in the wheelchair is being pushed over it by a helper. Where the threshold has an internal drop, as in houses there usually is for the placement of a loose mat inside the door, what can happen is that the castor wheels may catch it and skew so that the wheelchair stalls when the wheels hit the floor, the occupant then being liable to fall forwards and the helper having to go back and start again[26]. When special housing for wheelchair users is designed, there are appropriate means of achieving unobstructed access at entrance doors. But in respect of general needs housing and provision for wheelchair users there is not, it would seem, a wholly satisfactory and universally applicable solution to the threshold problem.

Accessible housing - planning policy guidance

The idea that private sector developers should be pressed to produce accessible housing began to emerge around 1990, with the Access Committee for England's campaign for a Part M housing regulation and the drafting of the plan policies which local authorities were required to develop under the terms of the Town and Country Planning Act of 1990. In their development plans local authorities could highlight the importance they attached to using the planning system to procure accessible housing, and when planning officers set about drafting them attention to the special concerns of disabled people was consistently high on the agenda. The policy statements in development plans would themselves be material planning considerations, and as such they would have considerable authority.

In cooperation with the Royal Town Planning Institute the Access Committee produced *Access Policies for Local Plans*[27], a guidance document which was issued and distributed to local authorities in early 1993. In it, with informative explanations and relevant background data, were a series of model policy statements which local authorities could adopt and incorporate in their development plans. Across England, local authorities welcomed the practical and political assistance which the Access Committee's guidance document gave them. Some drafted policy plan statements which replicated the models, others sought to make them more demanding, and few were inclined to make them less forceful. Where the Access Committee's draft policy statement for accessible housing was not copied, a relatively common line was to ask for housing to mobility standard (citing HDD Occasional Paper 2/74) or mobility-type housing.

With regard to how planning conditions should be applied by local authorities, the Department of the Environment issued official guidance in the form of planning policy guidance notes, which local authorities needed to have regard to when drafting their development plans. In March 1992 the Department of the Environment issued a revision of PPG3 – *Planning Policy Guidance: Housing*[28]. In its 14 pages three topics were raised of relevance to the provision of accessible housing – the mix of houses in a development; the matter of 'affordable' housing; and the scope of planning control with regard to design standards.

In March 1997, the time that this is written, the 1992 text of PPG3 is current. The advice in its paragraph 6 is that local authorities might need to control aspects of the design of new developments, but functional requirements within a development should be a matter for the marketing judgement of developers. Planning authorities should not attempt to prescribe rigid formulae: 'they should regulate the mix of house types only where there are specific planning reasons for such control, and in doing so they should take account of marketing considerations'. Paragraph 8 advises that development plans should show how future requirements for new housing could best be met, having regard to other planning objectives.

Paragraph 38 advises that a community's need for affordable housing is a material planning consideration which can be taken into account in formulating development plan policies, and that planning authorities could seek to negotiate with developers for the inclusion of affordable housing in their schemes. Affordable housing is low-cost housing; it can be housing for rent or for sale, but because there are wide variations in house prices and earnings between different areas of the country there is no single national measure of need for it.

On the planning side, there are thus three considerations which could constrain the imposition of conditions aimed at procuring housing in line with the Access Committee's model policies – that account should be taken of marketing considerations; that affordable housing should be a feature of housing schemes; and that there should be regard to other planning objectives. The provision of housing for the disabled is considered in PPG3[29]:

> Developers should already be considering whether the internal design of housing, and access to it, can meet the needs of the disabled, whether as residents or visitors. To the extent that regulation is justified the Government looks to the Building Regulations and not the planning system to impose requirements. . . . the Department is assessing the practicality of extending the requirement of Part M of the Building Regulations to new dwellings. However, where there is clear evidence of local need, a local planning authority could include in a local plan a policy indicating that it would seek to negotiate elements of housing, accessible to the disabled, on suitable sites. . . . The plan should not seek to impose detailed standards.

The message here was that planning controls should be limited to planning considerations, and planning conditions ought not to be employed to control housing design standards. The expectation in 1992 was that a Part M housing regulation would be forthcoming, and that its effect could be to prevent planning control encroaching into the realm of building control. Without it, there was no discipline. In their development plans local authorities could assert firm policies for the provision of accessible housing, cite sources of detailed guidance and prescribe design standards and design conditions. The Department of the Environment's guidance could tell them that their development plans should not *seek* to impose detailed standards, but it could not prevent local authorities imposing planning conditions for which compliance could only be tested by checking that there was conformity with appropriate design standards.

It was private developers who came under most pressure when local authorities brought their plan policies into operation. Planning authorities could point to their policies, ones, for example, which said that mobility-type housing should be the norm for all new housing developments, and tell developers that planning permission would be subject to compliance with the policies. In pressing for all new housing to be so designed as a matter of course, they were, however, being unreasonable. In the late 1970s, when local housing authorities were responding with enthusiasm to the idea of producing mobility housing, they never came near to designing all their housing to mobility standard – as has been noted, the best they could achieve, in 1979, was 7.8 per cent. And, as the House Builders Federation was to report, there were occasions when planning authorities' insistence on mobility-type housing would dismay private sector housebuilders. Not until the promised Part M building regulation was introduced, it seemed, would the demands of planning authorities be constrained.

6 The prospective Part M housing regulation

On 12 January 1995, the day that the government presented its Disability Discrimination Bill, the Department of the Environment issued formal proposals for extending the Part M building regulation to cover new housing[30]. The controls which it was proposed should be introduced were to apply equally to new housing built by housing associations and by private developers, and with a draft approved document, *Access and facilities for disabled people: New Dwellings*, the January 1995 consultation paper proposed two regulatory requirements:

M5 Reasonable provision shall be made for disabled people to gain access to and use the entrance storey of the dwelling.

M6 Reasonable provision shall be made for sanitary conveniences on the entrance storey of the dwelling which allow access and use by disabled people.

Drawing on the Access Committee's criteria for accessible general housing, the stated objectives were to allow the occupiers of new dwellings (a) to be able to invite disabled people to visit them in their homes without undue hazard or inconvenience; and (b) themselves to be able to cope better with reducing mobility, and to 'stay put' longer in their own homes[31]. With regard to these objectives, the draft Approved Document said that where sites were reasonably level, wheelchair users should be able to gain access to the dwelling without assistance, with thresholds being no higher than 15mm above the floor on either side; that within the dwelling, access to habitable rooms on the entrance storey should be facilitated; and that, where reasonable, there should be a wc at entrance level, one that should be accessible to wheelchair users.

As with the Part M requirements for public buildings, the draft Approved Document relied on the premise that a set of formula prescriptions to be applied nationally could be held to constitute reasonable provision. Associatedly there would be national rules for application conditions, and for M6 the proposed rule was that there must be an entrance level wc in two-storey houses where the entrance storey, with at least one habitable room, had a floor area of 35m^2 or more; this had, it seemed, been determined with reference to public sector housing. The Housing Corporation's rule was that HAG-funded three-bedroom five-person houses must have an entrance level wc, but not two-bedroom four-person houses. Given that floor spaces in HAG-funded housing were commonly some 10 per cent below Parker Morris standards[32], a typical five-person house would have an area of 37m^2 on each floor, and a four-person house 32m^2. The proposed requirement would not trouble housing associations, but it did not appeal to private sector housebuilders.

The response from the House Builders Federation

Comments on the proposals were requested by 30 April 1995, by which time the House Builders Federation (HBF), the national organization representing the interests of some 750 commercial housebuilding companies, had marshalled its response[33]. Drafted by Roger Humber, the Federation's director, it was severely critical: the proposals were too heavily oriented to wheelchair access; they represented a wholly disproportionate response to a very limited problem; there was no need for most of them; and their effect would be to add to the cost of dwellings in key sectors of the market. Popular house types would become non-viable, and, with a series of knock-on effects, the output of new houses for sale would be reduced.

The HBF view was that the design standards proposed in the draft approved document were not reasonable. The requirement for a level or suitably ramped approach to dwellings was felt to be particularly unreasonable: it was incompatible with good building practice, and on sloping sites it would mean pushing dwellings back on their land, so impeding access to gardens and increasing excavation costs. The wc requirement was also considered unreasonable. Most of the larger housebuilders had good-selling small three-bedroom house types without a ground floor wc and a ground floor area exceeding $35m^2$; these houses had an important place in the market, and for developers to continue building them the cut-off point would need to have been set at around $40m^2$.

The requirement for extra space at dwelling entrances (300m additional width by the door to allow wheelchair access) would, the HBF warned, have a major impact, with the cost of small starter homes going up significantly. An important factor here was land prices, regarding which I was personally advised by a private sector house-builder active in the south of England. At public auction in 1958 he had bought three acres of land with planning permission for £2,000 per acre; in late 1996 similar land with planning permission would fetch between £500,000 and £600,000 per acre. In 1958 land had been cheap enough to build semi-detached houses with an internal width of 8 metres, whereas his typical 1996 semi-detached house had a width of 4.8 metres. The effect of high land prices had been 'jamming in', and, as the HBF had warned, a regulatory requirement for greater widths at entrance doors would mean increased dwelling areas and reduced site densities.

On plots with perhaps only 17 houses where before there could have been 18, the HBF reckoned there could be an additional cost per dwelling of around £2,500, on top of an additional cost of up to £1,500 for direct construction works to meet the regulatory requirements. The impact would be on the lower end of the market where sales prices were particularly inelastic; first-time buyers did not have the flexibility, due to mortgage factors, to opt for products priced to recover such costs. The production of affordable housing, low-cost housing for sale which developers were encouraged to market, would diminish.

The HBF, while being extremely critical of the January 1995 proposals, was not in principle opposed to the Part M idea, and indeed positively favoured it. The reasoning was that, with a Part M regulation in place, local planning authorities would no longer be free to impose unreasonable conditions on housebuilders seeking planning permission for proposed new housing developments. The Department of the Environment's advice in Planning Policy Guidance Note 3 was that, should the regulation of the internal design of housing and access to it to meet the needs of disabled people be justified, it ought to be for Building Regulations and not the planning system to impose requirements. So were the January 1995 proposals to be dropped and new proposals then put forward, and were the outcome to be a Part M regulation with requirements for access and internal design which the HBF considered acceptable, that would be agreeable.

The Access Committee for England's response

The Access Committee predictably responded in a rather different way from the HBF. It welcomed the government's intention to extend Part M to cover new housing, while saying that revisions – ones which would make the requirements more demanding – should be made to the proposals in order for the objectives to be fully achieved. The revised package which it proposed would not, the Access Committee believed, put an unreasonable burden on housebuilders; its argument[34] was:

> The cost of implementing these regulations is tiny in relation to the total building costs. Builders will obtain a competitive advantage in relation to the existing housing stock; purchasers should find houses built to these standards more attractive and more flexible. Building to these regulations would lower the level of subsidies required later for adaptations and other community care facilities. There is no reason why public money in the future should pay for avoidable inadequacies in design today.

Backed by the Joseph Rowntree Foundation with its Lifetime Homes initiative, the Access Committee lobbied organizations and individuals to press the Department of the Environment to accept its case. On the other side, the HBF lobbied its members to press the government to completely reconsider the form a Part M housing regulation should take. In early 1995 the Access Committee and other disability lobbyists could, however, feel confident that they would get a housing regulation of the kind they wanted. The government's proposals represented a firm intention, and in line with established procedures the understanding was that regulations would be forthcoming; if they could not be brought into effect by revisions to the initial proposals there would, with new proposals, have to be a further consultation round.

Six months after the end of the comment period there had been no indication from the government as to which course it would pursue, and a written parliamentary question was put by Nick Raynsford, the Labour MP who was Shadow Minister for Housing. Robert Jones as Minister for Housing replied on 23 November 1995[35]:

> 'Over a thousand responses have been received to the consultation paper on possible changes to Part M of the Building Regulations issued earlier this year. These are at present being analysed. The Building Regulations Advisory Committee will be considering this analysis in due course and will be making recommendations to ministers on the way forward.'

Two months later Mr Raynsford tried again, asking the Secretary of State what advice he had given to the Building Regulations Advisory Committee (BRAC) on the likely timetable for implementing proposed amendments to Part M. The reply was that papers on various aspects of work on building regulations had been discussed at BRAC meetings held in the previous June and October[36]: 'These papers included possible implementation dates taking into account, among other things, the time needed for consultation and analysis. Decisions on the timetable for individual items will depend on the rate of progress achieved at each stage.'

In July 1996 when the Housing, Construction and Regeneration Bill returned to the Commons at report stage, Peter Thurnham, formerly a Conservative MP and at that time an Independent, put down an amendment asking that within three months of the enactment of the Bill the Secretary of State for the Environment should extend the scope of the Part M building regulation to cover new housing. The government was prepared, and on 8 July, when a division was called after a short late-evening debate, the amendment was lost by 247 votes to 270[37]. Disability lobbyists continued to protest angrily, but to get their Part M housing regulation they would have to wait until after the general election scheduled for May 1997.

I speculate from here on. The starting presumption is that the Department of the Environment will come up with revised proposals for a Part M housing regulation and put them out to consultation. Next, the regulatory requirements, it may be assumed, will continue to be in the form 'Reasonable provision shall be made for disabled people'. And in the light of reactions to the 1995 proposals, the guidance in the draft Approved Document will not so markedly be based on the characteristics of public sector housing; it will, for example, take into account the complaints made about the 1995 proposals by the HBF.

The divide between public and private sector housing

My next prediction is that when it emerges in final shape, the new Part M housing regulation will be geared almost entirely to treating private sector concerns, with little or no attention being given to the characteristics of public sector housing. With low-cost housing in mind, a relevant factor here is that requirements which would be acceptable to the private sector would suit the public sector, whereas the converse would not (as the 1995 proposals demonstrated) be the case. That is one consideration, and there are others.

For public sector housing a Part M housing regulation would, in effect, be superfluous, the reason being that there are already national rules for reasonable provision, in the form of the accessibility criteria set out in the Housing Corporation's *Scheme Development Standards.* They are for provisions which the Corporation deems to be reasonable, and administratively and organizationally the system is sound. The Corporation monitors the performance of housing associations, who have incentives to satisfy the criteria. The design standards are kept under review, and could be elaborated or refined – if the Corporation were to consider it appropriate, it could, for example, incorporate full Lifetime Homes criteria in its standards for normal provision. And it could, were a future government content for it to do so, bring in minimum overall space standards on Parker Morris lines. In summary, given that the Housing Corporation is effectively controlling the accessibility of new public housing, a Part M regulation serving the same purpose would be unwanted.

The proposition that there should be a Part M housing regulation was fostered by the disability lobby and then taken on board by government. But had the idea been widely debated before it became crystallised, and had it in particular been debated with private sector housebuilding agencies, a different course could have been followed. The preferable way to tackle accessibility on the private sector side would be, it might have been felt, to have gone down the same path as the Housing Corporation; on the model of the Corporation's criteria for accessibility (or the Rowntree Foundation's criteria for Lifetime Homes) an authorised accessibility checklist for private sector developments could have been produced, with incentives for implementation and ongoing monitoring of its operational effects. That could, I believe, have been wiser than launching uncritically into government-decreed regulations.

A further consideration is pertinent to the principle that a Part M regulation should defer to the interests of private sector housebuilders. It is that the great preponderance of new housing built in Britain today is private sector housing. Relevant information comes from the official housing statistics issued quarterly by the Department of the Environment; for completions in England, the figures for the years 1992 to 1995 show that approaching 80 per cent of all new houses are currently built speculatively by private developers; the actual proportions for private sector completions being 83.2 per cent in 1992, 79.0 per cent in 1993, 79.4 per cent in 1994 and 79.6 per cent in 1995[38]. Social housing – the provision made by housing associations – accounts for less than 20 per cent.

Complications come with the shift in focus from public to private. Social housing – low-cost government-subsidised housing – comes in the form of standardised products, and in consequence the designing of it is amenable to certain common rules. Private sector housing products are quite different; they come in a whole variety of shapes and sizes, from little two-storey boxes for first-time buyers of limited means to large luxury houses for wealthy customers. In consequence, there cannot, for private sector housing, be a neat package of generally applicable rules for accessibility. In large houses the planning parameters of reasonable provision for disabled people are expanded; there will be an entrance level wc, perhaps with a shower, and a downstairs room which can be used as a bedroom. In small speculatively built houses the parameters are much more confined, often more so than with housing association units. So if for new housing there is to be a Part M regulation, what, for the purposes of mandating accessibility for disabled people, does 'accessibility' mean? What broad rules should there be for setting Part M requirements?

The comparison between public buildings and housing

In the business of setting broad rules for what should be deemed to constitute accessibility, housing poses problems that public buildings do not. In the case of new public buildings, there is not as a rule any difficulty: it is, virtually always, reasonable and practicable to apply the three basic accessibility conditions: (1) that there is a level or suitably ramped approach to the building entrance; (2) that all public areas of the building are reachable without having to negotiate steps or stairs, making them wheelchair-accessible; and (3) that toilets for the use of the public are accessible. In the case of new housing, corresponding conditions are not viable. First, because houses are built on small plots, and where the terrain slopes there have to be steps to the dwelling entrance. Second, because the standard product is a two-storey box, with half of it being reachable only by climbing stairs. Third, because in small houses the ground floor has all to be living, cooking and eating space, and the only wc in the house is upstairs in the bathroom.

For Part M purposes there could not, in other words, be generally applicable core conditions for the accessibility of new housing in the same way as there can be for public buildings. There could only be limited core conditions, ones which could be ordered in particular circumstances, ones where it was appropriate, reasonable and practicable to apply them. I postulate four, of which the first two would relate to houses of two or three storeys:

1 Circumstances where a wc would be required on the ground floor of the dwelling.
2 Circumstances where, as well as a wc, a shower or bath and a bedroom would be required on the ground floor of a dwelling.

The third would relate to terrain:

3 Circumstances where level approach to the front entrance to the dwelling would be required.

The fourth would relate to single-storey dwellings (flats) in multi-storey buildings:

4 Circumstances where the requirement would be that all areas within dwellings should be suitably accessible, with no-steps approach and access to all dwelling entrances.

The premise is that on these lines there would be core conditions for meeting Part M requirements, with the approved document prescribing, as precisely as could be, the circumstances where they would be applicable. I consider first the circumstances where there would be a requirement for an entrance level wc in two- or three-storey houses; my view is that, as was proposed in the 1995 consultation papers, these would relate to the area of the ground floor of the dwelling.

The entrance level wc core condition

The proposal in the 1995 consultation round was that 35m^2 should be the cut-off point – there would have to be an entrance level wc where the area of the ground floor was 35m^2 or more. That did not please the HBF; marketing considerations indicated, they said, that 40m^2 would be more appropriate. I express personal views on the matter. As a person with a severe physical disability, what most concerns me when I visit other people's houses is the availability of a downstairs wc. I consider that any three-bedroom family house ought, as a matter of course, to have a downstairs wc, and for new houses the 35m^2 cut-off point would seem to be sensible. But I would not feel that the government ought to introduce a legislative mandate, a Part M regulation with a strict 35m^2 cut-off point, which could deny a family of limited means the right to buy a new three-bedroom house without a downstairs wc if that was what they wanted. In this connection, I review the character of small public versus private sector houses.

Small two-storey houses without a downstairs wc are a standard product of today's housebuilding industry. In respect of internal planning, the private sector product is usually different from the public, the reason being that it is aimed at first-time buyers. These are often young couples looking for a low-cost house which will see them through for five years or so until, with children on the way, they will be able, they hope, to afford to move to something more spacious. They want maximised living space on the ground floor, and are content for the only wc to be upstairs in the bathroom, along with a decent-sized bedroom and perhaps two other small rooms.

Comparative information on private versus public sector space and amenity standards is to be found in *New Homes in the 1990s*, the report by Valerie Karn and Linda Sheridan of a survey commissioned by the Joseph Rowntree Foundation and published in 1994[39]. In three-bedroom five-person housing association houses, the finding was that nearly all households were families with children, and of these 88 per cent had two or more children and 32 per cent had three or more. Comparable occupancy data for new private sector houses drawn from a related study made in 1989 had found that 34 per cent of the households in family homes consisted of families with children; this compared with 69 per cent of the housing association family homes examined by Karn and Sheridan. In low-price private sector houses, there were children in only 16 per cent of the households. A related finding was that a typical two-storey public sector unit having an overall floor area of some 75m^2 was, on average, occupied by 3.2 people, giving each person 23.4m^2 floor space; by contrast, a private sector unit of the same size was occupied by 2.2 people, giving each 34.1m^2 floor space.

In the context of an entrance level core condition under a 'reasonable provision shall be made for disabled people' mandate, the inference to be drawn from this analysis is that it would be appropriate for the cut-off point for market-driven, speculatively built houses to be set at a higher level than that for government-subsidised 'welfare' housing for families. There is not a 'level playing field'. On the public sector side, it could be reasonable to require that four-person two-bedroom houses should have a ground floor wc, with the cut-off point set at, say, 30m^2. On the private sector side, it could be reasonable, if there is to be an absolute criterion rather than one with an 'exceptional circumstances' qualification, for the cut-off point to be at 40m^2.

The two-storey house livability core condition

For disabled people, the ground floor wc requirement would as a rule make two-storey houses visitable, but without an accessible bathroom or bedroom there would not be livability. In the case of public sector housing with its welfare function and the vision of Lifetime Homes, it could be reasonable in five-person houses to require that it be potentially practicable to install a through-floor lift as insurance against a household member who became severely disabled. That would not be reasonable in the case of private sector houses whatever their size, but for large family houses which are built speculatively suitable livability provision for disabled people could be made, and in appropriate circumstances it might be reasonable to require that it should be. The relevant core condition for meeting Part M requirements might read as follows:

> In a house where a room which it is intended should be usable as a bedroom is provided on the ground floor, the entrance level wc facility should be supplemented by a shower or bath.

A way of meeting this requirement could be by having an en-suite bathroom to the bedroom.

The level approach core condition

The core condition for making the approach to dwelling entrances convenient for wheelchair users might read as follows:

> Where a house with an entrance level wc is constructed on level terrain, the approach to an entrance to it from the place where visitors arriving by car are set down should be level or suitably ramped.

In my view, it would not be appropriate to apply the level approach condition to small two-storey houses without a downstairs wc. Where at the front entrance to a house there is a ramp and a flush-threshold door, the implication is that special care has been taken to make the house wheelchair-accessible. But what matters most for visitability is the entrance level wc, and without it the 'here is a wheelchair-accessible house' message would be fraudulent.

With the only houses covered by the condition being those with a ground floor area of more than 35m^2 or so, the reasonable assumption is that, as well as having a front entrance door, all will have a door at the rear of the house giving onto the garden. Where the condition was applied, it could be standard practice for it to relate to the rear entrance, with the front entrance being in conventional form with a couple of steps.

The core condition for flats with lift access

For flats in multi-storey blocks with lift access, the core condition would be that there should be no-steps access to all areas of all flats. As a matter of course, related conditions would be (1) that there is a level or suitably ramped approach to communal entrances from nearby car parking spaces; (2) that all dwelling units at ground floor level are to have a level approach; (3) that lifts are to be wheelchair-accessible; (4) that on all storeys the approach to any flat from a lift is to be level (other than penthouse flats, subject to local agreement); and (5) that all dwelling units are to have level access with no upstanding thresholds at dwelling entrance doors.

The coverage of the Part M housing regulation

It would not in my view be sensible for single architect-designed bespoke houses to be subject to the Part M housing regulation. The regulation would cover all other new housing developments and new dwellings provided by the conversion of existing buildings such as warehouse and office buildings. It would defer to private sector interests, and, with private housebuilders working to less rigorous criteria than housing associations, the consequence would be differential provision. That would not be out of order – there is not a level playing field.

Planning controls

I return to the issue of planning controls and the tendency of local planning authorities, licensed by development plan policies which emphasise the importance of catering for the special needs of disabled people, to seek to impose demanding conditions when planning permission is sought for proposed new housing schemes. This troubled the HBF, whose view was that a Part M regulation was needed to curtail the extent to which planning controls could stray into the realm of building control.

The same issue was considered in Chapter 25 with regard to planning controls and alterations to existing buildings used by the public. To deal with it, the line put forward was that all accessibility control measures ought to be concentrated on the building control side, with planning conditions typically coming in the form 'Planning permission is granted, subject to accessibility provision being in compliance with the requirements of the Part Z building regulation'. For new housing developments it would not, in the same fashion, be feasible for planning and building control functions to be merged for accessibility purposes; there are planning matters which impinge on accessibility provision for which planning authorities may properly apply conditions – these relate, for example, to the mix of houses in a new development, the layout of housing, the disposition of dwellings on the site, the type of dwelling units that should be provided and the provision to be made for car parking.

Essentially, the argument focuses on building features, on the accessibility provision made within dwellings and the approaches to dwelling entrances within plots. The enforcement under Part M of the four according-to-circumstances core conditions could, I suggest, have a remedial effect, in that they could, given their operational parameters, serve to circumscribe the remit of planning control. And although planning matters could not all be absorbed into building control, there could, on the same lines as for public buildings, be a similar standard planning condition. For new housing schemes, it might say, 'Planning permission is granted subject to accessibility provision within and around individual dwellings being made in compliance with Part M requirements'.

The Approved Document and the supporting guidance documents

The Approved Document for a Part M housing regulation issued by the Department of the Environment would sensibly restrict itself to prescribing core conditions; it would not, as I have indicated, be feasible for it to present comprehensive guidance on the detail design of the component features of new housing. But since there would be an overall 'reasonable provision' requirement, such guidance would have to be produced. In two parts, it would, I envisage, be presented in an officially authorised supporting document, one that could perhaps be issued by a non-government agency.

The housing feature conditions which it would be appropriate to apply to private sector schemes in order to meet the overall 'reasonable provision' Part M requirement would be different from those applicable to public sector schemes. Either combined or separately, there could be two supporting guidance documents, perhaps prepared by an independent outside agency. On the one hand, there would be practical guidance amplifying the Housing Corporation's criteria for accessible housing (Table B.3); on the other, there would be guidance for private sector housebuilders.

As was noted in Chapter 23, the advice in the official manual to the Building Regulations is, 'You can choose whether or not to use the Approved Documents or you can follow some or parts of them. You are obliged only to meet the requirements of the Regulations'. While the supporting documents would present design guidance on housing features for meeting Part M requirements, they would not, without the insignia of the Crown on them, be 'Approved Documents'. They could, however, be authorised by the Secretary of State for the Environment and would then become 'approved documents'. A merit of having an independent agency prepare them would be that the recommendations could be regularly reviewed, revised and updated in the light of experience.

Core conditions and housing feature conditions

The four core conditions would be nationally applicable; they would be for requirements which, in prescribed circumstances, would be deemed to be reasonable provision under the Part M mandate. The housing feature conditions would as a rule be ones which need to be determined locally, in the light of the circumstances of the particular case under consideration. The matter is illustrated by stepped approaches to buildings and wc provision.

As noted earlier, the Housing Corporation's criteria for accessible housing did not include design conditions for stepped approaches to dwelling entrances where houses are built on sloping plots, and this I felt was a regrettable omission. Owing to the variability of relevant circumstances and the impracticability of setting national rules, it is not an item which could be the subject of a core condition. But it would be a matter which could be covered in the supporting guidance documents, perhaps with menu options; the preferred norm, I suggest, might be a condition for a handrail on at least one side of the steps, with the goings of treads being say 300mm and the height of rises 170mm*. In any particular case it would, however, be for the building control inspector to agree what would be appropriate.

The core condition for an entrance level wc would simply be a requirement for there to be a wc; there would not in the Approved Document be advice on its size, layout, door position, door width or how wheelchair-accessible it should be. Again, the supporting guidance could present menu options for conditions, all of which would require a wash basin to be provided alongside the wc. While in any particular case the normal rule could be for the building control inspector to agree the proposed provision shown on plan drawings, there could be occasions when he might, having regard to the 'reasonable provision for disabled people' requirement, request changes.

The entrance level wc is a feature where 'reasonable provision' could commonly be differently interpreted for public as against private sector housing schemes. For housing association two-storey family units, it could well be reasonable to have a wheelchair-accessible facility, whereas for low-cost private sector units it would not be. Again, it would be for the building control inspector to agree or not the proposed provision. Where I surmise there could be arguments would be in respect of a housebuilder's house type where the wc was not at all wheelchair-accessible, and a local

*Data of relevance to the application of conditions for external steps to public buildings are in Annex A, page 336.

authority building control officer insisted that it ought to be. This brings the National House-Building Council into the reckoning.

The status of the NHBC

The National House-Building Council (NHBC) is a self-regulatory body of the private housebuilding industry; it provides technical and inspection services to its members and an insurance policy to purchasers of newly built and converted houses which have the NHBC Buildmark warranty. Some 90 per cent of all new private sector houses currently built in Britain are insured against structural defects by the Buildmark warranty.

NHBC builder members agree to comply with NHBC standards, ones which, as codes of practice, set technical requirements and present guidance on practical design, suitable materials and quality of workmanship. As mentioned earlier, the NHBC was planning in 1992 to issue a code of practice presenting guidance on making new private sector houses accessible to disabled people, but deferred proceeding with it until the terms of the proposed Part M regulation had been finalised.

For the purposes of the Building Act 1984 the NHBC is a corporate approved inspector. This gives the company authority to check designs for new and converted housing, inspect sites and grant approval under the Building Regulations throughout England and Wales. The current score is that some 45 per cent of all new private sector houses are, through a network of local offices, inspected by NHBC technical staff for building control purposes. The other 55 per cent are handled by local authority building control departments. Independent approved inspectors do not deal with housing. Were a Part M housing regulation to be introduced, it would be the duty of NHBC building control inspectors to be satisfied, for compliance certification purposes, that in each case reasonable provision had been made for disabled people. NHBC inspectors are not, however, free agents; they are agents of the corporate approved company, the NHBC. Where an NHBC inspector was uncertain about some particular Part M provision in a case he was dealing with, he would look to the national company for advice and guidance.

In whatever way the new Part M housing regulation were presented, the NHBC would be dominant in the enforcement business, and for that purpose it would need to have a guidance document to advise its member housebuilders about the interpretation of the Part M 'reasonable provision' edict and the practical ways in which suitable provision for disabled people ought to be made. So if for Part M purposes there were to be a DOE-approved supporting guidance document on housing feature conditions issued by an agency, its recommendations would need to be ones which the NHBC could endorse. And the NHBC, in conjunction with the housing trade associations, the HBF and the Federation of Masterbuilders, would have substantial influence on the advice and recommendations contained in the guidance document.

The NHBC has its own type approval scheme, one which parallels LANTAC, the Local Authority National Type Approval Scheme. It operates to the benefit of housebuilders; where a national housebuilder has a standard house type for which he has obtained building control approval in one location, it can be given NHBC type approval, meaning that it can be used elsewhere without on each occasion needing to check that it satisfies Building Regulation requirements. Were there to be a Part M housing regulation, the NHBC could, in cooperation with its member housebuilders, develop a substantial bank of standard house types which met Part M requirements.

As noted earlier, some 55 per cent of all new private sector housing schemes are dealt with by local authorities for building control purposes. I hypothesise what might occur with the introduction of a Part M housing regulation. The typical local authority building control department, influenced by the authority's plan policies relating to housing provision for disabled people, could tend, when it checked proposed new housing schemes, to adopt a more rigorous line than the NHBC with regard to housing feature conditions and the interpretation of the advice in the guidance document. An effect of this might be that housebuilders accustomed to using the local authority for building control purposes could be inclined to switch to the NHBC.

Should events take the course I have indicated, it could be that around 1999 the Part M housing regulation will be made and laid (though not brought into operation), and its Approved Document with its according-to-circumstance core conditions will be issued at the same time. Following that, the agency commissioned to prepare the two supporting guidance documents will draft proposals and consult with the Housing Corporation, the NHBC, housebuilding associations, construction industry bodies, local authority associations, disability organizations and others. Reaching agreement on the final terms of the documents could be a protracted and problematical business. And when, with Department of the Environment approval, the documents had been published, housebuilders would need a long lead-in time, say three years or so, to adjust their construction programmes and bring the design of their house types into line with Part M criteria. Only after all that, perhaps around the year 2005, could the Part M housing regulation be brought into operation.

I acknowledge that in the course of this discussion I have been immensely speculative. It might happen that the idea of a Part M housing regulation could be dropped; though that I doubt, given the force of the disability lobby. Or the Department of the Environment might devise a less cumbersome process for instituting the regulation. Or others concerned might come up with attractive and realistic ideas for expediting preliminary procedures. I write this in March 1997; perhaps by the time this book is published the prospective scenario will be clearer.

Appendix 1
Wheelchair users in European and English towns

Listed below are the counts I made of people in wheelchairs in towns in Europe and England between August 1986 and October 1989. They were not conducted systematically; to obtain them, I kept a mental score while in a town, usually for a period of two hours or so. On most occasions a colleague who was with me helped do the counting.

Europe

Belgium: Bruges 4 and 1; Malmedy 0; Tongeren 0; Tournai 0; Veurne 4.
France: Aix-en-Provence 0; Avignon 1; Beaune 0; Besançon 0; Charleville 3; Colmar 0; Dijon 2; Dinan 0; Dinard 0; Dole 0; Nancy 0; Nîmes 2; Quimper 0; Reims 1; Rouen 0; St Malo 2; Sedan 0 and 0; Strasbourg 2.
Germany: Bad Kreuznach 4; Bingen 2; Freiburg 2; Trier 21.
Italy: Bergamo 1; Bologna 0; Faenza 0; Ferrara 1; Mantua 0; Padua 0; Venice 3, 0 and 0; Verona 1.
Luxembourg: Echternach 1 and 0; Luxembourg 1 and 0.
The Netherlands: Amsterdam 4; Breda 2; Gouda 0, 0, 0 and 1; Leiden 4, 0, 0 and 1; Middelburg 3 and 2; Zierikzee 1.
Switzerland: Berne 0; Biel 2; Brunnen 0; Interlaken 0; Lucerne 2; Neuchatel 0.

England

Arnold 6; Barnsley 23; Bolton 8; Cambridge 4; Cheltenham 10; Chester 2 and 10; Coventry 10 and 10; Doncaster 28; Ealing 15; Hereford 7; Manchester 0; Melton Mowbray 13; Milton Keynes 21; Nottingham 2; Peterborough 31; Plymouth 5 and 7; Reading 2; St Albans 2; St Helens 4; Saffron Walden 0; Salisbury 7; Shrewsbury 2 and 0; Slough 11; Swindon 1; Telford 25; Wakefield 8; Wigan 7; Winchester 6; Wolverhampton 2.

Appendix 2
Building users, user subgroups and building usage

The premise underlying the methodology of the Department of the Environment's sanitary provision research project was that the shopping centre user population could serve as a surrogate for the population of building users generally. There are, however, differences between the two populations. The shopping centre user population can be defined as all those people who visit an urban shopping centre during the course of say a year. The population of building users generally is much less easy to define. What kind of buildings, other than their own home, do people have to visit to become building users? How many building users are not shopping centre users? They could include, for example, those disabled people who never go to shopping centres but who occasionally walk to local shops or the pub, go to a hospital, or are taken out by car for occasional outings and in doing so use a public toilet or have tea at a cafe.

For the purposes of the project it did not, however, much matter that the surveys excluded building users who were not shopping centre users. The principal purpose was to generate data which would inform decision-making when public buildings were planned and designed, and for this purpose those who were interviewed in the four project locations were asked about their usage of 13 types of buildings: these were department stores/supermarkets; cafes/restaurants; pubs; hotels; cinemas/theatres; museums/art galleries; swimming pools/leisure centres; sports stadia; railway stations; airport terminals; motorway service stations; other petrol service stations; and doctors' surgeries. With the possible exception of doctors' surgeries in respect of some disabled people, an admissible assumption is that all the people who happened to use these building types would be people who in the course of a year would be shopping centre visitors. For a survey of the user populations of different types of public buildings, the population of shopping centre users can therefore be held to be a reliable population to examine.

The selection of interview locations

The selection of locations for the interview survey was affected by consideration of the *would use* factor. Disabled people, it may be contended, cannot use buildings or environments which are not accessible, but would use them if they were accessible. This was not a proposition to be ignored; had, for example, the four locations all been on hilly terrain, the reasonable complaint would have been that, particularly in respect of wheelchair usage, project findings were unreliable and unrepresentative.

With regard to interview locations for the project, a deliberate decision was made to select towns which had uncommonly good accessibility characteristics. Relevant

Table A2.1 Population counts
The table below is based on the results of all population counts undertaken in shopping centres in towns around England between 21 August 1989 and 15 September 1990, and in Carlisle, Eastbourne, Hereford and Peterborough (CEHP) between 28 August and 1 September 1990.

	England	CEHP
number of half-hour counts	54	60
total number of people counted	114,991	119,571
	%	%
regular people	96.0	95.4
pushchair users	3.4	3.7
stick/crutch users	0.4	0.6
wheelchair users	0.2	0.3
blind people	*	*
total	100.0	100.0

*Less than 0.05
Source: bibliography item **471**, Table 2.1, p.112

criteria were that the central shopping area of each should be on level terrain, with ample parking facilities convenient for disabled visitors, a covered shopping centre to which disabled people could resort in the event of rain, and well-sited for-the-disabled public toilets. In addition, each town should have an extensive pedestrianised area and examples of the principal public buildings about which questions would be asked. In the event, the four towns virtually chose themselves – they were Carlisle, Eastbourne, Hereford and Peterborough. They came with bonuses. In Hereford and Peterborough there was a shopmobility scheme, and the possibility that an adequate sample of blind people might not be found was avoided – Eastbourne, Hereford and Peterborough had respectively a hotel, a school, and a training centre and workshop for blind people.

Speculations were in order. These were towns where 'would use' disabled people would not, on access grounds, have any excuse for not being 'do use' people. Hypothetically, the project towns might therefore proportionately display perhaps five or ten times more wheelchair users than less congenial towns elsewhere. That could be checked by the population counts which were to follow the interviewing, the simple test being the proportion of wheelchair users among all those observed in the four project towns as against those in towns elsewhere across England. The findings, shown in Table A2.1, demonstrate that although the four towns displayed relatively more wheelchair users than others, the hypothesis that many times more are to be found in 'accessible' towns than elsewhere is not supportable.

Population subgroup quotas

The presentation of estimates of the proportion of people with special needs among the total population of building users and the users of particular building types was based on the application of quotas; these were for each of the seven population subgroup categories, expressed in each case as the estimated proportion of the total national population of building users on a typical day. The base for calculating the quotas, listed in the left-hand column of Table A2.5, was Saturday population counts, the principal factors involved being (a) the removal of the age 15 or under population; (b) the difference between the age distribution of Saturday shopping centre users and the population generally; and (c) the tendency of wheelchair users, stick/crutch users and blind people to visit shopping centres relatively more frequently than others on weekdays than Saturdays, and, relatedly, for pushchair users to do so less frequently.

In the case of pushchair users, stick/crutch users, wheelchair users and blind people, the quota estimates were drawn from population count data. The estimate for the division among regular people between regular able-bodied people and regular disabled people was derived from the finding that 11.5 per cent of the 1954 regular people interviewed in the four project locations identified themselves as 'disabled'. In the four towns where interview samples were drawn, the proportion varied; in Hereford it was 9.9 per cent, in Carlisle 10.1, in Eastbourne 14.6 and in Peterborough 15.4[1]. From an analysis of related variables, the conclusion presented in the report was that there was no reason why the overall 11.5 per cent result should not, for national purposes, be considered representative. But even granting this, the small size of the sample brought with it a wide margin of possible error, with the actual national amount probably being somewhere between 10 and 13 per cent.

In the case of stick/crutch users and wheelchair users, the base for the quota estimates was the aggregates of counts made on Saturdays in towns around England between September 1989 and September 1990. Further counts were made on the same basis between August 1991 and July 1994, and the results are compared in Table A2.2. The comparative differences are so marginal as to give no cause for rejecting as unreliable the Table A2.5 by-the-day quotas which inform the discussion in Chapters 18 and 19.

Table A2.2 Saturday population counts

The table below compares the results of the Saturday population counts undertaken in shopping centres in towns around England between 2 September 1989 and 15 September 1990 (on which the findings of the sanitary provision research project were based) and subsequent Saturday counts made between 3 August 1991 and 9 July 1994.

period	2.9.89–15.9.90	3.8.91–9.7.94
number of half-hour counts	36	31
total number of people counted	87,606	63,527
	%	%
regular people	96.49	96.17
single pushchair users	2.97	3.30
double pushchair users	0.11	0.12
stick/crutch users	0.26	0.23
wheelchair users	0.16	0.17
blind people	less than 0.005	0.01
total	100.0	100.0

Source: bibliography item **471**, Table 2.1, p.112 and unpublished data

The distribution of users of public buildings

Table A2.3 records the proportions of people interviewed in Carlisle, Eastbourne, Hereford and Peterborough who said they had used respective building types at least once during the previous 12 months. Table A2.4 lists the estimated proportions of those who were users of the building types on a typical day. As for all other estimates, the figures relate to adult people only; had they been for all users, including children aged 15 or under, the results would have been different, particularly in respect of swimming pools. In Table A2.4 blind people are included among 'all disabled people', but the contribution they made was negligible and is not recorded separately. The estimates for an 'average' public building at the foot of Table A2.4 represent the average of the public building types for which project data were obtained, with the exception of doctors' surgeries.

Noting that data were obtained for adult people only, the mean ages of disabled people in the interview samples were wheelchair users, 54; regular disabled people, 65; and stick/crutch users, 70. The calculations for determining building user subgroup quotas indicated that among people in the youngest age band – those aged between 16 and 44 – wheelchair users were twice as prevalent as stick/crutch users[2]. Unsurprisingly, therefore, Table A2.4 shows that proportionately more wheelchair users than stick/crutch users had used most types of public buildings.

Table A2.3 Public building types: 'had used' proportions

	Regular able-bodied people	Regular disabled people	Single pushchair users	Double pushchair users	Stick/ crutch users	Wheelchair users	Blind people
total number in interview sample	1714	240	104	49	182	174	43
	%	%	%	%	%	%	%
department stores/ supermarkets	98	96	97	98	95	96	93
cafes/restaurants	89	83	88	76	80	86	81
pubs	66	37	33	24	38	54	42
hotels	43	29	15	12	35	37	47
cinemas/theatres	47	26	2	2	22	28	7
museums/art galleries	37	28	14	10	24	17	7
swimming pools/ leisure centres	51	29	62	49	15	37	7
railway stations	53	45	44	41	28	26	30
airport terminals	35	29	16	8	15	16	14
motorway service stations	62	44	35	24	40	41	33
doctors' surgeries	72	82	83	73	82	52	65

Source: bibliography item **471**, Table 2.6, p.119

Table A2.4 Public building types: distribution of users on a typical day

	Regular able-bodied people %	Regular disabled people %	Stick/ crutch users %	Wheelchair users %	All disabled people %	Pushchair users %
Proportion of total population of shopping centre users	84.8	11.0	0.5	0.2	11.7	3.5
department stores/ supermarkets	84.6	11.3	0.4	0.2	11.9	3.5
cafes/restaurants	84.5	11.4	0.4	0.2	12.0	3.5
pubs	92.0	6.2	0.3	0.1	6.6	1.3
hotels	88.4	9.7	0.3	0.1	10.0	1.6
cinemas/theatres	94.9	4.9	0.1	*	5.0	0.1
museums/art galleries	90.2	8.2	0.3	0.1	8.5	1.3
swimming pools/ leisure centres	87.5	7.6	0.1	0.2	7.9	4.6
railway stations	90.5	7.0	0.2	0.1	7.2	2.3
airport terminals	93.3	5.6	0.1	0.1	5.8	0.8
motorway service stations	91.7	6.6	0.3	0.1	6.9	1.4
doctors' surgeries	74.1	18.7	0.9	0.2	19.8	6.1
'average' public building	90.7	7.1	0.3	0.1	7.4	1.9

* less than 0.05
Source: relevant tables in bibliography items **471** and **472**

Attitudes to amenities and facilities in the four towns

Carlisle, Eastbourne, Hereford and Peterborough were selected as project survey locations on the basis that they rated highly as towns which were conveniently accessible to disabled people. To ascertain whether it was felt they were, eight attitudinal propositions were put to interviewees. From the responses – in all, more than 2500 – mean ratings as shown below were calculated, based on a score of 100 for 'agree strongly', 75 for 'tend to agree', 50 for 'neither', 25 for 'tend to disagree' and 0 for 'disagree strongly'. For each item the 1/2/3/4 rank of the four towns is shown in the column on the right.

The pedestrianisation of the streets here makes it easier to get around*	84.7	C/H/E/P
It is an attractive town to visit	83.5	E/H/C/P
It is easy to get around here*	81.1	E/C/P/H
I enjoy coming here to shop	79.4	E/P/H/C
There are good places here to have a cup of tea or a meal	70.2	P/C/H/E
The car parking facilities here are good	68.0	P/H/E/C

Public transport to get here is good	67.3	E/P/C/H
The toilet facilities here are good	61.8	E/C/P/H

* According to whom the questions were put, these included terms such as 'with a pushchair', 'with my wheelchair' or 'for blind people'.

Pedestrianisation

Listed below for the seven user subgroups are the mean ratings of the responses given to the proposition 'The pedestrianisation of the streets here makes it easier to get around'.

stick/crutch users	86.9	E/C/H/P
regular disabled people	86.0	H/E/C/P
regular able-bodied people	85.8	C/H/E/P
wheelchair users	81.8	H/C/P/E
single pushchair users	80.5	C/P/H/E
blind people	79.7	H/C/P/E
double pushchair users	78.2	C/E/P/H

The by-the-year population of building users

To convert by-the-day into by-the-year data, weightings were attached to interviewees according to how frequently they visited their local shopping centre whether it was about once a week, once a month, three or four times a year or once a year. Many of the once-a-year visitors had not travelled to the shopping centre from their home, suggesting they could be holiday visitors. There was also a remarkably high correlation (in statistical terms, plus 0.96) between responses to the proposition 'It is an attractive town to visit' and once-a-year shopping centre visitors[3]. On account of these factors, the once-a-year visitors could have included many who regularly used a shopping centre elsewhere, and for that reason were excluded from the conversion analysis.

The by-the-year calculations of subgroup proportions were therefore drawn from data for those who said they visited once a week or more, about once a month, or three or four times a year, with results which are shown in Table A2.5. Broadly, there is little difference between the by-the-day and by-the-year figures, and the data ought to be treated cautiously. Pushchair users tend to go to shopping centres relatively frequently, so proportionately there are fewer of them in the by-the-year than the by-the-day population. The hypothesis that in the by-the-year population there would proportionately be many more disabled people is not confirmed. For regular disabled people, stick/crutch users and blind people, the differences are negligible. For wheelchair users, where for every 20 in the by-the-day there are 26 in the by-the-year population, the difference is more substantial. But the supposition that wheelchair users go to shopping centres much less frequently than others, and that there are proportionately many times more of them in the by-the-year than the by-the-day population, is a hypothesis that fails.

The figures in Table A2.5 do not indicate that, among all building users, the generality of disabled people use buildings about as frequently as others; as Table A2.4 shows with reference to an 'average' public building, they do not. They suggest only that those disabled people who go to their local shopping centre visit that shopping centre about as frequently as others, the exception being wheelchair users. A proviso is that the figures in Table A2.5 strictly relate only to the shopping centres in Carlisle, Eastbourne, Hereford and Peterborough; in less conveniently accessible towns

Table A2.5 Estimated proportions of by-the-day and by-the-year shopping centre visitors

	By-the-day proportion %	By-the-year proportion %
regular able-bodied people	84.775	85.802
regular disabled people	10.988	10.998
single pushchair users	3.403	2.334
double pushchair users	0.131	0.098
stick/crutch users	0.480	0.484
wheelchair users	0.205	0.263
blind people	0.019	0.021

Source: bibliography item **471**, Table 8.6, p.165

elsewhere, the by-the-day and by-the-year proportions could be found to be further apart.

Building users: the missing disabled people

For the purposes of the sanitary provision research project, the measure applied to distinguish people with disabilities from others was a measure of architectural disability, of difficulties caused by stairs in the way of getting to toilets. Where they had a medical disability, architecturally disabled people thus had a disability of the kind described by the Office of Population Surveys and Censuses (OPCS) as locomotor disability.

Locomotor disability was one of 13 types of disability which a person interviewed in the course of the OPCS survey could be found to have, and which, with a complex scoring system, could, on its own or in combination with others, be decreed to be an above-the-line 'disability' for national counting purposes. The tendency was for certain types of disability to occur together so that, for example, people with a reaching or dexterity disability commonly also had a locomotor disability. Reflecting the way in which they tended to bunch, the 13 disabilities were grouped for analysis purposes into five main areas: physical, mental, seeing, hearing and 'other'. In the physical area were locomotion, reaching and stretching, dexterity, personal care, and disfigurement; in the mental area were behaviour and intellectual functioning; in the seeing area there was seeing disability only; in the hearing area were hearing and communication; and in the 'other' area were consciousness, continence, and eating, drinking and digestion disabilities[4].

Broadly, what we may reasonably suppose is that a person who has only a locomotor disability is more likely to be a regular user of buildings than a person who has one or more other disabilities as well, and in this connection the age factor is significant. The OPCS finding was that young people predominated among those with a disability in the physical area only; as age increased, a physical disability tended to be associated with a disability in another area as well, and among physically disabled people aged 75 some three-quarters had disabilities in one or more of the other areas[5].

The hypothesis that the non-use of public buildings could be positively correlated with multiple disability was supported by the findings of the sanitary provision project. Based on an analysis of the prevalence of disability by age the finding was that the prevalence line for building users closely followed the line for OPCS-disabled people until age 60, after which the two lines diverged[6]. The building user line rose to reach 35 per cent at age 80, meaning that an estimated 35 per cent of 80-year-old building users were putative architecturally disabled people. The OPCS disability line rose much more steeply, and, at 60 per cent at age 80, indicated that an estimated 60 per cent of all 80-year-old people were disabled people.

Appendix 3

Public buildings: toilet users with special needs

Level access need

Table A3.1 summarises the responses of interviewees in the shopping centres of Carlisle, Eastbourne, Hereford and Peterborough to the question 'If you are trying to use a public toilet, how important is it for you to have level access so that you don't need to use steps or stairs to get there?'

Table A3.1 Access to public toilets: the need for level access

	Regular able-bodied people	Regular disabled people	Single pushchair users	Double pushchair users	Stick/crutch users	Wheelchair users	Blind people
sample number	1714	240	104	49	182	174	43
	%	%	%	%	%	%	%
essential	2	28	57	71	38	68	53
important	9	73	38	27	36	25	40
not very important	25	n/a	6	2	19	5	5
not at all important	63	n/a	0	0	7	2	2

Source: bibliography item **471**, Table 3.4, p. 125

Public buildings: toilet users with special needs

From the findings of the Department of the Environment's sanitary provision research project, Table A3.2 lists by particular building types the estimated proportions of toilet users with special needs. Regular disabled people, stick/crutch users, blind people and regular able-bodied people with special needs were classed as having a need for level access only. Single and double pushchair users and wheelchair users were classed as having a need for lateral space as well as a need for level access.

Male/female usage of public toilets

Drawn from an analysis of sanitary project interview findings, and emphasising again that the data relate only to adult people, the first column in Table A3.3 lists estimates of the ratio of male to female usage of toilet facilities in certain public buildings. The second column lists parity ratios, based on the assumption that women take

Table A3.2 Toilet users with special needs: estimated proportions by building type

	Men %	Women %
Department stores/supermarkets		
level access need only	12	20
lateral space as well as level access need	1	6
Cafes/restaurants		
level access need only	9	19
lateral space as well as level access need	*	6
Pubs		
level access need only	6	8
lateral space as well as level access need	*	3
Hotels		
level access need only	9	10
lateral space as well as level access need	*	3
Cinemas/theatres		
level access need only	3	9
lateral space as well as level access need	*	*
Museums/art galleries		
level access need only	5	13
lateral space as well as level access need	1	2
Swimming pools/leisure centres		
level access need only	8	15
lateral space as well as level access need	1	8
Railway stations		
level access need only	4	12
lateral space as well as level access need	1	3
Airport terminals		
level access need only	4	13
lateral space as well as level access need	*	2
Motorway service stations		
level access need only	6	11
lateral space as well as level access need	*	4
Doctors' surgeries		
level access only	28	38
lateral space as well as level access need	3	13

*less than 0.5
Source: bibliography item **471**, Table 6.5, p.149

twice as long and ought therefore to have twice as many amenities. Taking department stores as an example, the calculation is 38:62 = 38:124 = 25:75.

Pushchair users

One hundred and fifty-three pushchair users were interviewed in the course of the DOE sanitary provision project; 104 (94 women and 10 men) were in the single pushchair sample and 49 (43 women and 6 men) in the double pushchair sample. The first photograph they were shown illustrated a cloakroom where it was not

Table A3.3 Individual public building types: male/female toilet usage

	Male/female usage ratio	Male/female amenities: provision parity ratios
department stores/supermarkets	38:62	25:75
cafes/restaurants	45:55	29:71
pubs	62:38	45:55
hotels	62:38	45:55
cinemas/theatres	53:47	38:64
museums/art galleries	56:44	39:61
swimming pools/leisure centres	46:54	30:70
railway stations	62:38	45:55
airport terminals	67:33	50:50
motorway service stations	65:35	48:52
doctors' surgeries	25:75	14:86

Source: bibliography item **471** p.188

possible to get a pushchair through the lobby leading to the wc compartments, as shown in Figure 19.2 on page 180. Interviewees were asked what they would do, their responses being set out in Table A3.4. The same base was used when pushchair users were asked about the importance of lateral space in wc compartments (Table A3.5).

Table A3.4 Pushchair users: coping with inaccessible wc compartments

	Single pushchair users		Double pushchair users	
	Respondent needs toilet %	Child needs toilet %	Respondent needs toilet %	Child needs toilet %
leave child/ both children in pushchair outside	9	n/a	6	n/a
leave other child in pushchair outside	n/a	n/a	n/a	4
take child/children inside, leave pushchair outside	73	67	43	61
fold the pushchair up and take it and child/children into wc compartment	5	8	16	16
would not go/would find somewhere else	7	1	27	10
other/don't know	7	6	8	8

Source: relevant tables in bibliography items **471** and **472**

Table A3.5 Pushchair-accessible wc compartment: importance of lateral space

	Single pushchair users	Double pushchair users
	%	%
essential	36	59
important	55	33
not very important	10	6
not at all important	0	2

Source: bibliography item **472**, single pushchair users Table 22; double pushchair users Table 20

Grabrails

The base of table A3.6 on the the use of grab rails was wheelchair users who when interviewed for the sanitary provision project had said they had used a BS5810 toilet; for public buildings the sample was 132 and for employment buildings 84.

The base for the data in Table A3.7 on wheelchair users and wc transfer was the 45 wheelchair users who, when interviewed for the sanitary provision project, had said that they usually transferred laterally when using a BS5810-type toilet.

Table A3.6 BS5810 toilet: grabrails used by wheelchair users

	Public buildings %	Employment buildings %
side horizontal rail on wall by wc	64	56
drop-down rail on open side of wc	36	15
vertical rail on side wall by wc	21	14
low horizontal rail behind wc	14	14
vertical rail on rear wall on open side of wc	8	12
none	14	29
don't know/not stated	4	2

Source: relevant tables in bibliography items **471** and **472**

Table A3.7 Wheelchair users: transfer to and from wc

	%
Able to transfer either to left or right	60
prefer left	11
prefer right	13
no preference	36
Not able to transfer to both left and right	22
able to transfer to left only	13
able to transfer to right only	9
Not able to transfer without assistance	18

Source: bibliography item **471**, Table 5.20

The peninsular layout compared with BS5810

There were 149 wheelchair users who, when interviewed for the sanitary provision project, said that they sometimes or always took their wheelchair into public toilets. Table A3.8 summarises their responses when they were shown the model of the BS5810 toilet and a card illustrating the peninsular layout and asked to rate the two for convenience. The vote in favour of BS5810 was confirmed when the same interviewees were asked which they preferred: 57 per cent said the BS5810 toilet, 34 per cent the peninsular layout and 8 per cent said 'no difference'[1]. The peninsular layout scored higher among paraplegics/tetraplegics (7 to 6 in favour) and the users of powered wheelchairs (8 to 5 in favour).

Table A3.8 Convenience of BS5810 toilet layout versus peninsular layout

	BS5810 %	Peninsular %
very convenient	27	28
quite convenient	51	38
not very convenient	15	26
not at all convenient	4	7
don't know	3	2

Source: bibliography item **471**, Table 5.22, p.46

The question asked of the 66 people who said they preferred the peninsular layout or that there was no difference between the two was, 'Imagine that the toilet like this model [the BS5810 toilet] had a lot more space, so there was enough space to turn your wheelchair right round; which would you prefer, a larger version of the model, or one like this card [the peninsular layout]?' In response, 34 people – 55 per cent of the 66 – switched their preference to the larger version of BS5810[2]. Fourteen people, or 8 per cent of all the 174 wheelchair users who were interviewed, still preferred the peninsular layout[3]. Relevant data indicated that these tended to be people who were severely handicapped; of the 14, ten were in a chair which had to be pushed, three were in a powered chair, and only one was in a chair which could be propelled manually[4].

People with ileostomies

People with ileostomies are those who, following an operation to remove their large intestine, wear a bag under their clothes in which, via a tube through the abdominal wall, bodily waste matter is collected. The bag, which is reusable, is unclipped before its contents are emptied into a wc, and what the ileostomist would wish to find in a wc compartment in a public toilet is, along with a wash basin, a shelf on which the bag clip and a jug of water (used to wash the bag out) can be placed and the bag wiped clean before it is reclipped and put back into its cotton cover. The Ileostomy Association estimates there to be some 20 000 people in Britain and Ireland with a permanent ileostomy – about one in 30 000 of the total population[5]. They would be catered for by a for-the-disabled unisex toilet with a shelf in it, and, failing that, would be helped were it customary for there to be a wash basin in all wc compartments in public buildings.

Appendix 4

Comparative dimensions and areas of wc compartments

For British, American and European accessibility standards, the minimum dimensions of wc compartments are listed below. The dimensions of Annex A wc types are shown for comparison.

		Width	Depth	Area	Plan diagram, page
1	1961 American Standard A117.1 ('at least one' toilet stall)	915mm	1420mm	1.30m^2	15
2	1967 British Standard CP96 (unisex, wheelchair-bound)	1370mm	1750mm	2.40m^2	26
3	1979 British Standard 5810 (unisex, wheelchair users)	1500mm	2000mm	3.00m^2	48
4	1979 British Standard 5810 (ambulant disabled)	800mm	1500mm	1.20m^2	–
5	1980 American Standard A117.1 (standard 'accessible' toilet stall)	1525mm	1420mm	2.17m^2	79
6	1987 British Part M building regulation (unisex, wheelchair users)	1500mm	2000mm	3.00m^2	48
7	1990 European Manual (moderately accessible facility)	900mm	1500mm	1.35m^2	119
8	1990 European Manual (integrally accessible facility)	1650mm	1800mm	2.97m^2	119
9	1993 European Manual (integrally accessible facility	1650m	2000m	3.30m^2	–
10	1991 Americans with Disabilities Act Accessibility Guidelines (ADAAG) (standard 'accessible' toilet stall)	1525mm	1420mm	2.17m^2	79
11	1991 ADAAG (alternative (a) for alteration work)	915mm	1675mm	1.53m^2	–
12	1991 ADAAG (alternative (b) for alteration work)	1220mm	1675mm	2.04m^2	–
13	1992 British Part M building regulation (unisex, wheelchair users)	1500mm	2000mm	3.00m^2	–

		Width	Depth	Area	Plan diagram, page
14	1992 British Part M building regulation (ambulant disabled)	800mm	1500mm	1.20m^2	48
15	Annex A, WC1A	850mm	1500mm	1.27m^2	323
16	Annex A, WC3A	1000mm	1500mm	1.50m^2	323
17	Annex A, WC4B	1500mm	1000mm	1.50m^2	324
18	Annex A, WC5C	1500mm	1200mm	1.80m^2	324
19	Annex A, WC6B	1500mm	1500mm	2.25m^2	325
20	Annex A, WC7B	2000mm	1500mm	3.00m^2	325
21	Annex A, WC8B	2200mm	1700mm	3.74m^2	326
22	Annex A, WC9	2500mm	2000mm	5.00m^2	326

Appendix 5
Lobbies to public toilets

Prior to 1985 building regulations were ordered under Public Health Acts, a requirement of the Building Regulations 1976 being that no sanitary accommodation should open directly into (a) a habitable room unless the room was used solely for sleeping or dressing purposes; (b) a room used for kitchen or scullery purposes; or (c) a room in which any person was habitually employed in any manufacture, trade or business[1]. Reference was not made to public toilets, but the understanding was that the regulatory requirement applied to them, and the common interpretation of it was that an enclosed lobby was necessary. That was the position when, under the provisions of the 1984 Building Act, the 1985 Building Regulations became operative. Part G was the hygiene regulation, and the requirements it made in respect of access to sanitary conveniences (meaning wcs and urinals) were affected by the findings of the Mant and Muir Gray inquiry.

In 1985 the Building Research Establishment, as part of a review of technical requirements for building regulations, commissioned a report, *Building Regulation and Health*, from two medical specialists, D.C. Mant and J.A. Muir Gray. The brief was to advise on whether building fabric and design services features controlled or controllable by regulations could influence health, and the report was published in 1986. With regard to health hazards associated with wc usage, the finding was that the risk from airborne micro-organisms caused by splashing was negligible. The risk from hand contamination of flushing handles, tap handles and door handles was greater, but could be contained by hand washing. The infection risk from urinals was negligible. The major conclusion was, 'The most important single feature in the prevention of spread of infection is the provision of adequate and convenient hand-washing facilities'[2].

The related advice in the Mant and Muir Gray report was, 'The risk from direct communication of wcs with kitchens derives from airborne contamination of surfaces and the possibility of wc users washing their hands in sinks used for food preparation. The risk is small but is unnecessary and should be avoided'[3]. This was reflected in the requirement for Regulation G1(1) of the 1991 Building Regulations, which reads, 'Adequate sanitary conveniences shall be provided in rooms provided for that purpose, or in bathrooms. Any such room or bathroom shall be separated from places where food is prepared'[4].

There is thus no requirement to separate sanitary conveniences rooms from public circulation areas or rooms other than where food is prepared. With regard to places where food is prepared, the advice in section 1 of the Part G Approved Document is, 'A space containing a closet or urinal should be separated by a door from a space used for the preparation of food (including a kitchen and any space in which washing up is done)'[5]. This was a change from previous guidance, the associated note confirming that the purpose was to make it clear that a lobby was *not* required to separate a space containing a sanitary convenience from a space used for the preparation of food[6]. The position was subsequently clarified in a technical report which stated that the intention of regulatory requirement G1(1) was that a wc should not open directly onto a kitchen *immediately adjacent* to areas where food was stored or prepared[7].

Aside from building regulations, the Food Safety Regulations 1995 are pertinent; the requirement is that an adequate number of flush lavatories must be available in food premises, and 'Lavatories must not lead directly into rooms in which food is handled'[8]. The Workplace (Health, Safety and Welfare) Regulations 1992 do not materially affect the issue; with regard to sanitary conveniences, the only relevant requirement is that any wc should be situated in a separate room or cubicle, with a door which can be secured from the inside[9].

Appendix 6
Height criteria for building fixtures and fittings

In the context of the facilitation of building usage and the expansion of the accommodation parameters of normal provision, the level at which fixtures and fittings are placed to suit the needs of building users presents problems for the architect of a kind not posed by space considerations. Relevant anthropometric data can inform height criteria, but in many circumstances the interpretation of them cannot yield universally 'right' solutions. Examples are the levels at which lift controls, wash-hand basins and urinal bowls are fixed.

For building users, the convenient positioning of fittings and equipment is governed by body and reach dimensions. In the hypothesized case of a building which will be used solely and exclusively by normal able-bodied people, appropriate height criteria can be drawn from relevant anthropometric data; this is because normal able-bodied people are a homogeneous population, presenting body and reach characteristics which, when measured, enable reliable predictions to be made of the level at which a particular item (a bookshelf, for example) ought to be placed so that it is convenient for say 95 or 99 per cent of the population.

The problems posed by wheelchair users

The population of building users with which Annex A is essentially concerned excludes normal able-bodied people, and it is when the needs of wheelchair users are considered in conjunction with the needs of standing people that appropriate height criteria become particularly problematical. The issue is illustrated by the height at which fittings and equipment ought to be placed so that they are reachable by people seated in wheelchairs.

More so than any other building user population subgroup, people who, for mobility purposes, are confined to wheelchairs are heterogeneous. A sizeable proportion of them have upper limb impairments which prevent them from using their arms to reach any fittings or equipment at all. Among those who can stretch their arms, the range of reach is very variable. In consequence, there cannot be any 'reaching to use' situation where provision can be made for all wheelchair users to tackle independently the task which is involved.

With regard to buildings subject to the Part M building regulation there is a further complication. In the case of other building user subgroups, for example ambulant disabled people, children and pushchair users, the reach characteristics of those who use buildings will broadly be the same in respect of all types of buildings. Not so in the case of wheelchair users: different types of buildings when used by wheelchair users display different types of wheelchair users; those who work in office

Table A6.1 Upward oblique reach
Other than for the wheelchair user examples, the data below relate to standing people wearing shoes. For wheelchair users and children,m the data are for individuals of average height. With regard to wheelchair users and the interpretation of the data in the context of setting the positions of fixtures and fittings, the understanding should be that the wheelchair user will reach upwards to the side of the chair, not forwards.

	mm
tall man	2150
tall woman	1990
average-height adult man	1940
average-height adult woman	1790
short man	1730
boy/girl age 13	1670
short woman	1590
paraplegic man in wheelchair	1580
paraplegic woman in wheelchair	1470
boy/girl age 10	1470
boy/girl age 7	1270
boy/girl age 4	1040

buildings will, for example, have quite different reach characteristics from those who go to churches, department stores or art galleries.

Tracing history back to the 1950s, to Tim Nugent's work on the Champaign-Urbana campus of the University of Illinois and the formulation of the design specifications in the 1961 American Standard, it has always been paraplegic-type wheelchair users who have determined the presentation of reach criteria for disabled people in guidance documents issued in Britain, America and elsewhere. It was on that basis, for example, that relevant anthropometric data were presented in the third edition of *Designing for the Disabled*[1].

The Americans with Disabilities Act mandates rights for people with disabilities, and many of the provisions prescribed in its accessibility guidelines (ADAAG) are geared to the accommodation of independent wheelchair users. As first presented in 1991[2], the maximum height of the generality of fixtures and fittings was set at 54in (1370mm) for unobstructed situations and 46in (1170mm) for side reach over an obstruction. In 1996, in response to representations from national organizations of people of short stature, the decreed maximum height reach was reduced from 54in to 48in (1200mm)*.

The flaws in the concept of universal design – the idea that for the generality of building features normal provision can be designed to suit all building users – are exposed when the matter under consideration is the height of fixtures and fittings. An illustrative example is lift controls; if they are placed within the reach of small children, people of short stature and disabled people seated in wheelchairs, the effect will be to inconvenience regular able-bodied adult people.

* See page 105.

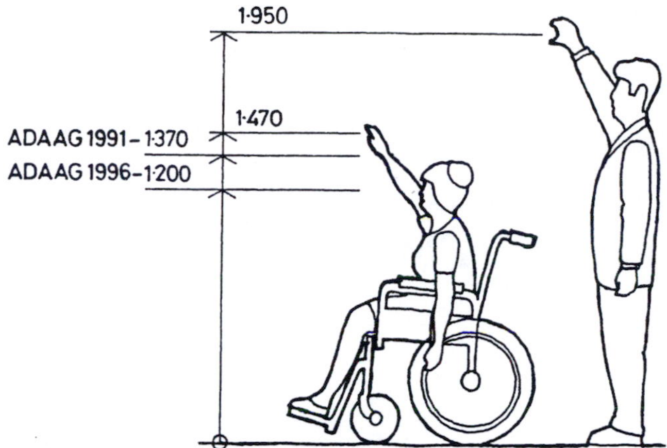

Ap6.1 The oblique upward reach of a paraplegic woman and an average-height man compared with the maximum height reach prescribed for the purposes of the Americans with Disabilities Act

Upward oblique reach

With regard to height criteria for building features whose usage involves the handling of goods or equipment (such as lift controls, window controls, storage shelves and bookshelves), the important anthropometric measure is upward oblique reach. Relevant data, derived principally from the authoritative American publication, Dreyfuss's *The Measure of Man and Woman*[3], are in Table A6.1.

For wheelchair users, the model is a notional paraplegic person, a chairbound person whose upper limbs are unimpaired, and for whose upward reach measures an average-height person seated in a standard wheelchair is assumed. This notional wheelchair user cannot, however, be held to be representative of all wheelchair users; in respect of the totality of wheelchair users who comprise the by-the-day or by-the-year population of wheelchair users of any particular type of public building, his or her attributes and capabilities will correspond to those of only a small minority.

For comparison with the ADAAG maximum height reaches, Figure Ap6.1 indicates the levels to which the notional paraplegic woman and an average-height man can reach obliquely.

Eye level

Eye level data are in Table A6.2. This is the anthropometric measure which affects the positioning of information notices and signage, the presentation of exhibits in buildings such as museums and art galleries, the placing of goods on display shelves, and the height of lift control labels.

The height at which mirrors should be fixed is a direct function of the eye levels of the users concerned. Figure Ap6.2a shows a tall man whose height is 1910mm (6ft 3in) and a short woman whose height is 1470mm (4ft 10in). Figure Ap6.2b shows an average-height woman in a wheelchair; the eye level of an average-height man in a wheelchair is 1220mm, and for all seated people a mirror with bottom and top levels at 900 and 1300mm will be suitable.

A mirror with bottom and top levels at 800 and 1820mm (type MR3 in Annex A) suits wheelchair users and all standing people, including small children.

Urinal bowls

The level at which the rims of urinal bowls are convenient for their users is a function of the height above floor level of penises. Discussion around the issue of the height

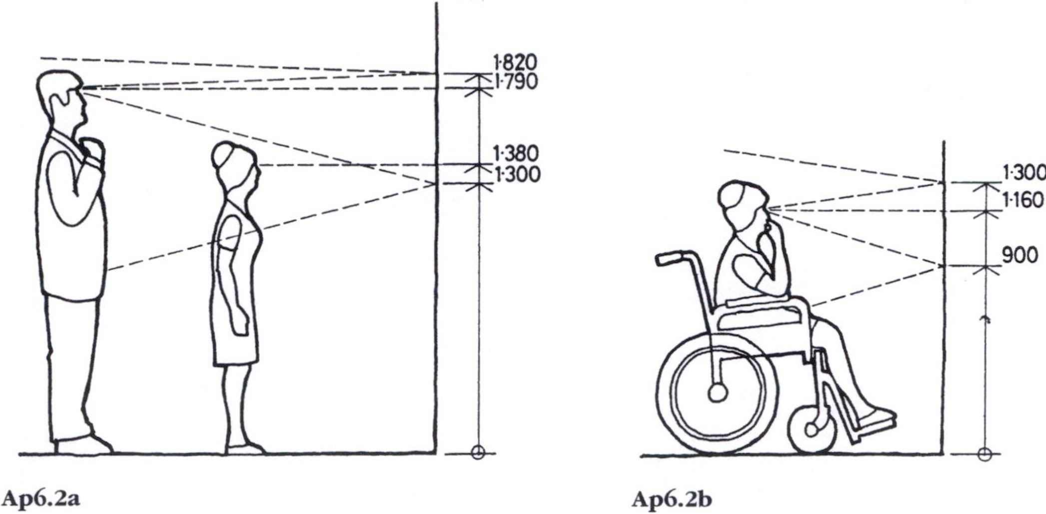

Ap6.2a **Ap6.2b**

of urinal bowls is on page 187, and, as noted there, no research data which could reliably inform design guidance would seem to be available. The data in the left-hand column of Table A6.3 are estimates drawn from relevant data in Dreyfuss's *The Measure of Man and Woman.*

Wash-hand basins

Discussion around the issue of the height of wash basins is on page 188; as noted there with regard to public buildings, the customary height of basin rims of about 820mm above floor level is unduly low for the convenience of standing adult users. On the premise that to suit their users the basin rim ought to be at about 150mm

Table A6.2 Eye level

Other than for the wheelchair user examples, the data below relate to standing people wearing shoes. For wheelchair users and children, the data are for individuals of average height.

	mm
tall man	1790
tall woman	1670
average-height adult man	1650
average-height adult woman	1540
short man	1490
boy/girl age 13	1460
short woman	1380
boy/girl age 10	1290
paraplegic man in wheelchair	1220
paraplegic woman in wheelchair	1160
boy/girl age 7	1130
boy/girl age 4	930

Table A6.3 Urinal bowls: preferred rim heights for different users

	p height when standing with footwear mm	Subtraction for vertical dimension between p height and height of urinal bowl rim mm	Preferred height of urinal bowl rim mm
tall adult man	840	160	680
average-height adult man	735	150	585
short adult man	640	140	500
average-height boy age 10	560	70	490
average-height boy age 7	465	60	405
average-height boy age 4	315	50	265

below elbow level, relevant data for standing adults and children are presented in Table A6.4.

The elbow height of a paraplegic person seated in a wheelchair is typically approximately 690mm[4], suggesting that a basin rim at 820mm could be uncomfortably high. But as Figure Ap6.3 shows, the frontal approach to a basin by a wheelchair user is obstructed by the front of the wheelchair arm at the point where the thigh crosses it, usually at about 610mm above floor level. If 660mm is allowed for comfortable clearance below the underside of the basin, the height of the rim, given that the basin has a vertical depth of about 140mm, will be about 800mm above floor level. A rim height of approximately 820mm is therefore about as convenient as can be for wheelchair users, even though elbows have to be raised for washing purposes.

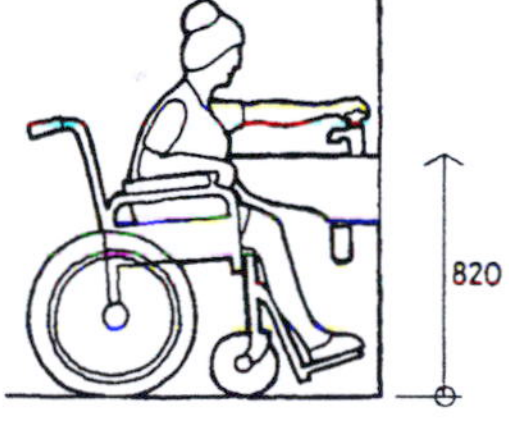

Ap6.3

Table A6.4 Wash-hand basins: suitable rim heights for different users

	A Standing person with footwear: height of elbow above floor level mm	B Suitable level for rim of wash basin, ie 150mm below dimension A mm
tall adult man	1250	1100
tall adult woman	1155	1005
average-height adult man	1130	980
average-height adult woman	1050	900
short adult man	1020	870
average-height boy/girl age 13	980	830
short adult woman	930	780
average-height boy/girl age 10	865	715
average-height boy/girl age 7	755	605
average-height boy/girl age 4	610	460

Appendix 7
Steps and stairs

For public buildings, there are no established design norms for the configuration of steps and stairs. Such studies as have been made in Britain, America and elsewhere of appropriate relationships between going and rise dimensions have yielded diverse and sometimes contradictory results[1]. A common feature of them is that they are based on the characteristics and capabilities of normal able-bodied people, and in practice that seems to be the rule which governs design decisions made by architects; a quick inspection of a random selection of steps and stairways in and around public buildings will confirm the impression that they are essentially geared to catering for fit able-bodied people.

For all building features, the precept for enhancing accessibility and usability is the extension of the accommodation parameters of normal provision. Applying this to steps and stairs, the people who would benefit most would be ambulant disabled and elderly people, with, according to circumstances, other beneficiaries being small children, people carrying luggage or heavy bags, people carrying infant children, people with infants in pushchairs, and sight-impaired or blind people.

In the case of existing buildings and the steps and stairs to be found in and around them, the only helpful intervention that may be made short of reconstruction will be the fixing of handrails where formerly there were none, or provision on one side only. And also in the case of new buildings it is the provision of suitable handrails which matters most, irrespective of the configuration of steps and stairs.

For stairways within buildings, the 'normal provision' base is usually less inclusive, on account of rises being high and goings shallow, than for steps at building entrances, where rises are lower and goings deeper. The vulnerability of external steps to rain, ice and snow is good cause for different design norms, although it could be that the horizontal movement factor has a greater effect on architectural decision-making. As against vertical movement, horizontal movement is often more important for external steps than it is for internal stairways, and for external steps it is standard practice for goings to be deeper than for internal stairs.

For steps and stairs generally, the advice in the approved document for the Part K building regulation is that 2R + G (twice the rise plus the going) should be between 550mm and 700mm, and for ambulant disabled people the application of this formula could entail unduly high rises or shallow goings. The advice in the 1992 Part M approved document is maximum 150mm for rises and minimum 280mm for goings; for internal stairs, the corresponding figures are 170mm and 250mm[2]. For reasons discussed below, the application of the minimum dimensions for goings may not suit ambulant disabled people.

For ambulant disabled people, as for others for whom extended design parameters for normal provision would be beneficial, there are two considerations: first, for comfort, that risers should be relatively low, and second, for safety and convenience, that goings should be relatively deep. In this connection, my own experiences as a user of steps and stairs were reported in Chapter 21 (page 218).

A stairway user is more at risk of stumbling and falling when coming down stairs than going up, a relevant factor being the depth of treads. When climbing, a typical user places only part of the foot on the treads, whereas when descending, the whole foot, or most of it, is placed on each tread. The narrower the tread, the more the user will twist the foot sideways when descending. With overall shoe lengths near to 300mm not being uncommon[3], and recognizing that ambulant disabled people need to place their leading foot securely on each tread as they descend a stairway, the going ought to be not less than 300mm for safety and convenience, and preferably of the order of 350mm or more.

Table An9.1 in Annex A (page 336) indicates appropriate going/riser relationships for different circumstances, the proviso to them being that from authoritative studies made of stair design, noting in particular John Templer's *The Staircase: Studies of Hazards, Falls and Safer Design*[4], no findings have emerged which indicate definitively correct configurations.

Appendix 8
Blind people

The prevalence of blind people among building users

To inform estimates of the prevalence of blind people among building users, population counts were made in the course of the Department of the Environment's sanitary provision research project; these were carried out in the four project locations and in towns elsewhere around England. People classified as blind people were those who when seen walking were using a white stick or cane as a mobility aid, were carrying a white wand or were accompanied by a guide dog. Of all the 234 562 people counted in all locations, 54 were blind people, for 52 of whom the mobility aid was noted. They were distributed as follows[1]:

white stick users	34
white cane users	13
white wand users	4
guide dog users	1

For the purposes of drawing national estimates of by-the-day building usage from the project data, the quota attached to blind people was 0.019 per cent, ie 1 in 5300 (Table A2.5, page 372). This was based on Saturday data for towns around England, adjusted to take account of the higher prevalence of blind people among shopping centre users on weekdays. The cumulative result of Monday-to-Friday counts was 7 out of 27 385, ie 1 in 3900, and for Saturday counts 4 out of 87 606, ie 1 in 21 900[2]. The result of subsequent Saturday counts, not included in the project report and unpublished elsewhere, was 8 out of 63 527, ie 1 in 7900.

Reliance on sight or feeling

'When you use public toilets, do you rely on your sight or on feeling your way with the help of your cane or guide dog?' was the question put to the 43 blind people interviewed in the course of the sanitary provision project. The responses, when analysed, gave the following results[3]:

rely entirely on sight	0
rely mostly on sight/partly on feeling the way	5
rely mostly on feeling the way/partly on sight	16
rely entirely on feeling the way	22

A point to note is that the question said 'When you use public toilets'. On a very-light to very-dark scale of the ambient light in and around places where public buildings and their facilities are used, public toilets are customarily at the very-dark end of the scale. Among blind people with some residual sight, the need to feel the way is, predictably, much more frequently occasioned in respect of toilet usage than it is, for example, in respect of walking along streets and crossing roads. Had the question been 'When you use pedestrian crossings', the responses could have been quite different.

Independent blind people

When population counts were carried out, no attempt was made to distinguish blind people who were travelling independently from those who were not, but relevant questions were asked when blind people were interviewed. The 43 people in the sample were asked which types of buildings they had used and then, 'When you are going out and about, visiting these kinds of places, do you always go with someone else, sometimes with someone else, sometimes by yourself, or are you always by yourself?' Responses were as follows[4]:

always with someone else	22
sometimes with someone else, sometimes by myself	15
always by myself	6

Obstacles to the mobility of blind people

Data regarding the mobility of blind people are to be found in two reports: one issued in 1965, the other in 1967. The question asked in the course of the survey reported by D. Liddle for the Royal National Institute for the Blind in 1965 was, 'Amongst the common obstacles to be met with outdoors, which do you find the greatest menace, and why?' In rank order, the obstacles most frequently mentioned were 1 bicycles; 2 roadworks; 3 prams; 4 toys; 5 ladders; 6 scaffolding; 7 overhanging branches, awnings, etc.; 8 tricycles; 9 children; and 10 dogs[5]. All the principal hazards were thus temporary, insubstantial, moving or unpredictable obstacles, the point to note being that to protect blind people against them there cannot as a rule be any physical warning signals of a kind which an architect could provide.

Facial vision

Some 3 per cent of registered blind people in Britain have a guide dog[6]. Others who are able to get about without the help of another person to guide them tend to do so by what is known as facial vision, by sensing the pressure of nearby objects against the skin. This pressure is a combination of touch and hearing, felt by the pores around the ears. In Liddle's survey there were people who claimed that they could detect walls at 20 metres, buildings at 15 metres and trees at 10 metres. These findings were amplified in the Gray and Todd Government Social Survey report *Mobility and Reading Habits of the Blind*[7] published in 1967, which surveyed a large sample of registered blind people. It focused in particular on the capabilities of totally blind people of working age who travelled unguided when they went out. Of the sample of 114 of these people, 71 per cent said they would, unguided, cross roads with traffic; 87 per cent claimed that when walking along a pavement they could sense the presence of a lorry with the engine off, and a similar number the position of lamp-posts; and 66 per cent responded with an unqualified yes and a further 15 per cent a qualified yes when asked whether they would be prepared to do a half-mile journey unguided along an unfamiliar route.

Appendix 9
Tactile pavings

Through the 1980s and into the 1990s the Department of Transport commissioned a series of research inquiries to do with tactile pavings. With the contractor for most of them being the Transport and Road Research Laboratory (TRRL) at Crowthorne in Berkshire, the aim of the first, undertaken during 1981 and 1982, was to assess how textured pavement surfaces could be used to help blind pedestrians locate zebra and pelican-controlled crossings[1]. For blind pedestrians, three main requirements were posited; these were (1) that the texture needed to be readily detectable underfoot; (2) that the pattern used should be distinguishable from those used to warn of danger, so that the single message 'You have arrived at a pedestrian crossing' was conveyed; and (3) that the texture should stretch right across the pavement, with its limits along the edge of the pavement coinciding with those of the crossing.

Blind people versus sight-impaired people

The hope was that a ramp with a textured surface and flush kerb would suit wheelchair users and at the same time provide sufficient surface contrast to satisfy the needs of blind pedestrians[2]. That was the first potential conflict of interests needing to be addressed, but another came with the texture requirement; this was that, as an aid to partially sighted people, the textured surface should preferably be distinctively coloured. I avoid using the term 'partially sighted', but my understanding is that for the purposes of the TRRL study it referred to what I call sight-impaired people, meaning those with a visual impairment who for mobility purposes rely entirely or predominantly on their ability to see. In the case of pavings at pedestrian crossings, it follows that sight-impaired people may be helped by distinctive colouring but not as a rule by tactile surfaces, and indeed, given that a tactile surface for the blind could be uncomfortable for them to walk on, they would not wish the surface of pavings to be tactile. Contrarily, blind people may be helped by a tactile surface – one which, to be detectable, will have to be knobbly – but not as a rule by colour distinctions.

There was here a further conflict of interest, indicating that for relevant research inquiries the two groups should have been examined separately. On one side, the focus should have been on blind people who travelled independently – not those who, when they went out, were always accompanied by another person. On the other, it should have been on sight-impaired people and, along with them, other pedestrians. Only on this basis would the merits and demerits of tactile pavings at street crossings have been properly evaluated. It was not, however, by way of this methodology that the TRRL projects were conducted; the user studies which were made and reported were all of a bunched mix of blind and sight-impaired people, or a mix of blind, sight-impaired people and others. In the account which follows of the Department of Transport's research inquiries, the terms 'visually handicapped' and 'partially sighted' are used where those were the terms adopted in official reports.

The rounded domes surface

For the 1981 study TRRL conducted experimental trials with 16 different surfaces. The subjects who did the initial testing were mainly TRRL staff, with 20 people who wore blindfolds acting as surrogates for blind people. Further assessments were made by representatives of outside organizations, blind people being included among them. The outcome was a consensus on the form that tactile paving should take: the paving slabs, of concrete 400mm square, would have a surface pattern of rounded domes 25mm in diameter and 6mm in height, with the centres of the domes being 67mm apart (Figure Ap9.1a).

Experimental installations using tactile pavings to the agreed pattern were then discussed with local highway authorities who had expressed an interest, the plan being that some 20 crossings would be converted. Reactions from local authorities and crossing users would be assessed, with more objective assessments being based on filmed records[3]. Set up in cooperation with Westminster City Council and six other local authorities, the on-the-streets evaluation project followed; one of the locations where prototype tactile pavings were laid was on the pedestrian crossing in Parliament Square close to the Houses of Parliament, and it was there that the programme was launched in July 1983.

Circular DU 1/86

In October 1986 the Department of Transport issued Disability Unit Circular 1/86 *Textured footway surfaces at pedestrian crossings*[4]; it came in the form of a letter to local authorities over the signature of the head of the Department's Disability Unit. It confirmed that, following the initial inquiries, a suitable tactile surface had been developed, and with three pages of instructional diagrams it advised local highway authorities on how tactile pavings should be laid at controlled crossings.

Paragraph 6 of the circular reported that the chosen surface had been installed at more than twenty sites around the country to assess its suitability and acceptability, and then continued:

> Further consultation with local organisations, together with site observations, led to three clear conclusions. First, that although the surface is uncomfortable, the great majority of people who walk across it pay no attention to it. Secondly, because it is uncomfortable, the surface should be restricted to the minimum area necessary to achieve its purpose. And, thirdly, blind people and wheelchair users generally found the experimental installations helpful.

Beyond that, no record of the site observations was published; it was left unclear whether any blind people had participated in controlled trials on the test sites, and how, in practice, they had performed had they done so.

The shaving of the domes

With authorised official guidance, local authorities around the country set about laying tactile pavings at controlled pedestrian crossings in accord with the Department of Transport's instructions. Some received complaints from members of the public that the prominent domes were unpleasantly uncomfortable[5], and the conflict of interests was apparent. If blind people walking along a street were to readily detect the pavings, the knobs on them had to be prominent. If, in response to the concerns of others, they were not, they would not be detectable and would not serve their purpose. The compromise solution which emerged was to shave off the round tops of the domes so that they would come with flat tops; from tests made at the Cranfield Institute of Technology, the report was that these were found to be easily detectable to blind people without causing discomfort to others[6].

Ap9.1 Tactile pavings

9.1a Rounded dome as advised in 1986

9.1b Flat-top dome as advised from 1991

Shared cyclist/pedestrian routes

A related research project was set up in 1986, its purpose being to develop tactile markings which would enable blind and partially sighted pedestrians to locate themselves on the correct side of shared cyclist/pedestrian routes[7]. The outcome was paving slabs with bar markings, laid to a ladder pattern on the pedestrian side and a tramline pattern on the cyclist side, and these were tested on six shared-route sites. The trials were reported in 1990; 36 blind and partially sighted people took part in them, of whom 24 could detect the markings, seven could sometimes detect them, three could not detect them and two did not want to use them[8]. The conclusion was that the markings were effective, and in December 1990 the Department of Transport issued a Traffic Advisory Leaflet *Tactile Markings for Segregated shared use by cyclists and pedestrians*[9], with detailed instructions to local authorities on how they should be laid.

Testing the scope for different surfaces

The major research project which followed was commissioned in November 1988. Its purpose was not to test further the principle of the advisability of tactile pavings as an aid for blind people – that had already been determined. Instead, with a contract placed with the Centre for Transport Studies at Cranfield Institute of Technology (now Cranfield University), its aim was to find out how many different surfaces could effectively and reliably be distinguished by blind and visually handicapped people when they walked over them.

The first stage was a literature review and an inquiry from which 20 different tactile surfaces were selected for testing. The second stage, an interview survey of the travel habits of 204 visually handicapped people drawn from areas of the south Midlands and south east of England, was intended to give a measure of the extent to which blind and sight-impaired people went out, the modes they used, whether or not they went out alone and what sort of problems they encountered[10].

With 50 participants selected from the 204 travel survey respondents, the third stage was conducted on the Cranfield campus. Its purpose was to choose from the 20 different first-stage surfaces the six which would be used in the fourth stage, the learning experiment. The idea was that for different practical purposes there would be different surfaces, and that the configuration and meaning of each surface could be learnt and then recalled by visually handicapped people. At the conclusion of the third stage six surfaces were designated for testing at the fourth stage: one was for pedestrian crossings with a dropped kerb; one was for guidance along a path; one was to warn of steps or stairs; one was to warn of the edge of railway platforms; and two had an information meaning, to indicate features such as bus stops and telephone boxes.

For the fourth stage, courses were laid out on the Cranfield campus and tested by 43 participants. Each was instructed by a researcher: 'The aim of the experiment is to see how easily different surfaces can be remembered. I shall ask you to walk across each surface and try to remember what it feels like and what message it gives. We will cross each one in turn.' On the first day the trial was repeated until each participant did all the remembering correctly; after six trials, there were still three who did not. The trial was repeated a week and then a month later, and still there were participants who could not remember what each surface meant[11].

For pedestrian crossings the choice at the third stage had been between the 1986 approved round dome surface and the proposed flat-top replacement. As with other surfaces, a check was made on how readily they were recognised when participants walked across them, and here the round tops scored better than the flat tops[12]. Participants were also asked to rate them for comfort, and on this the flat tops scored appreciably better than the round tops[13]. But of the 48 participants who assessed the flat tops, there were 15 who rated them 'uncomfortable'. The flat-top surface was chosen for the learning experiment.

Of the 50 third-stage participants with whom the fourth-stage learning experiment was undertaken, 21 were totally blind[14]. But those who travelled independently were not separated from those who did not, and when the participants' assessments of the 20 different surfaces were recorded the blind people were bunched with the others. There was thus no record of whether independent blind people found it significantly easier to detect and recognise round tops by comparison with flat tops.

Circular DU 1/91

During 1990 the Department of Transport consulted on guidance in Draft Disability Unit Circular 1/90 *Tactile footway surfaces at uncontrolled crossings*[15], which, with slight revisions, was issued in May 1992 as Disability Unit Circular 1/91 *The use of dropped kerbs and tactile surfaces at pedestrian crossing points*[16]. With a series of informative layout diagrams, the guidance in it was informed by the findings of the Cranfield project, and the recommended paving surface now had 'blisters' with a flat top at a height of 5.0mm, plus or minus 5mm (Figure A9.1b). Circular 1/91 remains operative in 1997.

The Wolverhampton project

A full report of the 1988 Cranfield project was issued in 1991[17], along with a two-page digest and a guidance leaflet illustrating the patterns of the paving surfaces which for five different purposes were available for trials on public sites[18]. An on-site follow-up project, again conducted by the Cranfield Institute of Technology, was undertaken in Wolverhampton. For the different practical purposes, appropriate tactile surfaces had been laid at locations in the town. The principal objectives were (a) to establish if the selected surfaces were useful to visually impaired people; and (b) to examine the extent to which tactile surfaces might cause problems for other groups of footway users, particularly wheelchair users and ambulant disabled people. The report, *Tactile surfaces in the pedestrian environment: Experiments in Wolverhampton*[19], was issued in 1992.

On the experiment at the pedestrian crossing where tactile pavings had been laid, the note in the report was that the usefulness of the experiment was reduced because the profiles of the flat-top blisters were below the recommended specifications and therefore less easy to detect than they might have been. Thirty-six people were selected to participate in this experiment, of whom 12 were familiar with the site and 12 were totally blind. They were asked to walk onto the pavings from a position behind the pavings, stop at the edge of the road and then cross to the other side. Twenty-eight detected the tactile pavings and stopped; five, of whom four were blind, did not locate them, among them one blind person who got lost; and three, all blind people with a guide dog, walked unknowingly across them and then had to be restrained by the researcher from walking straight across the road. Five people overshot the tactile pavings on the central reservation, and six, having veered when crossing the road, did not find the tactile pavings on the other side[20].

Guidance paths for blind people had been laid across St Peter's Square in the centre of Wolverhampton. Three blind people with guide dogs who were invited to participate in the experiment on the site refused to do so, their reason being that they would be asking their dogs to do what their training had taught them not to do. Forty-five visually handicapped people participated in the experiment, of whom 12 were totally blind; of these 12, nine failed to locate the tactile pavings on the guidance path[21]. To supplement the tests, video recordings were made on the site over a period of four weeks; of the 301 pedestrians observed, none was a visually handicapped person[22].

Twenty-five people who were wheelchair users or ambulant disabled people participated in one or other of the Wolverhampton experiments. When asked whether the tactile surfaces posed problems, the response from 23 was that uneven pavements around the town were much more of a problem[23].

The 1996 consultation document proposals

In March 1996 the mobility unit of the Department of Transport invited comments on a consultation document *Guidance on the use of tactile paving surfaces*[24]. With 37 pages of text and 36 illustrative diagrams, it presented proposals on the application and use of different tactile surfaces for a range of purposes, of which there were now seven. The note in the document was that research had determined that visually impaired people could reliably detect, distinguish and remember a limited number of different tactile paving surfaces and the distinct meanings assigned to them[25].

Surface 1 was the modified blister surface for pedestrian crossing points. *Surface 2* was a 'corduroy' surface, its purpose being to warn of the presence of hazards such as stairs, level crossings or the approach to on-street light rapid transit platforms. It conveyed the message 'hazard, proceed with caution'. *Surface 3* was the guidance path surface, its purposes being to guide visually impaired people along a route where cues such as kerb edges are not available, to guide pedestrians round obstacles such as street furniture in a pedestrian precinct, to help specific locations to be found and to guide people between facilities in transport terminals. It had a corrugated surface like that of the paving tiles laid in Wolverhampton, and very similar to the tactile pavings laid in the Dutch town of Gouda[26]. *Surface 4* was the information surface, its purpose being to help visually impaired people locate amenities such as telephone boxes, bus stops or ticket offices. It was simply to be a soft surface, a surface which would be detectable because it would feel slightly softer underfoot than conventional paving materials. *Surface 5* was the platform edge (off-street) warning surface, its purpose being to warn people of the presence of the edge of railway platforms. It was virtually identical to the modified blister surface for pedestrian crossings, the marginal difference being that alternate rows of domes were offset. *Surface 6* was the platform edge (on-street) warning surface, its purpose being to warn people that they were approaching the edge of an on-street platform serving a light rapid transit system. The surface had rows of 'lozenge' shapes. *Surface 7* was the segregated cycletrack/footway surface, its purpose being to protect blind people on routes shared with cyclists. With 'ladder' pattern tactile pavings on the pedestrian side and 'tramline' pattern pavings on the cycle side, it was in accord with the guidance issued by the Department of Transport in December 1990[27].

The consultation document noted that the successful use of tactile paving depended on visually impaired pedestrians understanding the meanings assigned to different paving surfaces and being made aware of the presence of tactile paving facilities in their area. Local authorities were advised to investigate how this information could most effectively be disseminated, and to assist with this a self-instructional training pack was being developed in cooperation with the Royal National Institute for the Blind. In March 1997, the time when this was written, advice from the Department of Transport on which of the various proposed surfaces would be officially approved was still awaited.

Appendix 10
The Audit Commission's measure of accessible local authority buildings

A duty of the Audit Commission for England and Wales is to promote 'best practice' in the delivery of local authority services[1], and for certain particular services local authorities are required to report their performance each year against a series of indicators. One is the accessibility of their buildings to disabled people, the measures being (a) the number of the authority's buildings open to the public; and (b) the number of such buildings in which all public areas are suitable for and accessible to disabled people.

On definitional criteria, the Commission's advice was that 'accessible' and 'suitable' were as defined in the approved document for the 1992 Part M building regulation. This posed interpretation problems; first, because the definitions in the approved document were not themselves precise, and second, because Part M mandated 'reasonable provision', the effect of which was that for different buildings what constituted reasonable access provision was variable. A complicating issue was that buildings which had been deemed to be accessible under the terms of the 1987 Part M regulation were, on account of the 'sensory impairments' factor, not accessible by the 1992 regulation. So local authorities had to determine their own rules when scoring their buildings, the unsurprising outcome being that measures were inconsistent.

When scores for the year 1994/95 were published in 1996[2], the modal number of accessible buildings reported was zero, reflecting a rigorous interpretation of Part M requirements on the part of the local authorities concerned. Among the authorities which recorded zeros were Kent (which had 262 'open to the public' buildings), Warwickshire (214), Calderdale (199), Kirklees (197) and Lewisham (178). These zero-per-cent ratings contrasted with the claims of local authorities which apparently applied less demanding (and perhaps more sensible) criteria; these included South Kesteven, which reckoned that 11 of its 12 'open to the public' buildings were accessible, Derby (26 out of 36), West Sussex (44 out of 66), Lancaster (15 out of 26), Hampshire (96 out of 182) and Suffolk (80 out of 169).

Appendix 11
The current (1997) Part M Building Regulation

The following requirements are in Part M of Schedule 1 to the Building Regulations 1991.

Requirement	Limits on application
Interpretation **M1** In this part, 'disabled people' means people who have – (a) an impairment which limits their ability to walk or which requires them to use a wheelchair for mobility, or (b) impaired hearing or sight.	1. The requirements of this Part do not apply to – (a) an extension which does not include a ground storey; (b) a material alteration; (c) a dwelling, or the common parts of a building which are intended for the exclusive use of two or more dwellings; (d) any part of a building which is used solely to enable the building or any service or fitting in the building to be inspected, maintained or repaired.
Access and use **M2** Reasonable provision shall be made for disabled people to gain access to and use the building.	
Sanitary conveniences **M3** If sanitary conveniences are provided in the building, reasonable provision shall be made for disabled people.	
Audience or spectator seating **M4** If the building contains audience or spectator seating, reasonable provision shall be made to accommodate disabled people.	

References and Bibliography

As well as listing sources of information referred to in the body of the book, the Bibliography (pages 406–20) includes ancillary material consulted in the course of the book's preparation; generally this is either relevant technical information or background material which has informed the drafting of the text. The Bibliography is set out under subject headings (as listed below), with individual items being coded with a three-digit number. Source material and other matters cited in the text are numbered sequentially for each chapter, annex or appendix. They are keyed to the list of references, and (in most cases) through that to the bibliography.

Two publishers feature more frequently than others in the Bibliography. One is HMSO, Her Majesty's Stationery Office, now known as The Stationery Office; its current (1997) publications address is Publications Centre, PO Box 276, London SW8 5DT. The other is the Centre for Accessible Environments, known until December 1989 as the Centre on Environment for the Handicapped. The title of its journal was *Design for Special Needs* until December 1989, and from January 1990 has been *Access by Design*. Its current address is Nutmeg House, 60 Gainsford Street, London SE1 2NY.

Bibliography subject headings

References

Preface
1 **708**
2 In this connection, see *303* Table 13.1 and associated commentary, pp. 43–6
3 **712** p. 15
4 **712** p. 35

Chapter 1
1 The report here was informed principally by personal communications with Duncan Guthrie.

Chapter 2
1 **113** p. 29; **114** p. 1
2 **116**
3 **113** p. 8
4 **113** p. 9
5 **101** 5.1.1 p. 8
6 **101** p. 10
7 A footnote to 5.6.2 stressed the importance of the design and mounting of the wc; its bowl should be shallow at the front of the seat and turn backwards more than downwards to allow the individual in a wheelchair to get close to the wc with the seat of the wheelchair.
8 pp. 10, 11
9 **101** p. 3
10 **113** pp. 3–4

Chapter 3
1 **805**
2 **311**
3 **231**
4 **211**
5 **807**
6 **806**, **808**
7 **303** p. 28
8 **303** p. 29
9 **303** p. 36
10 **303** p. 36
11 **301** p. 127
12 **462**, **463**
13 **231**
14 **301** p. 195
15 **301** p. 13
16 **302** p. 193
17 In correspondence with me, Tim Nugent has stressed the significance of Leon Chatelain's role in securing the realisation of the 1961 A117.1. Mr Chatelain died a few years after the event reported here
18 **461**

Chapter 4
1 This report is informed by **121**
2 **192**
3 **114** p. 23; *115* p. 35
4 **116**
5 **115** p. 35
6 **113** p. 15
7 **115** p. 36
8 **194** p. 7

9 **114** p. 12
10 **195** pp. 20–2; **125** pp. 49–52

Chapter 5
1 **762** p. 9
2 **213** paras 35–6
3 **213** para 24
4 **241**, p. iii
5 **241**, p. 4
6 **241**, p. 45

Chapter 6
1 **232**
2 **821**
3 **213** para 26
4 **303** p. 349
5 **221** p. 11; **222** p. 21
6 **221** p. 5
7 **222** pp. 20–1
8 **191** p. 1
9 **124** p. 108

Chapter 7
1 **125** p. 53
2 **125** p. 53
3 **125** p. 62
4 Exemplified by lack of mention in **123**
5 **125** p. 67
6 This report informed by personal communications and **143** pp. 56–8 and **124**
7 **125** p. 66
8 **143** pp. 41–5
9 **143** pp. 45–7
10 **143** pp. 47–8; **171** p. 19
11 **143** pp. 48–9
12 **143** pp. 50–1
13 **143** pp. 52–4, **171** p. 19
14 **143** pp. 54–5
15 **171**
16 **171** p. 46
17 **143** p. 49
18 **143** pp. 66–9; **127** p. 3

Chapter 8
1 **764**
2 For example, **744** p. 28
3 **221** p. 10; *222* p. 15
4 See for example **783**
5 See for example **778** p. 326
6 **721** p. 1
7 **721** p. 67
8 **721** p. 9
9 **721** pp. 54–5
10 **721** p. 9

Chapter 9
1 Reported in **322**
2 *Lords Hansard*, 2 June 1981, col 1210
3 **214** para 7.1
4 Relevant comment is in **323**
5 *Commons Hansard*, 11 February 1983, col 1276

Chapter 10
1 **122** p. 22676
2 **122** p. 22677
3 **122** p. 22681
4 **122** p. 22680
5 **125** p. 55
6 **143** p. 72
7 **143** p. 73
8 **124**
9 **102** p. 38
10 **102** p. 11
11 **102** p. 26
12 **125** p. 111
13 **125** p. 113
14 **125** p. 114
15 **125** p. 114
16 **125** p. 113
17 **131**
18 **132**
19 **135**
20 The report here on the feud surrounding the Access Board during 1981 is informed by **133**, **134** and a series of other press articles copied to me by the National Center for a Barrier Free Environment
21 **125** p. 116
22 **106**
23 *Congressional Record* 1 August 1981, quoted in **125** p. 119
24 **125** p. 122; **107** p. 33864
25 **107**
26 **105**

Chapter 11
1 Reported in **361** p. 7
2 Reported in **361** p. 8
3 **234**, **235**
4 **102**, pp. 15, 62
5 **325**, p. 4
6 **325**, p. 5

7 **326**
8 **311**
9 Published as **312**
10 **314**
11 **362** p. 16
12 **464**
13 **465**
14 **466** p. 13
15 **466** p. 20
16 The report here was checked when in draft with John Dobinson and Sarah Langton-Lockton

Chapter 12

1 See for example **162**
2 **143** p. 120
3 **143** p. 121
4 **128**
5 **129**
6 **143** p. 124
7 **125** p. xi
8 **151**
9 **141** p. 35586
10 **141** p. 35552
11 **157** p. 2
12 **141** p. 35557
13 **141** p. 35625
14 **148** p. 5
15 **148** p. 1
16 **142** p. 35709
17 **156** p. 19
18 **156** p. 22
19 **146** p. 165
20 **146** p. 182
21 **143** p. 140

Chapter 13

1 **221** p. 2
2 **341**
3 See, for example, **331**, **332**, **334**, **335**, **341**, **342**
4 **343** p. 10
5 **345** p. 2
6 **345** p. 3
7 **222** p. 2

Chapter 14

1 **611**
2 **344** p. 22
3 **621**
4 **612**
5 **613**
6 **616**
7 **617**
8 **618**

Chapter 15

1 **768**, p. 317
2 *Commons Hansard*, 11 February 1983, col 1266
3 *Commons Hansard*, 11 February 1983, col 1267
4 *Commons Hansard*, 11 February 1983, col 1268
5 *Commons Hansard*, 11 February 1983, col 1267
6 *Commons Hansard*, 11 February 1983, col 1294
7 *Commons Hansard*, 11 February 1983, col 1295
8 *Commons Hansard*, 11 February 1983, col 1275
9 *Commons Hansard*, 8 March 1988, col 162
10 *Commons Hansard*, 31 January 1992, col 1235
11 *Commons Hansard*, 31 January 1992, col 1259
12 *Commons Hansard*, 5 February 1992, col 287
13 *Disability Now*, February 1990
14 *Disability Now*, August 1993
15 *Commons Hansard*, 11 March 1994, col 526
16 *RADAR Bulletin*, April 1994, p1
17 *Commons Hansard*, 11 March 1994, col 538
18 *Commons Hansard*, 11 March 1994, col 537
19 *Commons Hansard*, 11 March 1994, col 536
20 *Commons Hansard*, 11 March 1994, col 541
21 *Commons Hansard*, 31 January 1992, col 1236
22 *Commons Hansard*, 6 May 1994, col 989
23 *Commons Hansard*, 10 May 1994, col 155
24 **792**
25 **791**
26 **722**
27 **141** p. 35553
28 **722** pp. 42, 43
29 **723** para 4.3, p. 22
30 **725**
31 **727**
32 **726**
33 **725** *Timetable Proposals* para 2.7, p. 6
34 **725** *Timetable Proposals* para 3.5, p. 8
35 **725** *Timetable Proposals* para 4.5, p. 10

Chapter 16

1 **157** p. 44
2 **141** p. 35648/9
3 Relevant reports are **315**, **316**
4 **444**
5 **401**
6 **401**
7 **471** p. 27

Chapter 17

1 **911**
2 **721** p. 55
3 In **753**
4 **741** p. 3, quoted in **755** p. 22

Chapter 18

1 **701** p. 18
2 Examples are reported in **512**, **513**, **514**, **515**
3 See, for example, **501** p. 13
4 **511**
5 **472** section 9.3
6 **472** regular disabled, Table 10/1
7 **471** Table 6.9, p. 58
8 **471** p. 125
9 **471** Tables 6.3 and 6.4, p. 148
10 **471** Table 4.5, p. 138
11 **472** regular disabled, Table 10/1
12 **471** p. 148
13 **472** wheelchair users, Table 20, p. 59
14 **472** wheelchair users, Table 21, p. 60
15 **472** wheelchair users, Tables 110–17
16 **704** Table 5.3, p. 49
17 **707**
18 **471** p. 182
19 **471** pp. 179–82
20 **471** Table 7.2, p. 74; Table 3.2, p. 20
21 **471** Table 11.7, p. 206
22 **471** pp. 205–6
23 **301** p. 38

Chapter 19

1 **471** p. 189
2 **473**
3 **913** p. 48
4 **222** p. 21
5 **472**: stick/crutch users, Table 13; blind people, Table 12; regular disabled people, Table 11
6 **471** Table 6.1, p. 50
7 **472** wheelchair users, Tables 68 and 69
8 **472** wheelchair users, Table 108
9 **303** p. 349
10 **481**, **482**, **483**
11 **472** wheelchair users, Table 78
12 Derived from an inspection of wcs in 11 public building locations in England; bowl rim heights ranged from 380 to 420mm
13 Derived from an inspection of normal provision urinals in 36 public building locations in England; rim heights ranged from 590 to 690mm
14 Derived from an inspection of 'odd' low-level urinals in 14 public building locations in England; rim heights ranged from 440 to 560mm
15 Derived from an inspection of wash basins in 13 public building locations in England; rim heights ranged from 770 to 900mm
16 **472** wheelchair users, Table 95; other relevant tables are 96, 106 and 107

Chapter 20

1 **704** Table 2.9, p. 4
2 **911** p. 41
3 **222** diagram 6, p. 10
4 The measure here is the reflectancy of different hues. As reported in **563** p. 79, yellow reflects 71 per cent of the white light that it strikes back to the viewer's eye, compared with 17 per cent for green, 15 per cent for blue and 13 per cent for red. For white and black, the respective figures are 85 per cent and 8 per cent
5 **707** pp. 133, 123
6 **525, 526**
7 **231** p. 20
8 **232** p. 2
9 **624**
10 **141** p. 35659
11 **552** p. 6
12 **143** p. 126
13 **552** p. 6
14 **552** p. 6
15 **551**
16 **553**, **554**, **555**
17 **556**
18 See, for example, 1987 Report pp. 36–7; 1988 Report para 121; 1989 Report para 80; 1992 Report para 17; 1993 Report p. 13; 1994 Report p. 24
19 **535**
20 **222** p. 8
21 **532**
22 **534**
23 **281**, **282**
24 **283** pp. 477–9
25 **222** p. 19
26 **141** p. 35658, 35670
27 *Disability Now*, June 1995, p. 3

Chapter 21

1 **222** p. 9
2 **521**
3 **411** p. 9

4 **221** p. 9; **222** p. 18
5 **426**
6 **222** p. 19
7 **222** p. 18
8 *The Times*, 20 June 1995, p. 21
9 Of relevance here are **365** and **367**
10 **303** p. 59

Chapter 22
1 For example, **501** p. 13
2 **261**
3 Information supplied by Newark and Sherwood District Council, January 1997

Chapter 23
1 **225** p. 13
2 Information supplied by Manchester City Council, January 1997
3 **407**
4 **341** p. 3; **344** p. 2
5 **404**
6 **405** p. 1
7 **252** para 37
8 **351**
9 **352** ENV 22 and ENV 30; **355** is also relevant
10 **353**
11 **354**

Chapter 24
1 **725**
2 **725** *Timetable Proposals*, para 4.8
3 Aimed at generating data to inform the presentation of a new British Standard which would replace BS5810 (**232**) and BS5619 (**821**), a number of ergonomic research contracts sponsored by the Department of the Environment were placed in early 1997
4 In this connection, a video (**271**), made with the support of the Department of Social Security on behalf of the Minister for Disabled People, was produced by the Centre for Accessible Environments and distributed in late 1996

Chapter 25
1 **253** para 33
2 **215** p. 1
3 By virtue of the requirements in article 22 of the Town and Country Planning (General Development Procedure) Order 1995
4 **215** para 10, p. 8
5 **215** para 14, p. 9. Cited for example in **356**, there are three established legal tests against which a condition of planning permission may be judged: (1) it must fairly and reasonably relate to a planning purpose; (2) it must fairly and reasonably relate to the permitted development; and (3) it must not be so unreasonable that no reasonable planning authority could have imposed it
6 **215** para 114, p. 34
7 **215** para 14, p. 9
8 **471** Table 6.7, p. 152
9 **472**: regular able-bodied, Table 9, p. 22; regular disabled, Table 9, p. 22
10 **471** Table 7.2, p. 74; Table 3.2, p. 20
11 **601**
12 **472** wheelchair users, Table 20

Chapter 26
1 With regard to improving access for the disabled in historic buildings generally, the advice in **255** is that a flexible and pragmatic approach should be taken

Annex B
1 *Commons Hansard* (Written Answers), 25 February 1992, col 427
2 **827**
3 **862** p. 44 and Table A5.14, p. 187
4 **801**
5 Sources for data in Table B.2 are **804** and **814**
6 **812**
7 **813**
8 **812** p. 46
9 **812** p. 48
10 **891** Tables 6.1 and 6.7; **892** Tables 6.1 and 6.7
11 **825**
12 **843**
13 **844**
14 **841** p. 9
15 **872**
16 **875**
17 **841** p. 8
18 **831**
19 **832**. Minor changes were subsequently made to the 16 criteria; Table B.4 lists them as set out in **834** when it was first introduced in 1987, p. 8
20 **852** paras 5–6
21 **834**
22 A *vox pop* survey was made by the NHBC and reported in a video production
23 **833**
24 **824**

25 **822**, **823**
26 **821** p. 8; **822** unnumbered page
27 **351**
28 **881**
29 **881** para 7
30 **851**
31 Noted in covering letter to consultation proposals from Paul F. Everall, 12 January 1995
32 **861** Table 3.7, p. 35
33 **852**
34 **853**
35 *Commons Hansard* (Written Answers), 23 November 1995, col 236
36 *Commons Hansard* (Written Answers), 23 January 1996, col 197
37 *Commons Hansard*, 8 July 1996, col 128
38 **892** Table 6.1, **893**
39 **861**; most of the findings which follow are reported on pages 30–2.

Appendix 2

1 **471** Table 3.3, p. 124
2 **471** Table 4.5, p. 138
3 **471** Table 8.5, p. 164
4 **704** p. 5
5 **704** Table 2.15, p. 7
6 **471** Figure 9.2, p. 180

Appendix 3

1 **472** wheelchair users, Table 106
2 **472** wheelchair users, Table 107
3 **471** pp. 47–8
4 **471** wheelchair users, Table 107
5 Personal communication from Ileostomy Association

Appendix 5

1 **226** P3(2)
2 **456** p. 15
3 **456** p. 15
4 **223** p. 3
5 **223** para 1.2, p. 3
6 **223** inside cover page
7 **457** p. 4
8 **454**, Schedule 1, Chapter 1
9 **455** p. 33

Appendix 6

1 **303** pp. 122–3
2 **141** p. 35625
3 **901**
4 **303** pp. 122, 123

Appendix 7

1 See for example **376** p. 37
2 **222** pp. 8, 16
3 **376** p. 36
4 **376**

Appendix 8

1 **472** mobility aids, Table 7
2 **472** Table 6, p. 9.3
3 **472** blind people, Table 19/2
4 **472** blind people, Table 7
5 **526** p. 147
6 **707** p. 183
7 **525**

Appendix 9

1 **531**
2 **531** p. 1
3 **531** p. 2
4 **532**
5 Reported in **543** p. 1
6 **543** p. 1
7 **544**
8 **545**
9 **536**
10 **541** pp. 5–18
11 **541** pp. 39–54
12 **541** Table 22
13 **541** Table 25
14 **541** Table 16
15 **533**
16 **534**
17 **541**
18 **543**
19 **542**
20 **542** pp. 29–36
21 **542** pp. 19–24
22 **542** p. 41
23 **542** p. 38
24 **535**
25 **535** p. 1
26 **624** p. 10
27 **536**

Appendix 10

1 **284**
2 **283** pp. 114–23

Bibliography

1 America

10 Access standards, Guidelines

101 ASA A117.1-1961 *American Standard Specifications for Making Buildings and Facilities Accessible to, and Usable by, the Physically Handicapped*, American Standards Association, New York, 1961

102 ANSI A117.1-1980 *American National Standard Specifications for Making Buildings and Facilities Accessible to, and Usable by, Physically Handicapped People*, American National Standards Institute, New York, 1980

103 ANSI A117.1-1986 *American National Standard for Buildings and Facilities – Providing Accessibility and Usability for Physically Handicapped People*, American National Standards Institute, New York, 1986

104 CABO/ANSI A117.1-1992 *American National Standard – Accessible and Usable Buildings and Facilities*, Council of American Building Officials, Falls Church, Virginia, 1992

105 General Services Administration, Department of Defense, Department of Housing and Urban Development, US Postal Service, *Uniform Federal Accessibility Standards* Federal Register, Washington DC, August 7 1984

106 US Architectural and Transportation Barriers Compliance Board, *Minimum Guidelines and Requirements for Accessible Design* Federal Register (46 FR 4270), Washington DC, January 16 1981

107 US Architectural and Transportation Barriers Compliance Board, *Minimum Guidelines and Requirements for Accessible Design* Federal Register (36 CFR 1190), Washington DC, August 4 1982

108 US Department of Justice, *Americans with Disabilities Act Accessibility Guidelines for Buildings and Facilities (ADAAG)* Federal Register (28 CFR 36), Washington DC, July 26 1991 (Appendix A to Part 36)

11 Application of A117.1

111 'Design of buildings to permit their use by the physically handicapped', Timothy J. Nugent, *New Building Research*, USA, Fall 1960, p. 51

112 'The campaign to eliminate architectural barriers in the United States', Edmond J. Leonard (printed in *Congressional Record*, Vol. 111, No. 126, Washington DC, July 13 1965)

113 *Proceedings of the National Institute on Making Buildings and Facilities accessible to and Usable by the Physically Handicapped, 21–24 November 1965*, National Society for Crippled Children and Adults, Chicago, 1965

114 A Report of the National Commission on Architectural Barriers to Rehabilitation of the Handicapped (Leon Chatelain Jr, Chairman), *Design for ALL Americans*, US Government Printing Office, Washington DC, 1967

115 'Architectural barriers for the handicapped – A survey of the law in the United States', Robert Dantona and Benjamin Tessler, *Rehabilitation Literature* (Chicago), February 1967, p. 34

116 Edmond J. Leonard, unpublished paper for Architectural Barriers Symposium, Washington DC, August 1988

12 Disability Civil Rights

121 'Strachan and the limits of Federal Government', Edward Berkowitz (University of Massachusetts, Boston), *International Review of History and Political Science*, February 1980, p. 65

122 US Department of Health, Education and Welfare, *Nondiscrimination on Basis of Handicap: Programs and Activities Receiving or Benefiting from Federal Financial Assistance* Federal Register (Vol. 42, No 86), Washington DC, May 4 1984

123 *Rehabilitation Act of 1973 – Public Law 93-112 Rehabilitation Gazette* (St Louis, Missouri), 1974, p. 13

124 *Campaigning for Disability Rights in America*, Judy Heumann (text of talks, April 1988), London Boroughs Disability Resource Team, London, 1988

125 *Disability, Civil Rights, and Public Policy – The Politics of Implementation*, Stephen L. Percy, University of Alabama, Tuscaloosa, 1992

126 'US national surveys reveal strong support for disability rights and services', *The Coalition* (journal of the American Coalition of Citizens with Disabilities), Washington DC, Spring 1979

127 'Human rights for the handicapped', *International Exchange News*, Washington DC, Spring 1978

128 *Toward Independence: An Assessment of Federal Laws and Programs Affecting Persons with Disabilities, with Legislative Recommendations*, National Council on the Handicapped, Washington DC, 1986

129 *On the Threshold of Independence*, National Council on the Handicapped, Washington DC, 1988

13 The Access Board

131 US Architectural and Transportation Barriers Compliance Board, *Notice of Intent to Issue Proposed Rules* Federal Register (45 FR 12167), Washington DC, February 22 1980

132 US Architectural and Transportation Barriers Compliance Board, *Notice of Proposed Rulemaking* Federal Register (45 FR 55010), Washington DC, 10 August 1980

133 'A story of runaway rule-making in an attempt to do good', Walter Pincus, *The Washington Post*, 5 January 1981, p. A3

134 'Here's one "Midnight Regulation" that's slipped through Reagan's net', Timothy B. Clark, *National Journal* (Washington DC), 2 July 1981, p. 221

135 *Comparison of technical provision differences between the A&TBCB Guidelines and Requirements and the ANSI 117.1 (1980)*, National Center for a Barrier Free Environment, Washington DC, 1981

14 The Americans with Disabilities Act

141 US Department of Justice, *Nondiscrimination on the Basis of Disability by Public Accommodations and in Commercial Facilities; Final Rule* Federal Register (28 CFR Part 36); Vol. 56, No. 144; Friday July 26 1991, Part III, Washington DC, 1991

142 US Department of Justice, *Nondiscrimination on the Basis of Disability in State and Local Government Services; Final Rule* Federal Register (28 CFR Part 36); Vol. 56, No. 144; Friday July 26 1991, Part IV, Washington DC, 1991

143 *No Pity – People with Disabilities Forging a New Civil Rights Movement*, Joseph P. Shapiro, Times Books, New York, 1993

144 'The Americans with Disabilities Act', Roger Andersen, *Access by Design* 55 (London), May/August 1991, p. 11

145 *Lessons from America – A study of the Americans with Disabilities Act*, Victoria Scott Royal Association for Disability and Rehabilitation, London, 1994

146 *Complying with the Americans with Disabilities Act – A Guidebook for Management and People with Disabilities*, Don Fersh, Peter W. Thomas, Quorum Books, Westport, Connecticut, 1993

147 *Implementing the ADA – Rights and Responsibilities of All Americans*, Lawrence O. Gostin, Henry A. Beyer, Paul H. Brookes, Baltimore, 1993

148 'Moving within reach', *Universal Design Newsletter*, Rockville, April 1966, p. 1

149 'The quest for "Equivalent"', *Universal Design Newsletter*, Rockville, July 1966, p. 6

15 ADA guidance

151 US Architectural and Transportation Barriers Compliance Board, *Americans with Disabilities Act (ADA) Accessibility Guidelines for Buildings and Facilities; Proposed Rule* Federal Register (36 CFR 1191), Washington DC, January 22 1991

152 US Architectural and Transportation Barriers Compliance Board, *Americans with Disabilities Act Accessibility Guidelines for Buildings and Facilities (ADAAG)*, The Board, Washington DC, 1992

153 US Architectural and Transportation Barriers Compliance Board, *Americans with Disabilities Act – Accessibility Guidelines Checklist for Buildings and Facilities*, The Board, Washington DC, 1992

154 ADA Access Facts Series, *Readily Achievable Checklist: A Survey for Accessibility*, Adaptive Environments Center, Boston, 1991

155 ADA Access Facts Series, *Achieving Physical and Communication Accessibility*, Adaptive Environments Center, Boston, 1991

156 The Americans with Disabilities Act *Title II Technical Assistance Manual*, Civil Rights Division, US Department of Justice, Washington DC

157 The Americans with Disabilities Act *Title III Technical Assistance Manual*, Civil Rights Division, US Department of Justice, Washington DC

16 Reports on access issues

161 'An American dream?', Andrew Lacey, *Design for Special Needs* 43 (London), May/August 1987, p. 10

162 'The Massachusetts method', Pauline Nee, *Access by Design* 53 (London), September/December 1990, p. 12

163 'Happenings in America', Selwyn Goldsmith, *Design for Special Needs* 35 (London), September/December 1984, p. 12

164 'Physical disability and public policy', Gerben DeJong, Raymond Lifchez, *Scientific American*, June 1983, p. 40

17 Independent living

171 *Design for Independent Living – The Environment and Physically Disabled People*, Raymond Lifchez, Barbara Winslow, Watson-Gupthill, New York/Architectural Press, London, 1979

172 'The independent living paradigm', Selwyn Goldsmith, *Design for Special Needs* 33 (London), January/April 1984, p. 11

18 Design issues

181 *Rethinking Architecture – Design Students and Physically Disabled People*, Raymond Lifchez, University of California Press, Berkeley, 1987

182 'The differences between accessibility and universal design', *Universal Design Newsletter*, Rockville, July 1994, p. 2

183 'Evaluating universal design', *Universal Design Newsletter*, Rockville, January 1996, p. 2

19 Other references

191 The American Institute of Architects, *An Architect's Guide to Building Codes and Standards*, The Institute, Washingon DC, third edition, 1991

192 *25 Years of Volunteers in Partnership*, President's Committee on Employment of the Handicapped, Washington DC, 1972

193 *FDR's Splendid Deception*, Hugh Gregory Gallagher, Vandamere Press, Arlington, Virginia, 1994

194 'Vocational Rehabilitation Act, Amendments of 1965', Mary E. Switzer, *Employment Service Review* (US Department of Labor), September 1966, p. 7

195 *Institutional Disability – The Saga of Transportation Policy for the Disabled*, Robert A. Katzmann, Brookings Institution, Washington DC, 1986

2 Britain: Access issues (1)

20 Statutory instruments

201 Statutory Instruments 1985 No. 1065 Building and Buildings: The Building Regulations 1985

202 Statutory Instruments 1985 No. 488 The Building (Fourth Amendment) Regulations 1985

203 Statutory Instruments 1987 No. 1445 Building and Buildings: The Building (Disabled People) Regulations 1987

21 Departmental circulars

211 Joint Circular: Ministry of Housing and Local Government 71/65, Ministry of Health 21/65 *Access to public buildings for the disabled*, HMSO, London, 1965

212 Department of the Environment Circular 11/85 *The Building (Fourth Amendment) Regulations 1985: Access and Facilities in Buildings for the Benefit of Disabled People*, HMSO, London, 1985

213 Department of Health and Social Security Circular 12/70 (Joint Circular from DHSS, DES (13/70), MHLG (65/70) and Ministry of Transport (20/70)) *The Chronically Sick and Disabled Persons Act 1970*, HMSO, London, 1970

214 Department of Health and Social Security Local Authority Circular (82)5 (Joint Circular from DHSS, DOE (10/82), DES (2/82) and DoT (1/82)) *Re: Disabled Persons Act 1981*, HMSO, London, 1982

215 Department of the Environment Circular 11/95 *The Use of Conditions in Planning Permissions*, HMSO, London, 1995

22 Building Regulations, official guidance

221 The Building Regulations 1985, Part M Approved Document *Access for disabled people*, Department of the Environment and the Welsh Office, HMSO, London, 1987

222 The Building Regulations 1991, Part M Approved Document, 1992 edition *Access and facilities for disabled people*, Department of the Environment and the Welsh Office, HMSO, London, 1992

223 The Building Regulations 1991, Part G Approved Document *Hygiene*, Department of the Environment and the Welsh Office, HMSO, London, 1992

224 The Building Regulations 1985, Part K Approved Document *Stairways, ramps and guards*, Department of the Environment and the Welsh Office HMSO, London, 1985

225 Department of the Environment and the Welsh Office, *Manual to the Building Regulations 1985*, HMSO, London, 1985

226 Department of the Environment and the Welsh Office, *The Building Regulations 1976*, HMSO, London, 1976

23 Codes and Standards

231 CP96:1967 *Access for the Disabled to Buildings Part 1, General Recommendations*, British Standards Institution, London, 1967

232 BS5810:1979 *Access for the Disabled to Buildings*, British Standards Institution, London, 1979

233 Design Note 18 *Access for Disabled Persons to Educational Buildings*, Department of Education and Science, London, 1984

234 BS5588: Part 2: 1983 *Fire precautions in the design and construction of buildings: Code of practice for shops*, British Standards Institution, London, 1983

235 BS5588: Part 3: 1983 *Fire precautions in the design and construction of buildings: Code of practice for office buildings*, British Standards Institution, London, 1983

236 BS5588: Part 8: 1988 *Fire precautions in the design and construction of buildings: Code of practice for means of escape for disabled people*, British Standards Institution, London, 1988

237 Health Building Note 40 *Common Activity Spaces*, Department of Health (NHS Estates), London, 1995

24 Reports

241 *Can disabled people go where you go?* Report by the Silver Jubilee Committee on Improving Access for Disabled People (chairman Mr Peter Large), Department of Health and Social Security, London, 1979

242 PD6523:1989 *Information on access to and movement within and around buildings and on certain facilities for disabled people*, British Standards Institution, London, 1989

243 'How reasonable is Part M?' (criticism of the Tate Gallery at St Ives), Sabrina Aaronovitch, *Access Action* (Access Committee for England), January 1994

25 Planning guidance

251 DOE Development Control Policy Note 16 *Access for the disabled*, Department of the Environment/Welsh Office, London, 1985

252 DOE Planning Policy Guidance Note 1 *General policy and principles*, Department of the Environment/Welsh Office, London, 1992

253 DOE Planning Policy Guidance Note 1 (Revised) *General policy and principles*, Department of the Environment/Welsh Office, London, 1997

254 DOE/DNH Planning Policy Guidance Note 6 *Town Centres and Retail Developments*, Department of the Environment/Department of National Heritage, London, 1994

255 DOE/DNH Planning Policy Guidance Note 15 *Planning and the historic environment*, Department of the Environment/Department of National Heritage, London, 1994

26 Historic buildings

261 *What Listing Means – A Guide for Owners and Occupiers*, Department of National Heritage, London, 1994

262 English Heritage Guidance Note *Easy access to historic properties*, English Heritage, London, 1995

27 The Disability Discrimination Act

271 *Access by Design* (video), Centre for Accessible Environments, London, 1995

272 'Accommodating the disabled', Ann Sawyer, *Architects' Journal*, 30 January 1997, p. 58

28 The Audit Commission

281 *The Publication of Information (Standards of Performance) Direction 1993*, The Audit Commission for Local Authorities and the National Health Service in England and Wales, London, 1993

282 *The Publication of Information Direction 1995: Performance indicators for the financial year 1996/97*, The Audit Commission for Local Authorities and the National Health Service in England and Wales, London, 1995

283 *Local Authority Performance Indicators 1994/95: Appendix to Volumes 1 and 2*, The Audit Commission for Local Authorities and the National Health Service in England and Wales, London, 1996

284 *Auditing Local Services*, The Audit Commission for Local Authorities and the National Health Service in England and Wales, London, 1994

3 Britain: Access issues (2)

30 Technical guidance

301 *Designing for the Disabled*, Selwyn Goldsmith, London, RIBA Publications, first edition 1963

302 *Designing for the Disabled*, Selwyn Goldsmith, London, RIBA Publications, second edition 1967

303 *Designing for the Disabled*, Selwyn Goldsmith, London, RIBA Publications, third edition 1976

304 *Designing for Accessibility*, Tessa Palfreyman, Centre for Accessible Environments, London, 1993

305 *Barrier-Free Design*, James Holmes-Siedle, Butterworth-Heinemann, Oxford, 1996

306 *Buildings for ALL to use*, Sylvester Bone, Construction Industry Research and Information Association, London, 1996

307 *Access Audits – a guide and checklists for appraising the accessibility of buildings for disabled users*, Denis Fearns, Centre for Accessible Environments, London, 1993

31 Access policy

311 'Designing for the Disabled', Frank Duffy (book review), *Design for Special Needs* 11, September/December 1976, p. 22

312 *The ideology of designing for the disabled*, Selwyn Goldsmith, in *Proceedings of the Fourteenth International Conference of the Environmental Design Research Association, 1983*, p. 198, edited by Doug Amedeo, James B. Griffin and James J. Potter, University of Nebraska, Lincoln, USA, 1983 (an edited version of this was published in *Design for Special Needs* 31, May/August 1983, p. 10)

313 'Defining the task of the Access Committee for England', John Dobinson, *Design for Special Needs* 34, May/August 1984, p. 8

314 'Micro or macro – how should we treat disabled people?', Selwyn Goldsmith, *Design for Special Needs* 38, September/December 1985, p. 6

315 'Groups' infighting obscures purpose', Adrian Barrick, *Building Design*, 23 June 1989, p. 8

316 'Government steps in over disabled design group', Adrian Barrick, *Building Design*, 18 August 1989, p. 3

317 'Architectural education: what about access?', Joanne Milner, Dennis Urquhart, *Access by Design* 56, September/December 1991, p. 17

32 Access regulations, history (1)

321 'Architectural barriers to the disabled' (report of 9 October 1962 RIBA meeting addressed by Professor Nugent), Selwyn Goldsmith, *Architects' Journal*, 17 October 1962, p. 909

322 'Access to public buildings' (report of 15 March 1978 seminar), *Design for Special Needs* 15, January/April 1978, p. 12

323 'The Government has second thoughts', Sarah Langton-Lockton, *Design for Special Needs* 30, January/April 1983, p. 19

324 'CEH Report', Sarah Langton-Lockton, *Design for Special Needs* 33, January/April 1984, p. 3

325 Proceedings of Access Committee for England conference, 26 March 1985 *Implementing Accessibility*, Centre on Environment for the Handicapped, London, 1985

326 'Schedule 2: the breakthrough we all wanted', Andrew Lacey, *Design for Special Needs* 39, January/April 1986, p. 9

327 'Recasting the access regulation', Stephen Thorpe, *Design for Special Needs* 41, September/December 1986, p. 10

33 Access regulations, history (2)

331 'Disabled rules "incompetent"' (news note on 1987 Part M regulation), *Architects' Journal*, 28 October 1987, p. 9

332 'Can the Part M Approved Document be made to work?', Sarah Langton-Lockton, *Design for Special Needs* 44, September/December 1987, p. 14

333 'Tired of waiting in the lobby', Robert Cowan (news feature on 1987 Part M regulation), *Architects' Journal*, 4 November 1987, p. 14

334 'British Columbia does it better', Robert Cowan (news feature on 1987 Part M regulation), *Architects' Journal*, 11 November 1987, p. 16

335 'When four walls make a prison', John Penton (news feature on 1987 Part M regulation), *Architects' Journal*, 9 December 1987, p. 17

34 Access regulations, history (3)

341 *Can the Part M Approved Document be made to work?* Report of Centre on Environment for the Handicapped seminar, 21 January 1988

342 'Difficult entry for document M', Robert Cowan (news feature), *Architects' Journal*, 27 January 1988, p. 17

343 'Unhappy birthday, Part M', Stewart McGough, *Design for Special Needs* 47, September/December 1988, p. 10

344 *The development of access regulations and the move towards 1992.* Report of Centre for Accessible Environments conference, 23 November 1990

345 *The revision of Part M.* Report of Centre for Accessible Environments seminar, 14 December 1990

346 'The revision of Part M', Tessa Palfreyman, *Design for Special Needs* 54, January/April 1991, p. 20

35 Planning issues

351 *Access Policies for Local Plans,* Access Committee for England in conjunction with Royal Town Planning Institute, London, 1993

352 Borough of Richmond upon Thames *Unitary Development Plan* (1) Deposit Draft, March 1992; (2) Inspector's Report (Shortened Version), October 1994; (3) Response to Inspector's Report, December 1994; (4) Proposed Modifications, December 1994

353 Letter of 2 December 1993, DOE Planning Inspectorate, Bristol to A.F. Davies & Associates, Richmond

354 Notes of Cases *Richmond upon Thames London Borough Council v Secretary of State for the Environment and Dahaga Establishment* (Queen's Bench Division, Mr R.M.K. Gray QC sitting as a Deputy Judge, 28 June 1994), *Journal of Planning and Environment Law*, August 1995, p. 700

355 *Design for Maximum Access – Design guidelines for people with restricted mobility*, London Borough of Richmond upon Thames, 1995

356 Law Reports 1981, *Judgment of House of Lords in Newbury District Council versus Secretary of State for the Environment*, The Incorporated Council of Law Reporting for England and Wales, 1981

36 Egress for disabled people

361 'Access versus Egress', John Dobinson, *Design for Special Needs* 34, May/August 1984, p. 7

362 'Means of escape for disabled people: defining a realistic approach', John Dobinson, *Design for Special Needs* 39, January/April 1986, p. 14

363 'Assisted escape: principles into practice', Philip Gartshore, *Design for Special Needs* 47, September/December 1988, p. 14

364 *BS5588 Part 8, Part B and means of escape for disabled people.* Report of Centre for Accessible Environments seminar, 27 March 1992

365 *Fire and disabled people in buildings*, T.J. Shields Building Research Establishment, Garston, 1993

366 'Fire escape strategies for disabled people', Chris Harrowell, Su Peace, *Access by Design* 60, January/April 1993, p. 17

367 'Fire and disabled people in buildings', Andrew Z. Lisicki (review of **365**), *Access by Design* 61, May/August 1993, p. 22

368 *Emergency Egress Plans for Disabled Users of Museums and Galleries.* Report of Centre for Accessible Environments seminar, 27 July 1994

37 Life safety

371 *Safety in the Built Environment*, Jonathan D. Sime (ed.), E. & F.N. Spon, London, 1988

372 *Elevator use for egress: The human-factors problems and prospects*, Jake Pauls, Albert J. Gatfield, Edwina Juillet (Paper presented at symposium on elevators and fire, Baltimore, 1991), American Society of Mechanical Engineers, New York, 1991

373 *Recent Social and Technical Developments Influencing the Life Safety of People with Disabilities*, Jake Pauls, Edwina Juillet, *Building Standards* (International Conference of Building Officials), May–June 1990, p. 7

374 *People Movement in Buildings and Public Places: Design, Management and Safety for*

Individuals and Crowds, Jake Pauls, John J. Fruin, Butterworth, London, 1991

375 *Are Functional Handrails within our grasp?*, Jake Pauls, *Building Standards* (International Conference of Building Officials), March–April 1991, p. 25

376 *The Staircase Volume 2 Studies of Hazards, Falls and Safer Design*, John Templer, Massachusetts Institute of Technology, Cambridge, USA, 1992

4 Britain: Access issues (3)

40 Alterations to existing buildings

401 *Historic buildings: Access provision for disabled people.* Report of Centre on Environment for the Handicapped seminar, 12 May 1989

402 *Historic buildings: Accessibility and/or conservation?* Report of Centre for Accessible Environments seminar, 31 October 1990

403 *Access provision: Alterations and extensions to existing public buildings.* Report of Centre for Accessible Environments seminar, 25 April 1990

404 'Research: Access to existing buildings', Stephen Thorpe, Ann Alderson, *Access by Design* 58, May/August 1992, p. 18

405 *Improving access when altering existing public buildings.* Report of Centre for Accessible Environments seminar, 29 March 1993

406 'Monumental changes ahead?', Lisa Foster, *Access by Design* 65, September/December 1994, p. 14

407 'National Portrait Gallery: Orange Street Openings', Sarah Langton-Lockton, *Access by Design* 66, January/April 1995, p. 12

41 Hotels

411 'Little Chef Lodges – the better place to stop?', Vivien Szitasi, Anne Davies, John Penton, *Design for Special Needs* 44, September/December 1987, p. 7

412 *Hotels and Resorts: Planning, Design and Refurbishment*, Fred R. Lawson, Architectural Press, Oxford, 1995

413 *Providing for disabled visitors*, John Penton, English Tourist Board, London, 1985

414 *Design for hospitality – Planning for Accessible Hotels and Motels*, Thomas D. Davies, Kim A. Beasley, Paralyzed Veterans of America, with assistance from the American Hotel and Motel Association, Nichols Publishing, New York, 1988

415 *Accommodating all Guests – The Americans with Disabilities Act and the Lodging Industry*, John P.S. Salmen, American Hotel and Motel Association, Washington DC, 1992

416 'CAE Design Sheet *Hotel bedrooms*', Stephen Thorpe, *Access by Design* 68, September/December 1995, p. 19

42 Stadia, leisure centres, swimming pools

421 *On the Sidelines: Football and Disabled Supporters*, edited by Callum Murray, Football Stadia Advisory Council, London, 1992

422 *Designing for Spectators with Disabilities*, edited by Callum Murray, Football Stadia Advisory Council, London, 1992

423 'Three nil!' (access to football stadia). Robert Trent, *Access by Design* 59 September/December 1992, p12

424 'In a league of their own' (Molineux Stadium, Wolverhampton). Richard Taylor, *Access by Design* 65 September/December 1994, p12

425 *Stadia: A Design and Development Guide*. Geraint John and Rod Sheard, Architectural Press, Oxford, 1997

426 'The Latchmere Leisure Centre'. Selwyn Goldsmith, *Design for Special Needs* 44 September/December 1987, p10

427 'A day at the Dome' (Leisure centre, Doncaster). Tessa Palfreyman, *Access by Design* 52 May/August 1990, p18

428 'CAE Design Sheet *Swimming pools*'. Stephen Thorpe, *Access by Design* 53, September/December 1990, p20

43 Shops, shopping centres

431 *Access in the High Street*, Stephen Thorpe, Centre on Environment for the Handicapped, London, 1981

432 'Gateshead Metrocentre: an environment of belonging', John Smith, *Design for Special Needs* 50, September/December 1989, p. 18

433 'Shopmobility – the Redditch experience', Rod Hoy, *Access by Design* 54, January/April 1991, p. 9

44 Transport buildings

441 *Accessible Public Transport Infrastructure: Guidelines for the Design of Interchanges, Terminals and Stops*, Philip Barham, Philip Oxley, Tony Shaw, Mobility Unit of the Department of Transport, 1994

442 'Stansted Airport, Essex', Tessa Palfreyman, *Access by Design* 55, May/August 1991, p. 6

443 'Waterloo International Terminal', George Stowell, Andrew Walker, *Access by Design* 63, January/April 1994, p. 6

444 'Epic Journey' (report on the reconstruction of Liverpool Street Station), Robert Thorne, Christopher Haddon, *Architects' Journal*, 6 May 1992, p. 24

45 Sanitary facilities (1)

451 BS6465: Part 1: 1984 *Sanitary installations Part 1. Code of practice for scale of provision, selection and installation of sanitary appliances*, British Standards Institution, London, 1984

452 BS6465: Part 1: 1994 *Sanitary installations Part 1. Code of practice for scale of provision, selection and installation of sanitary appliances*, British Standards Institution, London, 1995

453 BS6465: Part 2: 1995 *Sanitary installations Part 2. Code of practice for space requirements for sanitary appliances*, British Standards Institution, London, 1996

454 Statutory Instrument 1995 No 1763 *Food: The Food Safety (General Food Hygiene) Regulations 1995*, HMSO, London, 1995

455 Health and Safety Commission Approved Code of Practice and Guidance L24 *Workplace (Health, Safety and Welfare) Regulations 1992*, HMSO, London, 1992

456 Building Research Establishment Report *Building regulation and health*, D,C. Mant, J.A. Muir Gray, Department of the Environment (BRE), Watford, 1986

457 'Is a lobby required between toilet and food preparation room?', Arthur W. Clarke (DOE Building Regulations Division), *Building Engineer*, June 1994

46 Sanitary facilities (2)

461 Joint Circular: Ministry of Housing and Local Government (33/68); Welsh Office (28/68), *Design of Public Conveniences with Facilities for the Disabled*, HMSO, London, 1968

462 *Public convenience design for the disabled*, John and Lorna Angell (unpublished thesis), Birmingham School of Architecture, 1966

463 'Designing a public convenience for the disabled', S. Goldsmith, P.J.R. Nichols, B. Rostance, J. Angell, L. Angell, *Annals of Physical Medicine*, Vol. VIII No 8, 1966, p. 307

464 *Design of public lavatories with provision for the disabled.* Report of Centre on Environment for the Handicapped seminar, 4 October 1978, *Design for Special Needs* 17, September–December 1978, p. 9

465 'Is the unisex loo ideologically sound?', Selwyn Goldsmith, *Design for Special Needs* 42, January/April 1987, p. 13

466 *Public lavatory provision for disabled people.* Report of Centre on Environment for the Handicapped seminar, 19 June 1987

47 Sanitary facilities (3)

471 *Sanitary provision for people with special needs Volume 1: Part 1 The practicalities of toilet usage; Part 2 Population needs estimates*, Department of the Environment, London, 1992

472 *Sanitary provision for people with special needs Volume 2: Part 3 Tabulated project data*, Department of the Environment, London, 1992

473 'The queue starts here: a raw deal for women', Rebecca Goldsmith, *Access by Design* 57, January/April 1992, p. 10

474 *The Bathroom*, Alexander Kira, Penguin Books, Harmondsworth, 1976

475 *Good Loo Design Guide*, Stephen Thorpe, Centre on Environment for the Handicapped, London, 1988

476 *At Women's Convenience: A Handbook on the Design of Women's Public Toilets*, Sue Cavanagh and Vron Ware, Women's Design Service, London, 1990

477 'CAE Design Sheet *Showers and changing cubicles*', Stephen Thorpe, *Access by Design* 56, September/December 1991, p. 19

478 'CAE Design Sheet *Level access showers*', Stephen Thorpe, *Access by Design* 58, May/August 1992, p. 12

48 Sanitary facilities (4)

481 'The Barnsley super loo', Mike Clover, *Design for Special Needs* 46, May/August 1988, p. 14

482 *Toilets for the disabled – Design specifications*, Portsmouth City Council in conjunction with Portsmouth Handicap Action Committee, City of Portsmouth Directorate of Engineering, 1990

483 'Portsmouth, public toilet mecca', Selwyn Goldsmith, *Access by Design* 55, May/August 1991

49 Building features

491 CAE Specifier's Handbook 1 *Electrical Controls*, Tessa Palfreyman, Centre for Accessible Environments, London, 1990

492 CAE Specifier's Handbook 2 *Wheelchair Stairlifts and Platform Lifts*, Stephen Thorpe, Centre for Accessible Environments, London, 1993

493 CAE Specifier's Handbook 3 *Automatic Door Controls*, Ann Sawyer, Centre for Accessible Environments, London, 1995

494 'Induction loops and infrared systems', Tessa Palfreyman, *Access by Design* 54, January/April 1991, p. 17

495 'Banking on the future' (cash dispensers)', Charles Rohan, *Access by Design* 60, January/April 1993, p. 15

496 CAE Design Sheet *Door ironmongery*, Stephen Thorpe, *Access by Design* 61, May/August 1993, p. 16

5 External environments, blind people, wayfinding

50 External environments

501 *Guidelines for Providing for People with a Mobility Handicap*, The Institution of Highways and Transportation, London, 1986

502 *Revised Guidelines for Reducing Mobility Handicaps*, The Institution of Highways and Transportation, London, 1991

503 'Access and the spaces that link buildings', Tessa Palfreyman, Barry Fitzgerald, *Access by Design* 56, September/December 1991, p. 13

51 Pedestrianisation

511 Local Transport Note 1/87 *Getting the right balance – Guidance on vehicle restriction in pedestrian zones*, Department of Transport, London, 1987

512 *Pedestrianised areas.* Report of Centre on Environment for the Handicapped seminar, 4 November 1986

513 *The way ahead.* Report of Centre on Environment for the Handicapped seminar, 21 November 1986

514 *Pedestrianisation and disabled people.* Report of Centre for Accessible Environments seminar, 10 December 1991

515 'The cancer invading our town centres', Douglas Campbell, *The Magic Carpet* (Disabled Drivers' Association), Summer 1990, p. 19

516 Transport and Road Research Laboratory Contractor Report 184 *An ergonomic study of pedestrian areas for disabled people*, G.R. Leake, A.D. May, T. Parry, Department of Transport, 1991

52 Blind people

521 *Building Sight*, Peter Barker, Jon Barrick, Rod Wilson, Royal National Institute for the Blind, London, 1995

522 *Designing for People with Sensory Impairments*, Stephen Thorpe, Centre on Environment for the Handicapped, London, 1986

523 *Improving the usability of public buildings for people with sensory impairments.* Report of Centre for Accessible Environments seminar, 25 April 1991

524 *Wayfinding without Vision: An Experiment with Congenitally Totally Blind People*, R. Passini, G. Proulx, Sage Publications, London, 1993

525 *Mobility and Reading Habits of the Blind*, P.G. Gray, Jean E. Todd, Government Social Survey, London, 1967

526 'Mobility: Report of a survey of the mobility of blind people in the external environment', D. Liddle, *New Beacon* (Royal National Institute for the Blind): (1) May 1965, p. 115; (2) June 1965, p. 142; (3) July 1965, p. 170

53 Tactile pavings (1)

531 Transport and Road Research Laboratory Leaflet LF 954 *Textured pavements to help blind pedestrians*, Department of Transport (TRRL), Crowthorne, 1983

532 Disability Unit Circular 1/86 *Textured footway surfaces at pedestrian crossings*, Department of Transport, London, 1986

533 Draft Disability Unit Circular 1/90 *Tactile footway surfaces at uncontrolled crossings*, Department of Transport, London, 1990

534 Disability Unit Circular 1/91 *The use of dropped kerbs and tactile surfaces at pedestrian crossing points*, Department of Transport, London, 1992

535 Draft Guidance Note *Guidance on the use of tactile paving surfaces*, Department of Transport, London, 1996

536 Traffic Advisory Leaflet 4/90 *Tactile markings for segregated shared use by cyclists and pedestrians*, Department of Transport, London, 1990

537 Traffic Advisory Leaflet 4/91 *Audible and tactile signals at pelican crossings*, Department of Transport, London, 1991

538 Traffic Advisory Leaflet 5/91 *Audible and tactile signals at signal controlled junctions*, Department of Transport, London, 1991

54 Tactile pavings (2)

541 Transport and Road Research Laboratory Contractor Report 257 *Tactile footway surfaces for the blind*, Christine Gallon, Philip Oxley, Barbara Simms, Department of Transport (TRRL), Crowthorne, 1991

542 Transport and Road Research Laboratory Contractor Report 317 *Tactile surfaces in the pedestrian environment: Experiments in Wolverhampton*, Christine Gallon, Department of Transport (TRRL), Crowthorne, 1992

543 Transport and Road Research Laboratory Published Article PA 2059 *Tactile markings for the guidance of visually handicapped pedestrians*, Marian Williams, Department of Transport (TRRL), Crowthorne, 1991

544 'Tactile markings for the guidance of blind pedestrians on facilities shared with cyclists', Marian Williams, (Transport and Road Research Laboratory), *Traffic Engineering and Control*, March 1987, p. 124

545 'Monitoring tactile markings on shared pedestrian/cycle routes', Marian Williams (Transport and Road Research Laboratory), *Traffic Engineering and Control*, December 1990, p. 655

546 *Guidelines for Dropped Kerbs and Tactile Paving*, Acer Consultants Ltd (October 1994 Draft for Consultation), City of Westminster, 1994

547 *Guidelines for Dropped Kerbs and Tactile Paving*. Report to Planning and Transportation Committee on results of consultation, City of Westminster, April 1995

548 *Dropped Kerbs and Tactile Paving – Further Work*. Report to Planning and Transportation Committee on results of consultation, City of Westminster, November 1995

55 Tactile pavings (3)

551 US Architectural and Transportation Barriers Compliance Board *Bulletin 1: Detectable Warnings*, The Board, Washington DC, 1993

552 'Access Board proposes two-year delay for detectable warnings', *Universal Design Newsletter*, Rockville, USA, April 1993, p. 6

553 *Detectable warnings: Safety and negotiability on slopes for people who are visually impaired*, B.L. Bentzen and others, Project Action, Washington DC, 1995

554 *Detectable warnings in transit facilities: Safety and negotiability*, B.L. Bentzen, Project Action, Washington DC, 1995

555 'Impact of curb ramps on the safety of persons who are blind', B.L. Bentzen, J.M. Barlow, *Journal of Visual Impairment and Blindness* (USA), July–August 1995, p. 319

556 'Trouble for truncated domes', *Universal Design Newsletter*, Rockville, USA, January 1995, p. 1

557 Australian Standard 1428.4 – 1992 *Design for access and mobility. Part 4: Tactile ground surface indicators for the orientation of people with visual impairment*, Standards Association of Australia, North Sydney, NSW, 1992

56 Symbols, signs, wayfinding

561 *A symbol for disabled people/Symbol application manual*, Selwyn Goldsmith, Peter Rea, RIBA Publications, London, 1969

562 *Wayfinding in Public Buildings: A Design Guideline*, R. Passini, G. Shiels, Architectural and Engineering Services, Public Works Canada, 1987

563 *Orientation and Wayfinding in Public Buildings: An Overview*, Paul Arthur, Newton Frank Arthur, Architectural and Engineering Services, Public Works Canada, 1988

564 *Wayfinding – People, Signs and Architecture*, Paul Arthur, Romedi Pasini, McGraw-Hill Ryerson, Whitby, Ontario, Canada, 1991

6 Europe and Canada

60 European Union Directives

601 European Parliament and Council Directive 95/16/EC *On the approximation of the laws of the Member States relating to lifts*, Official Journal of the European Communities, No. L213/1, 1995

602 Council Directive 89/654/EEC *Council Directive of 30 November 1989 concerning the minimum safety and health requirements for the workplace*, Official Journal of the European Communities, 30.12.89

61 European Manual

611 *European Manual for an Accessible Built Environment*, Central Co-ordinating Committee for the Promotion of Accessibility (CCPT), Rijswijk IG-Nederland, Utrecht, 1990

612 *European Manual for an Accessible Built Environment* (Part A, Draft revision Concept 1), CCPT, Rijswijk, 1993

613 *European Manual for Accessibility* (Draft revision 1), CCPT, Rijswijk, 1995

614 *European Concept for Access* CCPT, Rijswijk, November 1995

615 *European Concept for Access: written remarks*, CCPT, Rijswijk, February 1996

616 *European Concept for Accessibility*, CCPT, Rijswijk, March 1996

617 *Proceedings of the International Seminar 'European Approaches to Accessibility'* Gehandicaptenraad, Utrecht, 1996

618 'Talking Point', Sarah Langton-Lockton, *Access by Design* 69, January/April 1996, p. 3

62 The Netherlands

621 *Geboden Toegang*, Stichting Nederlandse Gehandicaptenraad Utrecht, 1989 (9th edition)

622 *Handboek voor Toegankelijkheid (voorheen Geboden Toegang)*, Maarten Wijk and others, CIP – Gegevans Koninklijke Bibliotheek, The Hague, 1995

623 *Dutch research and standards on accessibility*, Theo J.M. van der Voordt, Delft University of Technology, 1995

624 *Gouda Demonstration Project: Safe traffic provisions for people with a mobility handicap*, Gemeente Gouda, 1986

63 Scandinavia

631 *The physically disabled and their environment.* Report of the Proceedings, ISRD Conferences, Stockholm, 12–18 October 1961, Swedish Central Committee for the Care of Cripples, Stockholm, 1961

632 *Rörelsehindrades stadsbygdsbygdsmiljö – en studie från Högdalen*, Henrik Muller, Statens råd för byggnadsforskning, Stockholm, 1961

633 The Nordic Committee on Disability, *Accessibility in the Built Environment – The Nordic Approach*, The Committee, Vällingby, Sweden, 1994

64 Canada

641 CAN/CSA-B651-M90 *Barrier-Free Design – A National Standard of Canada*, Canada Standards Association, Toronto, 1990

642 Public Works Canada, *Barrier-Free Design: Access to and use of buildings by physically disabled people*, Public Relations and Information Services, Ottawa, 1985

643 *The Section 3.7 Handbook: Building Requirements for Persons with Disabilities Including Illustrations and Commentary 1984*, Ministry of Municipal Affairs, Province of British Columbia, Victoria, 1984

644 *The Building Access Handbook: Building Requirements for Persons with Disabilities from the British Columbia Building Code 1992*, Ministry of Municipal Affairs, Province of British Columbia, Victoria, 1995

7 Britain: Disabled people

70 Population surveys

701 OPCS surveys of disability in Great Britain, Report 1 *The prevalence of disability among adults*, Jean Martin, Howard Meltzer, David Elliot, HMSO, London, 1988

702 OPCS surveys of disability in Great Britain, Report 2 *The financial circumstances of disabled adults living in private households*, Jean Martin, Amanda White, HMSO, London, 1988

703 OPCS surveys of disability in Great Britain, Report 3 *The prevalence of disability among children*, Margaret Bone, Howard Meltzer, HMSO, London, 1989

704 OPCS surveys of disability in Great Britain. Report 4 *Disabled adults: services, transport and employment*, Jean Martin, Amanda White, Howard Meltzer, HMSO, London, 1989

705 *Handicapped and Impaired in Great Britain, Part I*, Amelia I. Harris, Office of Population Censuses and Surveys, HMSO, London, 1971

706 *Work and Housing of Impaired Persons in Great Britain*, Judith R. Buckle, Office of Population Censuses and Surveys (Part II of **705**), HMSO, London, 1971

707 *Blind and Partially Sighted Adults in Britain: the RNIB Survey Volume 1*, Ian Bruce, Aubrey McKennell, Errol Walker, HMSO, London, 1991

708 Office for National Statistics, *Communicable Disease Statistics 1994*, HMSO, London, 1996

709 *Registered blind and partially sighted people, year ending 31 March 1994*, Department of Health, London, 1994,

71 Disabilities

711 World Health Organisation, *International Classification of Impairments, Disabilities and Handicaps*, WHO, Geneva, 1980

712 *The Residue of Poliomyelitis*, Michael Lee, Office of Health Economics, London, 1965

713 *A Summer Plague – Polio and its Survivors*, Tony Gould, Yale University Press, New Haven and London, 1995

72 Disability discrimination, official reports

721 *Report by the Committee on Restrictions against Disabled People* (The CORAD Report, chairman Mr Peter Large) issued by the Department of Health and Social Security, London, 1982

722 *A Consultation on Government Measures to Tackle Discrimination Against Disabled People*, The Disability Unit, Department of Social Security, London, 1994

723 *Ending discrimination against disabled people* (Command Paper presented to Parliament by the Minister for Disabled People), HMSO, London, 1995

724 Disability Discrimination Act 1995, *A Consultation on the Employment Code of Practice, Guidance on Definition of Disability and Related Regulations*, Department for Education and Employment, London, 1996

725 Disability Discrimination Act 1995, Consultation Package *Access to Services (i) Timetable Proposals; (ii) Proposals for Regulations Rights of Access to Goods, Services and Property, Proposals for a Code of Practice*, Department of Social Security/National Disability Council, London, 1996

726 Disability Discrimination Act 1995, *Code of Practice for the elimination of discrimination in the field of employment against disabled persons or persons who have had a disability*, HMSO, London, 1996

727 Disability Discrimination Act 1995, *Code of Practice: Rights of Access. Goods, Facilities, Services and Premises*, HMSO, London, 1996

728 Disability Discrimination Act 1995, *Guidance on matters to be taken into account in determining questions relating to the definition of disability*, HMSO, London, 1996

73 Commentaries on legislation

731 *The Role of Non-Governmental Organisations in the Legislative Process, Legislation by Disabled People for Disabled People: The UK experience since 1970* (Paper for International Expert Meeting on Legislation on Equalisation of Opportunities for Disabled People, Vienna, June 1986), Peter Mitchell, Royal Association for Disability and Rehabilitation, London, 1986

732 *Disabled People in Britain and Discrimination: A case for anti-discrimination legislation*, Colin Barnes, Hurst and Co, London, 1991

733 *Equal Rights for Disabled People – The case for a new law*, Ian Bynoe, Mike Oliver, Colin Barnes, Institute for Public Policy Research, London, 1992

74 The disability movement

741 Union of the Physically Impaired Against Segregation, *Fundamental Principles of Disability* London, 1976

742 International Exchange of Information in Rehabilitation Monograph 5 *Attitudes and disabled people*, Victor Finkelstein, World Rehabilitation Fund, New York, 1980

743 *The Politics of Disablement*, Michael Oliver, Macmillan Education, Basingstoke, 1990

744 *Disabled Lives*, Jenny Morris, BBC Education, London, 1992

745 *Disabling Barriers – Enabling Environments*, edited by John Swain, Vic Finkelstein, Sally French, Mike Oliver, Sage Publications, London, 1993

746 *Removing Disabling Barriers*, edited by Gerry Zarb, Policy Studies Institute, London, 1995

747 'The disability movement has run out of steam', Vic Finkelstein, *Disability Now*, February 1996, p. 11

748 *Disability Politics*, Jane Campbell and Mike Oliver, Routledge, London, 1996

749 *Exploring the Divide: Illness and disability*, edited by Colin Barnes and Geof Mercer, The Disability Press, Leeds, 1996

75 Sociology, psychology

751 *Physical Disability – a psychological approach*, Beatrice A. Wright, Harper and Row, New York, 1960

752 *Disability: Whose Handicap?*, Ann Shearer, Basil Blackwell, Oxford, 1981

753 *The Handicapped Person: a new perspective for social workers?*, edited by J. Campling, Royal Association for Disability and Rehabilitation, London, 1982

754 *Social Work: Disabled People and Disabling Environments*, edited by Michael Oliver, Jessica Kingsley, London, 1991

755 *Understanding Disability – From Theory to Practice*, Michael Oliver, Macmillan, Basingstoke, 1996

756 'Disability models . . . or muddles?', Colin Low, *Therapy Weekly* (London), 1 February 1996, p. 7

76 Biographical and autobiographical material (1)

761 *Stigma – The Experience of Disability*, edited by Paul Hunt, Geoffrey Chapman, London, 1966

762 *No feet to Drag – report on the disabled*, Alfred Morris, Arthur Butler, Sidgwick & Jackson, London, 1972

763 'I truly believe that my disaster was the best thing that ever happened to me', Mike Oliver, *The Guardian*, 24 February 1982

764 'When red tape is better than sympathy', Susan Beattie, *The Guardian*, 29 December 1981

765 *The World Walks By*, Sue Masham, William Collins, London, 1986

766 *Well, I forget the Rest*, Quentin Crewe, Hutchinson, London, 1991

767 *Pride Against Prejudice*, Jenny Morris, Women's Press, London, 1991

768 *Acts of Defiance*, Jack Ashley, Penguin, Harmondsworth, 1992

769 *Declarations of Independence: War Zones and Wheelchairs*, John Huckenberry, Penguin, London, 1996

77 Biographical and autobiographical material (2)

771 'Paul Hunt – A Tribute from UPIAS' *Cheshire, Smile* (London), Spring 1980

772 *Able Lives – Women's experience of paralysis*, edited by Jenny Morris, Women's Press, London, 1989

773 *Living Independently*, Ann Shearer, Centre on Environment for the Handicapped/Kings Fund, London, 1982

774 *On a Clear Day*, David Blunkett, Michael O'Mara Books, London 1995

78 Journal features

781 'The day I denounced Daddy' (Valerie Grove interview), *The Times*, 13 May 1994, p. 19

782 'A family split apart by politics' (Profile, Nick and Victoria Scott), *Sunday Times*, 15 May 1994, News Review, p. 3

783 'From the Chair – A Tribute to Alf Morris', Joe Hennessy, *The Magic Carpet* (Disabled Drivers' Association), Summer 1979, p. 4

8 Housing

80 Housing provision, the 1960s

801 Report of the subcommittee of the Central Housing Advisory Committee under the chairmanship of Sir Parker Morris, *Homes for today and tomorrow*, HMSO, London, 1961

802 Ministry of Housing and Local Government Circular 36/67 *Housing standards: Costs and subsidies*, HMSO, London, 1967

803 Ministry of Housing and Local Government Circular 82/69 *Housing Standards and Costs – Accommodation Specially Designed for Old People*, HMSO, London, 1969

804 Ministry of Housing and Local Government Circular 27/70 *Metrication of Housebuilding: Progress*, HMSO, London, 1970

805 *Towards housing the disabled* (Commentary to exhibition at the Royal Society of Health, October 1962), Central Council for the Disabled, London, 1962

806 Ministry of Housing and Local Government

Design Bulletin 1 *Some aspects of designing for old people*, HMSO, London, 1962

807 Ministry of Housing and Local Government Design Bulletin 2 *Grouped flatlets for old people, a sociological study*, HMSO, London, 1962

808 Ministry of Housing and Local Government Design Bulletin 11 *Old people's flatlets at Stevenage*, HMSO, London, 1966

81 Mobility and wheelchair housing

811 Department of the Environment Circular 74/74 *Housing for People who are Physically Handicapped*, HMSO, London, 1974

812 Housing Development Directorate Occasional Paper 2/74 *Mobility housing*, Selwyn Goldsmith, Department of the Environment, London, 1974 (reprinted from *Architects' Journal*, 3 July 1974, p. 43)

813 Housing Development Directorate Occasional Paper 2/75 *Wheelchair housing*, Selwyn Goldsmith, Janis Morton, Department of the Environment, London, 1975 (reprinted from *Architects' Journal*, 25 June 1975, p. 1319)

814 Department of the Environment Circular 92/75 *Wheelchair and Mobility Housing: Standards and Costs*, HMSO, London, 1975

815 'Mobility housing: more flexibility in housing for the disabled', E.F. Cantle, N. A. Sharp, *Design for Special Needs* 11, September/December 1976, p. 15

816 *Housing Design Brief: Housing for Disabled People*, Institute of Housing/Royal Institute of British Architects, RIBA Publications, London, 1988

817 *Housing for People with Disabilities – A Design Guide*, Stelios Voutsadakif, Islington London Borough Council, 2nd edition, 1989

82 'Accessible' housing

821 BS5619:1978 *Design of housing for the convenience of disabled people*, British Standards Institution, London, 1978

822 'The gestation of 'X' housing', Selwyn Goldsmith, *Design for Special Needs* 39, January/April 1986, p. 6

823 Report of Disability Workshop Meetings at Bracknell. *Visitability in new private sector housing*, Phippen Randall and Parkes Architects (unpublished)

824 NHBC Advisory Note 2 *How to make houses more suitable for elderly and handicapped people*, National House-Building Council, Amersham, 1987

825 Habinteg Housing Association Design Guide *A design guide and technical manual for accessible new build housing*, Habinteg Housing Association, London, 1992 (3rd edition)

826 *Every house you'll ever need – A design guide for barrier-free housing*, Edinvar Housing Association, Edinburgh, 1992

827 *Building Homes for Successive Generations – Criteria for Accessible General Housing*, Access Committee for England, London, 1992

828 'Accessible housing' (Jack Ashley Court, Colindale)', Stephen Thorpe, *Access by Design* 70, May/August 1996, p. 15

83 Lifetime Homes

831 *Lifetime Homes – Flexible Housing for Successive Generations* (Seminar report on all-age housing edited by Andrew Rowe), Milgate Publishing for Helen Hamlyn Foundation, London, 1990

832 *Lifetime Homes*, Joseph Rowntree Foundation, York, 1993

833 *Incorporating Lifetime Homes standards into modernisation programmes*, David Bonnett, Joseph Rowntree Foundation, York, 1996

834 *Designing Lifetime Homes*, edited by Julie Brewerton and David Darton, Joseph Rowntree Foundation, York, 1997

835 *Costing Lifetime Homes*, Kim Sangster, Joseph Rowntree Foundation, York, 1997

836 *A Cost Benefit Analysis of Lifetime Homes*, Christopher Cobbold, Joseph Rowntree Foundation, York, 1997

837 Findings Housing Research Paper *Lifetime Homes in Europe and the UK*, Joseph Rowntree Foundation, York, 1997

84 Housing Corporation

841 *Scheme Development Standards* (August 1995), The Housing Corporation, London, 1995

842 Housing Corporation Policy and Research Report *Housing for people with disabilities – The needs of wheelchair users*, The Housing Corporation, London, 1991

843 *Housing for visually impaired*, The Housing Corporation, London, 1995

844 *Housing for older people*, The Housing Corporation, London, 1996

85 1995 proposed Part M regulation

851 *Access and facilities for disabled people: New dwellings*, The Building Regulations 1991, Draft Part M Approved Document, consultation proposals, Department of the Environment, January 1995

852 *The application of Building Regulations to help disabled people in new dwellings in England and Wales* (response from the House Builders Federation to the Department of the Environment's January 1995 proposals)

853 *Extending the Building Regulations to improve access to new dwellings* (response from the Access Committee for England to the Department of the Environment's January 1995 proposals)

854 'Access to new dwellings', John Miller, Trisha Gupta, Jon Watson, Peter Randall, *Access by Design* 66, January/April 1995, p. 8

86 Surveys

861 *New Homes in the 1990s – A Study of Design, Space and Amenity in Housing Association and Private Sector Housing*, Valerie Karn and Linda Sheridan, Joseph Rowntree Foundation, York, 1994

862 Department of the Environment, *English House Condition Survey 1991*, HMSO, London, 1993

863 *Living Independently: A Study of the Housing Needs of Elderly and Disabled People*, Paul McCafferty, Department of the Environment, London, 1995

87 Adaptations, adaptability

871 Department of the Environment, *House adaptations for people with physical disabilities – A guidance manual for practitioners*, Rosemary Statham, Jean Korczak, Philip Monaghan, HMSO, London, 1988

872 'Adaptable housing in the Netherlands', Sarah Langton-Lockton, *Design for Special Needs* 49, May/August 1989, p. 13

873 *Building Adaptable Housing*, Nationale Woningraad (National Housing Council), Almere, The Netherlands, 1989

874 *Adaptable Housing*, Disability Action Access Committee, Disability Action, Belfast, 1993

875 US Department of Housing and Urban Development, *Fair Housing Accessibility Guidelines* Federal Register, Vol. 56 No. 44, Washington DC, March 6 1991

88 Planning guidance

881 DOE Planning Policy Guidance Note 3 (revised), *Housing*, Department of the Environment, London, 1992

882 DOE Circular 13/96 *Planning and affordable housing*, HMSO, London, 1996

89 Housing statistics

891 Department of the Environment, *Housing and Construction Statistics 1978–1988*, HMSO, London, 1989

892 Department of the Environment, *Housing and Construction Statistics 1984–1994*, HMSO, London, 1996

893 Department of the Environment, *Housing and Construction Statistics, June Quarter 1996*, HMSO, London, 1996

9 Other references

90 Anthropometrics, design data

901 *The Measure of Man and Woman – Human factors in design*, Alvin R. Tilley (Henry Dreyfuss Associates), Whitney Library of Design (Watson-Guptill Publications), New York, 1993

902 *New Metric Handbook – Planning and Design Data*, Patricia Tutt and David Adler (eds), Butterworth-Heinemann, Oxford, 1979

91 Other references

911 *The Modulor*, Le Corbusier (translation: Peter de Francia, Anna Bostock), Faber, London, 1961

912 Health and Safety Commission Consultative Document *Proposals for Workplace (Health, Safety and Welfare) Regulations and Approved Code of Practice*, Health and Safety Executive, London, 1992

913 'Birthday bores', Jeffrey Bernard, *The Spectator* (London), 4 June 1994, p. 47

Index